CW01500351

List of Illustrations

Colour Plates (between pages 160 – 161)

Part One – The Fundamentals

Chapter 1 – Organisation and Tactics

British Napoleonic
Field Artillery

BRITISH NAPOLEONIC

FIELD ARTILLERY

THE FIRST COMPLETE ILLUSTRATED GUIDE
TO EQUIPMENT AND UNIFORMS

by

C.E. Franklin

SPELLMOUNT

This book could not have been written without the unstinting help of M.P. Evans BSc the librarian of the James Clavell Library, Royal Artillery Historical Trust, Woolwich; the Tøjhusmuseet in Copenhagen and the host of re-enactors and enthusiasts who have spent hours researching and showing the way for the author to follow, particularly George Bauman and Torstein Snorrason. Particularly thanks are due to Philip A. Magrath MA, the Curator of Artillery, at the Royal Armouries at Fort Nelson who painstakingly worked his way through the manuscripts and corrected many errors.

To Barbara and Lindsey
and all the gunners with whom
I had the privilege to serve.

First published 2008
This paperback edition published 2012 by
Spellmount, the military history imprint of
The History Press
The Mill, Brimscombe Port
Stroud, Gloucestershire, GL5 2QG
www.thehistorypress.co.uk

© C.E. Franklin, 2008, 2012

The right of C.E. Franklin to be identified as the Author
of this work has been asserted in accordance with the
Copyrights, Designs and Patents Act 1988.

All rights reserved. No part of this book may be reprinted
or reproduced or utilised in any form or by any electronic,
mechanical or other means, now known or hereafter invented,
including photocopying and recording, or in any information
storage or retrieval system, without the permission in writing
from the Publishers.

British Library Cataloguing in Publication Data.
A catalogue record for this book is available from the British Library.

ISBN 978 0 7524 7652 0

Typesetting and origination by The History Press
Production managed by Jellyfish Print Solutions; printed in India

Contents

Part Three – Uniforms

List of Tables

Preface

The first phase of the Napoleonic War began when France declared war on Britain, Spain and Holland in February 1793 and continued until the peace of Amiens in March 1802. The peace was not destined to last and in May 1803, Britain declared war on France and the second phase of the war continued until after June 1815 when Napoleon abdicated. The history of any famous regiment invariably considers the men, the theatres of operation and usually in a much smaller way, the equipment. In the case of the Royal Artillery this is due to the apparent absence of any surviving gun carriages and limbers and most of the previous studies have limited themselves to the comparisons with the anachronistic material of earlier and later periods. This compendium draws together new and existing contemporary information that provides new insights into the field equipment and uniforms of the period. While some of the material has been published before much is placed into the public domain for the first time.

The ordnance considered by this book is limited to the field artillery and the supporting equipments. The role of field artillery was to support the army in the field and in this context the Royal Regiment of Artillery had two fighting arms, the Royal Artillery and the Royal Horse Artillery. The Royal Artillery supported the infantry and was formed into 'Brigades', the gunners marching with the guns. The Royal Horse Artillery supported the cavalry and was formed in 'Troops', with all the gunners mounted or riding on the equipment. The field pieces of this period were bronze, smooth-bore weapons and the inventory of the field artillery was made up from the light and heavy 3-pr, the light, heavy and long 6-pr, and the medium 12-pr. Later, after 1808, came the 9-pr; also included in the field inventory were the light and heavy 5.5-inch howitzers and the iron 24-pr howitzer. There were trials with other ordnance but none was taken into full service, so these are not considered nor is the ordnance associated with the garrison and siege artillery. In addition to field equipments, this book also addresses the different gun carriages, limbers, ammunition wagons, other supporting equipment, the drills and exercises, and the uniforms of the period.

The Duke of Richmond, the Master General of Ordnance, had proposed a new design for the gun and limber when it was decided to introduce horse artillery into the British service. Generally attributed to General Congreve (1st Bart) it probably owed more to General Desaguliers. He had designed a block trail carriage and a double draught limber for experimental service of a heavy 3-pr gun in 1779. This was based upon a French gun carriage captured at Martinique in 1761 and followed the principles of Prussian horse artillery. As a result, new equipment was introduced which included many of the latest ideas. The wheels of the gun and limber were the same size, 60 inches in diameter and interchangeable; iron axles of the same length were fitted to both the gun and limber so the wheels of the gun could follow in the tracks of the limber. A new design of gun carriage, the block trail, was adopted and the limber was fitted to carry the first-line ammunition. The advantages of this new equipment were so apparent, it was issued to the rest of the field artillery as soon as it became available. In Spain, where there was a constant re-supply of new wheels and carriages as the war progressed, the changeover took some time and there were several different styles of gun carriage and limber in use by the foot brigades, some going back to the 1760s, but the horse artillery was fully equipped with the new designs from the start.

Thus, it can be seen, at the beginning of the Napoleonic War that British field artillery was in transition. The short-comings of the earlier field systems had become self evident and with the introduction of the new equipments for the horse artillery, the ordnance had taken the opportunity to sweep up all the desired changes into the new designs and there was an immediate and progressive replacement of the older equipments in the foot artillery brigades. The programme of replacement began with the introduction of the larger wheels and iron axles and there is some evidence to suggest that the bracket trail carriages were used in conjunction with the new style of limber but with an extended rear bolster to carry the pintle for the trail transom. This evolution progressed throughout the war. By 1814 all of the bracket trail carriages, and the old limbers of the field artillery engaged in the European conflict had been replaced, although Woolwich placed less emphasis on upgrading equipment in the Colonies. One thing has become clear, the introduction of the block trail carriages to the foot artillery was much sooner and on a more comprehensive scale than generally considered.

Information is given on the different guns, howitzers and carriages used by the British field artillery during the Napoleonic Wars and, where the information is available, details of their performance is included. It is clear, during the war the field artillery used other types of ordnance not covered by this book; this omission is due to the lack of contemporary information or that their use was more a trial or on a temporary basis rather than an adoption into service. In every case, where the information has been available, the ordnance is represented and fully illustrated.

In spite of the unremitting help of the James Clavell Library. The Royal Artillery Museum, Royal Armouries, National Archive, British Library, Tøjhusmuseet in Copenhagen and many others, no research, however intensive, is ever the final word on any subject and it may well be further information has yet to be placed into the public domain. Some of the drawings contained in this book are reconstructions based on the information available and the practices of the period. Added to this must be an understanding that troop and brigade commanders were very much their own men and individual practices and modifications were not at all uncommon. These factors need to be considered when referring to the drawings with no specific attribution.

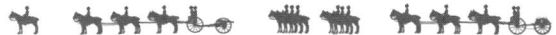

PART ONE

The Fundamentals

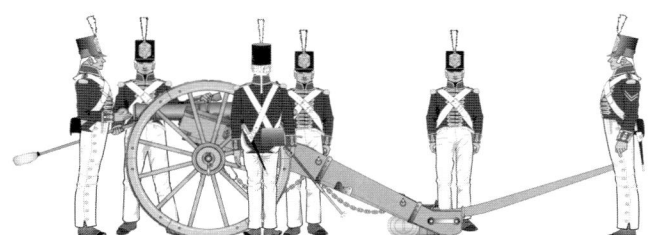

Introduction to Part One

The first part of this book contains the main elements to be considered in any study of the British field artillery of this period. The following chapters address each of these topics and each explains the techniques used and the terms adopted at the time. It should be remembered that the terminology in use during the period, like the spelling, varied from person to person and from country to country and it would be quite wrong to interpret any other artillery arm from the basis of this material.

The chapters consider the organisation and tactics of the field artillery, albeit in limited form, as this is well covered elsewhere. It addresses the different types of gun carriage and the different limbers in use during the period. It also gives a detailed assessment of the ammunition used and discusses the forms of draught harness employed by the artillery to move their equipment. In each instance, every effort has been made to cover all the aspects of the techniques in question, but in spite of all the research some omissions will have occurred. Chapter 7 considers the more common aspects of the drills and procedures used by the field artillery of the period, but the reader will no doubt be aware that these are just a sample of a much more comprehensive and detailed series of exercises and drills intended to cover every possible event or circumstance.

In each case, the tables of data relating to the following chapters are included in Appendix A at the end of Part One.

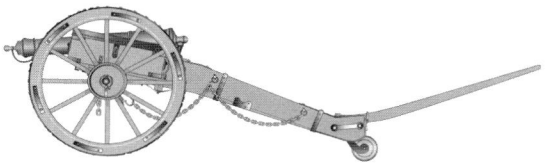

Organisation and Tactics of the Field Artillery

Organisation of the Royal Regiment of Artillery

At the beginning of the period, the field artillery was divided into two main types. The Royal Horse Artillery, intended for the support of cavalry and the Royal Artillery, which could be allocated to support the infantry or siege duties as the needs dictated while others served garrison and coastal artillery. When artillery was deployed on campaign, there was usually an additional grouping, the 'Park of the artillery'. This used to be the area where the guns were parked when not in action but evolved into the area headquarters where the staff, specialist personnel, spare guns and manpower, reserve ammunition, spare horses and other supporting wagons and carts were encamped to support the artillery in the field or the guns at siege.

Organisation of the Royal Artillery

The Royal Artillery was divided into battalions, each of ten companies notionally 145 men strong, but usually less. There were no specific roles and each company was posted to whatever duty was required; they could be employed on duties relating to artillery of the park, field artillery, siege artillery or garrison artillery as needed and often changed roles in theatre to meet operational requirements. In 1793, there were four battalions, a fifth was raised in 1794, a sixth in 1799, a seventh in 1801, an eighth in 1803, a ninth in 1806 and the tenth in 1808. The number of officers in 1791 was 274; by 1814, this number had increased to 727. The establishment of a company in 1808 was five officers, four senior NCOs, 13 junior NCOs, 116 gunners and 3 drummers plus attached drivers from the Corps of Artillery Drivers.[1] The gun crews usually marched with the guns, although they rode on the limbers and ammunition wagons when required.[2]

Battalion Guns

At the start of the war field brigades were usually split into two gun groups and allocated to support a particular infantry regiment or battalion with one wagon to carry reserve ammunition; in this role the artillery strength was usually one subaltern, two NCOs, eight gunners, three drivers and nine horses. The limbers were primitive, usually with limited ammunition and the draught usually two horses in single file under the control of a driver. This practice had many drawbacks; the guns were advanced or retired by the marching infantry and as such they were either too light to have much effect upon the enemy or if larger, they encumbered the infantry and slowed their advance. This began to change and as early as 1799 advancing and retiring the gun by horse instead of infantry manning the drag ropes was being implemented.[3] The experiences of the field were beginning to tell, in the Peninsula, the opinion was to brigade the guns, and by 1802, this was being put into effect.[4] In England, practices were also changing but at a slower pace, 'the allocation of field pieces to be two pieces per Regiment of the Line but artillery to act with militia is to be continued in Brigade and a proportion of men of each regiment instructed in the exercises of field artillery'.[5] The term 'battery' was only used during this period to denote a collective group of guns for siege or garrison purposes, the term for the foot artillery was a 'brigade'.[6] This was only applied when a group of guns was allocated to a specific company. The company without any guns was officially known by the captain's name, for example 'Captain Lawson's Company of the 8th Battalion, Royal Artillery'. Only when the guns were attached did it become known as 'Captain Lawson's Brigade of light 3-pr guns', the captain's name and the nature of the ordnance being the essential features. Companies often exchanged their ordnance as the situation demanded and during the period, there were many such examples.[7]

When brigaded each unit was organized in a similar way to the horse artillery. The six guns were numbered off from the right. Guns 1, 2, and 3 were the right half brigade and operated under the command of the Captain; guns 4, 5 and 6 were the left half and operated under the command of the 2nd Captain. Two guns formed a division; guns 1 and 2 formed the right division under the command of the senior subaltern, 3 and 4 formed the centre division under the command of the next senior subaltern with guns 5 and 6 forming the left division under the command of the junior subaltern. Guns 1, 3 and 5 were the right guns of their division and 2, 4 and 6 the left. The howitzer, when used, was usually the number 3 gun, the gun of direction.[8] When required the divisions could be split into sub-divisions each consisting of one gun and the supporting wagons.

The establishment for a Brigade of 4 long 6-pr guns to be employed in the Low Countries in 1793 is given in a paper by General Sir William Congreve (see Figure 1.1). It notes in addition to the 3 officers, 1 drummer, 7 NCOs and 65 gunners, it required 2,120 rounds of ammunition, over 40 assorted carriages, limbers and wagons, 199 horses plus 94 drivers and 15 other civilian staff and artificers.

The 4 long 6-pr guns and carriages required 24 horses and 12 drivers; the 4 spare limbers with 240 rounds, 16 horses and 8 drivers; 4 new pattern ammunition wagons with 720 rounds, 24 horses and 12 drivers. There were 8 old pattern ammunition wagons with 960 rounds, 32 horses, 16 drivers; there were 11 assorted supporting wagons with 39 horses, 19 drivers; 5 baggage wagons with 36 horses and 18 drivers, plus spare horses in the ratio of 1 to 10, and 9 spare drivers. The logistic tail and personnel to support just 4 guns is clearly demonstrated and it should be

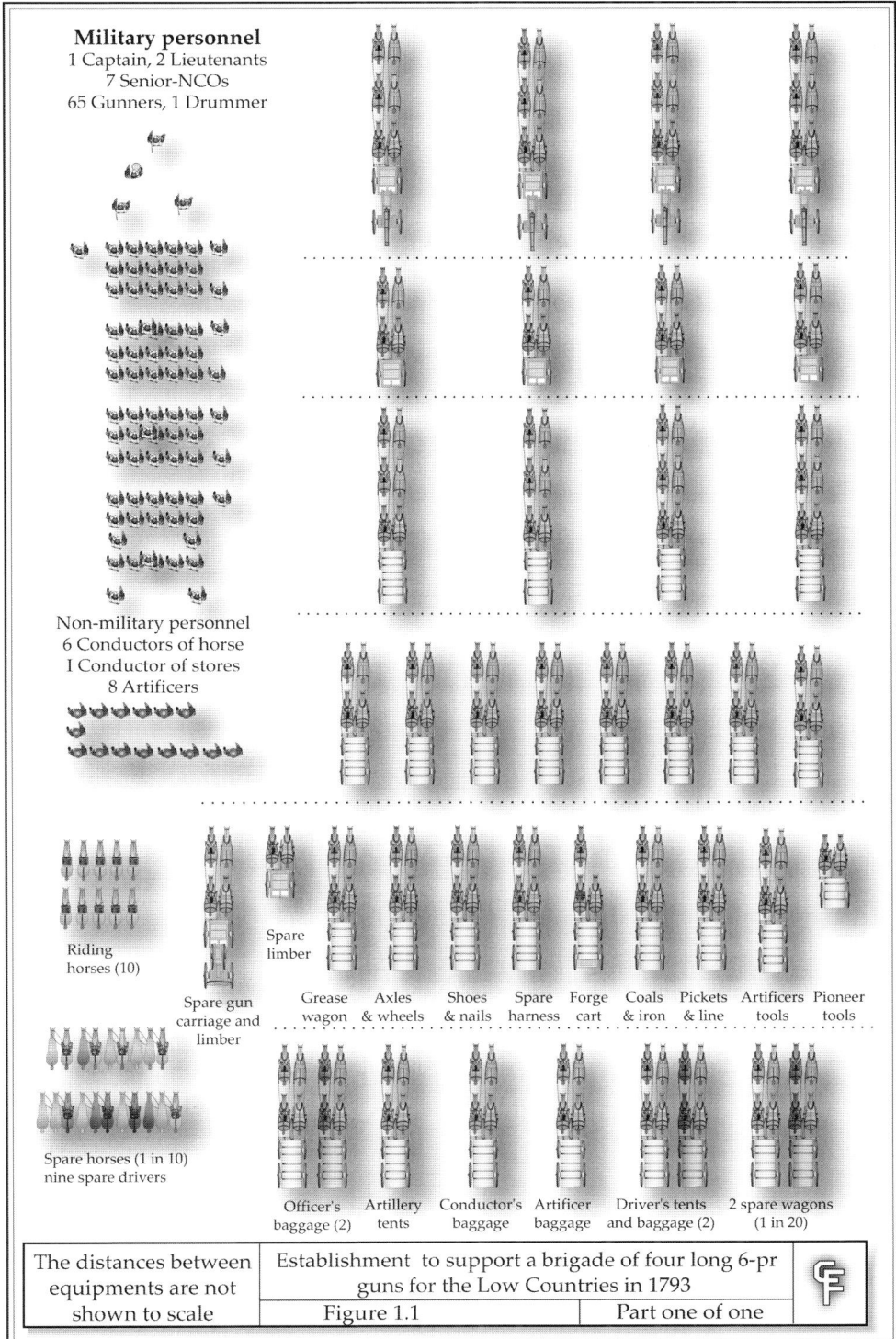

Military personnel
1 Captain, 2 Lieutenants
7 Senior-NCOs
65 Gunners, 1 Drummer

Non-military personnel
6 Conductors of horse
I Conductor of stores
8 Artificers

Riding horses (10)

Spare gun carriage and limber

Spare limber

Grease wagon

Axles & wheels

Shoes & nails

Spare harness

Forge cart

Coals & iron

Pickets & line

Artificers tools

Pioneer tools

Spare horses (1 in 10) nine spare drivers

Officer's baggage (2)

Artillery tents

Conductor's baggage

Artificer baggage

Driver's tents and baggage (2)

2 spare wagons (1 in 20)

The distances between equipments are not shown to scale	Establishment to support a brigade of four long 6-pr guns for the Low Countries in 1793	
	Figure 1.1	Part one of one

Figure 1.1. Visual representation of the establishment necessary to support a brigade of four long 6-pr guns for the Low Countries in 1793 after a paper by General Sir William Congreve.

remembered it does not include the extra personnel and equipment required for the park of artillery or carts and wagons for rations and forage. [9]

All this began to change with the introduction of the horse artillery in 1793. It was not that the shortcomings of the system had been appreciated before, but this event provided the catalyst for a series of changes that were to sweep through the whole of the field artillery. By 1813 most foot brigades were organized along the lines of the horse artillery with the attached drivers coming under the direct command of the Brigade Captain, the officer of drivers being responsible only for pay and subsistence.[10] Adye notes, 'since the abolition of the battalion guns, the foot artillery were equipped with either five medium 12-pr guns and one heavy 5.5-inch howitzer, five 9-pr guns and one heavy 5.5-inch howitzer, five long or heavy 6-pr guns and one heavy 5.5-inch howitzer, 5 light 6-pr guns and one 5.5-inch howitzer or in the mountains 3-pr guns',[11] but the picture from the Peninsula shows that units changed their ordnance and mixed brigades were equally common.

At Waterloo, the British foot brigades were all organized on the same lines and with similar equipments to those of the horse artillery. The use of the block trail had become standard, as had the size of the wheels, the limbers and the ammunition wagons. To all intents and purposes the old system of the battalion gun had been abandoned and the guns and limbers had been replaced with the same much improved patterns introduced for the horse artillery.

Organisation of the Royal Horse Artillery

The Royal Horse Artillery was a separate arm within the Royal Regiment of Artillery. It was divided into 'troops', named after the cavalry they were initially intended to support; collectively they were called Horse Artillery Brigades. They were designated by letter, 'G Troop, Royal Horse Artillery', but more commonly known by the Captain's name – Mercer's 'G' Troop etc. The armament and establishment of the troops varied considerably, initially each troop was intended to have two 5.5-inch howitzers, two long 3-prs and two long 6-prs. In reality, the first troops only had four guns, and this was increased to six and then eight in 1794. In 1804, they reverted to six guns but the combination and disposition was often changed to suit the circumstances.[12] During the Peninsula War (1807–14), some had two 9-pr guns, two heavy 6-pr guns, three light 6-pr guns and one 5.5-inch howitzer; these were supported by six ammunition wagons, three reserve ammunition wagons, a forge, a spare wheel carriage and a curricle.[13] In 1813 the Duke of Wellington ordered that each Troop should have one long 6-pr, four light 6-pr and one heavy howitzer.[14] At the end of the Peninsula War, each troop had six pieces, usually five 6-pr guns and one 5.5-inch howitzer and all the detachment members were mounted or rode upon the limbers. After 1808 about half the horse artillery units had been re-equipped with the heavier 9-pr guns and one, heavy 5.5-inch howitzer. Each division was supported at first line by ammunition wagons and their limbers with further ammunition reserve at second line, usually carried in four-wheeled wagons. The troop establishment also listed a forge cart, spare wheel cart, and miscellaneous other vehicles.

The establishment of a troop also changed frequently, and was regularly supplemented by the attachment of drivers and horses from the Corps of Drivers.[15] In 1808 the establishment was a troop Captain, his deputy usually a 2nd Captain,

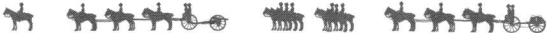

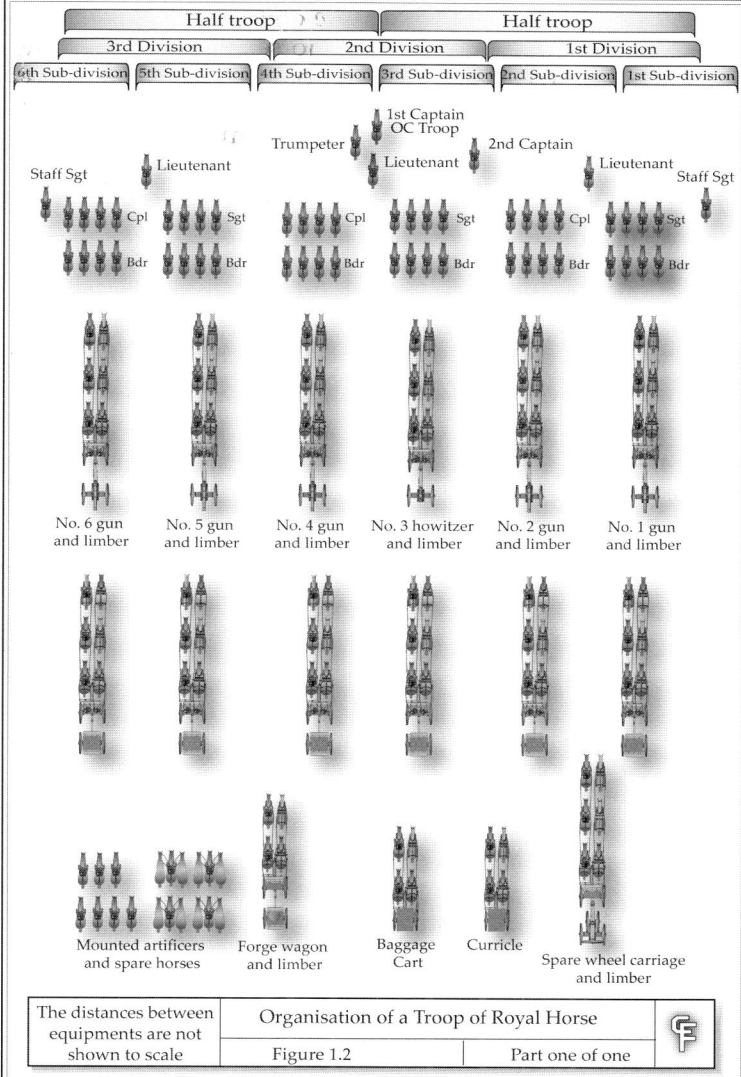

*Figure 1.2.
Organisation of a 6-pr
Royal Horse Artillery
Troop, circa 1809. (The
distances between the
equipments are not
to scale.) The drivers
of the horse artillery
served with the arm
throughout their service
and were dressed in
the same way as the
gunners.*

two 1st Lieutenants and one 2nd Lieutenant; each to command one division. The non-commissioned officers consisted of two Staff Sergeants, three Sergeants, three Corporals and six Bombardiers. There were eighty gunners and sixty drivers, with 7 artificers and 1 trumpeter; in all 167 men with 56 riding horses and 108 draught horses. This establishment is difficult to resolve, but it appears each gun was allocated eight draught horses and each wagon six and the forge curricle and baggage wagon four each. Even so there appears to be a surplus of six drivers probably needed to control the spare horses. The establishment of 80 gunners is also difficult to reconcile, but as the actual strength of a unit varied and rarely matched the establishment, this surplus may well have been non-existent. In any event, there were ample duties where extra personnel could be deployed.[16] In 1813, the horse artillery was equipped with five light 6-pr guns and one light 5.5-inch howitzer.[17] Mercer gives his establishment at Waterloo as five 9-pr guns and one heavy 5.5-inch howitzer (the right gun of the centre division), each with 8 draught horses. He had nine ammunition wagons with six horses each, one spare wheel carriage with six horses and a forge, curricle and an officers' baggage cart each with four draught horses. This gave 120 draught horses. He had six detachments of eight men, two senior NCOs, two farriers and one collar maker, all mounted. This gave 53 riding horses not including the 17 officers' mounts. There were also 30 spare horses whose type is not specified and six mules used to carry officers' baggage, a total of 226 animals in all.

His manpower consisted of five officers and one Surgeon, a Sergeant Major, a Quarter Master Sergeant, three Sergeants, three Corporals, six Bombardiers, one farrier, three shoeing smiths, two collar makers, one wheeler and two trumpeters with eighty gunners and 84 drivers, 198 personnel in all; plus Mr Coats the Commissariat officer and his country drivers and wagons to carry the rations and forage. His troop was supplemented with extra drivers when re-equipped with 9-pr guns each with eight horses, but it did not receive the additional gunners the 9-pr guns warranted. Here again it may be that the extra drivers were used to control the horses.[18] Details of the establishment of a horse artillery troop in 1813 are given in Table A1 of Appendix A at the end of Part One.

Royal Artillery Drivers

At the start of the war the Royal Artillery hired civilian drivers and horses to move the guns of the foot and siege artillery, but this proved so unsatisfactory that in September 1794 a permanent corps of 'Captains, Commissaries and Drivers' was established. Parties of men and horses of this corps were attached to field artillery brigades as the situation demanded and throughout the period the foot artillery had to rely upon horses and drivers that belonged to another corps. The horse artillery soon recruited their own drivers and horses as an integral part of the troop. In 1801, a Royal Warrant ordered the 366 drivers of horse artillery to be mustered and paid as horse artillery, although drivers from the corps were still often attached to horse artillery units to provide additional personnel, but from this point on the horse artillery drivers were an inherent part of the troop.[19]

The corps of Captains, Commissaries and Drivers was disbanded in 1801 and replaced by a similar body, the 'Corps of Gunner Drivers'. The strength of this corps in 1792 is given as seven troops consisting of 1 Captain Commissary, 2 Lieutenants Commissary, 2 Staff Sergeants, 4 Sergeants, 6 First Corporals, 6 Second Corporals, 6 farriers, 3 smiths, 4 collar makers, 150 drivers, 25 riding horses and 328 draught horses.[20]

This corps proved equally unsatisfactory and was disbanded and replaced in 1806 by the 'Corps of Royal Artillery Drivers' who, while adopting the artillery style of dress, still remained as a separate corps to the artillery. They now came more fully under the auspices of the military side of the Board of Ordnance and their Commandant, General Douglas, was quartered at Woolwich.[21] This corps had its own officers and NCOs but when serving in the field it answered to officers of the unit in which they served. In 1808, there were eight troops of drivers each of some 554 men of which 450 were drivers, and 1,020 horses of which 75 were riding and 945 for draught. In 1815, this corps was reduced by four troops, and four more in 1816 when all the officers were placed on half pay and officers of the horse artillery placed in command. The Corps of Royal Artillery Drivers was disbanded in 1822 and their duties were taken over by the artillery.

Known by the nickname the 'Wee Gee Corps' the drivers were not highly regarded by the artillery with whom they served and artillery personnel often resented the similarity of dress. A brigade inspection of 1798 notes each gun was drawn by three horses in file with hired drivers in white smocks with blue collar and cuffs. Mercer remarks:

> The first brigades … were formed by Major Spearman in 1800 … They consisted of medium 12-prs, I think six each (there were two brigades), drawn by six horses each, two and two, the drivers (then a new corps) mounted as postillions – quite a novelty … At the same time Lieutenant (now Colonel) Wallace was drilling another brigade of light 6-prs for the same destination, but to be attached as battalion guns to the Guards. The equipment of these was entirely different from Spearman's brigades. The guns were drawn by three horses each, with common cart harness and chain traces. These were conducted by contract drivers, dressed in canvas frocks, like our gunners' undress, with blue fall-down collars. One walked by the leader, the other by the wheelers, and both carried long waggon whips. [22]

Details of the manning for drivers and horses serving in foot brigades at home and abroad are given in Tables A.2 and A.3 of Appendix A at the end of Part One.

Artillery Strengths

The history of the units within the artillery, the horse artillery 'troops' and foot artillery 'brigades', is well covered elsewhere and the following information is given in order that the lay reader may gain some insight into the artillery placed into field use. British artillery was in limited supply throughout the Napoleonic Wars and particularly in the opening stages of the Peninsular War. Even during the final stages, the French usually had superiority artillery, but the standards of British artillery had improved greatly and the horse artillery had come to represent the very best of its type. In 1798 the total number of field guns available in England was 126 light 6-pr guns for the battalion role, 30 light 6-pr guns for the horse artillery, 41 medium 12-pr guns, 66 long 6-pr guns and 40 5.5-inch howitzers. [23]

The first British artillery units in the Peninsula were the foot brigades of Geary and Raysford, each equipped with five 6-pr guns and one light 5.5-inch howitzer plus a reserve brigade with five 9-pr guns and one heavy 5.5-inch howitzer. These were supplemented by Lawson's half brigade with a further five 6-pr guns and one light 5.5-inch howitzer. They were split into half brigades and allocated out to the various line brigades of infantry. In November 1808, two troops of horse artillery arrived (Downman's 'B' Troop and Evelegh's 'C' Troop), these were each equipped with five 6-pr guns and one light 5.5-inch howitzer. Apart from a reserve maintained at Lisbon these were all withdrawn to England after the retreat to Corunna in January 1809.[24] In 1809 Wellington's total British artillery in the Peninsula was five medium 12-pr guns, five long or heavy 6-pr guns, nine light 6-pr guns, two heavy 5.5-inch howitzers and five light 5.5-inch howitzers. This included the ordnance of the two troops of horse artillery. (It is interesting to note that the carriages of the howitzers and the 3-pr guns were reported as being of the 'old pattern' and 'unsuited for the country').[25] All together at the end of 1809 there were two troops of horse artillery and five companies of foot artillery.[26]

The artillery of the New Orleans expedition in 1814 was equipped with only twelve field guns; two 9-prs, four 6-prs, one heavy 5.5-inch howitzer, one light 5.5-inch howitzer and four light 3-prs and Captain Lane's rocket equipment. There were also three 5.5-inch brass mortars under the command of the Royal Marine Artillery. [27]

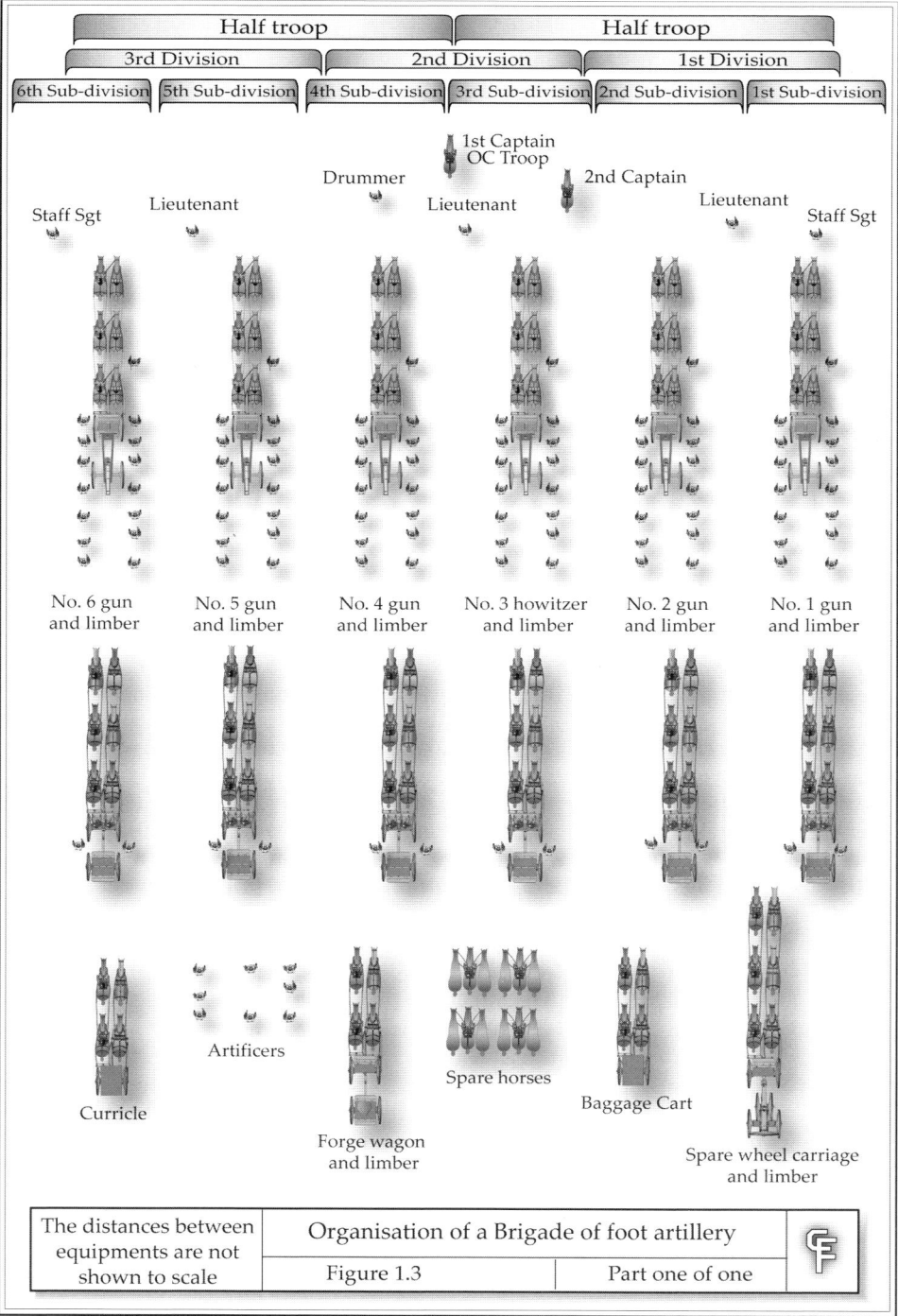

Half troop				Half troop		
3rd Division		2nd Division		1st Division		
6th Sub-division	5th Sub-division	4th Sub-division	3rd Sub-division	2nd Sub-division	1st Sub-division

1st Captain
OC Troop

Drummer   2nd Captain

Staff Sgt   Lieutenant   Lieutenant   Lieutenant   Staff Sgt

No. 6 gun and limber   No. 5 gun and limber   No. 4 gun and limber   No. 3 howitzer and limber   No. 2 gun and limber   No. 1 gun and limber

Artificers

Spare horses

Curricle

Baggage Cart

Forge wagon and limber

Spare wheel carriage and limber

The distances between equipments are not shown to scale	Organisation of a Brigade of foot artillery	
	Figure 1.3	Part one of one

Figure 1.3. Foot artillery brigade, circa 1810. Now grouped along the lines of the horse artillery, the foot brigades were equipped and operated in a similar manner except that the detachment personnel were not mounted and marched with the guns. The use of 15-men detachments was being phased out and at Waterloo the foot artillery units were equipped in this manner, and most were manned to the more usual 9 men per gun supplemented by extra personnel when available.

At Waterloo there were eight troops of Royal Horse Artillery: Ross's 'A' Troop had five 9-pr guns and one heavy 5.5-inch howitzer as did Mercer's 'G' Troop and Ramsay's 'H' Troop. Bean's 'D' Troop had five 6-pr guns and one heavy 5.5-inch howitzer as did Gardiner's 'E' Troop and Webber Smith's 'F' Troop. Bull's 'I' Troop had six heavy 5.5-inch howitzers and Whinyates 2nd Rocket Troop had five 6-pr guns as well as rockets and one rocket cart. There were also seven brigades of British foot artillery: Bolton's Brigade (Alm's Company, 9th Battalion) with four 9-pr guns and two heavy 5.5-inch howitzers. The brigades of Roger, Sandham (Roger's Company and Sandham's Company, both of the 3rd Battalion), the brigade of Sinclair (Gordon's Company, 3rd Battalion) and Lloyd (Lloyd's Company 10th Battalion), was each equipped with five 9-pr guns and one heavy 5.5-inch howitzer. Unett's and Brome's brigades, each with five 9-pr guns and one heavy 5.5-inch howitzer were detached. It should be noted there is some disagreement among the sources regarding the ordnance shown for each unit. [28]

The Piece

The manufacture of guns or more properly the 'pieces' of the period have been well covered in other books. As the ordnance itself usually outlasted the carriages, there are many surviving examples of the different pieces, although none relating to the long 6-pr have been traced. In brief then, guns are designed to achieve the greatest muzzle velocity for the projectile within the limits imposed by weight and length. The howitzer was designed to fire explosive shells and was much shorter in the barrel, being a compromise between a mortar and the gun with the ability to fire a larger round, but without the weight penalty of the larger weapon and the longer bore. It was used to fire at high elevations to facilitate plunging fire over the heads of friendly forces, something a gun could not do unless placed on elevated ground. The design of brass (more properly bronze or gun-metal in the proportions of 8 or 10 parts of tin to 100 parts of copper[29]), smooth bore, muzzle-loading guns had settled into a standard pattern by the start of the century. The rigid adherence to a set of mathematical proportions allocating the metal to each part of the gun was no longer used and the pieces of the period were built to meet their purpose rather than to a set of rules, although there were many different, and some much older, patterns and types in use throughout the empire.

The parts of the piece were known by specific terms and names. Starting at the muzzle of the piece (A), there were muzzle mouldings of two different diameters (b) (notionally three for a gun and two for a howitzer or mortar), these lead to the lip of the muzzle swell (c). The muzzle swell then reduced the diameter towards a raised band, flanked by two smaller bands, and known as the muzzle astragal and fillets (d). These marked the end of the muzzle and the start of the chase (BC), which widened to a maximum at the second reinforce (C). The chase usually carried the appropriate crest and cipher of the Master General of the Board of Ordnance (1784 to 1795, Charles, Duke of Richmond; 1795 to 1801, Charles, Marquis Cornwallis; 1801 to 1806 and 1807 to 1810, John, Earl of Chatham; 1806 to 1807, Francis, Earl of Moria; 1810 to 1818, Henry Earl Mulgrave). On some pieces partway along the chase were a chase astragal and fillets (e), which separated the chase from the chase girdle (f). The thickest part of the piece was divided into the second reinforce (CE) and the first reinforce (EH). After the second reinforce ring and ogee (g) came the trunnion and shoulders (D). These used to be a calibre in diameter and length but guns of this period no longer adhered to these proportions, but the trunnions were still placed with their centres aligned with the bottom axis of the bore and positioned to ensure there should be more weight at the rear – to prevent the gun kicking up when fired.

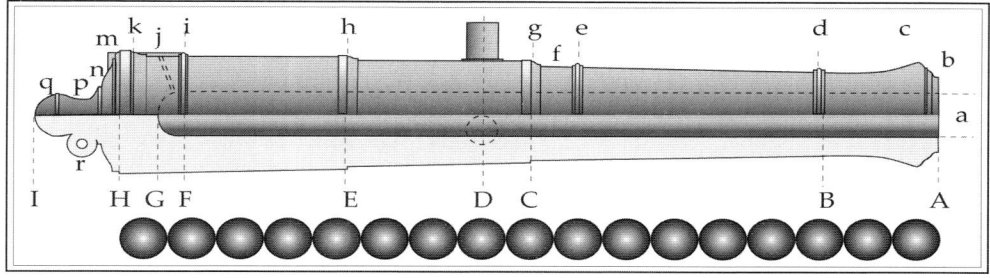

Figure 1.4. The parts of the piece and the scale of calibres. The muzzle (AB), the chase (BC), the second reinforce (CE), the first reinforce (EH) and the cascable (HI). The trunnions are at (D) and rings for the elevation mechanism have been added below the neck cascable (r). Note on a British gun, the top of the trunnions align with the centre of the bore. The first reinforce ogee (h) and the chase girdle astragal and fillets (e) were not fitted on pieces of Blomefield design.

The next band was the first reinforce ring and ogee (h). The first reinforce (EH) carried the crest and cipher of the monarch and had the thickest metal round the bore. It was divided by the vent field astragal and fillets (i), behind which was the vent field (j). The vent field (FG) and the breech (GH) were followed by the 'base ring and ogee' (k), which formed the largest diameter of the piece. The length of the piece was measured from the rear of the base ring to the muzzle (AH), behind the base ring were the cascable (HI), with fillets and breech mouldings (n) decreasing the diameter of the piece to the neck (p) and the button of the cascable (q). The button was designed to take one end of a sling for lifting the gun, the other end being attached to a handspike inserted in the bore. Also fitted to the underside of the cascable were the attachment rings for the elevating mechanism (r). The upper part of the breech moulding also carried a block and screw for the attachment of a tangent sight (m). The length of the bore reached from the muzzle to the rear of the chamber (AG).

The vent was a most important part of the piece. It was a small hole in the vent field inclined at some 101 degrees to the axis – so designed that the pressure of the charge would blow the remains of the tube or quill clear of the gun, the internal diameter was 0.2 inch but the gas of the burning powder soon enlarged the vent. When this happened, the vent was drilled out and a copper screw or bush, which was much less prone to burning, inserted; a process termed bouching. A gun could be put out of action by spiking; a metal spike about 4 inches long was driven into the vent and snapped off close to the vent field. [30]

Mortars and howitzers were constructed in a rather different manner to guns. A mortar was a short piece with a large bore and was primarily intended to fire shells from a high angle with the trunnions at the breech end of the piece. Their use was usually restricted to siege trains, bomb ketches and fortresses.

The pieces usually survived a lot longer than the carriages and it was quite common to find much older ordnance on the inventory particularly in the Colonies. Some pieces, including some of the 5.5-inch howitzers and the medium 12-pr guns, were fitted with handles placed at the point of balance – these were called dolphins after the earlier pieces, as they were often cast in the shape of the animal.

The howitzer was similar to the mortar in construction, but it had the trunnions in the centre of the piece, and, unlike the gun, they were aligned level with the axis of the bore.

Like the mortar, the howitzer was intended to fire shells, but where the mortar had a fixed quadrant elevation of 45 degrees (the range being adjusted by altering the weight of the charge or a different size of quoin), the howitzer could be fired at variable elevations and azimuth against targets in the field. They were often fitted with a dispart patch or sight moulded to the muzzle. Dispart was a measure of the difference in distance of the muzzle from the axis of the bore to the larger diameter base ring. It provided the gunner with a direct line of sight parallel to the bore of the piece. [31]

Brass guns continued to be the preferred armament for the field artillery in spite of their expense when compared with iron guns. Brass guns weighed less for a given nature, were considered to be cooler with constant fire and more durable. Generally, brass guns were expected to last about 3,000 rounds while those of iron would reveal stresses much earlier. As an interesting aside, bronze or 'gunmetal' was an expensive commodity and the senior Royal Artillery Officer had the long-standing right to claim the bells of any place and its dependencies captured by siege, or compensation in lieu. As the value of scrap brass at the time was £84 17s per ton, it is understandable why this policy was carried out with some enthusiasm. [32]

Windage

This was the difference in the size of the bore of the piece and the diameter of the shot. In guns of this period, a windage of 0.2 inches was not uncommon and this would have increased with the use of the piece. The difference in size was necessary to allow for rust, inaccuracies of casting, fouling of the bore of the gun and the thickness of any tin straps attaching shot to a wooden bottom. The difference in size and the weight of the shot caused it to sit on the bottom of the bore with all the windage above it; the first action of the charge was to force the shot down and forwards and this produced ring-like indentations in the bore over time. In practice, the ball would bounce from one side of the bore to the other as it travelled down the barrel. This zigzagging motion meant that as it exited the barrel it would tend be to one side or the other. It was rarely in line with the axis of the piece and the resultant trajectory could be quite different to that intended.

Point Blank and the Line of Metal Range

The term 'point blank', originally from the French 'blanc' and referring to the white centre of a target, had different meanings, usually dependant on the nation concerned. The British definition of point blank during this period was the same as that used to define the line of metal.[33] In the British artillery, the definition of point blank during the Napoleonic era is defined as follows. A line is drawn through the centre of the bore and parallel to the ground. On leaving the bore, the round rose in a notional parabola and descended under gravity to a point where it passed back through the axis. This was the point blank range, also known as the 'line of metal' range. The range at which it occurred varied for each nature of piece. Other interpretations of point blank considered it to be the distance where the shot first struck the ground, which in the British service of the period was the point of 'first graze'.

To engage targets beyond point blank, elevation was required and to engage targets before it, depression. How much elevation or depression was usually a matter of experience, although gunner officers were given lists of range tables while under training at Woolwich and these were copied with great care into personal notebooks.

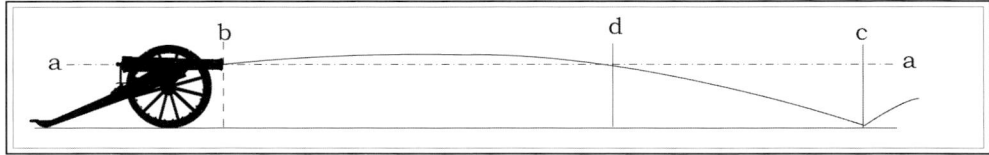

Figure 1.5. Point blank. A line 'aa' is drawn through the centre of the bore and parallel to the ground. On leaving the bore at 'b', the round rose in a notional parabola and descended under gravity to a point where it passed through the axis at point 'd'. Other interpretations of point blank considers it to be the distance where the shot hit the ground at 'c'.

It was quite possible to fire out to ranges of 4,000 yards with a smooth bore gun and 45 degrees of elevation. However, such fire would have been effectively useless in the field artillery as the extra weight required for the carriage to achieve this elevation would have been prohibitive and the ability to observe the fall of shot practically impossible.[34]

Aiming the Gun

The aiming of a gun in the vertical axis was quite straight forward. The trail of the gun was moved until the axis of the barrel was aligned with the target, usually achieved by moving the trail of the gun carriage so that the centre of the bore aligned with a vertical through the target; for siege work a plumb line was often used. There are no records of any allowances to be made for cross winds, but later trials showed that in order to hit a target at a mile distance it was necessary to point the gun some 400 yards to the right or left of the target, depending upon the nature of the cross wind.

The most advantageous distance for a field gun firing round shot was considered to be the line of metal range and siege guns were often placed at this range to achieve the maximum impact on walls. In the field a 6-pr gun would have a first graze at 500 yards and pass a maximum elevation of some 6 feet – an effective dispart of 58 minutes 27 seconds. The 9-pr was 600 yards, an effective dispart of one degree, 5 minutes and 56 seconds.

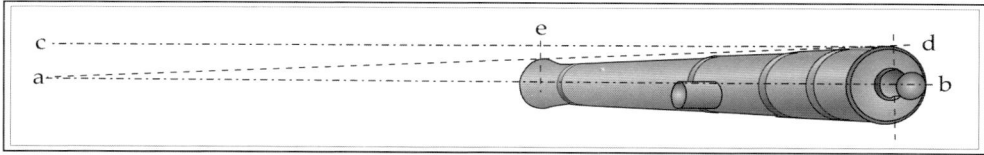

Figure 1.6. The main axis of the piece was a line taken through the centre of the bore (line ab) and a parallel line from the end of the base ring (line cd). The line of metal was (line ad) from the base ring to the muzzle lip (e) and intersected the axis (a). The natural dispart was the vertical distance between the lines (ab) and (cd) at the muzzle (e) and represented the height of a dispart sight often found on howitzers.

The elevation could only be changed by adjustment of the elevating screw. The elevation required to achieve a given range could be a matter of judgment or found by the use of a range table and quadrant. Every officer had his own set of range tables, carefully kept and maintained. The type of ammunition and the size of the cartridge each required consideration in the elevation of the gun. To assist in the application of elevation, each field piece had three notches cut in the lip of the muzzle, aligned to the axis of the bore and a series of lines cut in the base ring. These were known as quarter sights and were used to elevate the gun up to 3 degrees, each line usually representing a quarter of a degree. Higher elevations were applied using tangent scales attached by a small screw into the block at the top of the breech mouldings. Tangent scales were in general use after 1790 and were issued with each gun, the scales being issued in wood as well as brass.[35] The later versions were of a semi-circular brass rod with a notched bracket at the top, the back of the rod had the flat surface marked off in half degrees up to six or seven degrees. When spherical case was introduced in 1803 the rear face was also engraved with the corresponding letter for the fuse to be used and on the round part was engraved the required length of the fuse in tenths of an inch and the range spread over which the spherical case would be effective. Howitzers were often fitted with a dispart patch or sight moulded to the muzzle – dispart was the measure of the difference in distance of the muzzle from the axis of the bore to that of the larger diameter base ring. It provided the gunner with a direct line of sight parallel to the bore of the piece.[36]

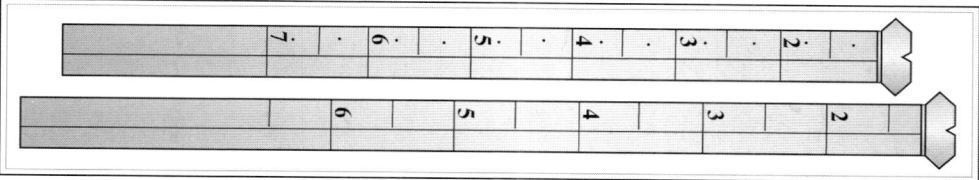

Figure 1.7. Early tangent scales used before the introduction of spherical case. Those shown are for the light 6-pr and the 9-pr gun, the scale for the other ordnance was similar. The flat face was marked with the elevation in half-degrees. The scale was slotted in the rear of the base ring and secured by a screw, when not in use it was carried in the limber.

In field artillery while tangent sights were available, they were rarely used; the gun was first aimed at the target in azimuth – the horizontal plane. Then the elevation was adjusted so the gun was aimed at the target in the vertical plane with a further elevation applied to compensate for the distance the round fell under gravity during the time it took to reach the target. This sequence was known as the 'laying' of the gun. Smooth bore guns in the field were often aimed by eye and the experience of the NCO was a critical factor.

Field Artillery Tactics

In the Napoleonic period the term 'direct fire' was used for a round striking the target without first grazing the ground, while in modern parlance it means the target is visible from the gun position. During the Napoleonic period indirect techniques where the target is not visible from the gun were in their infancy and rarely used. It was essential that the gunner could see the effect of his shot to correct it. This was only achievable with the target in sight and the effective range of the gun was limited accordingly, and while most guns could achieve a much longer range they were usually limited to the visible distance and then only while the target was not obscured by a cloud of smoke, dust, men or horses. The exception was where howitzers and mortars were employed to send plunging fire, spherical case or shells, over the heads of friendly troops into areas or buildings. A practice regularly adopted by the mortars on ships and at Waterloo where 'Bull's' Troop were equipped with six heavy 5.5-inch howitzers used with great effect to fire over the defenders of Hougoumont.

Thus, most field artillery of the Napoleonic period was applied where the target was visible from the gun position and elevation was usually restricted to a few degrees. This gave a flat trajectory and meant the guns were only able to fire over the heads of friendly forces if the guns were elevated on higher ground or on the flanks. In practical terms the effective range for light equipments was limited to some 1,500 yards – or the visible distance and range table were produced giving the graze points of the different guns at various elevations and charge sizes.

Engagement Parameters

The main application of fire from field artillery was against the massed ranks of infantry or cavalry, counter battery fire being rarely practiced and often against orders. The general parameters used to consider the type of engagements were based upon experience of the time and specific trials conducted in Hyde Park in 1802 and in Jersey during 1805.[37] (During this trial the effective range of a light 6-pr gun was considered as 600 yards as the use of spherical case had not been introduced.) The speed at which infantry advanced was based upon a man walking at a moderate pace of 200 yards in one minute (7 mph). In quick time, they were expected to cover the 200 yards in half a minute (14 mph); but where infantry were advancing in line, it was generally considered that, depending upon the terrain, it took at least 5 minutes to cover 500 yards (between 3 and 4 mph).

Infantry were considered to form up at some 1,200 yards, they then advanced in line or column at a notional rate of 100 yards in one minute and this transit would expose them to artillery fire for some 11 to 12 minutes. The speed at which cavalry advanced was also studied. They were considered to walk at 3 mph, trot at 7 mph and gallop at 14 mph; this is slower than modern figures but it should be remembered that the light cavalry horse carried a load of some 280lb and it was required that they never arrived at the charge, blown.[38] The form of engagement would vary but General Regulations for the Cavalry proposed they advance at the walk to 400 yards from their target.

They would then advance at the trot for a further 150 yards, the next 170 yards were at the gallop and finally the last 80 yards at the full charge. Assuming they formed up at 1,200 yards the cavalry would be at the walk for 800 yards, some 9 minutes of exposure time, the trot for some 44 seconds, the gallop for 25 seconds and the charge, a further 8 seconds. This would place them in the line of fire for just over ten minutes, but in the test carried out the cavalry actually covered the distance from 600 yards in 115 seconds, although more generally they were expected to cover 500 yards in under two minutes. [39]

During the trials the artillery fired every 8 seconds, but this time must be considered with caution. While there is ample evidence to support this rate of fire if the cartridge and shot were rammed together, the records of the trial make it clear the time did not allow for any change of elevation.

When under attack from infantry the artillery were expected to commence firing at 5 degrees of elevation and a range to first graze of some 1,200 yards. They would have some 11.5 minutes to fire upon closing infantry and 5 minutes to fire upon cavalry. In this time, it was expected with a 3-pr gun that '37 rounds could be fired at infantry and 15 rounds at cavalry, allowing 5 rounds or 7 case can be fired in one minute by the lighter ordnance'. A 3-pr field piece was expected to be loaded and

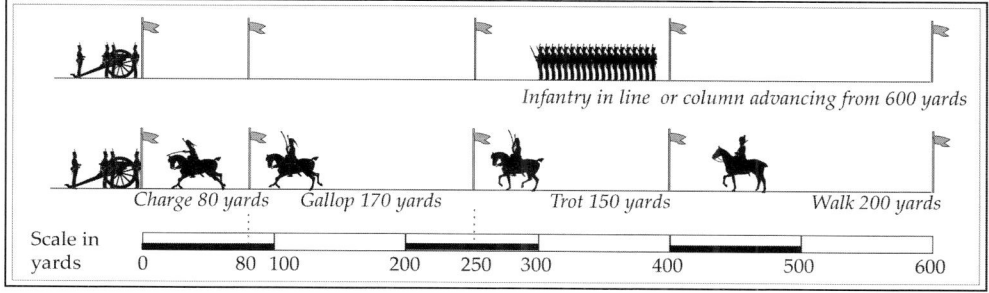

Figure 1.8. Trials were carried out to determine the time taken by attacking cavalry and infantry to cover the ground in front of an artillery piece and the number of times the gun could fire when under such attack. Tests were also carried out to determine the number of times the infantry could fire when under attack from cavalry or other infantry.

fired 8 times in a minute but it was observed 'as the smoke cannot clear from before the gun in that time, the before mentioned allowance is thought a good one to do execution'.

Heavier guns took a longer time to load and a 6-pr was expected to fire 11 rounds against cavalry and 28 against infantry.[40] In later engagements, after the introduction of spherical case shot, it was practice to fire seven spherical case or shell at a range of 1,500 yards to 600 yards; then as the enemy closed, two round shot at a range of 650 yards to 350 yards followed by two common case at a range of 350 yards and below. When the attack was by infantry, the detachment fired nineteen spherical case or shell at a range of 1,200 yards down to 650 yards followed by seven round shot at a range of 650 yards to 350 yards. Between 350 yards and 100 yards they fired eight heavy common case and as the enemy closed to under 100 yards, the gun fired two further light common case. [41]

In the field tests conducted in Hyde Park in 1802, a dragoon commenced his attack at 600 yards. He walked his horse 200 yards in 95 seconds, trotted a further 150 yards in 28 seconds, galloped 170 yards in 13 seconds and charged the last 80 yards in 8 seconds. During this transit, a light 6-pr gun fired 13 times some at 9 seconds per round and in later experiments in Jersey the gun fired 14 times in 117 seconds. This is a round every 8 seconds, which seems to be an accepted figure for a light 6-pr gun but it represents an unattainable rate of fire where the limbers are 25 yards to the rear as the ammunition men would have to run a 50-yard round trip to collect each round in the same 8 seconds.[42] Where the infantry trials were concerned, the infantry formed at 250 yards and marched towards the gun; the last 80 yards were carried at 'step out and charge'. This transit took 117 seconds in which time the gun fired 14 times.

Muller gave the following casualty figures from a 6-pr gun against cavalry:

1,600 yards to 800 yards	four killed, two wounded
800–400 yards	six killed, four wounded
Under 400 yards	nine killed, twenty-three wounded

Against infantry the figures were:

1,600–1,200 yards	four killed, four wounded
1,200–800 yards	eight killed, two wounded
800–400 yards	sixteen killed, ten wounded
Under 400 yards	thirty killed, ninety wounded

General Firing Performance

A fully trained detachment could fire and sponge a light 3-pr gun 8 times in a minute. In good conditions a crew could sponge, load and fire a 6-pr in less than 15 seconds, but this could not be sustained and running up the carriage after firing often took much longer. (The average recoil for a light gun was some 3.5 feet.) Working flat out, a crew could achieve eight or nine rounds a minute but this was deliberately slowed to prevent accidents. In battle a 6-pr would fire three rounds a minute for common case and two rounds a minute for round shot; for a light 3-pr, 5 round shot and 7 case were the norm. These figures would probably be improved upon as the enemy closed and light case was used.[43] At close range, the 3-pr could be double shotted, but it was common practice to fire with case in front of shot. The effect of such fire was recalled by Mercer in his *Journal of the Waterloo Campaign*:

> 'Every man stood to steadily at his post, the guns ready, loaded with round shot first and case over it; the tubes were in the vents; the portfires glared and spluttered behind the wheels; and my word alone was wanted to hurl destruction on that goodly show … I … allowed them to advance unmolested until the head of the column might have been about fifty or sixty yards from us, and gave the word, 'Fire!'. The effect was terrible. Nearly the whole leading rank fell at once; and the round shot penetrating the column, carried confusion throughout its extent … the fall of every shot was followed by a fall of men and horses like that of grass before a mower's sythe'.[44]

No recorded rates of fire have been found for the 9-pr, but it would have been at a slower rate than the light 6-pr which also carried an immediate supply of round shot in the right axle box of the gun, something the 9-pr did not. However, as the cartridges were carried in the limber, the number 12 brought up the cartridges in a cartouche to provide an immediate supply of ammunition and this practice is alluded to during the Battle of Waterloo, as is the carrying of both cartridges and round shot in the same cartouche and the practice of loading case over round shot. It was common practice to speed up the rate of fire by only sponging out the bore after every third or fourth round. Details of ranges firing two round shot are given in Table A4 of Appendix A at the end of Part One.

Colour of Artilllery Equipment

There is some dispute between the different authorities regarding the colour of artillery equipment. The contemporary paintings show a dark grey colour, but modern artists seem to prefer a blue-grey. As far as can be determined, during the Napoleonic period all wood and ironwork of artillery equipment was painted to protect it and the brass guns were polished when circumstances warranted but were usually left dull on campaign.[45] There are several indicators that the carriages were painted; Dickson recorded in December 1809 that his brigade had been sent to Quinta Nova for just that purpose.[46] The facilities in the Royal Carriage Department included 'painters stores and sheds for the painting of carriages' and there are several references to the cost of paint colours and oil.[47] One reference in 1812 specifically refers to gun carriages painted in a 'lead' colour.[48] One of the few paintings to show such equipment is David Morier's 'Royal Artillery in the Low Countries'; this shows a darkish grey, which matches the description 'lead'.[49] According to later records of 1858 when white zinc oxide had replaced white lead, all wood was painted a grey, called 'lead', later 'white lead':

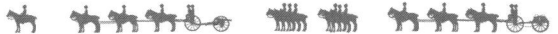

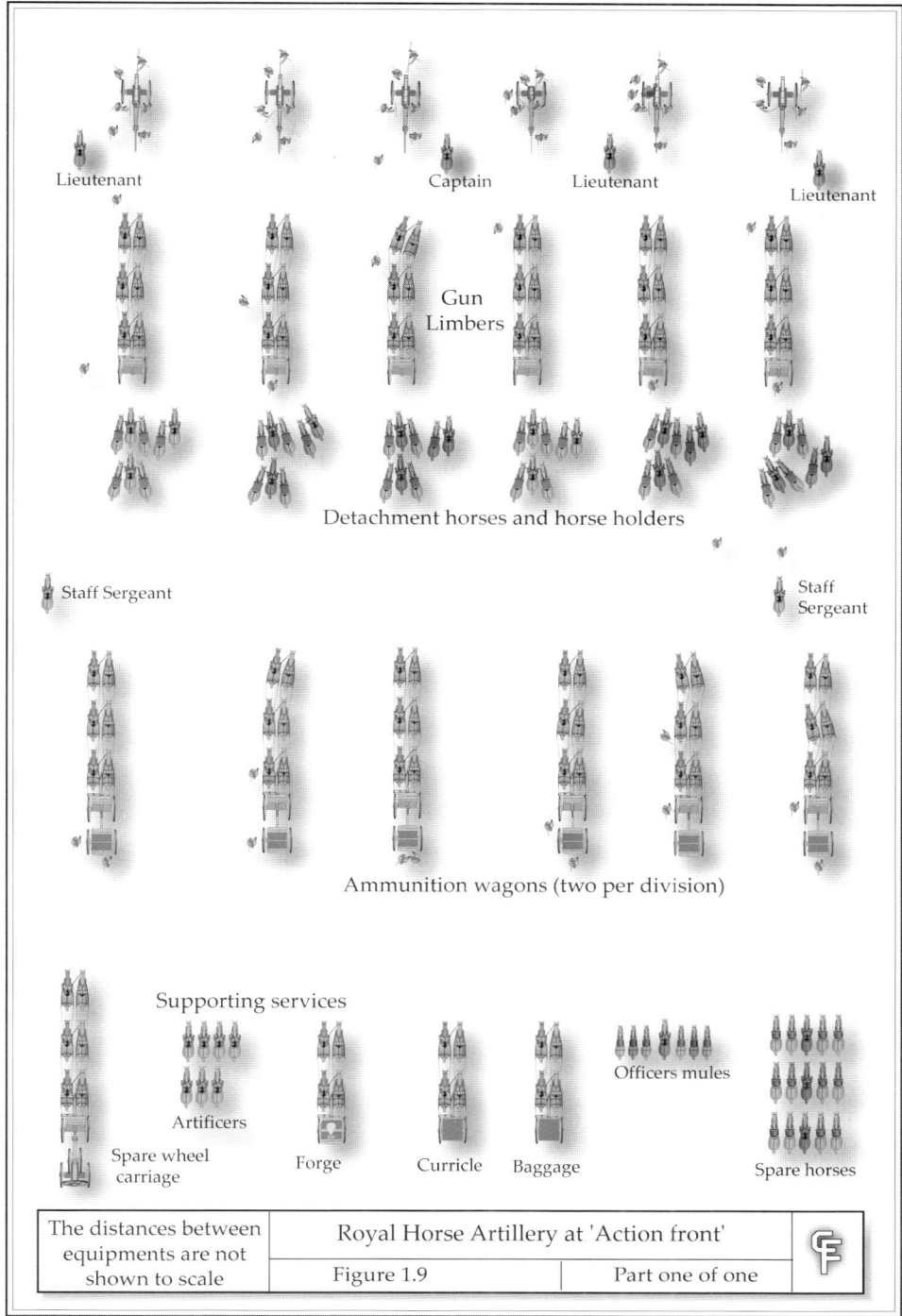

Lieutenant   Captain   Lieutenant   Lieutenant

Gun
Limbers

Detachment horses and horse holders

Staff Sergeant   Staff
                                                      Sergeant

Ammunition wagons (two per division)

Supporting services

Officers mules

Artificers

Spare wheel   Forge   Curricle   Baggage   Spare horses
carriage

The distances between equipments are not shown to scale	Royal Horse Artillery at 'Action front'	
	Figure 1.9	Part one of one

Figure 1.9. 6-pr horse artillery troop in 'action front'. (The distance between the equipments is not to scale
and should be 15 yards between guns and 15 yards from gun to leading horse muzzle with the support carts
and wagons further to the rear.) The limbers are under the command of the Senior NCOs who also control
the movement of the ammunition wagons back to the ammunition park as the ammunition in the limbers was
expended. The distance to be covered by the ammunition numbers is clearly considerable.

The principal ingredient, used in making paint in this Department, is the oxide of zinc. The raw oxide is mixed with raw linseed oil, in the proportion of two gallons of oil to one cwt. of oxide, it is then incorporated in a pug mill, and afterwards passed between stone rollers until it acquires a uniform consistency; in this state it is termed 'ground white zinc', and is stored in kegs until required for use. The proportions of the ingredients for making the several kinds of paint used in the service are as follows:

For Carriages, &c. for Home Service

Ground oxide, of white zinc	112lb
Lamp-black	6lb
Oil (boiled), for grinding	3 quarts
Manganese, as a drier	8 ounces
Raw linseed oil, for mixing	2.5 gallons
Boiled linseed oil, to give body and gloss	2.5 gallons
Turpentine, for thinning and drying	2.5 gallons

The above ingredients are carefully incorporated and strained through a wire sieve to make 197lb. For tropical climates, where a lighter colour is required, the lampblack is reduced to 1lb mixed with one pint of boiled oil.

Black Paint, for Iron Work

Lamp-black	56lb
Boiled oil, for grinding	8 gallons
Boiled oil, for mixing	4.5 gallons
Turpentine	1 quart
Red lead for drying	2lb
Litharge for drying	4lb

The above ingredients are carefully incorporated and strained through a wire sieve to make 164lb. [50]

There is no evidence to support the use of any other colourant and while ironwork was painted black the metal ends of the shafts, the elevating mechanism, trunnion bearings, inside of the capsquares, axletree arms, linchpins and washers were not painted but 'kept bright' and lightly oiled. Tests conducted with the relevant pigments and oils give two quite different tones of grey.

The re-enactor or modeller should note when lead white is mixed to the above recipe it produced a colour very similar to Dulux, Ebony Mist 3. The zinc white, used after the period, produced a darker grey similar to Dulux Ebony Mist 2. Analysis of the sample of the earlier paint using white lead was sent to the NCS Colour Centre and they provided Natural Colour System reading of 'S 6000-N'. NCS colours can be obtained at a variety of outlets including Dulux, Crown, Johnston and Leyland. A similar analysis was carried out by DG Colour using the 'Munsell' system and this gave a grey scale reading that is nearest to N4.5. A further sample was sent to Humbrol Modelers Paints. The modeller will find their nearest equivalent is Matt Ocean Grey 106, which is equivalent to Revel 47.

In 1861, the colour of British artillery equipment was changed to green, to make the equipment less conspicuous, but this was abandoned in December 1862, and the colour reverted to the original lead colour.

Endnotes to Chapter 1

1. Leslie, 1912: pp. 11, 28–31.
2. Adye, 1813: p. 157.
3. Duncan, 1872: p. 55.
4. Duncan, 1872: pp. 94–5.
5. National Archive, WO 3/36: p. 81 dated 8 June 1802
6. Ibid: p. 54.
7. Dickson, 1908: p. 535.
8. Mercer, 1870: p. 87.
9. WO 1/167: p. 227 dated 6 October 1793
10. Duncan, 1872: pp. 342–3.
11. Adye, 1813: p. 3.
12. Duncan, 1892: pp. 34–6
13. Duncan, 1892: p. 35.
14. Duncan, 1908: p. 902.
15. Ibid: p. 41.
16. Leslie, 1912: p. 2.
17. Adye, 1813: p. 3.
18. Mercer, 1870: pp. 88, 89, 160, 270.
19. Duncan, 1872: p. 136.
20. Ibid: p. 136.
21. Hogg, 1963: p. 541.
22. MacDonald, 1985: p. 56.
23. Duncan, 1872: p. 86.
24. Leslie, 1912: pp. 11, 28–31.
25. Ibid: pp. 74– 5.
26. Ibid: p. 100.
27. Dickson, 1929: p. 93.
28. Siborne, 1993: pp. 184–241; Mercer, 1870: p.87 et al; Duncan, 1892: p. 418.
29. Adye, 1810: p. 218; Adye, 1813: p. 218.
30. Hughes, 1969: pp 34–5.
31. Rogers, 1971: pp. 90
32. Duncan, 1872: p. 167.
33. Adye, 1813: p. 288; Caruana, 1980: pp. 86–94.
34. Hughes, 1969: p. 34.
35. Dickson, 1908: p. 701.
36. Rogers, 1971: p. 90.
37. Russell, 1806: et al.
38. Adye, 1813: p. 219.
39. Russell, 2005: p. 19.
40. Carauna, 1980: pp. 12–14.
41. Hughes, 1969: p. 78.
42. Russell, 1806: pp. 1–3.
43. Hughes, 1969: p. 78.
44. Mercer, 1870: pp. 175, 176.
45. Mercer, 1870: p. 333.
46. Dickson, 1908: pp. 126, 130, 142, 145.
47. Hogg, 1963: pp. 485, 527.
48. Henry, 2003: p.16.
49. Morier, D. *Royal Artillery in the Low Countries*. Royal Collection, catalogue no. 125.
50. HMSO, 1858: p.11.

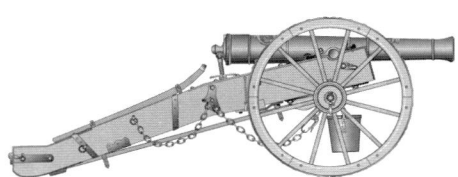

CHAPTER 2

Bracket Trail Gun Carriages

Introduction

The design criteria of the gun carriage for the field artillery was primarily intended to provide the mobility needed to support the army in the field while still meeting the needs and necessities of the function of the piece. The travelling gun carriage had been developed over the years and at the start of this period it had evolved into a gun or piece, mounted upon a trail composed of two long planks or brackets, which were connected to each other by cross pieces called transoms. The brackets were mounted on an axletree with two wheels. This travelling carriage had to be robust enough to carry the weight of the piece, move over rough ground and absorb the energy of the recoil. They were tail heavy and difficult to move, two men were needed to traverse the gun and movement over short distances was achieved by the addition of a small castor wheel, a Hanoverian truck, fitted to the trail and the efforts of at least six men working on drag ropes. When it became necessary to move a gun carriage any significant distance they were attached to a limber consisting of shafts at the front for the draught horse, two wheels and an axletree with a vertical pintle over which the gun carriage was hooked. When joined together, the gun and limber created an articulated four-wheeled vehicle intended to give good traction, manoeuvrability and mobility.

On bad roads and over rough ground the system had several shortcomings. The axles were made of wood and were prone to failure, the wheels for the gun and limber were of different sizes and if one was damaged it was not possible to use the wheels of the other as a spare. The size of the bracket trail has been considered by some to limit the turning circle, but analysis has shown the bracket carriage allowed tighter turns than those of the later block trail carriage, but the small diameter of the limber wheels meant the shafts were set low, putting a great load on the wheel horse. This style of limber left no facility for the carriage of ammunition and a limited supply of ready use ammunition had to be carried at the gun. Many of these problems had been addressed by the introduction of the new light 6-pr battalion gun of 1776,[1] but it was not until the new equipments ordered by the Duke of Richmond in 1793 for the horse artillery came into general use that the later changes to the foot brigade carriage, limber and draught were implemented.

Bracket Carriage Design

The situation regarding the design of field artillery bracket trail carriages at the start of the Napoleonic War is difficult to define, as no surviving examples or detailed illustrations have been located. While the evidence suggests the designs illustrated by Muller[2] and Rudyerd[3] were being replaced, little can be found to confirm this. It is known the design of bracket gun carriages changed in 1776 when a new carriage and limber were introduced into service for the 6-pr battalion gun.[4] These are the same pattern depicted by Rudyerd in 1792 and it is assumed, in the absence of any information to the contrary, at the start of the war this may have been the pattern used by the foot artillery brigades, and they were still being issued to the Colonies as late as 1812.[5] There is an example of this carriage, *circa* 1796, at The Museum of Artillery at Woolwich, England. One part of this puzzle is the shape of the bracket trail; Muller and Rudyerd both show a trail where the cheeks conform to the shape of the piece and widen towards the rear, and this is the style prevalent among the drawings in the sketchbooks of the gentlemen cadets at Woolwich. There is some evidence to suggest this was not always the case and some drawings indicate a bracket gun carriage with parallel cheeks had been introduced similar to those shown in later publications.[6]

Contemporary sketches by Atkinson and Pyne suggest this may be the case but research has failed to find any drawings or equipment to support this, although it is claimed that there are such drawings on the Continent to show a 9-pr gun so mounted. There are illustrations in the *Aide Memoire to the Military Sciences*, which clearly show parallel cheeks, but these are dated 1840 and cannot be relied upon to portray the situation twenty-five years earlier.[7] At the same period, the style of the limber had also been updated; but it is not possible to determine if this is the case for the Napoleonic period.

The author has been unable to locate any contemporary drawings of the medium 12-pr and the carriage for this gun is still something of an enigma. The lack of drawings may be due to the fact the weight of the medium 12-pr meant it effectively went out of use with field artillery before the end of the Napoleonic era. One thing is clear, all the current field guns of the foot artillery brigades were equipped with the bracket trail prior to 1793. They were progressively replaced as the block trails became available, with the possible exceptions of the long 6-pr and medium 12-pr gun, although as they both continued in service after the war, albeit not as light equipments for the field artillery, there is some evidence they too may have been placed on block trail carriages.[8]

Bracket Trail Gun Carriage

The wood used for gun carriages and limbers was always well seasoned with fittings of iron, generally welded to give added strength. The British bracket gun carriage of this period consisted of two shaped, wooden planks called cheeks or brackets, each made from a single piece of wood. These were placed on edge and connected

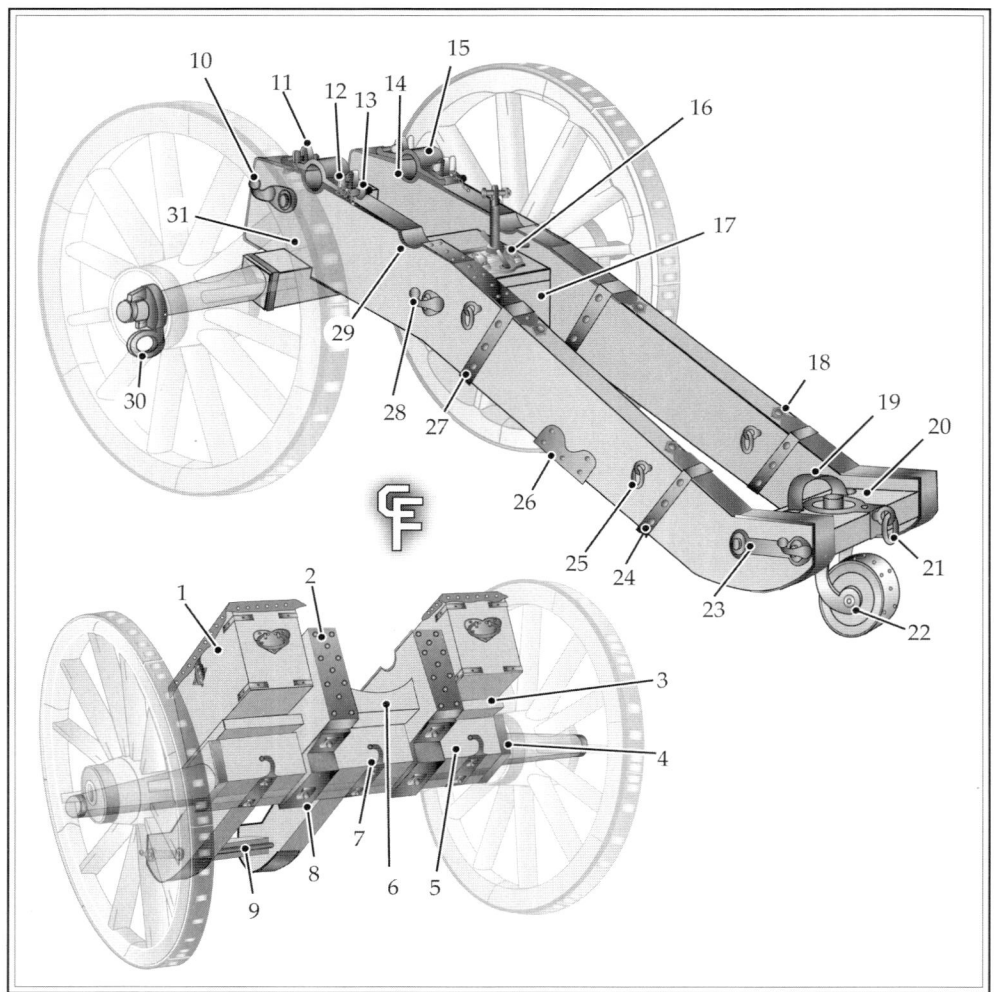

Figure 2.1. Component parts of generic bracket trail carriage with wooden axles. Ammunition side boxes (1), breast or head plate (2), side box shelf (3), axletree hoop (4), axletree (5), breast transom (6), advance or breast hooks (7), axletree band (8), trail transom bolt (9). On the upper drawing the breast transom hook (10), eye bolt (11), double keys with chains and staples (12), joint bolt (13), trunnion plate (14), capsquares (15), elevation mechanism (16), centre transom (17), trail plate (18), traversing hoop, pin and chain (19), pintail plate (20) and traversing ring (21). Hanoverian truck (22), trail transom bolt plate and hook (23), rear side plate (24), side arm or lashing ring (25), locking plate (26), front side plate (27), centre transom bolt and hook (28), transporting trunnion plate (29) drag washer and linchpin (30) and bracket or cheek (31).

together by wooden transoms or cross pieces. The transoms were usually placed in four places: at the trail end of the carriage, at the centre, one supporting the bed and at the front, as the breast transom. Muller and Rudyerd confirm the size and dimensions of the brackets and transoms were prescribed in relation to the calibre of the gun. Adye records the cheeks were lengthened from 94 inches to 104 inches when the elevation became adjustable over a wider 16.5-degree range,[9] but the design still made for a trail heavy carriage requiring considerable effort to move and traverse. The brackets, shaped to facilitate handling of the piece, were angled down at the

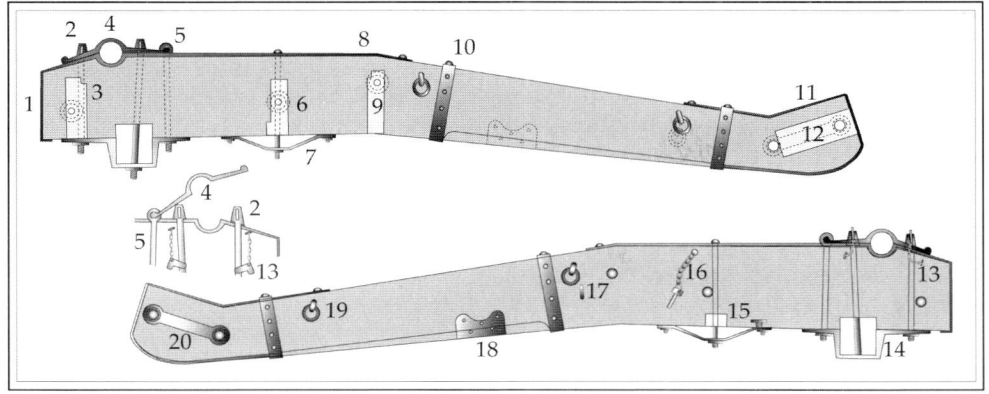

Figure 2.2. Side views of a bracket trail. The breastplate (1), eyebolts (2) the captive capsquare (4), hinged on the ringbolt (5). Breast transom and bolt (3), first centre transom (6) carried a support for a side box shelf (15) assisted by the bracket (7), garnish plate (8) and side plates (10). Trail strapping (11) and the trail transom (12) carried the pintle hole and strengthening side plates (20). Spring keys and chains (13), axletree band (14), the side boxes chained pins (16) and the locking chain was hooked up (17) when not in use. The locking plates (18) and various ringbolts (19).

breech and then straightened out again at the trail where they were rounded off on the lower edge to take the recoil. Metal strapping, with the semi-circular recesses to hold the trunnions, protected the top of the brackets and extended from under the front, around the breast and back to the breech of the gun. The strapping was held in place by garnish and shaped rose bolts. The trunnions were secured to the carriage by curved iron straps termed capsquares. The capsquares were secured to the gun carriage by double layer 'spring keys' driven through eyebolts and the ends opened out locking the capsquares into position. It was noted that:

> Capsquares must always be keyed down, to prevent the key shaking out; they must be opened after they have been driven through the eyebolts.

The eyebolts and ringbolt passed down through metal strapping and the bracket to protrude below where they were fitted with square nuts that also retained the axletree band.[10] The sides of the brackets were fitted with ringbolts and hooks for drag ropes and locking rings for side arms.

Locking plates were placed on the outer face to protect the bracket from the metal tyres of the limber in a tight turn. There is some suggestion parallel brackets had come into service by this period, but it has not been possible to confirm this. Joining the two brackets were the transoms set into mortises on the inside faces and secured in place by transom bolts passing through the brackets and terminating each side with a hook. At the front, the breast transom was usually just wide enough to allow the trunnions to fit into the brackets and was shaped at the top to receive the chase of the gun during transportation. The trail transom was usually wider to accommodate the shape of the piece. The axletree was placed beneath the bracket, just behind the breast transom with the front face aligned with the rear of the trunnions. The function of the bed and centre transom had changed by this time and the bed transom acted to support the improved elevating mechanism. The centre transom acted to support the brackets and in earlier carriages carried an extra storage box on the rear face.

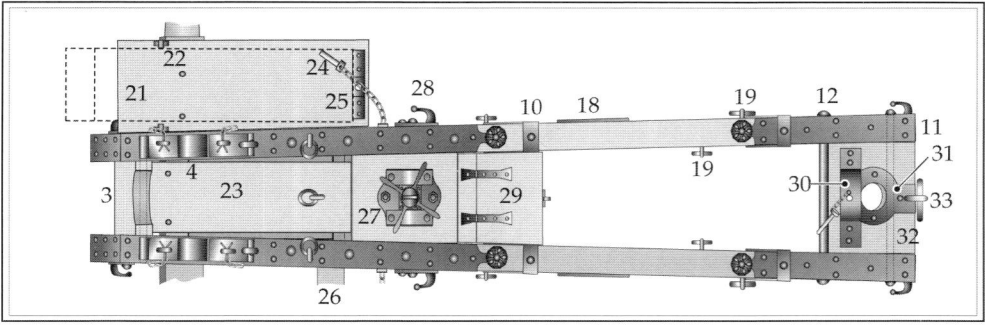

Figure 2.3. Plan view of bracket carriage. The front transom (3), the side box shelf (21) fitted with retainers for the side boxes (22). The side boxes were fitted with metal plates to engage the side lugs and rear bracket (25) where they were secured by a chained pin (24). The centre was fitted with a locker (23) for the carriage of dragropes and pulley blocks. When side boxes were fitted, the first centre transom was extended to form supports (26). The elevation mechanism shelf (27) sat between the first and second centre transom. Bolt hooks were fitted to the brackets for the attachment of dragropes (28) and on early gun carriages; a centre locker was fitted on the rear face of the second centre transom (29). The traversing loop, pin and chain (30), the pintle plate and hole (31) and the traversing ring (33) were fitted to the trail transom (32)

The top face of the trail transom was fitted with a loop and ring to accept the traversing lever and pierced by the pintle hole, which was protected by upper and lower pintle plates nailed to the trail transom. The bracket carriages were issued with a Hanoverian truck – a small, metal tyred, wooden wheel mounted on an iron spindle. When required, to assist manoeuvre in the field, the trail was raised and the castor spindle was inserted into the pintle hole of the trail transom to act as a castor.[11]

Some bracket carriages had a locker between the breast and a centre transom to carry drag ropes; in emergencies, it was used to carry round shot. The side arms were carried strapped to the ringbolts on the brackets. The general arrangement meant the sponge staff was carried on the outside of the right bracket and the handspike and traversing lever on the left. The linstock was strapped to the inside of the right bracket and any fork levers or other side arms on the left. The gun bucket was carried under the axle of the gun and a leather bucket for watering the horses under the limber. Initially, the limber carried no ammunition and side boxes were fitted on shelves over the axles, but as the new pattern limbers came into service, this practice was generally abandoned.

Elevating Mechanism

The method of elevation had also evolved into a more sophisticated mechanism for the field artillery. The old system, by which a screw was passed through a brass block and was allowed to move, had been replaced. The ring of a brass elevating screw (two threads per inch) was now attached by a nut and bolt to circular brackets on the underside of the cascabel button and the elevation applied by a four-spoke hand wheel acting on the screw thread. The hand wheel now sat upon a swinging block made of two pieces through which the elevating screw was free to pass. The box pivoted on two trunnions passing through the horn plates fixed on either side of the base plate by two bolts and the base plate was bolted to the cushion of the trail. As the gun elevated and the cascabel prescribed an arc about the trunnions the box pivoted on the horns to provide a constant vertical. In this manner some 12 degrees of

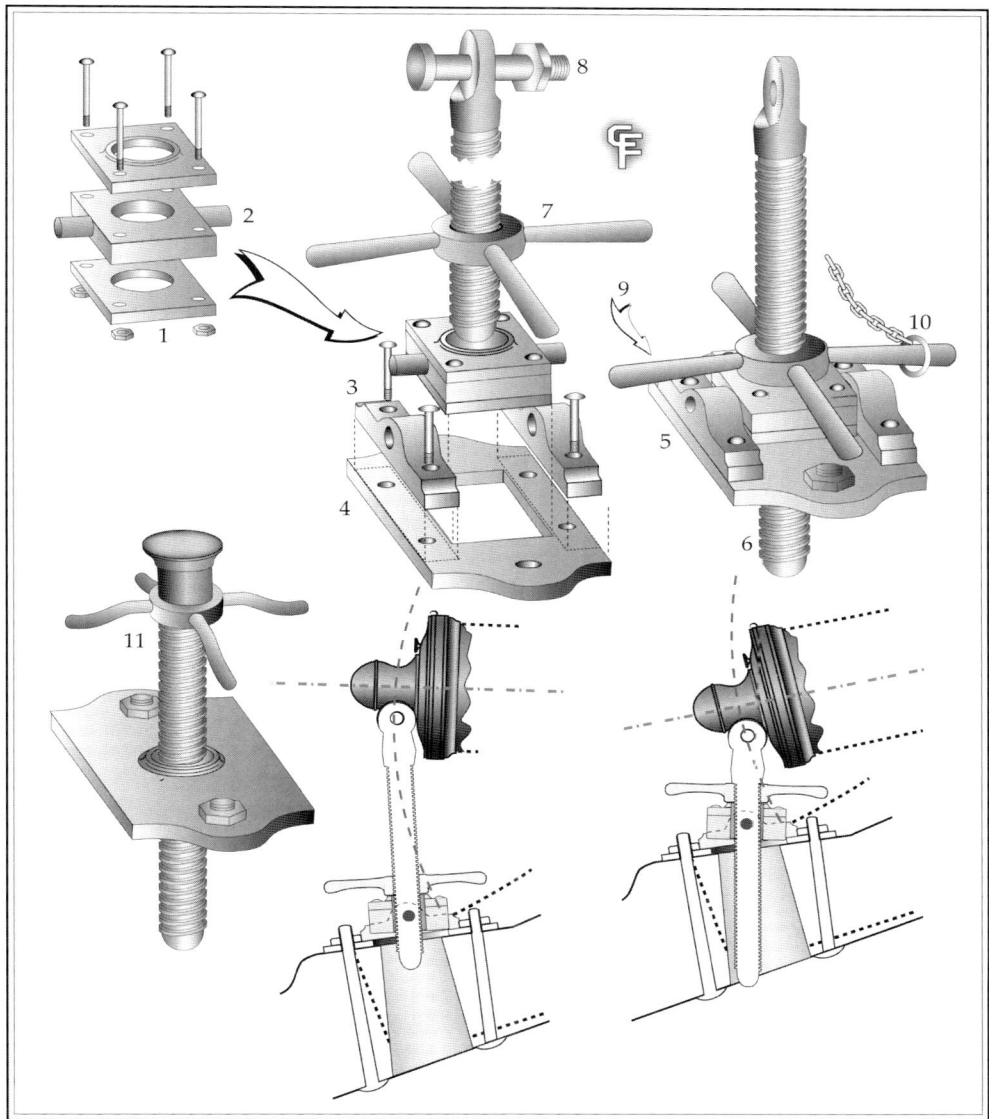

Figure 2.4. Elevating mechanism for both bracket and block trail field carriages. The unthreaded elevation screw box (1) swings on the horns (2) to allow for the change in angle as the gun rotates about the trunnions. The horn plates (3), base plate (4) and complete assembly (5.) The elevating screw (6), hand wheel (7) and the elevation screw nut and bolt (8). The hand wheel (9), locking chain ring (10) looped over one arm of the hand wheel. The elevating mechanism for some pieces had no elevation box and the elevation screw was not attached to the piece (11).

elevation and 6 degrees of depression was possible. To allow for the change in angle of the elevating screw an ovoid hole was cut through the cushion. When the gun was on the move the piece was placed at a high angle of elevation and a chained metal ring was placed over an arm on the hand wheel to prevent it moving. It was noted that:

> All guns when drawn over rough ground shake the box of the elevating screw so much so as to occasion the breech of the gun to sink down as low as the thread of the screw

will allow. A small chain is fixed to the left cheek of the carriage with a ring at the end, which is to be slipped over one of the handles of the hand wheel, and prevents the screw running down. The ring is removed when the gun is pointed by the right hand of the person who elevates the gun.[12]

This elevation mechanism is not to be confused with that often shown where the elevating screw passed through a metal olive rotating in a cupped bed bolted to the trail. This design was not adopted until 1864 when the elevating mechanism for most field ordnance was modified with the exception of the 12-pr guns.[13]

Wooden Axletrees

Prior to the introduction of iron axles for the new equipment of the horse artillery, wooden axletrees were the standard fitting to all the field artillery carriages and limbers. They were of a common design but the sizes depended upon the purpose and the weight of the wheel and the load to be moved. Each type of gun and limber usually had a different axletree and this could cause serious problems when interchangeability became an issue.

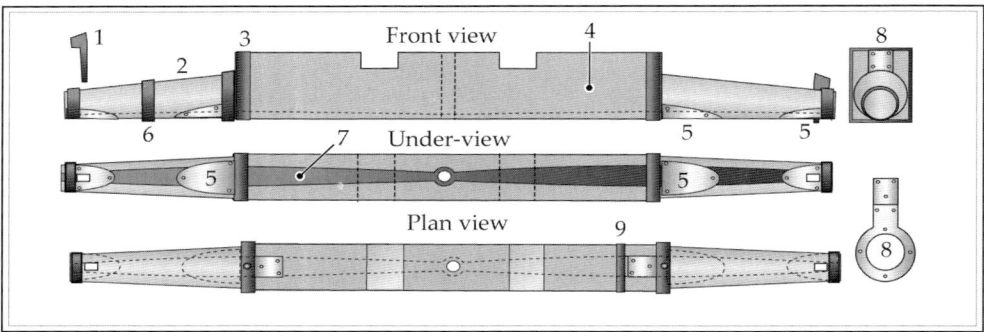

Figure 2.5. Views of a wooden axletree. The linchpin (1) keeps the wheel on the axletree arm (2). Axletree hoop (3) and the body of the axletree (4) mortised to receive the brackets. Clouts (5) fitted at the linch and shoulder end of the arm. Axletree hoops (6), hurters (8) and plan view (9). The axles and bed formed a straight line across the bottom and the axles were supported by an iron axletree bar (7) set into the bottom of the axletree.

The wooden axletree was formed from one piece of timber with the axles turned on a lathe and the top of the axle sloped so the axletree arms were effectively inclined downwards. This caused the lower spokes of the wheel to be nearer the vertical, the inclination being known as the 'hollow or let', usually an angle of about four degrees. The hollow also caused the top of the wheel to lean away from the sides of the vehicle thus increasing the load carrying capability. The gait of a walking horse set up a lateral motion, this was passed to the shafts and thence to the wheels. This caused the wheels to run 'off and back' on the axle arms and caused wearing by the nave hoops on the shoulder of the axle and a force working against the linchpin at the other. To counter this, washers were used to protect the linchpin and sheet metal 'hurters' protected the shoulders from the rubbing action of the hind hoops. Iron axletree hoops were fitted to the axle at the linchpin ends and to provide strength and some axles had an additional hoop at the centre and shoulder of the arm. While wooden axles were considered weaker than those made of iron, any wear could be overcome by replacing the metal 'clouts' and 'hurters'. Dimensions of the wooden axles are given in Table A.5 of Appendix A at the end of Part One.

The Artillery Wheel

The gun carriage and limber of the field artillery was a mutually dependent system but one of the most vulnerable parts was the wheel, particularly the felloes. When damaged these could not only put a gun out of action but also rendered it immobile and at the mercy of the enemy. At the start of the period, the wheels of the guns and limbers were of different size and not interchangeable, later a standard wheel was introduced. The artillery wheel followed a well-established pattern and most wheels had twelve spokes and six felloes except those for the front of wagons: these usually had ten spokes and five felloes; there were other types for specialist vehicles. Generally by this period the smaller wheels were forty-eight inches in diameter and the larger, sixty inches. The major change came in 1793 with the introduction of the 60-inch diameter wheel as a 'standard' for both the gun and limber, only the thickness of the felloes, spokes and knave increasing for the heavier ordnance.

The description below describes the 60-inch diameter wheel introduced for the horse artillery but the general construction was similar irrespective of size and purpose. The wheel consisting of a wide nave or hub, the spokes and the felloes forming the rim of the wheel. Each part was made from a particular wood. The nave was made from a single block of seasoned elm; to resisted splitting when the tenon of the spoke was hammered in. The 60-inch wheel had a nave 13 inches long with a maximum diameter of 12.5 inches. It was turned to shape and size and bored to receive the nave box – this was not fitted until the last stage of manufacture. The nave was then hooped with two 2-inch wide metal bands, one on the linch face and one on the hind, on wheels intended for particularly heavy loading a centre hoop was often added. Next twelve 3-inch long by 1-inch wide mortises, were cut radially into the nave to receive the spokes.

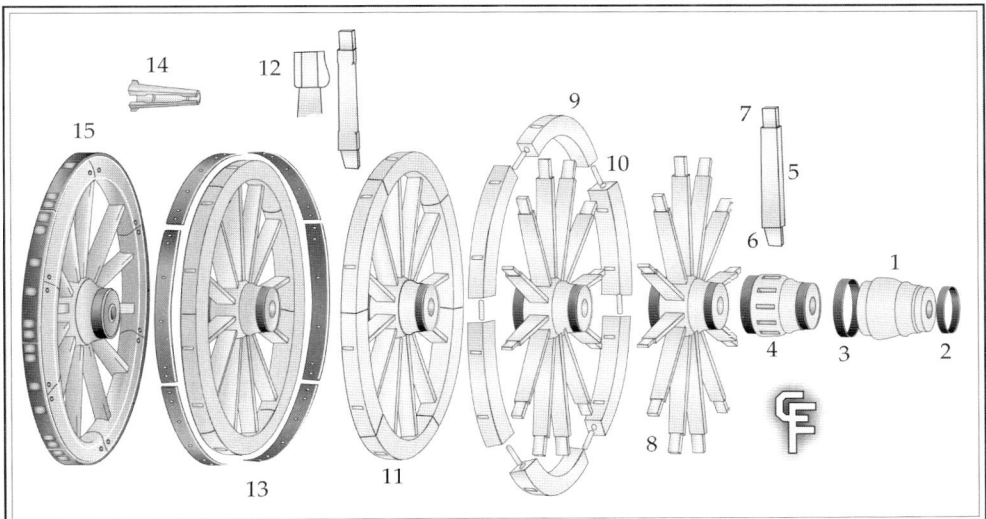

Figure 2.6. Construction of an artillery wheel. The knave (1) was fitted with linch (2) and hind hoops (3) and mortises were cut in for the spokes (4). The spokes (5) were driven with the foot (6) into the knave, the tongue (7) to the outside on the speech (8). The six felloes (9) were cut to basic shape and the holes for the dowels (10) and the mortises for the tongue of the spoke cut in. At this stage, the wheel was termed 'on the wedge' (11) and left to season. When the wheel had seasoned, the spokes and felloes were rounded to shape (12) and six iron streak tyres (13) were nailed into position across the join of the felloes and the wheel painted. The final task was to hammer the grease box (14) into the hind end of the knave and the wheel was complete (15).

The spokes of the wheel were made of oak to withstand longitudinal stress, they were 20 inches long from shoulder to shoulder with a 4-inch tenon at the foot and a 3-inch tenon at the tongue; the feet of the spokes were fitted into the nave and the tongues into the felloes. The spokes at this stage of manufacture were rectangular in cross-section, 3 inches wide and 1 inch thick at the nave with the outer edge, the face, straight and the inner edge, the back, tapering to some 2 inches at the felly. They were not set in vertically but stood away from the vertical to enable the wheel to resist the lateral thrust tending to force the nave or hub outwards and to bring the working spoke to a nearer vertical position. This was called the 'dish' and normally 0.5 inch was allowed for each foot of wheel diameter. At this stage, where just the spokes had been fitted to the hub, the wheel was known as a 'speech'.

The next stage was to add the rim of the wheel. This was made up of six felloes or fellies made of resilient ash. Each curved felloe was some 30 inches long and mortised together with a dowel driven in half way into each at one end, leaving a hole for the dowel of the adjacent felly at the other. The concave face was termed the 'bosom' the convex the 'sole'. In cross-section, the felloes were rectangular at this stage, being 4 inches deep and, depending upon the load, 2.5 inches wide with each pierced by two mortises to receive the tongues of the spokes. The felloes were driven onto the speech ensuring the spokes and dowelling pins entered the mortises. Once the felloes were on, the tongues were split at the rim of the felly and wooden wedges driven in to hold them tight. On earlier wheels, metal plates called 'dowledges' were nailed over the joins of the felloes to reinforce them. At this stage, the wheel was termed 'on-the-wedge' and usually left for a time to season.

When the wheel was seasoned the outside face and 'bosom' of the felloes was rounded off. The sole was bevelled to reduce the diameter of the outer edge and ensure the rim of the wheel sat flat on the ground. It was at this stage the faces of the spokes were rounded off from the first 4 inches at each end.

The last stage was to add the nave box and the metal tyres. The tyres acted to protect the wheel from wear and to strengthen the assembly. At this time all artillery wheels were shod with six, separate iron streaks, sections of curved metal strip 0.5 inches thick and the same width as the felloe. (The artillery only adopted the one-piece circular metal tyre after 1868). Each streak covered half of two adjacent felloes to which they were fastened by tyre nails, two at each end, one into the end of each spoke and two between the spokes, forty-eight in all. In November, 1813 it was ordered all the tyres of gun carriages and wagon wheels of the next brigade ordered to the Peninsula should be fixed in place by bolts and nuts instead of nails; the bolts were 4 inches long and one quarter inch diameter. 'The additional expense would only be two shillings and five pence per pound and the felloes would be protected from damage since the nails when driven home had a tendency to split them. These wheels made in the Portuguese manner were so successful that on 31 March 1814 it was adopted as standard practice.[14]

The nave was lined by a metal box or pipe. This was the same inner shape as the axle but bore on only 3 inches at each end of the axle, the larger diameter centre forming a grease trap and acting to reduce the wearing surface. It was held in position in the nave by two protruding 'feathers' integral with the casting. It was usually fitted during the final stages of manufacture.

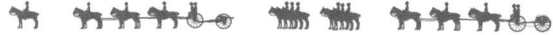

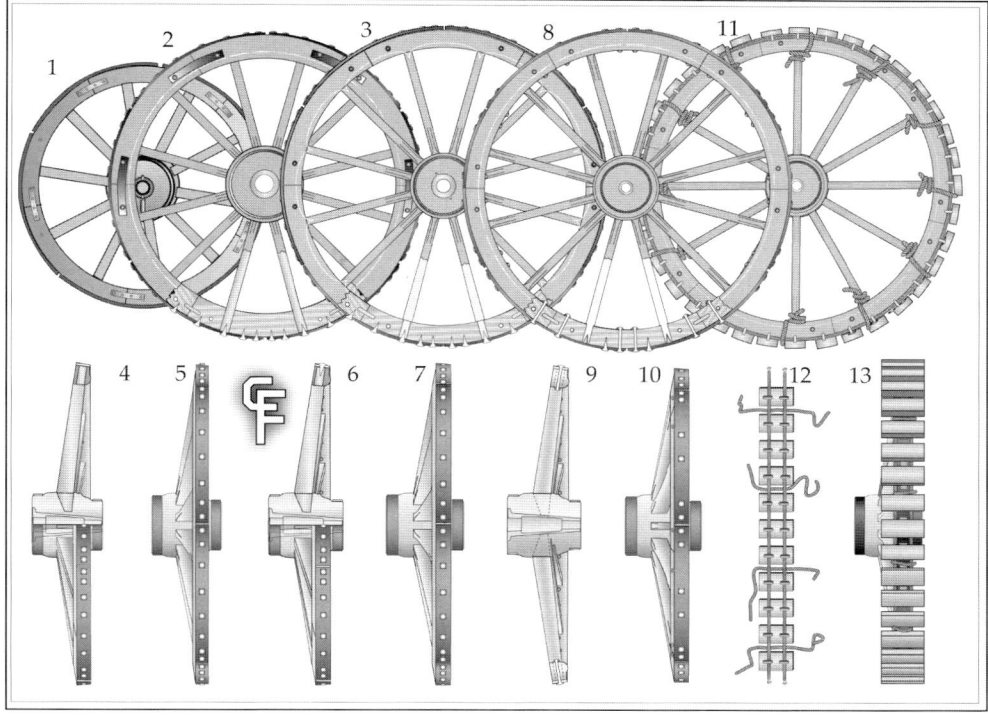

Figure 2.7. Types of field artillery wheels. At the left is a ten-spoke wheel of 48 inches diameter (1) and a 60-inch diameter, twelve-spoke wheel (2) both pre-1793 and fitted with dowledges to reinforce the junction of the felloes. Next is the inner face of a 60-inch diameter wheel (3) post-1793 but before 1813 with nails securing the tyre with the light (4 & 5) and heavy equipment wheels (6 & 7). Post-1813 wheels were fitted with tyre bolts (8) this view shows the outer face. The construction remained unchanged and both light and heavy equipment wheels were issued (9 & 10). The method to widen the footprint of the wheel when travelling over gravel or sand (11) as adopted by General Lawson during the Egyptian Campaign: staves from casks were cut into short, eight-inch lengths and secured together with staples and ropes (12). The whole was lashed around the circumference of the wheel and around the spokes (13).

The term track was generally accepted as the distance between the opposing wheels, but some consider it to mean the distance to the outer edge of the wheels. Where the set of the wheels is discussed, all measurements are given in Chapter 14.

The introduction of the new wheels was such that by 1801 it was noted 60-inch diameter wheels and iron axles were now fitted to most field artillery carriages. [15]
* All horse artillery carriages and limbers
* Long 3-pr carriages and limber
* Light 6-pr foot brigade carriages
* Heavy 6-pr carriages and limber and the light 5.5-inch howitzer carriage

The smaller wheels of 56-inch diameter and iron axles were fitted to:
* Limbers of foot brigade light 6-pr of 4ft 6in
* Heavy 5.5-inch howitzer gun and limber
* Medium 12-pr guns and limbers

By 1813, the status had stabilised for the field artillery and there were just three wheels in general use as shown in Table A.6 of Appendix A at the end of Part One.

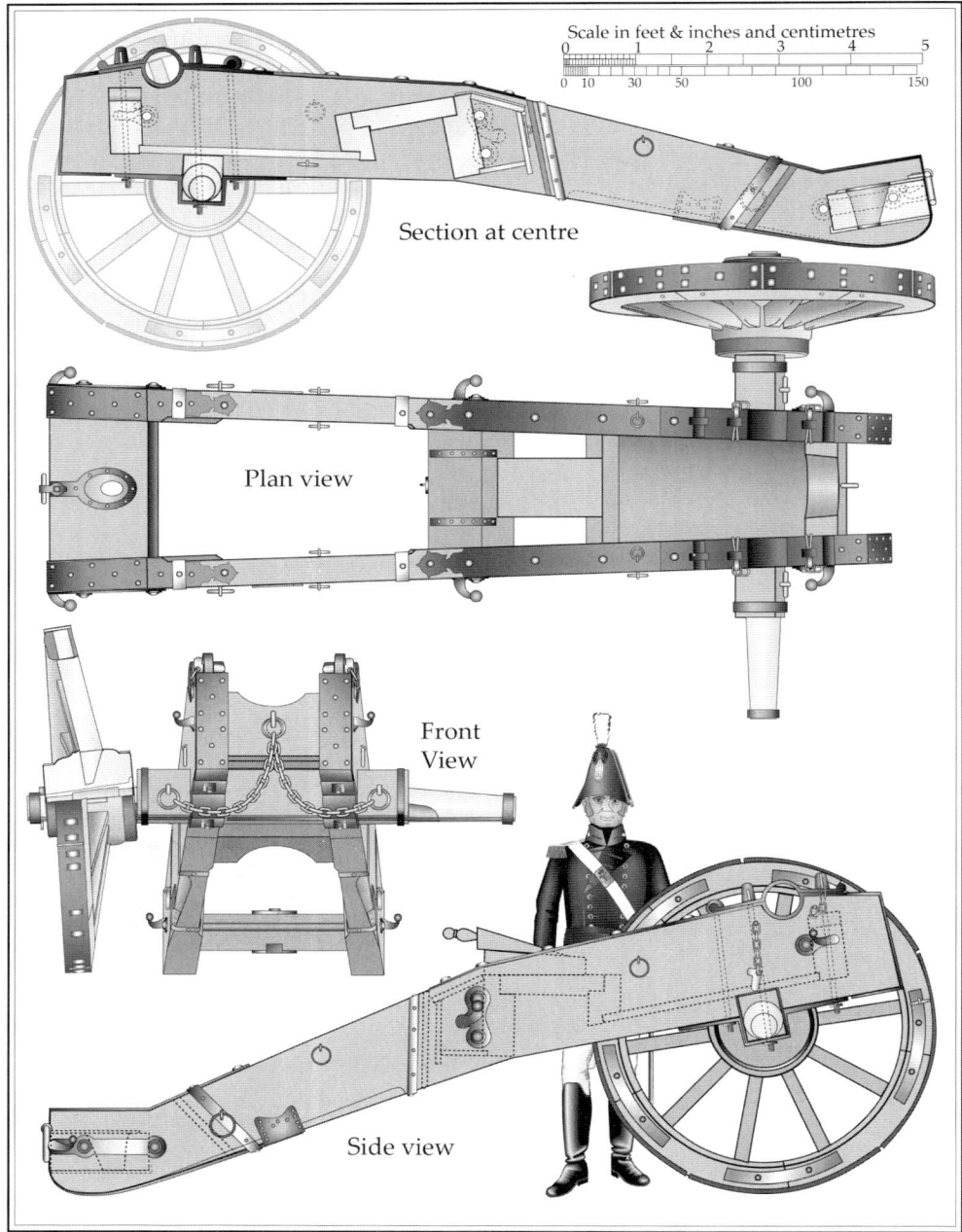

Scale in feet & inches and centimetres

Section at centre

Plan view

Front View

Side view

Figure 2.8. Construction of a divergent trail, gun carriage, circa 1792. It is fitted with wooden axles and 58-inch wheels, a form of carriage in general use at the start of the war. This carriage, made for an 18-pr gun, has the earlier form of quoins and quoin bed more usually associated with siege or garrison artillery. This means of elevation was replaced by a screw elevation mechanism for field artillery gun carriages and the centre lockers went out of use.

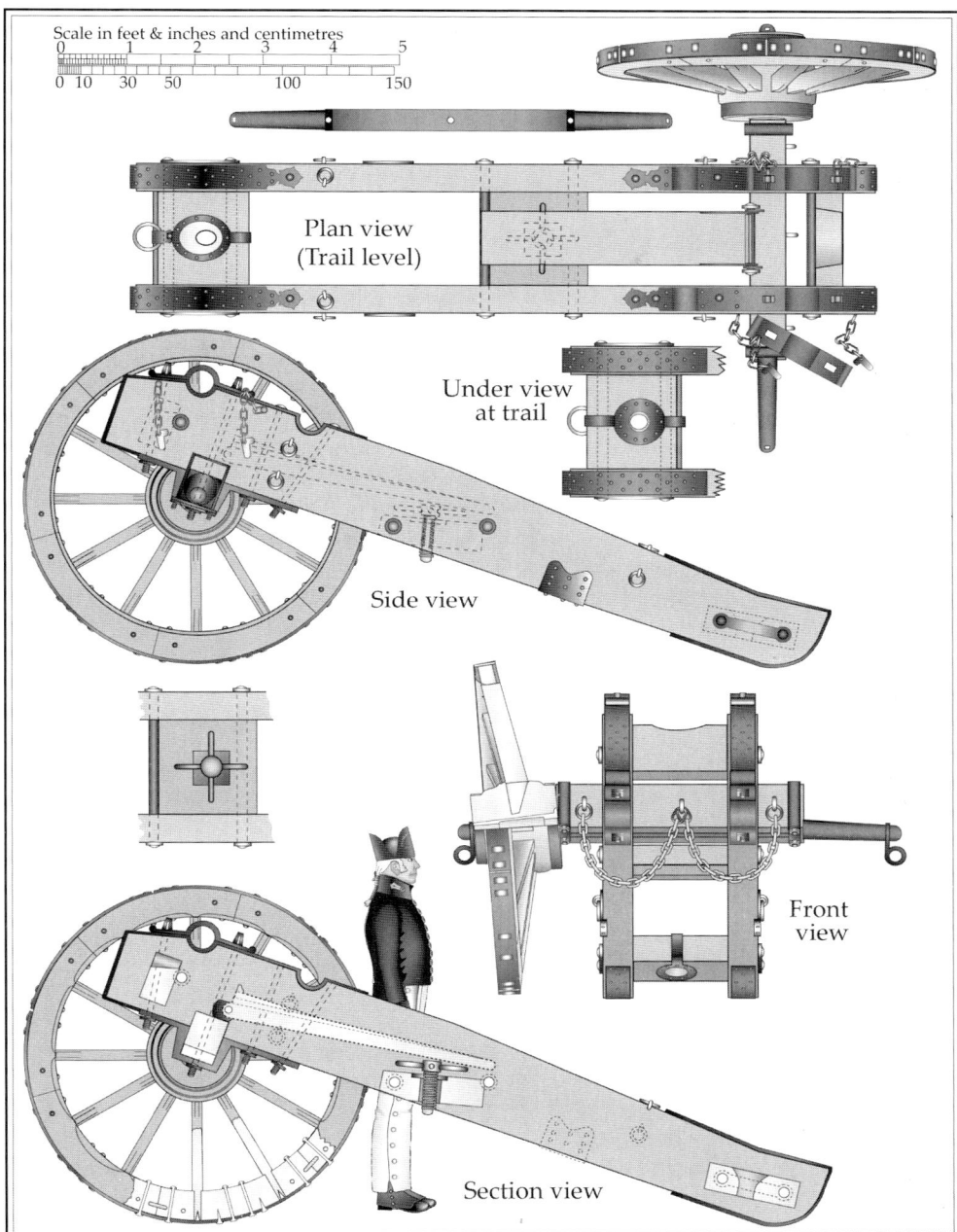

Scale in feet & inches and centimetres

Plan view
(Trail level)

Under view
at trail

Side view

Front
view

Section view

Figure 2.9. Construction of a parallel trail gun carriage, circa 1815. This form of carriage was introduced for field service later in the period and is fitted with iron axles and 60-inch wheels. While also sized for an 18-pr gun, it has the additional trunnion holes to allow the gun to be moved rearwards when travelling and has been fitted with an elevation mechanism working against the bottom of a swinging elevation board. The wheels followed the standard form but were of heavier and stronger construction.

The advantages of the new 60-inch wheels and iron axles for the horse artillery were quickly recognized and the foot artillery rapidly adopted the same concept. The size of the new wheel was chosen for several reasons. Most artillery equipment had to be constantly moved by hand and one of the most efficient ways of using manpower was by applying it to the spokes of the wheel. These had to be of a length and height that could be readily grasped by a man of normal stature (5 feet 8 inches in the horse artillery) and so designed that the power applied to the upper spokes would exert a two-to-one leverage on the axletree, the fulcrum being the part of the wheel on the ground. Another significant advantage was that the height of the wheel enabled a better angle on the traces of the horses and this meant far less of their effort was wasted; for the heavier equipments the strength of the wheel and the thickness at the rim was increased from 2.5 to 3.5 inches.[16] This change in wheel was applied to most field guns the exception being the light 3-pr which had a 56-inch wheel. It seems by 1808, all the guns sent to the Peninsula from England had been fitted with block trails and only the medium 12-pr and the guns from Gibraltar were on the old-style carriages.

The wheels used on guns of position or garrison artillery still followed the earlier sizes, as did the guns of the specialist equipment not covered in this book. There were special sizes and widths for siege limbers, sling, and devil wagons or carts used to transport artillery equipment. Guns of position were normally mounted on garrison carriages with metal or wooden trucks of the appropriate size and thickness according to the nature of the piece. Usually the hind wheel was the smaller and varied between 10 and 16 inches, the front wheels between 14 and 19 inches.

Endnotes to Chapter 2

1. Caruana, 1977: et al.
2. Muller, 1780: et al.
3. Rudyerd, 1970: et al.
4. Caruana, 1977: et al.
5. Caruana, 1982: p. 129.
6. *Aide Memoire*, 1847: *Aide Memoire*, 1853: et al.
7. *Aide Memoire*, 1847: plates 16–18.
8. Hughes, 1996: pp 28–9.
9. McConnell, 1988: p. 198.
10. Caruana, 1977: p. 25.
11. Pyne, 1802: show the truck in use.
12. Caruana, 1977: p. 28.
13. List of Changes: change no. 907 of 27 April 1864.
14. Hogg, 1963: p. 540; National Archive WO/47, 2,640, p. 1,248; Dickson, 1908: pp. 1,054, 1,180.
15. Adye, 1801: p. 57; 1802: p. 76.
16. Adye, 1802: p. 76.
17. Duncan, 2005: pp. 115, 120, 121.

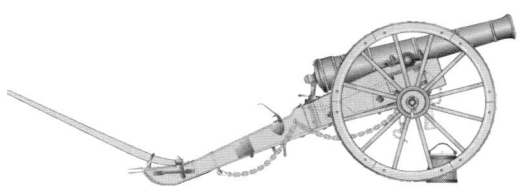

CHAPTER 3

Block Trail Gun Carriages

Introduction

The design of the new equipment for the horse artillery in 1793 acted as a spur for major change throughout the British field artillery. The new design of carriage and limber had been proposed by the Duke of Richmond and the process of selection had involved the most eminent British gunners of the day. The story of the selection of the equipment for the horse artillery has already been well written about and there is little point in repeating it, although the first choice in ordnance was soon changed to five light 6-pr guns of five feet and one 5.5-inch howitzer.[1] The gun carriages for the horse artillery were made with the block trail, a new pattern limber and a new form of draught; so effective were the improvements, the new equipments were soon being issued to the foot brigades as well. The workload on the Royal Arsenal in re-equipping the field artillery imposed a requirement for a more efficient practice than the Constructor of Artillery Carriages and his jobbing carpenters had previously used in the construction of gun carriages and limbers, and by 1800 block trail carriages were being issued for use in the foot brigades.[2] In April 1803, the warrant for the establishment of the Royal Carriage Department was issued and thereafter all gun carriages, limbers and associated vehicles were manufactured by this department, which due to the demands of the service was the first to have a steam-driven saw pit and planer, the first fully mechanized facility at the Royal Arsenal.[3]

It has not been possible to determine when each field brigade changed from one style of carriage to the other but the progress was rapid and continual, with fresh supplies being sent to the Peninsula to replace worn-out equipment.[4] Woolwich replaced the older bracket trail as block trails became available, but their priority seems to have been Europe, so the Colonies were only supplied when the immediate requirements had been met. It seems that in the foot artillery brigades both the long and light 6-pr guns and the medium 12-pr guns may have been first modified to take iron axles and larger wheels. As early as 1794 some 6-prs and 5.5-inch howitzers were being issued 'upon new pattern carriages'.[5] In 1804, the policy of replacement was:

> Carriages of 'other construction will be furnished as soon as they can be prepared. As soon as cavalry brigades arrive an equal number of similar pieces not so equipped with their carriages and appointments to be returned to Woolwich in lieu of those supplied from thence'[6]

The 9-pr guns brought into service in 1808 were all issued on block trail carriages and the new pattern limbers were in general service as early as 1794;[7] by 1815 most field guns were mounted on them and all the field brigades at Waterloo were equipped with block trails.[8] By 1812, even the artillery in Canada had received some of the new pattern carriages.

In spite of the new design, gun carriages like everything else, soon wore out in the difficult terrain of the Peninsula and Dickson wrote in 1811:

> ... that the 3rd – Light 6Pr – brigade of my division is in immediate want of a new set of gun carriages, the old ones being very nearly unserviceable; and I have to add that the 1st – Light 6Pr – brigade will in the course of two or three months also require a complete set of carriages.[9]

The Block Trail Gun Carriage

The wheels and axles of the limber and gun were now of the same size which gave better mobility as the hind wheels of the gun could follow in the ruts of the wheels of the limber. It also meant the wheels, the most vulnerable part of the system, were now interchangeable. The increased size of the limber wheels also made the draught easier as experience had shown the best angle was about 6.5 degrees. The design of the gun carriage placed the centre of gravity well forward so that unlimbering, with the trail lifting handles, was an easy task for two men. With the handspike inserted into the traversing stay and loop on the trail plate, one man could traverse and lay the gun. The parts of gun carriages were officially interchangeable, but as each troop had their own artificers and wheel makers, local improvements and modifications were not uncommon.

In the Egyptian Campaign of 1800, General Lawson recalled that 'These block-trail carriages, from their lightness, short draught, and quick turning, passed over the inundation dykes and desert with great ease, while the framed carriages with more horses were attended with difficulty and delay, and once in the desert, were obliged to be left behind'.[10]

The block trail carriage consisted of the following main parts, a single trail, two cheeks or brackets, an iron axletree an axletree bed and two wheels. The dimensions of the trail were determined by the recoil of the gun and usually set to provide an angle of 22 degrees and long enough to prevent any tendency for the gun to flip backwards when fired.

The trail was of oak, usually in one piece, and fitted with a metal trail plate at the rear carrying the traversing stays and the steeled towing eye for attachment to the limber. At the front the trail was pierced horizontally for three transom bolts and

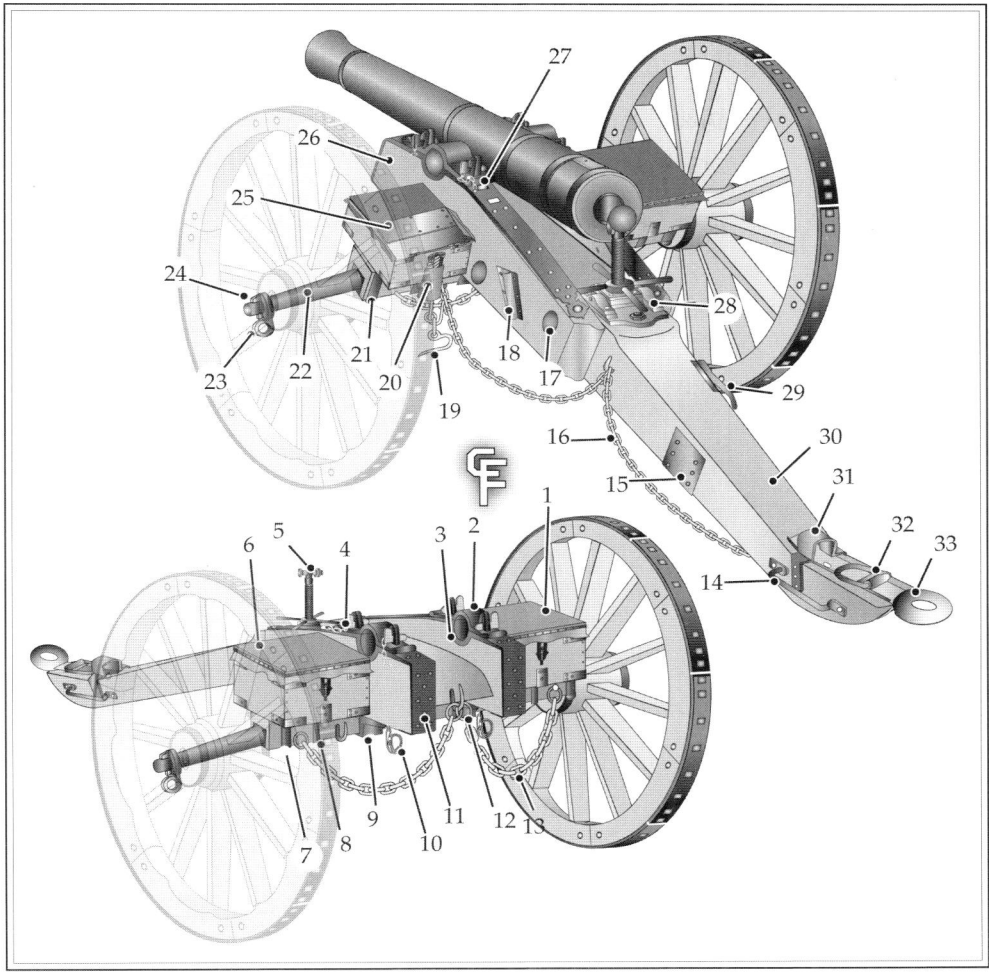

Figure 3.1. Component parts of a generic block trail carriage. The axle box for slow match (1), capsquare (2), trunnion plate (3), double key and chain (4), elevating mechanism (5), ammunition/small stores box (6), axle hoop (7), axle box bracket (8), axletree band (9), side arm strap and staple (10), breast plate (11), trail breast hook (12) and advance or breast chain (13). Trail handles (14), locking plate (15), wheel or locking chain (16), transom bolts (17), portfire holder bracket (18), 'snake' or 'dog' hook (19), slow match guard (20), axle hoops and coupling plates (21), iron axle (22), drag washer (23) and linchpin (24). The slow match protector (25), carriage bracket or cheek (26), bracket bolt (27), elevating hand wheel (28), portfire cutter (29), block trail (30), traversing loop and pin (31), traversing ring (32), and towing eye (33).

vertically for the axletree bolt. The sides were fitted with locking plates to protect the trail from the iron tires of the limber in a sharp turn and at the rear end there were two handles to assist the manhandling of the trail.

Mounted on the cushion of the trail was the elevating gear described in Chapter 2. Passing through the trail cushion was a vertical hole, which allowed the movement of the elevating screw, this hole was an elongated, some 4 inches by 2.5 inches, to allow for the movement of the elevating screw as the angle to the cascabel changed when the gun was elevated or depressed. A portfire clipper was attached on the right side, as was a hook for the locking chain. The rear end of the trail was

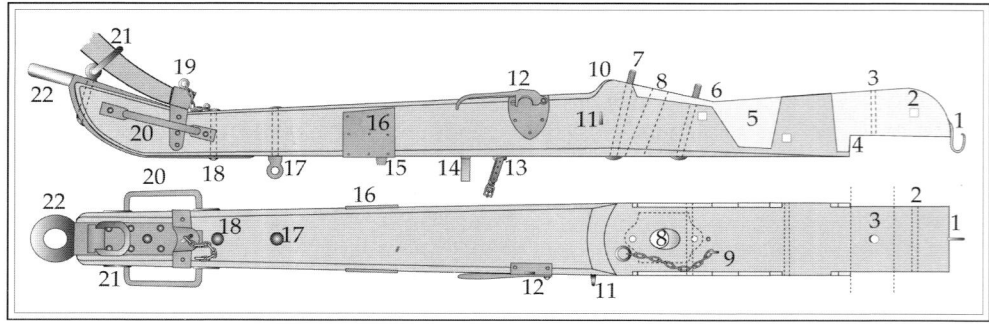

Figure 3.2. Block trail, side and plan view with the main parts identified. The hook for the advancing or breast chains (1), hole for the transom bolt (2), hole for the axletree bolt (3) and the notch for the axletree bed (4). The tenon for the brackets (5), neck of the trail (6), elevation mechanism bolts (7), hole for the elevation screw (8), elevation locking chain (9) and the cushion of trail (10). The locking chain hook (11), portfire cutter (12), side arm staple and strap (13), rammer hoop (14), rammer stop (15), locking plate (16), locking chain eyebolt (17) and the trail plate bolt (18). At the rear of the trail metal strapping prevented undue damage from the recoil and fitted to this were the traversing loop, pin and chain (19), trail handles (20), traversing ring or loop (21) and towing eye (22).

protected by a metal trail plate and the top of the trail carried a shoe and ring for the handspike. The underside carried an eyebolt for the locking chain and joining the two locking plates, a stop against which the head of the rammer rested. The trail was cut in elaborate mortise on each side to fit the matching tenon of the brackets; these elaborate joints provided strength to resist the action of the gun and a watertight seal to prevent the ingress of moisture.

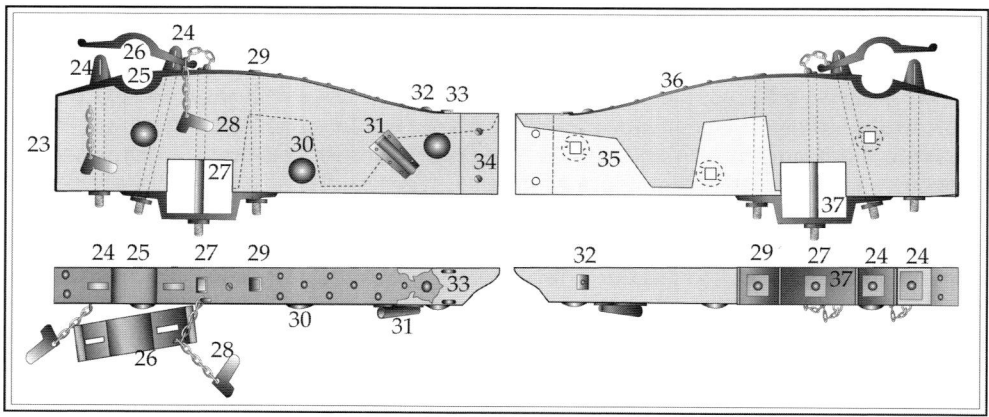

Figure 3.3. Block trail carriage left side bracket or cheek with the main parts identified. Breast plate (23), eye bolt (24), trunnion plate (25), captive capsquare (26), axletree band bolt (27), double or spring key and chain (28), bracket axletree band bolt (29), transom bolt (30), portfire holder bracket (31), bracket or garnish bolt (32), side arm staples (33), bracket screws (34), bracket tenon (35), garnish plate or bracket strapping (36) and axletree band (37).The right is similar except item 31 is not fitted.

The sidepieces or brackets, sometimes called cheeks, were of elm of sufficient height to allow the required depression and elevation of the gun (notionally some 12 degrees of elevation and 10 degrees of depression) and sufficient depth over the axletree. The holes for the trunnions were positioned so that the trail would remain on the ground when the gun fired but still allowed for the ease of traverse of the trail by one man and the limbering and unlimbering by two. The inner face of the bracket was cut in an elaborate tenon to fit the mortise cut in the trail. The front face and top of the brackets were bound with iron secured by nails back to the breech of the piece where they were secured by garnish bolts. The upper faces were shaped to accept the trunnion plates and secure the trunnions. Passing vertically down through the brackets were three bolts, protruding underneath. Two were the capsquare or eyebolts mounted either side of the trunnion mounting and the third was a bracket bolt mounted just behind them.

Secured to the trunnion plates by a small chain at the rear were the capsquares holding the trunnions in place. These fitted over the eyebolts where they were secured by a new design of chained spring keys. A portfire holder was screwed to the side of the left bracket to align with the vent. This was used to carry the portfire holder when the gun was being run up after recoil or when the portfire had been extinguished but the gun was still at the firing point. Three transom bolts were bolted, from the left side, through the brackets and trail and acted to secure the brackets to the trail. (On post-Napoleonic carriages the brackets were modified, being longer and higher with the trunnions and axle moved to the rear to improve the stability of the carriage; similarly the thickness of the waist of the trail in front of the elevating mechanism cushion was increased to overcome an inherent weakness.)[11]

Iron Axletrees

The iron axletrees had been specified for the horse artillery from the very beginning in 1793. They were much stronger, simpler to make, easier to change and more durable in the field. They also did away with the need for the 'clouts' on the wooden axle. Their advantages were such, and they were quickly adopted by the field artillery as soon as availability permitted. Tests had been made with iron axles arms inserted into each end of the axle bed,[12] a practice used in country wagons, but they were apparently unsuccessful, as by 1801 most foot brigade carriages were fitted with iron axles and by 1813 all had them.[13] With the introduction of iron axles the washers were retained to protect the linchpins but the 'hurters' were discarded as the shoulder of the axle was now of iron. Iron axletrees were cast in one piece and the arms turned on a lathe. The size of the axle varied with the load to be carried, and except for special equipment the limber and gun used the same axle, but there were different sizes for light and heavy equipments. The size of the different iron axles is given in Table A.7 of Appendix A at the end of Part One.

The axletree arms were inclined downwards by 0.375 inches for the 'hollow or let'. A further setting was the 'strut'. This was the inclination of the working spokes, (when on level ground) to the vertical. This set the wheel nearer the vertical to the surface of the ground when the vehicle was at a slant or a wheel fell into a rut. Due to these settings, the wheel had to be made to give a cone to the tyre so it would sit squarely on the ground, and this set a constant pressure against the washer and linchpin and further negated the need for hurters. The arms were also aligned with the linchpin ends slightly forward by 0.125 inches; this was called the 'lead' and it put the front part of the wheel and the leading spokes forward by one degree in a better position to meet obstacles.[14] With iron axles, unless regular greasing was carried out, dried-up grease could cause seizure and the friction could make the iron so brittle, a sudden jolt could cause it to fracture. The early brigade establishments had always included a grease wagon, but with the introduction of the horse artillery and the new pattern ammunition wagon with its large grease boxes and grease keg,

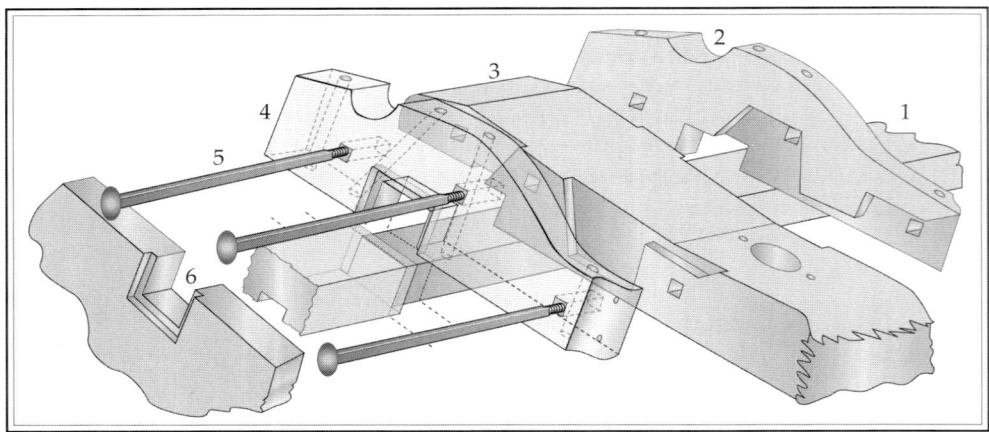

Figure 3.4. Axle, trail and bracket joints. To prevent the ingress of moisture and to provide additional strength during the shock of firing the axle, brackets and trail were joined by a complex system of mortises. The brackets (4) were notched to provide a mortise for the axle (1) and the trail (3) was also notched to provide a mortise for the axle. The trail and brackets were joined together by a set of shaped mortises and bolted together by three 'transom bolts' (5). These square bolts were passed through the trail and brackets from the left side and secured on the right. The bracket to the axle joint is also shown (6). The vertical holes through the brackets are for capsquare bolts.

the requirement became unnecessary. In 1810, the overall length of a gun carriage axle was similar to that of the limber, 76 inches. The breadth between the wheels at the top was 65 inches, at the bottom 57 inches, but it must be remembered, wheels could shrink by as much as 2 inches in diameter as they weathered so these figures are arbitrary and based upon two new wheels of 60 inches in diameter. The full dimensions of the wheel set-up are given in Chapter 14.

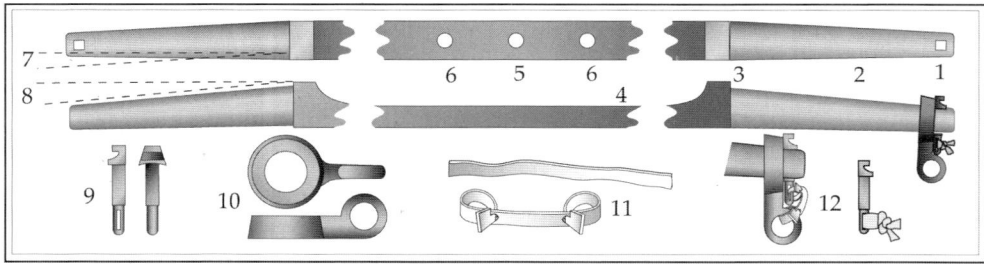

Figure 3.5. Plan and front view of an iron axletree. The linchpin hole (1) and axletree arm (2) form an integral assembly with the shoulder (3). The body (4) was cut away to save weight and was pierced by three holes, one for the axletree bolt (5) and two for the bracket bolts (6). The angle of lead (7) was small and the angle of let or the hollow (8) was some four degrees. The washer (10) prevented the nave of the wheel working on the linchpin (9), which was secured by a leather lace or tie (11). One end of the tie passed through the slot of the linchpin and the other end through the drag loop (12).

Each wheel was retained on the axletree by a linchpin and washer. The washer was fitted to prevent the knave of the wheel working against the linchpin; there were three different types of washer, plain, drag and loop for the attachment of drag ropes or chains. During the Napoleonic period there were different sizes of washer to fit each type of axle, the size of the larger plain washers for the light equipments was 4 inches in diameter and just over 1 inch thick. It was bevelled to the outer face and was 3.75 inches in diameter with a central hole of 2.5 inches. Drag washers were similar but with a 2 inch loop to receive the hook of a drag rope. The drag loop, set at ninety degrees to the washer, was 2 inches in diameter on an extended shank. The drag washer had an overall length of 6.75 inches and weighed some 3.25 pounds. The loop washer was only used on siege equipments for the attachment of outrigger stays when multiple draught was required.

Linchpins

The body of the linchpin was rectangular in section and long enough to fit the different sizes of axle, with a rounded section at the lower end with a slot for a leather tie or toggle connected through the linchpin at one end and the drag ring at the other. The head was rectangular in section and notched on the front face so it could be easily knocked out if it became a tight fit in the axletree.

Axletree Bed

Iron axletrees were secured into a slot along the bottom of an ash axletree bed, where they were secured by bolts and at each end by yoke hoops and coupling plates. Later guns had the axletree bed tapered to the rear so that the bottom face and the hollow of the iron axle were more effective when the gun was being towed. The bed was fitted under the cheeks to align just behind the trunnions and held in position by axletree bands. These clamped around the axle-bed and fitted over the protruding ends of the eye and bracket bolts and were secured by square nuts. A further bolt passed down through the trail to the centre of the axletree where it was fixed by a square nut. At each end the axle was strengthened by yoke hoops and coupling plates secured by octagonal nuts. The front face of the axle bed was fitted with two advancing or breast chains, which were looped up to a hook on the front of the trail. Staples for the leather straps holding the small arms were placed into the underside of the axle. The rear face was fitted with various hooks and attachment points as were required.

The axletree bed could be fitted with one or two axle boxes, one either side. Howitzers only had the box fitted on the left or off side. The boxes were secured by metal bands around the axletree and made from timber 1 inch thick and always

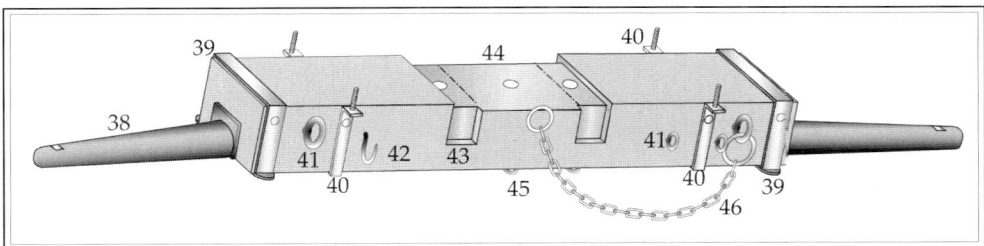

Figure 3.6. Block trail carriage axletree bed with the parts identified. Iron axletree (38), yoke hoops and coupling plates (39), axletree box brackets (40), breast chain ringbolts (41), hooks (42), mortise for the brackets (43), mortise for the trail (44), side arm staples (45) and advance or breast chain (46).

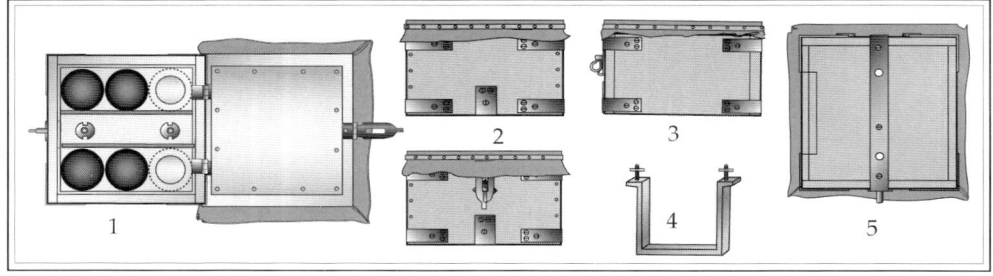

Figure 3.7. Right or near axle box fitted to the light 6-pr gun for the storage of ready use ammunition. The centre compartment was used for vent tools and other small stores (1). A front and rear view (2). A side view (3) and the axle bracket by which the box was secured to the axle (4). The under view showing the metal band through which the bolts of the axle band passed to be secured inside the box (5).

hinged at the rear with the staples facing forward. The tops were covered with canvas to preclude moisture. On the lighter equipments, the right axle box was used to store round shot for use in emergencies, but as it was on the wrong side of the gun for the loader, it must have been most inconvenient, particularly as the cartridges were carried in the limber. It was only after the Napoleonic period that the right axle box was used to carry fixed ammunition.

Slow Match Box

The left or off axle box provided the slow match to ignite the portfires and thus replaced the need for the linstock of the bracket trail carriage. The canvas on the lid of this box was prolonged at the rear to form an apron, the end of which was given weight by a riveted copper sheet. This acted to protect the canvas and the burning slow match from the weather. The box was divided into two parts; the left was used for small stores the other was copper lined and held the slow match. The slow match was coiled in the right-shand compartment. When action was expected both ends were fed through the hole in the rear of the box, down through the hinged metal feed tube and ignited. As the slow match burnt away, the firer pulled new match down from the box or called up new match from the limber. Mercer recalls that during the heavy rain preceding Waterloo, the slow matches were extinguished and he was unable to find a nearby fire to relight them.[15]

Side Arms, Small Stores and Special Tools

A wide variety of equipment or side arms were required to handle, load, fire, clean and service the guns. Some were mounted on the gun itself, others were carried in the axle boxes and others on the limber or ammunition wagon that accompanied each gun. The main side arms were strapped to the gun carriage where they were ready to hand and the small tools and other equipment were shared between the axletree boxes on the gun, the centre box and ammunition boxes on the limbers.

Advance or breast chains were used, with drag ropes, for manhandling the carriage. The chain was 2 feet long with 21 links, 0.75 inches wide by 1.5 inches long. They were fastened to the front face of the axletree by a 2-inch ring secured to a

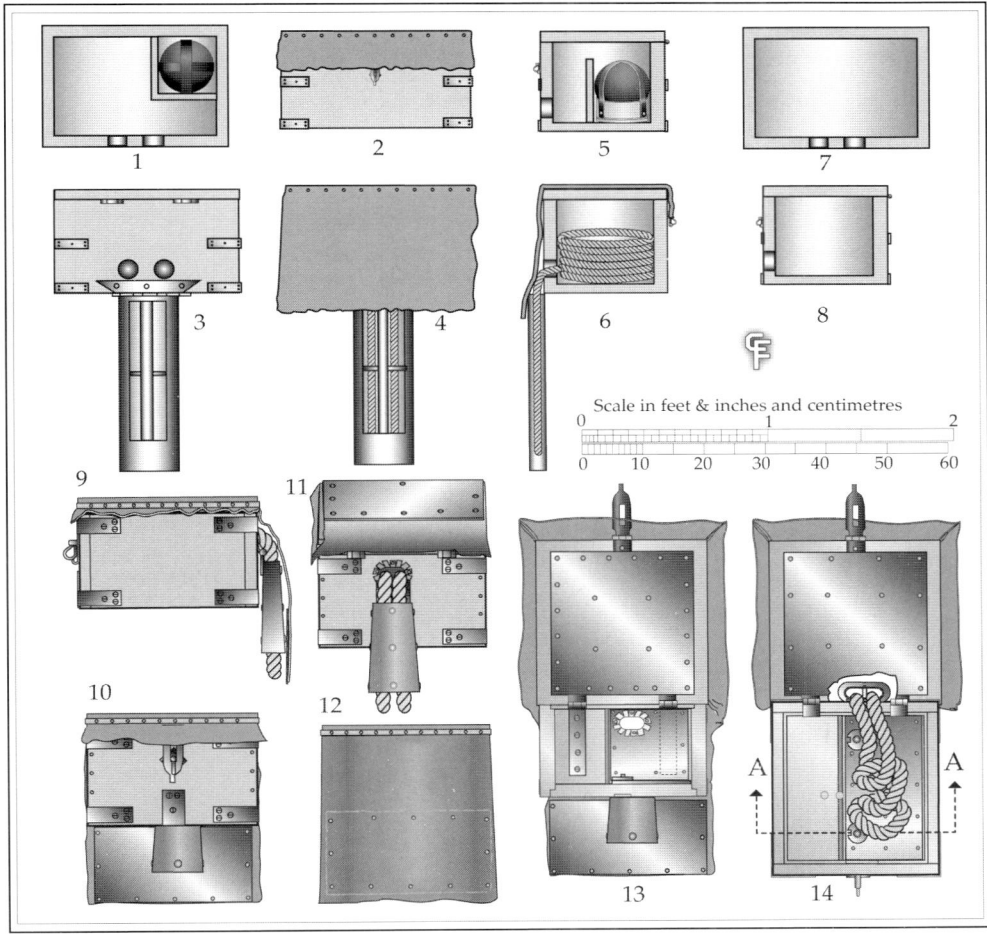

Figure 3.8. Slow match boxes. Early model, circa 1804. The plan section (1) and fore elevation (2). Two hind views showing the rear of the box (3) and the extended rear canvas to protect the slow match (4). Two side sections showing the storage of one round shot (5) and the slow match (6). The plan and side view for the 5.5-inch howitzer were similar (7), but without provision for ready use ammunition (8). Details of the slow match box carried after 1807. A side view showing the hinged rear slow match feed tube (9) and a front view showing the copper sheet protecting the canvas cover, hung down over the slow match feed tube to protect it from the rain (10). A rear view with the slow match fed through the feed tube and the protective cover folded over the top of the box (11) and a rear view showing the prolonged canvas that protected the feed tube (12). A sectioned view through 'AA' showing the metal-lined exit hole and the copper-lined compartment for the slow match (13) and a plan view showing the compartment for small stores or ready use ammunition (14).

2-inch ringbolt. The working end terminated in a 3-inch ring hooked up to the front of the trail.

There were two types of bucket issued. A leather bucket was issued for watering the horses and a wooden one was used to carry water to swab out the barrel. It was hung from a hook on the axletree bed when not in use and a spare was carried under the ammunition wagon. The wooden version, termed the 'French' model, was made from ten staves 10 inches long by 3 inches wide and 0.5 inch thick; these were bound together by three metal bands with a metal handle and a tight-fitting lid. The bottom diameter was 10.25 inches, and larger than the top diameter to make it very stable and unlikely to be upset. It was noted that

> The leather bucket at present in use for carrying water for field pieces will not last long, and from their figure [shape] are often thrown over and loose the water out of them; but the French Buckets being contrived to stand firm, and having Covers fitted to them, they preserve the water to the last drop, and are not more expensive than the former. [16]

A caps sponge was made of material such as woven hemp or canvas, and tied through a selvedge around the neck. It was made large enough to fit over and protect the sheepskin covering of the wooden end of the sponge-staff. They were hung on a hook on the right of the front of the gun axle when the sponge was in use.

Drag-rope and chain. A 3-inch rope, some 18 feet long, with a loop at one end and a 7.5-inch hook on a 3-foot length of chain, with eighteen links, at the other. To provide grip for the detachment three 12-inch wooden handles were attached through spliced loops; one at the centre of the rope and two others, each at 3 feet either side. Normally the hook was attached to the loop of the drag washer to manhandle the gun. They were used more by foot artillery battalion guns and were issued in pairs and stored on the limber. They weighed 26lb. [17]

Drag washers weres fitted on the axletree to act between the nave and the linchpin. They carried a metal loop used to provide an attachment for the gun drag ropes. They were not fitted to the off side of the limber where the shaft iron acted as a washer. The size of the different washers is given in Table A.24 of Appendix A at the end of Part One.

Fork levers were designed by William Congreve for the improved carriage of 1776, but they were not taken into use with the block trail carriages.

The grease used by the artillery of this period was composed of equal parts of tallow and coarse sweet oil melted together. It was packed in an 8-inch keg made from eleven 3-inch staves. It carried 28 pounds of grease accessed through a strapped door. It was carried on the ammunition wagon. [18]

Gun spikes were issued to each gunner to render the gun unusable in the event of capture; they were driven into the vents and the ends left flush. Their removal was a difficult process and in extremis required the breech of the gun to be heated to soften the metal of the spike and permit it to be drilled out. [19] There were two types, a sprung spike and a jagged spike; both were some 5 inches long and 0.2 inches in diameter. The cleft of the sprung spike started 2 inches from the bottom. The spikes were of different lengths for each nature of ordnance but in emergency, any could be used. During the early Napoleonic period the gun spikes were carried in the cartridge pouches of the gunners. It was only some years later, when it was no longer the practice for the gunners to leave the guns and shelter in the infantry squares, the gun spikes were carried in the off compartment of the slow match box on the left axle of the gun. [20] The sizes of the different gun spikes are given in Table A.8 of Appendix A at the end of Part One.

The handspike was a 6-foot long wooden lever weighing eleven pounds, the top of the shaft was round; 1.75 inches diameter and the lower 2-foot long section was

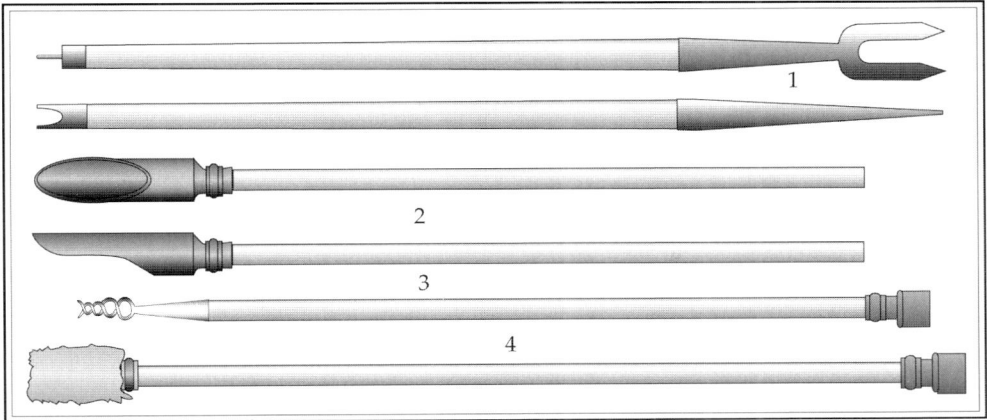

Figure 3.9. Gun side arms and equipment (part one). These items were peculiar to the early equipments and were probably not used during the period except for the older bracket trail carriages and guns deployed in the battalion role. The fork levers (1) were introduced by Congreve to assist in the manoeuvring of the gun. The copper ladle (2) was almost certainly out of use by the period as was the old-style wad hook (3) and the old-style rammer and sponge (4). The dimensions of the side arms varied to suit the ordnance being served.

3 inches square. The angled end was protected by a metal plate 3 inches wide and covering the end face and folded up 7 inches at the front and back.[21]

Hanoverian truck. Each bracket trail gun was supplied with a wooden, metal-tired wheel fitted with a metal spindle. This was designed to fit into the pintle hole of the trail transom and was used to facilitate manoeuvre in the field particularly when advancing or retiring battalion guns. It was not used with block trail guns.[22]

The ladle was originally used to hold powder when cartridges were not available. It was made from a wooden shaft with a copper ladle on the end. The length of the ladle was about three diameters and it was used to introduce a charge of powder into the gun or loosen a shot to withdraw it. Lades were little used by the start of the period and not supplied with bracket trail guns. There was a smaller version used in the magazines to fill cartridges.

A leather bucket was issued for watering the horses. They were hung from a hook on the axletree bed under the limber. Initially they had been issued to hold water for the gun but were soon replaced for this purpose by the wooden bucket.

Linchpins retained the washer and wheel on the axle. While they were of one common size for the field artillery, other sizes were issued for specialist equipment. The washer was essential to prevent the nave of the wheel working against the linchpin.

A general-purpose 1-inch rope, 30 feet long, wound into a skein 9.75 inches by 2.5 inches and secured with a small strap was carried in a limber box and known as a 'line seizing'. Heavier rope was often carried tied in a hank and strapped to staples on the platform board of the limber.

The linstock was used to carry the slow match for guns mounted on bracket trail carriages and two were issued to each gun. Several different patterns are known and it may be they were often embellished by the gun crew. They were not issued

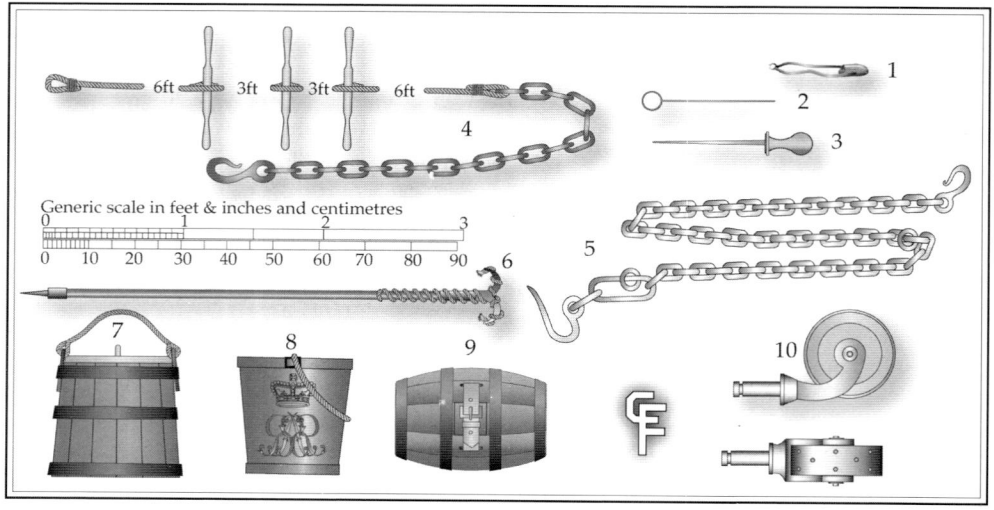

Figure 3.10. Gun side arms and equipment (part two). A thumbstall (1), vent pricker or priming wire (2) and vent bit or gimlet (3). The drag-rope and chain for manhandling the gun (4), locking chain and hook (5); the linstock (6) was only used on bracket trail gun carriages. The 'French-style' water bucket usually used at the gun (7) and the 'English-style' leather water bucket used to water the horses (8). The 28lb grease keg was carried on the ammunition wagon (9) and the Hanoverian truck fitted to the trail of a bracket trail gun to aid mobility (10).

to guns on block trail carriages as these had a copper-lined box on the left axle for the burning slow match.[23]

Gun carriages had no brakes and there were three circumstances when some method of arresting the progress was needed. Firstly, during ascent to prevent them running back. Secondly, during descent to prevent them over-running the horses, and thirdly when standing. To achieve this a 'locking or drag chain' was used to lock the wheel. It was usual to fit these chains on the near sides of the gun and each was usually made of one length of chain. This was passed through the spokes of the wheel and coupled back by a sliding 'dog and shake' hook, through a locking ring, on the body of the chain. When not in use, it was hooked up on the near side of the trail and the shake hook attached to a hook on the rear of the axletree bed. Locking chains were usually applied on the near side only, the off side wheel acting to stop the gun from moving sideways. It was never practice to lock the wheels when firing – the force generated would shatter the wheel. The 15lb locking chain was 6 feet long with forty-eight 2.5-inch links, 1.5 inches wide. The locking ring was on the twenty-first link and the end of the chain was attached to an eyebolt under the trail by a 6-inch hook. The chain terminated with a shake hook, loop and keeper at the working end. The dog loop was of 0.5-inch iron, 6.5 inches long and 2.5 inches wide and carried a further locking ring or keeper for the hook. Attached to the loop by a 3-inch ring was the 8-inch 'shake' hook. When going down steep inclines it was sometimes better to use drag ropes than the locking chain and in Spain, this was often the case.[24] While there is some evidence to suggest drag shoes were used during the period – particularly on country wagons – there is no evidence that they were general issue to the artillery until well after the war.[25]

A Portfire cutter was used to cut off the end of a burning portfire and extinguish it. On bracket carriages, this was carried separately as a small store; on a block trail carriage it was usually mounted on the right side of the trail.

Powder horns were not used in the field artillery after the introduction of the tube or quill and the carriage of the 1lb bag of priming powder on the gun limber. They continued in use with siege artillery where the powder was stored in budge barrels 10.5 inches deep and 13 inches diameter with leather covers that drew together like the mouth of a bag. Each contained 38lb of priming powder.[26]

A variety of small tools were carried on the hinged shelves under which the rounds were stored, most probably in a spare cartridge bag. The list of tools and their location varied with the type of ordnance and if both axle boxes were fitted. According to the lists of the period the tools would include, hammer, files, two needles and 1oz of worsted thread, pincers and scissors. Also issued for active ammunition were a funnel, mallet, fuse holder and saw. It is most probable that this set of tools was supplemented as experience required.

A 23-inch long portfire holder was issued to each piece to allow the firer to stand clear of the recoil, when firing the gun. It consisted of an 18-inch wooden handle with a round metal socket at the top with a screw to retain the portfire. It was usually carried in a holder on the left bracket of a block trail carriage.

Each ammunition wagon carried a spare bucket and a spare axletree, it is not clear if spare shafts were carried during this period. The centre box of each limber carried two spare drag washers, two spare linchpins and a spare rammer head. A spare sponge sheepskin and two spare thumb-stalls were carried in one of the limber boxes or gun axle boxes. What is puzzling is that there is no scale of spares, including those of the later periods, that lists any spare capsquare keys. A spare gun carriage fitted to carry spare wheels for the guns and limbers accompanied each troop or brigade.

Initially each gun was equipped with both a sponge-staff and a rammer, but by 1794 these were being replaced by a combined version.[27] This had a long ash staff, one end of which was fitted with a hollowed, wooden rammer and the other with a wooden cylinder covered with sheepskin used to sponge out the barrel of the gun and extinguish any smoldering residue. The sponge-staff was usually carried on the gun with the swab end strapped to a staple under the axle and the rammer end though a metal loop under the trail. It was important the sponge head completely filled the bore of the gun to exclude any air that could ignite any smoldering remains. A spare sheepskin was always carried and a spare rammer was carried in the limber centre box. When not in use the sponge head was protected by a canvas cap. It was common practice for the sponge man to mark the staff so that he could instantly tell if there was a round or cartridge in the bore if the mark did not align with the muzzle – in the heat of battle, it was all too easy to make a mistake. Each gun required a sponge-staff of the appropriate length and diameter and the different sizes are given in Table A.9 of Appendix A at the end of Part One.

Wooden tampions with collars were issued for each gun and howitzer. They were a push fit and often secured with seizing line. They were inserted into the muzzle of the piece to protect the bore from the ingress of foreign matter.[28]

A thumb protector known as a 'thumbstall' was made from leather and used by the vents man to protect his thumb from the hot metal when 'serving the vent'.

The traversing lever was a specially shaped curved pole some 66 inches long and weighing about 5 pounds. These provided leverage to the trail when traversing or

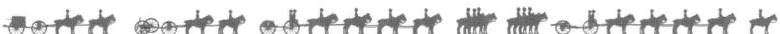

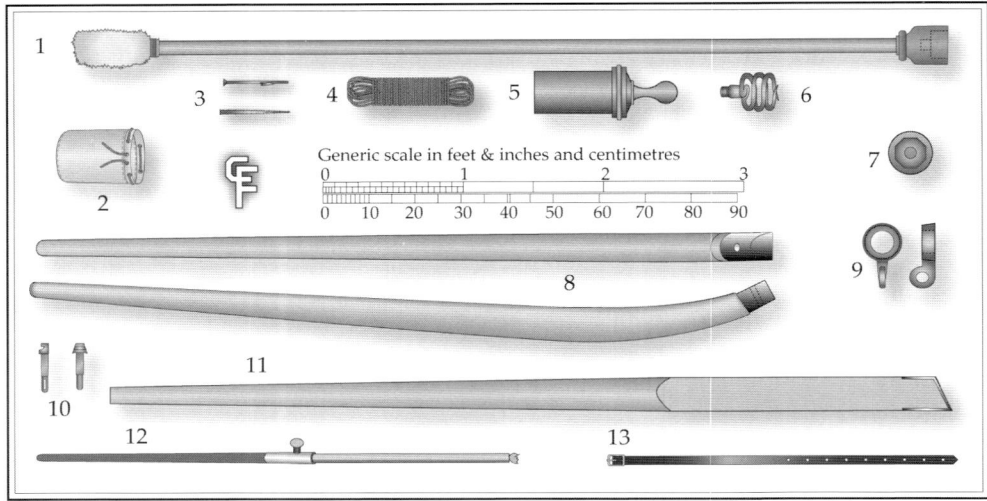

Figure 3.11. Gun side arms and equipment (Part Three). Combination sponge staff and rammer with the hollow end for the wad hook (1), sponge cap (2), spring and jagged gun spikes (3), 30ft of seizing line (4), wooden tampion (5) and the wad hook or worm (6) that screwed into the hollow end of the rammer (7). The traversing lever (8), drag washers (9), linchpins (10), 11lb handspike (11), portfire holder (12), and a side arm strap (13). The parts were common to both bracket and block trail carriages and the appropriate dimensions varied to suit the ordnance being served.

aiming the gun. Each gun carried at least one of these, and was usually strapped under the right side of the trail. When in use the curved, metal-clad end was fitted through the traversing ring and secured by a chained pin through the traversing loop. The exact size varied with the ordnance in use.

Priming wires were used to pass through the vent and pierce the cartridge to enable the quill to better ignite the powder of the cartridge; they were made from a 9-inch long wire, 0.1 inches in diameter and two were always carried.

The vent bit was used to clean the vent when it became fouled with powder residue or if a quill failed to blow clear. They were usually carried in one of the gun axle boxes or on the limber. They were made of square section to ream out the vent and were fitted with a wooden handle.

Wad Hook

The wad hook was initially issued as a separate side arm, usually with a rammer on the other end. It was used to draw charges or unburnt remnants from the bore of the gun. By 1794, a new combination version which attached to the new sponge-staff had been being introduced.[29] It consisted of a double helical hook welded to a shank, which screwed into a nut in the hollow end of the rammer. It was usually stored in the right axle box or the limber centre box. It was a standard item and the same size was used on all ordnance. The double helix hook had a diameter of 3 inches and was 3 inches long. It was welded to a threaded shank 1 inch in diameter, the overall length being 4.5 inches.

Endnotes to Chapter 3

1. Caruana, A. 'The Introduction of the Block Trail Carriage', *Arms Collecting*, Vol. 18, No. 1, 1980.
2. Duncan, 1872: p. 113.
3. Hogg, 1963: pp. 508-9, et al.
4. Dickson, 1908: p. 154.
5. National Archive, WO 1/168: p. 431, dated 16 August 1804.
6. Ibid: WO 3/37: pp. 73–7, dated 3 January 1794.
7. Lawson, C.P., *A History of the Uniforms of the British Army*, Vol. IV, Norman Military Publications, London, 1966: p. 80.
8. Leslie, 1912: p. 75.
9. Dickson, 1908: p. 407.
10. Duncan, 2005: p. 119.
11. *Aide Memoire*, 1847: plates 21 and 22; Royal Carriage Department: plates 13 and 14.
12. McConnell, 1988: p. 194.
13. Ibid: p. 192. (It is not clear if this means iron axles had been fitted to bracket trail carriages or if they were now equipped with block trail carriages.)
14. HMSO, *Treatise on Military Carriages*, 1868: p. 13.
15. Mercer, 1870: p. 150.
16. Caruana, 1979: p. 30.
17. Rudyard, 1793: plate 42; Adye, 1813: p. 219.
18. Adye, 1813: p. 195.
19. Dickson, 1908: p. 512.
20. Griffiths, 1839: pp. 30, 142, 153, 156.
21. James Clavell Library. Papers dated 1825 and Adye, 1813: p. 196: 1810: p. 219.
22. Rudyard, op cit.
23. Rudyard, op cit.
24. Webber, W., *With the Guns in the Peninsula*, Greenwood, 1991: p. 170.
25. Dickson, 1908: p. 863.
26. Dickson, 1908: p. 614.
27. National Archive, WO 1/68: p. 96
28. Rudyard, op cit.
29. National Archive, WO 1/68: p. 9.

CHAPTER 4

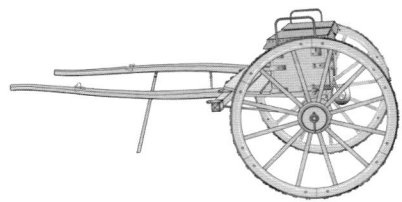

Limbers

Limbers

The limber was originally called the fore-carriage and was only used when the gun carriage was to be transported over distance. The early limbers used by the field artillery were of the basic type, consisting of an axletree, wheels, shafts and a bolster, which carried a vertical pintle over which the pintle hole in the tail transom of the gun was placed, where it was retained on the limber by the limber chain and hook. The limber wheels were generally smaller than those of the gun carriage in order to keep the trail of the gun carriage low to make limbering and unlimbering a less onerous task, but this propensity to use small diameter wheels caused a problem with the draught which is discussed in Chapter 6. The limber also provided a convenient method by which the horses were attached to move the gun. The first horse was placed in the shafts of the limber and preceded by double or treble draught for the larger ordnance, but more usually just one for the lighter battalion guns.

The simple pintle limber allowed the trail of the gun to move freely in the horizontal plane and, to a lesser extent, in the vertical plane, which gave good articulation over uneven terrain and often provided a tighter turning circle than the later patterns of limber. These limbers were made of a size to suit the ordnance to be moved, and with the exception of the shafts the dimensions varied from piece to piece except for the limited number of common parts.

The bolster was made in two parts, the lower section forming the axletree and the upper part, the bolster proper. Between the two sections were mortised the shafts and across the top was mounted an iron plate, strapped down each face to strengthen the wooden bolster and to prevent wear from the trail. At each extremity the bolster was fitted with iron hoops, adding strength to the bolster and axle. The iron pintle stood some three calibres tall above the bolster and the lower part bolted

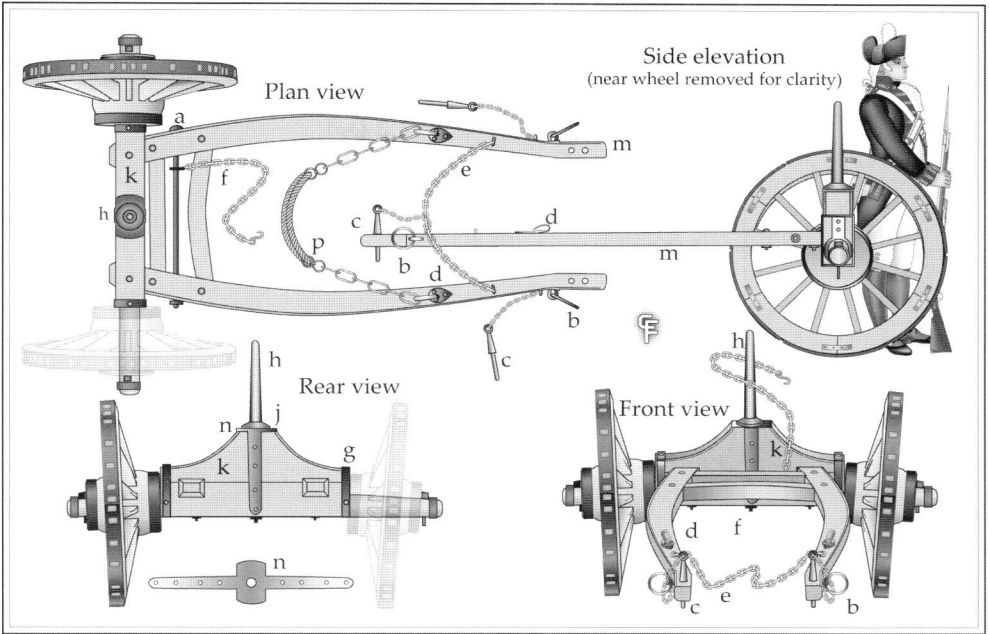

Figure 4.1. Early limber used for the movement of bracket trail gun carriages. The shafts (m) connect through the bolster (k), which also forms the axletree. The parts were named as the limber bolt (a), shaft rings (b), tug pins and chains (c), breeching hooks (d), ridge chain with hooks and loops (e) and the limber chain with hook (f) used to secure the carriage to the limber. The bolster hoops (g), pintle (h), pintle washer (j), bolster plate (n) and back band (p).

vertically through the body and was secured underneath by a square nut. The shafts at the front of the limber were strengthened by wooden fore and hind cross bars and a metal rod; the limber bolt, which also acted as a retainer for the 'limber chain with hook and rings', was used to retain the trail of the carriage to the limber when on the move. The shafts were also fitted with the various attachments for the draught harness and this aspect is discussed in more detail in Chapter 6. The design of these limbers had many disadvantages and most early Napoleonic field ordnance, the 3-pr and 6-pr guns in particular, carried first-line ammunition in side boxes mounted on the gun axles, the simple pintle limbers having no space available. It was also noted:

1. The limber is of no other use than to support the Trail of the Carriage, in the doing of which it is attended with the following inconveniences;
2. It will not allow the Carriage to turn so short as is frequently necessary to accompany the infantry.
3. The wheels are so low … and from the same cause the thrill [wheeler] Horse is sadly crippled by the draft of the fore Horse tending to bear the shafts down until they form a right line with his traces, which is prevented by the thrill horses back; on which, in bad roads, so great a stress is thrown, that it is with difficulty he can support himself beneath it; consequently must very much counteract the Power of the Fore Horse.
4. The naves of the Limber Wheels are too small to admit their being put upon the axletree of the Gun Carriage, to bring it out of the field, in case its wheels should be disabled; and from the Slightness and Construction of the Limber, it is impossible to bring the gun off upon it.[1]

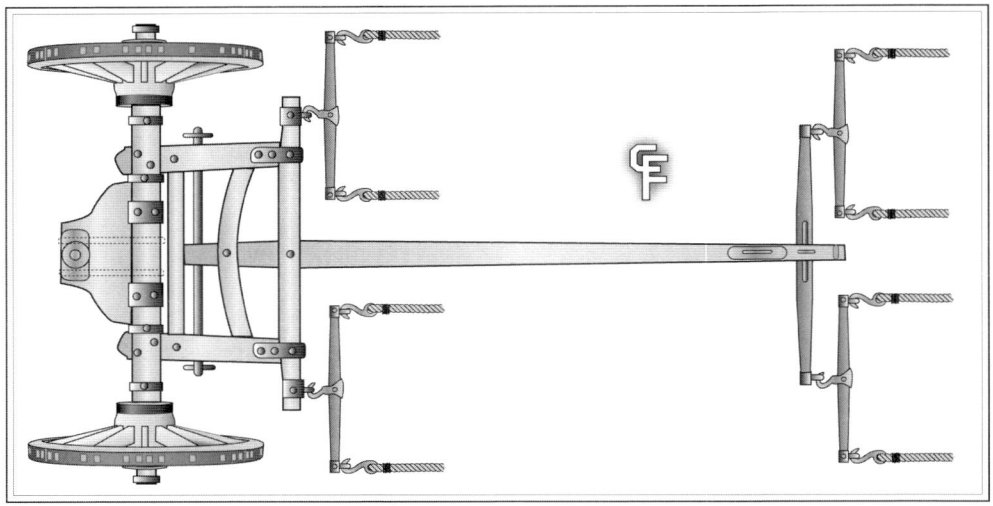

Figure 4.2. Early limber for the 3-pr gun modified by General Lawson during the Egyptian Campaign of 1800. The shafts have been cut off and replaced by a pole fitted for double draught. The pintle has been moved to the rear to provide space for one of the side ammunition boxes from the gun carriage to be carried on the limber.

The simple limber described above had gone out of general use with the field artillery by the start of the war, although the distant colonial outstations still had them, as did the heavier siege ordnance. General Lawson in the Egyptian Campaign of 1800 had four older-spattern 3-pr guns issued from Malta and these he modified by altering the limbers to pole draught and removing the side boxes from the gun carriage, placing one on the limber.[2]

The advantages of the introduction of the new pattern of limbers for the horse artillery and based upon the 'new pattern ammunition wagon'[3] were so apparent an immediate programme of replacement was begun; even some field guns on bracket trails were re-equipped with a version of the new pattern, albeit with extended rear bolsters to carry the vertical pintle for the gun. It is not possible to say exactly when ammunition boxes were placed upon the limber. Notes of 1778 by Congreve and those of Colonel Williams in 1781 show the horse teams in pairs and suggest the boxes were now on the limber. As early 1794, this programme had begun; a sketch by de Loutherberg for the Siege of Valenciennes shows a gun with ammunition boxes on the limber.

The shortcomings of carrying ready to use ammunition had long been a difficult one, and the use of side boxes on the old-style battalion guns meant the ammunition had to be moved from the gun and sent to the limber when action was expected. The new pattern limbers now carried the ammunition in boxes and by 1793, the 3-pr and 6-pr guns of the horse artillery had been modified to carry small amounts of round shot in the right axletree box, even though the cartridges were still carried in the limber. These problems had long been recognized and by the start of this period the field artillery had begun to replace the simple pintle limber as soon as new patterns became available, although they continued in use with distant outstations and for the heavier siege weapons.

The Congreve Limber of 1776 (see Figure 4.8)

The first major attempt to resolve the ammunition situation had come in 1776 with the introduction of the new light 6-pr battalion gun when a new pattern limber was introduced. This is the type illustrated by Rudyerd in his drawings of 1792, in which he provides two views of the new type of limber for use with the 6-pr gun. These drawings are of the limber that was introduced by Congreve in about 1776.[4] The improvements introduced included a vertical 'pintail' fixed upon a bolster placed 18 inches behind the axletree, which allowed the carriage to 'turn short', and more importantly, the ammunition could now be carried upon the limber where it was immediately available for use at the gun. The ammunition was stored in two boxes that could be easily handled and moved, but it was necessary to counter-balance the load on the axle of the limber, and for this purpose the boxes could be moved to the front or rear to affect the point of balance. Another advantage was that the limber axletree could carry entrenching tools and a locker under the shafts, which served to hold the tackles and ropes to move the gun over difficult ground. This limber still used only one wheel horse, but was usually preceded by one or two leaders in single file. The method of draught had also been improved to ease the loading on the wheel horse, the traces of the horse in front of the wheeler were now attached in a better line of draught to chains under the rear of the shafts rather than to the tug staples of the shafts themselves.

The New Limber of 1793 (see Colour Plates 5 and 6)

The new design of equipment for the horse artillery introduced a completely new limber for the block trail gun carriage and this design also formed the basis of the 'transitional' limber for guns mounted on bracket trail carriages. The new limbers were of a standard size for all puposes, but those for the larger ordnance were fitted with stronger wheels. the framework for the new limber was formed by the axletree bed at the rear, a splinter bar at the front and three longditudinal pieces, called futchells, at each side of the limber and one in the centre. Across the top of this framework were bolted a footboard raised by small brackets and two platform boards. The first platform board was bolted across the top of the futchells, behind the footboard and beyond this was the second platform board. This board was fitted with two box staples, or slots, to receive the iron nibs of the ammunition boxes.[5]

At the rear, in a groove under the axletree bed, an iron axle was secured by yoke hoops and coupling plates. Two further bolts were passed through the axletree bed and axle, one on each side of the centre, and the nuts secured a metal plate bolted to the underside of the axle to cover the unused centre hole. To give wider seating for the ammunition boxes the rear face of the axletree bed was fitted with two bolsters or shelves. The limber hook was also fitted to the lower edge of the rear face by three bolts passing through the axletree bed; attached to the bed by a chain was a 6-inch long keyed pin that fitted through a hole in the top of the limber hook to secure and retain the towing eye. At the front the splinter bar was fitted with trace bands on the top face, shaft irons on the lower face and two iron stays that supported the splinter bar from the underside of the axletree bed.

The shafts of the limber were transferable from one carriage to another. On top of each shaft were stapled the breech rings, one on the off shaft and two on the near. There were two shafts, an off shaft and a near shaft. The off shaft terminated in a

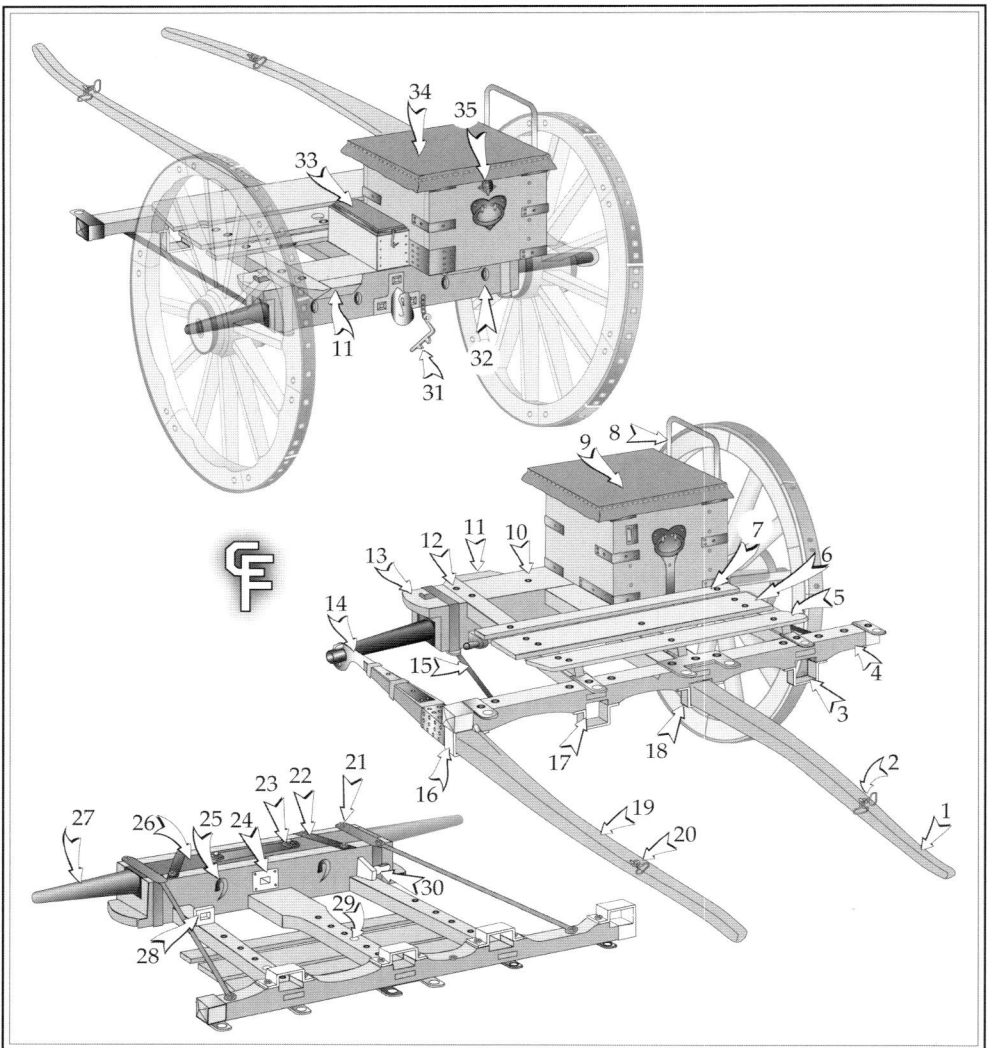

Figure 4.3. Component parts of a generic 'new pattern' limber. Near shaft (1), near shaft breeching rings (2), near shaft iron with the trace band above (3), splinter bar (4), footboard (5), platform boards (6 & 7). The guard iron (8) and near ammunition box (9). The axletree bed (10), shelf or bolster (11), futchell (12), lip of axletree bed and ammunition box stay (13), off wheel iron (14), splinter bar support stay (15), off shaft iron and trace band (16), off centre shaft iron and trace band (17), centre shaft iron and trace bands (18), off shaft (19) and off shaft breeching ring (20). The yoke hoop (21) and coupling plate (22), axle plate and bolts (23), near shaft plate and mortice (24), hooks for side arms (25), axle body (26) and axletree arm (27), near shaft stirrup iron (28), hole for shaft bolt (29) and off shaft pin, crutch and washer (30). The limber hook and key (31), iron staples for the ammunition boxes (32), the centre box for spares (33), off ammunition box (34) and ammunition box hasp (35).

metal ring known as a wheel iron and the part reaching between the splinter bar and the axletree was of iron, so it could be made thinner to allow more space for mud to work through. There was also a locating lug fitted to the top of the shaft to ensure it was correctly positioned when the shaft was passed through the shaft iron. The near shaft terminated in a metal tenon, this fitted into a metal plate set into the front of the axletree bed. If the off shaft of the limber was damaged, the near shaft could be fitted with a handspike or cross piece to permit the limber to be driven in

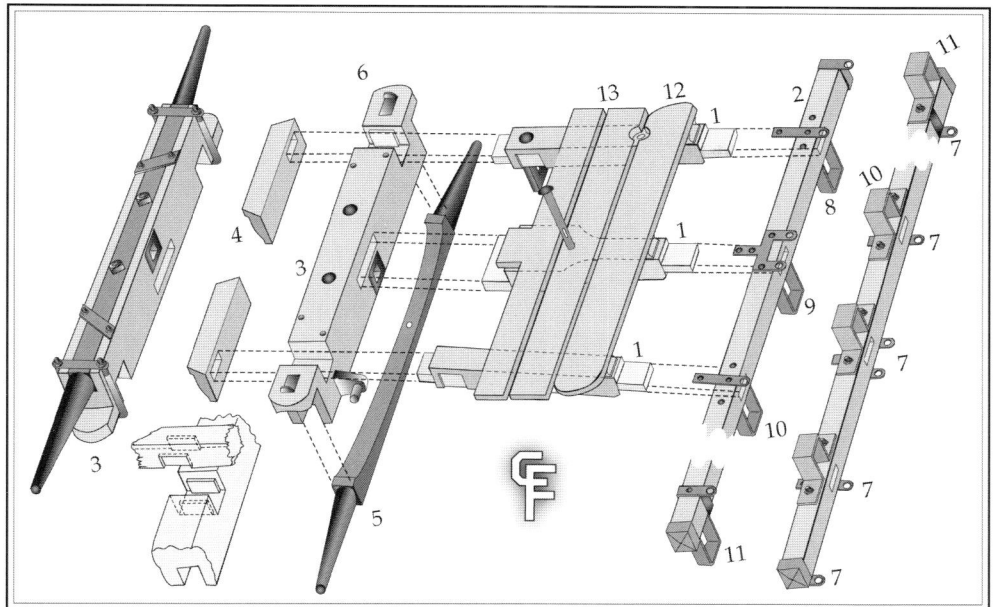

Figure 4.4. The construction of the new pattern limber of 1793. The futchells (1), splinter bar (2), axletree bed (3), shelves or bolsters (4) and iron axletree (5). Axletree bed extensions (6), widen the seating for the ammunition boxes. Trace irons (7), near shaft iron (8), centre shaft iron (9), off-centre shaft iron (10), off shaft iron (11), the foot board (12) and platform boards (13).

pole draft. The near shaft also carried a shaft prop, which was strapped up to the shaft when in draft and let down when the limber needed to stand with the shafts in the draft position.[5]

As with all wooden vehicles produced by The Royal Carriage Department the timber used was that providing the most appropriate strength and resilience. The axletree bed, footboard and brackets were of elm; the splinter bar, platform boards, bolsters and shafts were of ash and all the metal work of iron.

The new combination of gun and limber effectively provided an articulated four-wheeled wagon with a good turning circle, capable of moving weight at speed with excellent mobility over rough ground. By counterbalancing the weight of the gun carriage with the limber and ammunition, the load upon the shafts was more or less in balance and this gave the advantages of a four-wheeled vehicle while precluding the disadvantages of loading the wheeler in rough going. The same pattern of limber was used in conjunction with the forge, ammunition wagon, spare wheel carriage and store wagons, and the records show that by 1810 the new pattern limbers had been adopted for general use throughout the British field artillery in Europe.[6]

Double Draught (see Figure 4.6)

In normal usage, the new limbers were driven in double draught with a team of horses arranged in pairs. To operate in double draught the near shaft was passed through the near-centre shaft iron, under the centre futchells, with the tenon fitted into the axletree bed. An iron bolt passing down through the platform board, centre

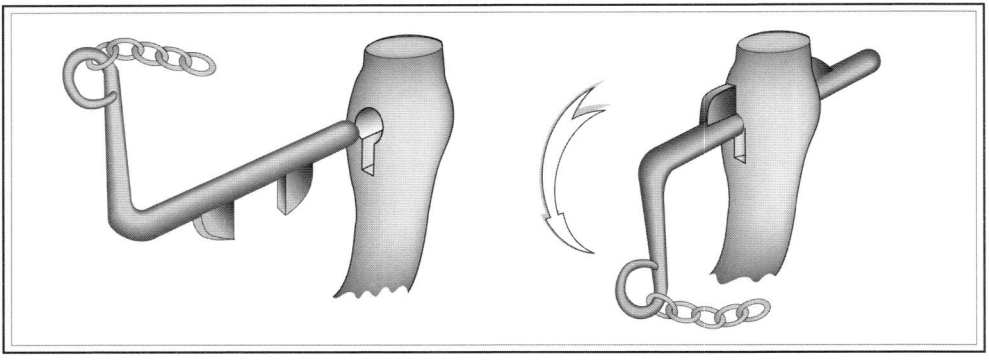

Figure 4.5. Limber hook and pin. The eye of the gun trail was locked on to the limber hook by a 6-inch long chained pin with a long arm and two integral keys protruding from the top. The pin was inserted upside down into the limber hook, passing through a shaped hole that accepted the protruding keys; the weight of handle caused the pin to drop down and rotate to engage the two keys around the upper part of the limber hook and lock into position.

futchell and the near shaft and keyed underneath, secured it in position. The off shaft was passed through the off shaft iron, with the wheel iron at the end fitted over the axletree arm, acting at the same time as a washer where it was secured by a linchpin.

Single Draught (see Figure 4.6)

Where narrow or bad roads necessitated single draught was used and the horses were arranged in single file, one behind the other with the off-wheeler staying between the shafts and preceded by the near-wheeler. In front of these the centre and lead hoses were similarly arranged. To accommodate this mode of draught the near shaft was placed through the near shaft iron and fitted into a mortise of an iron plate mounted vertically under the left futchell. The shaft was secured by the same iron bolt, but now passing through the gap between the platform board and footboard, down through the left futchell and keyed underneath. The off shaft passed through the off-centre shaft iron and the wheel iron fitted on an iron pin of a crutch fitted to the front of the axletree bed where it was secured by a linchpin. A washer, kept on the crutchpin in double draft, was transferred to the off axletree to act between the nave and the linchpin and replace the wheel iron of the off shaft.

Treble Draught (see Figure 4.6)

When the going was particularly difficult treble draught, with the horses three abreast, could be arranged. The shafts were set as for single draught and a swingletree added to the trace iron at either end of the splinter bar for the two outer horses.

Ammunition Boxes

Each limber carried two ammunition boxes placed either side of a small centre box fitted to carry spares. The first pattern ammunition boxes accepted fixed ammunition but were divided unequally.[7] These changed in about 1807 to boxes that were the

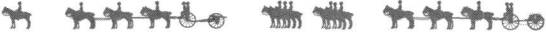

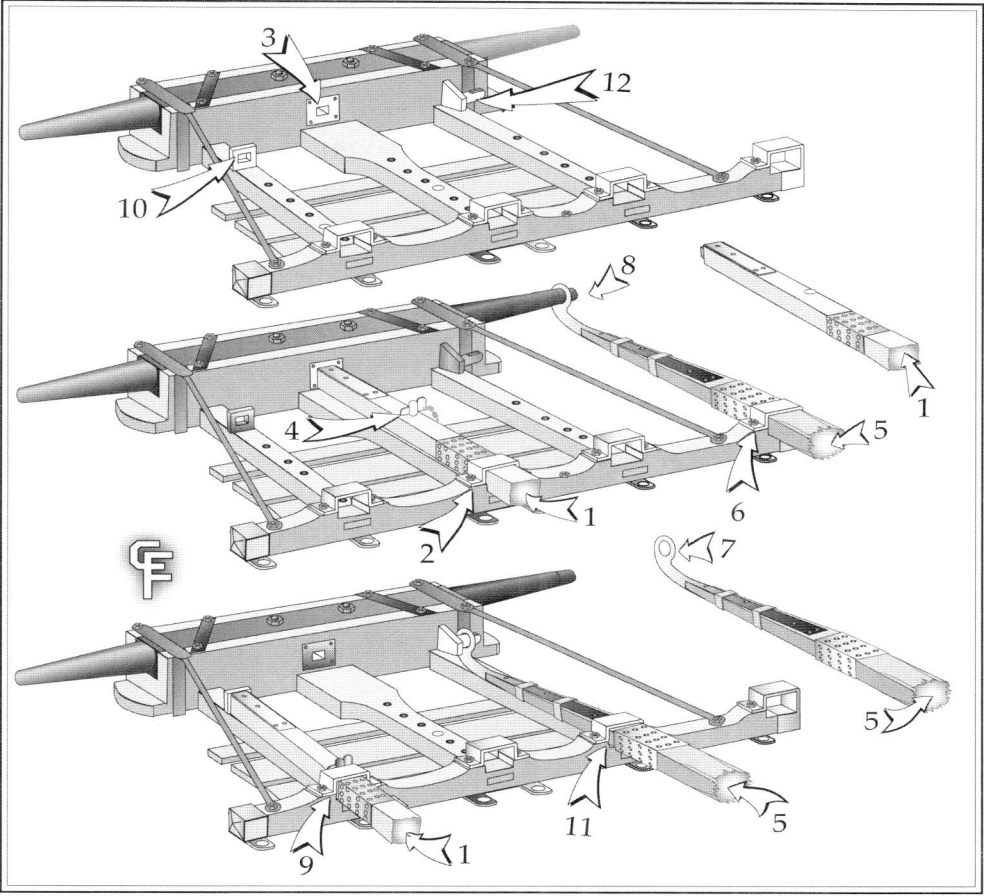

Figure 4.6. The limber fittings for different draughts. In double draught, the near shaft (1) slotted through the centre shaft iron (2) with the end of the shaft placed in the metal plate on the axletree bed (3) and secured by a bolt (4). The off shaft (5) passed through the off shaft iron (6) and the wheel iron (7) fitted over the off axle (8) and was secured by a linchpin. In single draught, the near shaft passed through the near shaft iron (9) and slotted into a metal stirrup under the near futchell (10). The off shaft passed through the off-centre shaft iron (11) and the wheel iron fitted over a metal pin (12).

mirror image of each other and were no longer fitted for fixed ammunition, but the limber of the gun and the limber of the ammunition wagon were always the same to ensure immediate interchangeability in the event of damage. The ammunition boxes were made of 1-inch plank, the sides of deal with elm ends and strengthened with squares of iron at the corners and a carrying handle at the front and rear face. Each had a guard iron on the outer face to act as a handhold for those detachment personnel who rode upon the limber. The top lid was was covered with canvas and prolonged on the inside to provide cover over the centre box. By 1810, with the exception of the medium 12-pr, the size of the boxes had standardized to a slightly larger 15.2 inches high, 20.6 inches wide and 16.75 inches from front to back.

The boxes were secured to the limber by an iron nib plate secured to the bottom of the front edge, which were keyed into staples or slots on the rear of the second platform board where they were secured with chained pins. The boxes were tied to the limber by ropes which passed through the rear carrying handles to iron staples fitted on the rear face of the axletree bed. The underside of the the lid was fitted with two leather straps, set in loops for the carriage of portfires, the off box also carried a saw used to cut fuses to the required length. The interior fittings of each box differed to suit the amount and nature of the ordnance to be carried, but where possible the projectiles were always placed to the outside of the carriages to protect them. In the foot artillery ammunition boxes were fitted with staples to the rear face of the boxes to accommodate straps for the carriage of the backpacks and greatcoats.

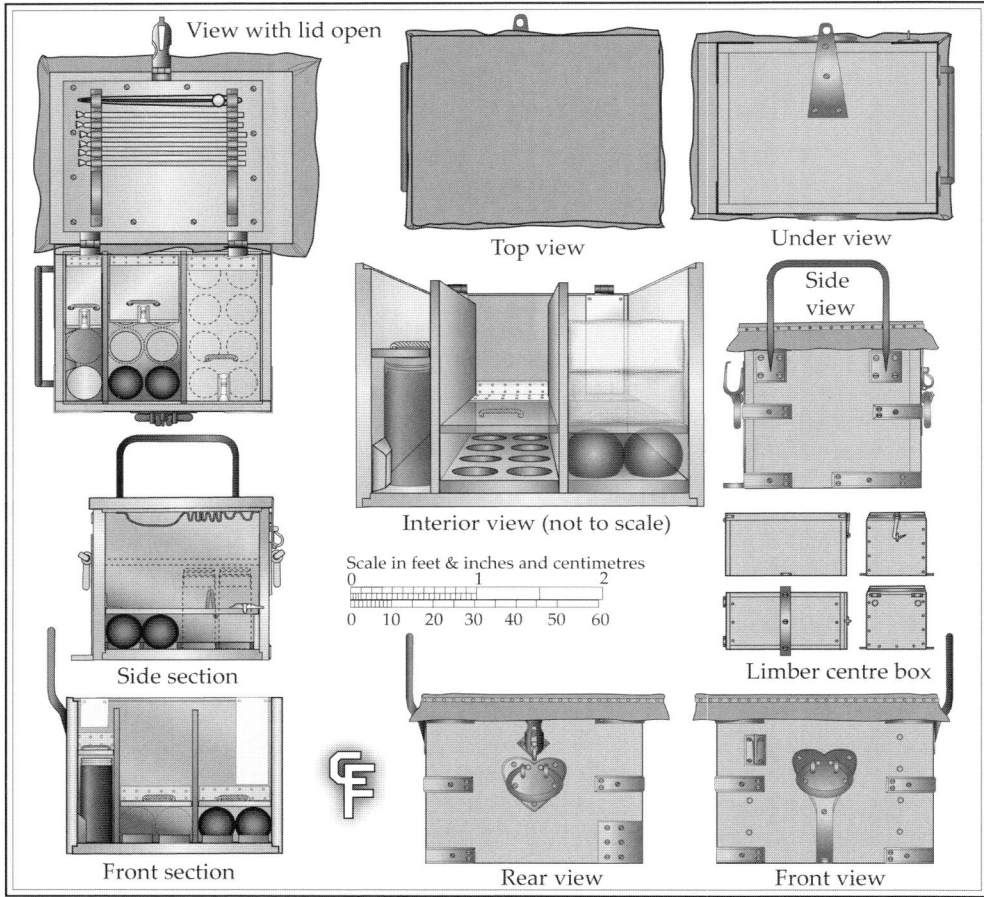

Figure 4.7. Typical limber ammunition boxes. The size was generally the same and the internal arrangement was altered to suit the nature of the ammunition carried. Where it was necessary to change the size of the box to carry larger calibre ammunition the width of the second platform board was modified to suit. The top view shows the box with the lid back to show the internal arrangement. This box carries four common case under the narrow shelf and eight round shot under each of the other two. The portfires are carried on the lid and the other box also carried a saw for cutting the fuses. The other views show the details of the general construction and were similar for all the boxes. The centre box, covered by the extended lids of the main boxes, carried selected spares. The nib screwed to the bottom of the box engaged in the bracket of the rear platform board where it was retained by a chained pin. The rear of the boxes was secured by ropes tied through the handles and eyebolts of the rear of the axle bed. Details of the specific ammunition carried for each gun is given in Appendix D at the end of Part Two.

In the British service it was practice to rezsuppply the limber with ammunition from the ammunition wagon, and there was a constant ferrying of ammunition between the two vehicles. The King's German Legion used a different approach and used the ammunition wagon limber to affect a direct exchange of boxes with the gun limber.

Each box was divided into compartments for the carriage of the appropriate ammunition, and over each compartment was a leather, hinged shelf. On top of the shelves were the cartridges, usually carried in canvas cartouches, the fuses and any separator charges for the spherical case. The fuses were often pre-cut to a given length and stored in marked bags. Round shot, spherical case or shells were stored under the shelves with their bottoms in circular wooden cutouts fixed to the floor of the box. It was common practice to place rounds in two tiers, one upon the other, separated by a wooden shelf. The records show that round shot could be carried unfixed or fixed, but spherical case and shells were always attached to wooden bottoms. Commomn case was usually stored upright, light case in one box and heavy case in the other, with the wooden bottom to the top and the rounds held tight by vertical wooden spacers. Usually, the shelf over the case shot was used to carry the small tools and stores, a tin container of quills and a supply of slow match. A detailed listing of the ammunition and tools carried is given in Part Two under the relevant type of ordnance.

The amount and nature of the ammunition carried in the limber boxes varied throughout the period. The records also show the contents, and the limber boxes were often modified to suit the local requirements and availability. The internal fittings were obviously changed to suit the needs of the moment, and there appears to be no set style or pattern. The figures quoted by Adye are generally low on spherical case and common shell when compared with the returns from the field, those from the Peninsula showing more spherical case allocated to the limbers with the corresponding round shot moved to the ammunition wagons.[8] Where such information is available, it is considered in Part Two with the respective field ordnance. Generic information on the ammunition carried is given in the Tables A.10 and A.11 of Appendix A at the end of Part One.

Transitional Limber for Bracket Trail Carriages (see Figures 4.9 and 4.10)

Contemporary illustrations show a new pattern of limber had been introduced before the start of the war. Designed by Congreve in about 1788 this new limber is illustrated in his note books and show a new style of limber with the horses in double draught and the off wheeler in the shafts.[9] It was either a forerunner to those of the horse artillery or a modification of it. The changes enabled this pattern of limber to be used with the bracket trail gun carriages of the brigades and battalion guns. The rate of change from one style to the other must have taken some time, as it was only after the introduction of the Royal Carriage Department at Woolwich in 1803 that the rate of construction became such as to allow a general re-equipping, but Congreve noted in 1797, battalion guns were being fitted with iron axles, five-foot wheels and four horses in double draught.[10]

The pattern of limber adopted for the bracket trail guns was similar to that adopted for the block trail carriage, but the rear was extended some 19 inches to provide a bolster fitted with a vertical pintle mounted in the same manner as the 1776 limber

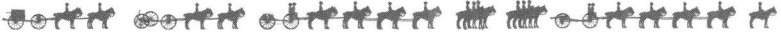

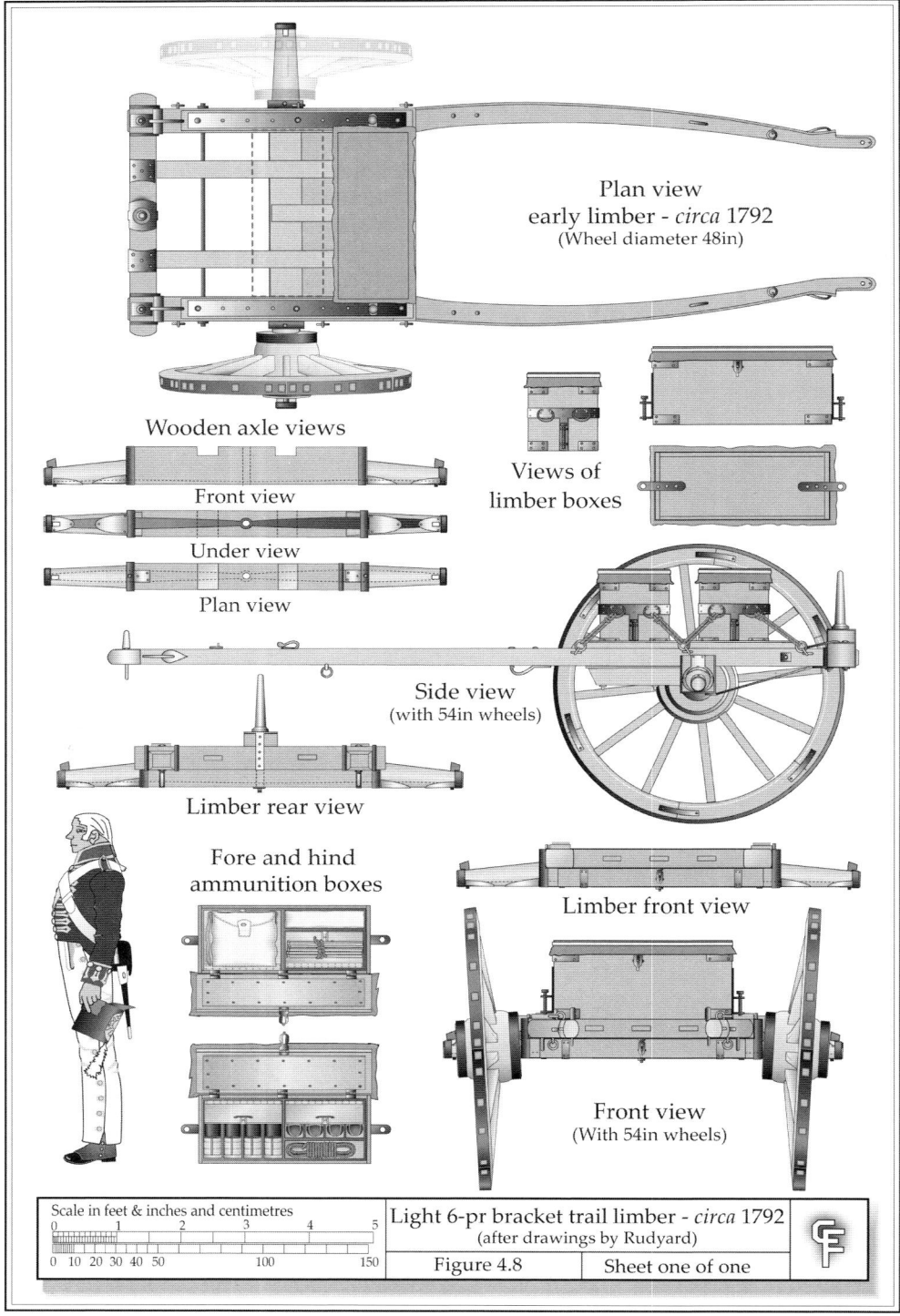

Plan view
early limber - *circa* 1792
(Wheel diameter 48in)

Wooden axle views

Front view

Under view

Plan view

Views of
limber boxes

Side view
(with 54in wheels)

Limber rear view

Fore and hind
ammunition boxes

Limber front view

Limber front view

Front view
(With 54in wheels)

Scale in feet & inches and centimetres

| 0 | 1 | 2 | 3 | 4 | 5 |

| 0 10 20 30 40 50 | 100 | 150 |

Light 6-pr bracket trail limber - *circa* 1792
(after drawings by Rudyard)

| Figure 4.8 | Sheet one of one |

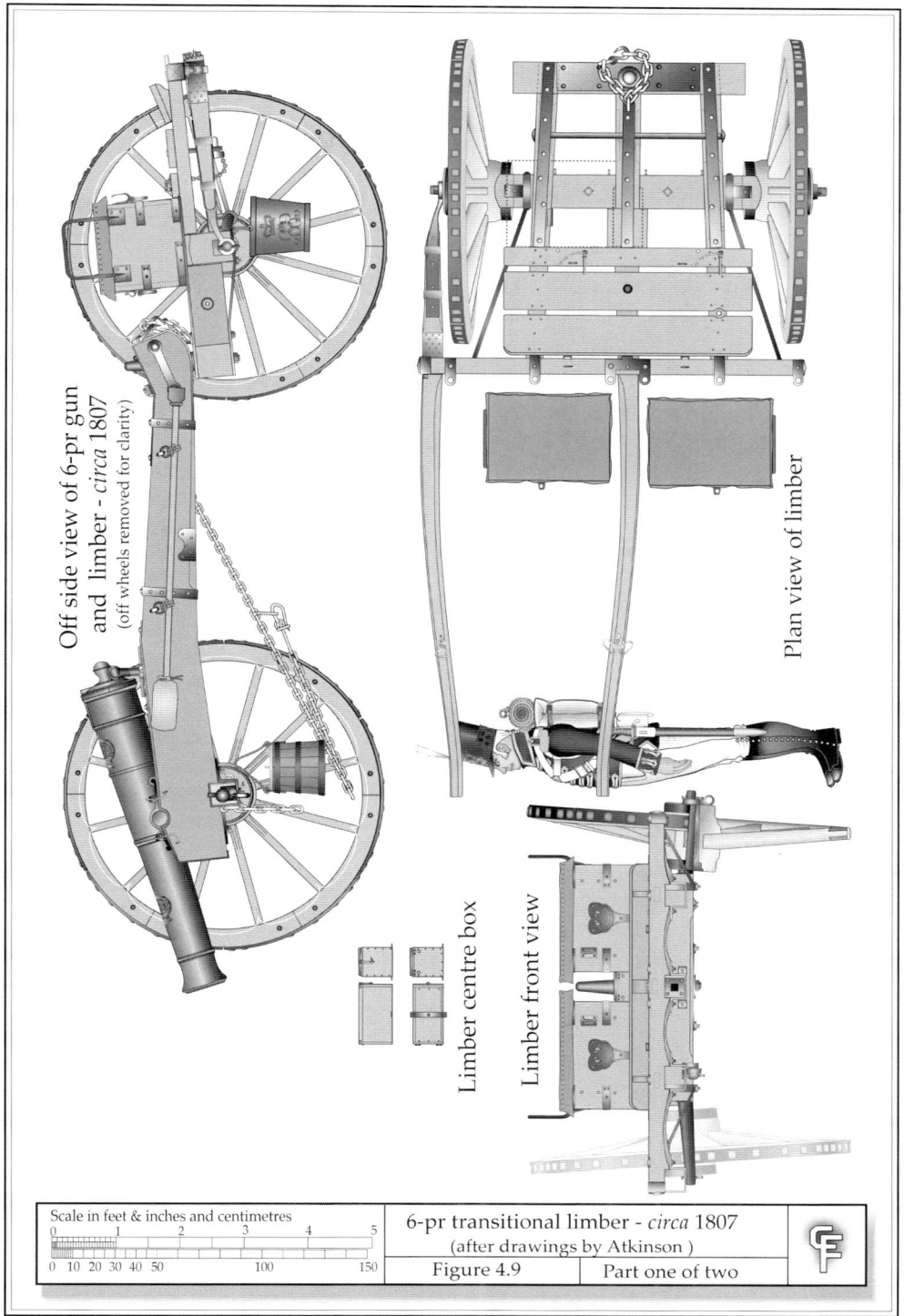

Off side view of 6-pr gun and limber - *circa* 1807
(off wheels removed for clarity)

Plan view of limber

Limber centre box

Limber front view

Scale in feet & inches and centimetres	6-pr transitional limber - *circa* 1807	
0 1 2 3 4 5	(after drawings by Atkinson)	
0 10 20 30 40 50 100 150	Figure 4.9	Part one of two

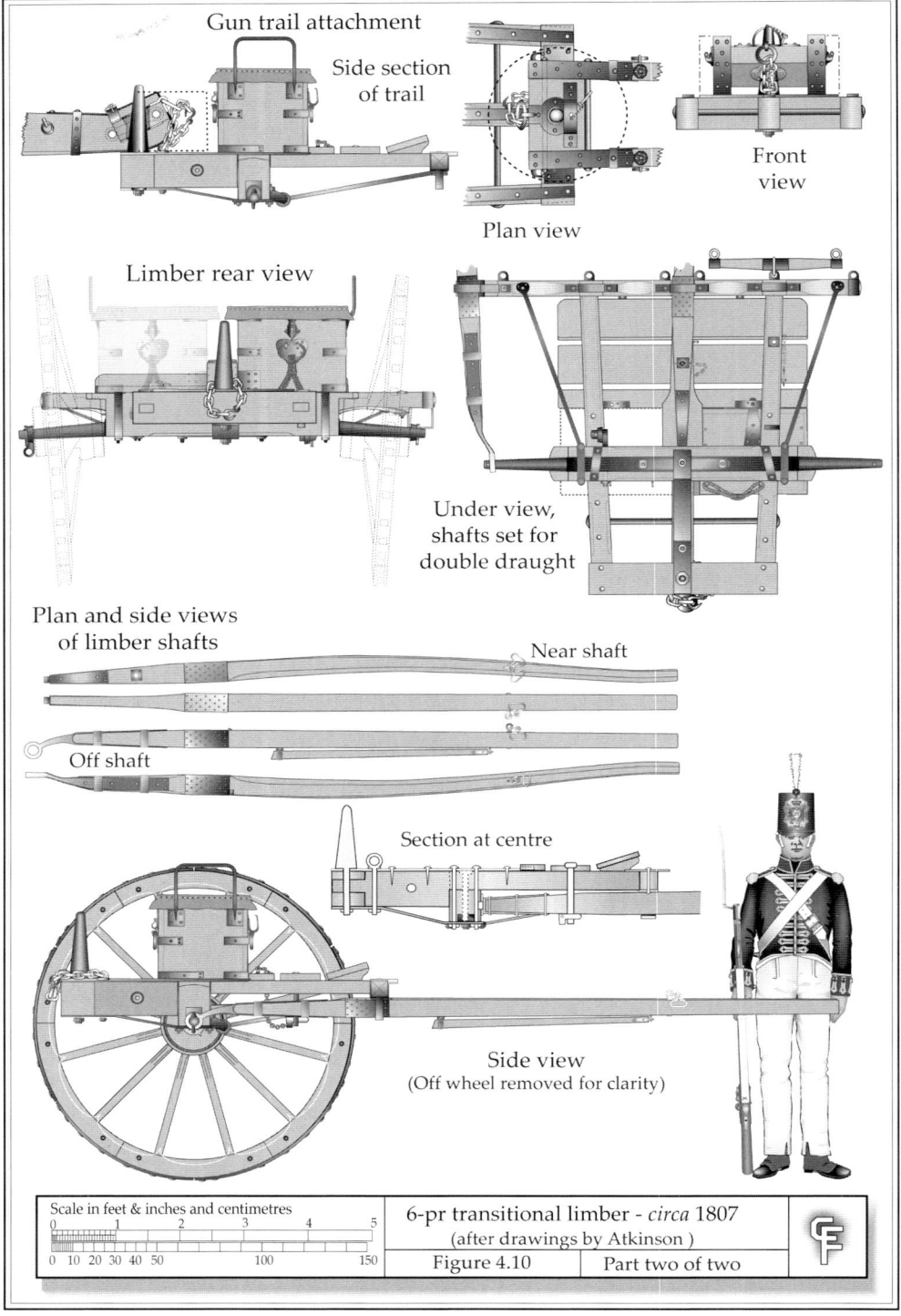

Gun trail attachment

Side section of trail

Front view

Plan view

Limber rear view

Under view, shafts set for double draught

Plan and side views of limber shafts

Near shaft

Off shaft

Section at centre

Side view
(Off wheel removed for clarity)

Scale in feet & inches and centimetres

0   1   2   3   4   5

0 10 20 30 40 50   100   150

6-pr transitional limber - *circa* 1807
(after drawings by Atkinson)

Figure 4.10 | Part two of two

described earlier. The need for this modification was the wider trail transom of the bracket trail carriage, which required a larger clearance around the pintle and could not fit on the towing hook of the standard limber. Consequently, the vertical pintle was retained but moved to the rear to provide the necessary clearance between the trail transom and the limber ammunition boxes. On some ordnance, the medium 12-pr in particular, the larger circle of clearance needed limited the size of the ammunition boxes, and the gun limbers were fitted with specially modified boxes. As with the previous limber, the bracket trail carriage was secured to the limber by a chain, but the transitional limber had a hook at one end and a link on the other. The chain was secured at its centre by a ringbolt attached to the extended centre futchell and the chain was passed through the traversing ring of the trail transom where the two ends were hooked together to secure the trail to the limber. In all other respects, the limber was of a similar pattern to that of the block trail gun with the same construction and draught.

By the end of the Napoleonic War, most British field guns in Europe had been equipped with block trails and the new pattern limbers. There were exceptions, and these may have included some of the long 6-pr and the medium 12-pr guns, which had not been modified to block trails and probably remained on transitional limbers for some time. The equipments at colonial outstations clearly varied between the old and new patterns of gun carriages and limbers but even so, some effort had been made to modernize these as ordnance returns from Canada show. [12]

Endnotes to Chapter 4

1. Caruana, 1977: pp. 17–19.
2. Duncan, 2005: pp. 118, 124; and Manuscript MD 3,054, Book 2, at the James Clavell Library, Woolwich.
3. Caruana, 1980: p. 4.
4. Caruana, 1977: pp. 12, 13, 17, 19; Rudyerd, 1793: plates 40 and 41.
5. Artillery Museum, Varde, Denmark and the Tøjhusmuseet, Copenhagen, Denmark. Surviving 6-pr gun limber made in 1810. *Aide Memoire*, op cit: plates 37 and 38.
6. Adye, 1813: pp. 12 to 14.
7. Dickson, 1908: p. 700.
8. Dickson, 1908: pp. 856–66.
9. James Clavell Library, MD213/3: pages not numbered.
10. Ibid, RA 20: pp. 268, 324.
11. National Archive, WO 44/245: p. 449 dated 30 June 1812; Graves, 1982: pp. 127–9.

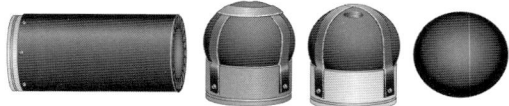

CHAPTER 5

Ammunition, Fuses and Igniters

Introduction

During the Napoleonic period covered by this book the use of shells was restricted to mortars and howitzers; it was only after the period that they were available for guns. Spherical case shot – later called Shrapnel after the man who introduced it into British service – was first used in the field in 1803, but the general availability of spherical case shot did not occur until after 1807. The figures given for the performance of the different types of ammunition are taken from contemporary sources, rather than the often-quoted later figures, where the powder, ammunition and methods of manufacture were different and no direct comparison can be assumed. The performance for the different ammunition and nature of ordnance is given in the tables of Appendix C, the ammunition carried at first line for each nature of ordnance is given in Appendix D, both at the end of Part Two.

Gunpowder

The propellant used for the guns of the period was gunpowder and the nature of this and the ratio to which it was mixed varied from country to country. The British powder of the period was notionally composed of 75 parts of saltpetre, 10 parts of sulphur and 15 parts of charcoal, but different mixtures existed where the circumstances demanded. The main source of powder was the Royal Powder Mills, but powder from civilian contractors was always needed and comparison with Royal Powder required it to be at least 95% effective or it was rejected. The process for the manufacture of gunpowder is well covered elsewhere, but it was mixed to the required proportions and then pressed into damp cakes which were forced through sieves to form the grain size. It was then rotated in a drum to corn the grains (round the edges) and coated with black lead to resist moisture. The gunpowder was provide from the mills in oak barrels, the largest was the 100lb whole barrel, next the 50lb half-barrel and lastly the 25lb quarter–barrel, each containing 90lb, 45lb and 20lb of powder respectively, the space being left to allow the powder to be 'better preserved'.[1] The powder, made up in different forms and grades, was identified by grain size and marked on the barrels in coloured paint, depending upon the type. Powder deteriorated in the field, some became 'shook' and had to be returned to be reformed while much became damp and had to be returned to be dried or re-stoved. In 1807, so much unserviceable gunpowder was being returned from units in the field that '200 of the most diligent boys' of the Royal Laboratory were employed to examine and break up the powder for re-stoving.[2] Dickson related:

> I have found so many cartridges shook, and the powder pulverized, occasioned principally by the length of time this ammunition has been with the Brigade, and in some degree from the wooden bottoms still remaining annexed to the cartridges … I have to add that no part of the ammunition is unserviceable but the cartridges of which the powder is pulverized of course have diminished in force.

In 1792, a new powder made from cylinder charcoal (charcoal baked in rotating cylinders) had been introduced into service. This was more powerful than the pit charcoal that preceded it and was designated red powder, the most powerful of which was 'Red LG' (red large grain). The power of this powder was so much greater. In 1793 trials were carried out to determine the new size of the cartridges for each ordnance, after great discussion the standard adopted was one quarter the weight of the shot for the lighter ordnance and one third for the heavier. This is the powder commonly used by the field artillery during the Napoleonic War.[3]

The new cylinder powder came in three main grades, each from different sieves, and the grade was identified by red lettering on the barrels:

'No ☐ LG'   Large grain of some 2 to 3 mm, and the most powerful of the powders. It was used by the field ordnance and specified for use by the artillery, later it became known as 'Ordnance Powder'.

'No 2 SG'   Small grain with a size of some 1.5 to 2 mm, it was easier to ignite but less powerful.

'No 3 FG'   The finest grain of powder of some 0.5 to 1.5 mm; it was the easiest to ignite but less powerful and used as musket or priming powder and the cartridges of mortars and howitzers.

'SA'   The dust from No. 3 and the fine grain cylinder.

'RA'   Special powder for rifled arms with a larger grain size to inhibit the initial rate of burning and make the delivery of power more gradual.

When powder became unfit or damp it was re-stoved (dried), but this process reduced the power and it was rarely used in its own right.

'RS No ☐ LG'   Painted in yellow letters inside a yellow diamond-shaped frame
'RS No 3 FG'   Painted in yellow letters inside a yellow diamond-shaped frame

Re-stoved powder was mixed with good powder for those purposes where the reduced quality was considered acceptable and designated white powder:

'White LG'   Large-grain powder used for saluting guns, the filling of shells and by the Navy for close-action engagements. It was made from a mixture of 4/7ths of red large-grain powder and 3/7ths of yellow large-grain powder, the cartridges were marked, 'No ☐ LG' painted in white letters.

'Blue LG'   This was a much less powerful powder (about 83% as effective) made from the conventional pit charcoal. This was the older powder used before the introduction of the new cylinder charcoal. In this period it was generally used in pyrotechnics and for the overseas market; 'No ☐ LG' and 'No 3 FG', both painted in blue letters.

In testing it was expected 2 ounces of red large-grain powder would give a range of 180 feet to a 64lb iron ball when fired from an 8-inch mortar, a similar amount of blue large-grain would give a range of 150 feet and re-stoved powder, 107 to 117 feet. The powder was also tested to see how much water it absorbed when exposed to the atmosphere; 100 pounds of powder was not expected to absorb more than 12 ounces of water in 17 or 18 days.[4] Later tests conducted by Boxer calculated the large-grain gunpowder exerted a force of 14.4 tons per square inch. The powder created a temperature of some 3,000°F in the chamber and expanded to fill a space 2,154 times greater than that of the powder.[5]

Fixed, Semi-fixed and Unfixed Ammunition

The term 'fixed' in this context meant when the round was assembled the amount of powder in the cartridge could no longer be adjusted, but this terminology was already anachronistic by this period, as the practice of adjusting the charges of field artillery had long gone out of service except for howitzers and mortars. The term fixed ammunition referred to a projectile attached by metal straps to a wooden bottom with a cartridge attached. To make fixed ammunition the appropriate cartridge was placed inside an empty cartridge and pushed into contact with the wooden bottom. The new bag was then re-tied with twine into two grooves on the base of the bottom or nailed with copper tacks to the wooden bottom. The gun crews could make up 'fixed' ammunition for ready use as required, but there is little evidence they did so, although needles and thread were carried in the near limber box and each unit was issued with a supply of empty cartridges for just this purpose.[6] The establishments of ammunition for the first phase of the war in 1793 make it clear it was usual to issue fixed ammunition for all field guns and howitzers,[7] but this practice appears to have been less in the Peninsula and there are no records to show the issue of fixed in-active ammunition to field artillery during the later period of the war. Dickson recorded he 'Commenced this day to separate the ammunition ... by sawing the wooden bottom in two, leaving a part attached to the cartridge, by which new cartridges are saved for the present, and the ammunition will be less liable to be broken in travelling'.[8] The surviving ammunition boxes and records of ammunition carried show no facility for storing this form of ammunition and there is nothing to suggest where it may have been carried, also there are no records or returns of any fixed ammunition being issued from Woolwich after the first phase of the wars. It was only after the Napoleonic period that the practice of placing fixed ammunition in the right axle box was adopted and there are no records of any such ammunition, activity or storage facility during the period.

Semi-fixed ammunition is regularly mentioned in the records during the period, this was supplied with the round already strapped to a wooden bottom but without the cartridge attached. Common shells and spherical case were always supplied so fitted,

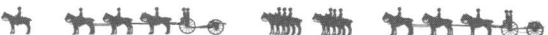

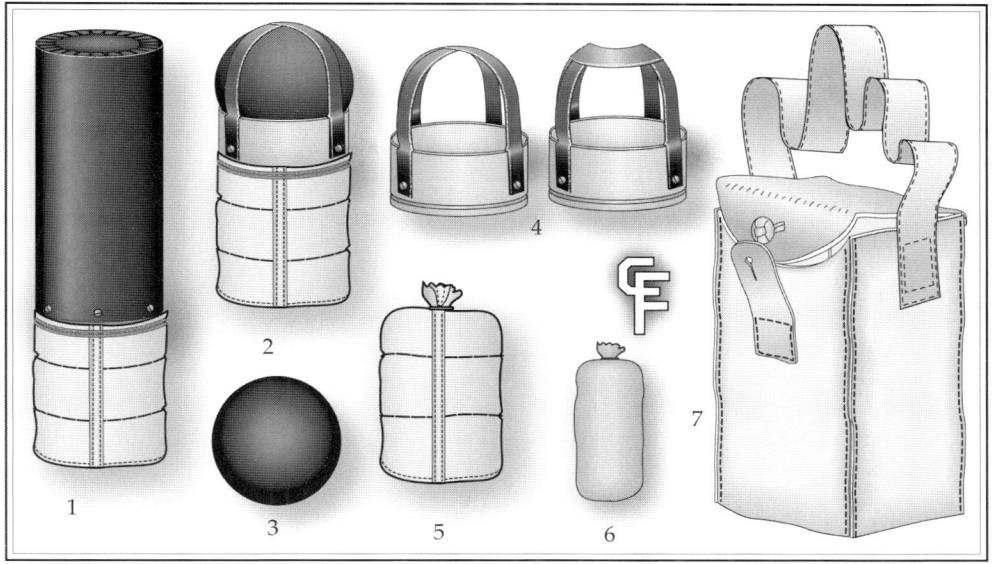

Figure 5.1. Ready use or fixed ammunition, canister or common case (1), round shot (2). Round shot was made of cast iron (3), the wooden bottoms (4) attached to round shot, shells or spherical case. Flannel cartridges of different sizes were pre- filled (5) and 1lb bags of priming powder (6) were used for howitzers. Canvas cartouches with leather bottom into which the cartridges were packed and stored in the limbers (7), they were often used to carry ammunition to the guns.

although round shot was issued both with and without bottoms. Mercer comments 'when on the move and expecting action' it was common to place a cartridge in the bore and hold it in position with a vent pin. It was under these circumstances that the axle box ammunition of the 3 and 6-pr, the only British guns so equipped, makes any sense, but as the cartridges were all carried on the limber the advantage seems dubious.

Wooden Bottoms

The bottoms were designed to prevent the spherical case or common shell turning in the barrel and damaging the fuse; they also tended to provide a higher muzzle velocity as they often fitted into the bore with less windage than the projectile.[9] Rounds issued with bottoms already attached were referred to as semi-fixed ammunition. The bottoms were made from wood, turned with the grain running along the axis of the bore and were hollowed on one face to receive the round. They were held to the round by two tin straps nailed by tacks to the bottom or by a more elaborate form for spherical case. Ammunition manufactured with bottoms pre-fitted by glue mixed with resin only came later, after the period.[10] Dimensions of the wooden bottoms are given in Table A.20 of Appendix A at the end of Part One.

Tubes and Quills

The use of priming powder to fire the gun was no longer used in field artillery of this period except in an emergency and a priming tube was normally used to ignite the charge. Early tubes were made of paper or tin, but this had shown a tendency to rust and the later version was made from the quill of a goose feather, but records show both were used over the period although the quill was the more common by the second phase of the war.[11] The interior of the quill was cleaned of pith, filled with mealed powder, and topped with a conical varnished paper or leather cap; the lower end was cut at an angle to assist in penetrating the bag of the cartridge. The tube had a flat cap at the top, this cap served two purposes, it provided a convenient flat surface for the palm of the hand when the quill was pushed into the vent and it also served to prevent the quill penetrating too far into the cartridge leaving the top below the level of the vent field of the gun. This did happen on occasion and priming powder carried in the limber boxes was for just such an emergency. When a quill failed to blow clear of the gun the number 9 had to ream it out of the vent. Quills were issued in boxes or tins of 100 and usually carried in the off ammunition box on the limbers and in the fore box of the ammunition wagon. The quills were two tenths of an inch in diameter, each of the appropriate length for the type of gun; 5.9 inches for the 3-pr gun and the 5.5-in howitzer; 6.8 inches for the 9-pr gun, 4.75 inches for the light 6-pr gun, 6.5 inches for the heavy 6-pr and 7.75 inches for the medium 12-pr.[12] Experiments were regularly made to determine the most effective material and in 1814, 5,000 brass tubes were authorized for field use.[13]

Cartridges

At the start of the period the use of paper cartridges by the field artillery had effectively ceased. This had been discarded in favour of flannel or serge, the paper having shown a tendency to split in use and a propensity to leave smoldering remnants in the chamber and block the vent. The new materials, although one fifth heavier and more expensive, were totally consumed in firing and rarely split. The flannel was boiled in glue to seal the weave and then hot pressed to keep out insects and stiffen the material, which if left too pliable could be difficult to insert into the bore of the piece. The bag was cut to size from a paper pattern and rolled on a wooden former then sewn into a tube with the ends overlapping. The 12-pr, 9-pr and 5.5-inch howitzer cartridges had seams of 1 inches with three rows of stitching; those for the 6-pr and 3-pr had seams of 0.75 inches wide with two rows of stitching. Each limber also carried a 1lb bag of priming powder (musket powder), which could be used to prime the gun in an emergency; they also served as cartridges for the 5.5-inch howitzers, although these were often supplied with cartridges made up at the artillery park. In 1806, there were two cartridges for the medium 12-pr, 4lb for shot and 3.5lb for common case; similarly, the light 6-pr had two, 1.5lb and 1.25lb.[14] By 1813, there were two cartridges for the 9-pr, one of 1.5lb and the other 3lb. There were three for the 6-pr of 12oz, 1lb and 1.5lb; two for the 3-pr of 9oz and 12oz and two for the 5.5-inch howitzers, of 1lb and 2lb. There was no longer a requirement for special cartridges for spherical case as the separators were now stored in the limber boxes.[15] Details of the cartridges are given in Table A.13 of Appendix A at the end of Part One.

Cartouches

Cartridges were stowed in cartouches carried in the limber boxes, usually stored on top of the hinged shelf covering the rounds. They were often used by the ammunition numbers to carry ammunition to the gun and Mercer recalls they were used to carry both cartridges and round shot, but they were often hung from the guard irons of

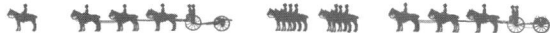

the ammunition boxes to give access to the rounds stored underneath the shelves. The cartouches were made of canvas or waterproofed linen with a buttoned, front flap and a carrying strap stitched to the sides. Dickson notes by 1813 that cartouches had been fitted with leather bottoms and the number of cartouches allocated to the limbers and ammunition wagons changed frequently over the period.[16] Details of the cartouches are given in Table A.12 of Appendix A at the end of Part One.

Wads

Wads were not used in field artillery of the period and their use was usually used for fortress guns, particularly those capable of firing heated round shot.

Slow Match

This was used to maintain a means of ignition for the portfires. It was made of twisted hemp boiled in a solution of lime water and wood ash (or saltpetre). It burnt at a rate of thirty-six inches in eight hours and was standard issue throughout the service. It had a circumference of 1.5 inches and was issued in 18 foot lengths. It was strapped in a hank 9.5 inches long by 2.5 inches and weighing 3lb. It was carried in the limber boxes and spare hanks were carried in the ammunition wagon limber and in the wagon boxes. On a block trail carriage a 30-inch long piece was cut off and placed in the copper-lined compartment of the left axle box. The match was coiled and each end fed through the hole in the rear of the box and down the flattened metal tube provided. It was protected from the weather by the extended canvas cover over the rear of the box and a copper plate was riveted to the inside of the canvas flap to protect it from the burning slow match. As the ends of the slow match were consumed, spare was pulled down from the box by the firer and replaced as necessary from the limber boxes. Where guns were mounted on bracket trail carriages, the length of slow match was wound round and through the ends of a linstock carried by the number 12.

Quick Match

Designed to burn at a fast rate and used to communicate rapid ignition from one point to another. At this time, made from a rope or thread soaked in a solution of fine grain gunpowder mixed with gum arabic and boiling water.

Portfire

The portfire provided the standard method of igniting the quill or tube and firing the gun. The portfire was a pale brown (flesh colour) stiff paper tube 16 inches long and about 0.75 inches diameter with the bottom turned in. The top had a small hole bored into the composition and was primed with mealed powder for easy ignition and it burnt for some 12 to 15 minutes. The portfire was filled with a composition of saltpetre, ground sulphur and mealed black powder to the proportions 24: 8: 5, respectively. They were a standard item issued in boxes containing a bundle of twelve portfires with the exposed ends covered by a paper cap secured with twine. They were carried in leather loops on the underside of the lid in each of the

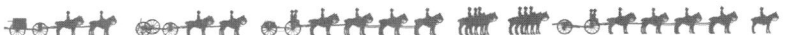

ammunition boxes on the gun and ammunition wagon limber. A portfire holder was also issued, to give a better reach and some protection to the firer from the efflux from the vent when the gun fired.

Round Shot

The most common projectile was round shot; it was used in howitzers but only when 'absolutely necessary'. It consisted of a solid cast-iron ball made to a given diameter and weight, but as this could vary with the density of the metal and the quality of the mould, maximum and minimum gauges were used to ensure the shot was of acceptable size. Round shot usually made up 75% of the ammunition for guns and was most effective at low elevations where it could arrive at the target with a high velocity and where any bounce or graze could be used to maximum advantage. Up to thirty men could be killed by one shot, but such occasions were rare as records of casualties to rounds fired show. In the main, round shot was used in two roles: against specific fixed targets such as walls, gateways of fortresses or against infantry and cavalry in the field where they were particularly effective if used against infantry or horses advancing en mass or in column.

It has been thought it was general practice to issue round shot attached to bottoms but the surviving records make it clear it was supplied both with and without.[17] It was also standard practice to double shot some guns either with two round shot or with canister in front of round shot. When two round shot were used the distance to first graze was different for each round; the details are given in Table A.4 and the dimensions of the round shot in Table A.17 of Appendix A.

When fired in ricochet mode, that is at low elevation, the ball would be travelling below the height of a man and thus it maximised the killing and maiming effect for troops advancing in column. When fire was opened at five degrees of elevation the plunging effect caused the ball to bounce over the heads of any advancing forces and cause few casualties, but if spherical case was used the result was much more effective. It was practice to open fire at longer ranges with spherical case, change to round shot as the enemy closed and change again to common case at shorter ranges, but in many instances the elevation was kept to a minimum where the ground favoured the used of round shot and artillery officers were advised not to fire directly at them but 'take aim rather before them, and in retreat beyond them'.

The ranges to first graze for each nature of gun are given in the Table of Performance for each field equipment. It was also common practice to fire shells in this manner so they bounded towards an enemy formation producing even more casualties before it exploded, although this could risk damage to the fuse.

Contemporary 'Directions, information and observations concerning the light 6-pr battalion gun' advised:

> To incommode the enemy as they advance it will be best to cannonade with round shot fired in ricochet along the ranks, so as to graze one or twice before it reaches the head of the columns, or front ranks of the lines, it often having been proved that soldiers have been more alarmed and put in confusion, by seeing shot hopping to them, than by having double the number of their comrades killed by their sides without seeing it. When the enemy is within 600 yards, round shot should be fired at one degree of

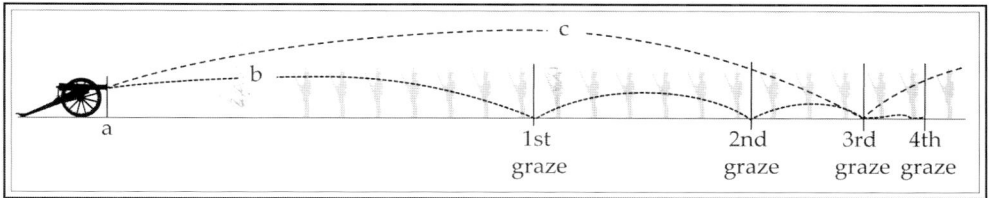

Figure 5.2. Ricochet fire. Round shot was usually fired at the flattest trajectory to achieve the maximum killing effect. A shot fired at point blank (a) would hit the ground at the first graze point a relatively short distance from the gun (b). It would then bounce approximately half the distance and strike the ground at the second graze point, rebound half as far again to strike the ground at the third graze point and then roll or bounce a little further; all very dependent upon the nature of the ground and the position of the gun.

> elevation and continued until they come within 350 yards, reducing the elevation to a quarter of a degree gradually when case shot must be fired, as it will do more execution to the centre of the enemy battalion opposite the gun.[18]

Tests carried out in 1780 with a light 6-pr of 4ft 6in firing in the ricochet mode showed, given the right terrain, a round shot could graze at least 10 times and still role a further 100 yards. With charges of as little as 3oz of powder the shots at point blank were reaching 579 yards and grazing seven times.[19]

Common and Tiered Case or Canister Shot

This was the standard anti-personnel weapon for close quarters. It was made from a thin cylindrical tin container or 'canister'; sealed at the top by a metal plate and at the lower end by a wooden bottom with two grooves for the thread of fixed ammunition. The container was packed with lead carbine balls and the spaces filled with sawdust. The size of the container and the number of balls depended upon the calibre of the gun, and there were considerable variations in the size and number of the shot contained, some having as many as 285. The case shot supplied for howitzers had a hemi-spherical wooden bottom. Heavy case ranged further than light case but had less shot, it was practice to use heavy case as the enemy neared the gun position and then change to light case as they closed upon the guns. Details of the tiered case are given in Table A.15 of Appendix A at the end of Part One.

When fired, the effect was to produce a swathe of bullets over the whole frontage of the gun position. Upon leaving the barrel, the container disintegrated and the balls continued forward forming an expanding cone, the lower balls of which struck the ground and the upper, passing over the heads of the enemy. The cone of effect varied with the ordnance involved and the elevation, but canister was rarely fired beyond ranges of 450 yards and double loading with case in front of round shot was fired at ranges of as little as 60 yards. Tests were made in 1806 against canvas targets 8 feet high and 90 feet long, hits on cavalry were calculated as target strikes up to 8 feet above the ground; those for infantry were limited to a height of 6 feet.[20] Double-shotting with canister over round shot was a regular practice by field artillery.[21] Details of the common case are given in Table A.14 of Appendix A at the end of Part One.

Common case was replaced by tiered case shot, originally introduced in the 1790s. This had 0.68-inch diameter musket balls stacked in an orderly fashion one row upon another. There was a heavy and light version for each type of gun; the medium guns

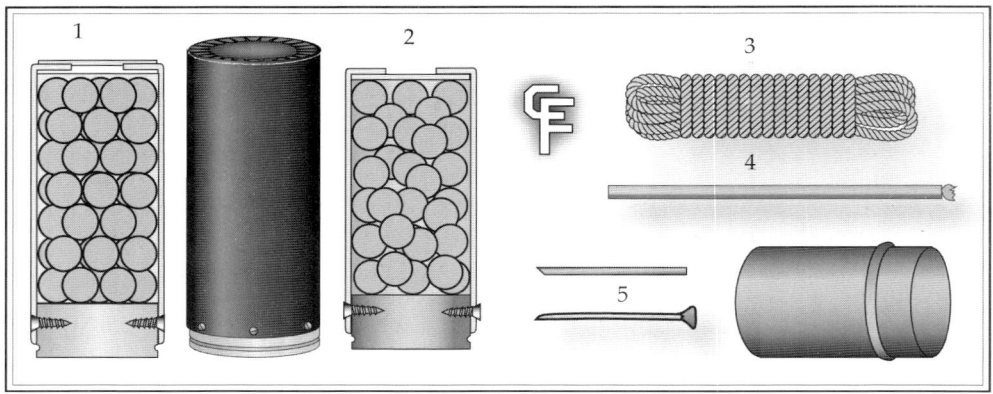

Figure 5.3. Tiered case where the musket balls were stacked in regular order (1) and common case or canister (2) where they were packed at random into sawdust. The slow match (3) used to ignite the portfires. The portfire (4) used to ignite the quill and fire the gun. Tubes or quills in a tin or box of 100 were also carried on the limber (5).

had either 15 or 41 balls and the light guns, 12 or 34 balls.[22] The data given in the tables is based upon contemporary descriptions, but it should be understood that the number and type of ball used in canister changed frequently. Dickson recalls in 1812, he used 'round seven' and canister at 800 yards. This is the colloquial name for the heavy tiered case for a light 6-pr gun.[23]

Grape Shot

This was a number of metal balls of about 1.5 inches diameter secured in a canvas bag tied with rope, through the centre of which ran an iron rod attached to an iron plate at the bottom. During this period, grape shot was not fired from brass guns as it tended to damage the barrel, so its use was restricted to iron guns. The only field pieces that may have used it were the iron 18-pr brigades introduced towards the end of the war.

Carcass

This was an incendiary device made from a hollow spherical shot with three to five holes to allow the egress of the flames from the burning composition. It was ignited by the flash of the charge and was only fired from mortars and howitzers. Carcasses were considered impossible to extinguish and those for the 5.5-inch howitzer burnt for about six minutes. They weighed about 1lb 12oz empty, the composition weighed 6lb 15oz and complete carcass 8lb 11oz.[24] The filling was made from a mixture of saltpetre (56%), sulphur (22%), antimony (5%), resin (11%) and tallow (6%).[25]

Common Shell

This was a cast hollow iron sphere of constant thickness, filled with a bursting charge. The case walls were about one sixth the diameter to ensure the greatest size of charge with the ability to withstand the stresses of firing. The explosion and

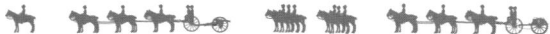

fragments of the bursting case could cause real injury to personnel and horses, but they were somewhat ineffective against hard targets.

During the period, shells were only fired from howitzers and mortars as the size of the cartridge of a gun usually caused premature detonation in or near the barrel; it was only after the period they were supplied to guns.[26] They were fitted with a fuse, which was ignited by the flash of the charge, and cut to a length calculated to explode the shell at the correct time and range. Each shell was fitted with a wooden bottom to prevent it turning in the barrel and damaging the fuse, and the fuse hole was usually aligned just off-centre and the metal straps for the bottom crossed across the top of the shell. Care had to be taken when ramming to prevent similar damage from the rammer head.

The setting of the fuse was critical if the burst was to occur at the correct range. The effective range of common shell was only between some 650 to 1,200 yards due to the uncertain nature of the fuses. Shells were painted to prevent corrosion with a mixture of 40lb of black lead to 5lb of red lead.[27] The performance of the shells has not been recorded for the period in question, but trials with shells conducted in 1819 observed that 82% took effect, 11% were dead and more alarmingly, 7% burst at the muzzle.[28] Details of the common shell are given in Table A.16 of Appendix A.

Fuses

There were two types of fuses, those for the common shell and those used for spherical case. The fuses used by the field artillery to initiate shells were made from boxwood with the outer body scored off at intervals equivalent to one second. The central bore was filled with a quick match composition that burnt for 18 to 21 seconds. In the cup at the top was a coil of quick match set in priming powder,

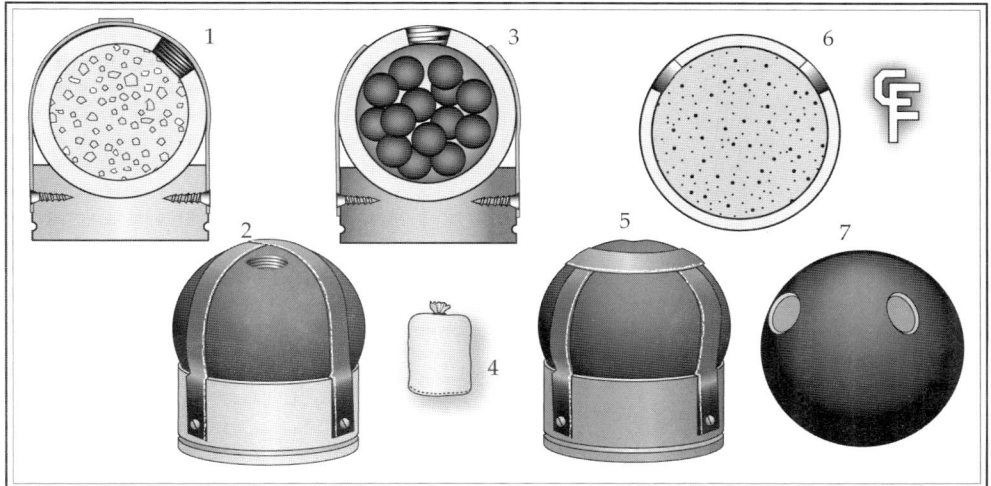

Figure 5.4. Different types of active ammunition. The common shell (1 & 2) was filled during manufacture and fitted with a wooden bottom. It was usually only fired by howitzers and mortars. Spherical case, later called shrapnel after its inventor, was filled with musket balls (3); the powder opening charge (4) was poured in just before use. It was fitted with a wooden bottom (5) and recognized by the different strapping. Carcass was incendiary ammunition (6) filled with a mixture and ignited by the flash of the charge (7).

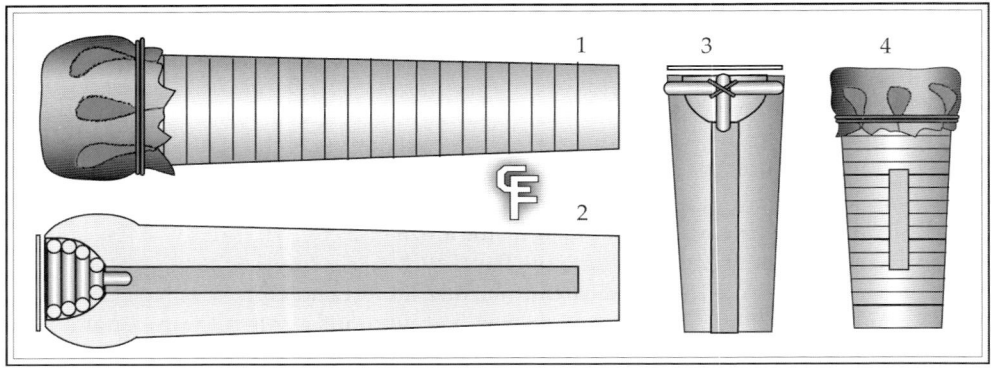

Figure 5.5. The two types of fuse used by field artillery. The 5.5-inch boxwood fuse (1) for the common shell and marked off in one second intervals and the internal construction (2) with the central length of quick match. The internal construction of the later 'catgut' version of the fuse introduced by Shrapnel for spherical case in 1810 (3). The outside was marked off in tenths of an inch (4).

covered by a paper disc. Over the head of the fuse was a brown paper cap, replaced by linen after 1800, and tied with twine. When assembly was complete, the cap was painted and marked with the date of manufacture. When the gun fired, the flash from the cartridge ignited the fuse, which burnt down during flight to ignite the burster charge of the shell. The fuses were carried in the gun limber boxes and the delay set by cutting the fuse with a saw to the required length, they were then driven into the round with a mallet. The fuses were made in several sizes; those for the field equipments were 5.5 inches long, with a lower diameter of 0.7 inches and the top diameter of 0.9 inches.

Spherical case required a fuse of greater accuracy. These were also made from boxwood in a similar way to those of the common shell but without the circular head, the shape of the fuse forming the frustum of a cone 1.5 inches wide at the top. There were two sizes but the field artillery only used the smaller with the shorter burning time. In the original instructions of 1804 for spherical case the length of the fuse was calculated by taking the range in yards, multiplied by two, divided by three, and the quotient gave the length of the fuse in decimals of an inch. This method lead to some inaccuracies and it was practice for the timing of fuses to be checked in the field. Dickson relates in January 1810, 'This day employed in burning fuses to establish a table for same'.[29] It should be noted, some officers prepared their fuses in advance and carried as many as 'six lengths of fuses'.[30] Initially the fuses followed a similar construction to those of the common shell but with the fuse marked off in tenths of an inch (equivalent to half a second). The fuses were often issued pre-cut to set lengths, for short, medium and long ranges and colour coded appropriate to the burning time. They were stored in different boxes or bags to save time and mistakes in the heat of battle and Mercer recalls the fuses were taken from either bag 'A or B' according to the length required.[31] No record of the colours used by Shrapnel to identify the fuses has been located; all that is known is one of the colours, probably the longest delay, was 'white'. Some fuses were pre-cut and marked with a letter corresponding to the letters on the rear of the tangent scale, 'B' represented the shortest range while 'M' the longest – 'A and J' were not used. The limited space within the limber boxes makes the storage of so many fuses for each round of spherical case difficult to understand and it may be these were issued to guns of position rather than field artillery.

Birch's manuscript in the James Clavell Library notes in the Gunner's Guide:

> Fuzes for short ranges, beginning at 350 yards, to be kept prepared, cut, and ready in bags, each bag containing fuzes for one range only, beginning at 350 yards, and fuzes kept ready cut for every one hundred yards afterwards, that is 450, 550, 650, 750, and 850 yards, after which distance they may always be prepared in the field … A certain number of lengths of fuze were carried in the limber boxes, distinguished by colours, and suitable for short and medium ranges; for longer ranges they had to be specially prepared. In order still further to facilitate the service of these shells, the tangent scales of the guns were marked with the letter of the fuze corresponding to the range, so that the gunner had only to guess his range when both fuze and elevation were shown to him, without troubling him degrees, minutes or rates of burning.[32]

In 1812, the system of fuses was improved and the size of the cartridges for the different guns settled to the extent that 'the same fuze will suit every kind of brass gun without varying the degree of elevation'.[33] The use of quick match in the central tube was generally dispensed with and priming powder adopted. Some quick match was used in the cup of the fuse where it was secured by catgut, known as catgut fuses; 6,000 were placed on general issue to each troop and brigade in 1813. These changes also meant that 'all natures of field ordnance may be fired with effect with the service charge for round shot'.[34]

Spherical Case Shot

Spherical case first saw service in 1803 and could be fired by guns, mortars and howitzers to exploit the effect of case at extended ranges. It was ideal for firing above or among a body of men gathered in dead ground or behind defences. The round consisted of a hollow sphere of cast iron, thinner than that of the common shell, being about one tenth the diameter with a threaded fuse hole, 1.5 inches in diameter and sealed by a brass plug. The shell was filled with carbine balls; 20 for the 3-pr, 50 for the 6-pr, 108 for the medium 12-pr and 208 for the 5.5-inch or 24-pr howitzer; in 1813 the carbine balls were replaced by a fewer number of larger musket balls.[35] The round was fitted with a wooden fuse which at the appropriate time and range initiated the opening charge. This was a small amount of powder used to open the case, not scattering the shot, but increasing the velocity in the original direction, the shot and splinters from the case forming an elongated cone with the apex at the point of opening.[36]

The early rounds had contained the opening charge pre-mixed with the bullets, but it was found the friction between the two often caused them to explode prematurely, both during transportation and in flight. By 1807, the burster charge was provided in a separate cartridge and only poured into the round just before use; the rounds were issued with a reduced size of cartridge in a further attempt to prevent premature explosions.[37] Spherical case, just like common shell, was usually carried by the ammunition number in the crook of the right elbow with the left hand over the fuse to protect it from sparks. The range of spherical case could be up to 2,500 yards and they were particularly effective when they burst about 50 yards short of the target, if this occurred at 600 yards the spread of shot reached 800 yards. It should be noted, as the elevation was increased the spread effect was reduced due to the angle at which the round was travelling when separation occurred.

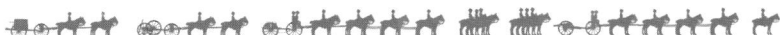

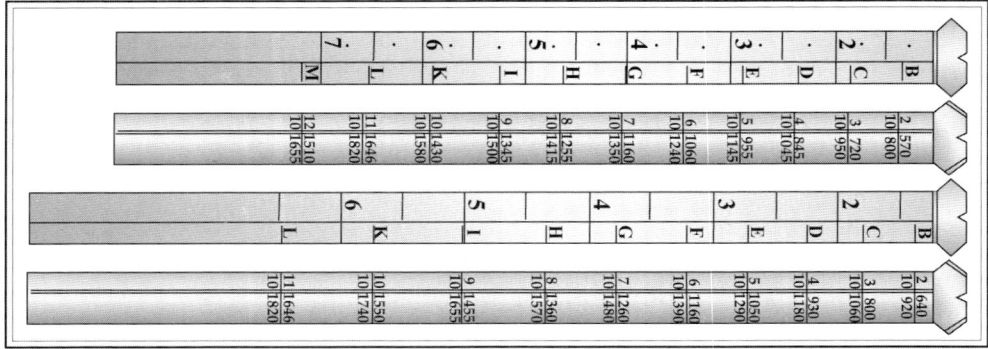

Figure 5.6. Light 6-pr and 9-pr gun tangent scale after 1804; the scales for the other ordnance were similar. The flat face was marked with the elevation in half-degrees and the required fuse designated by letter. The curved side was marked with the length of the fuse in tenths of an inch and the effective range spread for spherical case at each fuse setting. The scale was slotted in the rear of the base ring and secured by a screw, when not in use it was carried in the limber. The fuse settings and range spreads were introduced after 1803 and the introduction of spherical case into general service, prior to that only the flat face was marked.

The round was supplied attached to a wooden bottom and the gunner recognized a spherical case by the nature of the tin strapping; the common shell having two plain straps with the fuse offset to one side while spherical case had the more elaborate circular strapping with the fuse at the centre. In the early tests, the effect upon a target 54 feet long and 9 feet high (the frontage of a mounted unit) was impressive. The targets were placed at 700, 750 and 800 yards. Ten rounds were fired from each of two 5.5-inch howitzers, four light 12-prs and four light 6-prs, all in 13 minutes. The effects were the first target was struck by 1,489 balls and 38 splinters of metal; the second by 1,296 balls and 17 splinters and the third by 1,213 balls and 17 splinters; more than a third of those fired. In a similar test against a target nine feet square, 183 balls and 6 splinters hit when fired by a 5.5-inch howitzer at half a mile and with a shell containing 208 balls.[38] Details of spherical case are given in Table A.19 of Appendix A at the end of Part One. Continual experiments were undertaken at the Royal Arsenal to improve performance, but it was not until the Boxer modifications some years later that the problems of pre-ignition were finally overcome.[39]

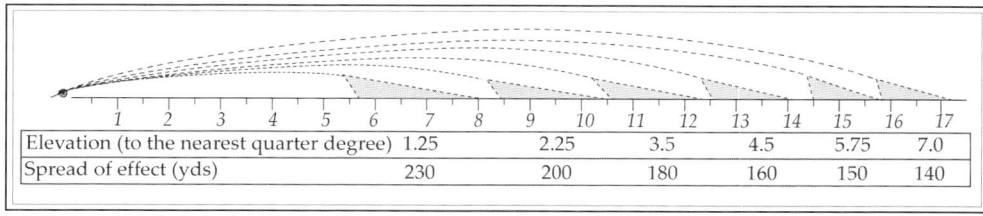

	1	2	3	4	5	6	7	8	9	10	11	12	13	14	15	16	17
Elevation (to the nearest quarter degree)	1.25								2.25		3.5		4.5		5.75		7.0
Spread of effect (yds)						230			200		180		160		150		140

Figure 5.7. Spherical case fire. The length of the fuse, range, elevation required and the spread effect were given on the rear of the tangent scale issued with each type ordnance. The figures above are those of a light 6-pr gun of 5 feet in 1803 and should not be confused with the later figures based upon the modifications to spherical case applied by Boxer. As with all the ammunition of this period, the figures given were arbitrary and greatly dependent upon the burning rate of the fuse, the state of the powder in the main charge and the wear and distortion of the barrel of the gun.

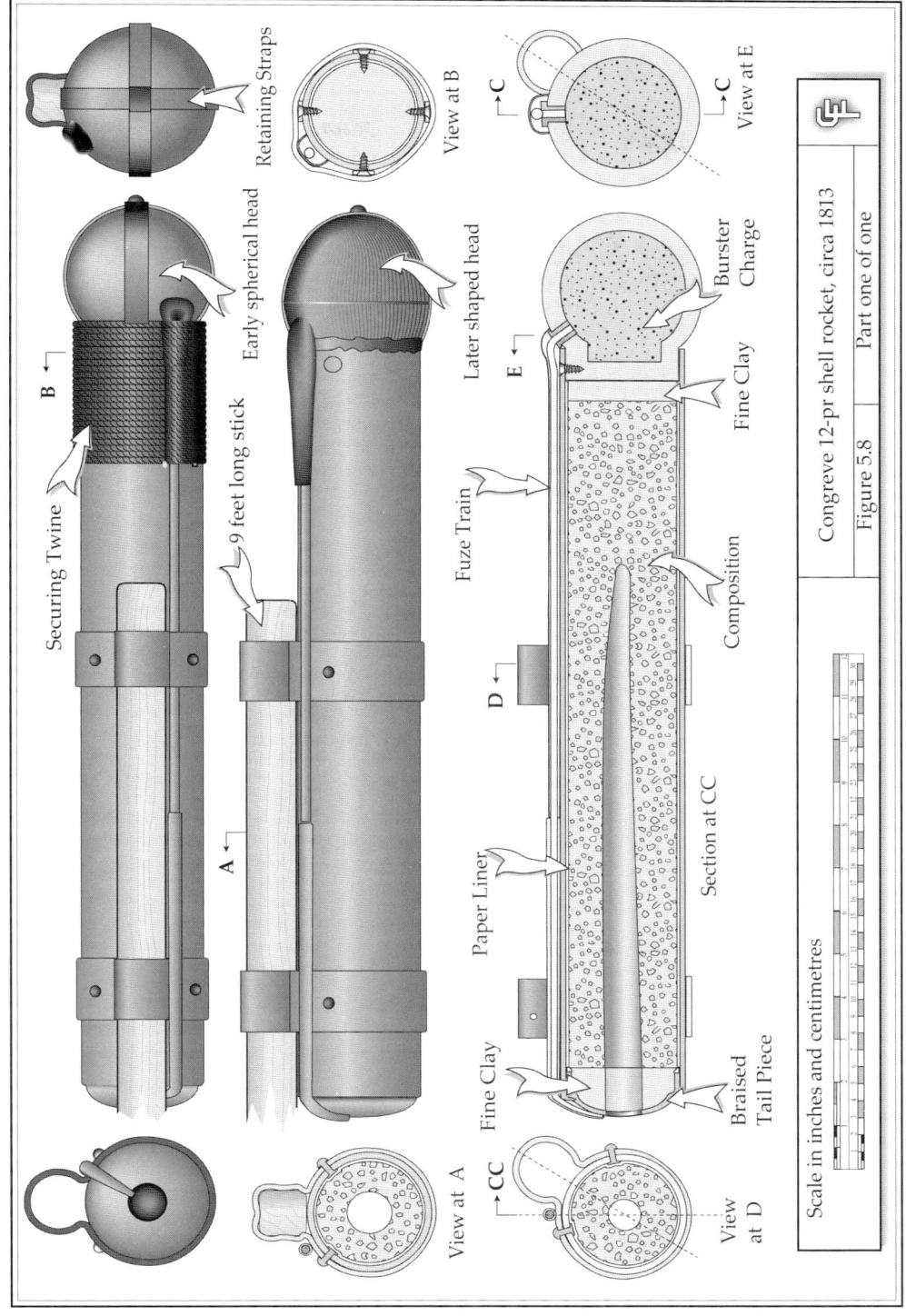

Retaining Straps

View at B

View at E

Early spherical head

Later shaped head

B

Securing Twine

9 feet long stick

Burster Charge

Fine Clay

E

Fuze Train

D

Composition

A

Paper Liner

Section at CC

Fine Clay

Braised Tail Piece

View at A

View at D

CC

Scale in inches and centimetres

Congreve 12-pr shell rocket, circa 1813

Figure 5.8   Part one of one

Rockets (see Figure 5.8)

The only field artillery units to use rockets were the specially formed detachments of the Royal Horse Artillery which evolved into the No. 1 and No. 2 Rocket Troops. They discharged the 12-pr shell rockets along the ground and the troops were equipped with a ladder frame rocket cart to discharge the 32-pr carcass rockets for bombardment purposes. These were used in the Peninsula War, at the Battle of Leipzig and at Waterloo. The rockets of this and later periods are covered in detail in *British Rockets of the Napoleonic and Colonial Wars*, also published by Spellmount.[40]

Endnotes to Chapter 5

1. Adye, 1802: p. 46.
2. Hogg, 1963: p. 555.
3. James Clavell Library. Ordnance correspondence, RA 20: pp. 225–9.
4. Adye, 1813: pp. 215–17.
5. Adye, 1806: p. 164: 1810, pp. 215-217.
6. Adye, 1813: p. 353.
7. National Archive, WO 1/167: pp. 227, 627; WO 1/168: pp. 89, 96.
8. Dickson, 1908: pp. 83, 91.
9. Caruana, 1979: p. 3.
10. James Clavell Library. Unpublished papers dated 1825.
11. Hughes, 1969: p. 49.
12. Adye, 1801: p. 210, Adye, 1813: p. 382.
13. Hogg, 1963: p. 599.
14. Adye, 1806: p. 81
15. Dickson, 1908: p. 107; *Proceedings of the Royal Artillery Institute*, Vol. 5: p. 417.
16. Dickson, 1908: et al.
17. National Archive, WO 1/167: p. 227; WO 1/168: pp. 89, 96; Dickson, 1908: pp. 143, 348.
18. Caruana, 1977: p. 27.
19. Caruana, 1977, p. 35.
20. Adye, 1806: p. 158.
21. Siborne, 1891: p. 218.
22. McConnell, 1988: p. 320.
23. Dickson, 1908: p. 692.
24. Adye, 1813: p. 87.
25. Adye, 1801: p. 50.
26. Adye, 1827: pp. 351, 347
27. Lefroy, 1854: p. 22; Griffiths, 1839: p. 148.
28. Ibid: p. 2.
29. Dickson, 1908: p. 145.
30. Proceedings of the Royal Artillery Institute, Vol. 5: p. 405.
31. Mercer, 1870: p. 151.
32. *Proceedings of the Royal Artillery Institute*, Vol. 5: p. 396.
33. Op. cit: p. 412.
34. Op. cit: p. 417.
35. *Proceedings of the Royal Artillery Institute*, Vol. 5: p. 416; Dickson, 1908: p. 907.
36. *Proceedings of the Royal Artillery Institute*, Vol. 5: p. 390.
37. Ibid: p. 424.
38. Shrapnel, 1803: p. 1.
39. Hogg, 1963: p. 586.
40. Franklin, 2005: et al.

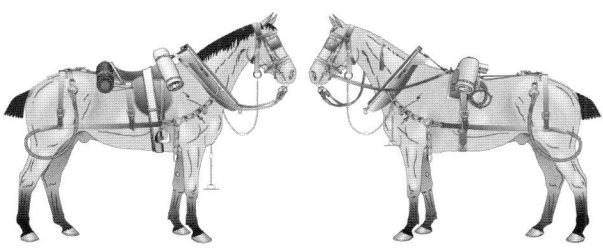

CHAPTER 6

Draught and Riding Harnesses

Artillery Draught Harness

The royal artillery used two distinctive aspects of draught harness, one was the neck collar the other was shaft draught. The strength of a horse is in the base of the neck and this can be utilised by the use of either a neck collar or a breast harness. The breast harness was considered to produce about half the effort obtained from the neck collar but was much easier to fit and was readily changeable if a horse was injured. The neck collar used throughout the British artillery of the Napoleonic period, while more efficient, required skilled fitting and was not usually interchangeable from horse to horse without the skilled services of a collar maker.

During the period, there were two main methods of connecting the horses to the load they were pulling. The most common was pole-draught where the steering and braking effort was applied via a central pole and this was the method used by most of the world's artillery, only the Royal Artillery and a few Russian equipments adopted shaft draught. It was generally considered that the use of shafts enabled the carriage to turn in a much smaller space and with greater speed, but it did require highly trained horses. Pole-draught, in spite of the drawbacks, was better adapted to the less well-trained horse. Many artillery officers advocated the use of pole draught and General Lawson, who was not in favour of shaft draught, remarked:

> Foreigners frequently observe the singularity of shafts being preferred in the British Artillery carriages to poles, made use of by all other nations as being simpler, lighter, and cheaper; added to which the experience of having traveled over the most difficult features of Europe, and ground of every description with them, fully evinces their perfect sufficiency. A strong instance of the inconvenience of shafts occurred to us at Rahmanich: just as one of the 6-pounders was limbering up, the shaft horse was killed by the enemy; much time was lost in clearing the carriage from him, and the harness being also damaged, rendered it difficult to apply another in his place.[1]

During the Egyptian Campaign of 1800 Colonel Lawson had the old pattern limbers of the 3-pr received from Malta modified to pole draught to overcome the problems of draught over sandy terrain and poorly trained horses.

In spite of these reservations shaft draught and neck collars continued in use by the field artillery until the end of the century, and by 1810 most foot brigades were also equipped in the manner of the horse artillery, and even guns in the battalion role were equipped with horses in tandem and transitional limbers. Throughout the early phases of the war and during the Peninsular Campaign in particular, the artillery were always short of horses due to poor supply and mules or bullocks were pressed into service whenever they could be found.

Early Draught Harness

Initially, before the introduction of the horse artillery, the draught was generally by two or three horses in single file with the rear horse between the shafts of the limber. This horse was known as the 'wheeler' or 'thrill' horse and any leading horse the 'leader' of which there were often two or more, in which case the middle horse was known as the 'centre' horse. When extra horses were needed, they were attached at the front of the file or to the shafts by outriggers. To prevent the rope or chain traces rubbing the flanks of the horses spreaders were used to spread the traces and keep them clear and when there were two leading horses the traces of the leader were attached to the spreader of the centre horse. This system of draught is well illustrated in the notebooks of the officer cadets at Woolwich and in the drawings of Pyne. Each leading horse had chain traces attached to a spreader and thence to the spreader of the following horse. The traces of the rearmost horse, the one before the wheeler, were attached to the front end of the shafts. This meant the wheeler spent most of its effort holding up the shafts while the leading horses tended to pull them down. Muller notes:

> The wheels of the limbers being but four feet high and the extremities of the shafts five, the draught of the shaft horse becomes so oblique, that the greatest part of his force is lost in supporting the fore end of the shafts, which the other horses draw down again, so as to bring the whole draught in a right line from the axle-tree to the breast of the fore horse; whereby the shaft horse is so shook that he is spoiled in a short time and rendered unfit for service.[2]

These remarks were echoed by Congreve (1st Bart) in 1776 when considering the weakness of the current limbers:

> The wheels are so low that the axletree often drags upon the ground in bad roads, and from the same cause the thrill horse [the wheeler] is sadly crippled by the draft of the fore horse tending to bear the shafts down until they form a right line with his traces, which is prevented by the thrill on the horses back; on which, in bad roads, so great a stress is thrown, that it is with difficulty he can support himself beneath it.[3]

The change adopted to overcome this problem was to connect the trace chains of the leaders to the underside of the rear of the shafts and give them a straight line of draught. These long chains were still kept clear of the horses by spreaders and were supported under the shaft by chain or leather trace bearers. The traces could now form a better 'right line' to the load without drawing down on the shafts, but the

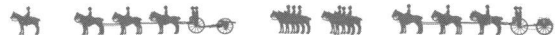

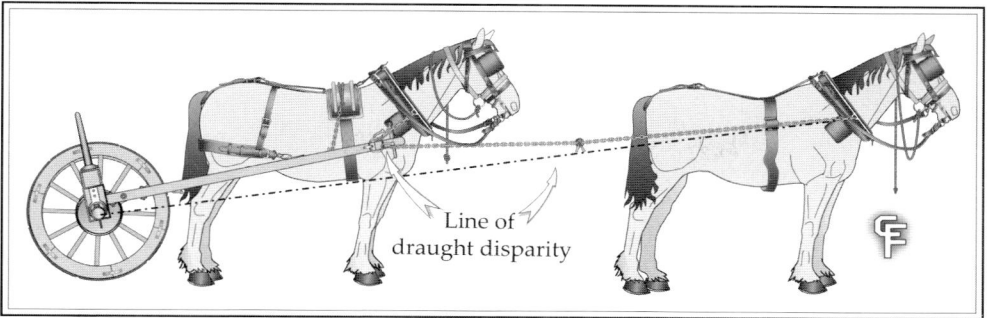

Line of
draught disparity

Figure 6.1. Early draught harness of the type used for battalion guns. The two horses were arranged in single draught one acting as leader the other as wheeler. The traces of the leader led to the shafts of the limber, while the wheeler was connected to the limber shafts by the breeching straps and a back chain. The traces of the leader attempted to form a straight line to the axle of the limber, pulling the shafts down while the wheeler expended great effort in attempting to keep the shafts up.

draught used for many of the country wagons, which were often hired from civilian contractors, still followed the old style.

It seems this style of harness continued in use for some time, as Mercer recalls:

> The first brigades (now called batteries) were formed by Major Spearman in 1800, and drilled by him at a set of manoeuvres of his own drawing up. They consisted of medium 12-prs, I think six each (there were two brigades), drawn by six horses each, two and two, the drivers (then a new corps) mounted as postillions – quite a novelty. These two brigades were destined for Swinley camp. (None of the gunners were mounted, but marched beside the carriages.) At the same time, Lieutenant (now Colonel) Wallace was drilling another brigade of light 6-prs for the same destination, but to be attached as battalion guns to the Guards. The equipment of these was entirely different from Spearman's brigades. The guns were drawn by three horses each, with common cart harness and chain traces.[4]

Artillery Horses

The draught horses of the artillery were hackney bays or chestnuts of at least 14.5 hands with docked tails.[5] In 1810 those for the horse artillery were to be 'from four to six years old (when bought), to be short-legged, open-chested, and broad-winded; not to exceed 15 hands 2 inches, nor – four years old – under 15 hands ⬜ inch; to have good bone and action, the colour to be bay, brown and dark chestnut'.[6] The price allowed was thirty guineas after a month's trial. In calculating the space required by horses the artillery assumed each required three feet in breadth, nine feet in length and 3 feet between nose and croup. Great care was taken to match the horses so they were used to best advantage and the horse artillery took great pride in the appearance and well being of the horses, even so the losses were considerable; in 1809 alone, the artillery in the Peninsula lost over 2,789 through sickness and fatalities.[7]

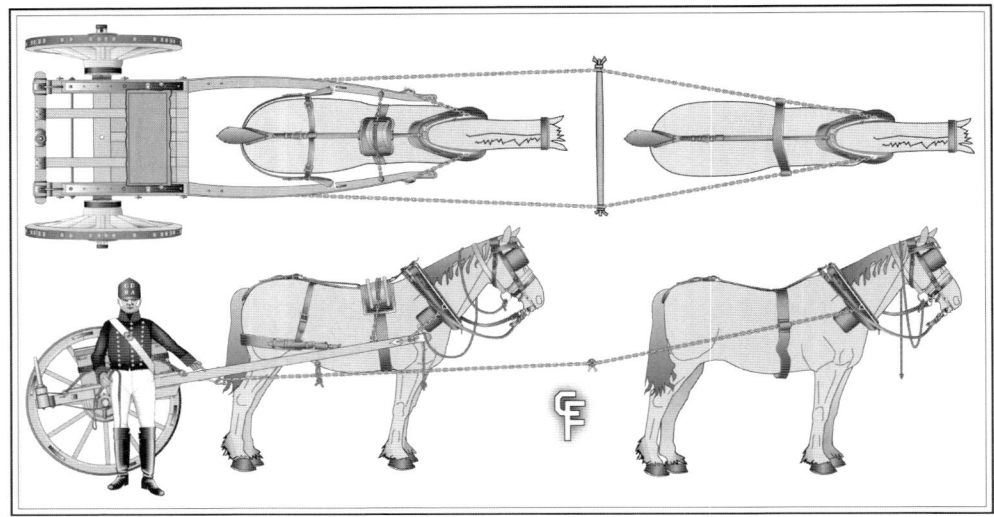

Figure 6.2. The early change in draught harness of the type used for battalion guns to improve the line of draught. The traces of the leader now passed via the spreader and the trace chain bearer to the rear of the shafts of the limber. The line of draught now more properly matched the efforts of the two horses and the effect on the wheeler was eased.

New Draught Harness

The two horses at the front of the team were termed the 'leaders', the two attached to the limber, the 'wheelers'. When extra horses were used, they were termed 'centre pairs' and were harnessed immediately behind the leaders. When there were eight pairs the leading centre horses were identified as 'centre leaders', those at the rear, 'centre wheelers'. All the horses to the right were the off horses and carried a light pad saddle. The horses on the left were the near horses and each was ridden by a driver who controlled both the near and off horse. The harness for the off and near horses differed as did that for the leaders and wheelers, but there was a similarity where the bridles, collars and saddles were concerned.

The colour of artillery harness at this time was black; the buckles were of brass and the bits of iron,[8] and all artillery draught horses wore blinkers.[9] No sizes for harness parts are given in contemporary sources and the dimensions shown are taken from later publications but, as the size of the artillery draught horses did not vary significantly, it is considered they are probably quite realistic.[10] The numbers in the following text and illustrations relate to those of the scaled illustration at Figure 6.13 and Table A.18 of Appendix A at the end of Part One.

During the Peninsular Campaign horses were in short supply and mules and even bullocks were often used in their place. Dickson recalls 'giving about 50 to each Light 6 Pr. Brigade, and 70 to the Heavy 6 Prs making up the number from the Portuguese horses and mules. Dickson noted, 'the 3 Prs have very fine mules and will not require any'. At the time, he had three brigades of light 6-pr, one Heavy 6-pr and one with light 3-prs. The usual practice was to use horses as wheelers and mules in the less demanding roles, whenever possible the guns were always given preference over the wagons.[11] The number of mules allocated to the different equipments is given in Table A. 22 of Appendix A at the end of Part One. A light

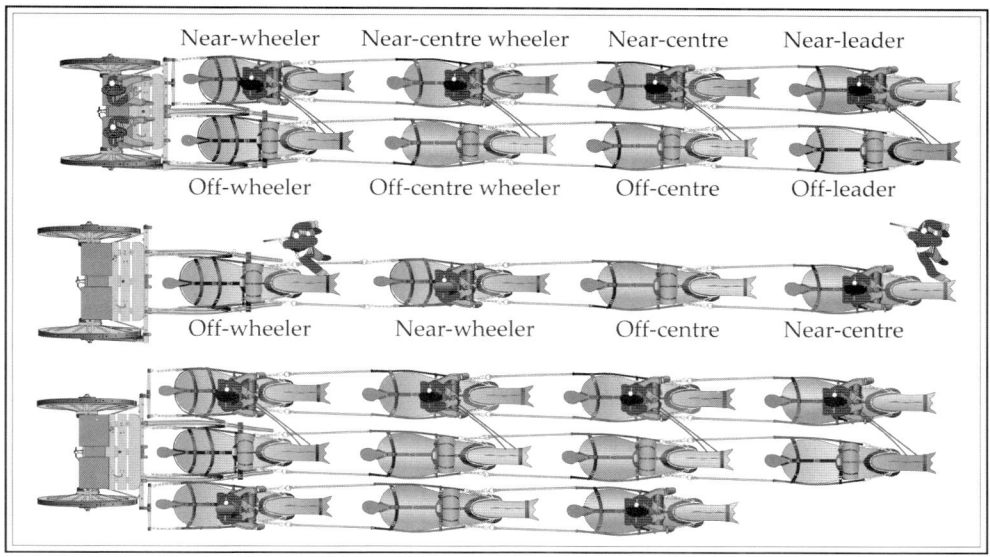

Near-wheeler Near-centre wheeler Near-centre Near-leader

Off-wheeler Off-centre wheeler Off-centre Off-leader

Off-wheeler Near-wheeler Off-centre Near-centre

Figure 6.3. Artillery draught, circa 1808. At the top, the eight-horse teams in double draught. In the centre a team in single draught, each pair with the near horse leading. When proceeding up hill or over difficult ground it was common to use additional horses taken from other teams. These were used in extended double draught or in treble draught; the exact configuration would have depended upon the horses immediately available, but most probably these would have been leader and centre horses.

6-pr gun team with six horses could march 50 to 60 miles in a day and at a hard gallop for some 6 miles.[12] In normal usage, the limber was driven in double draught with the horses arranged in pairs, and only the off-wheeler between the shafts of the limber.

To turn the team and carriage in narrow roads it was often necessary to 'Reverse by Unlimbering' to get the gun around. When crossing dubious bridges the traces of the leading horses were often unhitched and the carriage and limber taken over by the two wheelers, and when climbing steep inclines it was standard practice to put double teams on the guns and take them up one at a time.[13] When descending steep slopes it was practice to lock one wheel of the gun carriage with the locking chain, but this could cause a problem as Captain Webber recalls:

> We now began the descent of the hill and to prepare for accidents and disasters to our carriages. Although the road was paved and rather broad, it would have been impossible to have moved without infantry to hold the drag ropes. General Stewart gave us two Companies of the 71st and by great care we succeeded in reaching the valley without accident. Had we locked our wheels, as is the plan in some brigades, I think not a carriage would have escaped injury and perhaps several might have been totally disabled.[14]

The number of horses in a team depended upon the terrain and the load to be moved. Four horses were expected to draw 24cwt; and two more were required for each additional 6cwt. They were expected to cover 800 yards in 9 minutes at the walk, just over 4 minutes at the trot and in 2 minutes at the gallop. Peacetime

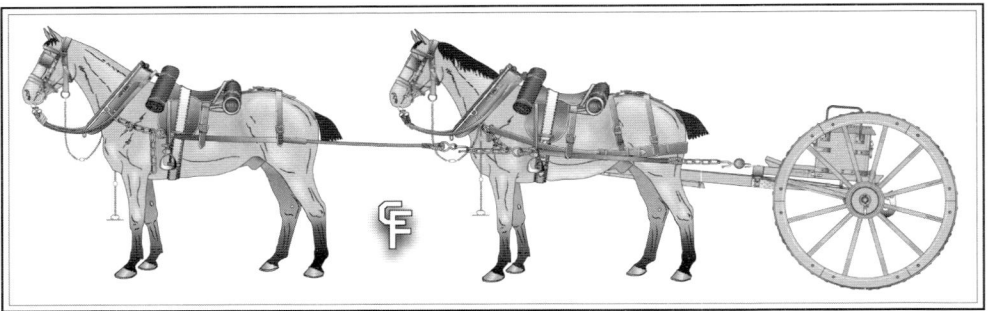

Figure 6.4. Improved artillery draught harness introduced with the horse artillery in 1793 and soon adopted by all the field artillery. Only the near horses were ridden. When braking, the long breaching strap of the wheeler acted to balance the load on the near side in the absence of a limber shaft. The off side of the near wheeler was harnessed to the limber shaft in the same way as the off wheeler.

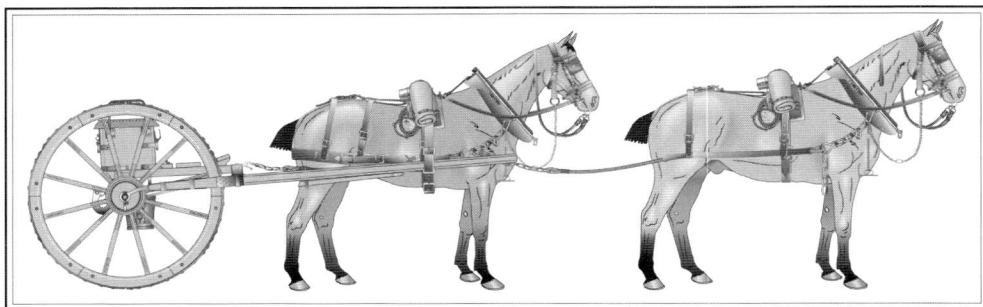

Figure 6.5. The two off horses of the improved artillery draught harness introduced with the horse artillery in 1793 (the other horses have been omitted for clarity). Only the near horses were ridden, the off horses carrying a light pad saddle. The off wheeler was the only horse between the shafts of the limber and was responsible for the direction of the limber via the tugs that passed over the shafts. Any centre horse had the same harness as the respective leader.

establishments often showed only four horses per equipment, but on active service most light guns and rocket carts required teams of at least six horses, eight for the 9-pr and heavy 5.5-inch howitzer, ten for the 12-pr and more for the 24-pr iron howitzer and the 18-pr iron gun.[15] In the Egyptian Campaign the block trail light 6-pr required ten horses to travel over sandy soil or shingle while those with a bracket trail required twelve.[16]

Draught Harness

Bridles (A) – All the draught horses wore a bridoon or double bridle. The first part consisted of a simple, two-part bridle head, buckled on the near side and fitted with a jointed and twisted snaffle bit on loose rings (8). Over this was worn the much more elaborate second bridle; this consisted of a head-piece (1), brow band (2), nose band (5), throat lash (9), harness bit (7), two cheek pieces (3) with billots (4) and blinkers (6). The head-piece was two inches wide, thirty inches long, and split some eight inches at each end to form two straps, both three-quarters of an inch wide; one to take the buckle of the cheek piece and the other the buckle of the throat lash.

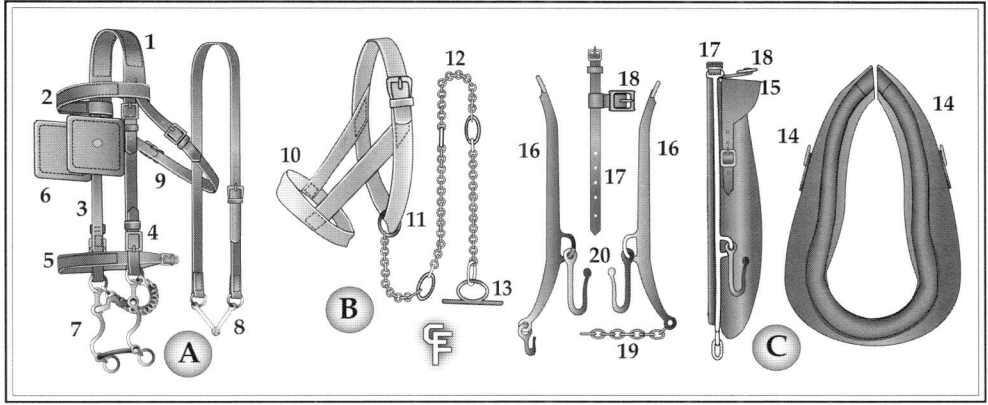

Figure 6.6. Artillery draught harness, circa 1800, bridles and collars. The bridoon bridle (A) was fitted with blinkers with a separate bridle head for the snaffle bit. The collar headstall (B). The neck collar (C) was used to transfer the effort from the horses neck and chest to the traces. The numbered items identified in the text are in the Table of Harness.

The brow band was 1.25 inches wide and 12 inches between the loops; the noseband was about 22 inches long and 1.5 inches wide; the throat lash was twenty-one inches long and three-quarters of an inch wide with a buckle at each end. The two cheek pieces were eight inches long from buckle to buckle, with seven-inch long billots, three and a half inches being turned up to the buckle after passing through the eye of the bit. (A billot is formed by a buckle with a further length of strap intended to fold back through the buckle.) Stitched to the cheek pieces were the blinkers. The harness-bit had a low port, loose rings and curb chain with a curved bar joining the bottom of the long swan-necked cheeks. No side rein was worn at this time and some earlier blinkers may have been supported by stiffening wires from the brow band.

Head-collar (B) – Under the bridles each of the horses wore a head-collar or 'collar, head, stall' buckling on the near side. It was made up of a throat lash (11), stitched to cheek pieces and a noseband (10). A chain rein (12) and 'T' iron (13) led from the ring of the throat lash and when in draught this was hooked up to the neck-collar. The head collar was worn with the full harness, but in stables it was mainly used on its own for watering parades and securing the horse in bivouac or in stalls.

Draught or Neck-collar (C) – Each draught horse wore the 'collar, neck, horse'; this transferred the effort from the horse to the traces. The leather collars were of one piece, open at the top where they were passed over the neck of the horse and then secured across the opening by a collar-housing (15) strapped to buckles on each side of the collar (14). Around the outside of the collar were fitted a pair of iron hames (16). These were secured at the top by a hames strap (17), which also served to carry the buckling-piece for the wither strap (18). Adjustment of the hames was at the bottom, by a breast-chain and hook (19) (to which the traces were attached). Below the centre of each hame was a shoulder link with a hook (20). Each neck-collar required skilled fitting and if one of the horses was killed or injured the collars were rarely interchangeable.

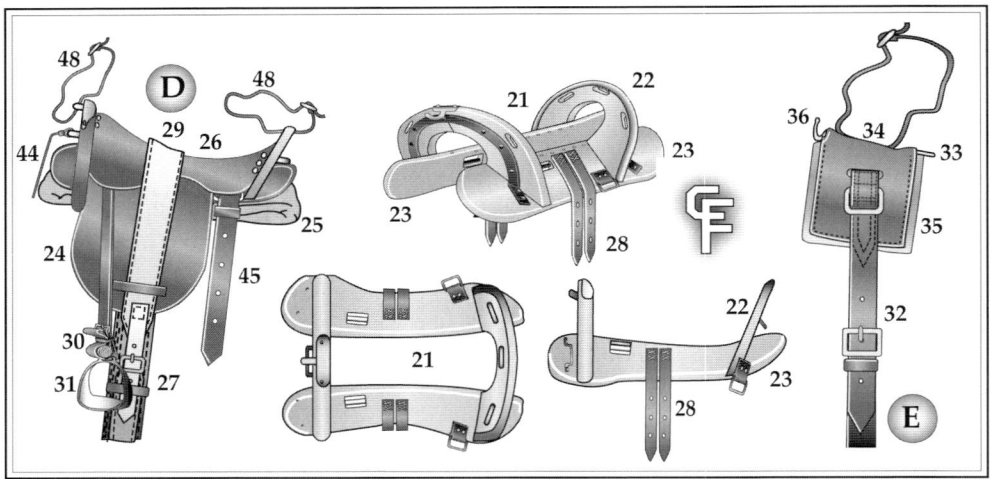

Figure 6.7. Artillery draught harness, circa 1800, saddles. The riding saddle (D) was of black leather and based upon the wooden 'Hungarian' saddletree. The pad saddle (E) was a light pad secured to the back of the horse. The saddle was used to carry various baggage items. The numbered parts are identified in the text and the Table of Harness.

Riding Saddle (D) – The artillery riding saddle was a leather-covered version of the Universal Saddle of 1805, also known as the 'Hungarian' or 'hussar' saddle. It was a wood-arch saddle (21) of one size with wooden sideboards (23) and short fans to the rear. The front arch was cut low and the cantle (22) edged in brass. The flank strap (45), wither strap (44) the cloak and valise straps (48) were attached through metal staples on the sideboards and arches. The leather seat (26), side flaps (24) and girth straps (28) were stitched to the unpadded sideboards. The saddle sat upon a folded blanket (25) of up to sixteen thicknesses and was held on the back of the horse by a web girth (27), buckled to the girth straps (28) and a surcingle (29).

Pad Saddle (E) – The light pad saddle was made up of a simple pad (35) and a saddle-flap (34). The pad was fitted with baggage straps (49) to secure the various items carried. The saddle was held in position on the back of the horse by a special girth strap (32), which also carried rings for the flank straps supporting the traces. The front of the pad carried a hook (36) for the bearing rein and a staple for the wither strap (44). At the rear, there was a further staple (33) for the strap of the crupper. The luggage saddle for the off horses was not introduced until 1856.

The Leaders

As has been noted the two horses at the front were termed the leaders; the near horse being ridden by a driver and the off horse carrying a luggage pad. The driver controlled the off horse with the aid of the leading rein and his whip but the two horses were not connected together in any way and the driver was responsible for ensuring that the two horses turned and acted together. In general terms the pattern of the bridles, collars and traces of the leaders were the same and the only significant difference was the saddle. When teams of more than four horses were used, the extra horses were placed immediately behind the leaders and termed centre-horses. They were harnessed in the same manner as the respective leading horse.

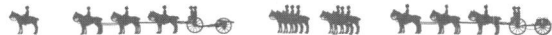

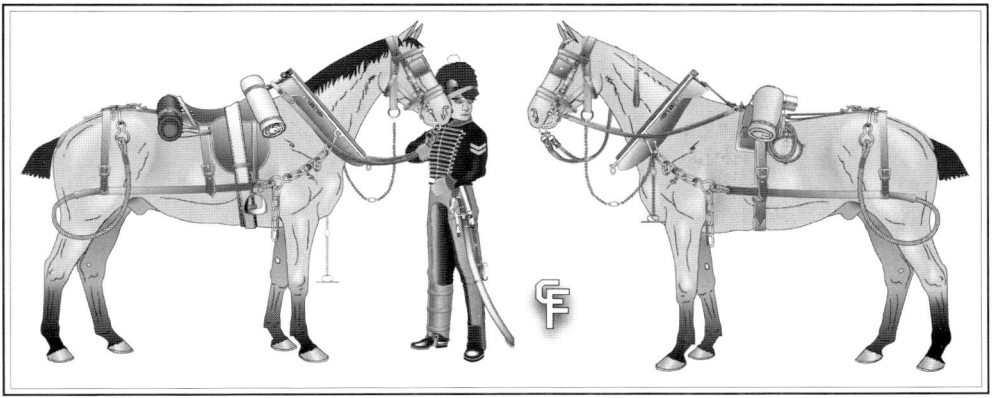

Figure 6.8. Artillery lead or centre horses. Off side view of the near leader and a near side view of the off leader. The traces were hooked to the crupper rings when not in draught. The harness of the near and off centre horses was the same as the respective leader.

Off-leader Harness (see Figure 6.9)

At the front of the team, on the right-hand side, was the off-leader. It wore the full bridles (A), head-collar (B), and neck-collar (C), as described above. A two-piece bearing rein (39) was buckled to the rings of the snaffle bit and led to the bearing hook (36), on the front of the pad saddle. A further two-part leading rein (40), was buckled to the rings of the harness bit and when in draught this rein was used by the driver to control the off-leader; when out of draught it was usually hooked to the neck-collar or draped over the neck of the horse. The off horses carried the light, pad saddle (E). The pad was fitted with baggage straps (49) to secure the various items carried. These could include sheepskins, picket and forage ropes, oil decks, horse cloths, nose and forage bags, canteens, valise, blankets and on campaign forage was carried secured to the saddle.[17] To prevent the saddle moving sideways it was secured to the back of the horse by a special girth strap (32) that carried rings for the flank straps supporting the traces. To prevent movement 'fore and aft' it was connected at the front by the wither strap (44) buckled to the buckling-piece (18) on the hames-strap (17). Like most of the others, a keeper secured this strap. (A keeper is a leather loop sewn to the end of the strap; a runner is similar but free to move: the strap is passed through the attachment point, then back through the keeper, and pulled tight, the free end being attached to the required buckle.) At the rear, the saddle was connected to the billot of the crupper (43) which passed through the staple on the rear of the saddle (33) and buckled back on itself.

Traces were used to transfer the effort of the horse to the load to be moved. The 96-inch long traces were made of rope (54), covered at the front part by a leather pipe (53), to prevent the rope chafing the horse. To prevent the horse's hooves striking the following horse when at the gallop, a yard was allowed between nose and croup. The traces were not long enough to allow for this and short, 36-inch long, rope traces were looped over the hook of the trace chains and a hook at the other end attached to the trace chains of any following horse. It seems, for parades and ceremonial these short traces were not used. At the front, the trace rope was looped through a trace-ring with two sets of chains (50). One set connected to the hook on the hame of the neck-collar, the other connected to the rear trace-hook of any leading horse (when there was no leading horse both chains were hooked to the collar). A ring and

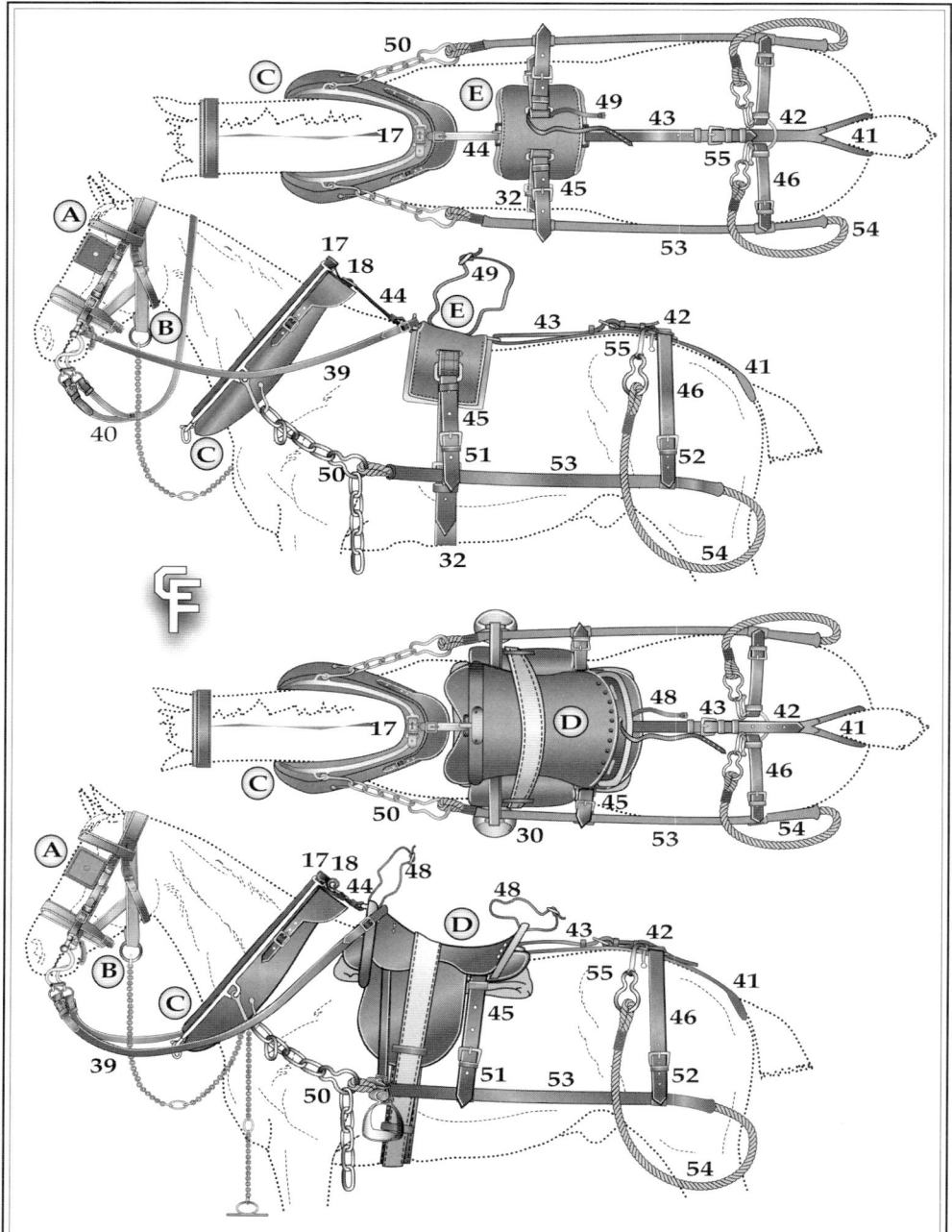

Figure 6.9. Artillery draught harness of the leader and centre horses. The upper view shows the near side of an off leader or off centre horse. The lower views show the harness of the ridden near leader or near centre horse, in each case the harness is similar on each side. The numbers in the illustration relate to those of the scaled illustration at figure 6.13 and the Table A.18 of Appendix A at the end of Part One.

hook (55) at the rear end of the trace-rope connected to the loop of a short trace or the trace-chains of any following horse. When not in draught the rear ends of the traces were often hooked to the front chains or to the ring of the crupper.

Each trace was held in position at two points. At the front, by a flank strap (45), secured through the ring on the pad saddle girth (32) and strapped down through the flank buckling-piece (51) to the trace. (A buckling piece is a buckle stitched to a piece of harness and intended to receive the strap of another harness part.) At the rear, a hip strap (46) similarly attached the buckling-piece (52) to the ring of the crupper (42). Each of these straps was fitted with a keeper.

Near-Leader Harness (see Figure 6.9)

The horse at the front, left-hand side, was the near-leader. The near horses had similar bridles (A), head-collar (B) and neck-collar (C), but the arrangement of the reins was different. The near horses were ridden on a single, two-piece bearing rein (39), buckled to the curb rings of the harness bit and leading to the saddle. Normally, the snaffle bit of the near horses had no reins attached and the leading rein was not worn. Each near horse was ridden by a driver, the saddle (D) was secured to the horse by the girth (27) and surcingle (29). To prevent movement 'fore and aft' it was connected at the front to the wither strap (44), which was connected in turn to the buckling piece on the hames strap (18). At the rear, the saddle was connected to the long billot of the crupper (43), this passed through the staple on the saddle and buckled back on itself. The cloak was rolled three feet long and secured over the front arch by a cloak strap (48); the valise was carried similarly strapped to the rear of the cantle (22). The stirrup irons (31) and leathers (30) were of light cavalry pattern with the buckle at the stirrup and the spare strap rolled up. The ridden horses carried the same traces as the off horses but usually carried the minimum of extra equipment. Drivers carried a short whip to control the off horse. They also wore a special reinforced legging on their right leg to protect it from being crushed between the horses. The leather legging was buckled around the leg by three straps and was reinforced on the outside face by a twenty-inch long iron strip encased in leather (see Figure 20.3).

Wheelers

The two horses immediately in front of the limber were the wheelers; in a similar way to the leaders the off horse carried the luggage pad and the near horse was ridden by a driver who controlled the off horse with the aid of the leading rein and his whip. In general terms the pattern of the bridles and collars of the wheelers were the same as those of the leaders and the only significant differences were in the traces and breeching.

Near-wheeler Harness (see Figure 6.11)

The horse at the rear, on the left-hand side, in front of the limber, was termed the near-wheeler. The near-wheeler had similar bridles (A), head-collar (B), neck-collar (C), reins and riding saddle (D) as the other near horse. The wheeler traces were not the same as those of the leader or centre horses. They were only sixty inches long with chains at the front (50) and rear (55), just long enough to keep the hindquarters clear of the splinter bar. Unlike the leader traces, they were only supported at the front by a flank buckling-piece (51). The trace-hooks (55) of the off-wheeler traces fastened into the trace-bands on the splinter bar of the limber. The breeching for

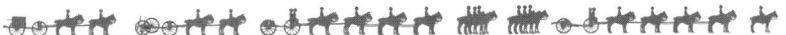

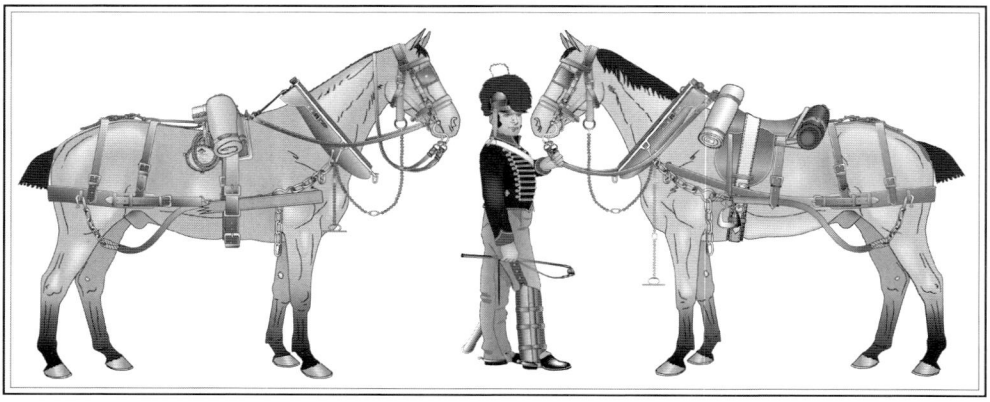

Figure 6.10. Artillery wheelers. Off side view of the off wheeler and a near side view of the near wheeler. The traces were hooked to the crupper rings when not in draught.

the near-wheeler, while similar, differed from the off-wheeler. The safe to the hip buckling-piece (59) was fitted on the off side of the horse – the side where the two horses could bump together. (A safe is a large flap of leather used to cover or replace a buckle and protect the horses from injury.)

Limbers had no brakes and in order to stop them, the wheel horses had to push backwards and to achieve this the wheel horses carried breeching harness. This was of four-inch wide leather (56), some 63 inches long, passing around the rear of the horse, about a foot below the root of the tail and supported, on each side, by two buckling-pieces (57 & 58); one for a hip strap (46) and one for a loin strap (47). The buckling-pieces were short straps with a buckle at one end and stitched to the breeching at the other. On the off side of the near wheeler, where there was a limber shaft, a standard breeching strap (60) connected to the limber shaft swivel ring, but on the near side, where there was no shaft, the near-wheeler had a special four-foot long breeching-strap with a hook (61). This buckled to the end of the breeching and led forward to the hook on the hame of the neck-collar. When braking, the unbalanced harnessing of the near-wheeler tended to cause a skew effect and to overcome this required a particularly well-trained and strong horse. When applying a braking force to the limber, the horses were said to be 'sitting back on the breechings'.

Off-wheeler Harness (see Figure 6.11)
The horse on the right in the shafts of the limber was termed the off-wheeler. The bridle (A), reins, head-collar (B), neck-collar (C), and saddle (E) of the off-wheeler were similar to those described for the off-leader.

In shaft draught, the off-wheeler was the only horse to be between the shafts but carried the same traces as the near wheeler. On the near side, between the two horses, the hip buckling-piece (59) was fitted with a large leather safe.

The breeching was supported in the same way as the near wheeler, hip straps (46) secured by their keepers to the ring of the crupper and by plain loin straps (47), which passed between the loops of the crupper strap (43). To connect the horse to the shafts of the limber, the off wheeler had a five-foot long breeching strap (60)

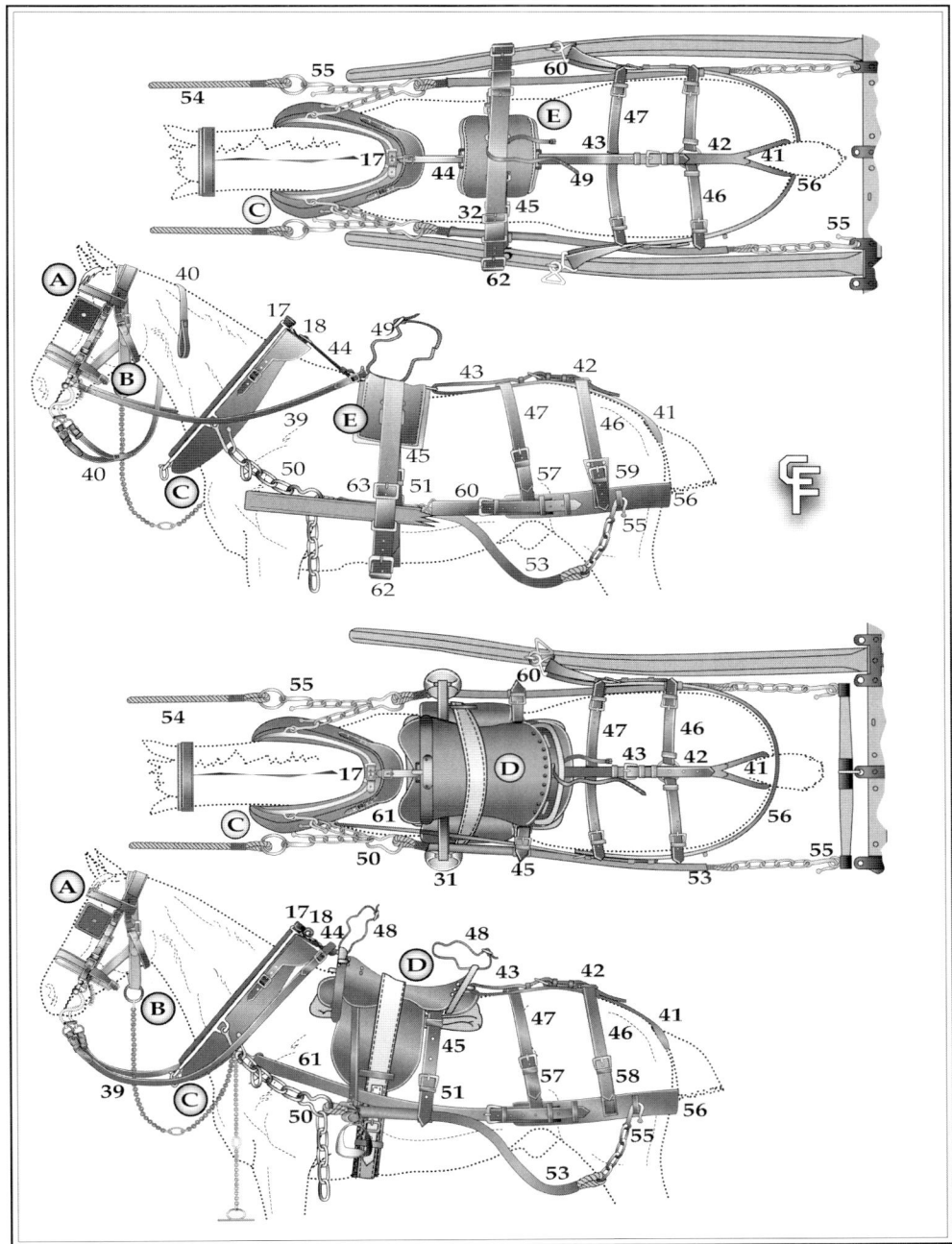

Figure 6.11. Artillery draught harness showing the top and the side views of the wheelers. The near side breeching strap (61) of the near wheeler is longer as the near wheeler is only connected to the limber shaft on the off side. The near wheeler harness on the off side is similar to the off wheeler. The off wheeler is the only horse to be between the shafts of the limber and to wear the back band (62); the harness was similar on both sides of the horse. The numbers in the illustration relate to those of the scaled illustration at figure 6.13 and Table A.18 of Appendix A at the end of Part One.

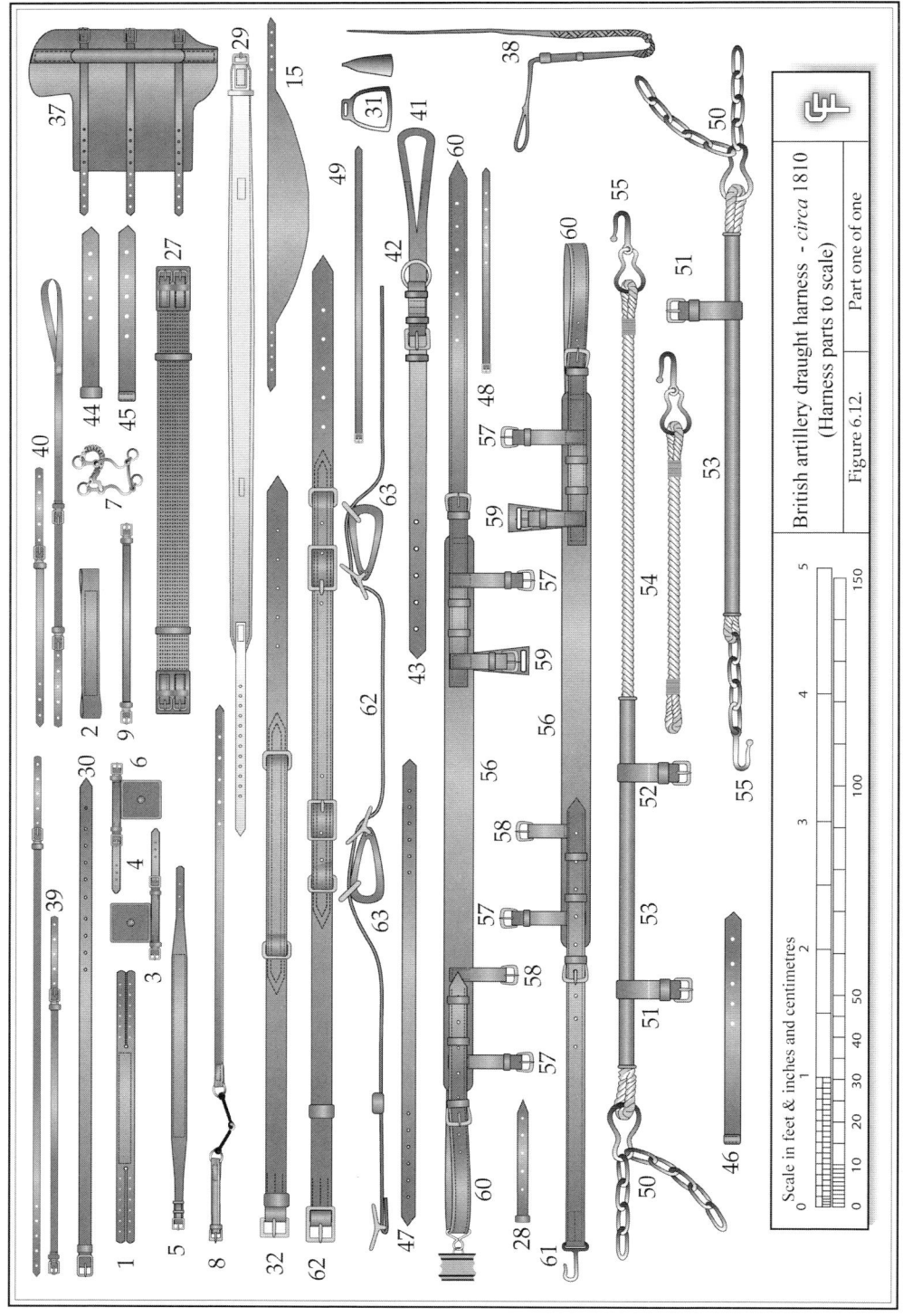

British artillery draught harness - *circa* 1810
(Harness parts to scale)

Figure 6.12.   Part one of one

Scale in feet & inches and centimetres

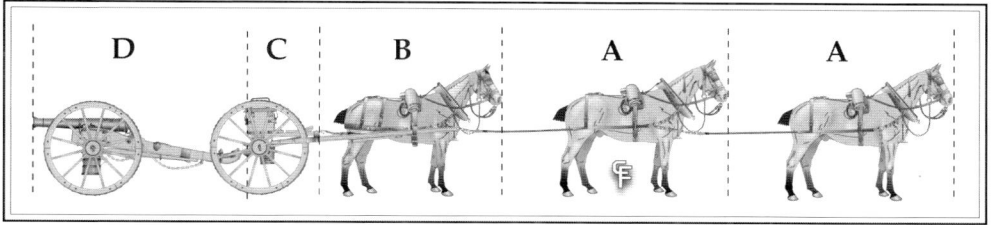

Figure 6.13. Artillery draught harness of a six-horse team showing the length of the line of march. The effective distance would vary with the different type of ordnance and the number of horses in the team. The effective distance between each horse with a yard between nose and croup (A) while the effective length of the limber (C) and that of the wheeler (B) would also remain a constant. The distance to the muzzle of the gun (D) would vary with the ordnance and length of the gun carriage.

stitched to each end of the breeching. The straps, one on each side, passed through the swivel (or breeching rings) on the shafts of the limber and buckled back onto themselves.

As the only horse in shafts, the off-wheeler was also fitted with a 'band, back and belly' (62), with 'tugs' (63). The back band was suspended over the pad saddle and passed around the horse like a loose girth with the shafts of the limber passing through the tugs on the inside of the back band. These supported the shafts in the vertical and horizontal planes and the back band was worn over the traces and outside the limber shafts. When single draught was required, the off-wheeler remained between the shafts of the limber, preceded by the near-wheeler; two additional short traces were required to extend wheeler traces and the distance between the two horses. The front rope loops were placed over the trace-hooks of the near-wheeler and the hooks connected to the trace-chains of the off-wheeler.

The work undertaken by the teams was hard and every effort was made to minimize the load on the horses. The near-wheeler harness weighed some 64 pounds and with the driver and saddle, carried a total weight of some 223 pounds. The off-wheeler carried a weight of some 88 pounds.[18] As a comparison, a cavalry or detachment horse, with a mounted gunner, carried a load of some 266 pounds without forage.[19] All of the harness parts listed and numbered in the preceding text and drawings are shown in the scaled illustration at Figure 6.12 and in Table A.20 of Appendix A at the end of Part One.[20]

Line of March

The length of the 'line of march' was the distance from the nose of the leading horse to the rearmost point of the vehicle or gun. While the length varied with the number of horses in the team, in general terms it can be considered the field distance of a four-horse team to the splinter bar of the limber was some 19 feet and for a six-horse team some 31 feet. Depending upon the adjustment of the harness a leader and a centre horse required some 11 feet from nose to nose. The short and long traces for the lead and centre horses when under load were about 135 inches long with the chains and hooks. The wheeler required some 9 feet from nose to the splinter bar depending upon the adjustment of the breeching straps and the limber hook was about 12.5 feet from the nose of the wheeler horse.

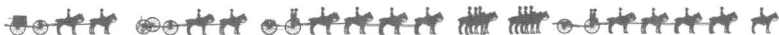

To this must be added the length of the gun and carriage projecting beyond this point and while this would have varied for each type of ordnance, as a rough guide a light 6-pr gun would be about 11 feet.

The total line of march for a 9-pr gun at Waterloo, where each was equipped with eight horses, can be considered to be some 19 yards, while similar pieces on parade with only four horses would be about 12 yards if short traces were used. More precise figures for the 'line of march' for the different equipments are given in Table A.21 of Appendix A at the end of Part One. It is noteworthy that the figures given in later sources are significantly similar, although they do allow a further distance of one horse length to any following equipment.[21]

Riding Harness of the Royal Horse Artillery

The horse artillery detachments were mounted on horses of some 15 hands. The horses were equipped in the style of light cavalry with a regimental pattern saddle and bridle; the colour of the harness for the riding horses of the detachments was brown with brass fittings and steel bits.[22] The descriptions given are based upon the few contemporary illustrations of horse artillery of this period. Mercer recalls when at bivouac the horses were secured to the wheels of the gun carriages.[23]

Bridles – In the same way as the light cavalry and draught teams, each horse wore three different and distinct sets of head harness, as has been described earlier and is shown in Figure 6.14. The standard method of holding the reins varied from country to country. The British light cavalry of the period when riding single handed, held the off curb rein between the first and second fingers of the left hand; the near curb rein was taken into the bottom of the hand, and the spare rein passed out of the top of the hand under the thumb. The snaffle bit was controlled with the off side rein passing between the second and third finger; the near side rein passing between the third and fourth finger. When riding two-handed the reins were held similarly, but with the snaffle reins in the left hand and the curb reins in the right.

Saddle – The horse artillery used the regimental pattern 'Hungarian' saddle. Made from beech, the stripped saddletree weighed some nine pounds eight ounces. It had a high front and rear arch attached by metal brackets to the two sideboards. A rawhide seat, to keep the man well above the horse's spine, was stretched and nailed between the two arches and the sides of the seat and the leather side flaps were stitched to the sideboards by leather thongs. The arches and sideboards were fitted with metal staples to take the various straps, accoutrements, and two straps for the girth were stitched to each sideboard. The saddle was usually placed on top of a folded blanket; this was some 6.5 feet wide and 8.75 feet long and folded into three equal parts in length and breadth to make a minimum of 9 folds, although this was varied to suit the horse and often some twelve to sixteen folds were needed. Bearskin flounces were worn over the front of the saddle to cover the pistol and cloak, although some preferred patent leather.[24] The saddle was held on the horse's back by the girth and a chest strap at the front, the crupper at the rear preventing the saddle sliding along the horse's back. A surcingle was also used to strap the saddle and any saddle cloth in place.[25]

Weapons – When the horse artillery was first formed, each mounted man carried 'one pistol and a pushing sword'.[26] This double-barrelled pistol with the additional

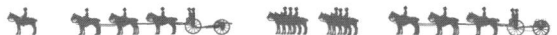

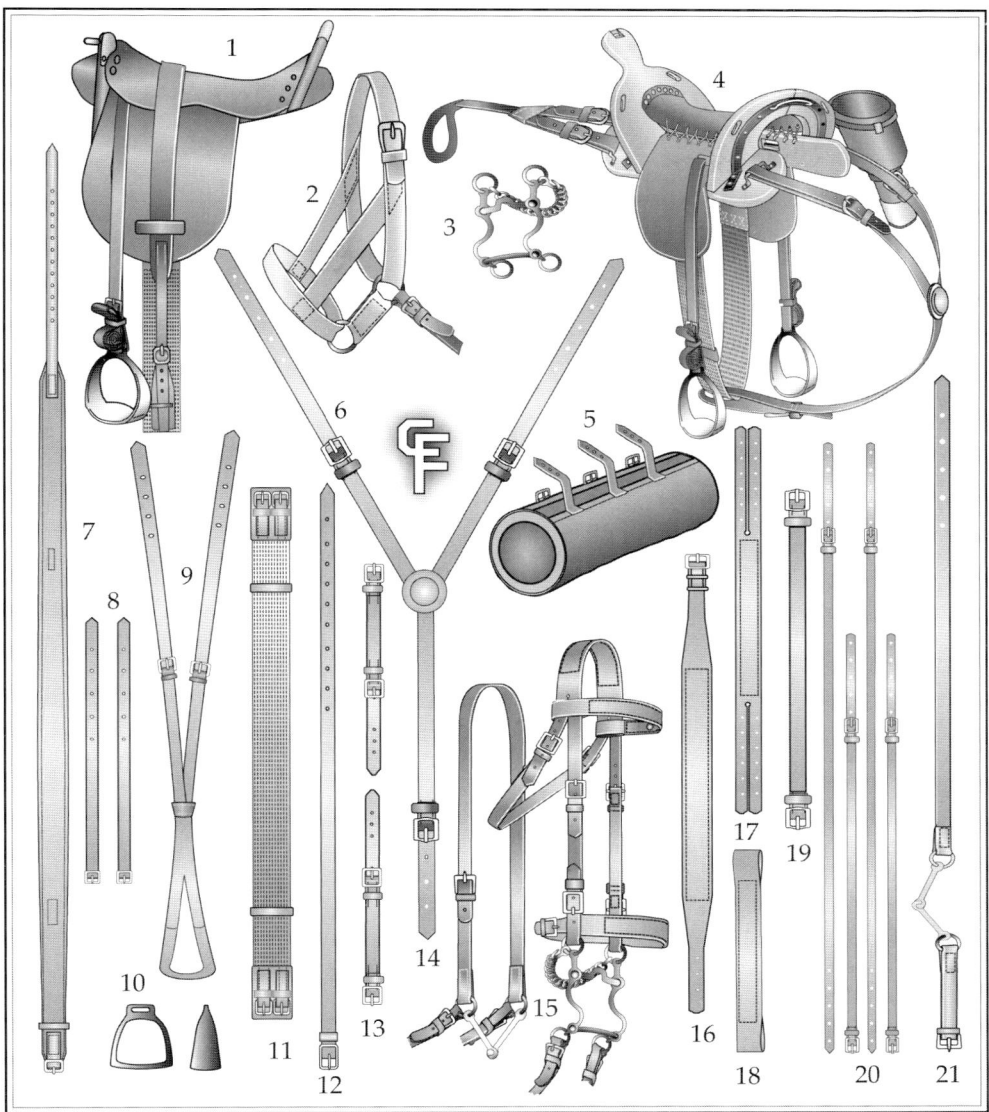

Figure 6.14. Horse artillery riding harness, circa 1810. The leather-covered horse artillery regimental saddle (1), collar headstall (2) and the general arrangement of the wooden 'Hungarian' saddletree and harness (4). The valise (5) was carried strapped to the rear of the saddle. The individual harness parts are the chest strap (6), surcingle (7), crupper (9), cloak and valise straps (8), web girth (11), stirrups leathers (12) and stirrups (10). The two-piece curb and snaffle reins (20) were strapped to the rings of the bits. The two-part bridle or bridoon (15) was formed from the headband (17) which passed through the loops of the brow band (18) and the straps buckled to the cheek pieces (13) and the throat lash (19). The billot ends of the cheek pieces (13) were strapped through the rings of the curb bit. The noseband (16) passed through the loops formed by the billots of the cheek pieces. Under this bridle was worn the bridle head for the snaffle bit (21). The sizes of these parts are the same as those shown in figure 6.13.

carbine butt is shown in Chapter 18. Later a standard light cavalry pistol replaced the special version and was carried in a holster strapped to the off side of the saddle and the pushing sword was replaced in 1796 by the light dragoon pattern sabre. Later illustrations suggest by 1813 that two pistols were carried in holsters on either side of the saddle.[27]

Stirrups – The brown stirrup leathers passed through a hole in the sideboard, under a metal runner, and back down to the stirrup. They were worn in light cavalry fashion, buckled at the stirrup with the ends rolled up – allegedly to prevent the leather being cut by a sword. The iron stirrups were of light cavalry pattern with a curved base, narrowed to the top. The stirrup leathers were adjusted so that the lower edge of the bar was two fingers above the upper edge of the heel of the boot.

Crupper – The crupper consisted of a rolled leather dock at one end and two straps with billots at the other. The dock passed under the tail of the horse and the other ends fastened to staples on the rear of the saddle to prevent it slipping forward. The dock was 14 inches long and the straps to the buckle 12 inches with the billot strap end a further 22 inches.

Breast plate – This prevented the saddle slipping backwards. It consisted of three leather straps, joined in the form of a 'Y' with a billot at each end. The two arms passed around the horse's neck and were strapped to metal staples on the sideboards. The third strap passed under the chest, between the front legs of the horse, and buckled around the girth. The centre of the 'Y' was at the chest of the horse and usually carried an ornamental boss. The length of each strap to the saddle was some 33 inches and to the girth, some 30 inches.

Shabraque – The other ranks used a square shabraque for dress; it was blue, laced red and showing a blue edge.[28] Senior NCOs used a plain blue long-tailed shabraque under a red-edged black sheepskin.[29] Officers in undress used a plain blue, light dragoon version with a long pointed and tasselled tail, but it seems most likely that a laced version would have been used for dress occasions, probably dark blue, laced gold and showing a blue edge with the rubbing plates of brown leather. Lined with leather or rawhide, it weighed some seven pounds. It was intended to prevent the equipment rubbing the sides of the horse and keep the horse warm over the loins. The shabraque was worn over the saddle and pierced to allow the cantle of the rear arch to protrude through. It was secured in place by the leather surcingle passing through loops in the girth and strapped over the shabraque. A narrow leather shabraque strap passed through loops on the inside of the surcingle, round the outside of the saddle holding the shabraque in place. The form of the shabraque for mounted officers of foot artillery are not known, but Pyne shows a mounted officer wearing a French-style 'bonnet de police' with a valise on the rear of the saddle and holstered pistol at the front.[30] A later print of 1815 shows a similar plain blue shabraque of the type used by the horse artillery.

Valise – This was the standard light cavalry, cylindrical, cloth baggage case and contained the spare kit and small gear of the rider. It was closed up by three straps and carried behind the rear arch of the saddle, resting on the fans and attached by straps passing through slots in the cantle. The colour was regimental dark blue with flat yellow lace around the circular face. It was common practice to carry a waterdeck folded and wrapped around the valise when on active service; the kit of the drivers was also carried in a blue valise in a similar manner, but where the two men who rode upon the limber placed their kit is not known, possibly on the off horses. The scale of riding harness issued to each horse artillery troop is shown in Table A.23 of Appendix A at the end of Part One.

Key to Colour Plate 16

Royal Horse Artillery – Mounts and harness
1. Mounted horse artillery gunner, *circa* 1802, after a painting in the Royal Collection.
2. Details of the shabraque ornamentation for Figure 1.
3. Details of the sabretache of the mounted gunner at Figure 1.
4. Mounted horse artillery officer, *circa* 1802, after a painting in the Royal Collection.
5. Details of the sabretache design of the mounted officer at 4.
6. Details of the shabraque ornamentation of the mounted officer at 4.
7. The detachment horse of a gunner of the horse artillery with a square shabraque and bearskin flounces over the pistol holsters.
8. Valisse carried at the rear of the saddle.
9. Mounted horse artillery officer in parade dress, *circa* 1815.
10. Riding horse for an artillery officer with the plain blue undress shabraque and black sheepskin saddle cloth.
11. Collar head stall of the horse artillery.
12. Chest strap worn to prevent the saddle moving backwards.
13. Horse artillery pattern double bridle or bridoon with light cavalry curb and snaffle bits.
14. The wood arched 'Hungarian' or 'Hussar' riding saddle upon which the artillery regimental saddle was based.
15. The crupper worn as part of the harness to prevent the saddle moving forward.

Endnotes to Chapter 6

1. Duncan, 2005: p. 124.
2. Muller, 1780: p. 118.
3. Caruana, 1977: pp. 17–19.
4. Macdonald, 1985: p. 56.
5. Adye, 1813: p. 220.
6. Duncan, 1872: p. 53.
7. Ibid: p. 276.
8. Ibid: p. 308.
9. Tylden, 1965: pp. 194–208.
10. James Clavell Library, *Artillery Harness*, plates 37, 38, Royal Carriage Department, 1870; *US Artillery Harness, circa 1848*. US Government, reprinted by Antique Ordnance Publishers, Michigan, 1992: et al.
11. Dickson, 1908: pp. vi–ix, 1.
12. Siborne, 1891: pp. 195–6.
13. Mercer, 1870: pp. 61, 133, 149, 254.
14. Webber, 1991: p. 170.
15. Ibid.
16. Duncan, 2005: p. 113.
17. Mercer, 1870: p. 227.

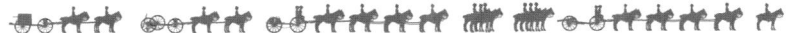

18. Tylden. op cit: p. 201.
19. Adye, 1813: p. 219.
20. The Royal Mews and The British Carriage Driving Society have been most generous in their advice and assistance, as has been the invaluable help and advice of T. Ryder Esquire of Huntingdon, who is probably one of the leading experts in the United Kingdom.
21. *Aide Memoire*, 1844: p. 8, table IV.
22. Adye, 1813: p. 308.
23. Mercer, 1870: p. 139.
24. Dickson, 1908: p. 411.
25. Adye, 1813: p. 359.
26. Carauna, 1980: p. 14.
27. Adye, 1813: p. 359.
28. Hamilton Smith, *Royal Horse Artillery, 1815*.
29. Campbell, 1971: plate VI.
30. Pyne, 1802: *Foot Artillery Detachment at Rest*.

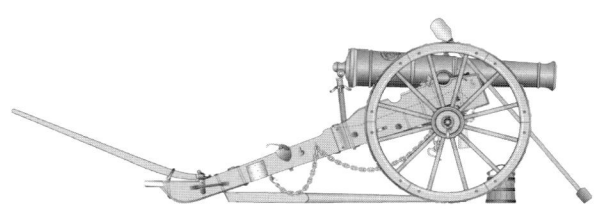

CHAPTER 7

Drills and Exercises

Introduction

The number of men in a gun detachment depended upon the arm of service and the nature of the ordnance. Where the field artillery were concerned the figure remained constant, but the heavier pieces of position and garrison artillery required more men to serve the gun – notionally one man was required for each 500 pounds of metal – but the records of the day clearly show the field artillery generally allocated the same number of men to all field pieces irrespective of their weight.[1] The foot artillery evolved through several modes of operation during the period. Early in the period, while brigaded by companies when allocated to the Park of Artillery, once in the field they were attached as one or two gun groups to infantry battalions to provide artillery support; in this role they were termed 'battalion' guns. The drills evolved through several modes as the war progressed, particularly as the new equipments introduced for the horse artillery became available to the foot artillery. Eventually, to counter the ever dominant weight of French artillery, the guns were brigaded into six gun groups on the same lines as the horse artillery; thus there were several different versions of drills for the field artillery, firstly for the battalion guns with the old form of draught, then the drills where the transitional limbers were involved. This was followed by the change necessitated as the foot artillery became equipped with block trail guns, which with their integral slow match boxes meant there was no longer a need for the man to carry the slow match, although the requirement remained for those guns mounted on bracket trails. The final change was the brigading together of the company guns in a similar way to the horse artillery. Meanwhile the horse artillery formed with their new equipment from the start soon adopted drills which closely followed those of the foot artillery, except the whole detachment was mounted and the horse holders absorbed the numbers previously used for the drag rope men.

Drills of the Foot Artillery

At the start of the war, the practice with a battalion gun relied upon men to manoeuvre the carriage. In this role the gun detachment required 15 men, six of whom were drag rope men who manhandled the gun. These were often supplied by the infantry and trained by the artillery in their duties; when this happened the artillery detachment required to operate the gun was nine men, although the detachments were trained to operate with less and were often required to do so. When expedient, the limber horses could be used to advance or retire the guns and drills existed for these circumstances; never-the-less the gun detachments stayed at nine or fifteen men throughout the war and it was not until the end of the Napoleonic period that the general practice of fifteen men to a gun was discontinued,[2] by 1813 it was noted 'the brigade exercises so resembles that of the horse artillery that little explanation is necessary. The officers are posted in the same manner and in all rapid movements, the gunners are mounted on the gun limber and ammunition carriage'.[3] There were no regulations laid down covering the disposition of horse artillery troops or foot brigades until after the period, but the note books of the cadets at Woolwich provide a clear insight to the practices taught. When in line the notional distance between guns was 15 yards from muzzle to muzzle, the distance to the wheel of the ammunition wagons was 50 yards.

When in action the limber was some 25 yards to the rear of the gun with the horses facing toward the front. Where the terrain allowed the ammunition wagons and limbers were a further 25 yards to the rear, usually under the command of the Quarter Master Sergeant. Where the nature of the ground afforded a degree of cover, the NCOs in charge of the limbers were justified in taking advantage of it where it did not effect the distances more than a few yards either way; the same principle was applied to the ammunition wagons. There was a multiplicity of drill and manoeuvre regulations covering every conceivable circumstance, but when the tactical situation or the disposition of the ground precluded their use, the brigade or troop commanders were expected to make the appropriate decisions and were fully responsible for the disposition of the unit and were expected to adopt whichever solution was appropriate.

It was only after 1853, when Chobham Camp was established, that the artillery had any opportunity to practice field training with other arms; prior to this they had to rely upon experience and whatever practice they received on Plumstead Marshes. At Waterloo, many of the artillery units were placed just in front of the Ohain Road, and there are some suggestions that the ammunition boxes were removed from the limbers and brought nearer the guns. This seems most unlikely, as their position would have rendered them liable to sparks from the gun and to enemy fire.[4]

The King's German Artillery, part of the King's German Legion, used the limbers of the ammunition wagons to ferry supplies to the gun limbers. This was eminently practicable as the ammunition boxes of the wagon limbers were identical to those of the gun, but whether they replaced the used ammunition or simply exchanged the boxes is not stated, although the latter would have been a much quicker procedure.[5]

At Waterloo, some artillery units withdrew from the field (Sandham's Brigade and Kuhlmann's Brigade of the King's German Legion) to replenish their exhausted ammunition and this involved moving away from the firing line. It may have been this that caused Wellington to write he was not pleased with the artillery at Waterloo accusing them that 'they ran off the field with their limbers and guns'.[6]

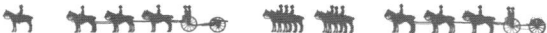

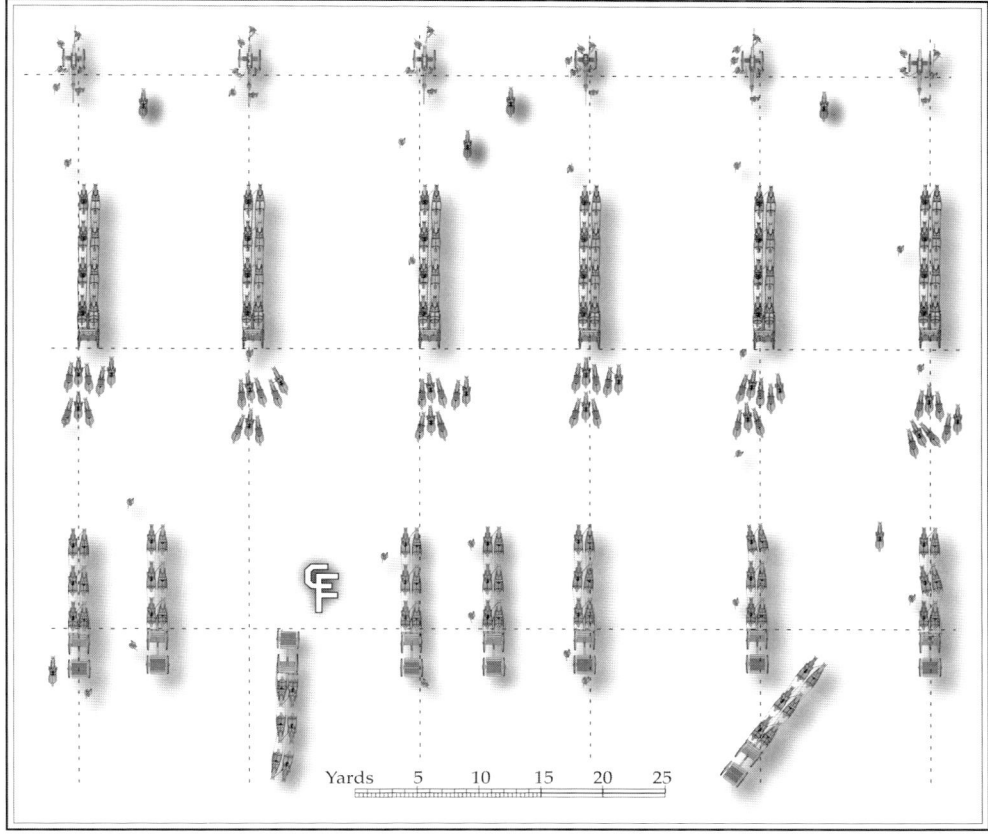

Figure 7.1. Royal Horse Artillery Troop equipped with 9-pr guns in 'action front'. The distances separating the guns, limbers and ammunition wagons are shown at the regulation 25 yards from wheel to wheel, but this would vary where the operational requirements or the terrain dictated otherwise, like the Ohain Road at Waterloo. In the front row are the six pieces, some 19 yards apart, with the howitzer as the gun of direction. The limbers are some 25 yards to the rear. Behind these are the detachment horses held by the mounted horse holders. On the third line are the ammunition wagons, a further 25 yards to the rear. Normally these would be shuttled between the reserve ammunition park and the battlefield with spare ammunition. The large distances covered by the ammunition numbers is evident as is the distance covered by the men from the ammunition wagons as they re-supply the gun limbers.

Position of the Limbers and Ammunition Wagons

In the drills of the period the limber is noted to retire some 25 yards to the rear of the gun; this distance being measured from the rear of the gun wheel to the front of the limber wheel. This would place the muzzle of the leading horses of a six-horse team only some 11 yards from the gun and for a four-horse team 15 yards (see Table A.21 in Appendix A at the end of Part Two). The notes of later drill instructions in which the distance to the limbers and ammunition wagons has been changed notes: [7]

Although ten yards is the distance nominally allowed the limbers in action, in the rear of their guns, yet it is to be observed, that when the nature of the ground is such as will in any degree cover them from the effect of the enemy's fire, a non-commissioned officer is perfectly justified in taking advantage of it, when the distance does not exceed a few yards either way. With respect to the ammunition wagons, no positive rules can be laid down as to their disposition in action, which, on service, must in a great measure, depend upon a variety of circumstances: when it is practicable, they should be under the charge of an officer, whose duty it will be to conform to the movement of the guns in such a manner as to enable him to supply them with ammunition before that which is in the limbers can be expended: the spare carriages should be under the charge of the Quarter Master Sergeant.

The ammunition numbers spent their time running the 25 yards or so to the limbers and back again. If one considers the rates of fire quoted it becomes clear that this could not be achieved without extra men and the gunners usually had 'cartouche-bags slung round them, containing ammunition'.[8] In battle, a 6-pr would fire some three rounds a minute for common case and two rounds a minute for round shot. When speed of loading was required, it was common to place the cartridge and projectile in the bore at the same time and ram them home together.[9]

The ammunition man had to run to the limber, prepare ammunition and run back to the gun; each a 50-yard round trip carrying a 6lb shot and cartridge. Even if the two men alternated, each needed to maintain a rate of some 50 to 75 yards for every minute in action, an impossible task. Similarly the men who manned the ammunition wagon were expected to re-supply the gun limber as the ammunition was consumed; again a most difficult task if the given rates of fire were actually achieved. To move the horses nearer the gun had clear disadvantages; but even if the distance was reduced the picture presented makes it clear how arduous the task would have been without additional manpower.

Allocating the Numbers

To assist in training and a total understanding of their task the specific duties of each man in the detachment was given a number. The method of allocating the numbers to the detachment duties changed several times between the late eighteenth century and middle of the nineteenth. Originally the artillery allocated the high numbers to the gun detachment and the low numbers to the supernumeraries and when the horse artillery were first formed they appear to have adopted the same system. In 1801, 1806 and 1808 Adye recorded that this was still the practice, but he shows the drills for the garrison artillery with the low numbers at the gun.

In 1813, Adye shows the numbering system in general use still allocated the high numbers to the gun. Mercer also relates at Waterloo, number 7 used the sponge staff and cadet notes at Woolwich confirm this, as does Lawson in 1821. By 1827, the system had changed to the low numbers at the gun and the higher numbers to the supporting supernumeraries and this is the system often erroneously quoted for the Napoleonic period.[10] The change in numbering may have been due, in part, to the insufficiency of numbers for a system requiring larger teams for heavier ordnance. However, during the period covered by this book the high numbers manned the gun. In either event, the numbering system used is somewhat academic, as it was the drills themselves that were the more important, but for correctness, the numbering system used throughout this chapter places the high numbers to the gun. When there were spare men available they were allocated at the discretion of the commanding officer. Mercer recalls:

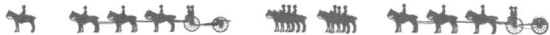

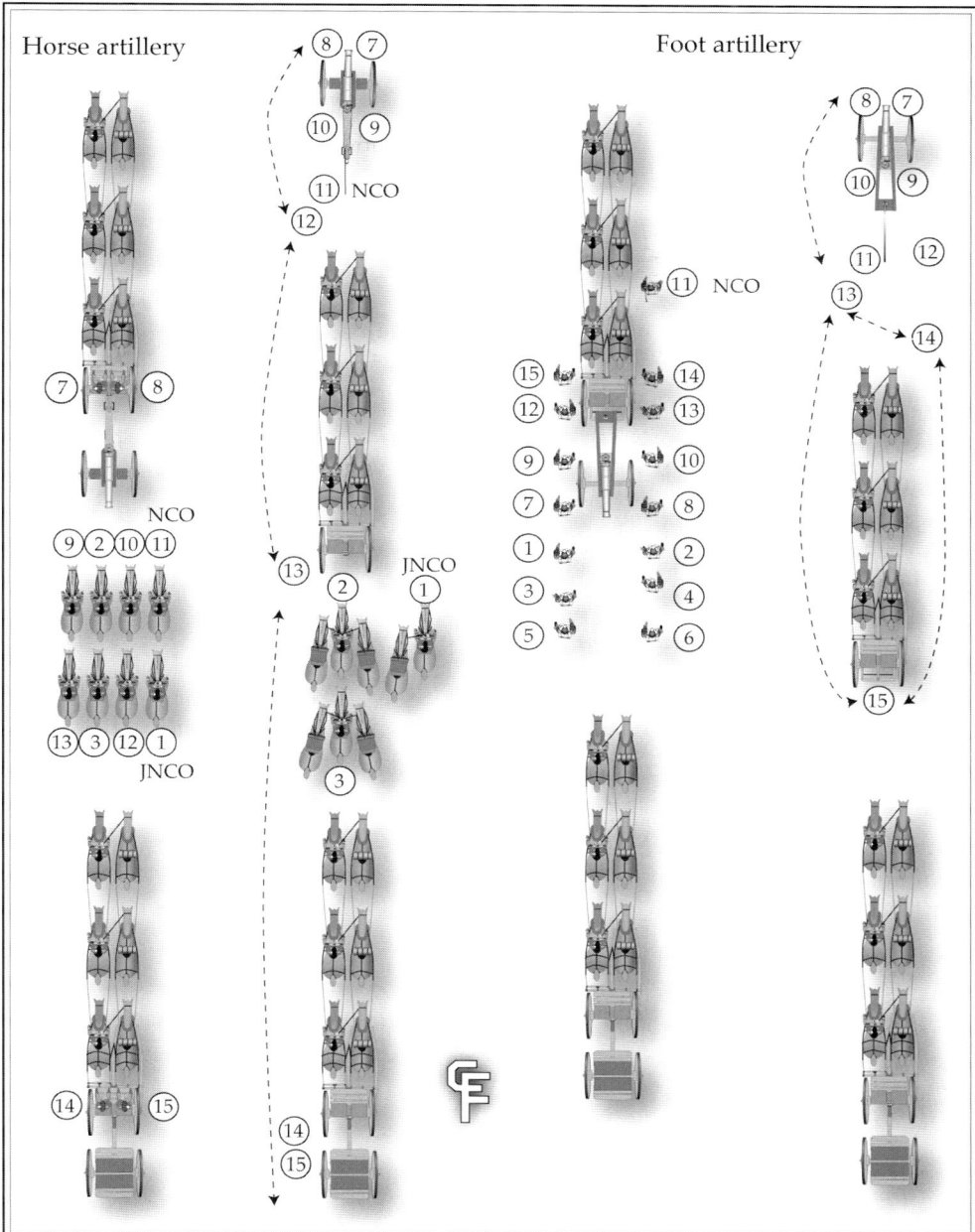

Figure 7.2. Key to detachment drill numbers and positions for brigade and horse artillery. (The size of the equipments is to a common scale but the distances between the equipments is not.) In the horse artillery, the numbers 1, 2 and 3 were allocated to the horse holders while 12 and 13 supplied the gun with ammunition from the limber. Numbers 14 and 15 were allocated to the ammunition wagon. In the foot artillery, numbers 1 to 6 were allocated to the men who manhandled the gun and 14 and 15 supplied ammunition, but when the block trail was introduced the duties more aligned to those of the horse artillery.

when I got my first commission, in 1799 … We had no system of field exercises for a battery ; even in the Horse Artillery every commanding officer drew up something of his own. In telling off numbers to guns, we differed entirely from the mode at present in use. For garrison guns, they went from 1 upwards – 1 sponges, 2 loads, etc. – For field guns, when there were drag-ropes they also began at 1, but then the first six were drag-rope men, and those serving the gun began at 7, which was the case when there were no drag-ropes ; so that with a field gun it always ran thus: 7 sponges, 8 loads, 9 serves the vent, 10 fires, 11 commands (non-commissioned officer), 12 holds the cartouche, 13 brings up ammunition, etc …[11]

Drill Duties

The drills for guns mounted on bracket trail carriage were different to those for guns mounted on block trails and the duties were different again where howitzers were concerned. When guns were used in the Brigade role or with the interim limbers the drills dispensed with the drag rope men and the limber and teams were used to advance and retire the gun. The horse artillery was equipped with guns mounted on block trail carriages and all the detachment were mounted. When the foot brigades were equipped with guns mounted on block trails their drills closely resembled those of the horse artillery, except that the detachment was not mounted and there were no horse holders. These differences should be borne in mind when considering the drills and exercises listed below, but it should also be remembered that these drills were practiced over and over again until each man in the detachment could not only perform his own duties but also those of all the others. During the drills, each of the steps was ordered by the NCO and repeated until the personnel performed them to perfection.

These orders included; 'Advance the sponge', 'Sponge', 'Prepare to load', 'Load', 'Advance the rammer', 'Ram cartridge', 'Spring rammer', 'Draw rammer', 'Ready' and 'Fire'. Many of these individual orders were unnecessary in action but the constant repetition and attention to detail served to prevent accidents in the heat of battle.

Allocation of Duties

Each detachment member undertook specific duties according to the number he was allocated:

Numbers 1 to 6	These numbers were allocated to drag rope men in the foot artillery. In the horse artillery numbers 1 to 3 were allocated to the horse holders with the numbers 4 to 6 not normally used in this period unless extra men were allocated to the gun.
Number 7	The man who sponged the bore and rammed the ammunition. His position in action was between the right wheel and the muzzle of the gun.
Number 8	The man who loaded the cartridges and rounds into the muzzle for 7 to ram home. His position was between the left wheel and the muzzle of the gun.
Number 9	The man who served the vent. His position was between the right wheel and the vent of the gun, but he retired outside the right wheel to avoid the recoil when the gun fired.
Number 10	The man who fired the gun. His position was in line with the vent of the gun and outside the left wheel to avoid the recoil.

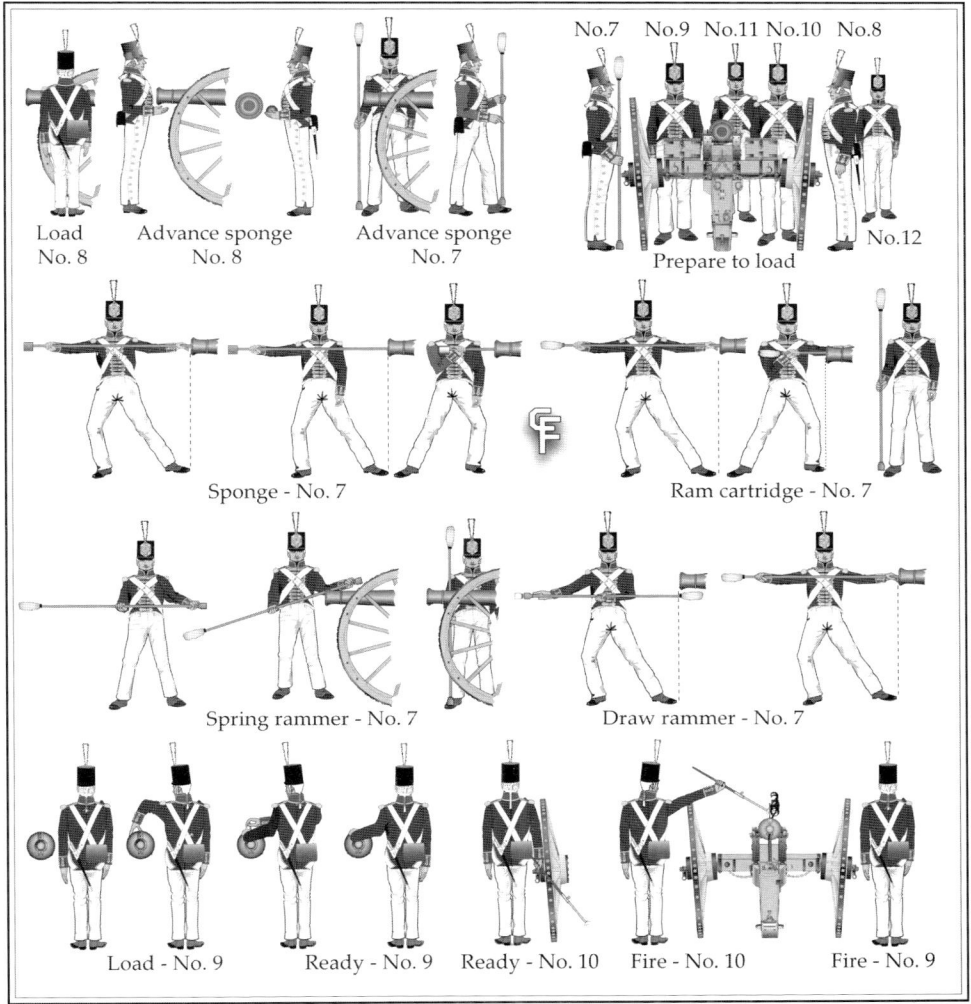

Load No. 8 — Advance sponge No. 8 — Advance sponge No. 7 — No.7 No.9 No.11 No.10 No.8 — Prepare to load — No.12

Sponge - No. 7 — Ram cartridge - No. 7

Spring rammer - No. 7 — Draw rammer - No. 7

Load - No. 9 — Ready - No. 9 — Ready - No. 10 — Fire - No. 10 — Fire - No. 9

Figure 7.3. Artillery drill positions and actions from a gun drill book (after later drawings but probably typical of the period). The rigorous attention to drills and constant practice could ensure the detachment achieved a rate of fire of eight rounds a minute in the heat of battle. Accidents due to mistakes were all too easy unless the drills were scrupulously followed and rotation of the duties and responsibilities was part of the regular practice.

Number 11 He was usually an NCO, he attended the left of the trail and was responsible for the aiming of the gun and command of the detachment.

Numbers 12 to 15 had different duties depending upon the type of gun carriage.

Duties with a bracket trail gun

Number 12 His duties were to attend the water, slow match and linstock. His position was on the left of 11, but clear of 9.

Number 13 He supplied 8 with ammunition, which he received from 14. His nominal position was five yards behind the left wheel.

Number 14 He supplied 13 with ammunition from the limber. He carried a cartouche and a battalion gun, and when 1 to 6 were not allocated he carried the drag ropes. His nominal position was 10 yards behind the right wheel.

Number 15   He attended the shaft horse of the limber. His position was some 25 yards to the rear of the gun.

Duties with a block trail gun

Number 12   He supplied 8 with ammunition collected from the limber. His nominal position was five yards behind the left wheel.

Number 13   Served at the gun limber and prepared ammunition for 12.

Number 14   He supplied the limber with ammunition from the ammunition wagon. His nominal position was at the ammunition wagon.

Number 15   He also supplied the limber with ammunition from the ammunition wagon. His nominal position was also at the ammunition wagon.

Duties with a howitzer

These drills only applied for the periods when howitzers or mortars fired common shell; they were not continued in the field artillery and were anachronous by the end of the war, but were still referred to in later drill books, most probably for use by guns of position. The object of these extra actions was to protect the powder and fuse of the shell from stray sparks.[12]

Number 7   Still sponged the bore and rammed the ammunition but he also uncapped the fuse of the shell and then fitted it in the shell.

Number 8   Still loaded the cartridge for 7 to ram home but he was also responsible for the sheepskin, which he took out of the barrel and laid upon the ground with the woollen side up. He wiped the bottom of the shell when 7 held it up and placed it into the bore. He then replaced the sheepskin, which he removed on the command 'Ready' and stopped the muzzle immediately after the piece had fired.

Numbers 9, 10, 11, 12, 13 and 15   Served as before

Number 14   Serves 7 with shells from the limber, which he places on the sheepskin, laid down by 8.

Rotation of Duties

Some of the duties were clearly more demanding than others and it was the usual practice to rotate the duties as the men tired. In action, the rotation would depend much upon casualties and who was best for the task to be done, but there was a procedure to follow: number 7 assumed the duties of 9, 9 of 15, 15 of 12, 12 of 13, 13 of 10, 10 of 8 and 8 of 7. Each man assumed the new duties and continued until they were rotated again.[13] A contemporary directive notes:

> It is to be observed that every man belonging to the artillery, even drummers, must be taught the several Motions of the Exercises, as well as every other Duty or Manoeuvre which may be required or can possibly occur in actual Service; picked men should not be allotted for particular Services, but the men are to be often changed, and to perform all the Duties in the Exercises alternately; nevertheless Officers should observe and mark those men who are most active, intelligent, attentive and careful, in ramming home, in

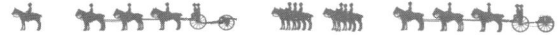

loading, and in firing, that such may be employed in those services, or any other in which they excel, upon important occasions.[14]

There were drills for every nature of events and for all foreseeable circumstances including dismounting the piece. A well-trained gun detachment could unlimber and bring the gun into action in about a minute. They could fire a light piece every 8 seconds but the rate of fire was slower for the larger guns and usually deliberately restricted.[15] This was done partly to conserve ammunition, but mainly to prevent rushed drills and avoid accidents. Each time the gun fired the gun carriage recoiled for some eight feet on level ground and the whole detachment were expected to run the gun back up to the firing position and re-lay it before the next round could be fired.[16] The need for the rotation of duties becomes clear when considering the efforts of the sponge man and the ammunition men compared to the relatively light duties of the vents man and firer. Any surplus manpower, spare drivers etc. would be brought into use in an effort to ease the workload.

Method of Distributing the Duties to a Smaller Number of Men

The detachments were trained to operate with reduced manpower, so casualties did not unduly affect their capabilities. The minimum number of men to operate a gun was considered as three. The usual manning was for nine, numbered 7 to 15, and this constituted a normal detachment. In the event of casualties the duties were reassigned as follows and the appropriate number took on the extra duties:

One casualty	The number 12 was not assigned and 11 did those duties.
Two casualties	On a gun, numbers 12 and 14 were not assigned. The cartouche was laid on the ground and 13 carried it when moving. On a howitzer, numbers 12 and 13 were not assigned, 8 served himself with cartridges.
Three casualties	The numbers 10, 12 and 13 or 14 were not assigned. Number 9 served the vent and fired the gun.
Four casualties	Numbers 9, 10, 12 and 13 or 14 were not assigned. Number 11 did all the duties of 9 and 12.
Five casualties	Numbers 9, 10, 12, 13 and 14 were not assigned. On a gun, number 8 collected the ammunition. On a howitzer, number 7 served his shells.
Six casualties	Numbers 8, 9, 10, 12, 13 and 14 were not assigned. Number 7 served and loaded all the ammunition. Number 7 and 15 changed duties when required.

As it can be seen, only 7, 11 and 15 were considered essential to operate a gun or howitzer.[17]

Line of Advance (see Figure 7.2)

When foot artillery advanced with a battalion gun, number 11 (the NCO), marched on the off side, in line with the shafts on the wheel horse. The number 7 and 8 marched in line with the muzzle of the gun; 9 and 10 marched in line with the breech; 12 and 13 marched opposite the trail and 14 marched in line with the axletree of the limber; 15 led the limber horse while the driver led the front horse. In each case the low number was on the off side, the higher on the near. When accompanied by drag

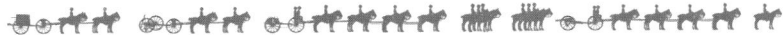

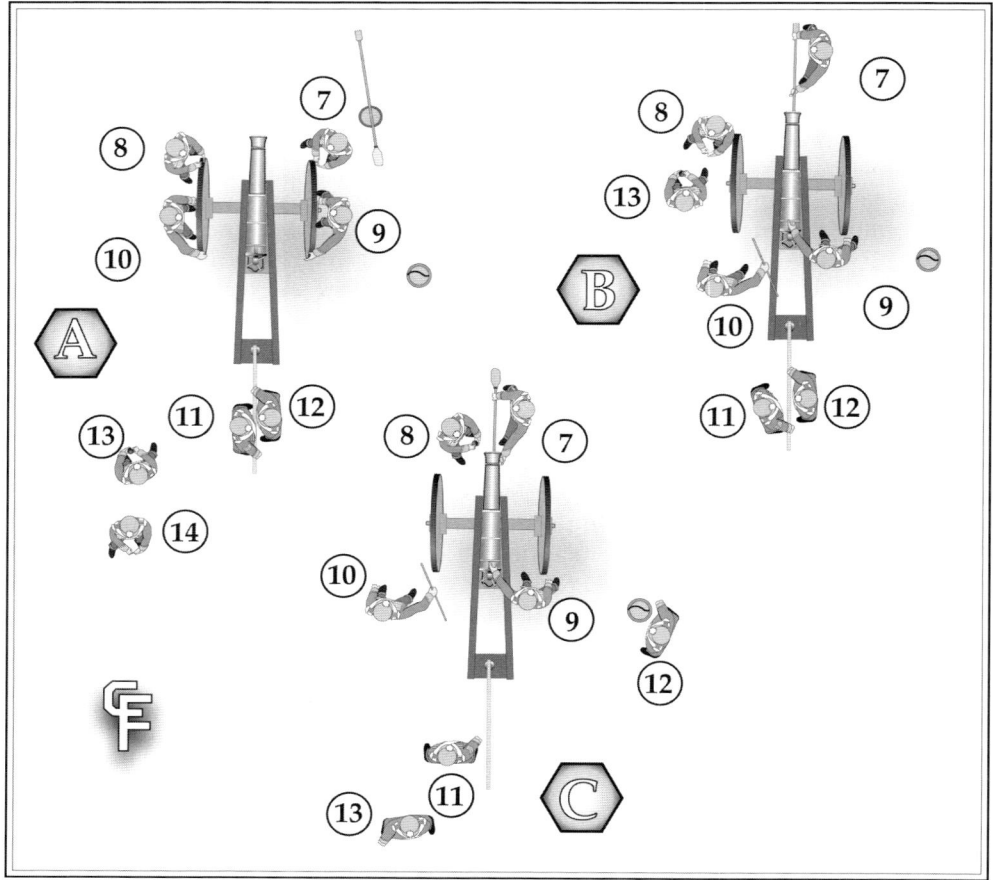

Figure 7.4. Detachment duties with a bracket trail gun carriage (part one). The bracket trail carriages required the number 12 to attend to the duties of the linstock and water. Additional numbers were often required to assist number 11 traverse the gun.

(A) The gun has fired and the detachment runs the gun back. Number 7 attended the front of the right wheel, 8 attended the front of the left wheel, 9 attended the rear of the right wheel, 10 attended the rear of the left wheel, 11 attended the trail, 12 assisted 11, 13 stood ready with ammunition from 14, 14 returned to the limber and 15 attended the limber horse.

(B) Reloading and sponging commenced. Number 7 sponged the bore, 8 received the next cartridge from 13, 9 served the vent, 10 took the portfire holder, 11 aimed the gun, 12 assisted 11, 13 stood ready with the projectile, 14 attended the limber and 15 attended the limber horse.

(C) Reloading, ramming commenced. Number 7 reversed the staff and rammed the cartridge, 8 stood ready with the projectile, 9 served the vent, 10 stood by with the portfire, 11 supervised, 12 attended the water and slow match while 13 returned for ammunition from 14. 14 left the limber with the next round and 15 attended the limber horse.

rope men, these marched behind the gun detachment, with 2, 4 and 6 on the near side and 1, 3 and 5 on the off.[18]

There were many different formations for advancing and retiring an artillery brigade and battalion guns, these usually depended upon the tactical situation at the time. When a brigade equipped with the new limbers advanced in column the number 11 marched on the off side in line with the head of the wheel horse; 7 and 8 marched in line with the muzzle of the gun; 9 and 10 marched in line with the breech of the gun. The ammunition men, numbers 12 and 13, marched in line with the axle of the limber and the limber men, 14 and 15, marched in line with the limber splinter bar. In each case the low number was on the off side, the higher on the near. At this time the foot artillery gunners could be mounted on the equipment when required, the number 11 rode on the gun limber off box and 7 the near; 8 and 9 on the ammunition wagon limber; 10 and 13 on the ammunition wagon fore box; 12 and 14 on the hind box with 15 (when present) between them.[19] Later, the numbers 7, 8 and 11 rode on the gun limber with 9 and 10 on the wagon limber, 13 and 12 on the wagon fore box and 15 and 14 on the hind box.[20] When marching in light order the greatcoats and blankets were carried strapped to the top of the ammunition boxes and the packs were attached to staples on their rear. The pack of number 11 was allocated the offside box of the gun limber, 7 the nearside box. On the wagon limber, 8 was allocated the off box, 9 the near. Number 10 the offside of the fore box; 12 the near side; 13 the offside of the hind box with 14 on the near side and 15 between them.[21]

When advancing in column the horse artillery mounted detachments could be at the front, rear or on the flank of the guns as appropriate to the 'Order of march'. Irrespective, their formation was in two rows of four with numbers 9, 2, 10 and 11 in the front row with 13, 3, 12 and 1, a junior NCO, in the rear. Numbers 7 and 8 rode upon the gun limber with 14 and 15 on the ammunition wagon limber.

Unlimber

With a battalion gun the detachment halted and turned to face the gun. Number 11 unchained the trail from the limber and 11 and 12 lifted the trail clear of the bolster pintle and set it on the ground assisted by 7 and 8 bearing down on the muzzle while 9 and 10 attended the wheels. Number 11 fitted the traversing handspike and the Hanoverian truck if required, while the detachment assumed the positions for action. The limber was led left about by number 15 and the driver retired some 25 yards to the rear where it turned left about and any leading horse was unhooked by the driver and tied to the rear of the limber. Where the weight of the gun carriage warranted 9 and 10 assisted 12 and 13 to raise the trail while 14 and 15 attended the wheels.[22]

With a brigade gun, the horses were halted facing the front and the detachment halted and turned to face the gun. Number 11 unkeyed or unchained the limber, 12 and 13 raised the trail and turned the gun to the right, assisted by 7 and 8 bearing on the muzzle and 9 steadying the right wheel while 10 worked the left, to spin the gun about. When the gun was unhooked and clear 11 ordered the limber to 'Drive on'. The limber turned left about and, depending upon the tactical situation, retired some 25 yards to the rear and turned left about to face the front.

When the gun was in position, 12 and 13 retired to the limber to remove the cartouches and hang them from the guard irons while preparing to supply the necessary ammunition, portfires or quills while 14 and 15 attended the wagon.

With the horse artillery, on the order the team halted facing the front. The detachment dismounted, the horse holders remaining mounted throughout the engagement to hold the horses of the dismounted personnel. Number 1 moved forward to hold the horse of 11 and that of the officer if dismounted; 2 held the horses of 9 and 10 and 3 held the horses of 13 and 12. At the same time 7 and 8 dismounted from the

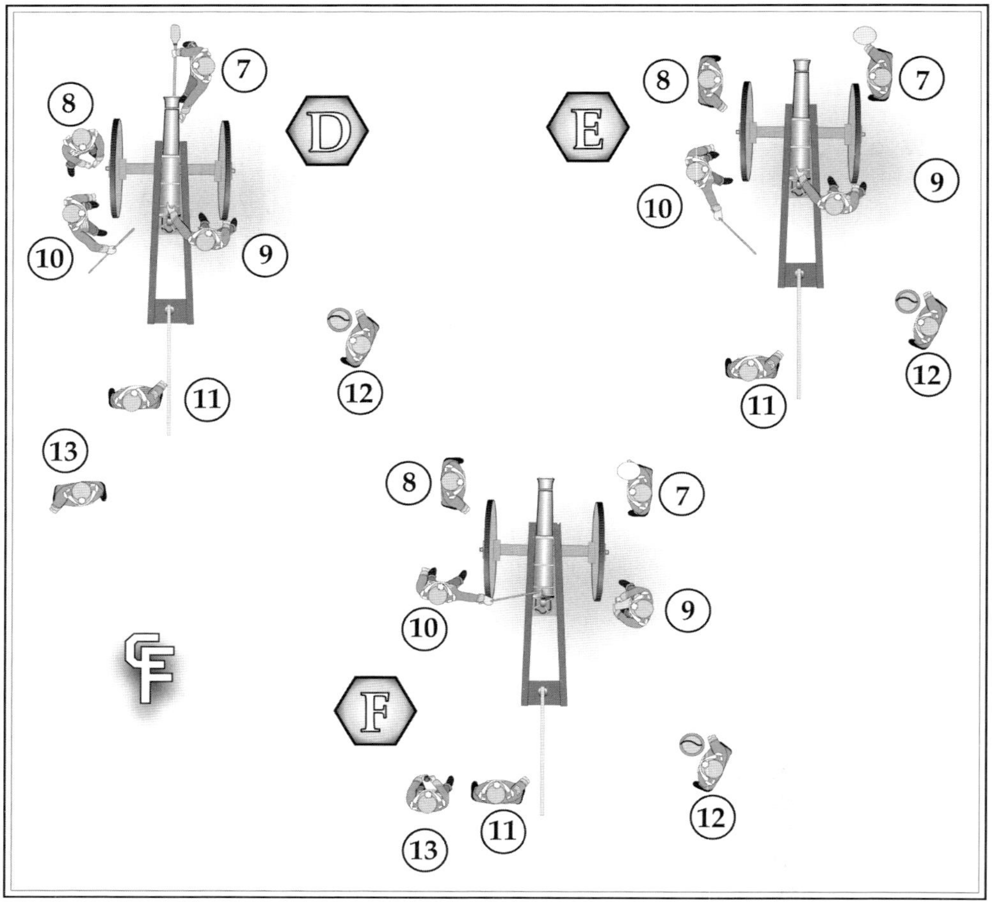

Figure 7.5. Detachment duties with a bracket trail gun carriage (part two).
(D) Reloading completed. *Number 7 rammed the projectile, 8 stood clear, 9 inserted the quill, 10 stood by with the portfire, 11 supervised, 12 attended the water and match, 13 went to meet 14, 14 came to meet 13 with ammunition and 15 attended the limber horse.*
(E) Prepare to fire. *Number 7 stood clear of the muzzle, 8 also stood clear with the rammer, 9 covered the vent from sparks, 10 moved outside the left wheel, 11 adjusted the elevation and traverse, 12 attended the water and match, 13 received the next round from 14, 14 then returned to the limber and 15 attended the limber horse.*
(F) Fire. *Number 7 stood clear, 8 stood clear, 9 uncovered the vent and stood clear of the right wheel, 10 reached over to fire the gun standing clear of the left wheel, 11 stood clear of the trail, 12 attended the water and match, 13 returned with the next cartridge, 14 returned to the limber and 15 attended the limber horse.*

gun limber; 11, unkeyed the limber, 12 and 13 raised the trail and turned the gun to the right assisted by 7 and 8 bearing on the muzzle and 9 steadying the right wheel while 10 worked the left wheel to spin the gun about. When the gun was unhooked and clear, 11 ordered the limber to 'Drive on'. Thereafter the drill was the same for the above except the horse holders also retired left about and turned left about behind the limber to face the front and remained mounted.

After the period, the field artillery adopted heavier ordnance and extra men were allocated, as were further horse holders. It may have been this that caused the numbering system to change, as there is no record of a 16 or 17 for this period and

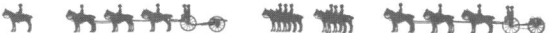

Mercer's troop was not reinforced with extra gunners when he was equipped with the heavier 9-pr guns for Waterloo.

Prepare for Action

With a block trail carriage, number 11 unhooked the elevation locking chain while 10 unstrapped the traversing lever and passed it to 11 who fitted it. 8 unstrapped the rammer head and went to his place, 9 removed the sponge head cover and passed the staff to 7; 8 then removed the bucket from the axle and removed the lid – water was an essential part of the operation and guns rarely fired without it. 9 checked the vent and collected his vent pins, thumb stall and quills from the right axle box or via 12 from the limber. 10 lit the slow match in the left axle box and fitted a portfire from 12 into the portfire stick. When ready, he lit the portfire from the slow match and fitted it in the holder on the cheek of the gun. 13 covered the left wheel stationed 5 yards to the rear of it, 14 covered the right wheel 15 yards to the rear of it. The reason for posting men in this manner was to prevent the enemy shot doing the execution it would if there were three or four men standing behind one another.

When the gun was mounted on a bracket trail, the number one would first remove the Hanoverian truck, if fitted, while 12 attended the water and the slow match. On receipt of the order, he lit the length of slow match on his linstock, pushed the spiked end into the ground and stood ready with a portfire in a stick to pass to 10 when his portfire was nearly burnt out. When side-boxes were fitted to the gun carriage, they were always removed to the limber when action was expected. Number 12 and 14 took off the right side-box and placed it upon the limber while 13 and 14 did the same for the left side-box. 14 then took a cartouche of ammunition from which he supplied 13. When his cartouche was empty, he was replaced by 15 with a full cartouche and retired to take charge of the limber horses.

Load the Piece

On the order to load, 12 ran to 13 and carrying a projectile in the crook of his right elbow and a cartridge in his left hand, returned to pass the cartridge to 8 (when firing spherical case or shell he held the round in the crook of his right arm with his left hand on top holding the fuse). 7 sponged the bore, to ensure it was empty (it was common practice to mark off the stave of the sponge staff so he could see in an instant if there was a cartridge or shot in the bore). At the same time 9, stationed behind the right wheel, 'served the vent' by placing his thumb – in a protective leather thumb stall - over the vent to prevent any rush of air which could cause any smouldering remains to ignite the cartridge.

The loader, 8, who had received a cartridge from 12, then placed it in the bore while 7 reversed the sponge staff and used the rammer end to push the cartridge home. Meanwhile, 8 stationed at the front of the left wheel, had received the projectile from 12 who then returned to the limber for more. 8 placed the projectile into the bore and 7 rammed it home (while the drills prescribe the round was rammed separately in battle it was common practice to ram the cartridge and shot as one movement). When 7 withdrew the rammer, 9 removed his thumb from the vent and inserted a vent pin down the vent to pierce the flannel bag of the cartridge. This was to ensure the priming powder in the quill would properly ignite the powder of the cartridge. He then placed a quill into the vent, which he covered with his left hand until the order to fire. Meanwhile, 10 had taken the portfire holder out of the socket on the left bracket and, taking hold of the end of the hinged slow match container under the extended apron of the left axle box had lifted it up and ignited the portfire from the smoldering slow match. Where a gun was mounted on a bracket trail, he lit the portfire from the linstock passed under the gun by 12.

The number 11 having attended to the traverse and elevation of the piece, the gun was now ready to fire.[23] When firing common shell or spherical case the process was different. Number 11 would order the cartridge and the timing or letter of the fuse required. At the limber, if common shell was to be used, the fuse was selected by letter or cut to length and fixed into the shell with the aid of a small mallet; if spherical case, the burster charge was poured in using the funnel from the tools and the appropriate fuse selected and hammered in. The ammunition number then returned to the gun, his right hand holding the cartridge and the other with the round held in the crook of his right elbow with his left hand over the fuse.

To Fire the Piece

On the order to fire, 9 removed his hand from over the vent and stepped clear of the right wheel as 10, standing clear of the left wheel, reached over and applied the burning end of the portfire to the quill. As the gun fired, the blast blew the remains of the quill clear of the vent. The whole was surrounded by a smog of burnt black powder and if the gun was to be fired again it was now the drills, so long practiced, that came into their own. Each man knew instinctively what was required of him. When the gun fired, it recoiled for some distance and the whole detachment was needed to manhandle the gun back to the firing point. Numbers 8 and 10 – who had placed his portfire stick in the holder on the left bracket of the gun – worked the left wheel and 7 and 9 worked the right wheel. Mercer recalls after the battle of Waterloo, where the guns fired on average 129 rounds per gun,[24] that his surviving men were so few and so tired at the end of the day that the guns were driven back and dangerously near the limbers and wagon drawn up behind them.[25]

Reload

Reloading could be an automatic function implemented by the detachment as soon as the gun had fired or as an ordered response, particularly if the nature of the ammunition was to be changed. Number 11 stationed behind the gun and slightly to the left, laid the piece in azimuth with the traversing lever; he then attended the elevation, often assisted by men at the wheels.

If the gun had just been fired, 7 stationed at the front of the right wheel, dipped the sponge end of the staff in the water bucket, knocked off the excess on the cheek of the gun and pushed the wet sponge down to the end of the bore; he then gave it a full twist to extinguish any smouldering remains. At the same time 9 stationed behind and to the right of the right wheel, 'served the vent' by placing his thumb over the vent to prevent any rush of air that might ignite any smouldering remains. Number 7 then withdrew the sponge staff, and 8 placed a cartridge in the muzzle

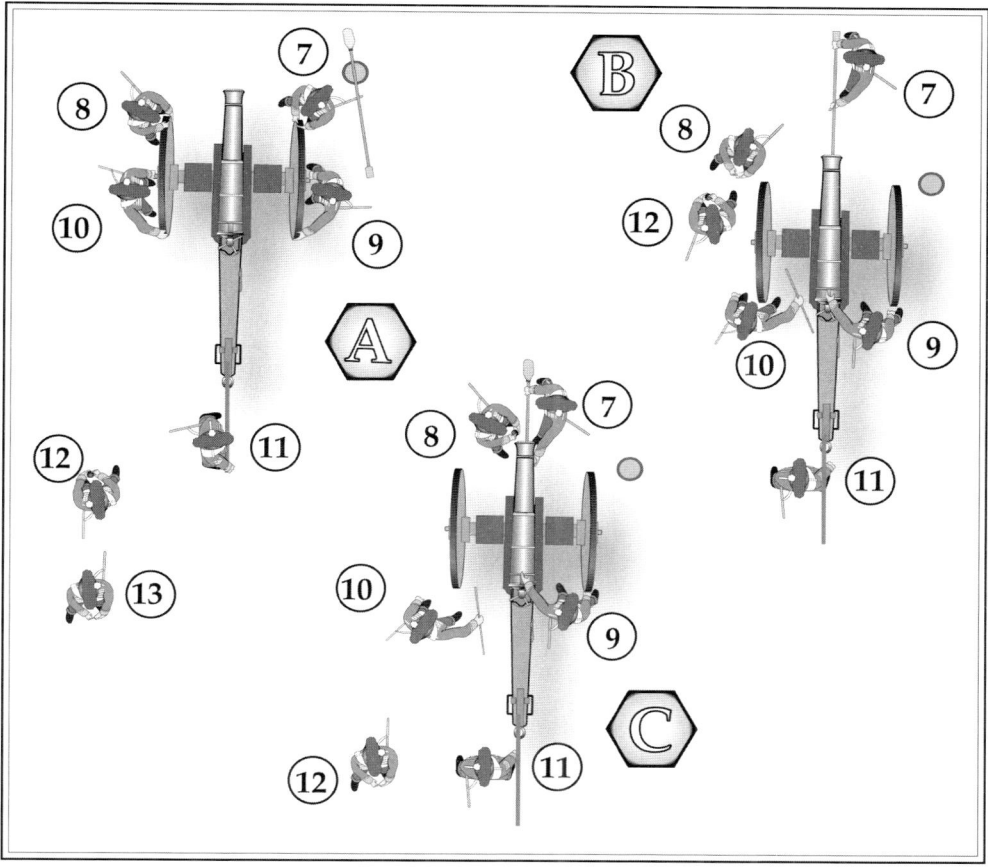

Figure 7.6. Detachment duties with a block trail gun carriage (part one). This was similar for both the brigade and horse artillery, generally the heavier the gun the larger the number of crew allocated and many units were supplemented with extra personnel and drivers.
(A) The gun has fired. The detachment runs the gun back. Number 7 laid aside the rammer and attended the front of the right wheel, 8 attended the front of the left wheel, 9 attended the rear of the right wheel, 10 placed his portfire stick in the holder and attended the rear of the left wheel, 11 attended the trail, 12 received the ammunition from 13, and 13 returned to the limber.
(B) Reloading commenced. Number 7 sponged the bore, 8 received with next cartridge from 12, 9 served the vent, 10 took the portfire holder, 11 aimed the gun, 12 stood ready with the projectile and 13 attended the limber.
(C) Reloading continued. Number 7 rammed the cartridge, 8 stood ready with projectile, 9 served the vent, 10 stood by with his portfire, 11 supervised, 12 returned for ammunition and 13 left the limber with the next round.

while 7 reversed the staff and rammed home the cartridge. Early records suggest round shot and cartridge could be, and often were, placed in the bore together and rammed at the same time.

Only when 7 had withdrawn the rammer, did 9 remove his thumb from the vent; he then pushed the vent pin down the vent to pierce the cartridge. Meanwhile 8, stationed at the front of the left wheel, placed the projectile into the bore and 7 rammed it home. (It was not uncommon for the cartridge and projectile to be placed in the bore at the same time and rammed home together.) Number 9 then placed a quill into the vent, which he covered with his left hand to protect it from sparks, until the order to fire. He also attended the vent with gimlet or bit when it became

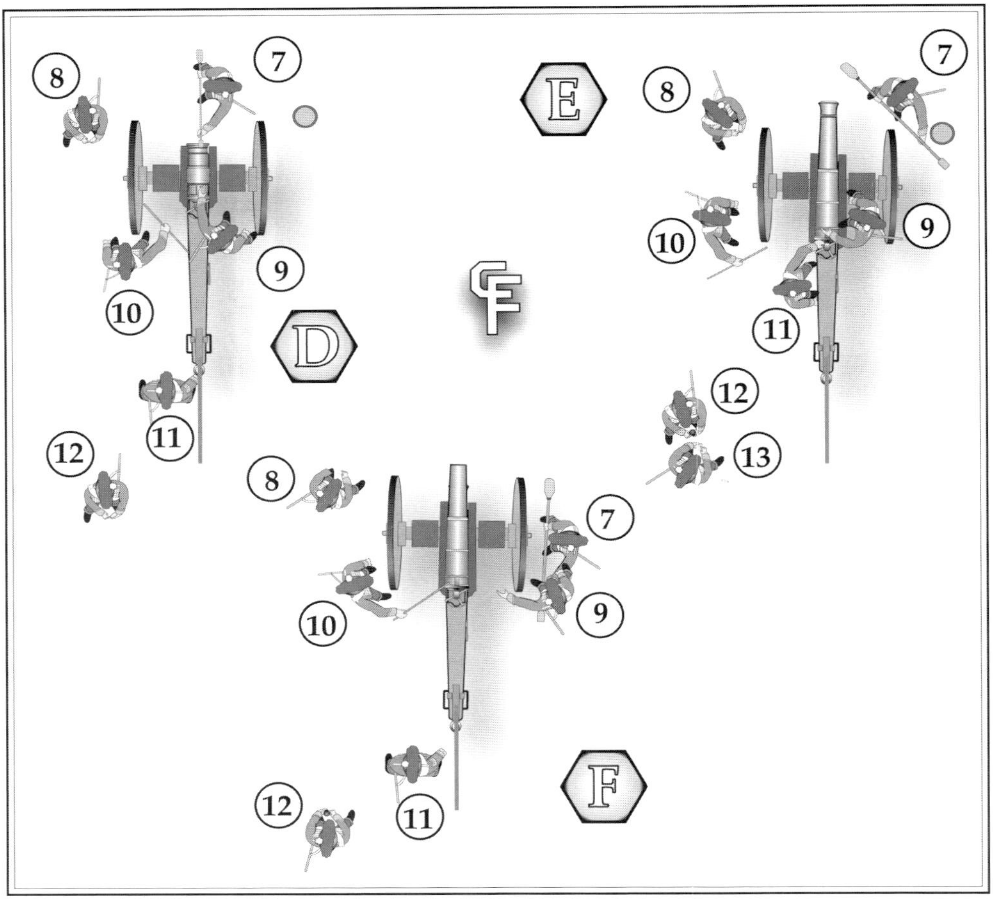

Figure 7.7. Detachment duties with a block trail gun carriage (part two).

(D) Reloading completed. *Number 7 rammed the projectile, 8 stood clear and awaited 12, 9 served the vent, 10 stood by with his portfire, 11 supervised, 12 awaited 13 and 13 came to meet 12 with ammunition. The piece shown is a howitzer, most units were equipped with one or more of these and the drills were fundamentally similar to those of the guns. The main difference was in the nature of the ammunition and the cartridges. The cartridges were supplied in 1lb bags of priming powder and when the heavy 5.5 inch howitzer was used, the 2lb cartridges were often made up in advance by the detachment. Howitzers could fire all natures of ammunition but the use shells and carcass was usually limited to these pieces.*

(E) Prepare to fire. *Number 7 stood clear, 8 stood clear, 9 inserted the quill, 10 moved outside the wheel, 11 adjusted the elevation, 12 received the next round from 13 and 13 returned to limber.*

(F) The gun was ready to fire. *Number 7 stood clear, 8 stood clear, 9 uncovered the vent and stood clear of the right wheel, 10 reached over to fire the gun standing clear of the left wheel, 11 stood clear of the trail, 12 waited with the next round and 13 returned to limber.*

fouled as well as carrying the gun spikes to render the gun unuseable in the risk of capture. On the order to fire, 9 stepped clear of the gun and wheels to avoid the recoil, as did the rest of the detachment. Number 10 took the portfire stick, and standing clear of the left wheel, reached over and ignited the quill in the vent of the gun with the burning end of the portfire, and so the cycle was repeated.

Mercer relates the sponge man was in some danger in the course of his duties. Having completed the ramming of the shot, a gunner was stepping back from the

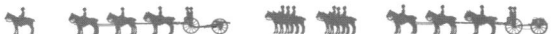

muzzle when his foot became stuck in the mud and he fell forward, just as the gun fired. Mercer recalled:

> As a man naturally does when falling, he threw out both of his arms before him, and they were blown of at the elbows. He raised himself a little on his two stumps, and looked up most piteously into my face. To assist him was impossible – the safety of all, everything, depended upon not slackening our fire, and I was obliged to turn from him.[26]

As the gun fired, 7 and 8, who had watched the muzzle of the gun to see the flash and knew it was safe to reload the gun, could then repeat the loading sequence with safety. (In action gunners were trained to watch the muzzle so they were not confused by the noise of other guns firing.) While the gun was in action 12 received the ammunition from the limber man 13, and passed it to 8. The man at the limber, number 13, sometimes carried cartridges in a cartouche to protect them; he also provided spare portfires and quills from the limber boxes as required, although this function was attended by number 12 when the gun was mounted on a bracket trail. Theoretically, the 9-pr needed an extra man to assist in manning the gun and the 12-pr a further two and this may be the reason the troops and brigades were often over-manned. Mercer gives the strength of his troop at Waterloo and although he had been re-equipped with 9-pr gun the extra men were not forthcoming, although he did have extra drivers. Dependent upon the circumstances the position of the ammunition numbers could vary particularly where operational requirements required the limbers moved further back. One of the duties of the Staff Sergeant or Junior Officer was to oversee such circumstances. Throughout the engagement 14 and 15 ferried replacement ammunition from the ammunition wagon to the gun limber.

Coming Out of Action or to Cease Fire

Upon the order to cease fire, 11 elevated the gun and secured the elevating hand wheel with the locking chain. Number 10, using the cutter mounted on the trail, cut the end off the burning portfire and replaced the portfire stick in the holder on the left bracket and, if no further action was expected, extinguished the slow match in the left axle box while 9 cleaned the vent. 7 passed the sponge over the gun to 9, and 7 then replaced the lid on the bucket, which he hung from the axle of the gun. 9 tied the protective cap over the sponge head and then fitted the rammer head end into the loop under the trail and buckled the sponge head end to the side arm strap under the axle of the gun. When the trail was correctly aligned, 11 unshipped the traversing lever and passed it to 10 who buckled it to the side arm straps at the trail and under the axle of the gun. 12 and 13 attended the gun limber while 14 and 15 attended the ammunition wagon. (Where the gun was on a bracket trail number 12 extinguished the slow match on his linstock, placed the lid on the bucket and hung it under the gun axle.)

To Limber the Gun

In the battalion role the men turned to face the gun while 11 removed the traversing handspike. 15 brought up the limber to the right of the gun then turned left about; when it was square with the trail of the gun, 11 called 'Halt, limber up'. 12 and 13 raised the trail of the carriage and placed it over the pintail of the limber assisted by 7

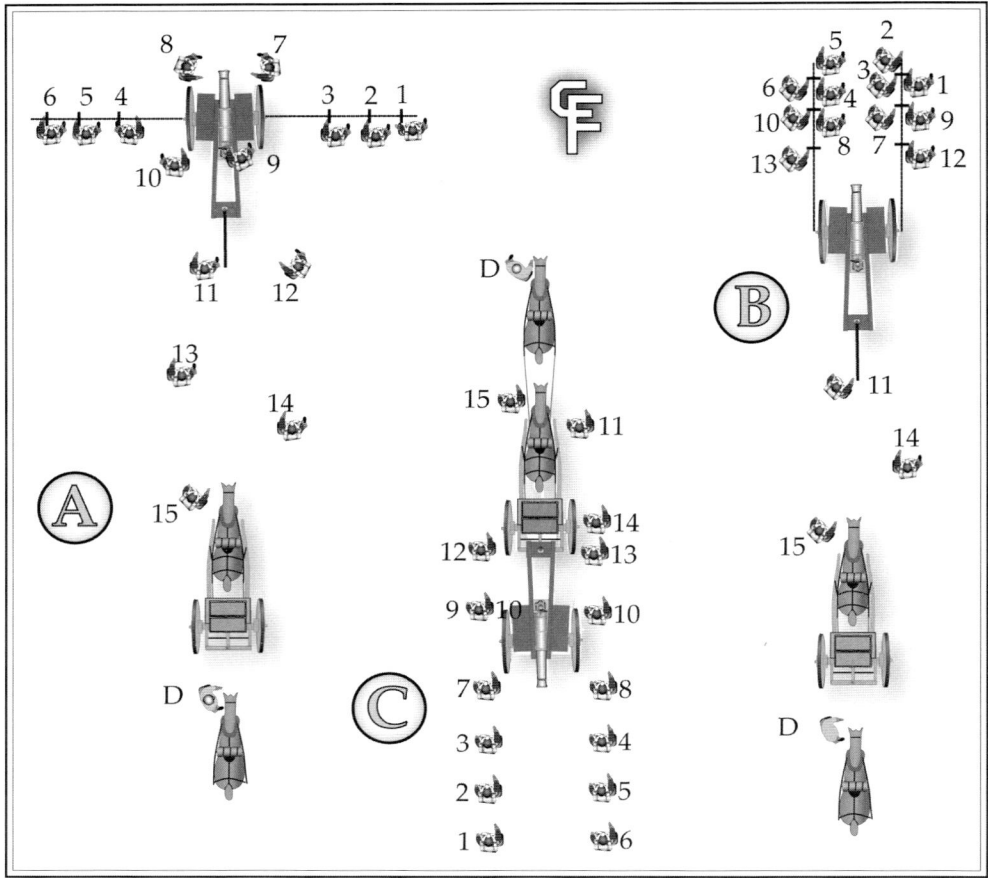

Figure 7.8. Artillery drill positions and actions with a battalion gun (part one).

(A) Positions in action with 15 men. *Numbers 1 to 6 are the drag-rope men, often seconded from the infantry. Number 7 attended the sponge staff, 8 loaded the cartridge and projectile, 9 attended the vent, 10 fired the gun, 11 commanded, 12 assisted 11 and attended the linstock and water, 13 supplied 8 with ammunition, 14 supplied 13 from the limber and 15 attended the limber horse.*

(B) Advancing 'quick' with Hanoverian truck. *Numbers 1 to 6 manned the drag-ropes assisted by numbers 7, 9 and 12 on the right rope and 8, 10 and 13 on the left rope. Number 11 fitted the Hanoverian truck in the trail transom, 14 carried a cartouche with ammunition and 15 attended the limber horse.*

(C) Advancing in enemy country with side boxes on. *Both horses were attached to the limber. Number 11 marched on the right of the wheeler, 14 & 15 in line with the front of the wheels, 12 & 13 in line with the rear. 9 & 10 marched in line with the axle of the gun, 7 & 8 in line with the muzzle followed by 1 to 6. Numbers 11, 14, 13, 10, 8, 4, 5, and 6 were on the right of the gun, the others on the left.*

and 8 bearing down on the muzzle while 9 and 10 assisted at the wheels. Number 11 then chained the trail to the limber and the detachment went to their positions for the 'line of march'. As with the unlimbering, where the weight of the carriage warranted, 9 and 10 assisted 12 and 13 to raise the trail while 14 and 15 attended the wheels.[27] With a brigade gun mounted on a bracket trail, the procedure was similar but if the gun was on a block trail, the procedure was slightly different. On the order, the men faced the gun while the drivers brought up the limber on the right side of the gun and turned left about as above. 12 and 13 raised the trail assisted by 7 and 8 bearing down on the muzzle while 9 and 10 served the wheels, the right wheel being run back the left forward. When the towing eye was in position it was placed over the limber hook and number 11 keyed the limber hook (if the gun had a bracket carriage he chained the gun to the limber). The detachment then took up their positions for the 'line of march'. In the horse artillery the procedure was similar. When the limber moved forward it was followed by the horse holders and horses of the detachment who halted at the right of the gun. On the order to 'Mount', 7 and 8 mounted the gun limber and the detachment mounted their horses while 14 and 15 mounted the ammunition wagon limber.

To Dismount the Gun and Carriage

This drill was regularly practiced to enable the carriage or wheels to be changed in the event of damage. On the order, 7 placed the rammer clear on the right while 12 did the same with the bucket. Number 11 placed the 'Hanoverian' truck to the right (bracket carriage only), removed the nut and bolt from the cascable rings and wound the elevating mechanism down. Number 13 brought up a drag rope from 14 and passed it to 9 and 10 who made a hitch at the cascable while 7 and 8 unkeyed and released the capsquares, and then bore down on the muzzle of the gun. Numbers 9 and 10 went to the front with the rope. Number 11, assisted by 14 and 15 raised the trail of the carriage until the muzzle of the gun was on the ground and free of the carriage while 9 and 10 took the weight and balance on the rope. The carriage was then run back and the gun lowered to the ground, breech towards the carriage. 12 and 13 removed the linchpins and washers, secured them and stood to the wheels while 7 and 8 stood to the front of the carriage, 9 and 10 to the rear. Numbers 7, 8, 9 and 10 raised the carriage while 12 and 14 removed the right wheel and 13 and 15 the left. The wheels were moved to the sides and the carriage lowered to the ground. All the detachment then laid down; 7, 8, 9 and 10 on the carriage; 12, 13, 14 and 15 on the wheels and 11 on the handspike.

To Mount the Gun and Block Trail Carriage

To mount the gun and carriage 7, 8, 9 and 10 raised the carriage while 12, 13, 14 and 15 fitted the wheels, washers and linchpins. Numbers 11, 14 and 15 raised the trail while 7, 8, 9 and 10 raised the gun on the muzzle while the carriage is run forward and aligned. Numbers 7 and 8 replaced the capsquares while 11, 14 and 15 lowered the trail. Number 11 then replaced the nut and bolt in the elevating mechanism while 7 and 12 replaced the rammer and bucket. Number 10 unhitched the rope and passed it to 13 who took it to the rear where 14 coiled it. The detachment then resumed its duties. Where the exercise involved a bracket trail carriage the duties were similar, except that number 11 would fit or remove the Hanoverian truck and 12 and 13 assisted to raise the trail of the carriage and move it to the rear and only 14 and 15 attended the wheels.

Changing Harness

When harnessing the horses to the gun and limber the drivers were assisted by the detachment members. The wheeler driver backed the off wheeler between the shafts and, on the off side, 8 assisted in fitting the tugs over the shafts and then the attachment of the breeching and rear traces on the off side while 7 attended the near side. The driver then positioned the near wheeler and 7 attended to the breeching and traces on the off side while 8, who had moved round, then attended to the near side. The wheeler driver controlled the wheeler horses while the centre driver positioned the off centre

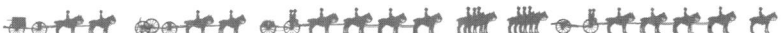

horse and 9 assisted with the traces. The next horse was the near centre and the driver was assisted by 10. This process was repeated until all the horses were in harness. When changing the shafts for double or single draught, the drivers unhooked the respective breeching and traces while numbers 7, 8, 12 and 13 changed the shafts of the gun limber and 9, 10, 13 and 14 changed the shafts of the ammunition wagon limber. In each case, the near shaft was moved first then the off shaft. In single draught the ridden, near horses preceded the off horses with the off wheeler remaining between the shafts.

Battalion Gun Drills

Where the guns were employed in the battalion role, there were special drills relying upon the use of manpower or the horses to manoeuvre the gun. The following drills are those used particularly in this role and were not used when the foot artillery were grouped into six-gun brigades as at Waterloo.

Advancing or Retiring the Gun

In the battalion role the gun was advanced or retired with the aid of men pulling on drag ropes attached to the rings of the washers on the axles or the advancing chains on the front of the axle. These men were often infantry personnel attached to the gun detachment for this purpose. They were trained by the gunners and assumed the numbers 1 to 6, 1, 2, and 3 being on the right of the gun and 4, 5 and 6 on the left. It was also practice to advance the gun by horse, in this event, the horse positioned at the rear of the limber was brought forward by the driver and the traces connected to the advance chains on the axle. To retreat the gun while in action the procedure was the same but the drag ropes were connected to the hooks on the trail transom.

In each of these manoeuvres, the NCO, number 11, could fit a Hanoverian truck into the tail transom to prevent the trail dragging on the ground. There were also drills for advancing and retiring a battalion gun without the aid of extra personnel.

Prepare to Advance

On the order 'Prepare to advance', 7 and 8 took three paces forward and faced in towards the gun, 9 and 10 took position at the gun axles while 12 and 13 brought up drag ropes from 14 and gave the chain ends to 9 and 10. Numbers 9 and 10 hooked the chains to the drag washers and manned the rear handles of the drag ropes; 7 and 8 manned the centre handles while 12 and 13 manned the front handles and loops. Number 11 mounted the Hanoverian truck in the trail transom and steered the carriage with the traversing handspike while the detachment pulled the gun forward.[28] Early brigade guns could be moved in a similar manner but by 1810, brigades had adopted the practices of the horse artillery where the guns were advanced or retired by limbering up and moving to the new location.

Advance with Horse

Number 7 passed the sponge to 9, 7 and 8 unhooked the breast chains and laid them across the spokes of the wheels. The driver brought up the horses by the right

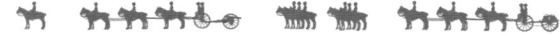

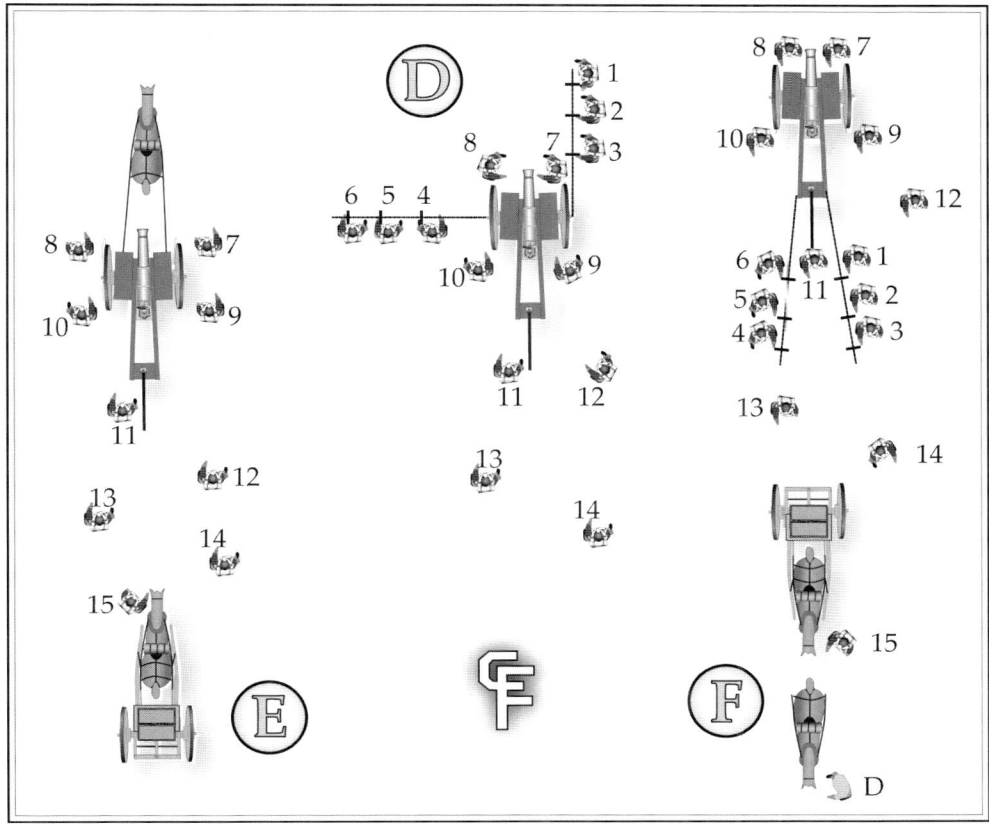

Figure 7.9. Artillery drill positions and actions with a battalion gun (part two).

(D) Disposition for wheeling a gun to the left. *Numbers 1 to 6 manned the drag ropes, 1, 2 and 3 took up handles on the right rope and 4, 5 and 6 the left. 7 attended the right of the muzzle while 8 attended the left, 9 attended the rear of the right wheel and 10 the left, 11 commanded, 12 attended the linstock and water, 13 and 14 carried cartouches and 15 attended the limber horse.*

(E) Advancing with horse in action. *The lead horse traces were attached to the advance chains on the axle of the gun. Each man assumed his position, 7 and 8 in line with the front of the wheels, 9 and 10 the rear. Number 11 commanded and steered the gun, 12 attended the linstock and water, 13 and 14 carried cartouches and 15 led the limber horse.*

(F) Prepare for action while retreating. *Numbers 1 to 6 manned the drag ropes attached to the trail transom hooks. 7 and 8 attended the muzzle of the gun, 9 and 10 the breech, and 11 commanded. 13 and 14 carried cartouches with ammunition and 15 attended the limber horse while the driver attended the lead horse.*

to the front of the gun. 7 and 8 hooked the breast chains to the traces of the horse and took post at the wheels after 7 had collected the sponge from 9. The rest of the detachment remained in their allocated positions.

Prepare for Action after Advance with Horse

Number 7 passed the sponge to 9, 7 and 8 unhooked the traces. The driver retired left about to the rear and 7 and 8 hooked the breast chains to the gun axle and 7 collected the sponge from 9 while 11 unshipped the Hanoverian truck. The rest of the detachment remained in their allocated positions.

Advance with Limber

The driver brought up the limber on the right to the front of the gun. 15 brought up a drag rope and laid the centre over the pintail of the limber while 7 and 8 unhooked the breast chains and attached them to each end of the drag rope. Number 11 fitted the Hanoverian truck. The rest of the detachment remained in their allocated positions. Upon the order 'Prepare for action', the process was reversed.

Retreat Slow

On this command, the detachment took post with 7 and 8 in line with the gun axle, 9 and 10 in line with the trail. Numbers 12 and 13 collected drag ropes from 14 and passed the chain ends to 7 and 8, 7 and 8 hooked the drag rope chains to the drag washers of the axle and then manned the rear handles of the drag rope. Numbers 9 and 10 manned the centre handle and 12 and 13 the front while 11 fitted the Hanoverian truck. Retreat fast was similar except the horses and limbers were connected to the rear of the gun.

Endnotes to Chapter 7

 1. Wilkinson-Latham, 1973: p. 63.
 2. Lawson, 1821: p. 39.
 3. Adye, 1813: p. 157.
 4. Siborne, 1993: pp. 185–241.
 5. Vigors, 1984: p. 137.
 6. Ibid: pp. 138–40.
 7. Wilkinson-Latham, 1973: pp. 71–2.
 8. Duncan, 2005: pp. 456, 457.
 9. Hughes, 1969: p. 48.
10. Spearman, 1828: pp. 174–80.
11. MacDonald, 1985: p. 56.
12. Adye, 1803: p. 102.
13. Griffiths, 1847: p. 102.
14. Caruana, 1979; p. 29.
15. Caruana, 1980: p. 13; Adye, 1813: p. 157.
16. Caruana, 1977: p. 29.
17. Adye, 1803: p. 103; Adye, 1813: p. 123.
18. Ibid: p. 101.
19. Adye, 1810: p. 157.
20. Adye, 1813: p.157.
21. Dickson, 1908: p. 701; Griffiths, 1847: p. 144.
22. Adye, 1803: p. 104.
23. Adye, 1827: p. 133.
24. Hughes, 1983: p. 17.
25. Mercer, 1870: p. 326.
26. Ibid: p. 173.
27. Adye, 1803: p. 104.
28. Lawson, 1821: p. 25.

Appendix A – Tables to Part One

Introduction

This appendix contains sets of tables relating to parameters referred to in the chapters of Part One.

Table A.1. Establishment of a horse artillery troop in 1813[1]															
Service	Captain	2nd Captain	Lieutenant	Staff Sergeant	Sergeant	Corporal	Bombardier	Gunner	Driver	Trumpeter	Farrier/smith	Collar maker	Wheelwright	Total	Horses
Foreign	1	1	3	2	3	3	7	90	60	1	4	2	1	178	164
Home	1	1	3	2	3	3	5	78	47	1	4	2	1	151	136

Table A.2. Number of drivers and horses to a foot brigade serving at home[2]					
	Officers	NCOs	Drivers	Riding horses	Draught horses
12-pr	1	4	57	12	92
9-pr	1	4	50	12	79
Heavy 6-pr	1	4	50	12	79
Light 6-pr	1	3	42	11	66

Table A.3. Number of drivers and horses to a foot brigade serving abroad[3]					
	Officers	NCOs	Drivers	Riding horses	Draught horses
12-pr	1	5	74	13	123
9-pr	1	5	74	13	123
Heavy 6-pr	1	4	53	12	84
Light 6-pr	1	3	44	11	70

Table A.4. Ranges of guns firing two round shot[4]				
Ordnance	Size of charge	Elevation (degrees)	Range in yards to first graze in yards	
			Front shot	Rear shot
Medium 12-pr	4lb	1.5	607	706
Long or heavy 6-pr	2lb	1.5	621	739
Light 6-pr	1.5lb	1.5	586	732
3-pr	1lb	1.5	523	638

Table A.5. Dimensions of wooden axletrees (inches)[5]				
Ordnance	Height	Width	Arm length	Length of bed
12-pr gun	7	5	18	45.5
12-pr limber	6	3.5	16	45.5
9-pr gun	6	3.5	16	42.5
Heavy 6-pr gun & limber	5 .5	3.5	13.5	40
Light 6-pr gun & limber	5	3	13	40
5.5-inch howitzer	5.5	5.5	13	40
5.5-inch howitzer, limber	4.5	5.5	11.5	40

Table A.6. Dimensions of wheels in 1813 (inches)[6]						
Ordnance	Wheel diameter	Nave length	Axle box diameter		Width of the tyre	Weight of wheel (lb)
			At body	At linch		
Gun and limber for the 12-pr, 9-pr, heavy 6-pr and heavy 5.5-inch howitzer	60	14	3.125	2.0625	2.75	237

Gun and limber for the light 6-pr, light 5.5-inch howitzer and heavy 3-pr	60	13	2.75	1.75	2.5	200
Light 3-pr (block trail) gun and limber	52	11	2.0	1.5	2.25	108
Note: All field equipments have brass axle boxes.						

Table A.7. Dimensions of iron axles (inches)[7]

Gun carriages	Axle overall length	Axle bed length	Axletree arms				
			Length To washer	Length To linch hole	Length of arm	Diameter at shoulder	Diameter at linchpin
Medium 12-pr gun, 9-pr gun, heavy 6-pr gun, heavy 5.5-inch howitzer	77	43	14.5	15.5	17	3.5	2.5
Heavy 3-pr gun, light 6-pr gun, light 5.5-inch howitzer	75	44	13	14	15.5	2.5	1.75
Light 3-pr gun	56	30.5	10.25	11.25	12.75	2.0	1.5
Limbers							
Medium 12-pr limber	77	43	14.5	15.5	17	2.75	2
9-pr limber, light & heavy 6-pr limbers, light & heavy 5.5-inch howitzer limbers, heavy 3-pr limber	75	44	13	14	15.5	2.25	1.75
Light 6-pr gun and limber (actual)							
Taken from surviving 6-pr gun carriages and limbers made in 1810	76	44	13.5	14.5	16	2.75	1.75

Note: The wheels of different ordnance were only interchangeable if the size of the nave box and axle arms was the same. The hole for the linchpin was 0.5 inches square and the washers 1 inch thick. Generally, there was a further 1 inch of axle beyond the linchpin.

Table A.8. Gun spike lengths (inches)[8]

Ordnance	Length of spike	Length of spring
12-pr	7.5	2.25

9-pr	7.0	2.5
Heavy & light 6-pr and light 5.5-inch howitzer	6.5	2.5
Heavy 5.5-inch howitzer	7.5	2.75
NB. All spikes were 0.20 inches in diameter		

Table A.9. Sponge-staff dimensions (inches)								
Ordnance	Rammer		Rammer hollow		Sponge		Staff	
	Length	Diameter	Depth	Diameter	Length	Diameter	Length	Diameter
6-pr	4.5	3.5	2.5	1.5	4.0	7.0	64	1.25
9-pr	4.5	3.75	2.5	1.5	4.5	7.5	76	1.25
12-pr	4.5	4.0	2.5	1.5	5.0	8.5	85	1.5
5.5-howitzer	4.5	5.0	2.5	1.5	5.0	9.0	24	1.25

Table A.10. Ammunition carried in horse artillery first-line wagons in 1801[9]						
Ordnance	Round shot	Case	Shell	Carcass	Spherical case	Totals
12-pr limber	12	4	4	-	-	-
Wagon & limber	52	10	10	-	-	92
Light 6-pr limber	32	8	-	-	-	-
Wagon & limber	97	13	-	-	-	150
5.5-inch howitzer limber	-	5	13	-	-	-
Wagon & limber	-	10	41	4	-	73
3-pr limber	6	6	-	-	-	-
Wagon & limber	100	240	-	-	-	135

Table A.11. Proportions of ammunition carried for different ordnance in 1813[10]								
Ordnance	Round shot	Heavy case	Light case	Spherical case	Common shell	Carcass	Cartridges	Totals
3-pr	210	23	23	24	-	-	280	280
6-pr	112	12	12	14	-	-	150	150
9-pr	82	9	9	10	-	-	110	110
12-pr	60	6	6	8	-	-	80	80
5.5-inch howitzer	-	-	8	8	60	4	80	80

Table A.12. Dimensions of cartouches (inches)[11]

Ordnance served	Cartouche details				Number carried			
	Cartridges carried	Width	Height	Depth	Gun limber	Wagon limber	Wagon fore box	Wagon hind box
3-pr	18	9.0	13.0	5.0	4	4	2	2
Light 6-pr	9	7.9	12.0	6.2	4	4	3	2
Heavy 6-pr	9	7.9	12.0	6.2	4	4	2**	2**
9-pr	7	9.4	12.0	6.2	2	2	2**	2***
12-pr	6	9.4	12.0	5.2	4	4*	2	2
Light 5.5-inch howitzer	18	12.0	16.0	4.0	2	2	1	1
Heavy 5.5-inch howitzer	18	12.0	16.0	4.0	2	2	1	1

Note: (*) Adye 1810, Page 94 gives none for wagon limber, ** this is given as one large and one small, *** two small.

Table A.13. Cartridge sizes for main charge and spherical case[12]

Ordnance	Main Charge (lb)	Cartridge length (inches)	Cartridge diameter (inches)	Charge for spherical case (oz)	Separating charge for spherical case (oz)
Light 3-pr	12oz	4.0	2.6	8.0	1.50
Heavy 3-pr	1.00	4.25	2.6	8.0	1.50
Light 6-pr	1.50	4.6	3.4	12.0	2.25
Heavy or long 6-pr	2.00	5.6	3.4	12.0	2. 50
9-pr	3.00	6.5	4.0	14.0	3.50
12-pr	4.00	6.5	4.4	16.0	4.50
Light 5.5-inch howitzer	1.00 (*)	2.625	5.75	16.0	6.00
Heavy 5.5-inch howitzer	2.00 (*)	2.625	5.75	32.0	6.00
Priming powder	1.00 (*)	4.0	2.62	-	-

Note: (*). Charges made up from 1lb bags of priming powder. Issued to both guns and howitzers. The charge for spherical case was increased to 24oz in 1811.[13]

Table A.14. Details of common case (inches) [14]

	Weight of ball	Musket balls	Total weight	External diameter	Case length	Length of bottom
3-pr, heavy case	1.5oz	31	3lb 3oz	2.77	4.0	1.55
3-pr, light case	1.25oz	34	2lb 15oz	2.77	4.0	1.55

6-pr, heavy case	2oz	40	5lb 10oz	3.55	4.9	1.97
6-pr, light case	1.5oz	56	5lb 14oz	3.55	4.9	1.97
9-pr, heavy case	3oz	44	9lb 6oz	3.52	6.0	2.05
9-pr, light case	2oz	63	9lb	3.52	6.0	3
Medium 12-pr, heavy case	4oz	42	11lb 12oz	4.4	6.25	3.5
Medium 12-pr, light case	2oz	84	11lb 12oz	4.4	6.25	3.5
5.5-inch howitzer	3oz	55	12lb 2oz	5.3	4.8	4

Table A.15. Details of tiered case shot or canister [15]				
Ordnance	Type of case	Weight of shot (oz)	Number of shot	Total weight (lb – oz)
12 -pr	Heavy	18.0	15	18 – 8
	Light	6.5	42	17 – 11
Heavy 6-pr	Heavy	8.5	15	9 – 0
	Light	3.5	42	8 – 14
Light 6-pr	Heavy	8.5	12	7 – 3
	Light	3.5	34	7 – 7
Heavy 3-pr	Heavy	4.5	15	4 – 10
	Light	1.5	42	4 – 6
Light 3-pr	Heavy	4.5	12	3 – 10
	Light	1.5	34	3 – 11
5.5-inch howitzer	-	3.0	55	12 – 8

Note: Total weight includes the weight of the tin container and the wooden bottom

Table A.16 – Dimensions of common shell (inches)					
	Weight	External Diameter	Firing Charge	Burster Charge	Height with Bottom
6-pr	3lb 2oz	3.568		1.77oz	4.14
9-pr	4lb 10oz	4.1		2.22oz	4.65
12-pr	5lb 15oz	4.476	2.8lb	5.5oz	-
5.5-inch light howitzer	16lb	5.25	1lb	10oz	-
5.5-inch heavy howitzer	16lb	5.25	2lb	10oz	-

Table A.17. Dimensions of common round shot (inches) [16]			
	Notional weight	Windage [17]	External diameter
3-pr	2lb 15oz	0.138	2.773–2.819
6-pr	5lb 13oz	0.17	3.494– 3.552
9-pr	8lb 12oz	0.20	4.000–4.067
12-pr	11lb 11oz	0.22	4.403–4.476
5.5-inch howitzer	23lb 6oz	0.20	5.4840–5.540
Note: The windage is nominal. The size variations for the round shot were changed in 1821.			

Table A.18. Draught harness of the Napoleonic period										
		Leader		Wheeler				Leader		Wheeler	
		Near	Off	Near	Off			Near	Off	Near	Off
		A. Bridle, horse						*E. Pad, luggage*			
1	Bridlehead	1	1	1	1	32	Strap, pad	-	1	-	1
2	Brow band	1	1	1	1	33	Ring, crupper	-	1	-	1
3	Cheek pieces	2	2	2	2	34	Flap, pad	-	1	-	1
4	Billets	2	2	2	2	35	Pad, luggage	-	1	-	1
5	Nose band	1	1	1	1	36	Hook, bearing	-	1	-	1
6	Blinkers, pairs	1	1	1	1		*Harness, draught*				
7	Bits, harness	1	1	1	1	37	Legging, driver	1	-	1	-
8	Bridle, snaffle	1	1	1	1	38	Whip, driver	1	-	1	-
9	Throat lash	1	1	1	1	39	Reins, bearing	1	1	1	1
		B. Collar, head, stall				40	Reins, leading	1	1	1	1
10	Nose band	1	1	1	1	41	Dock, crupper	1	1	1	1
11	Throat lash	1	1	1	1	42	Ring, crupper	1	1	1	1
12	Reins, chain	1	1	1	1	43	Strap, crupper	1	1	1	1
13	'T' iron	1	1	1	1	44	Strap, wither	1	1	1	1
		C. Collar, neck, horse				45	Strap, flank	2	2	2	2
14	Buckle, housing	2	2	2	2	46	Strap, hip	2	2	2	2
15	Housing, collar	1	1	1	1	47	Strap, loin	-	1	-	1

16	Hames, iron	2	2	2	2	48	Strap, cloak	2	-	2	-
17	Strap, hames	1	1	1	1	49	Strap, baggage	-	1	-	1
18	Buckling, wither	1	1	1	1		*Traces, leader and wheeler*				
19	Chains, breast	1	1	1	1	50	Chains, trace	2	2	2	2
20	Hook, hames	2	2	2	2	51	Buckling, flank	2	2	2	2
	D. Saddle, driver					52	Buckling, hip	2	2	-	-
21	Saddletree	1	-	1	-	53	Pipe, trace	2	2	2	2
22	Cantle	1	-	1	-	54	Rope, trace	2	2	2	2
23	Sideboard	2	-	2	-	55	Hook, trace	2	2	2	2
24	Flap, saddle	2	-	2	-	-	Trace, short	2	2	2	2
25	Blanket	1	-	1	-		*Harness, breeching*				
26	Seat, saddle	1	-	1	-	56	Breeching	-	-	1	1
27	Girth, saddle	1	-	1	-	57	Buckling, loin	-	-	2	2
28	Straps, girth	4	-	4	-	58	Buckling, hip	-	-	1	1
29	Surcingle	1	-	1	-	59	Ditto with safe	-	-	1	1
30	Leathers, irons	2	-	2	-	60	Strap, breeching	-	-	1	2
31	Irons, stirrup	2	-	2	-	61	Ditto with hook	-	-	1	-
						62	Band, back	-	-	-	1
						63	Tugs, shaft	-	-	-	2

Note: This table identifies the draught harness parts used by each horse and the numbers correspond to those used in the illustrations in Chapter 6. When the team was supplemented by centre horses each was equipped in the same manner and to the same scale as their respective leader.

Table A.19. Details of spherical case in 1813 [18]						
	Firing charge (oz)	Burster charge (oz)	Number of musket balls	External diameter (in)	Case thickness (in)	Height with bottom (in)
3-pr	8	1.5	11	2.79	0.283	3.22
6-pr	12	2.25	27	3.55	0.355	4.11
9-pr	14	3.25	41	4.05	0.405	4.84
12-pr	16	4.5	63	4.4	0.44	5.56
5.5-inch heavy howitzer	32	6	128	5.5	0.55	6.90
5.5-inch light howitzer	16	6	128	5.5	0.55	6.90

Table A.20. Dimensions of wooden bottoms (inches) [19]						
	Height	Overall height	Diameter of shot	External diameter	Depth under semi-circle	Depth of semi-circle
3-pr	1.26	3.22	2.77	2.77	0.45	0.81
6-pr	1.76	4.11	3.5	3.55	0.61	1.15
9-pr	2.22	4.84	4.0	4.0	0.84	1.38
12-pr	2.69	5.56	4.4	4.4	1.16	1.53
5.5-inch howitzer	3.57	6.90	5.3	5.4	1.60	1.97

Note: The figures for the 6-pr and 9-pr bottoms are given by Adye, the others are extrapolated.

Table A.21. Effective length of march for different ordnance (inches)									
Ordnance	Leader	Centre leader	Centre	Centre wheeler	Wheeler	Limber	Gun and carriage	Total	Total (yards)
Light 3-pr	134	-	-	-	109	44	97	384	10.66
Heavy 3-pr	134	-	134	-	109	44	149	570	15.83
Light 5.5-inch howitzer	134	-	134	-	109	44	151	552	15.33
Heavy 5.5-inch howitzer	134	134	134	-	109	44	134	689	19.13
Light 6-pr bracket trail	134	-	134	-	109	60*	118	555	15.42
Light 6-pr block trail	134	-	134	-	109	44	136	557	15.47
Long 6-pr bracket trail	134	134	134	-	109	60*	162	733	20.36
9-pr with six horses	134	-	134	-	109	44	147	469	13.02
9-pr with eight horses	134	134	134	-	109	44	147	702	19.50
Medium 12-pr bracket trail	134	134	134	134	109	60*	146	851	23.64
Medium 12-pr block trail	134	134	134	134	109	44	143	832	23.11
Ammunition wagon	134	-	134	-	109	44	116	537	14.92
Forge wagon	134	-	-	-	109	44	130	417	11.58

Note: * Transitional limber assumed. The distances for the leader and centre horses are given from nose to nose. The wheeler distance is from nose to the front of the limber splinter bar. The limber distance is from the front of the splinter bar to the limber hook. The figure for the carriage is the distance from the limber hook to the muzzle of the gun or to the wheel, whichever is the greater. The medium 12-pr was moved to the rear trunnion positions when travelling. In each case the adjustment of the harness would have caused minor variations.

Table A.22. Mule requirements in the Peninsula [20]			
9-pr gun	8	Ammunition wagon	6
5.5-inch heavy howitzer	8	Forge	6
Light 6-pr gun	6	Spare wheel carriage	6
5.5-inch light howitzer	6	Store carts	4
Iron 5.5-inch howitzer (24-pr howitzer)	8	2nd line ammunition wagons	6
Heavy 6-pr gun	8	-	-

Table A.23. Riding harness for a troop of horse artillery [21]	
Bearskin flounces for holsters	Scale according to the number of horses and the nature of the service
Breast plate	
Bridles bit and bridoon	
Bridles watering	
Cloaks	
Collar, head stall	
Corn bag	
Crupper	
Holsters (pairs)	
Irons, stirrup with leathers (pairs)	
Nose bags	
Picket rope	
Saddle bags	
Saddles, gunners, with web girth	
Sponges for cleaning harness	
Straps, baggage, double and single	
Straps, cloak (three to a set)	
Surcingle	

Carriage	Overall height	Drag washer		Thickness of washer	Washer		Internal (axle) diameter
		External diameter	Internal diameter		Front (linch) diameter	Rear (nave) diameter	
Medium 12-pr gun, 9-pr gun, heavy 6-pr gun, heavy 5.5-inch howitzer and medium 12-pr limber	6.75	1.9	1.0	1.0	3.75	4.0	2.5
Heavy 3-pr gun, light 6-pr gun, light 5.5-inch howitzer, light 3-pr gun and all other limbers	5.5	1.9	1.0	1.0	2.75	3.0	1.75

Table A.24. Dimensions of axle washers (inches) [22]

Endnotes to Appendix A

1. Adye, 1813: p. 380.
2. Adye, 1813: p. 72.
3. Adye, 1813: p. 72.
4. Adye, 1806: p. 157; Adye, 1813: p. 206.
5. Adye, 1801: p. 57
6. Adye, 1813: pp. 390–1.
7. McConnell, 1988: p. 459; Adye, 1801: p. 56.
8. Adye, 1810: p. 330
9. Adye, 1801: p. 16.
10. Adye, 1813: p. 14.
11. Adye, 1813: pp. 94, 104.
12. Ibid: pp. 98, 99.
13. Dickson, 1908: p. 864.
14. McConnell, 1988: p. 502; Caruana, 1979: p. 15.
15. Adye, 1801: p. 197; Adye, 1806: p. 257.
16. McConnell, 1988: p. 418.
17. Adye, 1827: p. 395.
18. Adye, 1813: p. 98.
19. McConnell, 1988: p. 418.
20. Dickson, 1908: pp. 627–8.
21. Adye, 1813: pp. 353–62.
22. McConnell, 1988: p. 459; Adye, 1801: p. 56.

PART TWO

The Field Equipments

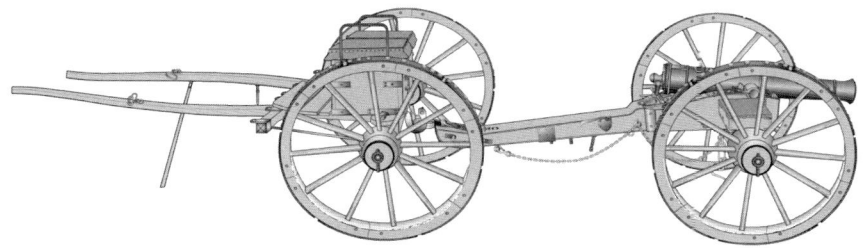

Introduction to Part Two

Part two provides information on the different guns, howitzers and carriages used by the field artillery during the Napoleonic Wars and where the information is available, on their dimensions, performance, weights and logistics. It is clear that in the early phases of the war the field artillery used other types of ordnance not covered by this book; this omission is due either to the lack of contemporary information or that their use was more a trial than an adoption into service. In every case, where the information is available, the ordnance is represented and fully illustrated. The reader should also remember that the allocation of ordnance to the brigades and troops was often changed and while they were more usually equipped with one type of gun, mixed ordnance was not at all unusual. A simple example is that in March 1810 Ross's and Bull's Troops were equipped with five 9-pr guns and one heavy 5.5-inch howitzer. In September of 1813 Ramsay's and Smith's Troops were each equipped with two long 6-pr guns, three light 6-pr guns and one light 5.5-inch howitzer, while Ross's troop was now equipped with five light 6-pr guns and one heavy 5.5-inch howitzer. At Waterloo Bull's Troop had six heavy 5.5-inch howitzers.[1]

The equipments are arranged by calibre and each chapter addresses the different ordnance and carriages within that nature. Also included are the details of the rocket equipment used by the Rocket Troop of the Horse Artillery and the supporting wagons and carts of the field artillery for which information has been obtained. In Chapter 14 are the detailed dimensions for a light 6-pr gun and limber of 1810.

In spite of extensive research and the unremitting help of the Royal Artillery Historical Trust, the James Clavell Library, the Royal Artillery Museum, the National Archive, the British Library, the Royal Armouries and the Tøjhusmuseet in Copenhagen, many of the drawings are reconstructions based on the information available and the practices of the period. Added to this must be an understanding that troop and brigade commanders were very much their own men and individual practices and modifications were not uncommon. These factors need to be considered when referring to the drawings that have no specific attribution.

Where ammunition is concerned, the figures given by contemporary sources show that the ammunition carried in the limbers and wagons was changed frequently throughout the period. This is confirmed by the information given in the contemporary documents of Dickson and Adye, all of which show a constantly changing allocation as the demands of supply and the tactical situation varied. The relevant tables and accompanying illustrations given in the following chapters are based upon recorded data, typical examples or surviving equipment, but are not intended to represent all the alternatives. Similarly, the performance figures are based only on information published during the period and the reader will realize that ranges given to the nearest yard were subject to considerable variation due to the uncertain nature of the powder, windage and the variations in the ammunition and fuses. The records are few but those of 1800 suggest range variations of up to 20% were not at all unusual.[2] In each case, the data given is believed to give a reasonable representation of the performance achieved during the period. The reader should also be aware that later figures, given after the period, should not be taken as a direct comparison due to the many improvements in powder and manufacturing accuracies achieved in the years after 1815.

All the tables relating to the field equipments are contained in the appendices at the end of Part Two:

Appendix B	Dimensions of the pieces
Appendix C	Recorded performance data
Appendix D	Ammunition carried at first line
Appendix E	Equipment weights
Appendix F	Supporting wagons and carts

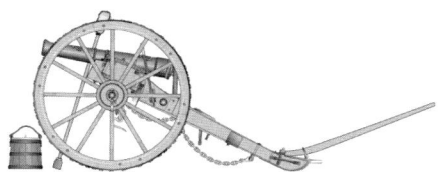

CHAPTER 8

3-pr Field and Mountain Guns

There were at least five different 3-pr guns used by the field artillery during the war:

* The Desaguliers heavy 3-pr of 6 feet
* The light common 3-pr of 3 feet 6 inches
* The Blomefield light or mountain 3-pr of 3 feet
* The Blomefield 3-pr of 4 feet
* Lord Townsend's light infantry 3-pr of 3 feet

The Desaguliers 3-pr became known as the heavy or long 3-pr and continued in use throughout the period. The 3-pr guns issued from Malta for use in the Egyptian Campaign and from Gibraltar to the Peninsula may well have been the light common 3-pr of 3ft 6in as they were described as being fitted with bracket carriages and single draught, but it has not been possible to provide a positive identification. The Blomefield 3-pr of 3ft, became known as the light 3-pr and may well have been used as mountain equipment. In the colonial arsenals the ordnance was often of an older stock and may well have included pieces not used in the European theatres of war: an example is the 'Lord Townsend's Light Infantry 3-pr'. It was thought that this had become obsolescent by 1800, but there is now evidence that this gun continued in use throughout the period, particularly in the West Indies, and was still in service there in 1811.

Desaguliers Heavy 3-pr Gun of 6ft

The heavy or long version of the 3-pr was a design by Desaguliers but was probably replaced by a similar piece of Blomefield design during the period.[3] The heavy 3-pr bronze piece is rated as weighing either 5.5cwt (616lb) or 6cwt (672lb), with a barrel length of 6 feet, some 25 calibres. It had a bore of 2.912 inches, a shot diameter of 2.775 inches and a windage of some 0.138 inches. In normal use, the gun fired a 1lb charge but for spherical case, the cartridge was initially reduced to 8 ounces with a separator charge of 1.5 ounces. Two of these guns were originally part of the armament of a horse artillery troop but were replaced by the light 6-pr of 5.5cwt. The weight may have been one reason why it was replaced in the horse artillery even though it matched or even bettered the performance of this gun in some areas.[4]

It was mounted on a block trail from the beginning in 1779, the carriage being based upon the principles of a French carriage taken in Martinique in 1761. This was the gun carriage that gave rise to the new design adopted by the horse artillery. The carriage axle was 75 inches long overall, with a 44-inch bed. The axle arm was 13 inches long with a diameter of 2.75 inches at the shoulder tapering to 1.75 inches at the linch end.[5] The wheels of the carriage were 60 inches in diameter with 2.5-inch wide tyres; the weight of two wheels was 399lb. The weight of the heavy 3-pr equipment is given in Table E.1 of Appendix E at the end of Part Two. The left-hand axle carried a slow match box while the right axle box was fitted to carry 12 round shot, eight in two tiers of four separated by a wooden shelf in the left compartment, and four more under a shelf in the right compartment. The centre compartment was used to store vent tools, worm, and spare sponge head.

Performance

In a letter to General Desaguliers, Congreve (1st Bart) claimed the following figures for the long 3-pr:

> With a 1lb cartridge, it achieved a muzzle velocity of 1,514 feet per second and at point blank, the first graze occurred at 300 yards; at one degree of elevation, the first graze was 700 yards; at two degrees of elevation, it was 800 yards and at three degrees of elevation, the first graze was 1,492 yards. The penetration into a bank of clay at 100 yards was nine feet. With common case shot against a target, at one degree of elevation and with case containing thirty-six 1.25oz shot, 11 shot hit the target; at 1.5 degrees of elevation, at 400 yards, 10 shot hit the target and at 2 degrees at 500 yards, 9 shot hit the target. With 72 shot (two case loaded together) at 500 yards, 30 shot hit the target.

It was advised that the 3-pr should begin to fire at infantry at five degrees of elevation, which would range one or even two rounds if double shotted, to upwards of 1,200 yards. In a normal engagement a 3-pr of six feet can fire 37 round shot at advancing infantry and 15 rounds at cavalry; changing to common case the light 3-pr can then fire 35 rounds at infantry and 14 rounds at cavalry; allowing only 5 round shot or 7 case shot to be fired in one minute. A 3-pr gun can be loaded and fired 8 times in one minute; but as the smoke cannot clear from before the gun in that time, the afore-mentioned allowance is thought a good one to do execution. If 74 round shot are fired, two at a time, and 35 rounds of case, 35 shot out of each case being supposed to hit a Battalion at 500 yards distance, and from 400 to 200 yards, 45 shot from each, great execution must be done before the atillery is in any danger of falling into enemy hands.[6]

From the beginning in 1779, it was mounted on a block trail, the carriage being based upon the principles of one taken in Martinique in 1761. This was the gun carriage that gave rise to the new design adopted by the horse artillery, and the limber was driven in double draught and carried two ammunition boxes side by side. The carriage axle was 75 inches long overall,with a 44-inch bed. The wheels of the carriage were 60 inches in diameter with 2.5-inch tyres, the weight of two wheels was 399lb and the axle was 13 inches long with a diameter of 2.75 inches at the shoulder tapering to 1.75 inches at the linch end.[7] The weight of the heavy equipment is given in table E.1 of Appendix E at the end of Part Two. The left-hand axle carried a slow match box while the right axle box was fitted to carry 12 round shot, eight in two tiers of four separated by a wooden shelf in the left compartment, and four more under a shelf in the right compartment. The centre compartment was used to store vent tools, worm and spare sponge head.

The performance figures given in the Tables C1 to C3 at the end of Part Two are those available from contemporary sources. Other figures often quoted are attributed to the Victorian period and these are not given as the powder, ammunition and manufacturing processes of the guns were different and no direct comparison can be assumed.

It was advised that the 3-pr should begin to fire at infantry at five degrees of elevation, which would range one or even two rounds if double shotted, to upwards of 1,200 yards:

> In a normal engagement a 3-pr of six feet can fire 37 round shot at advancing infantry and 15 rounds at cavalry; changing to common case the light 3-pr can then fire 35 rounds at infantry and 14 rounds at cavalry; allowing only 5 round shot or 7 case shot to be fired in one minute. A 3-pr gun can be loaded and fired 8 times in one minute; but as the smoke cannot clear from before the gun in that time, the before mentioned allowance is thought a good one to do execution. If 74 round shot are fired, two at a time, and 35 rounds of case, 35 shot out of each case being supposed to hit a Battalion at 500 yards distance, and from 400 to 200 yards, 45 shot from each, great execution must be done before the artillery is in any danger of falling into enemy hands.[8]

The ammunition carried at first line for the heavy 3-pr is given in Table D.1 of Appendix D, at the end of Part Two.

Light Common 3-pr Gun

The Light Common 3-pr bronze piece was of Desaguliers design and weighed 2.75cwt (308lb), it was 3 feet 6 inches long, some 14 calibres. It had a bore of 2.913 inches, a shot diameter of 2.775 inches and a windage of 0.138 inches. In normal use, the gun fired a 12-ounce charge of red large-grain powder but for spherical case, this was initially reduced to 8 ounces with a separator charge of 1.5 ounces. This piece was probably obsolete by 1800, but remained in service in the Colonies.[9] Surviving pieces were cast by the Verbruggens and Bowen. The gun was considered obsolete by 1815. During the Egyptian Campaign of 1800, four light 3-pr guns were received from Malta; these were probably the older light-common pieces as they were mounted on bracket trails with old-style limbers with shafts and single draught. They were modified in the field to make them and the method of draught more suitable.[10] Two pieces accompanied the Buenos Aires Expedition in 1807 and in the Peninsula the first four 3-pr car brigade received in 1808 came from Gibraltar. They were considered unsuitable:

> 'As the carriages of the light 3-pr are of the old pattern with single horse draught, they are totally inapplicable to the service of this country' and 'should be replaced by guns more adequate to the service'.[11]

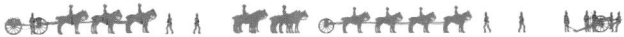

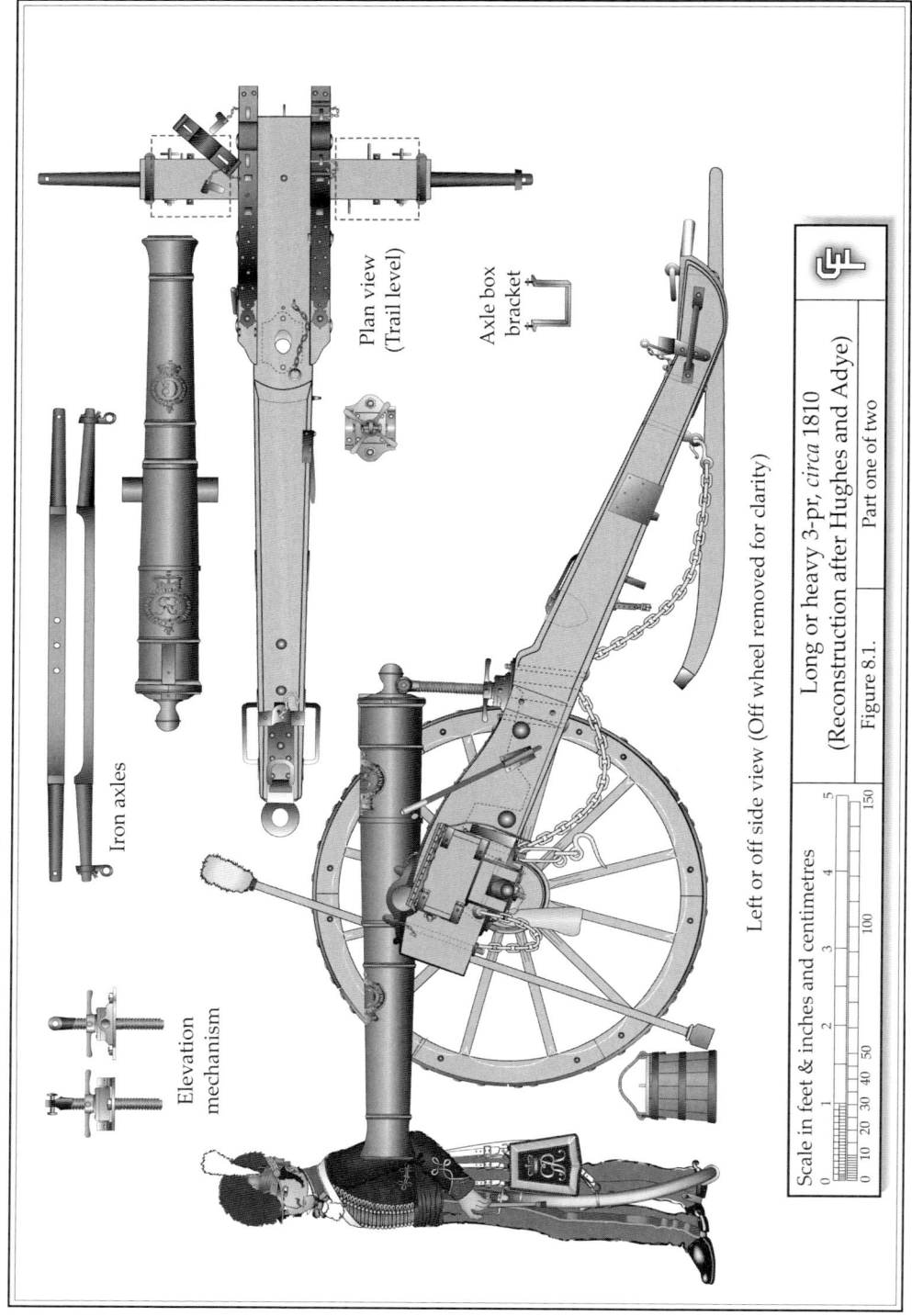

Plan view (Trail level)

Axle box bracket

Iron axles

Elevation mechanism

Left or off side view (Off wheel removed for clarity)

Scale in feet & inches and centimetres

Long or heavy 3-pr, *circa* 1810
(Reconstruction after Hughes and Adye)

Figure 8.1.   Part one of two

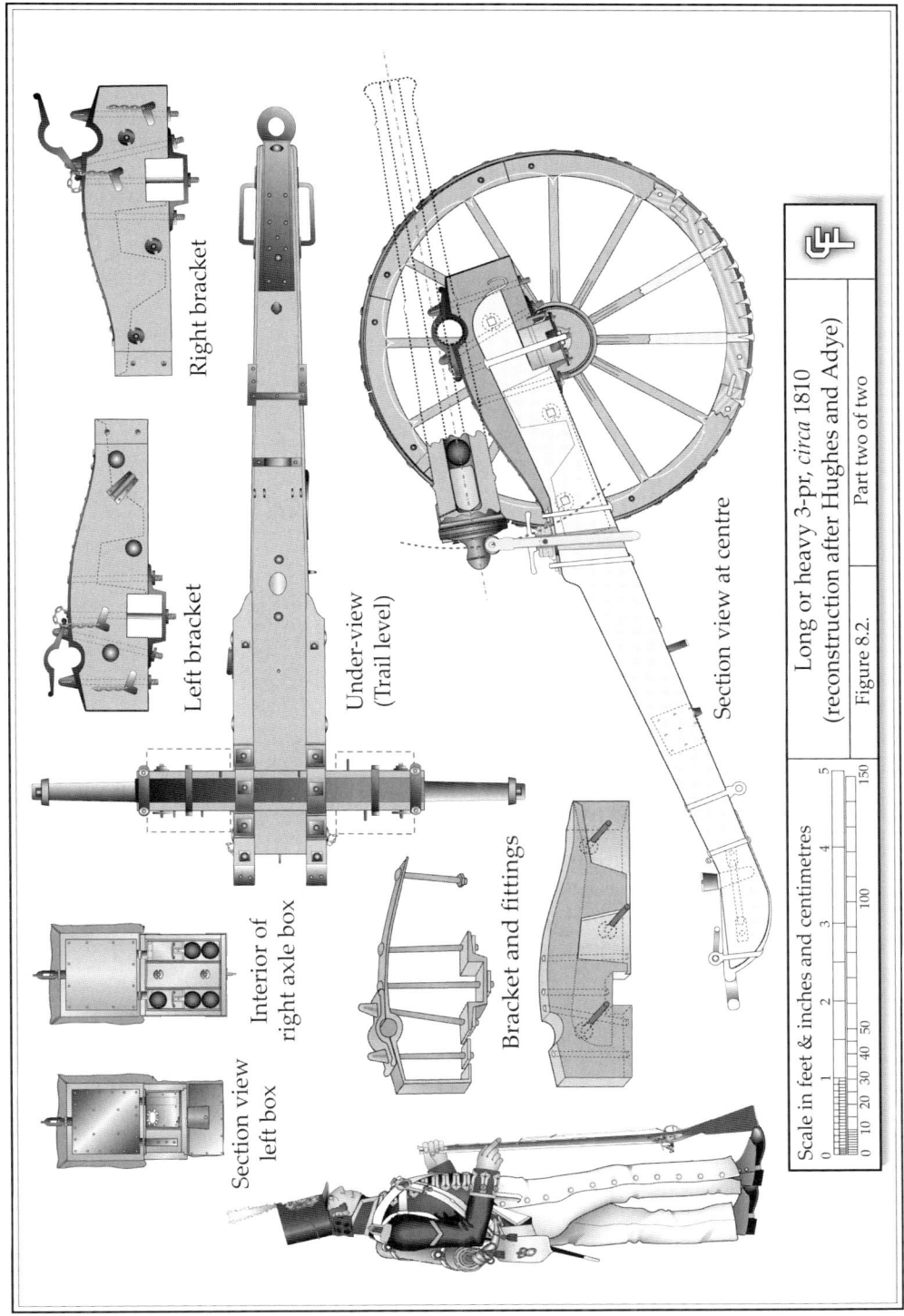

Right bracket

Left bracket

Under-view
(Trail level)

Interior of
right axle box

Bracket and fittings

Section view
left box

Section view at centre

Scale in feet & inches and centimetres

Long or heavy 3-pr, *circa* 1810
(reconstruction after Hughes and Adye)

Part two of two

Figure 8.2.

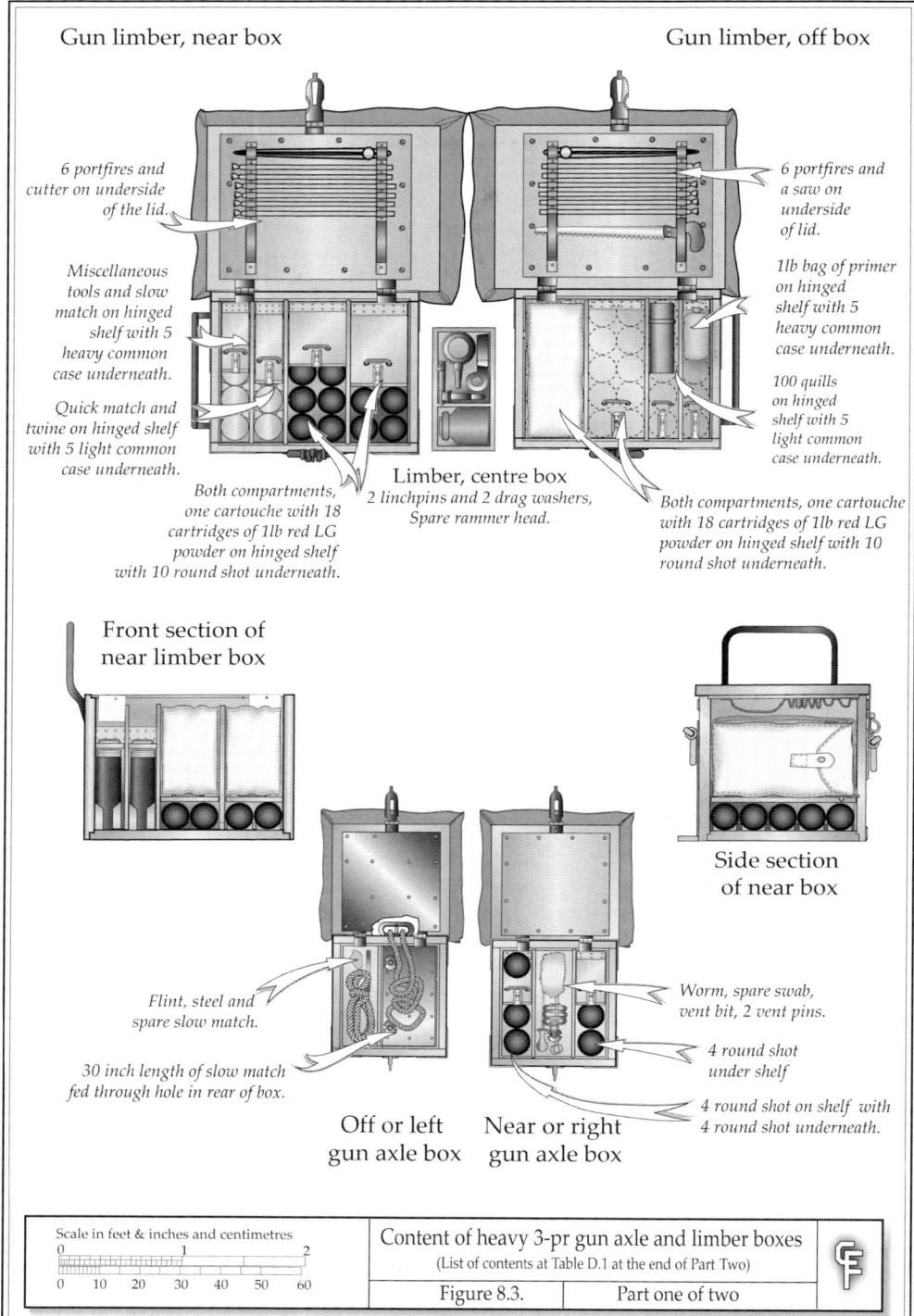

Gun limber, near box

Gun limber, off box

6 portfires and cutter on underside of the lid.

Miscellaneous tools and slow match on hinged shelf with 5 heavy common case underneath.

Quick match and twine on hinged shelf with 5 light common case underneath.

6 portfires and a saw on underside of lid.

1lb bag of primer on hinged shelf with 5 heavy common case underneath.

100 quills on hinged shelf with 5 light common case underneath.

Both compartments, one cartouche with 18 cartridges of 1lb red LG powder on hinged shelf with 10 round shot underneath.

Limber, centre box
2 linchpins and 2 drag washers, Spare rammer head.

Both compartments, one cartouche with 18 cartridges of 1lb red LG powder on hinged shelf with 10 round shot underneath.

Front section of near limber box

Side section of near box

Flint, steel and spare slow match.

30 inch length of slow match fed through hole in rear of box.

Off or left gun axle box

Near or right gun axle box

Worm, spare swab, vent bit, 2 vent pins.

4 round shot under shelf

4 round shot on shelf with 4 round shot underneath.

Scale in feet & inches and centimetres	Content of heavy 3-pr gun axle and limber boxes
0 1 2	(List of contents at Table D.1 at the end of Part Two)
0 10 20 30 40 50 60	Figure 8.3. Part one of two

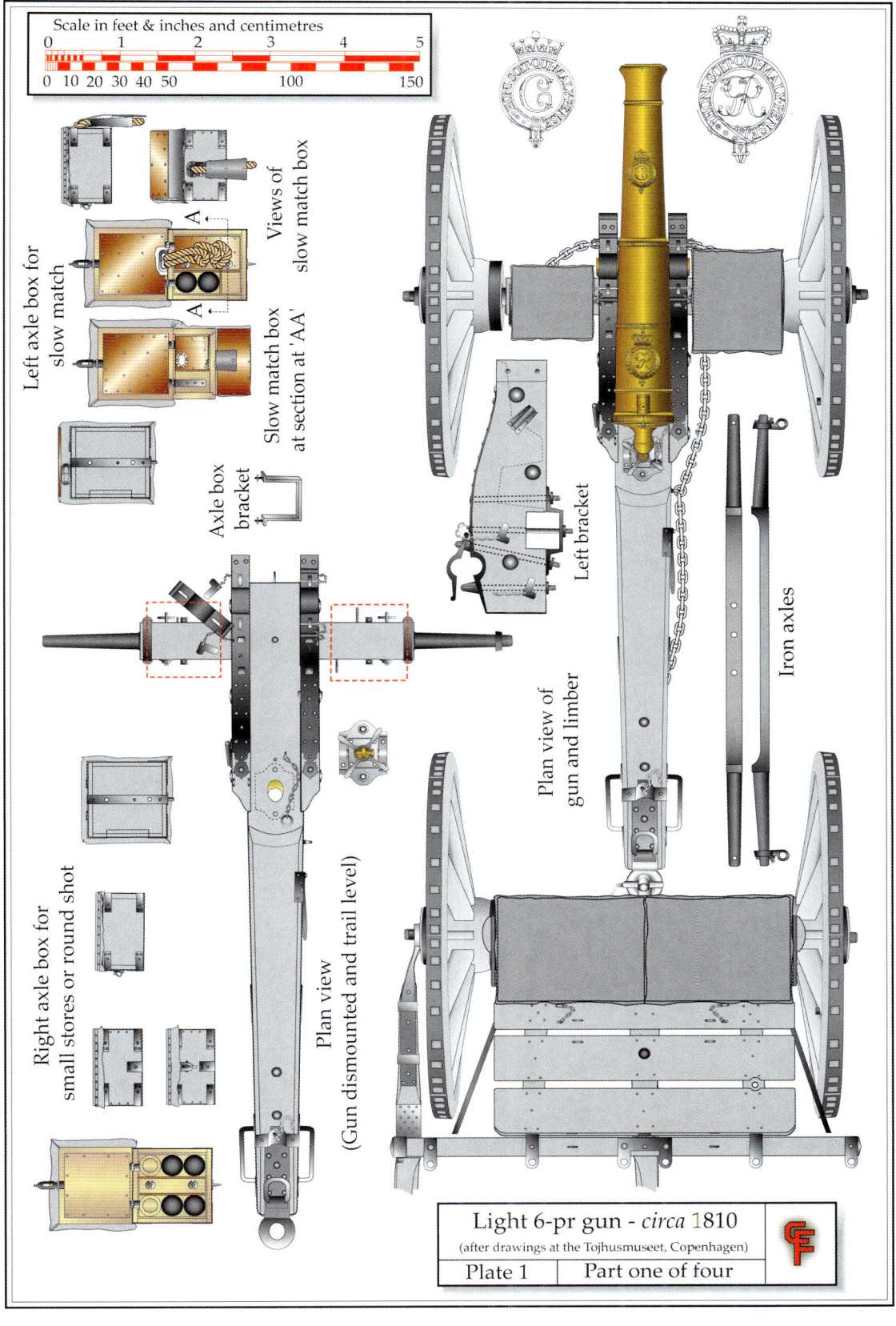

Scale in feet & inches and centimetres

0   1   2   3   4   5
0 10 20 30 40 50   100   150

Views of slow match box

Left axle box for slow match

Slow match box at section at 'AA'

Axle box bracket

Left bracket

Iron axles

Plan view of gun and limber

Right axle box for small stores or round shot

Plan view (Gun dismounted and trail level)

Light 6-pr gun - *circa* 1810

(after drawings at the Tojhusmuseet, Copenhagen)

Plate 1 | Part one of four

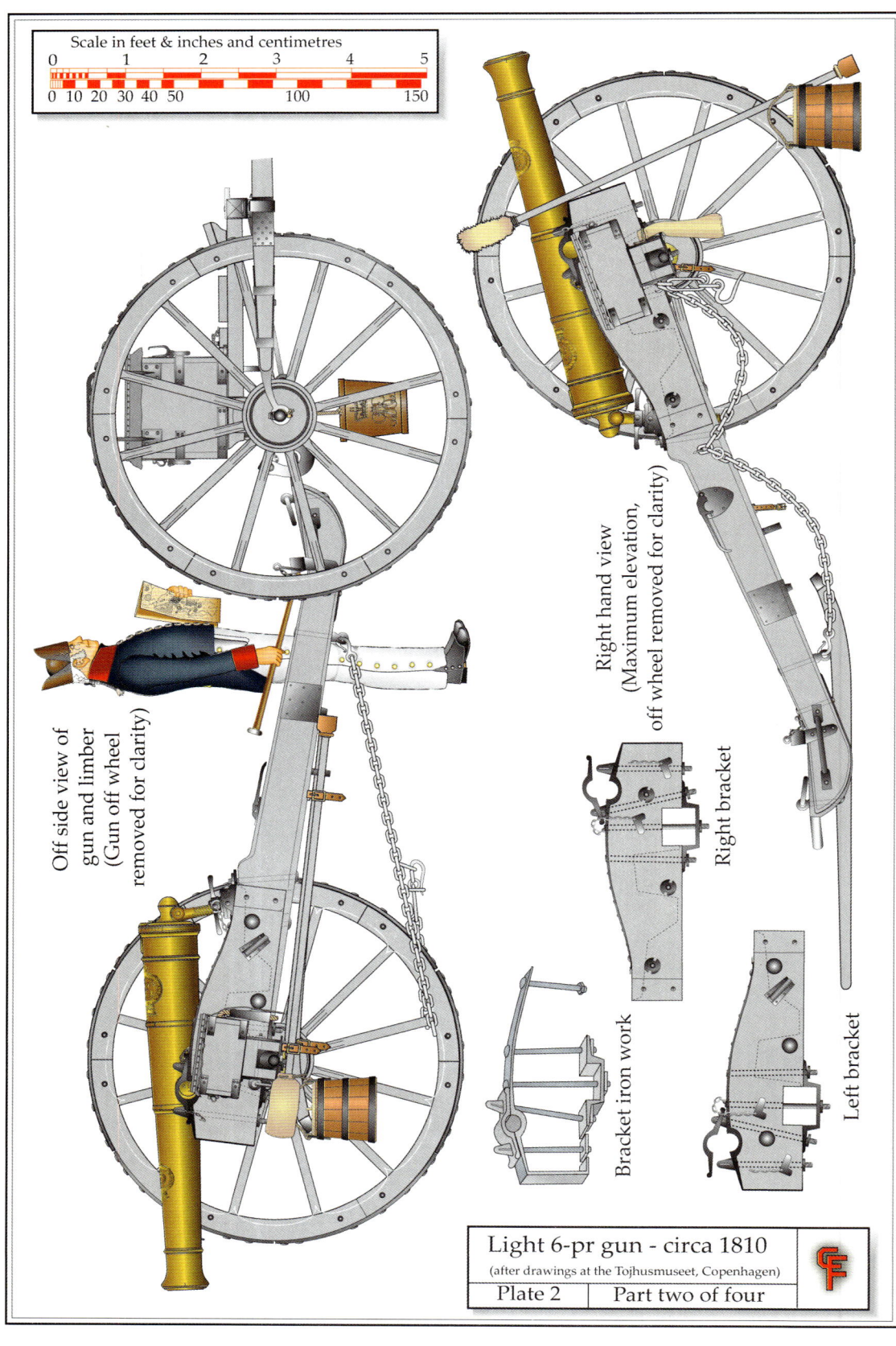

Scale in feet & inches and centimetres

0 1 2 3 4 5

0 10 20 30 40 50 100 150

Off side view of gun and limber (Gun off wheel removed for clarity)

Right hand view (Maximum elevation, off wheel removed for clarity)

Right bracket

Bracket iron work

Left bracket

Light 6-pr gun - circa 1810

(after drawings at the Tojhusmuseet, Copenhagen)

Plate 2 | Part two of four

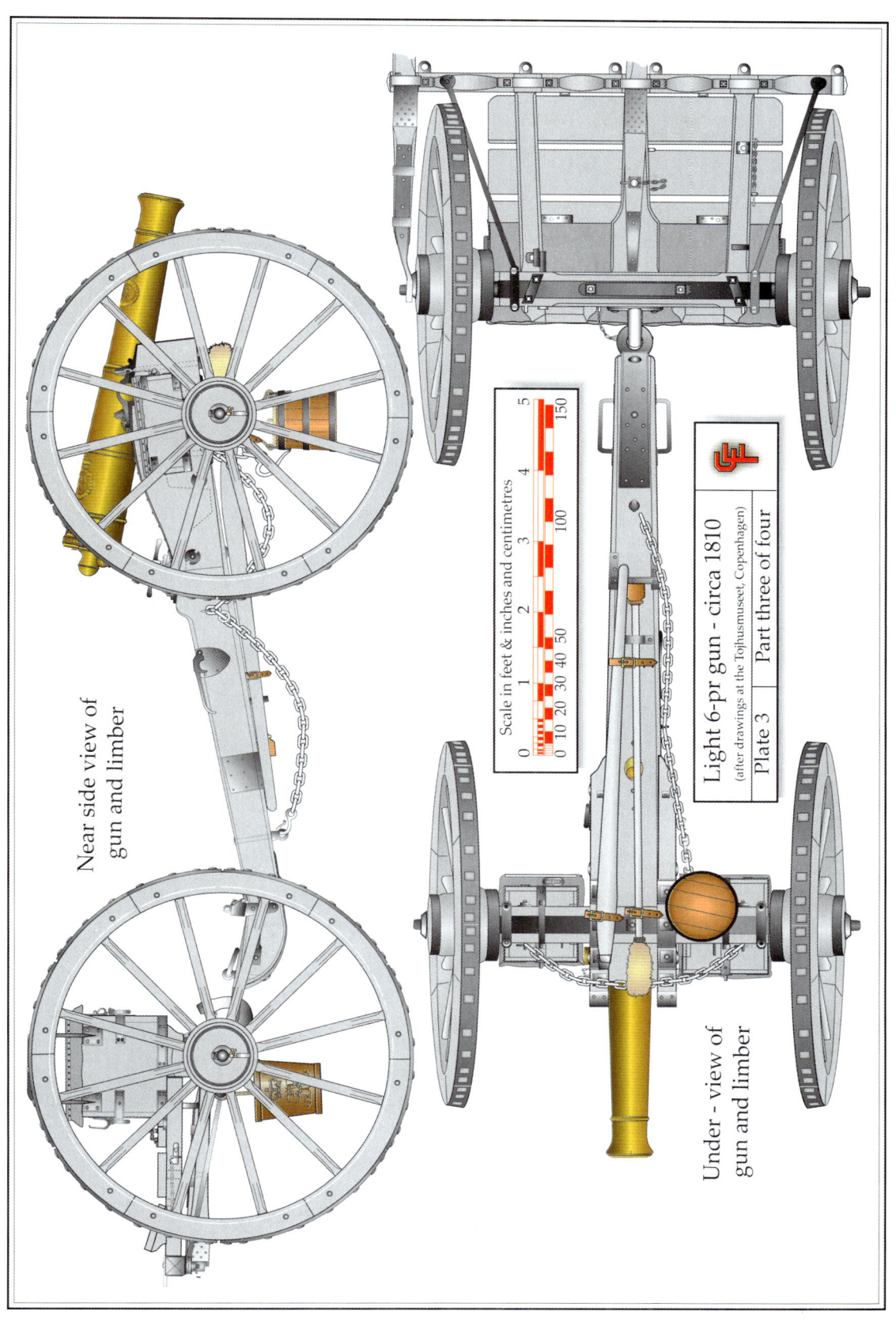

Near side view of
gun and limber

Under - view of
gun and limber

Scale in feet & inches and centimetres

0   1   2   3   4   5

0 10 20 30 40 50   100   150

Light 6-pr gun - circa 1810
(after drawings at the Tøjhusmuseet, Copenhagen)

| Plate 3 | Part three of four |

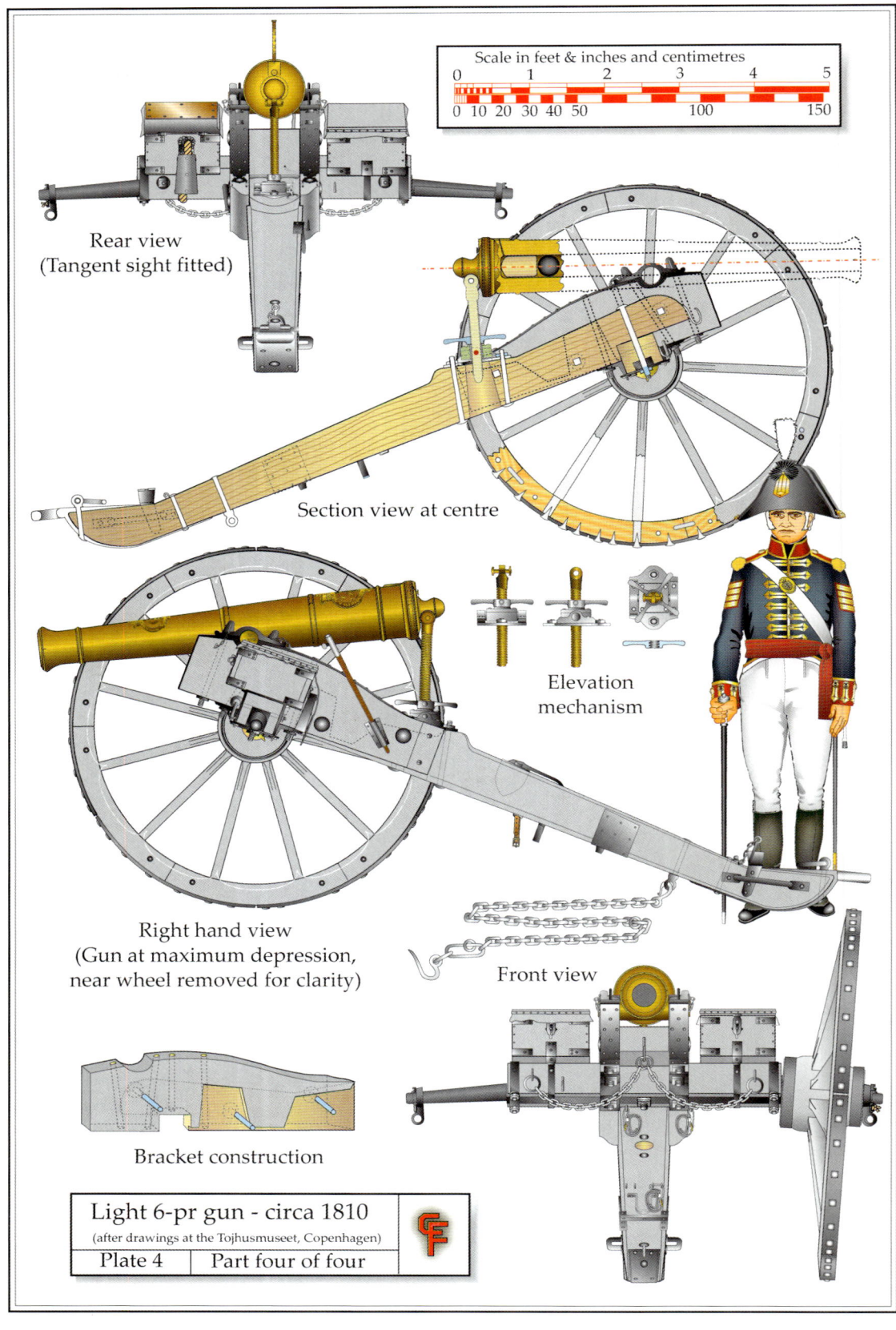

Rear view
(Tangent sight fitted)

Scale in feet & inches and centimetres

Section view at centre

Elevation
mechanism

Right hand view
(Gun at maximum depression,
near wheel removed for clarity)

Front view

Bracket construction

Light 6-pr gun - circa 1810
(after drawings at the Tojhusmuseet, Copenhagen)

Plate 4 | Part four of four

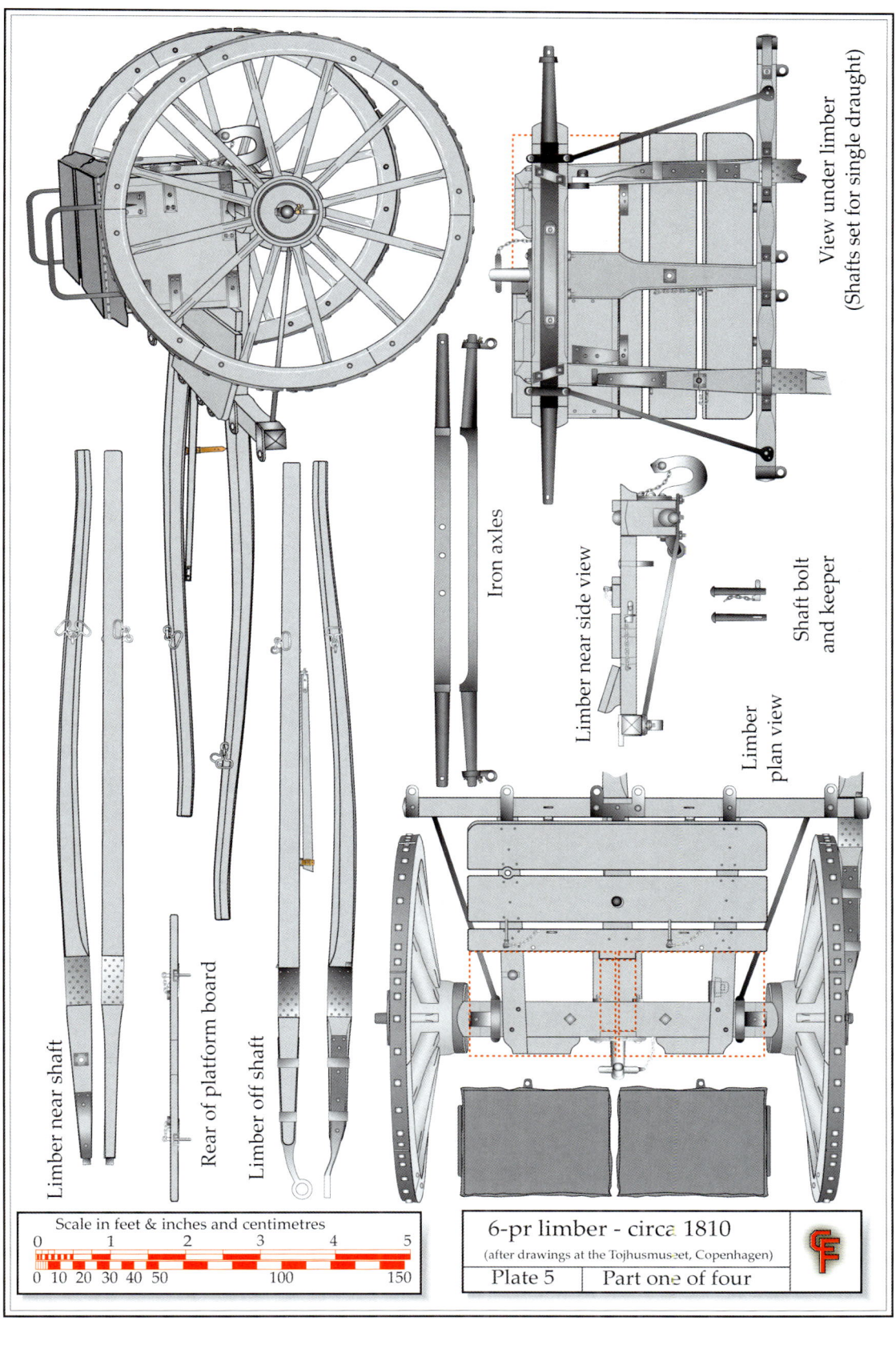

View under limber
(Shafts set for single draught)

Iron axles

Limber near side view

Shaft bolt
and keeper

Limber
plan view

Limber near shaft

Rear of platform board

Limber off shaft

Scale in feet & inches and centimetres

0   1   2   3   4   5

0 10 20 30 40 50   100   150

6-pr limber - circa 1810

(after drawings at the Tojhusmuseet, Copenhagen)

Plate 5   Part one of four

GF

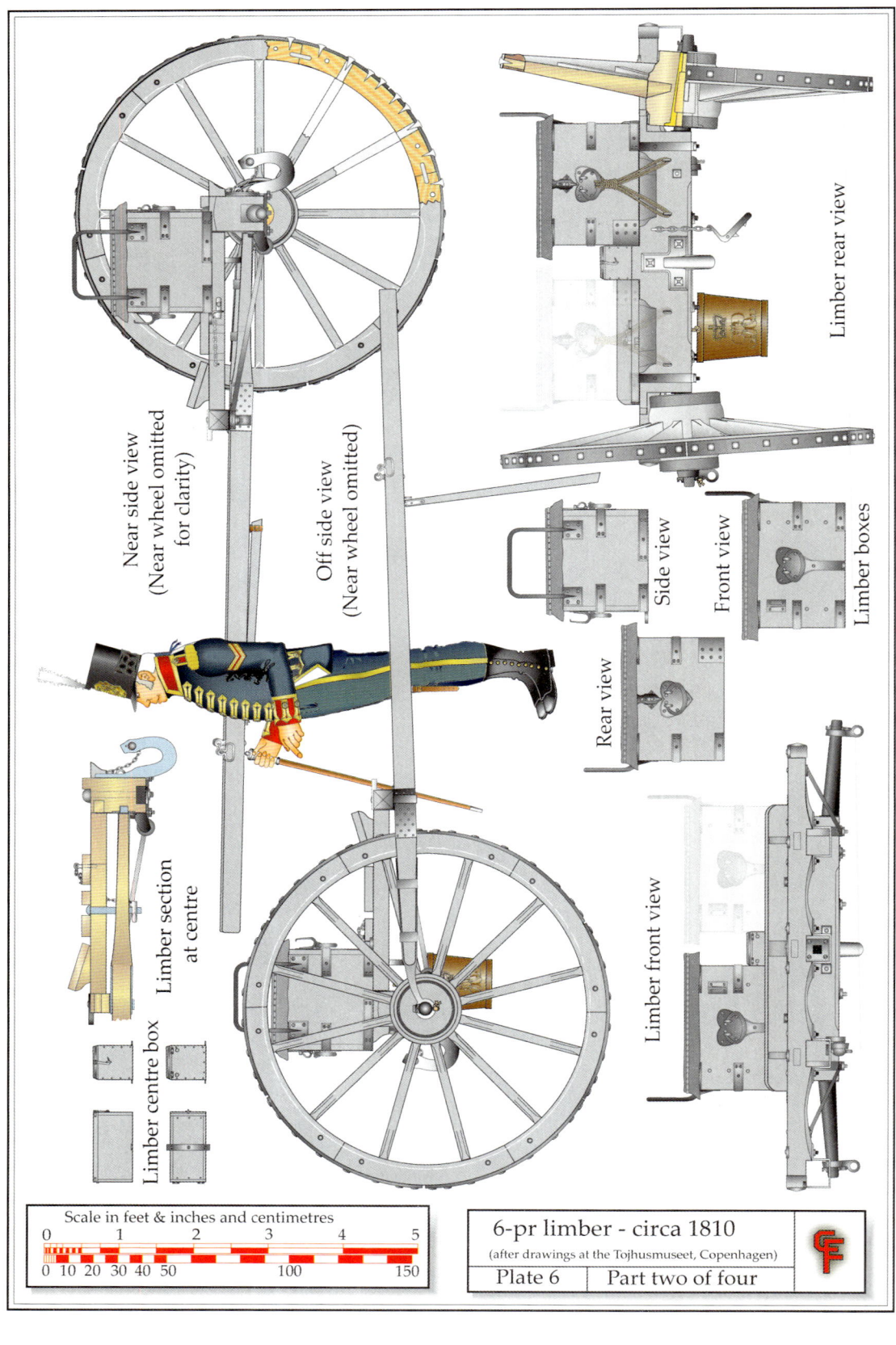

Near side view
(Near wheel omitted
for clarity)

Off side view
(Near wheel omitted)

Limber section
at centre

Limber centre box

Limber rear view

Side view

Front view

Limber boxes

Rear view

Limber front view

Scale in feet & inches and centimetres

0   1   2   3   4   5

0 10 20 30 40 50   100   150

6-pr limber - circa 1810

(after drawings at the Tojhusmuseet, Copenhagen)

Plate 6   Part two of four

Gun limber, near box

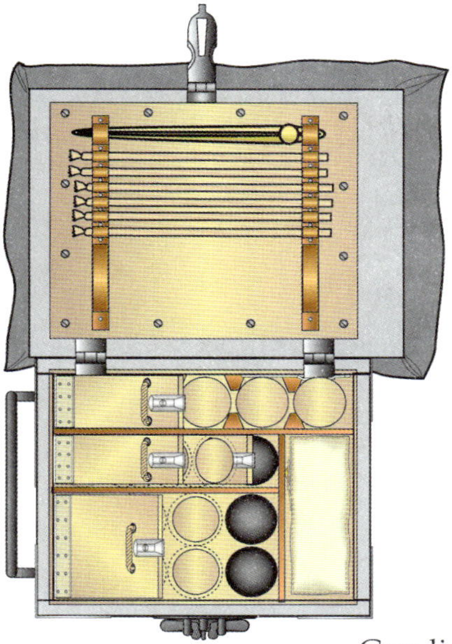

Gun limber, off box

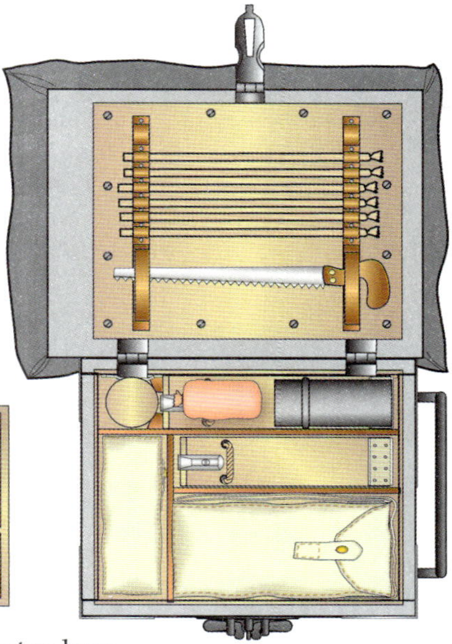

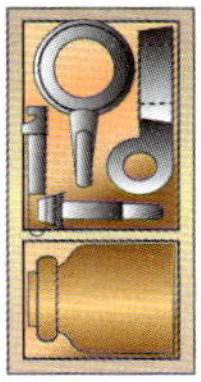

Gun limber, centre box
2 linchpins and 2 drag washers,
Spare rammer head.

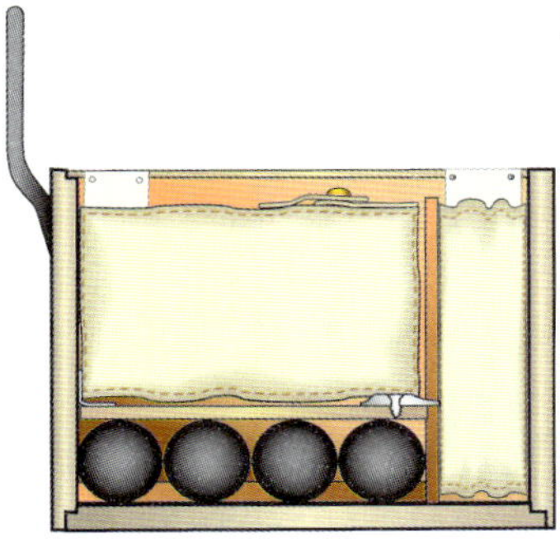

**For contents see
Table D.5.
at the end of Part Two**

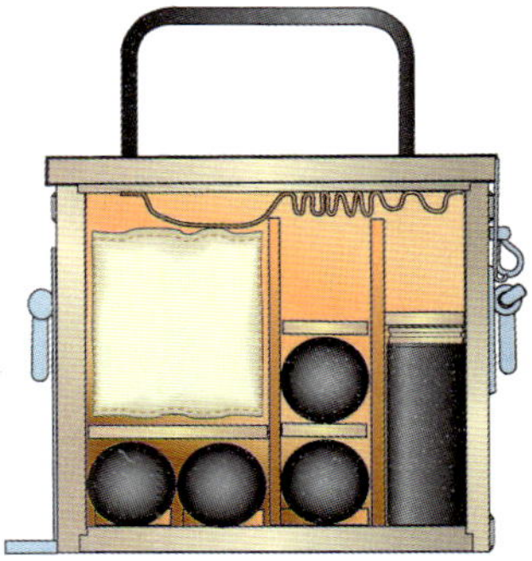

Front section of
near limber box

Side section
of off box

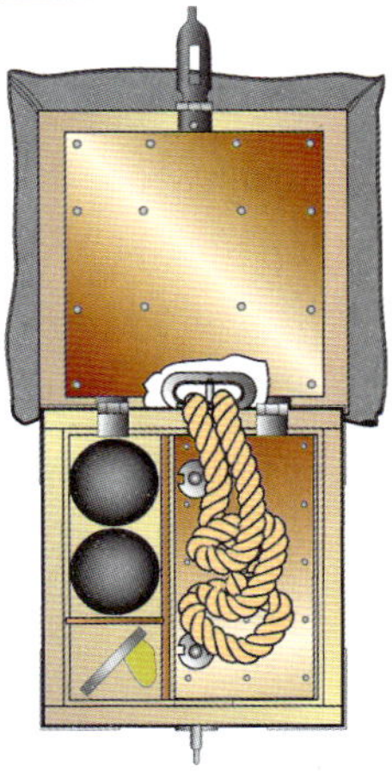

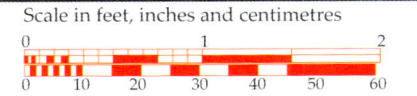

Off or left
gun axle box

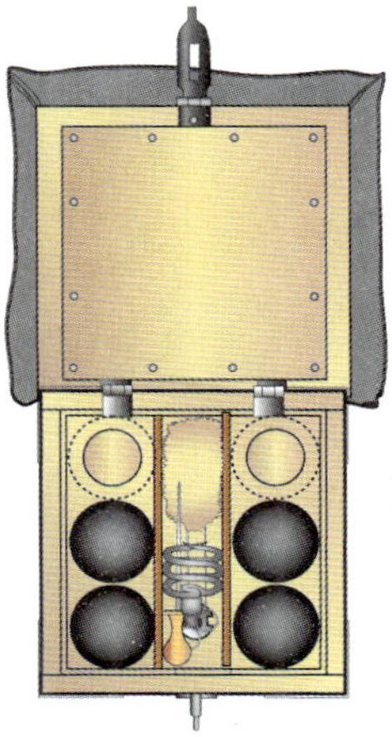

Near or right
gun axle box

Scale in feet, inches and centimetres

0   1   2
0   10   20   30   40   50   60

Light 6-pr gun - contents of the
axle and limber boxes (after Adye)

Plate 7   Part three of four

Ammunition wagon
limber, near box

Ammunition wagon
limber, off box

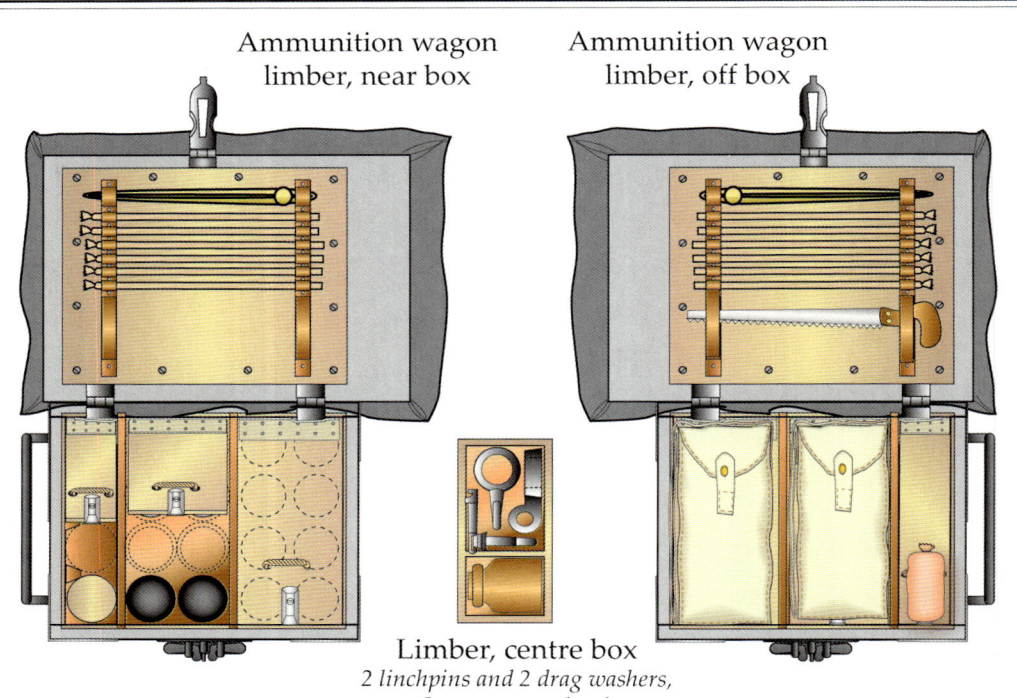

Limber, centre box
2 linchpins and 2 drag washers,
Spare rammer head.

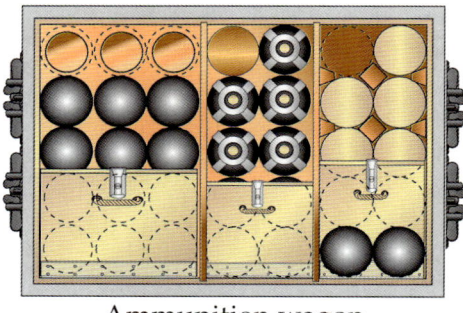

Ammunition wagon
fore box

**For contents see
Table D.5.
at the end of Part Two**

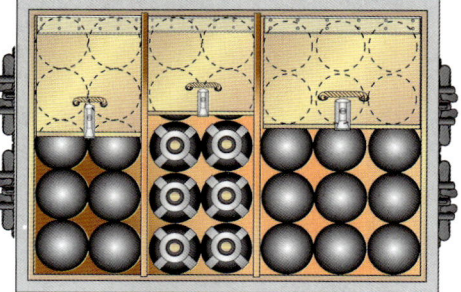

Ammunition wagon
hind box

Scale in feet, inches and centimetres

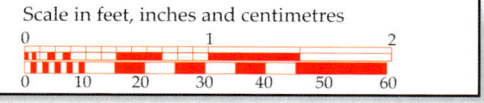

0   1   2

0   10   20   30   40   50   60

6-pr ammunition wagon and
limber - circa 1813

| Plate 8 | Part four of four |

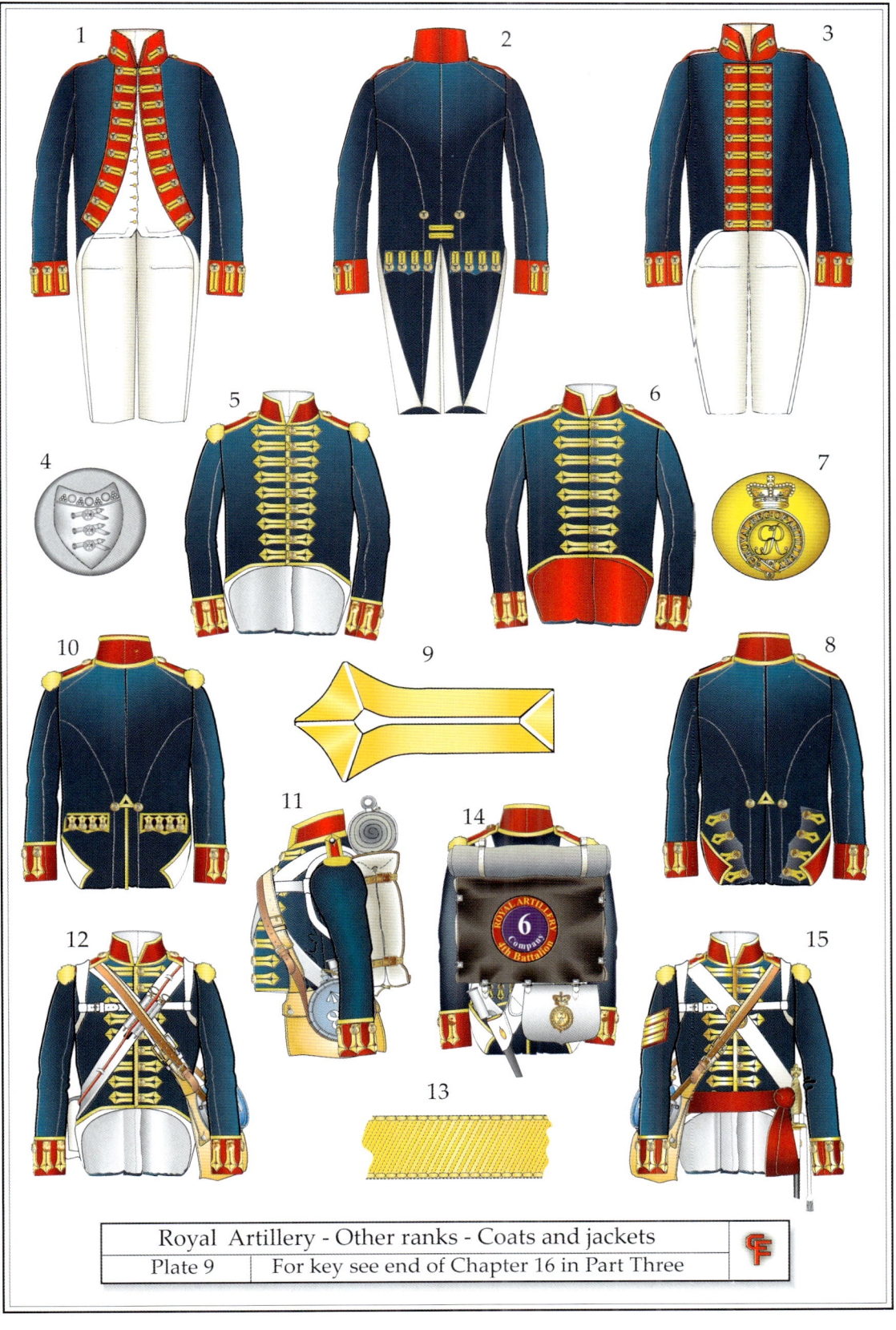

Royal Artillery - Other ranks - Coats and jackets

Plate 9   For key see end of Chapter 16 in Part Three

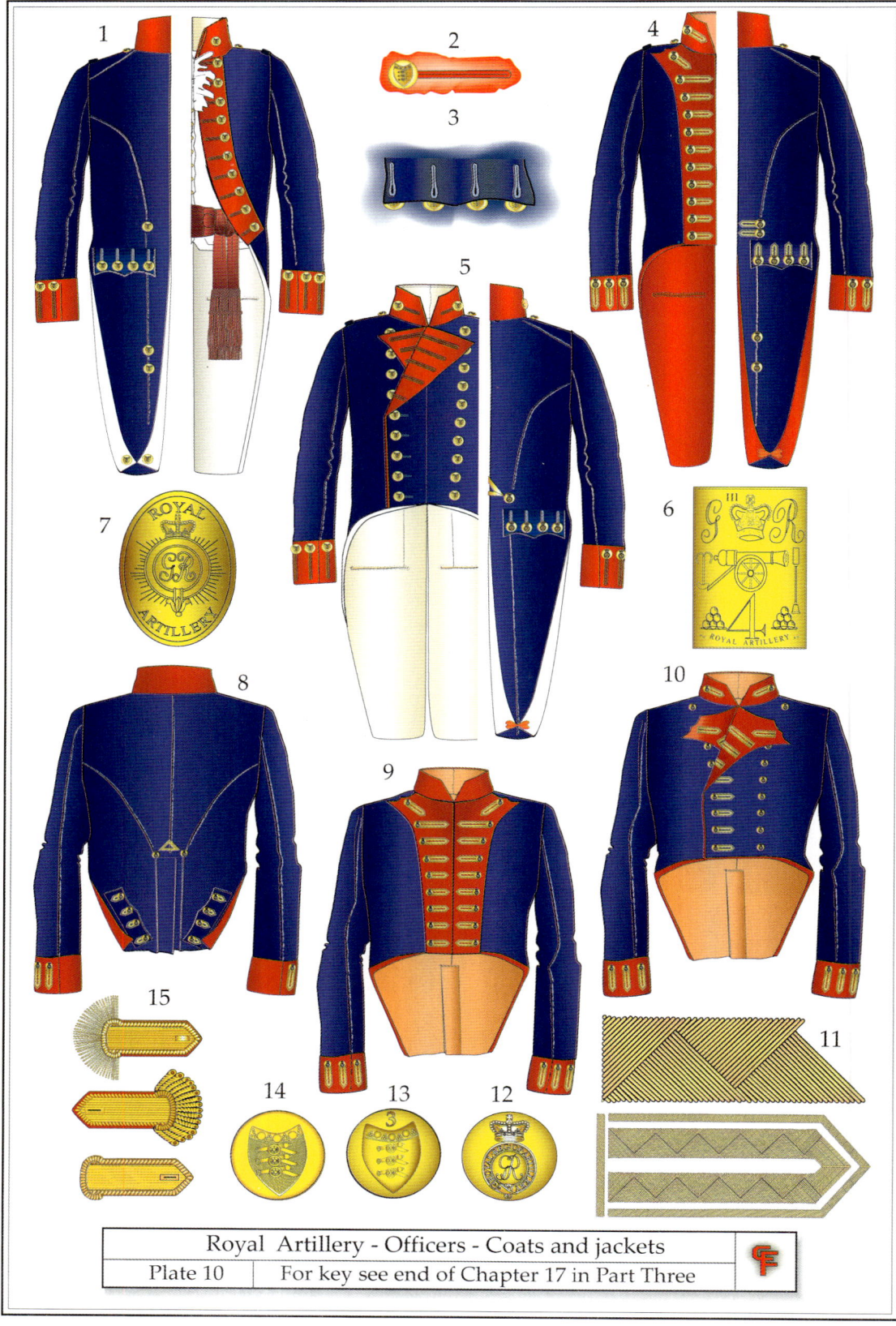

Royal Artillery - Officers - Coats and jackets

Plate 10 | For key see end of Chapter 17 in Part Three

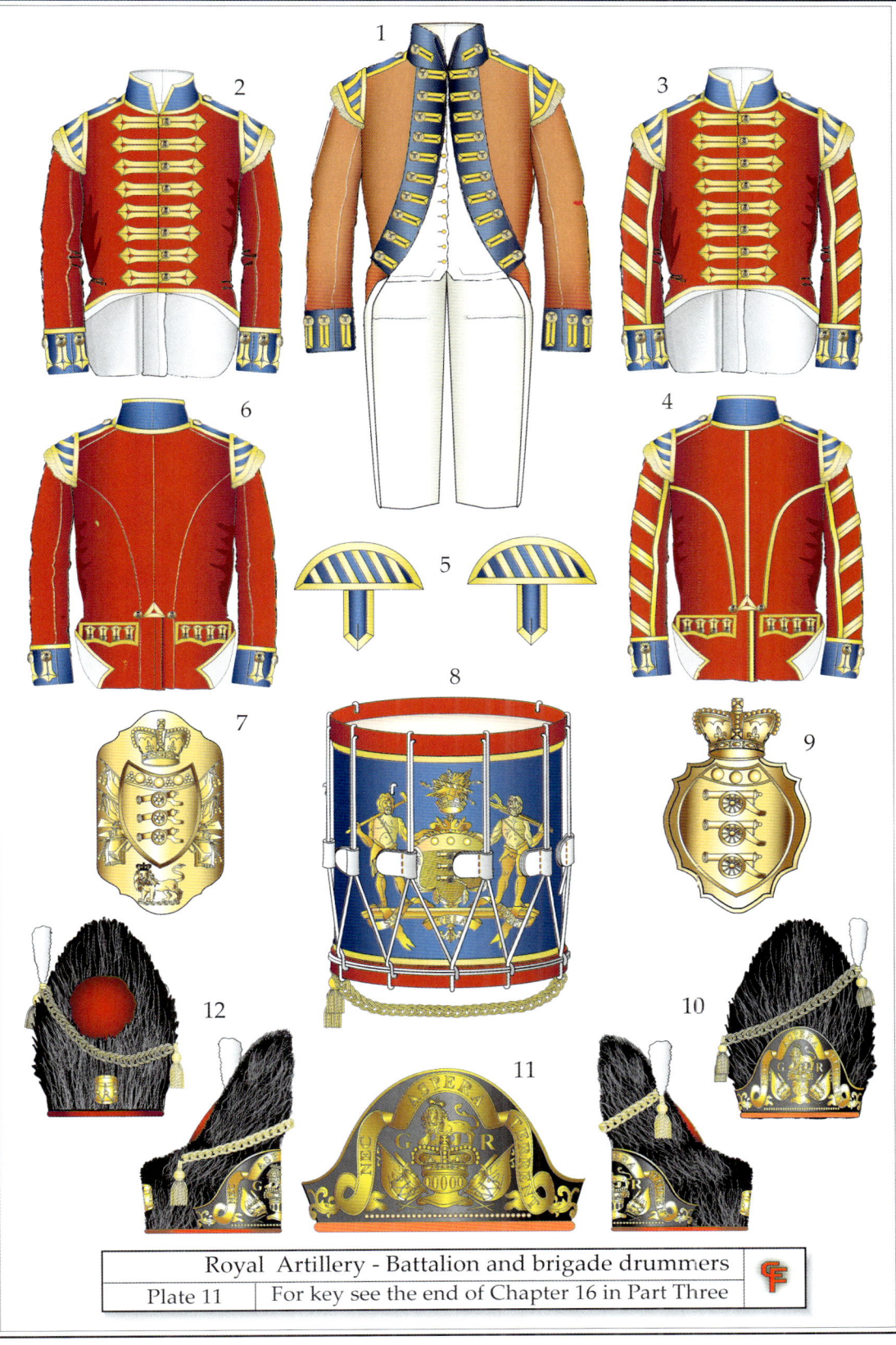

Royal Artillery - Battalion and brigade drummers

Plate 11   For key see the end of Chapter 16 in Part Three

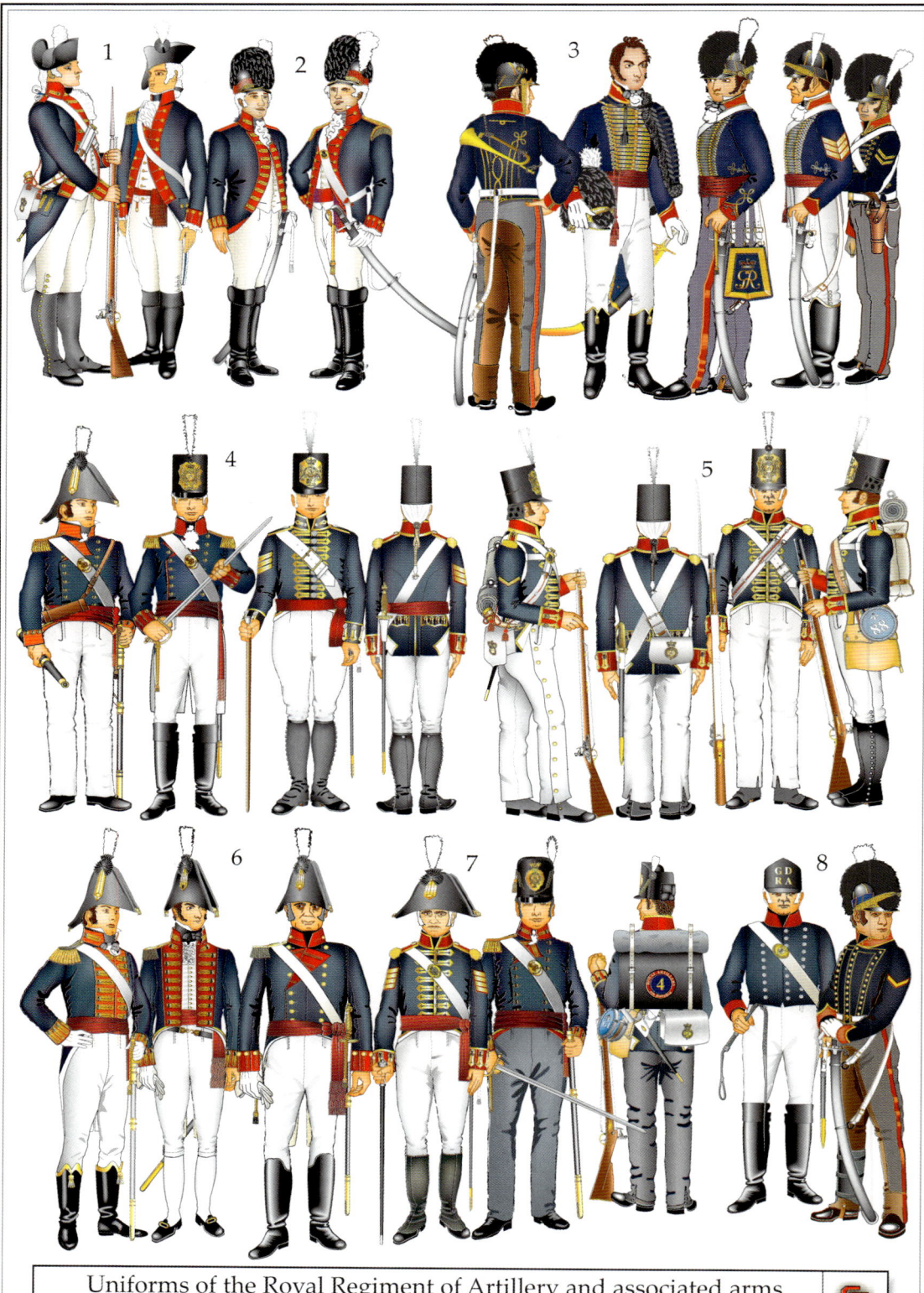

Uniforms of the Royal Regiment of Artillery and associated arms

Plate 12 · For key see end of Chapter 16 in Part Three

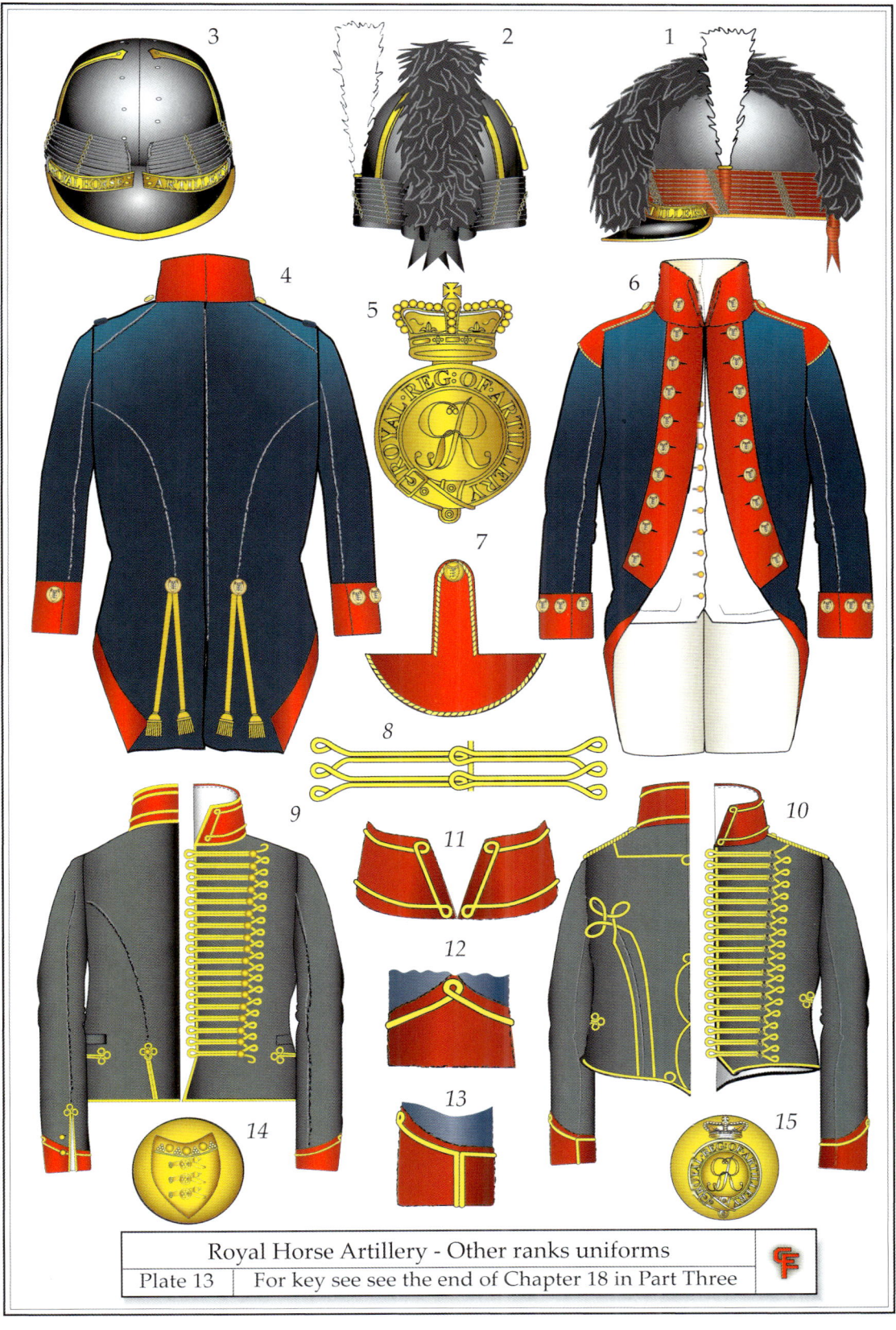

Royal Horse Artillery - Other ranks uniforms

Plate 13 | For key see see the end of Chapter 18 in Part Three

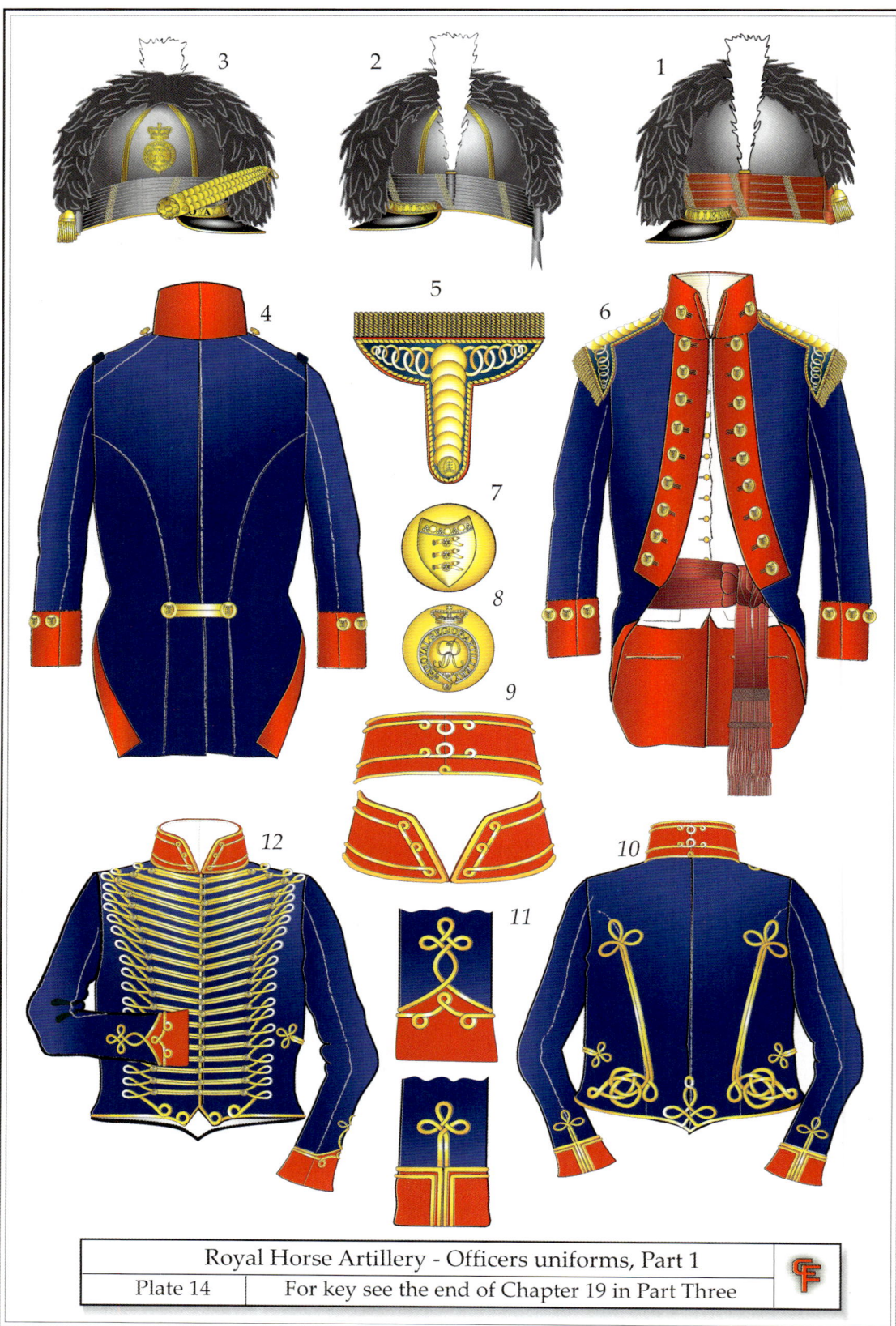

Royal Horse Artillery - Officers uniforms, Part 1

| Plate 14 | For key see the end of Chapter 19 in Part Three |

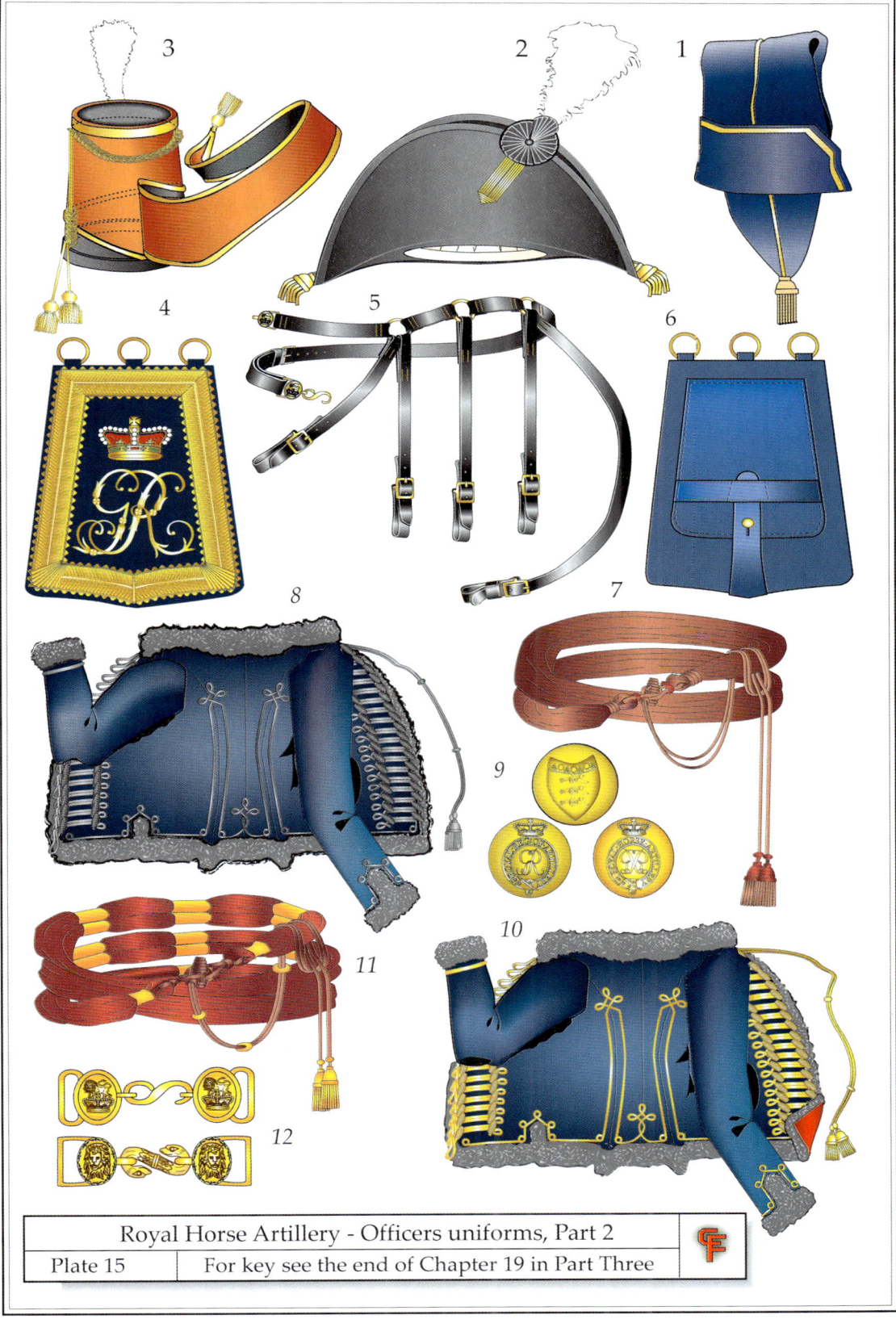

Royal Horse Artillery - Officers uniforms, Part 2

Plate 15 | For key see the end of Chapter 19 in Part Three

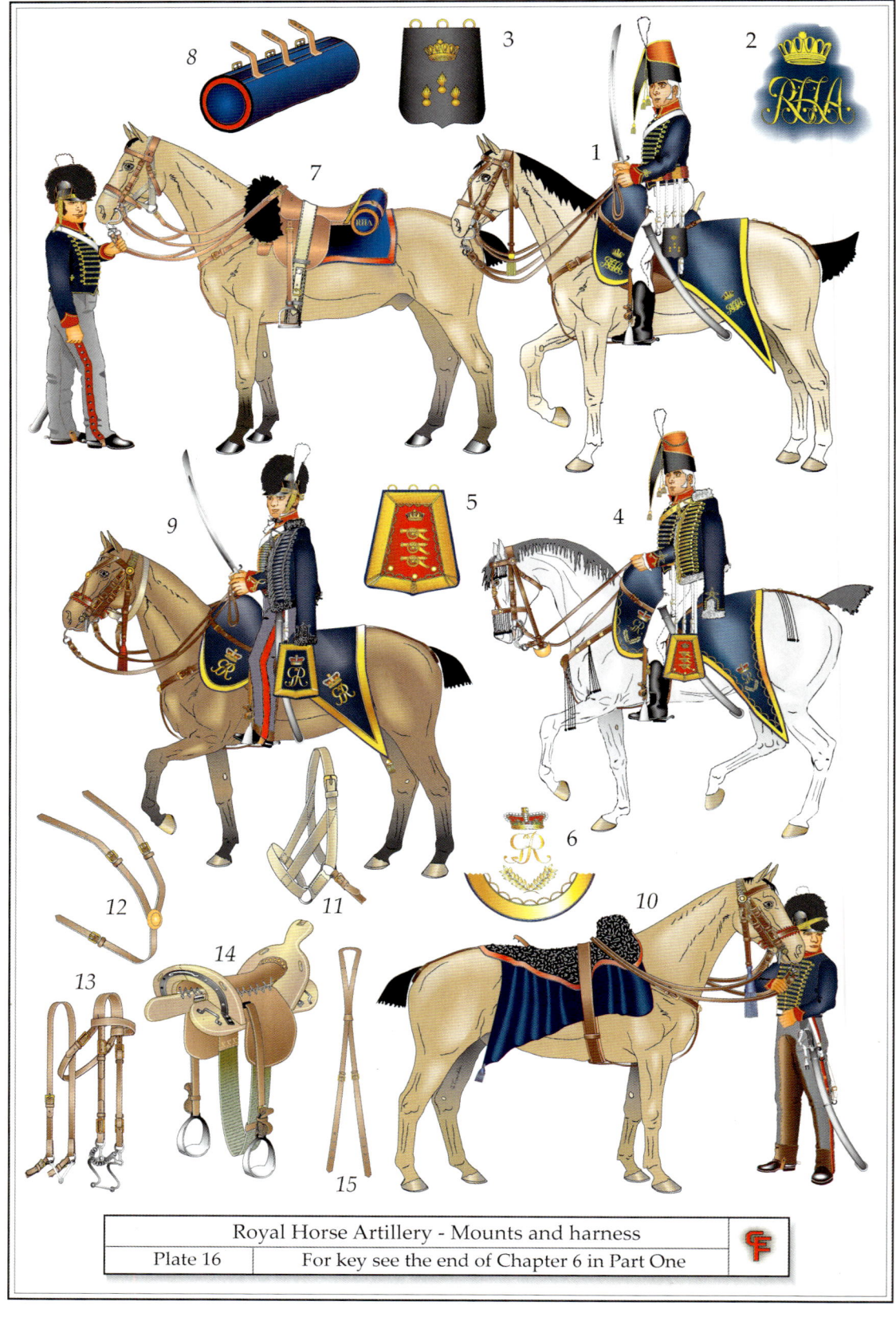

	Royal Horse Artillery - Mounts and harness	
Plate 16	For key see the end of Chapter 6 in Part One	

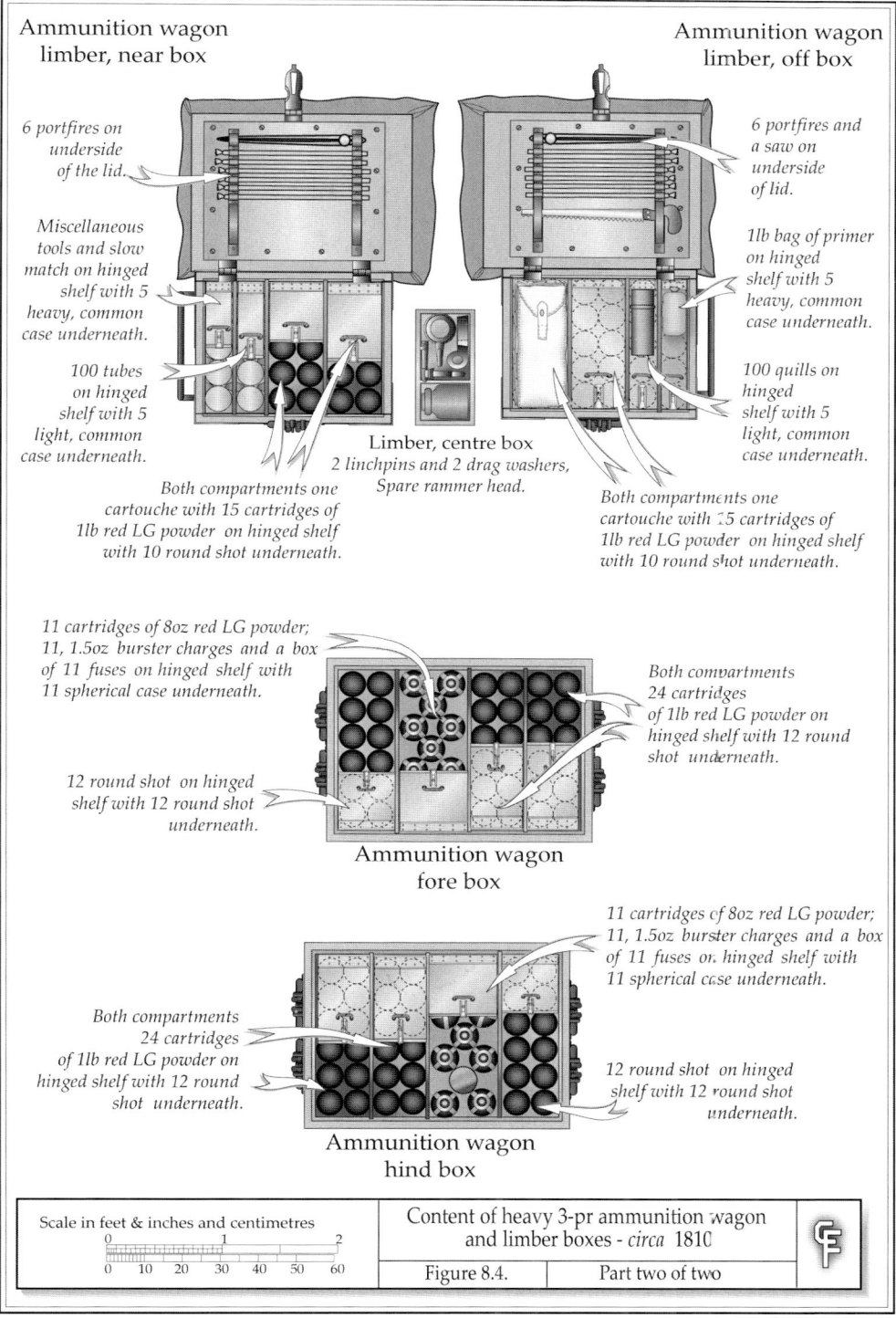

Ammunition wagon
limber, near box

6 portfires on
underside
of the lid.

Miscellaneous
tools and slow
match on hinged
shelf with 5
heavy, common
case underneath.

100 tubes
on hinged
shelf with 5
light, common
case underneath.

Both compartments one
cartouche with 15 cartridges of
1lb red LG powder on hinged shelf
with 10 round shot underneath.

Ammunition wagon
limber, off box

6 portfires and
a saw on
underside
of lid.

1lb bag of primer
on hinged
shelf with 5
heavy, common
case underneath.

100 quills on
hinged
shelf with 5
light, common
case underneath.

Both compartments one
cartouche with 15 cartridges of
1lb red LG powder on hinged shelf
with 10 round shot underneath.

Limber, centre box
2 linchpins and 2 drag washers,
Spare rammer head.

11 cartridges of 8oz red LG powder;
11, 1.5oz burster charges and a box
of 11 fuses on hinged shelf with
11 spherical case underneath.

Both compartments
24 cartridges
of 1lb red LG powder on
hinged shelf with 12 round
shot underneath.

12 round shot on hinged
shelf with 12 round shot
underneath.

Ammunition wagon
fore box

11 cartridges of 8oz red LG powder;
11, 1.5oz burster charges and a box
of 11 fuses on hinged shelf with
11 spherical case underneath.

Both compartments
24 cartridges
of 1lb red LG powder on
hinged shelf with 12 round
shot underneath.

12 round shot on hinged
shelf with 12 round shot
underneath.

Ammunition wagon
hind box

Scale in feet & inches and centimetres
0   1   2
0   10   20   30   40   50   60

Content of heavy 3-pr ammunition wagon
and limber boxes - circa 1810

Figure 8.4.   Part two of two

By March 1808, this battery was fully equipped with 162 rounds per gun and manned by Lawson's Company, but there is no further record of its use in the Peninsula after Talavera. In Quebec, the light 3-prs were still on the older-type carriages and were in the process of replacement with block trails in 1813,[12] and four unspecified pieces, on block trails, were used in the New Orleans Expedition.[13]

When these short pieces were mounted on a block trail carriage the standard form of elevation mechanism was too large to fit on the cushion of the trail, so a simpler form was adopted. The left-hand axle carried a smaller version of the slow match box but no right axle box was fitted. The wheels for the light 3-pr were 52 inches diameter and 2.25 inches wide and weighed 216lb. The length of the axle arm was 11 inches, 2 inches diameter at the shoulder and 1.5 inches at the linch end.[14] The performance of the light 3-pr is given in Table C.1 of Appendix C at the end of Part Two.

Blomefield 3-pr guns of 3ft

This gun was used throughout the period and pieces are known that were cast between 1801 and 1812. The piece weighed 2.25cwt (238lb); it was 3 feet long, some 14 calibres. It had a bore of 2.912 inches, a shot diameter of 2.775 inches and a windage of 0.138 inches. In normal use, the gun fired a 12-ounce charge, but for spherical case, this was initially reduced to 8 ounces with a separator charge of 1.5 ounces. This gun had no bracket for the tangent scale on the breech mouldings and may well have been used for the Cuppage or later mountain guns.[15]

Blomefield 3-pr Guns of 4ft

The piece weighed 3cwt (343lb); it was 4 feet long, some 16 calibres. It had a bore of 2.912 inches, a shot diameter of 2.775 inches and a windage of 0.138 inches. In normal use, the gun fired a 12-ounce charge, but for spherical case this was initially reduced to 8 ounces with a separator charge of 1.5 ounces. Examples are known cast by J&H King between 1799 and 1810. This piece probably replaced the light common of 3ft 6in.[16]

Lord Townsend's Light Infantry 3-pr

These guns were named after their designer, Lord Townsend and nicknamed the 'Butterfly'. They had seen service during the American War of Independence but they remained in use in the West Indies until 1811 and in Canada until 1812.[17] The main point of interest is that the gun could be packed on horses or mules and carried in panniers and they may well have been the instigation for the mountain brigade used in Spain. The piece was initially cast by Verbruggen and lasted in use for many years. A surviving example has the base ring engraved 'I & P Verbruggen Fecerunt', it is dated 1775. The piece was 3 feet long and weighed about 1.75cwt (196lb), the second reinforce carries a broad arrow and the breech is marked 1:2:20, indicating the weight. The elevating mechanism followed both the early and later form with a pin through the neck of the cascable. The detachment consisted of seven men and two drivers who were solely concerned in the transport. The gun fired fixed ammunition from a 6- or 8-ounce charge and a round of case with 36 shot. At an elevation of three degrees, the recoil on firm ground was five feet.[18]

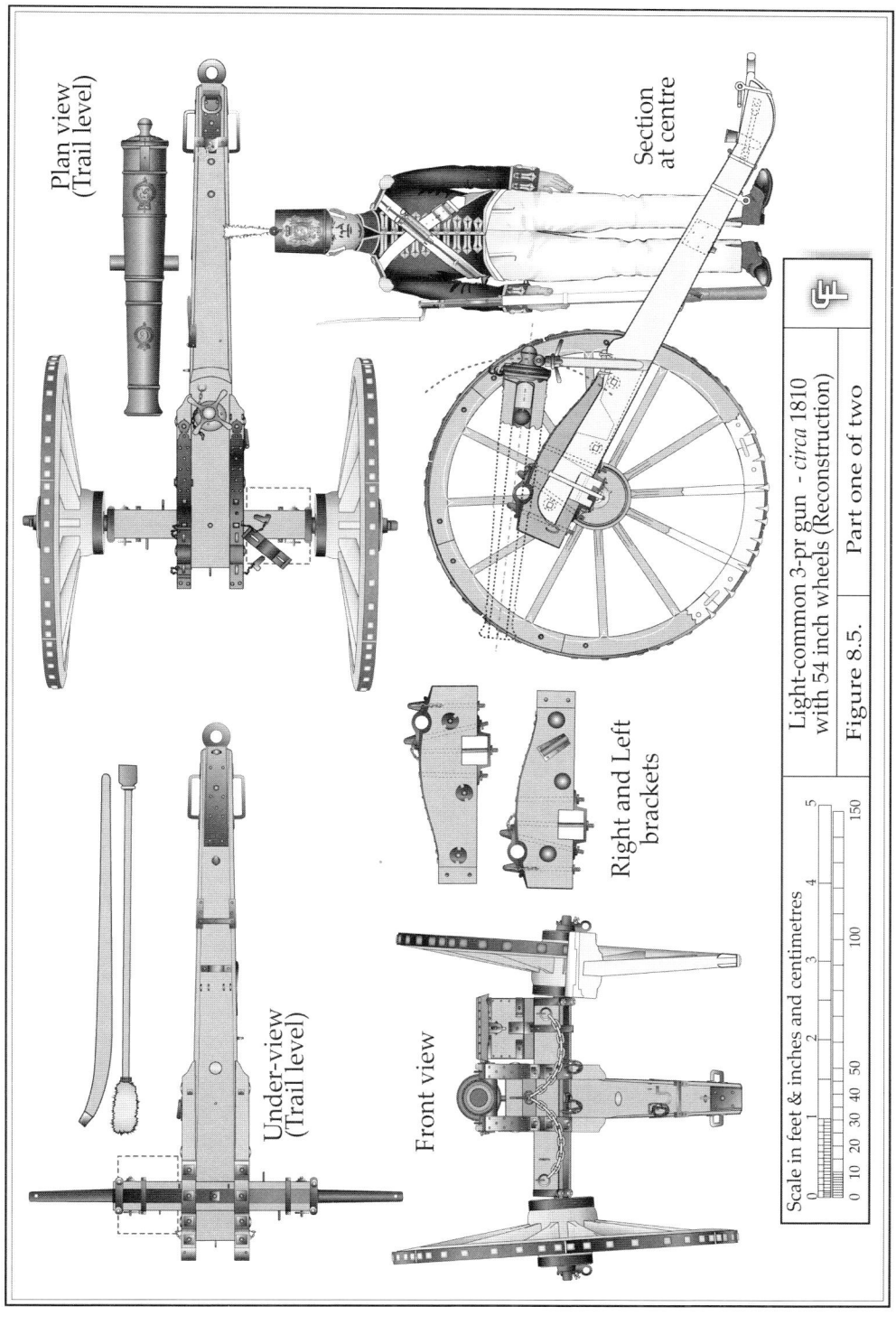

Plan view
(Trail level)

Section
at centre

Under-view
(Trail level)

Right and Left
brackets

Front view

Scale in feet & inches and centimetres

Light-common 3-pr gun - *circa* 1810
with 54 inch wheels (Reconstruction)

Figure 8.5.   Part one of two

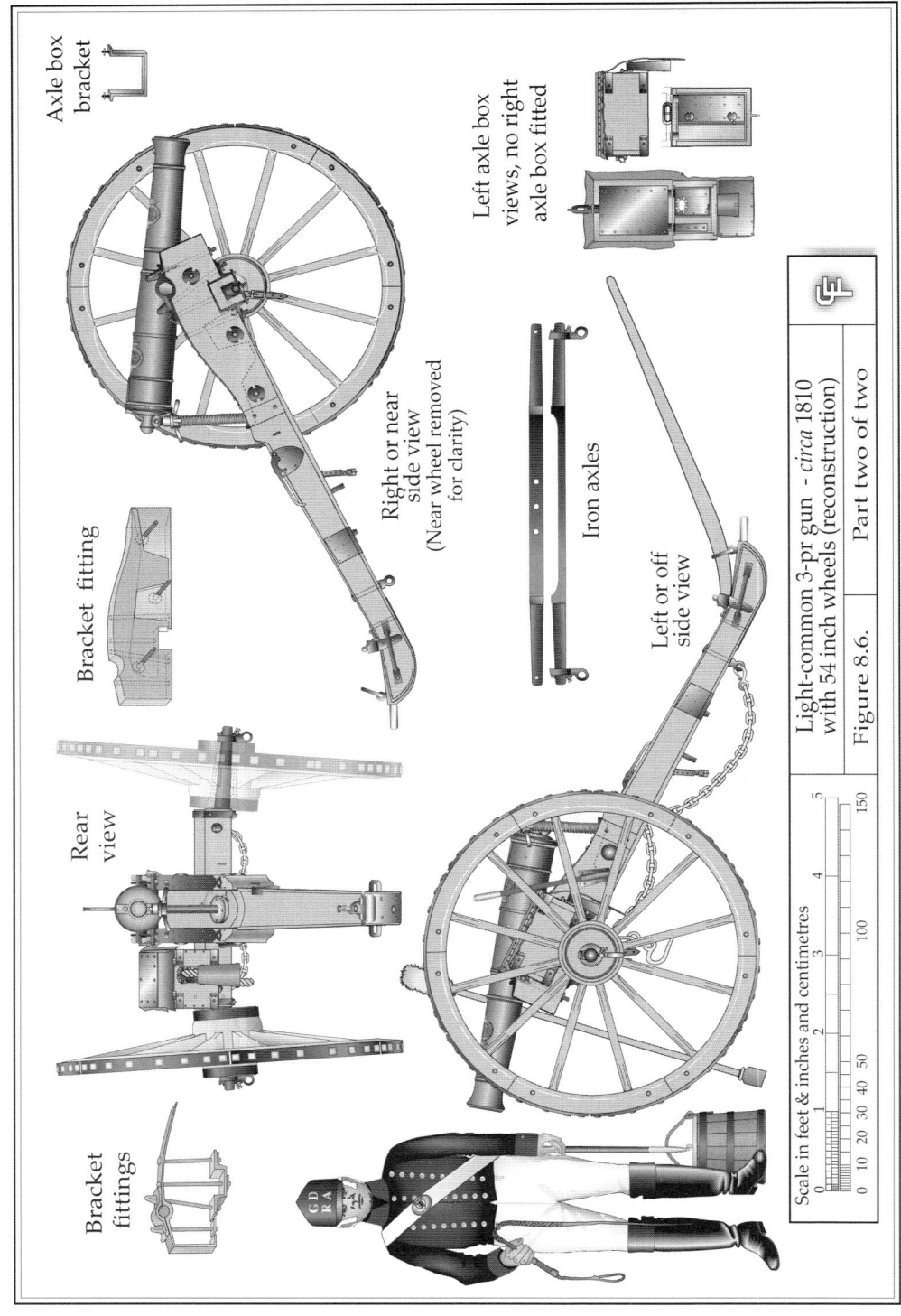

Axle box bracket

Left axle box views, no right axle box fitted

Right or near side view
(Near wheel removed for clarity)

Iron axles

Left or off side view

Bracket fitting

Rear view

Bracket fittings

Scale in feet & inches and centimetres

Light-common 3-pr gun - *circa* 1810 with 54 inch wheels (reconstruction)

Figure 8.6.   Part two of two

These guns were considered attractive for use in the Peninsula. In 1808 Captain Robe wrote:

> I mean to ask for a 3-pr brigade, for use of the light troops, those formed for the West Indies will answer very well in this country, only having the draught made double. The span of the wheels being less than common, but limber wagons should be formed for them of the same span of wheel and constructed to carry the same ammunition for the 3-pr as the 6-pr.[19]

There is no indication that his request was immediately satisfied, but light 3-pr guns were forthcoming in the following year.

Mountain Brigades

It was found that the terrain in the Pyrenees often precluded the use of conventional artillery. In response to this difficulty a mountain battery of 3-pr guns was designed by Colonel Cuppage of the Royal Carriage Department at Woolwich. The first batch arrived in Spain in May 1809 where it was noted that '*it travelled well*' and further supplies in December enabled the brigade to be fully equipped with six guns.[20] No further details of the equipment have been located.

In 1813 three 3-pr guns captured from the French were converted to single draught and placed under the command of Lieutenant Robe as the 1st Mountain Brigade – the nature of these captured French guns remains unclear. Three light 3-pr guns brought from Lisbon were equipped for mule transport and added to the command.[21] The guns were carried by one large country mule, the carriage on another and wheels by a third. The battery was disbanded at the end of the campaign and there are no surviving details of these carriages or the mule panniers used to carry them. The type of pack-saddles issued to the Peninsula in 1808 were called 'Devonshire crooks'. These were made by bending strong poles of willow saplings, cut green and bent into the required shape for the two arches. When dried out they were connected by sideboards like any other saddle.

The arches, or pommels and cantles, were known as the crooks and were connected with longer sideboards for loads like sheaves of wheat and shorter ones for heavier material; a similar type was also in use on the farms in central Spain.[22] These saddles weighed about 50 pounds and were the model upon which most of the army saddles were made, although these were probably made entirely from beech like cavalry saddles.

The Robe 1st Mountain Brigade was composed of both Royal Artillery and Portuguese gunners and members of the Corps of Drivers and probably local muleteers and guides. A mule at this time was rated to take a load of between 160 to 300 pounds for twenty to thirty miles a day.[23] Some authorities believe that the carriage was dismantled and loaded on two mules,[24] but one would be able to carry the gun, one the stripped carriage, one the wheels and side arms with the ammunition being carried on further mules. The lack of contemporary information makes it difficult to be certain, but later illustrations provide some insight. However, in these the carriage and wheels were carried on one mule, a load of 194.75lb,[25] but the carriage and wheels of 1810, based upon the weights of the Napoleonic period, were too heavy a load for one mule.

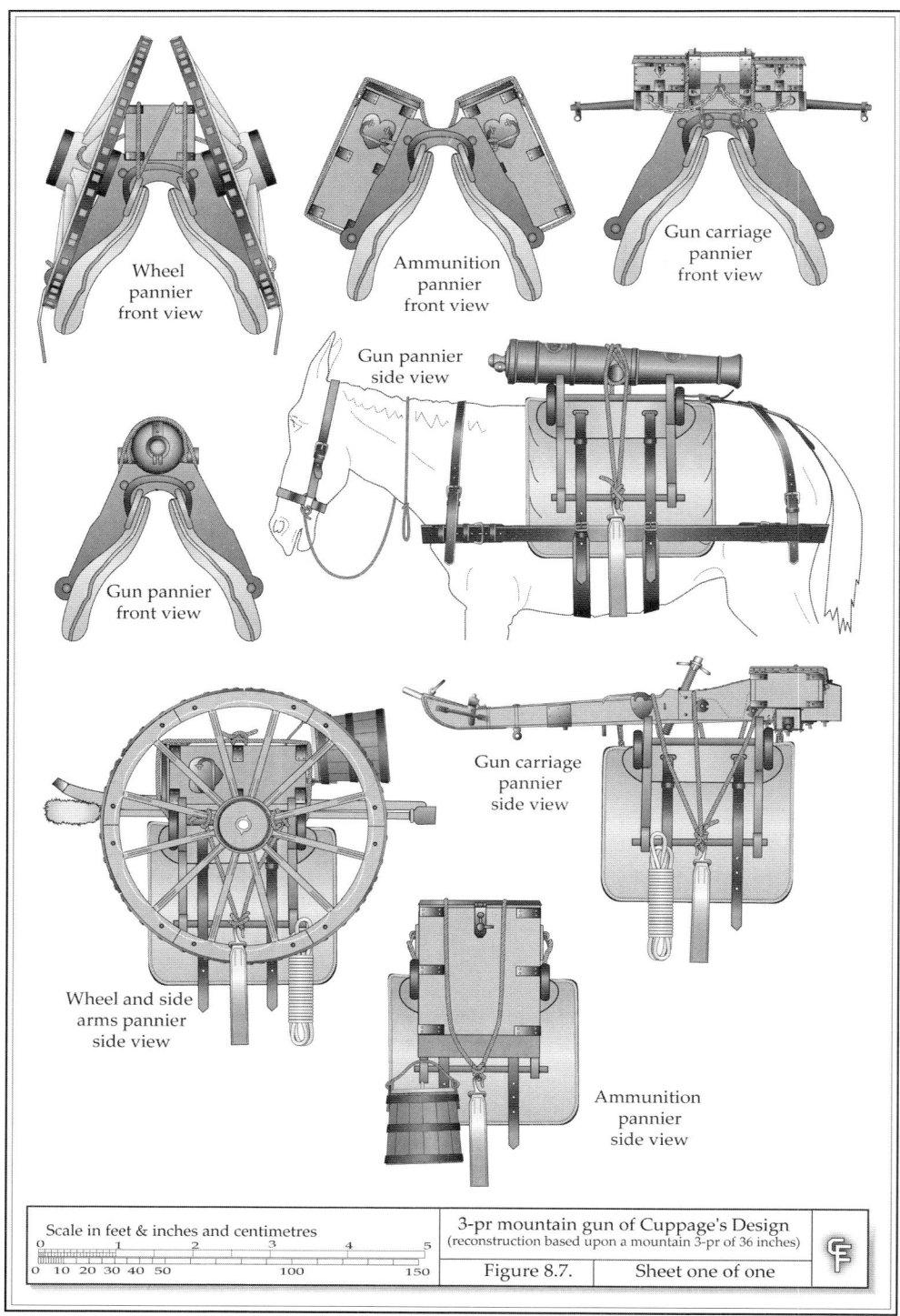

Wheel
pannier
front view

Ammunition
pannier
front view

Gun carriage
pannier
front view

Gun pannier
side view

Gun pannier
front view

Wheel and side
arms pannier
side view

Gun carriage
pannier
side view

Ammunition
pannier
side view

Scale in feet & inches and centimetres

| 3-pr mountain gun of Cuppage's Design |
| (reconstruction based upon a mountain 3-pr of 36 inches) |
| Figure 8.7. | Sheet one of one |

Later a brigade of Portuguese mountain guns was also equipped. It was manned by Portuguese artillerymen, British drivers and mules.[26] Dickson wrote of mountain artillery:

'… you ask my opinion respecting mountain guns. As yet we have not tried them much, but for general purposes I think it may be said, they are more useful from the confidence they give men, than from their own effect, which it is evident must be very uncertain except when employed at very short ranges ; soldiers like the noise of Artillery ; it gives them confidence when employed in their support, with however little effect, and in like manner it disquiets them when brought against them, and although perhaps the shot only pass over their heads, still they are not able well to judge how high, and feel that if they remain in the same position the practice may become more annoying. Were Armies from a peculiarity of Mountain Country, obliged to wage war for a length of time without being able to employ any other ordnance than the small pieces termed Mountain Guns, I have no doubt that the soldiers would very soon learn the inefficacy and uncertainty of these pieces when employed at a distance, and would grow indifferent about them … It is also to be observed that the report of small guns in a Mountainous Country appears louder, which serves to add to the illusion. In attack therefore, I think Columns should always in mountain war be supported by Mountain Guns if no other can be employed. The troops advancing are entertained by their noise, and the force attacked are incommoded by it, but when the attack becomes close the Ordnance of the defenders is then of real efficacy when probably the Guns of the assailants have not been able to keep pace with their Columns. I therefore think that either party would labour under a disadvantage were they without mountain guns. However, their utility may be confined to stage effect in a great degree. In thus approving of their employment, I would recommend at the same time that it should be as limited as possible, and every exertion should be made to bring forward heavier Ordnance, … To return to Mountain Guns, I have two kinds ; one carried on Mules, the other single draught. The former kind galls, and indeed ruins many animals, and the only advantage it possesses over the other is that the Ordnance can be conveyed by the narrowest footpaths, and up the most difficult steeps. The gun in draught does not injure the animals ; it is much easier to bring to action ; it can retire quicker, and as it will admit of being of greater length, its practice will be more exact than the other. I think these kind [draught] of guns might be useful in a close or woody country with Light troops …[27]

Endnotes to Chapter 8

1. Dickson, 1908: pp. 73, 174, 1,048.
2. Hughes, 1969: p. 76.
3. McConnell, 1988: p. 50.
4. Caruana, 1978: p. 59; McConnell, 1988: p. 201; Duncan, 1908: p. 34.
5. Adye, 1813: pp. 390–1.
8. Caruana, 1980: pp. 12–13.
9. McConnell, 1988: p. 50.
10. Duncan, 1908: pp. 118, 124.
11. Leslie, 1912: p. 75: Duncan 1908: p. 177.
12. Graves, 1982: pp. 128, 129.
13. Leslie, 1912: pp. 96, 98; Duncan, 1908: p. 398.
14. Adye, 1813: p. 392.
15. McConnell, 1988: p. 49.
16. McConnell, 1988: p. 49.

17. Caruana, 1982: p. 128.
18. Caruana, 1979: pp. 8–10.
19. Leslie, 1912: p. 79.
20. Dickson, 1908: pp. 25, 124.
21. Duncan, 1908: p. 376.
22. Tylden, 1965: pp. 181–3.
23. Ibid: pp. 90–1.
24. Rogers, 1971: p. 86.
25. *Aide Memoire*, 1847: plate 29; Royal Carriage Department, plate 1a and 1e of 1867 (pack saddles).
26. Dickson, 1908: pp. 1,079, 1,086, 1,088, 1093.
27. Dickson, 1908: p. 1,120.

CHAPTER 9

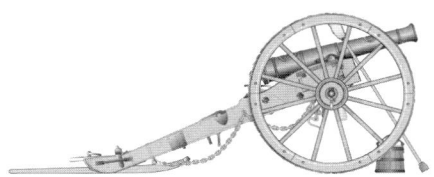

6-pr Field Equipments

Introduction

There were five different types of 6-pr gun in regular field use during the Napoleonic Wars not counting the variants maintained in the Colonies. As far as can be determined the main pieces used in the European theatre were:

- The Desaguliers medium 6-pr of 7 feet
- Congreve's light 6-pr of 4 feet 6 inches
- The Belford and Blomefield light 6-pr of 5 feet
- Blomefield heavy 6-pr of 5 feet 2 inches

To these must be added three further 6-pr pieces by Desaguliers: the long, of 6 feet weighing 5.5cwt; the heavy, of 5 feet 6 inches and 9cwt and the light, of 5 feet 6 inches and 8.25cwt. Research has failed to reveal any specific field references to these pieces and their use during the period is generally unclear, but it is considered that they were not obsolete until 1813.[1]

Desaguliers Medium 6-pr Gun

This bronze gun was designed by Desaguliers and weighed 12.25cwt (1,372lb), it was 6 feet long, some 14 calibres. It had a bore of 3.668 inches, a shot diameter of 3.5 inches and a windage of some 0.118 inches. In normal use, the gun fired a 2lb charge of red large-grain powder, but for spherical case this was initially reduced to 12 ounces with a separator charge of 2.5 ounces.[2] More commonly known as the long 6-pr, the references to the gun during the Napoleonic period are few and limited to the first part of the Peninsular Campaigns in 1809.[3] No surviving details of the piece or the carriage have been located and the gun appears to have been replaced by the Blomefield heavy 6-pr, at least in the European theatre, but the piece is mentioned by Dickson in the Peninsula and some may have survived in the Colonies. It is also referred to by General Congreve (1st Bart) in the establishment of a park of artillery for use in the Low Countries in 1793:

> Four long 6 prs with 50 rounds of ammunition to each gun in its limber boxes. 6 Horses and 3 Drivers each. Four spare limbers with 60 rounds of amm'n. Each 4 Horses and 2 Drivers. Four new pattern waggons, 180 rn'ds in each, 6 Horses and 3 Drivers.[4]

From this it may be assumed that the new pattern of ammunition wagon was already available for use at this date and that the gun limber was of the later style, as it carried 50 rounds of ammunition. If the transitional limber was in use, then the ammunition carried would be arranged in a similar way to that shown for the light 6-pr.

The nature of the carriage is unknown, but it seems unlikely that this gun was mounted on a block trail. The ammunition was the same as that for the light 6-pr and the bracket gun carriage is assumed to have followed the same design criteria as that of the Congreve light 6-pr. In the absence of surviving drawings or detailed information regarding this gun or its carriage, the drawings are reconstructions based upon the principles and practices of the time. While the piece was proposed as part of the initial armament of the horse artillery, there is no evidence to suggest that a block trail carriage was issued for these pieces.[5] It may be due to the weight of the piece that it was relegated to service as a gun of position by the introduction of the 9-pr in 1808. While the pieces had a similar performance, the extra weight of metal of the 9-pr would have made it favoured during the Napoleonic period when the British artillery were usually faced by the heavier French guns.

Congreve's Light 6-pr of 4ft 6in

This piece was introduced in 1778, it weighed 5.25cwt (588lb), and it was 4 feet 6 inches long, some 15 calibres. It had a bore of 3.668 inches, a shot diameter of 3.5 inches and a windage of some 0.118 inches. In normal use, the gun fired a 1.5lb charge of red large-grain powder, but for spherical case this was initially reduced to 12 ounces with a separator charge of 2.5 ounces. The records make it clear that this gun saw service in the early part of the Napoleonic War where it formed the mainstay of the battalion guns, but was rarely used in the European theatre after the first phase of the war. Hughes considers this piece obsolete in 1800,[6] however, there is clear evidence it survived much longer in the Colonies where bracket trail carriages for these guns were still being issued by the Royal Carriage Department as late as 1812 but the gun must be considered obsolete by the end of the period.[7]

While the majority of battalion guns were of this pattern, by 1800 the gun was obsolete and being replaced.[8] The original carriage was designed by Congreve and had been formally introduced into service about the same time; the piece was mounted on the older bracket trail carriage and rear pintle limber. No surviving examples of this carriage have been located and the drawings are reconstructions based upon the Rudyerd illustrations and the Congreve carriage of 1780, with the piece of 4ft 6in shown by Rudyerd. Adye records that the carriage was fitted with 60-inch diameter wheels and iron axles by 1801 and the new pattern limber was added, which dispensed with the need for the side ammunition boxes on the gun carriage axle. As the war progressed the light 6-pr of 4 feet 6 inches was replaced by the light 6-pr of 5 feet mounted on block carriages and more usually brigaded.

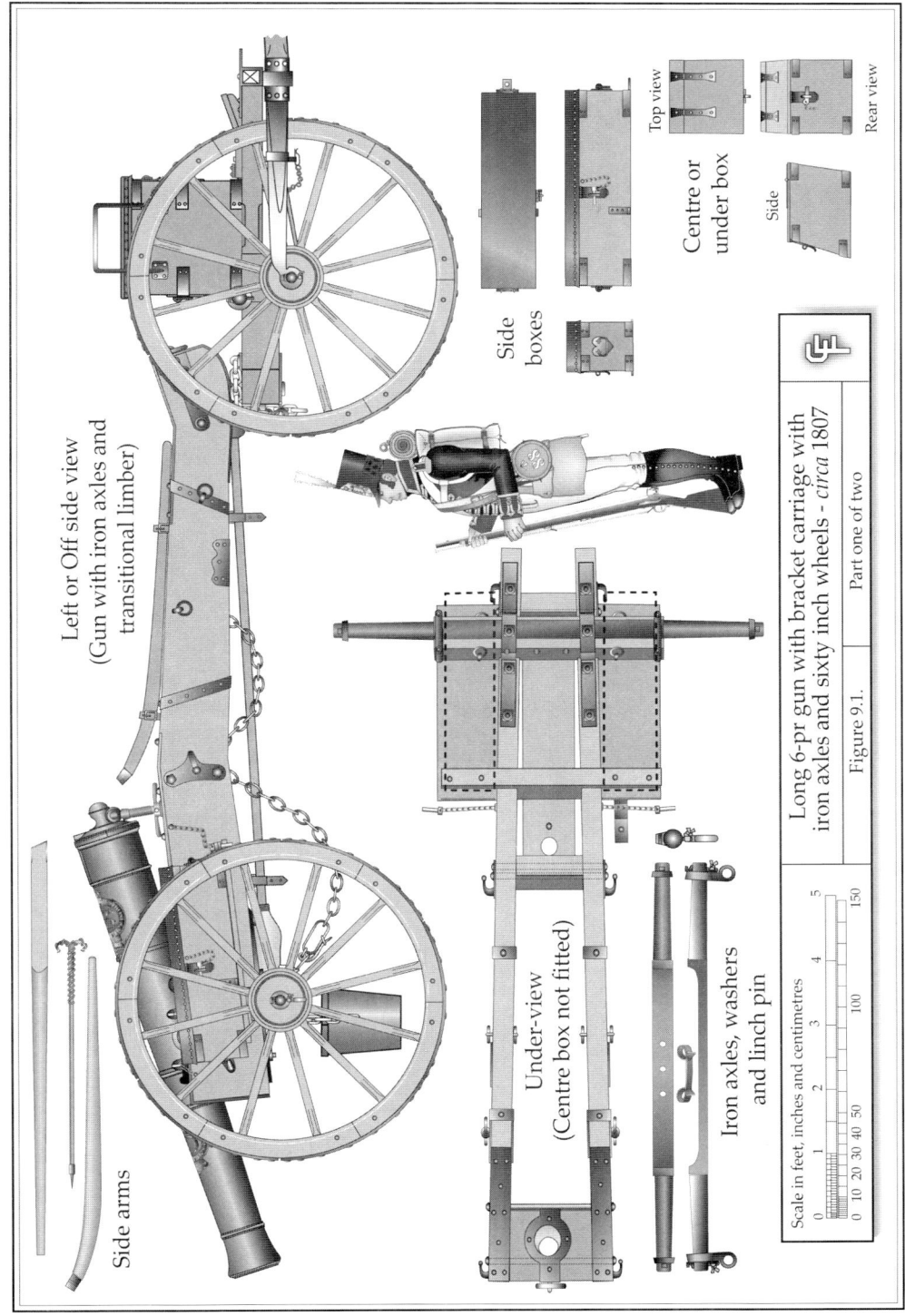

Side boxes

Top view

Rear view

Centre or under box

Side

Left or Off side view
(Gun with iron axles and transitional limber)

Side arms

Under-view
(Centre box not fitted)

Iron axles, washers
and linch pin

Scale in feet, inches and centimetres

Long 6-pr gun with bracket carriage with
iron axles and sixty inch wheels - *circa* 1807

Figure 9.1.

Part one of two

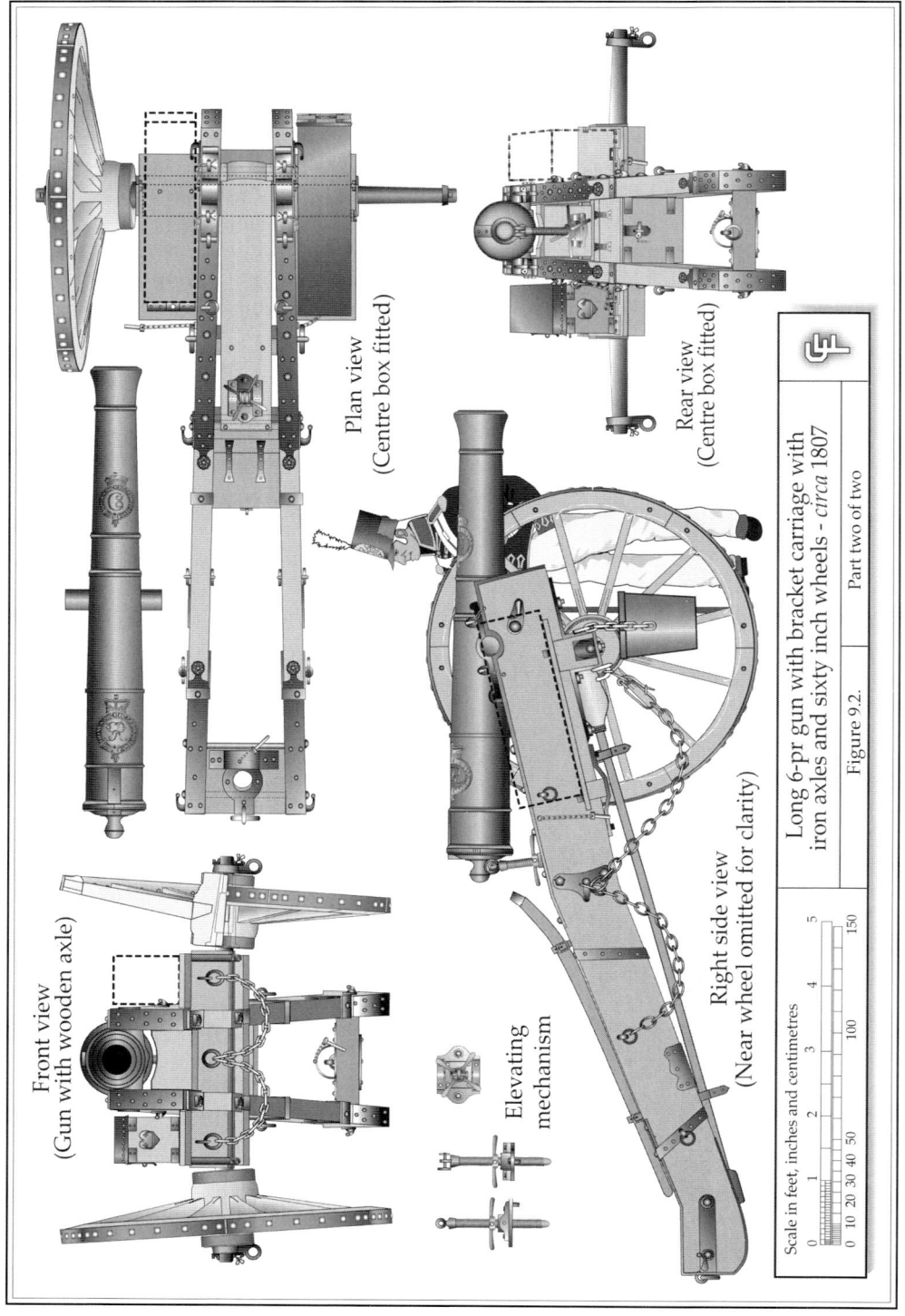

Plan view
(Centre box fitted)

Rear view
(Centre box fitted)

Front view
(Gun with wooden axle)

Elevating
mechanism

Right side view
(Near wheel omitted for clarity)

Long 6-pr gun with bracket carriage with
iron axles and sixty inch wheels - *circa* 1807

Figure 9.2.   Part two of two

Scale in feet, inches and centimetres

0   1   2   3   4   5
0 10 20 30 40 50   100   150

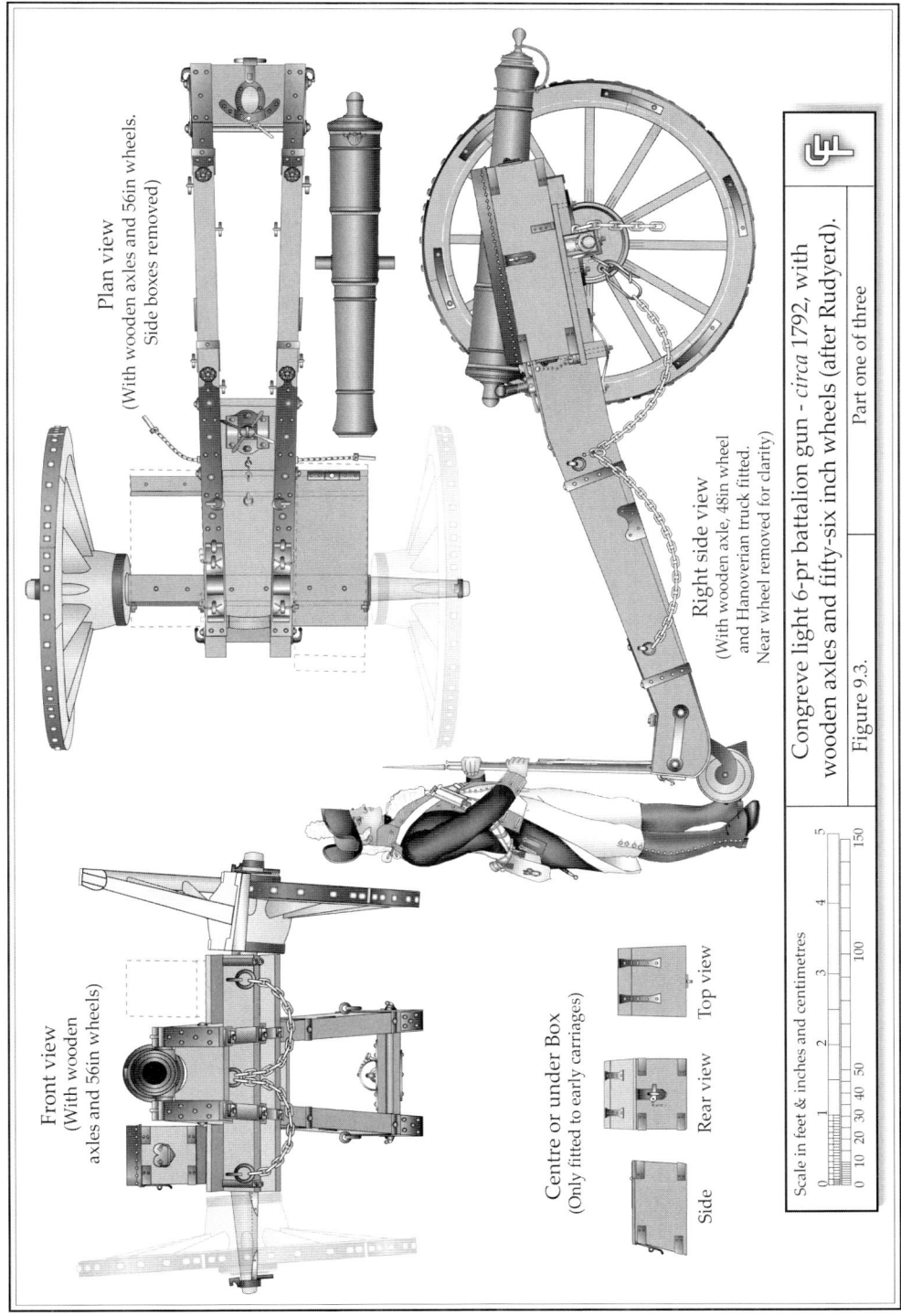

Plan view
(With wooden axles and 56in wheels.
Side boxes removed)

Front view
(With wooden
axles and 56in wheels)

Right side view
(With wooden axle, 48in wheel
and Hanoverian truck fitted.
Near wheel removed for clarity)

Centre or under Box
(Only fitted to early carriages)

Side

Rear view

Top view

Scale in feet & inches and centimetres

Congreve light 6-pr battalion gun - *circa* 1792, with
wooden axles and fifty-six inch wheels (after Rudyerd).

Figure 9.3.

Part one of three

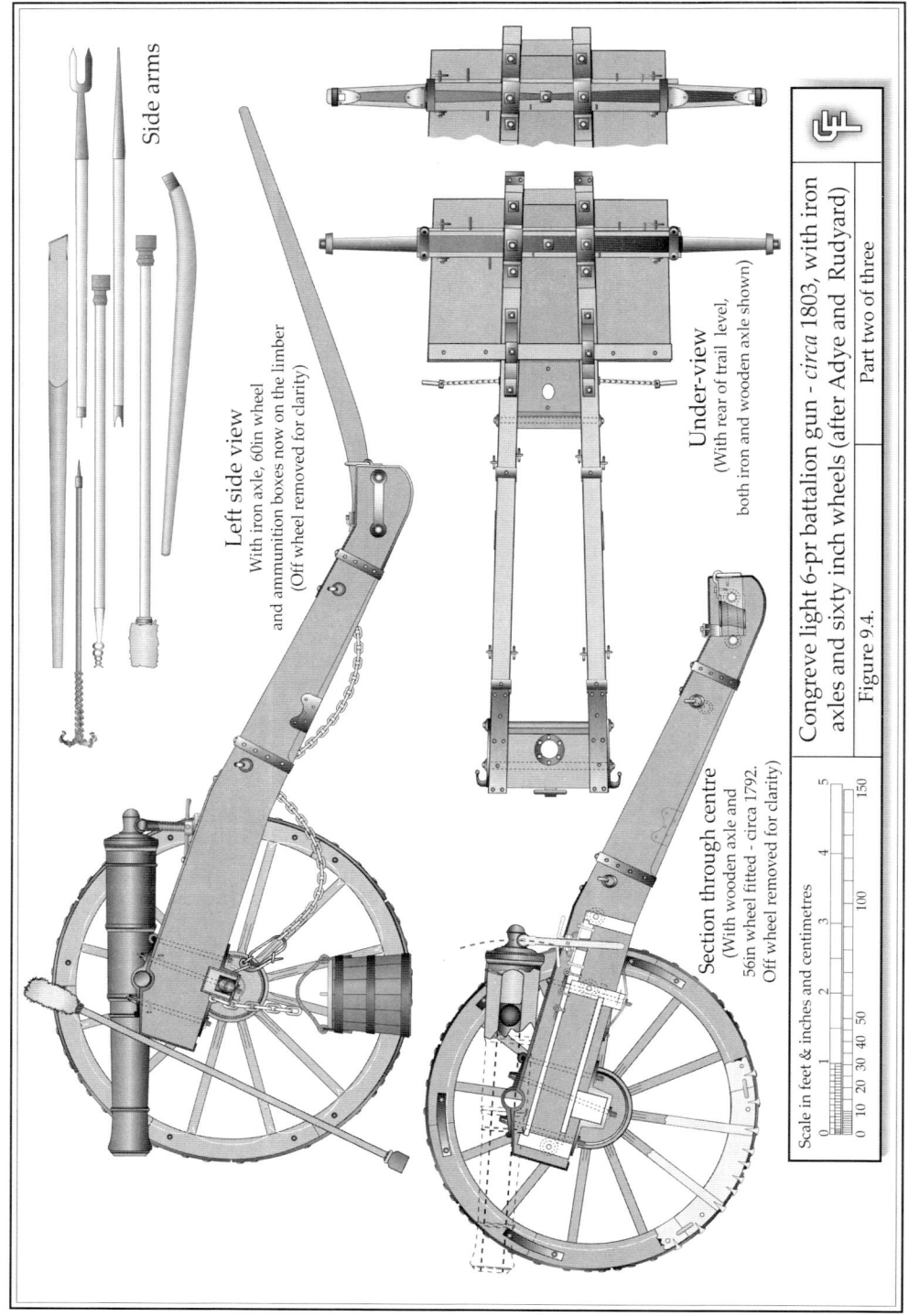

Side arms

Left side view
With iron axle, 60in wheel
and ammunition boxes now on the limber
(Off wheel removed for clarity)

Under-view
(With rear of trail level,
both iron and wooden axle shown)

Section through centre
(With wooden axle and
56in wheel fitted - circa 1792.
Off wheel removed for clarity)

Scale in feet & inches and centimetres

Congreve light 6-pr battalion gun - *circa* 1803, with iron
axles and sixty inch wheels (after Adye and Rudyard)

Part two of three

Figure 9.4.

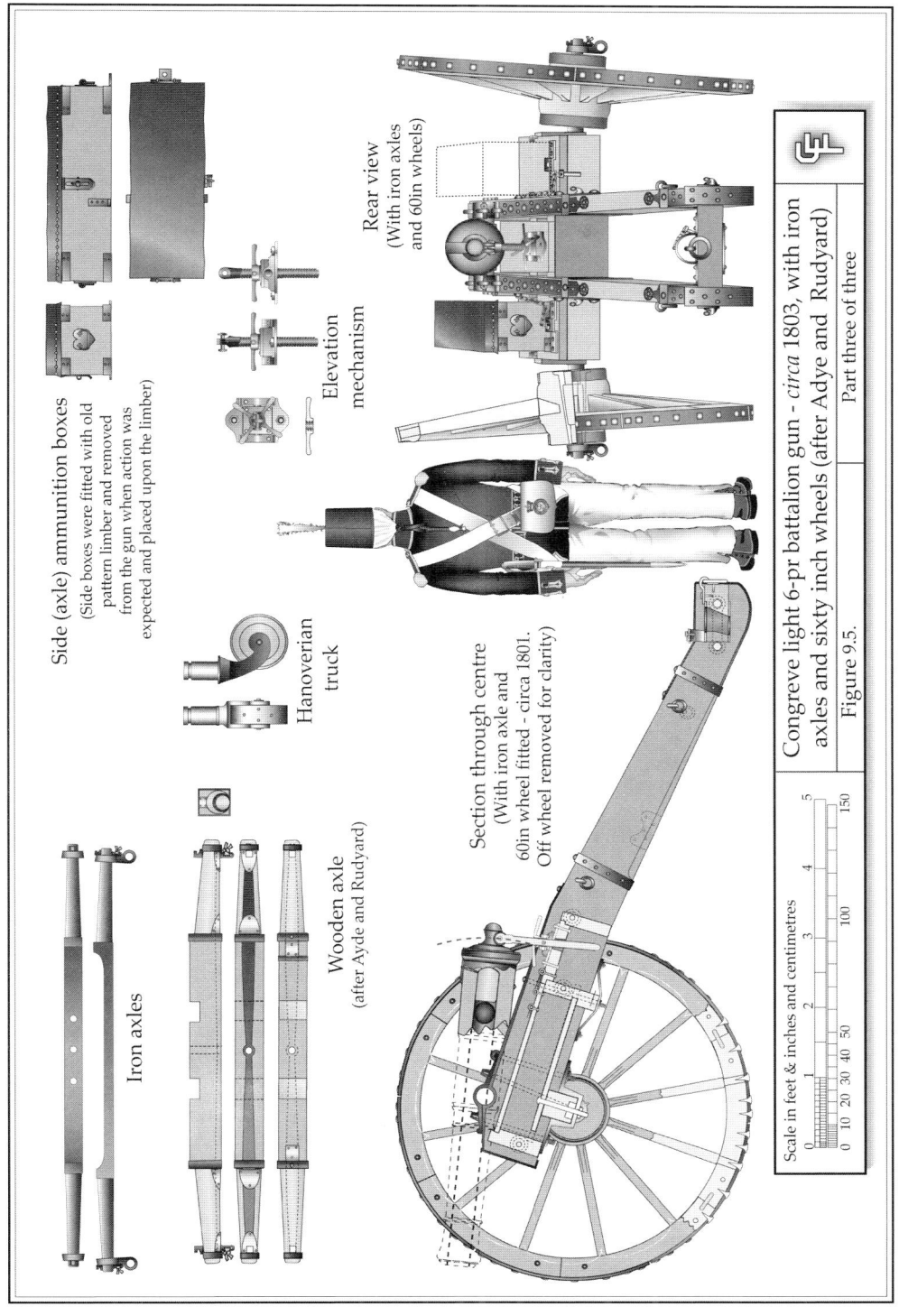

Side (axle) ammunition boxes
(Side boxes were fitted with old pattern limber and removed from the gun when action was expected and placed upon the limber)

Rear view
(With iron axles and 60in wheels)

Elevation mechanism

Hanoverian truck

Iron axles

Wooden axle
(after Ayde and Rudyard)

Section through centre
(With iron axle and 60in wheel fitted - circa 1801. Off wheel removed for clarity)

Congreve light 6-pr battalion gun - *circa* 1803, with iron axles and sixty inch wheels (after Adye and Rudyard)

Part three of three

Figure 9.5.

Scale in feet & inches and centimetres

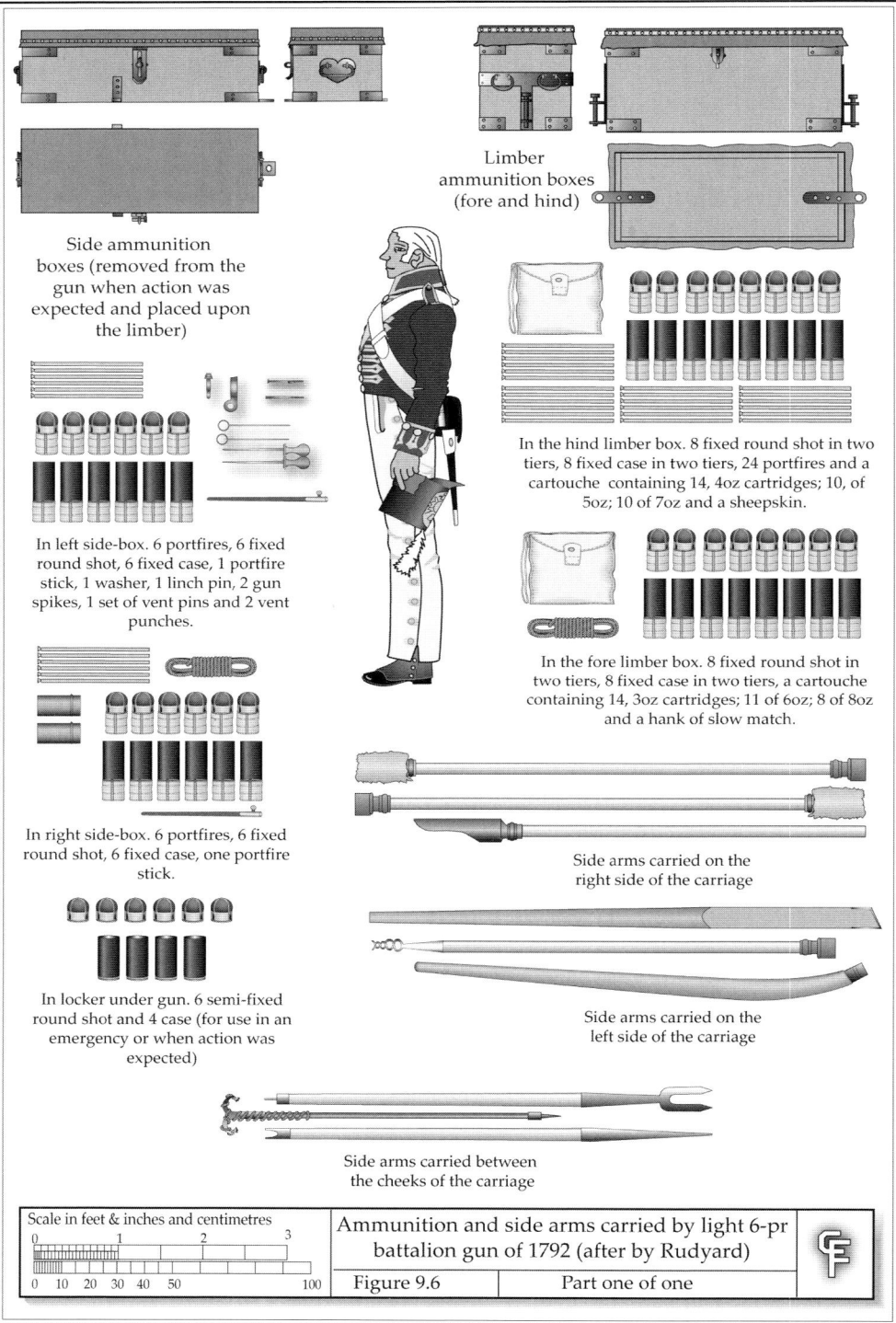

Limber
ammunition boxes
(fore and hind)

Side ammunition
boxes (removed from the
gun when action was
expected and placed upon
the limber)

In the hind limber box. 8 fixed round shot in two
tiers, 8 fixed case in two tiers, 24 portfires and a
cartouche containing 14, 4oz cartridges; 10, of
5oz; 10 of 7oz and a sheepskin.

In left side-box. 6 portfires, 6 fixed
round shot, 6 fixed case, 1 portfire
stick, 1 washer, 1 linch pin, 2 gun
spikes, 1 set of vent pins and 2 vent
punches.

In the fore limber box. 8 fixed round shot in
two tiers, 8 fixed case in two tiers, a cartouche
containing 14, 3oz cartridges; 11 of 6oz; 8 of 8oz
and a hank of slow match.

In right side-box. 6 portfires, 6 fixed
round shot, 6 fixed case, one portfire
stick.

Side arms carried on the
right side of the carriage

In locker under gun. 6 semi-fixed
round shot and 4 case (for use in an
emergency or when action was
expected)

Side arms carried on the
left side of the carriage

Side arms carried between
the cheeks of the carriage

Scale in feet & inches and centimetres

0		1		2		3

0	10	20	30	40	50		100

Ammunition and side arms carried by light 6-pr
battalion gun of 1792 (after by Rudyard)

Figure 9.6	Part one of one

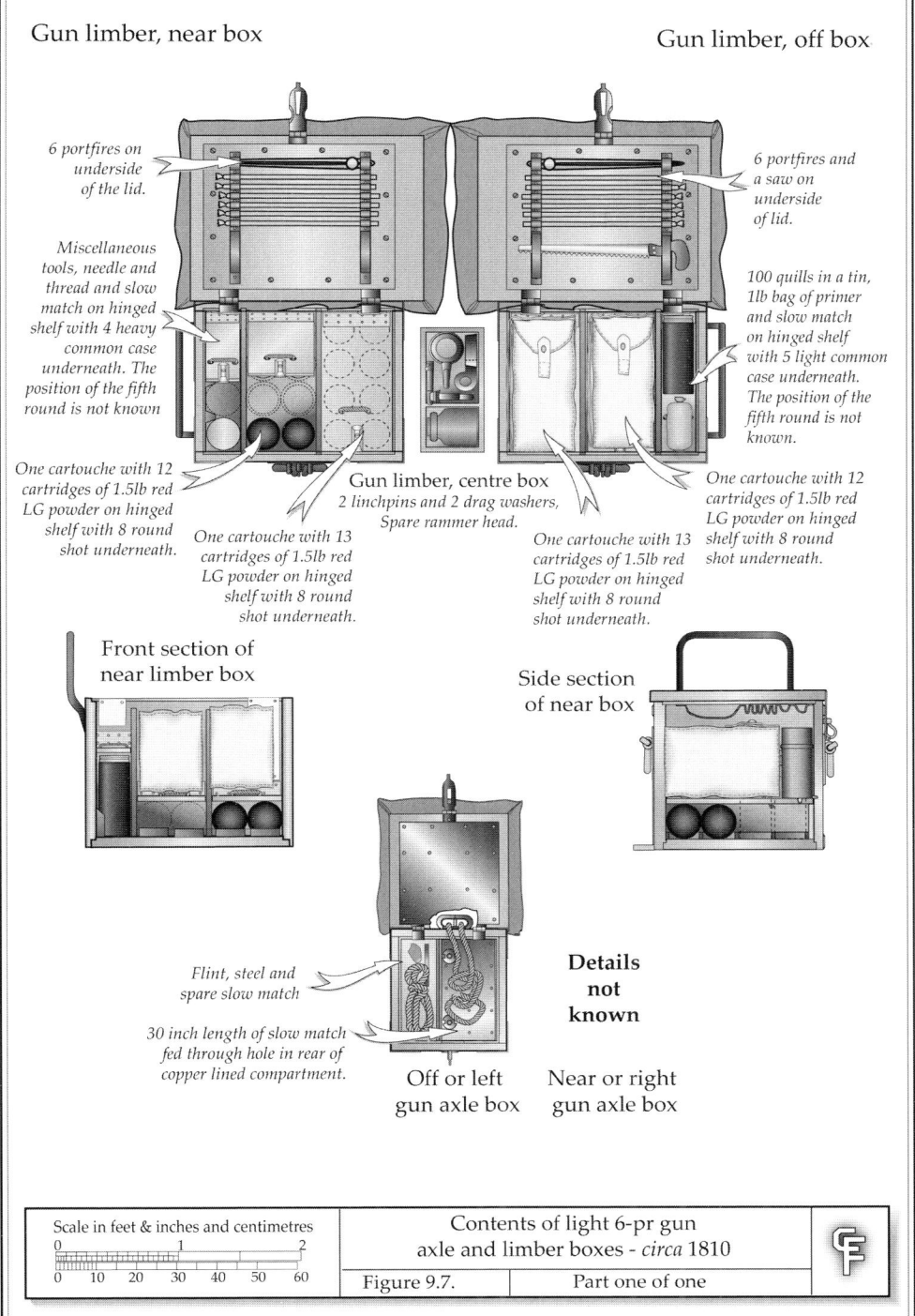

Gun limber, near box

Gun limber, off box

6 portfires on underside of the lid.

6 portfires and a saw on underside of lid.

Miscellaneous tools, needle and thread and slow match on hinged shelf with 4 heavy common case underneath. The position of the fifth round is not known

100 quills in a tin, 1lb bag of primer and slow match on hinged shelf with 5 light common case underneath. The position of the fifth round is not known.

One cartouche with 12 cartridges of 1.5lb red LG powder on hinged shelf with 8 round shot underneath.

Gun limber, centre box
2 linchpins and 2 drag washers, Spare rammer head.

One cartouche with 13 cartridges of 1.5lb red LG powder on hinged shelf with 8 round shot underneath.

One cartouche with 13 cartridges of 1.5lb red LG powder on hinged shelf with 8 round shot underneath.

One cartouche with 12 cartridges of 1.5lb red LG powder on hinged shelf with 8 round shot underneath.

Front section of near limber box

Side section of near box

Flint, steel and spare slow match

30 inch length of slow match fed through hole in rear of copper lined compartment.

Details not known

Off or left gun axle box

Near or right gun axle box

Scale in feet & inches and centimetres
0   1   2
0 10 20 30 40 50 60

Contents of light 6-pr gun axle and limber boxes - *circa* 1810

Figure 9.7.

Part one of one

The equipment carried with each gun was extensive, but as they usually operated with limited support in the battalion role, it is understandable. The guns were advanced and retired by hand as well as by horse and a complex series of drills was established to ensure they operated to the best effect. The drag ropes were often manned by infantry when gunners were in short supply and the Hanoverian truck was used to aid mobility.

In the original design, each side box carried six round shot and six common case with fixed charges and bottoms, six portfires and one portfire stick. The centre locker under the gun carried a hammer and rope; it was also used to carry four case and six round shot, but only when action was expected. The side arms carried on the right side of the gun were two sponges and a ladle. On the left side were a straight traversing handspike, a crooked traversing handspike and a wad-hook. Between the cheeks were two fork levers strapped to the right cheek and on the left cheek the linstock. A set of drag ropes was also carried under the breech of the gun or on the limber. A bucket was carried on the breast transom. This was the arrangement recorded in 1777, but with the introduction of the new pattern limber the disposition will have changed.

It is clear that this arrangement dates to the period before the introduction of the transitional limber when the gun was equipped with side boxes to carry the ready use ammunition and stores. Later with the new limber, the disposition of the ammunition would have been similar to that of the block trail limber. The ammunition carried on the gun and limber would probably have varied to suit the expected engagement, but as these guns were invariably employed in the battalion role, the type of ammunition would not have changed by much. Those guns deployed after 1803 may have been supplied with spherical case, but there are no records to support this. The details of the dimensions of the piece are given in Table B.1, the performance records for this piece in Tables C.4 and C.5 and the ammunition carried at first line is given in Table D.3. The weights of the equipment are given in Table E.2, all at the end of Part Two.

Belford and Blomefield Light 6-pr of 5ft
(see colour plates 1 to 8)

This piece was designed by General William Belford as early as 1757 and was subsequently widely used. It weighed 5.5cwt (616lb), was 5 feet long, some 16 calibres. It had a bore of 3.668 inches, a shot diameter of 3.5 inches and a windage of 0.118 inches. In normal use, the gun fired a 1.5lb charge, but for spherical case this was initially reduced to 12 ounces with a separator charge of 2.5 ounces. It can be distinguished from the Blomefield version in that it has an ogee to the front of the first reinforcement ring with a shorter chase and longer muzzle. This was the piece selected to equip the horse artillery, but it is clear from surviving equipments that pieces by Blomefield were also used. These were very similar to the Belford 6-pr, but more easily distinguished by the typical profile with a lack of an ogee on the first reinforcement ring and the shorter muzzle. These pieces were in use at the same time and were considered interchangeable; the Blomefield piece is mounted on the two surviving gun carriages made in 1810 and now in the Tøjhusmuseet, Copenhagen. The dimensions of the surviving Blomefield pieces as taken in 1813 are given in Chapter 14 and the later manufacturing figures are given in Table B.2 of Appendix B at the end of Part Two.[9]

The 6-pr gun for the horse artillery was equipped with the block trail carriage and field equipment limber from 1793, and this combination proved so successful that by the end of the Napoleonic War nearly half the horse artillery were still equipped with this gun and it continued in used until well after the period. The gun, carriage and limber had a rated weight behind the team, of 27.25cwt and six horses were required for the team (four for parades and peacetime establishments). The length between the axles of guns and limbers of 1810 has been measured at 9 feet, the length stored in a gun shed 22 feet 2 inches, while those made later are recorded as 8 feet 9 inches and 21 feet 10 inches respectively. The overall length in line of march, with team, was about 59 feet.[10] Adye records that the new gun complete with two men on the limber and 42 rounds of ammunition weighed just over 34cwt. The accompanying ammunition wagon, limber, with two men, one spare wheel, 2 spare shafts and 128 rounds weighed 39cwt.[11] Detailed, dimensioned views of a surviving block trail carriage and limber with a Blomefield 6-pr piece of 5 feet are given in Chapter 14. The weights of this equipment are included in Table E.4 of Appendix E at the end of Part Two.

The left axle box is intact and provides a clear understanding not hitherto possible. This box carries the slow match stored in a copper-lined compartment with two round shot in the left. The right axle box carried three round shot in the two outer compartments and spare vent tools, worm and sponge head in the centre,[12] but the right axle boxes of the original guns had been modified by the Hanoverian Artillery by the time of the drawings in 1813, and it is not possible to confirm what they carried. Adye recorded in 1801 that the limber for the light 6-pr of the horse artillery carried 32 round shot and 16 case, a further 97 round shot and 13 case were carried in the ammunition wagon. A further supply, carried at second line in the reserve wagons, was given for each gun as 34 case fixed to bottoms, 94 round shot, 190 cartridges, 280 quills or tubes and 31 portfires.[13]

The Tøjhusmuseet limbers show that in 1813 – the date the surviving limbers were measured and drawn – each box carried 16 round shot and 4 common case, with the same for the ammunition wagon limber (see Figure 9.7). In 1813 Adye wrote that the new limbers for the brigade light 6-pr carried 180 rounds of ammunition and noted they contained eight round shot in the right axle box and the number of cartridges given in his lists allow for this. He also claimed that the gun limber boxes carried five case shot but the wagon limber still carried four. It seems probable that this may be an error unless the boxes on the gun limber were no longer common, as it does not match with the surviving boxes. Such an arrangement is clearly possible if eight round shot was stacked in two tiers, perhaps the boxes were changed after 1810, but by 1822 they were back to the old pattern. The wagon itself carried a further 90 rounds, making 180 rounds in all.[14] The records from the Peninsula show a greater proportion of spherical case at the gun limber and on the wagon than that accorded by Adye.[15]

In addition to the main ammunition, each limber box also carried two cartouches, 25 gun cartridges, a bag of priming powder, 5 portfires, a hank of slow match, a hank of seizing line, wads, quills and associated ancillaries, etc. After the war the right axle box was modified to carry three round shot and three case shot, but the cartridges were still carried in the limber boxes.[16] Details of the ammunition carried are included in Tables D.4 and D.5 of Appendix D at the end of Part Two.

Performance

The effective percentage of hits for a light 6-pr gun are given thus; at 520 yards 82%, 950 yards 40% and at 1,200 yards 17%. The generic range limits were a maximum of 1,200–1,500 yards, out to an extreme of 1,700 yards; the maximum effective range for shot was 800–900 yards and 350–400 yards for canister. Adye gives the point blank range of the light 6-pr gun to first graze as 200 yards. This range increased by 100 yards for each quarter degree, up to one degree. Between one and three degrees the range increased by 50 yards for each quarter degree.

It must be noted that Congreve quoted the range to first graze at point blank as 312 yards, while at one degree it was 740 yards; at two degrees it was 850 yards and at three degrees 1,492 yards. He also quotes that at 100 yards the shot would penetrate 9.5 feet into a clay bank. With case shot at one degree and case of seventy-two 1.25 ounce shot, at 300 yards 27 shot hit the target; at 1.5 degrees at 400 yards, 21 shot hit the target; at two degrees and 500 yards, 11 shot hit the target.[17] In general terms with a charge of 1lb 8oz the light 6-pr at point blank ranged 200 yards, each quarter degree up to one degree, or the line of metal, increased the range by a further 100 yards. Each further quarter degree to three degrees increased the range by a further 50 yards. The performance of these early battalion guns is shown in Tables C.6, C.7, C.8 and C.9 of Appendix C at the end of Part Two.[18]

The Blomefield Heavy 6-pr Gun

Some artillery units, both foot and horse, were equipped with the heavy 6-pr gun which continued in service until the Crimean period. This was not the long 6-pr of 7 feet as shown by Hughes,[19] but a heavy 6-pr designed by Blomefield and was 15% larger overall. It weighed 8.75cwt (980lb); it was 5 feet 2.356 inches long, 17 calibres. It had a bore of 3.668 inches, a shot diameter of some 3.5 inches and a windage of some 0.118 inches. In normal use, the gun fired a 2lb charge of red large-grain powder, but for spherical case this was initially reduced to 12 ounces with a separator charge of 2.5 ounces. The later manufacturing figures are given as distances from the rear of the base ring and are shown in Table B.3 of Appendix B at the end of Part Two.[20]

The conversion to block trail carriages and new limbers had started in January 1794.[21] This is further confirmed, as they saw service in the Peninsula and Mercer recalled that his troop were due to be re-equipped with them on arrival in Europe before the Waterloo Campaign – in the event he was given 9-prs.[22] The carriage is to all intents similar to that for the light 6-pr but stronger and slightly larger to accommodate the larger piece and maintain the 22 degree angle on the trail. The distance between the brackets was wider and the cushion of the trail would be further to the rear. In 1813 both Ramsay's and Webber Smith's Troops were equipped with two heavy 6-prs, three light 6-prs and one light 5.5-inch howitzer. The brigades of Lawson and Brandreth also had heavy 6-prs.[23] The weights for the heavy 6-pr equipment are given in Table E.5 of Appendix E at the end of Part Two.

The ammunition carried generally corresponds to that of the light 6-pr, but the cartridges were longer to contain the extra 8 ounces of powder. In 1801, Adye noted that the heavy 6-pr carried 36 round shot and 14 case on the limber and the remaining 120 rounds in one wagon.[24] The total carried for each gun was given as 30 case fixed to bottoms, 120 round shot, 150 cartridges, 178 quills or tubes and 18 portfires.[25]

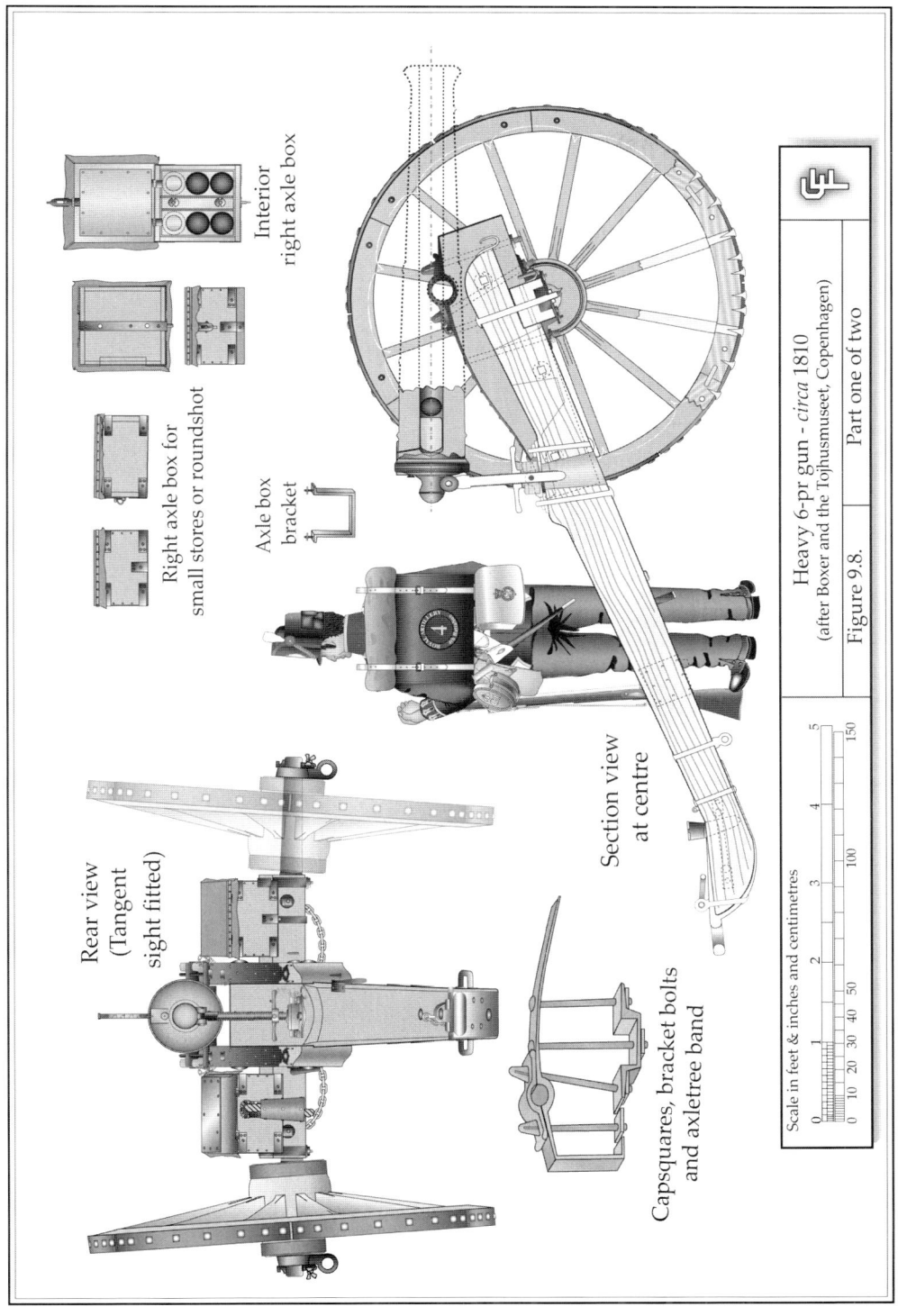

Interior right axle box

Right axle box for small stores or roundshot

Axle box bracket

Rear view (Tangent sight fitted)

Section view at centre

Capsquares, bracket bolts and axletree band

Scale in feet & inches and centimetres

Heavy 6-pr gun - *circa* 1810
(after Boxer and the Tøjhusmuseet, Copenhagen)

Figure 9.8.   Part one of two

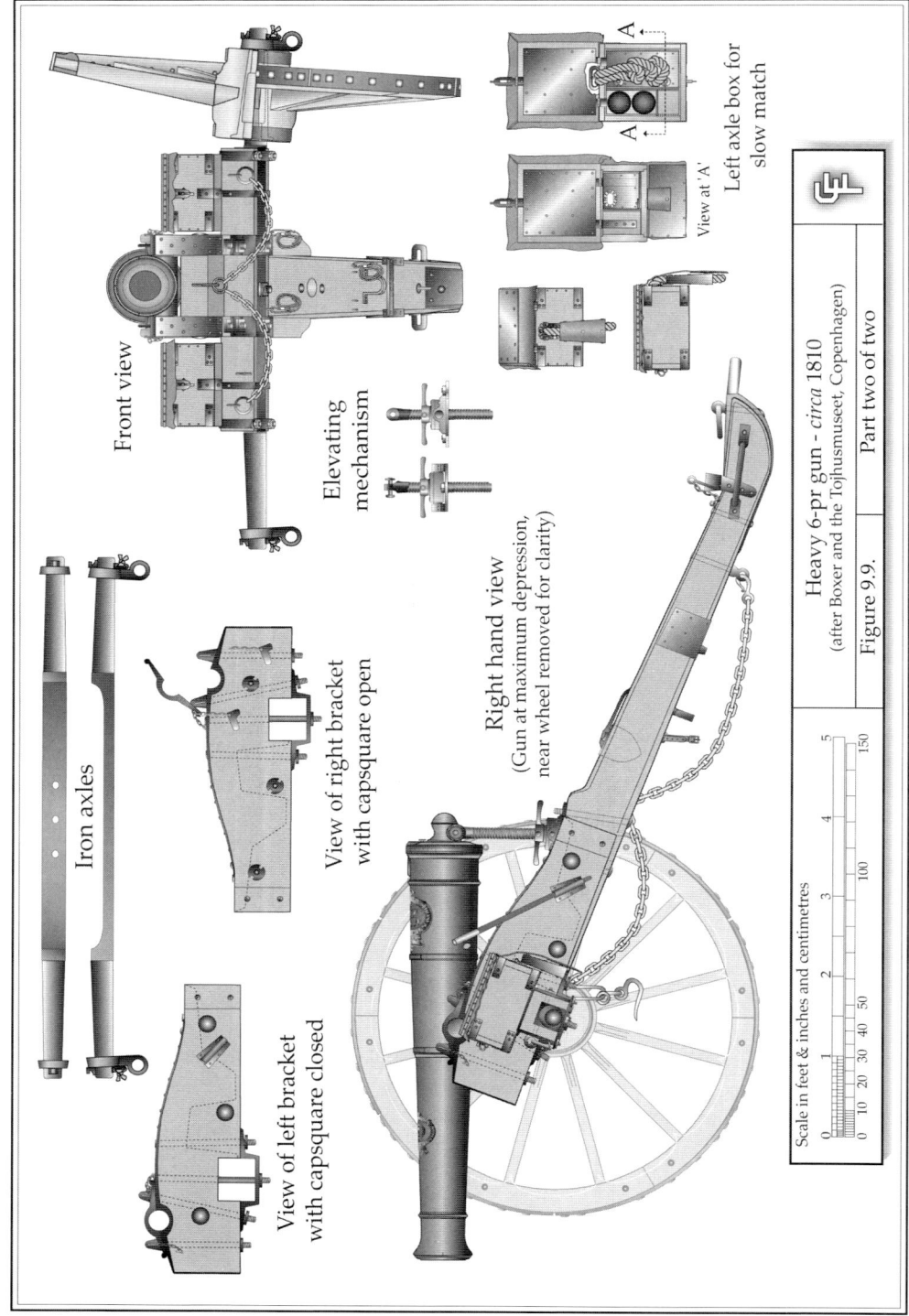

Front view

Left axle box for
slow match

View at 'A'

Elevating
mechanism

Iron axles

View of right bracket
with capsquare open

View of left bracket
with capsquare closed

Right hand view
(Gun at maximum depression,
near wheel removed for clarity)

Heavy 6-pr gun - *circa* 1810
(after Boxer and the Tøjhusmuseet, Copenhagen)

Part two of two

Figure 9.9.

Scale in feet & inches and centimetres

Gun limber, near box

Gun limber, off box

6 portfires on
underside
of the lid.

6 portfires and
a saw on
underside
of lid.

Miscellaneous
tools and slow
match on hinged
shelf with 5 light,
common case
underneath.

Priming powder,
100 quills in
container and
slow match on
hinged shelf with
5 heavy, common
case underneath.

5 round shot on
hinged shelf with
5 round shot
underneath.

5 round shot on
hinged shelf with
5 round shot
underneath.

One cartouche with
25, 2lb cartridges on
hinged shelf with 10
round shot underneath.

Limber, centre box
2 linchpins and 2 drag washers,
Spare rammer head.

One cartouche with 25, 2lb
cartridges on hinged shelf
with 10 round shot

Front section of
near limber box

Side section
of off box

Flint, steel and
two roundshot

Two compartments
with 3 roundshot under
shelves in each

30 inch length of slow match
fed through hole in rear of
copper lined compartment.

Vent bit, worm, 2 vent pins,
spare thumbstall

Off or left
gun axle box

Near or right
gun axle box

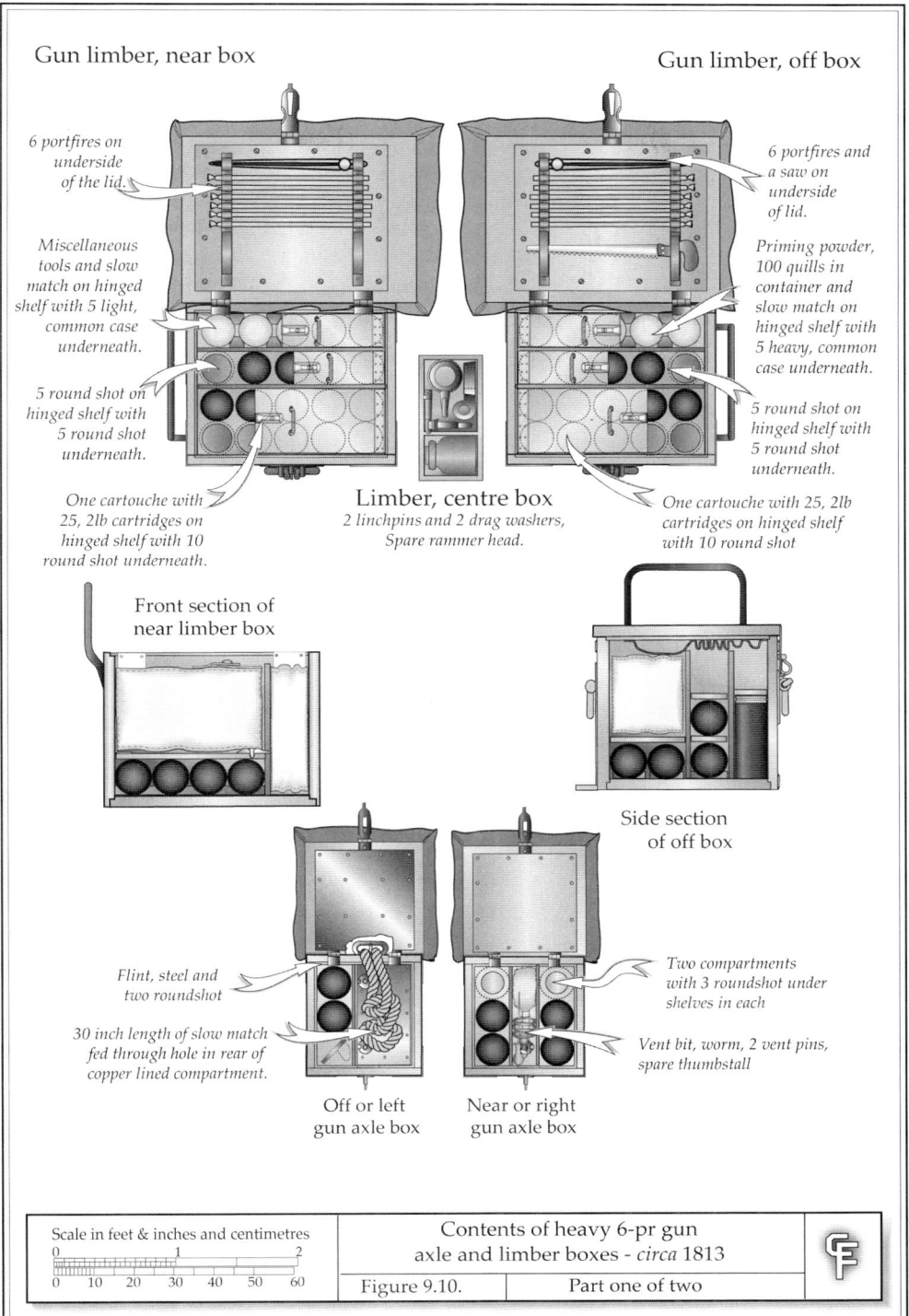

Scale in feet & inches and centimetres	Contents of heavy 6-pr gun axle and limber boxes - *circa* 1813	
0 1 2 0 10 20 30 40 50 60		
	Figure 9.10.	Part one of two

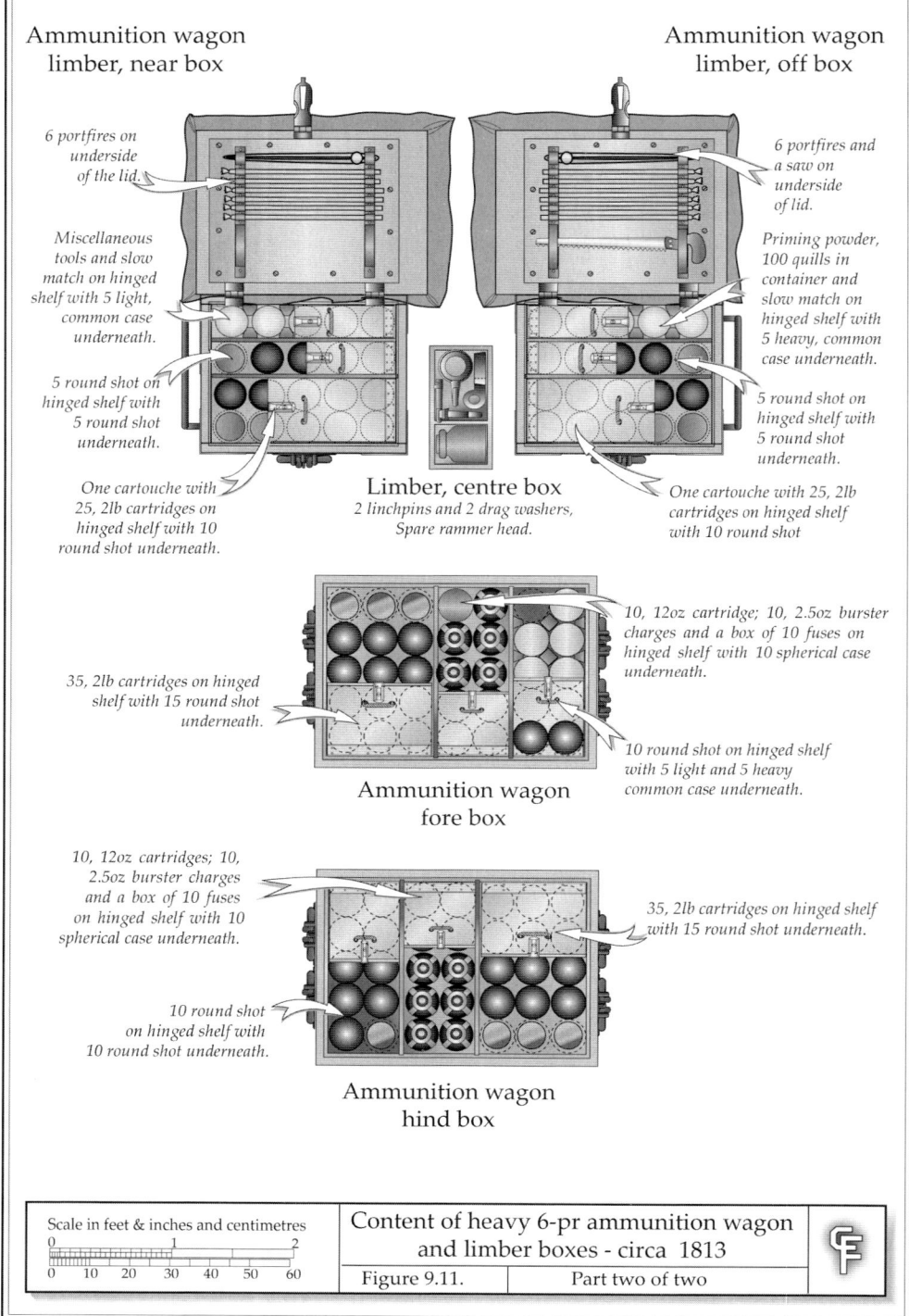

Ammunition wagon limber, near box

6 portfires on underside of the lid.

Miscellaneous tools and slow match on hinged shelf with 5 light, common case underneath.

5 round shot on hinged shelf with 5 round shot underneath.

One cartouche with 25, 2lb cartridges on hinged shelf with 10 round shot underneath.

Ammunition wagon limber, off box

6 portfires and a saw on underside of lid.

Priming powder, 100 quills in container and slow match on hinged shelf with 5 heavy, common case underneath.

5 round shot on hinged shelf with 5 round shot underneath.

One cartouche with 25, 2lb cartridges on hinged shelf with 10 round shot

Limber, centre box
2 linchpins and 2 drag washers, Spare rammer head.

35, 2lb cartridges on hinged shelf with 15 round shot underneath.

10, 12oz cartridge; 10, 2.5oz burster charges and a box of 10 fuses on hinged shelf with 10 spherical case underneath.

10 round shot on hinged shelf with 5 light and 5 heavy common case underneath.

Ammunition wagon fore box

10, 12oz cartridges; 10, 2.5oz burster charges and a box of 10 fuses on hinged shelf with 10 spherical case underneath.

10 round shot on hinged shelf with 10 round shot underneath.

35, 2lb cartridges on hinged shelf with 15 round shot underneath.

Ammunition wagon hind box

Scale in feet & inches and centimetres

Content of heavy 6-pr ammunition wagon and limber boxes - circa 1813

Figure 9.11.   Part two of two

In his 5th edition of 1810, Adye noted that the new style of limbers and ammunition wagons for the brigade heavy 6-pr carried 180 rounds of ammunition. The records from the Peninsula show a different allocation of ammunition with the spherical case available at the gun limber increased to 20, with 21 round shot and 9 common case. The limber for the ammunition wagons carried the same loading but the wagon only carried 66 round shot and 14 common case, a reduction of 20 rounds. Each troop or brigade was noted as having a further two spare wagons and limbers, the limbers carrying the standard loading but the wagons with just 80 rounds; 57 round shot, 19 spherical case and 4 common case.[26] Details of ammunition carried at first line, is given in Table D.6 and the performance in Tables C.10 and C.11 in Appendix C at the end of Part Two

Endnotes to Chapter 9

1. McConnell, 1988: pp. 42–5.
2. Hughes, 1969: p. 29.
3. Leslie, 1912: pp. 74, 75, 78.
4. WO 1/167, p. 227 dated 6 October 1792.
5. Caruana, 1980: pp. 6, 14.
6. Hughes, 1969: p. 29.
7. Graves, 1982: pp. 127–9; Caruana, 1982: p. 129; McConnell, 1988: pp. 42–5.
8. Hughes, 1969: p. 29, Caruana, 1977: p. 6.
9. Boxer, 1853: plate 21.
10. Nelson, 1972: p. 9.
11. Adye. 1801: p. 54.
12. Adye, 1813: p. 9.
13. Adye, 1801: p.10.
14. Ibid: p. 16 and surviving limber boxes of 1810 at Copenhagen.
15. Dickson, 1908: pp. 856–66
16. Lefroy, 1854: p. 23; Griffiths, 1839: pp. 156–7.
17. Caruana, 1980: p. 12.
18. Rudyerd, 1792: plate 44.
19. Hughes, 1996: p. 29.
20. Boxer, 1853: plate 21.
21. National Archive, WO 1/168: p. 70, dated 6 January 1794.
22. Mercer, 1870: p. 88.
23. Dickson, 1908: pp. 860, 1,048.
24. Adye, 1801: p. 14.
25. Adye, 1801: p. 10.
26. Dickson, 1908: p. 858.

CHAPTER 10

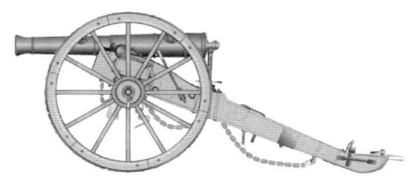

9-pr Field Equipments

9-pr Gun

The Belford 9-pr brass gun came into service with British artillery in 1807 to counter the heavier weight of the French 8-pr and 12-pr artillery. First used at the Siege of Copenhagen,[1] in the Peninsula they proved so successful that by the end of the Napoleonic period more than half the horse artillery and most of the field brigades were equipped them. The guns were introduced on block trail carriages from the start with the new pattern limbers and 60-inch wheels. As soon as availability permitted, the foot brigades were also supplied with them and at Waterloo, all the British brigades were so equipped. There is a suggestion that drawings exist showing a 9-pr mounted on a bracket trail but research has not provided any confirmation, though such may have been the case.

The 9-pr bronze piece was of Blomefield design and weighed 13.5cwt (1,512lb), it was 5ft 11.4in long, 17 calibres. It had a bore of 4.2 inches, a shot diameter of 4 inches and a windage of 0.2 inches; dolphins (handles) were not usually found on the bronze 9-pr gun of this period. In normal use, the gun fired a 3lb charge, but for spherical case this was initially reduced to 14 ounces with a separator charge of 3.5 ounces. The dimensions of the surviving Napoleonic pieces and the later manufacturing figures which closely tally are given below and are taken as distances from the rear of the base ring.[2] The dimensions of this piece are given in Table B.4 of Appendix B at the end of Part Two.

The block trail carriage was of similar design to that of the light 6-pr but generally larger, stronger and heavier to take the extra weight of the piece, the larger shot and heavier charge. It still maintained the 22-degree angle on the trail but was wider to accommodate the extra width of the piece and the brackets were longer to bring the elevating mechanism under the cascable. Extra reinforcement was provided by the addition of a central axletree support bolted through the trail and the axletree-bed and three bolts were used to secure the axletree brackets to the brackets of the carriage.[3] The limber was a standard item, but with larger ammunition boxes.

The 9-pr gun, carriage and limber had a weight, behind the team, of 38cwt and eight horses were required for the team (six for parades and peacetime establishments). Mercer notes that these guns were known as 'heavy drags' by the horse artillery,[4] and the weight of the 9-pr equipment is given in Table E.6 of Appendix E at the end of Part Two.

Ammunition

In 1813, Adye wrote that 116 rounds of ammunition were carried on the new-style limbers and ammunition wagons (16 in each of the four limber boxes and 26 in each of the two ammunition wagon boxes) and these figures match with the recorded returns.

Records from the Peninsula show that the ammunition allocated to the 9-pr made a greater use of spherical case than that indicated by Adye, and the ammunition boxes of the limbers must have been modified to accommodate this ammunition as it came with bottoms fitted. The standard limber box was some 16.75 inches from front to back, 21.5 inches wide and 16.5 inches deep. To accommodate the larger 9-pr ammunition the second platform board was reduced in size; this way the length of the limber ammunition box could be increased to 19 inches, but it was not possible to make the box wider or significantly deeper and the ammunition carried is always listed as permutations of 16 per box. The ammunition carried at first line is given in Tables D.7 and D.8 of Appendix D at the end of Part Two.

The ammunition allocation was later changed to increase the amount of spherical case available at the gun limber to 13, with 13 round shot and 6 common case; these numbers suggest that the round shot may have been carried in one limber box and the spherical case in the other. The ammunition wagon limber carried the usual identical loading, but the wagon now carried 44 round shot and 8 common case, still with a total of 84 rounds. Each of the two extra ammunitions wagons allocated to each troop or brigade carried the same limber lading but the wagon boxes now carried 38 round shot, 12 spherical case and 2 common case, again a permutation of 84 rounds.[5] At Waterloo, Mercer recalls that his guns had expended some 700 rounds and his ammunition was reduced to the 50 rounds carried on the limber.[6] Unfortunately, there are no records of any such ammunition distribution and all of the notes by Adye, Dickson, Spearman and Griffith show only 16 rounds for each limber box.[7] Mercer's statement is difficult to explain, as the limber boxes are not large enough to carry 25 rounds each. It may be that he was thinking back to his days with the 6-pr; if not the boxes on the limber must have been significantly deeper to carry the extra rounds and cartridges, particularly if spherical case was also carried in the limber boxes.

Performance

The effective percentage of hits for a 9-pr gun firing round shot are given thus; at 600 yards 87%, 950 yards 40% and at 1,300 yards 17%. The generic range limits were a maximum of 1,700 yards, but the maximum effective range for shot was 800-900 yards and 450 yards for canister. The recorded performance figures are given in Tables C.12 and C13 of Appendix C at the end of Part Two.

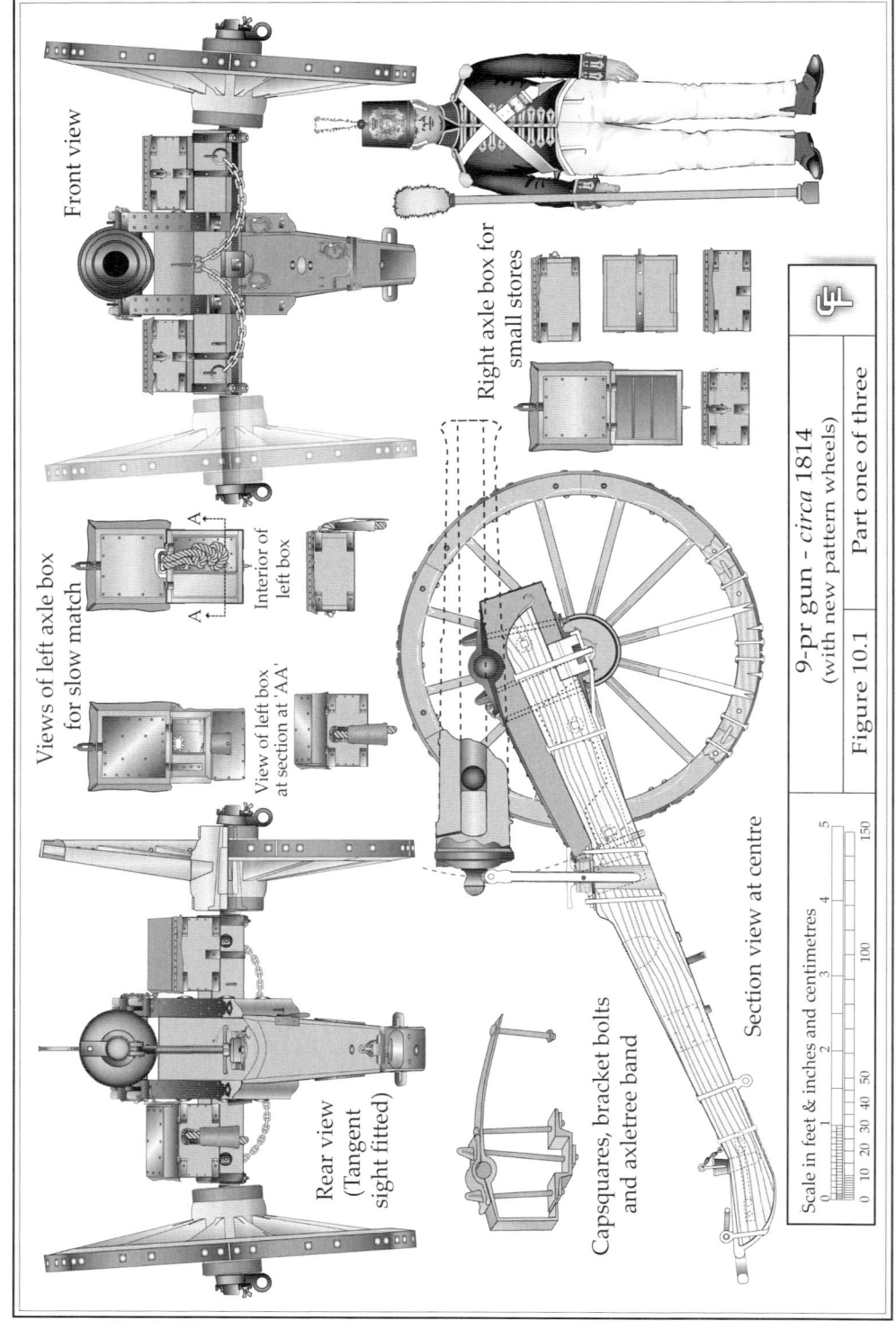

Front view

Views of left axle box
for slow match

Interior of
left box

View of left box
at section at 'AA'

Rear view
(Tangent
sight fitted)

Right axle box for
small stores

Capsquares, bracket bolts
and axletree band

Section view at centre

Scale in feet & inches and centimetres

9-pr gun - *circa* 1814
(with new pattern wheels)

Figure 10.1　　Part one of three

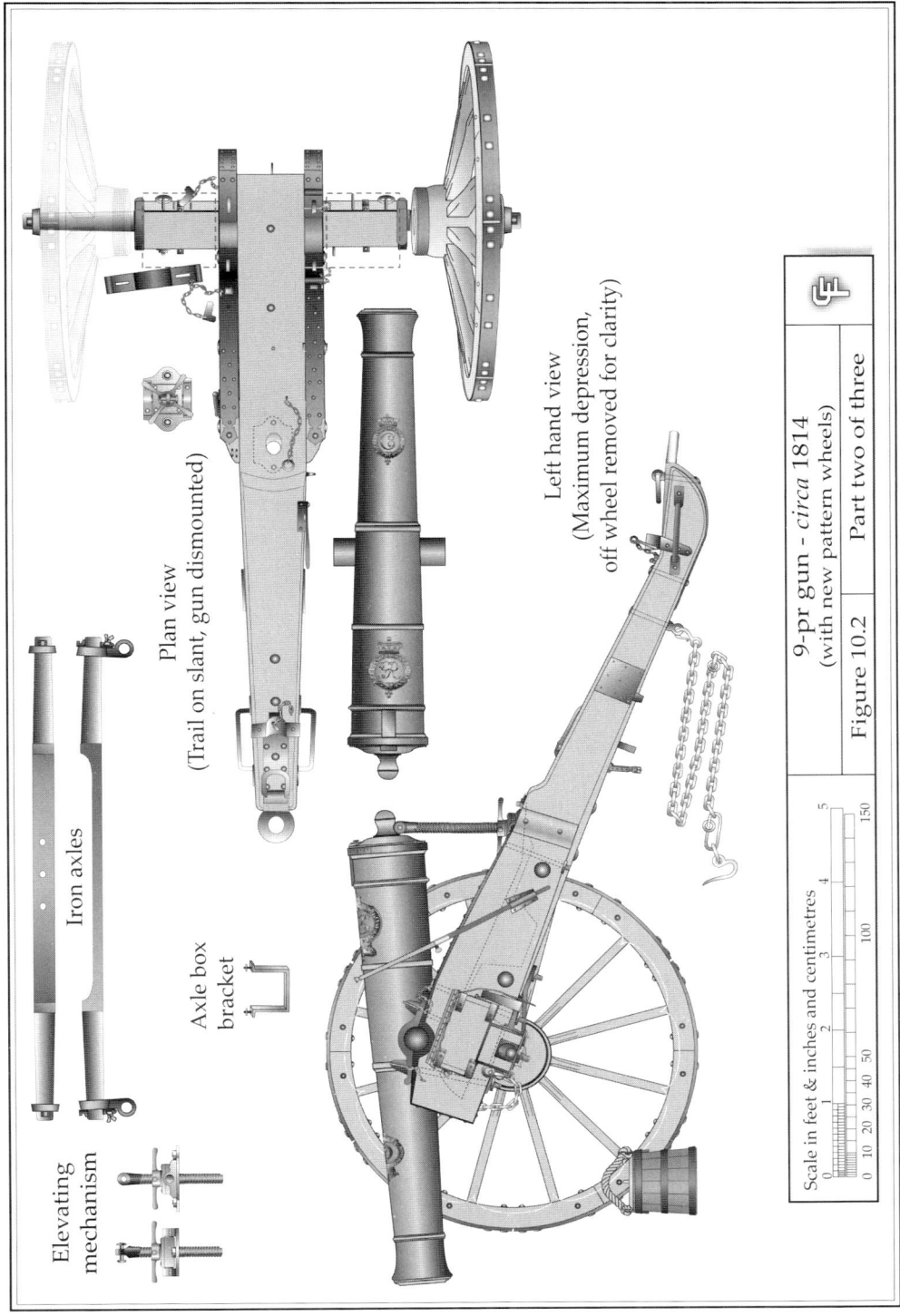

Plan view
(Trail on slant, gun dismounted)

Left hand view
(Maximum depression,
off wheel removed for clarity)

Iron axles

Axle box
bracket

Elevating
mechanism

Scale in feet & inches and centimetres

9-pr gun - *circa* 1814
(with new pattern wheels)

Figure 10.2   Part two of three

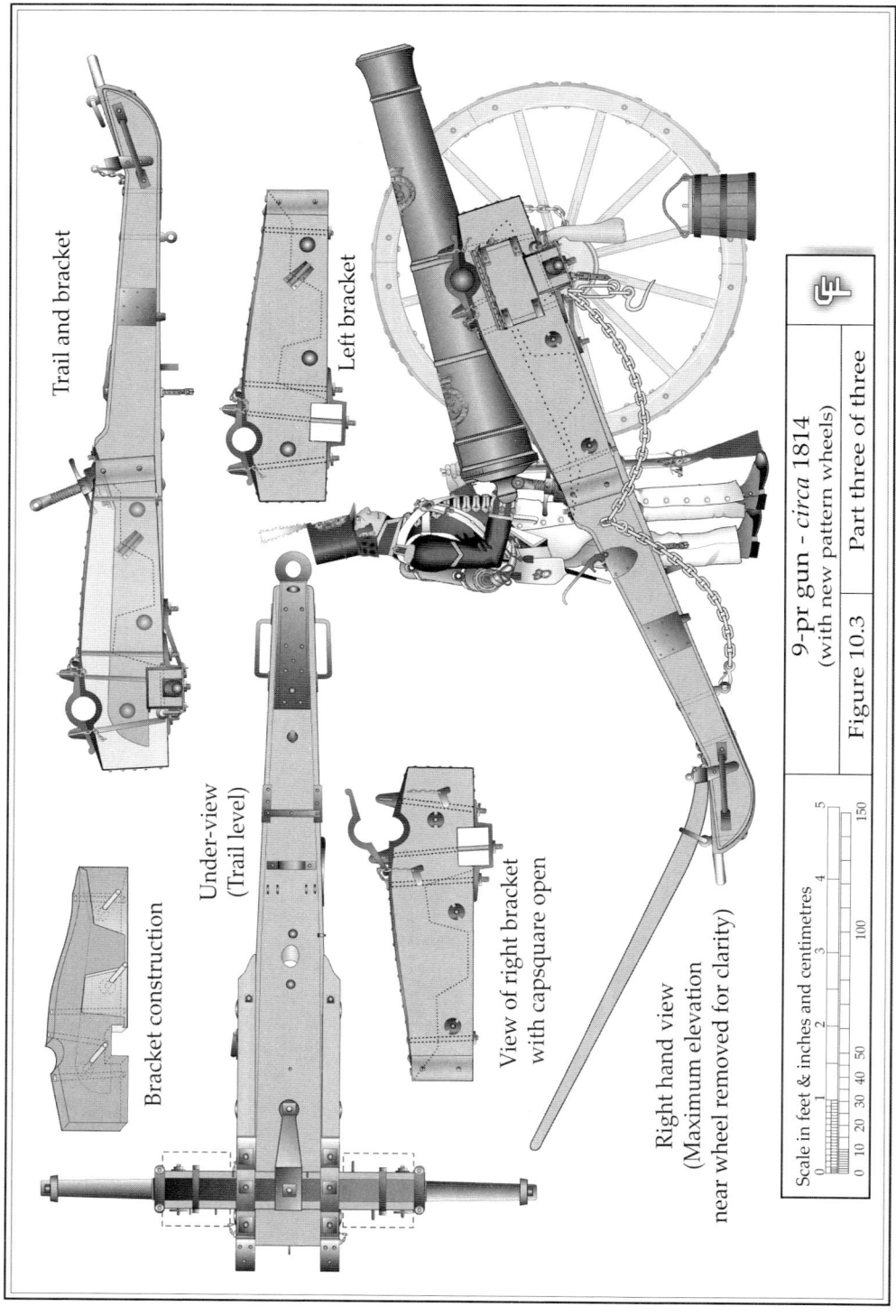

Trail and bracket

Left bracket

Bracket construction

Under-view
(Trail level)

View of right bracket
with capsquare open

Right hand view
(Maximum elevation
near wheel removed for clarity)

Scale in feet & inches and centimetres

9-pr gun - *circa* 1814
(with new pattern wheels)

Figure 10.3   Part three of three

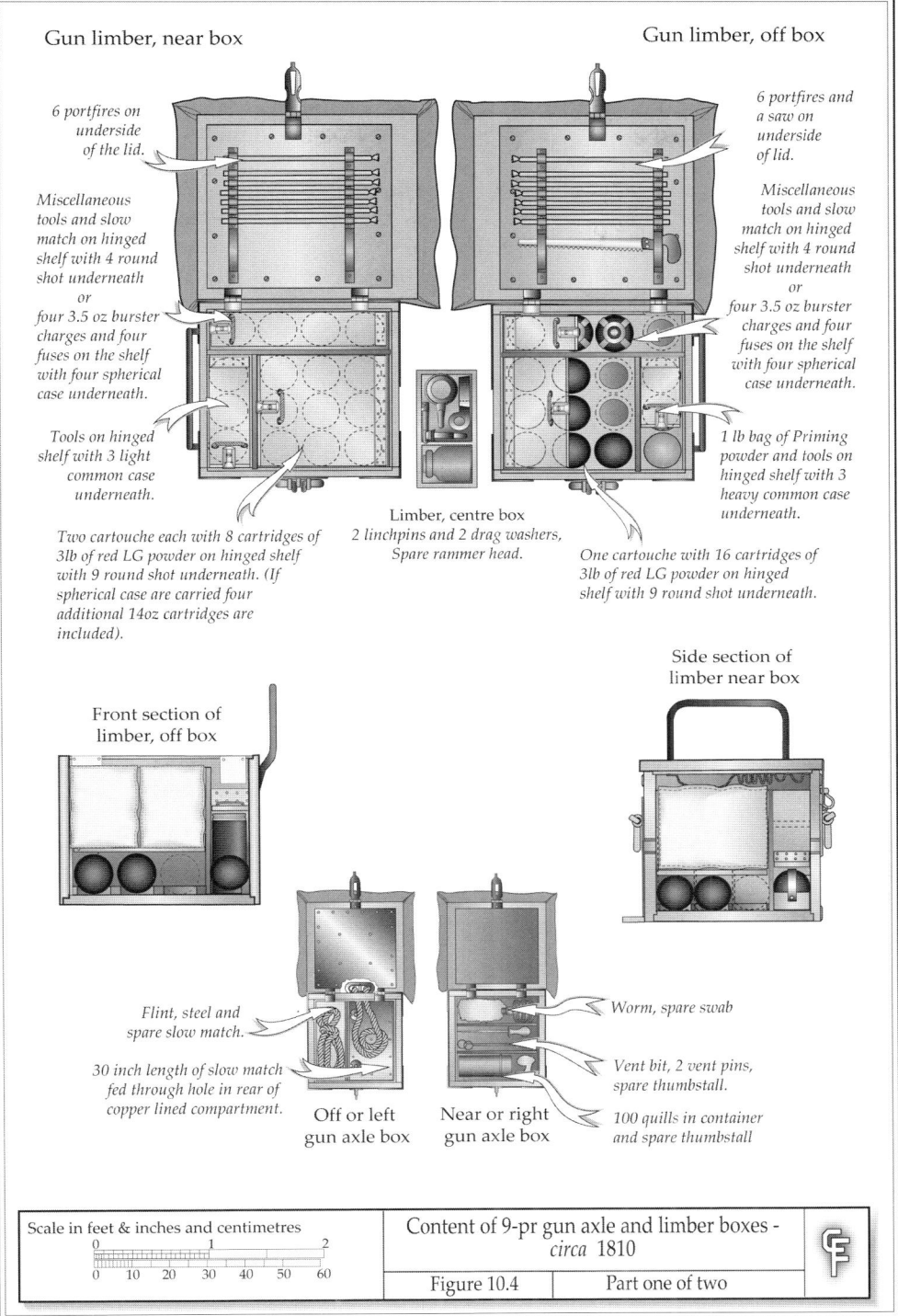

Gun limber, near box

Gun limber, off box

6 portfires on underside of the lid.

6 portfires and a saw on underside of lid.

Miscellaneous tools and slow match on hinged shelf with 4 round shot underneath or four 3.5 oz burster charges and four fuses on the shelf with four spherical case underneath.

Miscellaneous tools and slow match on hinged shelf with 4 round shot underneath or four 3.5 oz burster charges and four fuses on the shelf with four spherical case underneath.

Tools on hinged shelf with 3 light common case underneath.

1 lb bag of Priming powder and tools on hinged shelf with 3 heavy common case underneath.

Limber, centre box
2 linchpins and 2 drag washers,
Spare rammer head.

Two cartouche each with 8 cartridges of 3lb of red LG powder on hinged shelf with 9 round shot underneath. (If spherical case are carried four additional 14oz cartridges are included).

One cartouche with 16 cartridges of 3lb of red LG powder on hinged shelf with 9 round shot underneath.

Side section of limber near box

Front section of limber, off box

Flint, steel and spare slow match.

30 inch length of slow match fed through hole in rear of copper lined compartment.

Off or left gun axle box

Near or right gun axle box

Worm, spare swab

Vent bit, 2 vent pins, spare thumbstall.

100 quills in container and spare thumbstall

Scale in feet & inches and centimetres

0   1   2

0   10   20   30   40   50   60

Content of 9-pr gun axle and limber boxes - *circa* 1810

Figure 10.4 | Part one of two

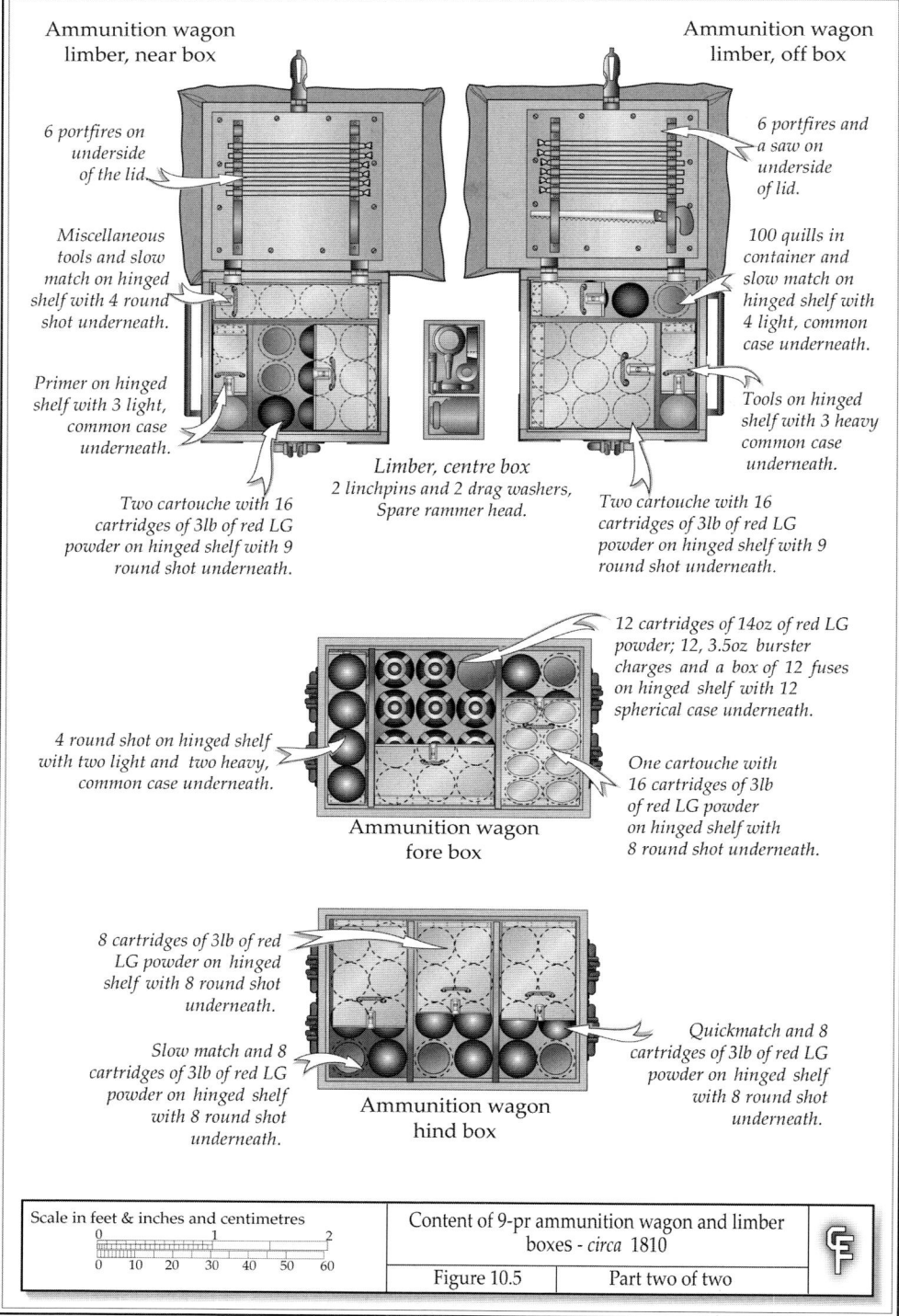

Ammunition wagon
limber, near box

Ammunition wagon
limber, off box

6 portfires on
underside
of the lid.

6 portfires and
a saw on
underside
of lid.

Miscellaneous
tools and slow
match on hinged
shelf with 4 round
shot underneath.

100 quills in
container and
slow match on
hinged shelf with
4 light, common
case underneath.

Primer on hinged
shelf with 3 light,
common case
underneath.

Tools on hinged
shelf with 3 heavy
common case
underneath.

Limber, centre box
2 linchpins and 2 drag washers,
Spare rammer head.

Two cartouche with 16
cartridges of 3lb of red LG
powder on hinged shelf with 9
round shot underneath.

Two cartouche with 16
cartridges of 3lb of red LG
powder on hinged shelf with 9
round shot underneath.

12 cartridges of 14oz of red LG
powder; 12, 3.5oz burster
charges and a box of 12 fuses
on hinged shelf with 12
spherical case underneath.

4 round shot on hinged shelf
with two light and two heavy,
common case underneath.

One cartouche with
16 cartridges of 3lb
of red LG powder
on hinged shelf with
8 round shot underneath.

Ammunition wagon
fore box

8 cartridges of 3lb of red
LG powder on hinged
shelf with 8 round shot
underneath.

Slow match and 8
cartridges of 3lb of red LG
powder on hinged shelf
with 8 round shot
underneath.

Quickmatch and 8
cartridges of 3lb of red LG
powder on hinged shelf
with 8 round shot
underneath.

Ammunition wagon
hind box

Scale in feet & inches and centimetres

0   1   2

0   10   20   30   40   50   60

Content of 9-pr ammunition wagon and limber
boxes - circa 1810

| Figure 10.5 | Part two of two |

Endnotes to Chapter 10

1. Duncan, 1872: p. 162.
2. Boxer, 1853: plate 21; two pieces at The Royal Armouries, Fort Nelson, cast by H & C King at the Royal Brass Foundry, Woolwich in 1813 and 1814, (XIX 631 and XIX 632).
3. *Aide-Memoire,* 1846: plate 22. Royal Carriage Department, plates 14 and 15 of 1867.
4. Mercer, 1870: p. 87.
5. Dickson, 1908: p. 858.
6. Mercer, 1870: p. 145.
7. Griffiths, 1839: p. 153; Spearman, 1828: p. 12.

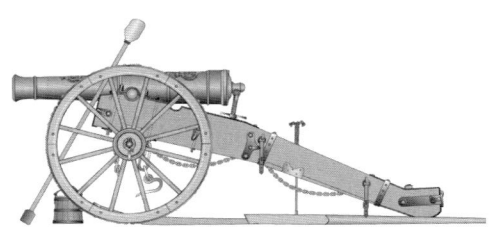

CHAPTER 11

Heavy Field Equipments

There were two heavy field equipments used during the period:

- Medium 12-pr
- Iron 18-pr

The medium 12-pr brass guns came into service with British artillery in 1760 and the 'New Medium' version remained in service with the foot artillery until after the Napoleonic period. The iron 18-pr was brigaded with the field artillery during the latter stages of the Peninsular Campaign and during the hundred days, but was probably used more as a gun of position.

Medium 12-pr

This piece was designed by Blomefield and weighed 18cwt (2,016lb), it was 6 feet 6.5 inches long, some 17 calibres. It had a bore of 4.632 inches, a shot diameter of some 4.4 inches and a windage of some 0.2 inches. In normal use, the gun fired a 4lb charge, but for spherical case this was initially reduced to 16 ounces with a separator charge of 4.5 ounces. The medium 12-pr is noted for being a field artillery weapon, but due to the difficulty in moving the weight of the gun and carriage over rough country, particularly during the Peninsular Campaign, the gun fell out of favour but remained as a field piece. Much of its work was as a brigade reserve and it was little used except as a gun of position or to supplement siege artillery.[1] Wellington had requested Horse Guards for 12-pr guns at the start of the hundred days, but never received them and his intentions for their use is unclear.[2] The service of this gun during the Napoleonic eras is something of an enigma, the records making little mention of them after the first few years of the Peninsular Campaign. The Peninsular artillery returns of November 1808 list one brigade, but by 1809 there is no further mention of them except for those of the 'German Artillery'.[3]

It has not been possible to determine with any accuracy the full details of this piece or the carriages and limbers used. The following illustrations are reconstructions based upon the available evidence and in order to ensure completeness an illustration of the medium 12-pr mounted on a bracket trail carriage and a block trail after Shuttleworth has been included, but it has not been possible to determine when, or if, these carriages came into use with the foot artillery. The horse artillery were originally equipped with the medium 12-pr and it is most probable that it was mounted on a block trail for this service. The guns saw service with the horse artillery in the Holland Expedition of 1799 but they were not used again by this arm after this date.[4] There are no surviving details for the piece of 18cwt but the later manufacturing figures for a piece of 17.5cwt closely tally.[5] The dimensions of the piece are given in Table B.5 of Appendix B and the weights for the equipment are given in Table E.7 of Appendix E, both at the end of Part Two.

12-pr Medium Gun on a Bracket Carriage

No surviving examples or contemporary illustrations of a bracket trail carriage have been located, but drawings by Pyne suggest it would have used a Hanoverian truck and the reconstruction is based upon the Congreve bracket trail of the period. The original wheels were 56 inches for the gun and 54 inches for the limber,[6] and the wooden axles for this gun are given as 7 inches tall by 4.9 inches wide with 18 inch arms and a bed of 45.5 inches. The limber axle was 6 inches tall by 3.3 inches wide with 16 inch arms and a bed of 45.5 inches.[7] The limber of the bracket trail was originally of the pintle type and had no limber boxes, but the limbers of the horse artillery are shown to carry them and this suggests they were of the new type.[8] The medium 12-pr gun, carriage and revised limber had a weight, behind the team, of 48cwt and ten horses were required for the team (six for parades and peacetime establishments) .[9]

The charge for round shot was 4lb, the charge for case was originally 3.5lb, but later changed to 3lb while that for spherical case was initially 1lb with a 4.5oz separator charge.[10] The accompanying ammunition wagon, limber, with two men, one spare wheel, 2 spare shafts and 78 rounds weighed 33.75cwt. The foot artillery version with a simple pintail limber weighed 42cwt.[11] In 1801 the 12pr limber of the foot brigades carried no boxes, but two supporting common ammunition wagons carried 144 rounds of ammunition comprising 24 case fixed to bottoms, 120 round shot, 144 cartridges, 172 tubes and 18 portfires.[12]

It seems that the interim limber was later used, as it is also recorded that there was a limber and the ammunition carried was 12 round shot, 4 case and 4 shells on the limber and a supporting wagon with 52 round shot, 10 case and 10 shells, a total of 92 rounds.[13] An additional small limber box which carried 6 shot and 2 common case with four cartridges of 4lb and two of 3.5lb was added in about 1806.[14] By 1813, Adye notes that 84 rounds of ammunition were carried on the new-style limbers and ammunition wagons with metal axles.[15] The details of the ammunition carried for the bracket trail carriage at first line is shown in Table D.9 of Appendix D at the end of Part Two.

Special Drills

When the gun carriage was fitted with two sets of trunnion holes and it was required to transport the gun over any distance it was necessary to move the piece further back in the gun carriage to improve the centre of gravity. This better spread the load more

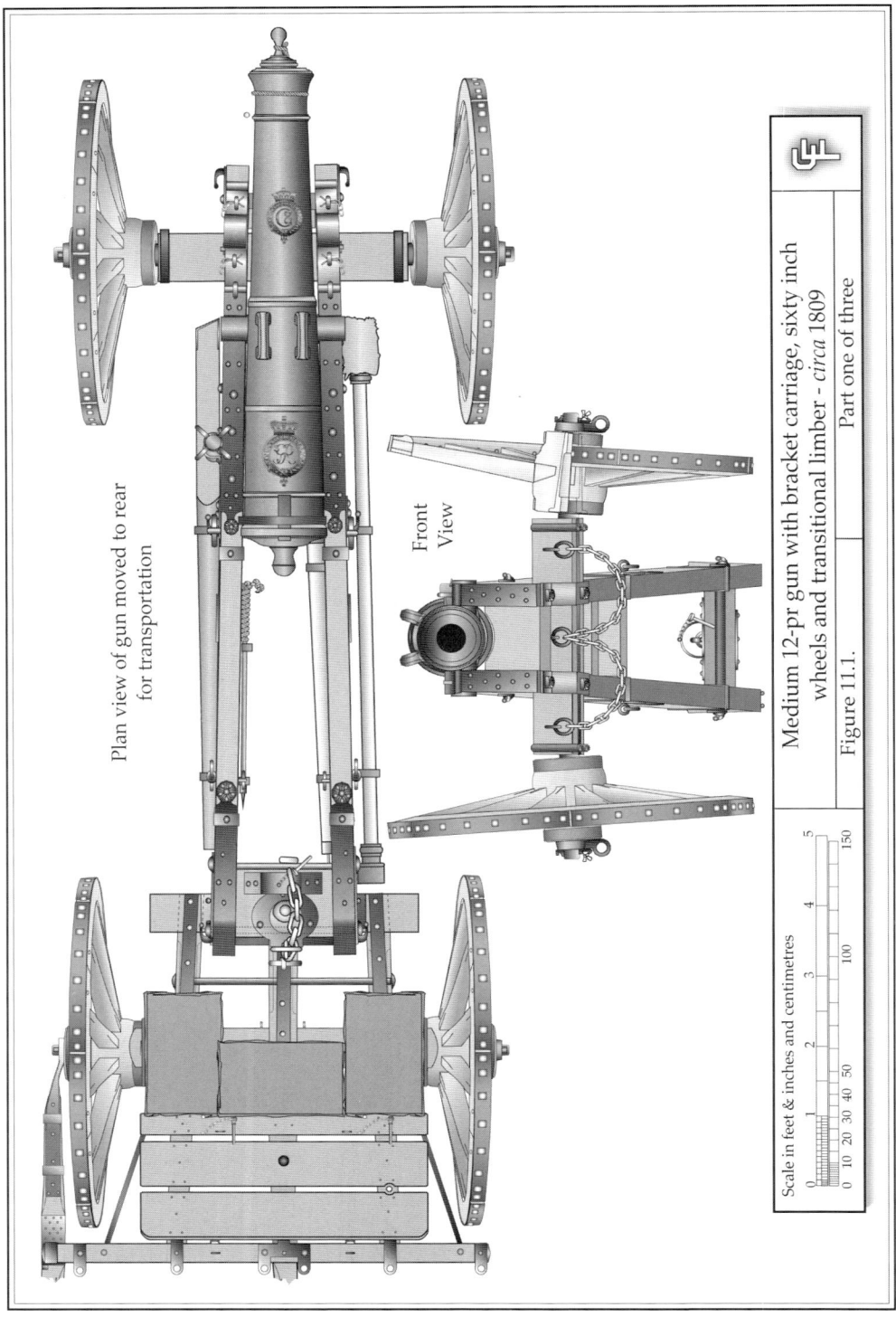

Plan view of gun moved to rear for transportation

Front View

Scale in feet & inches and centimetres

Medium 12-pr gun with bracket carriage, sixty inch wheels and transitional limber - *circa* 1809

Figure 11.1. Part one of three

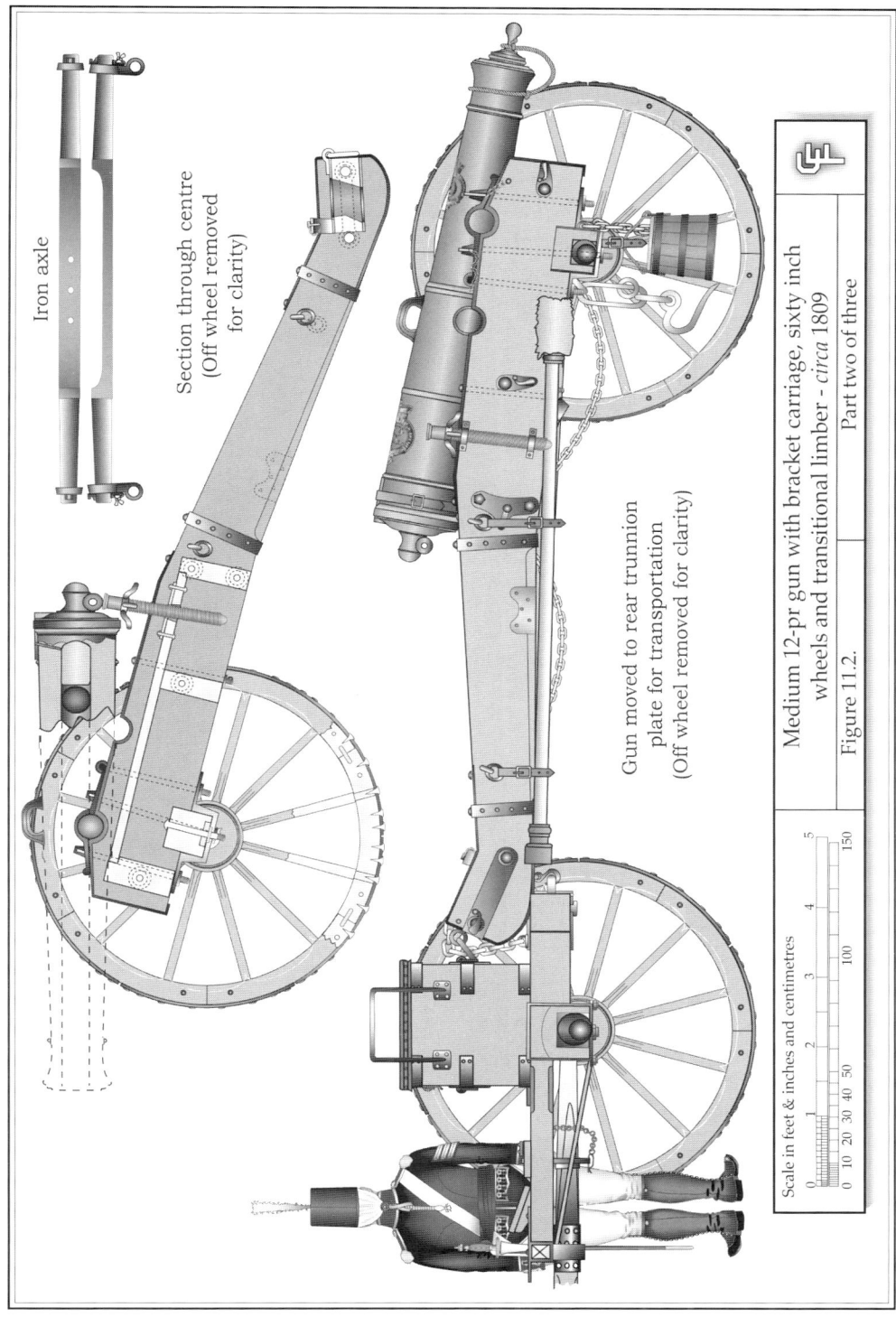

Iron axle

Section through centre
(Off wheel removed
for clarity)

Gun moved to rear trunnion
plate for transportation
(Off wheel removed for clarity)

Medium 12-pr gun with bracket carriage, sixty inch
wheels and transitional limber - *circa* 1809

Part two of three

Figure 11.2.

Scale in feet & inches and centimetres

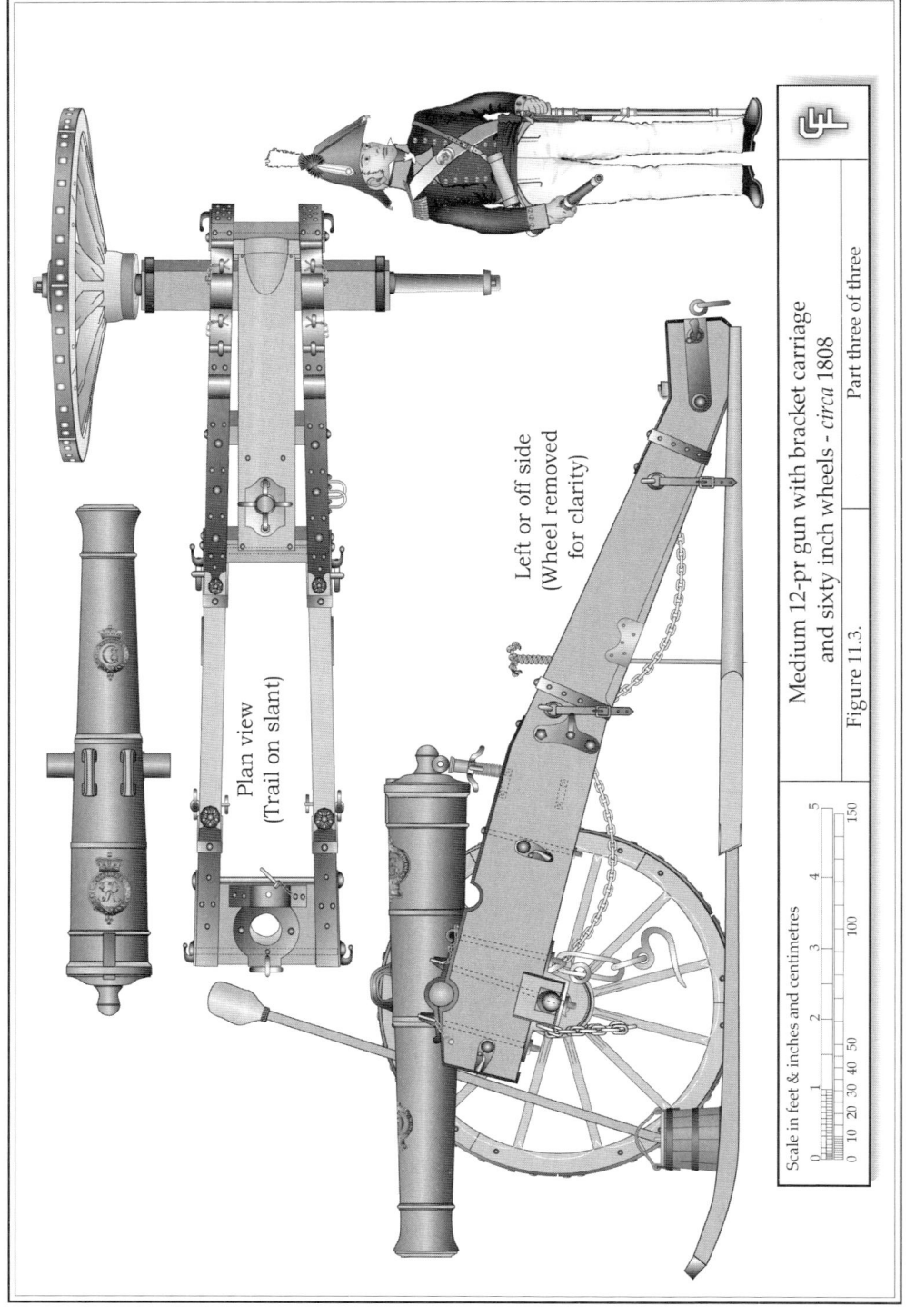

Plan view
(Trail on slant)

Left or off side
(Wheel removed
for clarity)

Medium 12-pr gun with bracket carriage
and sixty inch wheels - *circa* 1808

Figure 11.3.　　Part three of three

Scale in feet & inches and centimetres

0　　1　　2　　3　　4　　5

0　10　20　30　40　50　　　100　　　150

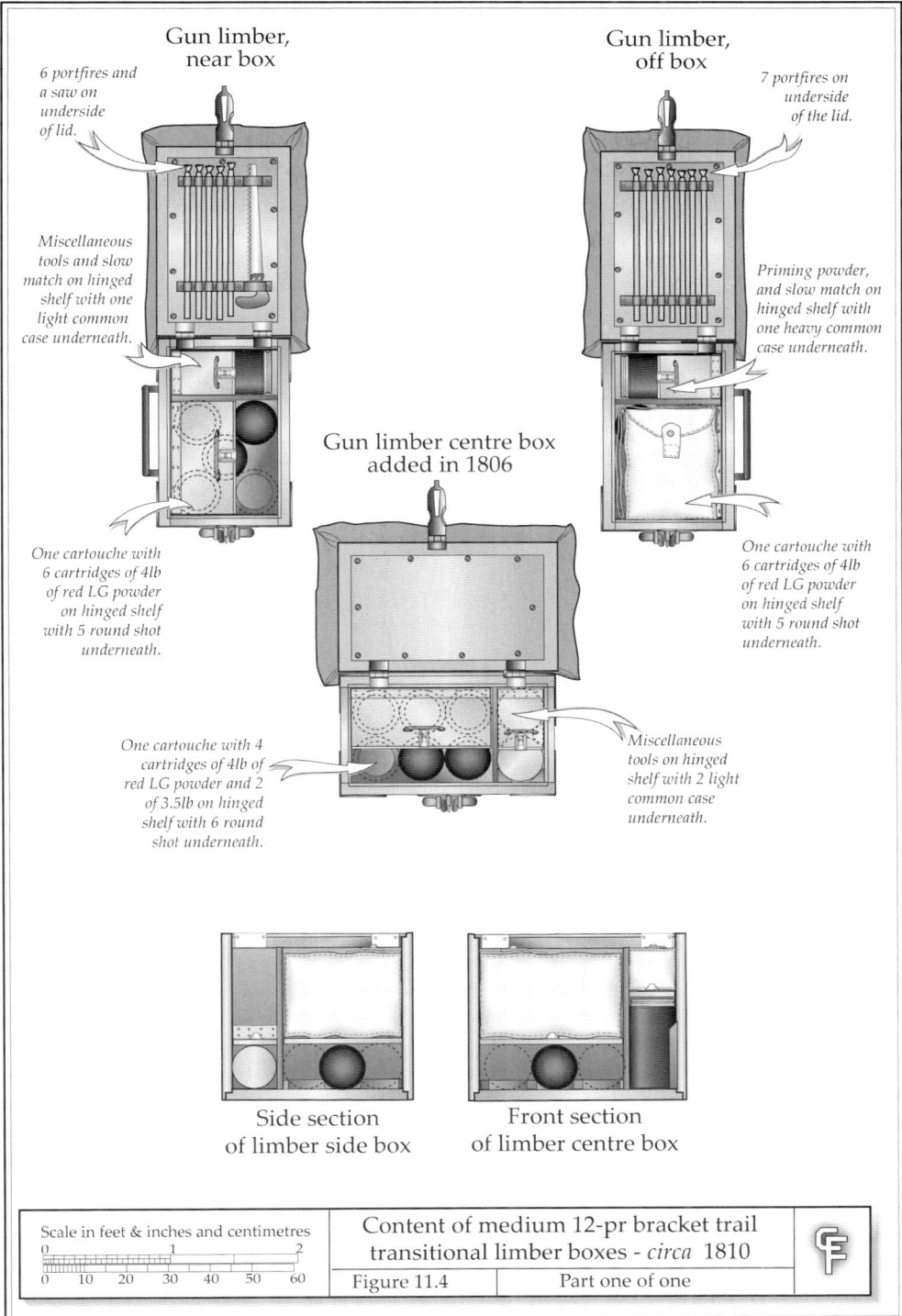

Gun limber,
near box

6 portfires and
a saw on
underside
of lid.

Miscellaneous
tools and slow
match on hinged
shelf with one
light common
case underneath.

One cartouche with
6 cartridges of 4lb
of red LG powder
on hinged shelf
with 5 round shot
underneath.

Gun limber,
off box

7 portfires on
underside
of the lid.

Priming powder,
and slow match on
hinged shelf with
one heavy common
case underneath.

One cartouche with
6 cartridges of 4lb
of red LG powder
on hinged shelf
with 5 round shot
underneath.

Gun limber centre box
added in 1806

One cartouche with 4
cartridges of 4lb of
red LG powder and 2
of 3.5lb on hinged
shelf with 6 round
shot underneath.

Miscellaneous
tools on hinged
shelf with 2 light
common case
underneath.

Side section
of limber side box

Front section
of limber centre box

Scale in feet & inches and centimetres	Content of medium 12-pr bracket trail transitional limber boxes - *circa* 1810	
0 1 2 0 10 20 30 40 50 60	Figure 11.4	Part one of one

evenly between the carriage and limber and applied to both the bracket trail and block trail carriages. The piece was moved with the gun carriage attached to the limber to provide a more level and easier passage and the locking chain was applied to the near wheel to keep the carriage stationary while the piece was moved. Numbers 7 and 8 removed the keys and the capsquares from the trunnions and they then pushed down on the muzzle to raise the breech while 11 removed the elevating mechanism from the elevation plate and placed it in the carriage brackets. (When in the travelling mode the elevation screw and hand wheel were removed from the base plate and carried in brackets on the right cheek of the gun carriage.) Meanwhile, 12 and 13 had brought up the handspikes. The common handspike was passed to 9 and 10 who placed the round handle under the raised breech of the piece. The traversing handspike was passed to 7 and 8 who had relaxed pressure on the muzzle and now inserted the handspike into the bore of the piece. With the aid of the detachment, 7 and 8 raised the muzzle until the trunnions were clear of the trunnion holes and above the eyebolts. Numbers 9 and 10 rolled the piece on the round section of the handspike to the rear trunnion grooves also assisted by the detachment. When the piece was safely in position it was lashed to ring bolts on the carriage; at the rear, rope was passed around the neck of the cascable and secured to two eyebolts on the trail. At the front, the muzzle was roped to two eyebolts on the inside of the brackets or cheeks of the carriage. To prepare a gun for action from the travelling mode the procedure was reversed.

12-pr Medium Gun on a Block Trail Carriage

The horse artillery were equipped with two 12-pr guns as part of their ordnance and this is confirmed by Adye in his 1801 edition where he lists the medium 12-pr as part of the their equipment. It may well be that while the 12-pr continued in use on the bracket trail for the foot artillery, the horse artillery were equipped with the gun on a block trail. When the horse artillery dispensed with these guns, they would have been allocated to the foot brigades and the 12-pr in the Peninsula may well have been mounted on block trails. Among the Shuttleworth papers is a drawing of a block trail carriage for the medium 12-pr and it is clear that this form of carriage was in use after the Napoleonic period as it is also included in the plates of the *Aide Memoire* to the Military Sciences.[16] The Shuttleworth drawings are registered as received in May 1819 or 1820 and probably predate this by a year or so, but it is of note that the wheels are of the pre-1813 pattern and thus the carriage depicted may have been in existence for some time.

General Lawson noted during the Egyptian Campaign of 1800 that

> In the marching of the 12-pounders to Grand Cairo … the want of double or travelling trunnion-boxes was much regretted. Some few carriages were formerly so constructed for the Horse Artillery, but why discontinued remains unknown, as they are undoubtedly advantageous to a heavy draught or indifferent horsess.[17]

The iron axles for the 12-pr were larger than the standard size used on the field equipments; the arms for the gun axles were 16.75 inches long, the linch diameter was 2.5 inches and 3.5 inches at the shoulder. The arms for the limber were 13.625 inches long with diameters of 2 and 2.75 inches respectively.[18] Adye records that the horse artillery gun complete with two men on the limber and 16 rounds of ammunition weighed just over 45cwt.[19] The ammunition carried for the block trail 12-pr is given in Table D.10 at Appendix D at the end of Part Two.

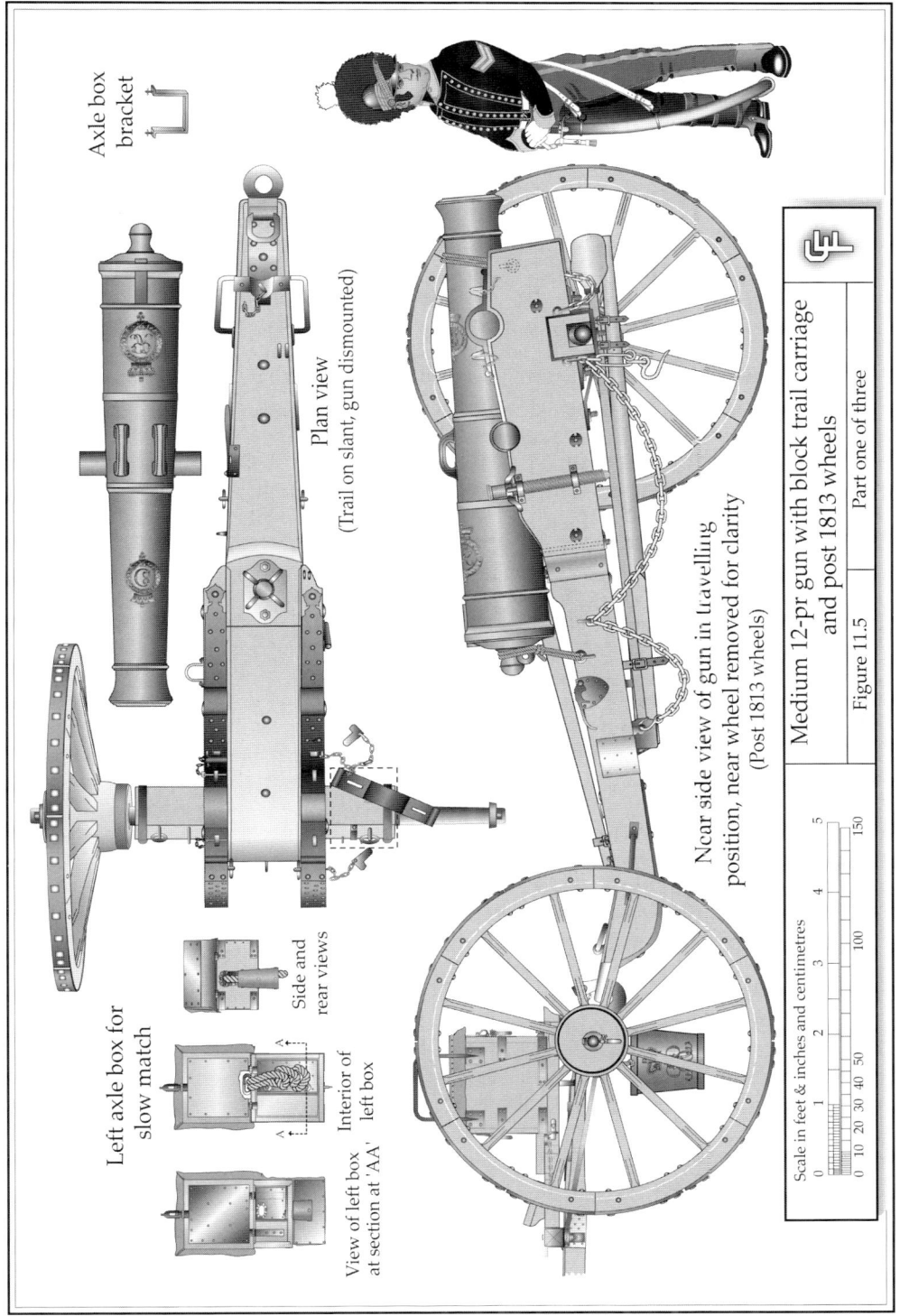

Axle box
bracket

Plan view
(Trail on slant, gun dismounted)

Near side view of gun in travelling
position, near wheel removed for clarity
(Post 1813 wheels)

Left axle box for
slow match

Side and
rear views

Interior of
left box

View of left box
at section at 'AA'

Scale in feet & inches and centimetres

Medium 12-pr gun with block trail carriage
and post 1813 wheels

Figure 11.5   Part one of three

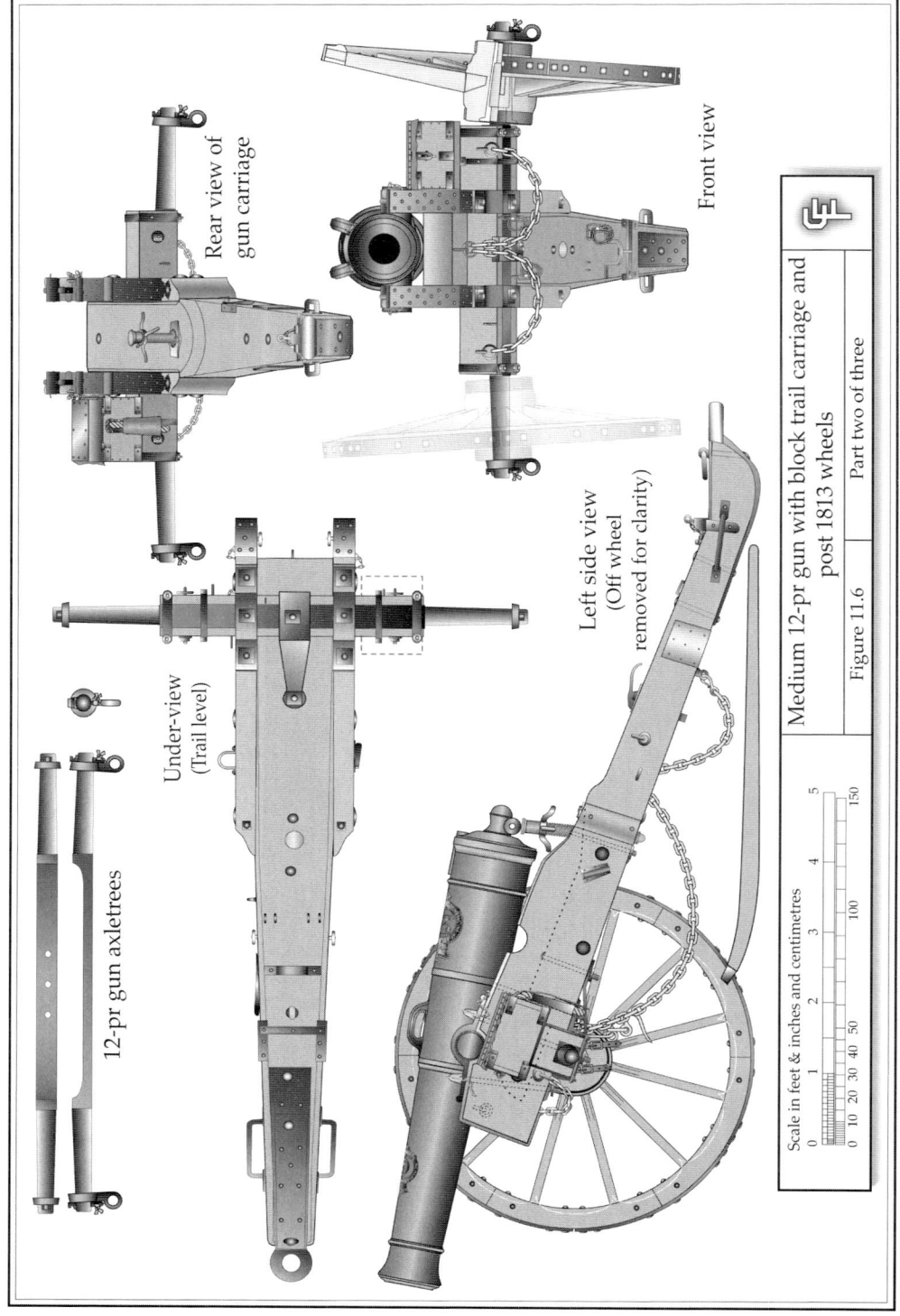

Rear view of
gun carriage

Front view

Left side view
(Off wheel
removed for clarity)

Under-view
(Trail level)

12-pr gun axletrees

Medium 12-pr gun with block trail carriage and
post 1813 wheels

Part two of three

Figure 11.6

Scale in feet & inches and centimetres

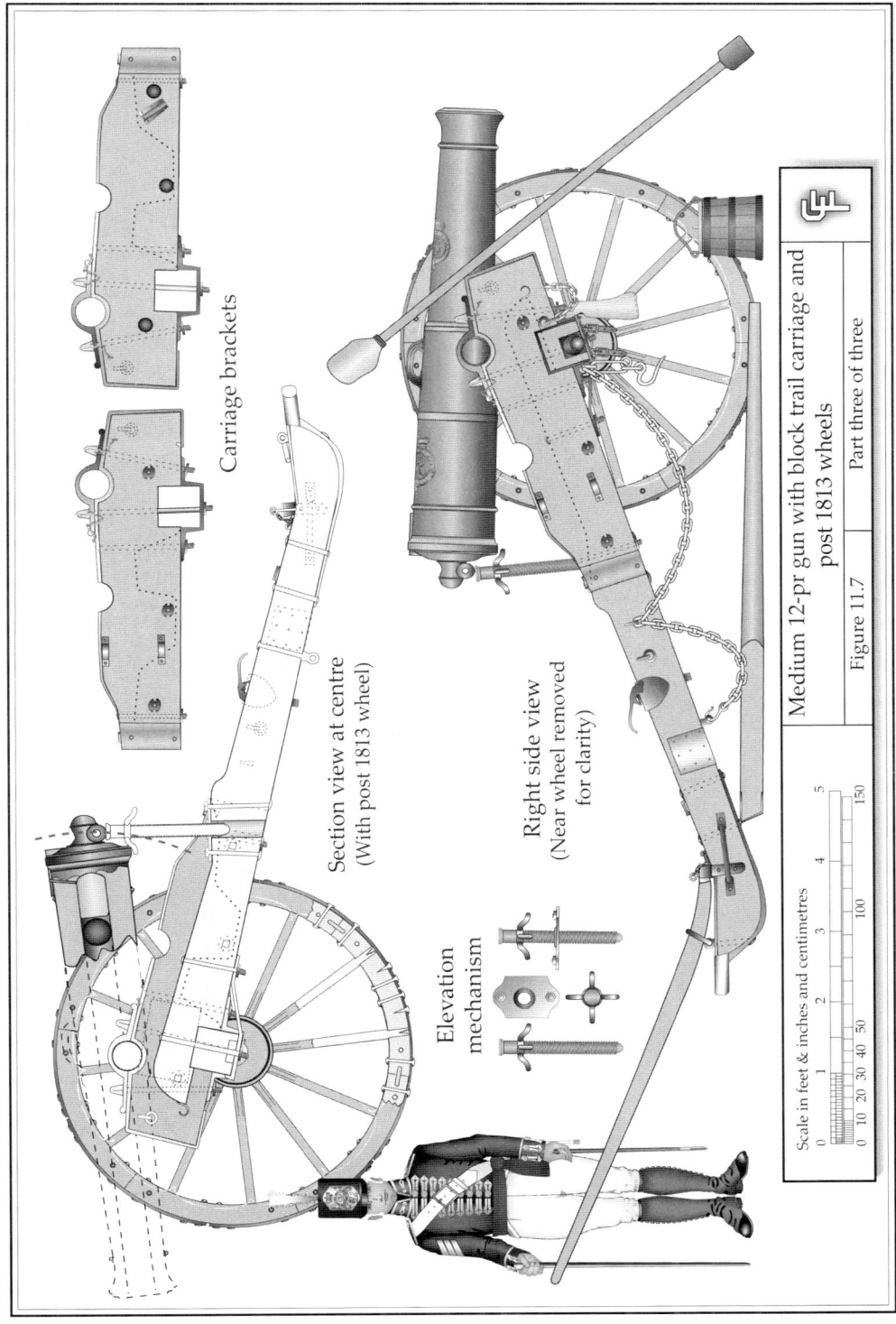

Carriage brackets

Section view at centre
(With post 1813 wheel)

Right side view
(Near wheel removed
for clarity)

Elevation
mechanism

Scale in feet & inches and centimetres

Medium 12-pr gun with block trail carriage and
post 1813 wheels

Figure 11.7 | Part three of three

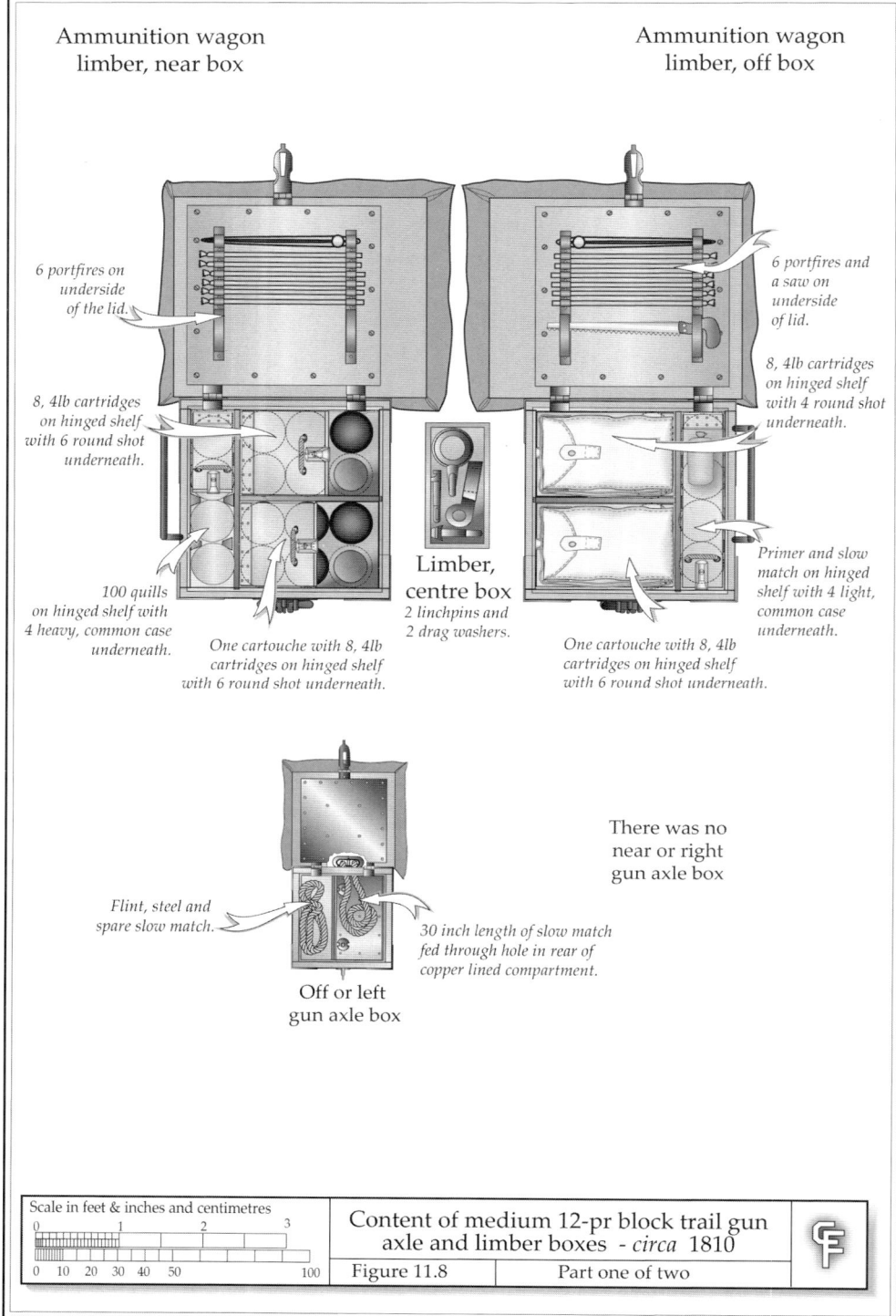

Ammunition wagon limber, near box

Ammunition wagon limber, off box

6 portfires on underside of the lid.

6 portfires and a saw on underside of lid.

8, 4lb cartridges on hinged shelf with 6 round shot underneath.

8, 4lb cartridges on hinged shelf with 4 round shot underneath.

Limber, centre box

2 linchpins and 2 drag washers.

100 quills on hinged shelf with 4 heavy, common case underneath.

One cartouche with 8, 4lb cartridges on hinged shelf with 6 round shot underneath.

Primer and slow match on hinged shelf with 4 light, common case underneath.

One cartouche with 8, 4lb cartridges on hinged shelf with 6 round shot underneath.

There was no near or right gun axle box

Flint, steel and spare slow match.

30 inch length of slow match fed through hole in rear of copper lined compartment.

Off or left gun axle box

Scale in feet & inches and centimetres

0   1   2   3

0   10   20   30   40   50   100

Content of medium 12-pr block trail gun axle and limber boxes - *circa* 1810

| Figure 11.8 | Part one of two |

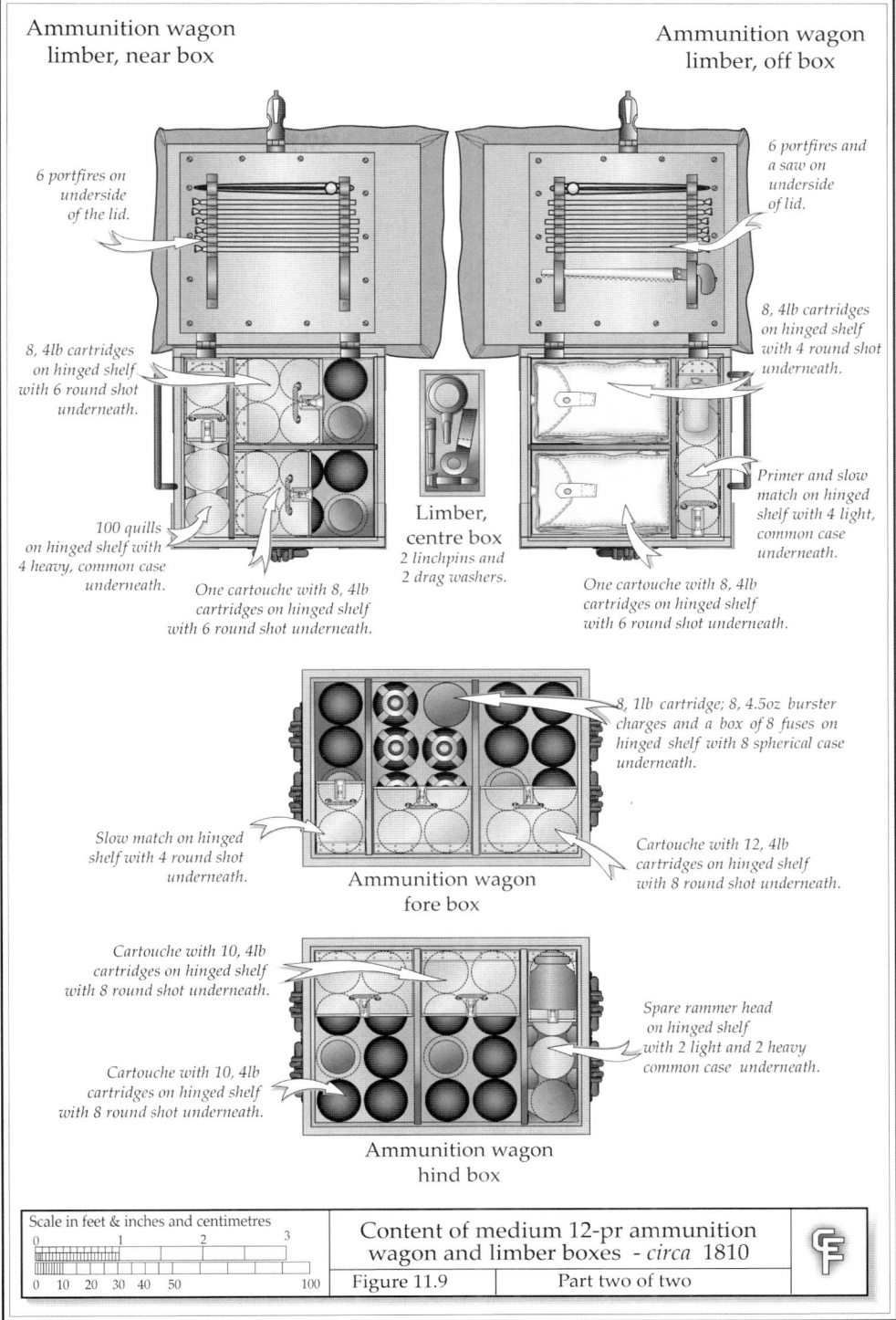

Ammunition wagon
limber, near box

Ammunition wagon
limber, off box

6 portfires on
underside
of the lid.

6 portfires and
a saw on
underside
of lid.

8, 4lb cartridges
on hinged shelf
with 6 round shot
underneath.

8, 4lb cartridges
on hinged shelf
with 4 round shot
underneath.

100 quills
on hinged shelf with
4 heavy, common case
underneath.

Limber,
centre box
2 linchpins and
2 drag washers.

Primer and slow
match on hinged
shelf with 4 light,
common case
underneath.

One cartouche with 8, 4lb
cartridges on hinged shelf
with 6 round shot underneath.

One cartouche with 8, 4lb
cartridges on hinged shelf
with 6 round shot underneath.

8, 1lb cartridge; 8, 4.5oz burster
charges and a box of 8 fuses on
hinged shelf with 8 spherical case
underneath.

Slow match on hinged
shelf with 4 round shot
underneath.

Cartouche with 12, 4lb
cartridges on hinged shelf
with 8 round shot underneath.

Ammunition wagon
fore box

Cartouche with 10, 4lb
cartridges on hinged shelf
with 8 round shot underneath.

Spare rammer head
on hinged shelf
with 2 light and 2 heavy
common case underneath.

Cartouche with 10, 4lb
cartridges on hinged shelf
with 8 round shot underneath.

Ammunition wagon
hind box

Scale in feet & inches and centimetres

| 0 | 1 | 2 | 3 |

| 0 | 10 | 20 | 30 | 40 | 50 | | 100 |

Content of medium 12-pr ammunition
wagon and limber boxes - *circa* 1810

| Figure 11.9 | Part two of two |

Performance

There is very little information on the performance of this piece, some sources have used the data from the 12-pr howitzer adopted after the Napoleonic period. This piece is very different and these figures cannot be taken as any indication of the performance of the medium 12-pr, nor can the later figures, which resulted from different guns, powder and projectiles. The recorded performance figures for the medium 12-pr guns are given in Tables C.14 and C.15 of Appendix C at the end of Part Two. The information contained in the tables is taken from the best contemporary sources available.

Iron 18-pr Gun

Little is known about this gun as a field piece. There were two versions, one of 9ft and one of 9ft 6in and it is assumed that the lighter would have been used in the field role. This was designed by Blomefield and weighed 40cwt (4,480lb), it had a bore of 5.292 inches, a shot diameter of 5.04 inches and a windage of 0.118 inches. It used a service charge of 6lb of powder and the range was noted as 1,800 yards at 5 degrees of elevation and 2,300 at 10 degrees. It is assumed that the gun was mounted on a bracket trail carriage, but the design is unclear as is that of the platform wagons that were included in the establishment, although they may well be similar to those illustrated after the period.[20] The wheel of the 18-pr carriage was 58 inches diameter, 4 inches wide and weighed 367lb. The axle arms were 17 inches long, 6.5 inches diameter at the shoulder and 5.5 at the linch.[21]

The brigade was formed in April 1813 and saw service in the later stages of the Peninsular Campaign under the command of Captain Morrison RA, although two companies, his and Captain Glubb's, were required to manage the guns. The brigade equipment consisted of 57 vehicles and carriages.[22] The inclusion of the six platform wagons suggests that the brigade was more intended for static use as guns of position, rather than the more usual field role. The establishment was given as:

6	18-pr guns on travelling carriages	2	spare carriages
18	ammunition (limber) wagons	150	round per gun
3	store wagons	6	platform wagons
20	bullock carts	2	forges

Three further brigades of 18-prs were also formed under the orders of the Duke of Wellington in 1815 just prior to Waterloo.[23]

Endnotes to Chapter 11

1. Hughes, 1969: p. 76.
2. Longford, 1971: p. 473.
3. Leslie, 1908: p. 29; Leslie, 1912: p. 96.
4. Duncan, 1782: pp. 91, 99.
5. Boxer, 1853: plate 21.
6. Adye, 1802: p. 76.
7. Adye, 1801: p. 57.
8. Ibid: pp. 14, 16.
9. Leslie, 1912: p. 77.

10. Adye, 1813: pp. 98, 99.
11. Adye, 1801: p. 55.
12. Ibid: pp. 10, 14, 15.
13. Ibid: p. 16.
14. Adye, 1806: pp. 11, 15.
15. Adye, 1813: p. 6.
16. Committee of Engineers, 1847: plate 19 and 20 of 1845.
17. Duncan, 1872: p. 124.
18. Adye, 1801: p. 56.
19. Ibid: pp. 54, 55.
20. *Aide Memoire*, 1846: plates 10 and 11, et al.
21. Adye, 1813: p. 390.
22. Duncan, 1872: p. 340.
23. Duncan, 1872: pp. 192, 415.

CHAPTER 12

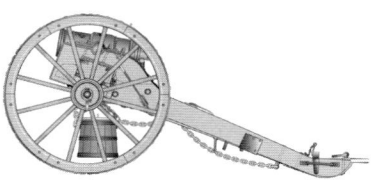

Field Howitzers

There were three howitzers used by the field artillery during the Napoleonic period:

- The brass, light 5.5-inch howitzer
- The brass, heavy 5.5-inch howitzer
- The iron 5.5-inch howitzer, also known as the 24-pr howitzer

The armament of the brigades and troops often changed but it was general practice to equip each brigade or troop with at least one brass howitzer. As the foot artillery were re-organized from battalion guns to brigades on the lines of the horse artillery it became general practice to equip each brigade of 6-pr guns with one light 5.5-inch howitzer while each 9-pr brigade was usually equipped with one heavy 5.5-inch howitzer. There were some clear exceptions to the general rule and at Waterloo the whole of Bull's Troop was equipped with heavy howitzers and Bolton's Brigade had two heavy howitzers and only four 9-pr guns.[1]

Howitzers were heavy and cumbersome weapons but their capability to fire at higher elevations was the deciding advantage that offset their weight. Howitzers not only fired round shot, common case and spherical case but common shell and carcass projectiles as well. They were considered capable weapons although the light 5.5-inch brass howitzer was considered short ranged and inaccurate. Some of these howitzers were used as mortars for siege work by removing the wheels from the gun carriage and elevating the carriage to 30 degrees.[2] In the later stages of the Peninsular Campaign the Duke of Wellington ordered the light howitzers to be laid aside and the heavy, brass, 5.5-inch howitzers were issued to the horse artillery and iron 5.5-inch howitzers to the foot brigades in an effort to counter the heavier weight of French metal which far outranged the light howitzers. The use of the light 5.5-inch howitzer seems to have ceased after this point and both were replaced immediately after the war by the 12-pr and 24-pr brass howitzers.

Some authors have expressed doubt that this howitzer was fitted to a block trail, although they accept that one was designed for the purpose.[3] However, there is clear evidence that they were; firstly, they had been considered as part of the ordnance of the horse artillery from the start,[4] and as early as 1794 the howitzers were to be mounted on the new pattern carriages.[5] Where the foot brigades were concerned the situation is less clear and it would appear that at the start of the war howitzers were mounted on bracket trail carriages similar to the type illustrated and it was noted in the Peninsula in November 1808 that:

> The howitzers, altho' their carriages are not in the present form, may be put to use here, by forming a reserve Brigade with the extra guns of the German Artillery.[6]

After the formation of the horse artillery and the introduction of the Royal Carriage Department the bracket trail carriages were progressively replaced and in 1811, even the artillery in Canada had requested block trail carriages to replace the old pattern with wooden axletrees.[7] Contemporary paintings of the foot artillery at Waterloo by Dighton show a heavy 5.5-inch howitzer mounted on a block trail; the gun axle has a slow match box on the left but no box on the right.

The powder for the howitzers was different from that of the guns. The howitzers used Red No. 3 FG (fine grain) priming powder, the same as that supplied for the infantry musket. This was supplied to the limbers in 1lb flannel cartridges; a sufficient charge for the light howitzer, but the heavy version used a 2lb charge. There is record of spare cartridges being supplied at this date, but it may well be that the heavy howitzer cartridges were made up by the detachment when time permitted.

Light 5.5-inch Howitzer

The light howitzers had a barrel length of 26.75 inches, 4.75 calibres, with a bore of 5.62 to 5.66 inches and weighed 4.75cwt, (532lb). Initially the chamber was conical in form, 6 inches long, with a larger diameter of 3.2 inches and a smaller one of 2.45 inches. Later versions had a cylindrical chamber. The diameter of shell was 5.3 inches and the windage 0.2 inches. In normal use, the gun fired a 1lb charge of priming powder and the same for spherical case with a separator charge of 6 ounces.

In 1801 Adye noted that the limber carried 13 shells, 5 case with wagons carrying a further 10 case, 41 shell, and 4 carcass, a total of 73 rounds.[8] The total carried for each howitzer was given as 24 case fixed to bottoms, 24 common shells filled, 120 empty, 4 carcass, 190 tubes or quills and 18 portfires, the amount of cartridges or powder is not given.[9] Adye records that the new gun complete with two men on the limber and 20 rounds of ammunition weighed just over 35.75cwt. The accompanying ammunition wagon, limber, with two men, one spare wheel, 2 spare shafts and 52 rounds weighed 39.5cwt.[10]

In 1813 he stated the new-style limber and wagon carried 84 rounds of ammunition and to complete the picture, in 1811 Quebec specifically ordered 'Carriages Travelling Block-Trail' for two 5.5-inch light howitzers.[11]

Records from the Peninsula show quite a different pattern of ammunition carried at first line and this is given in Tables D.11 and D.12 of Appendix D at the end of Part Two.

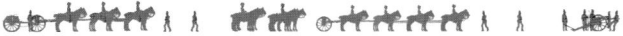

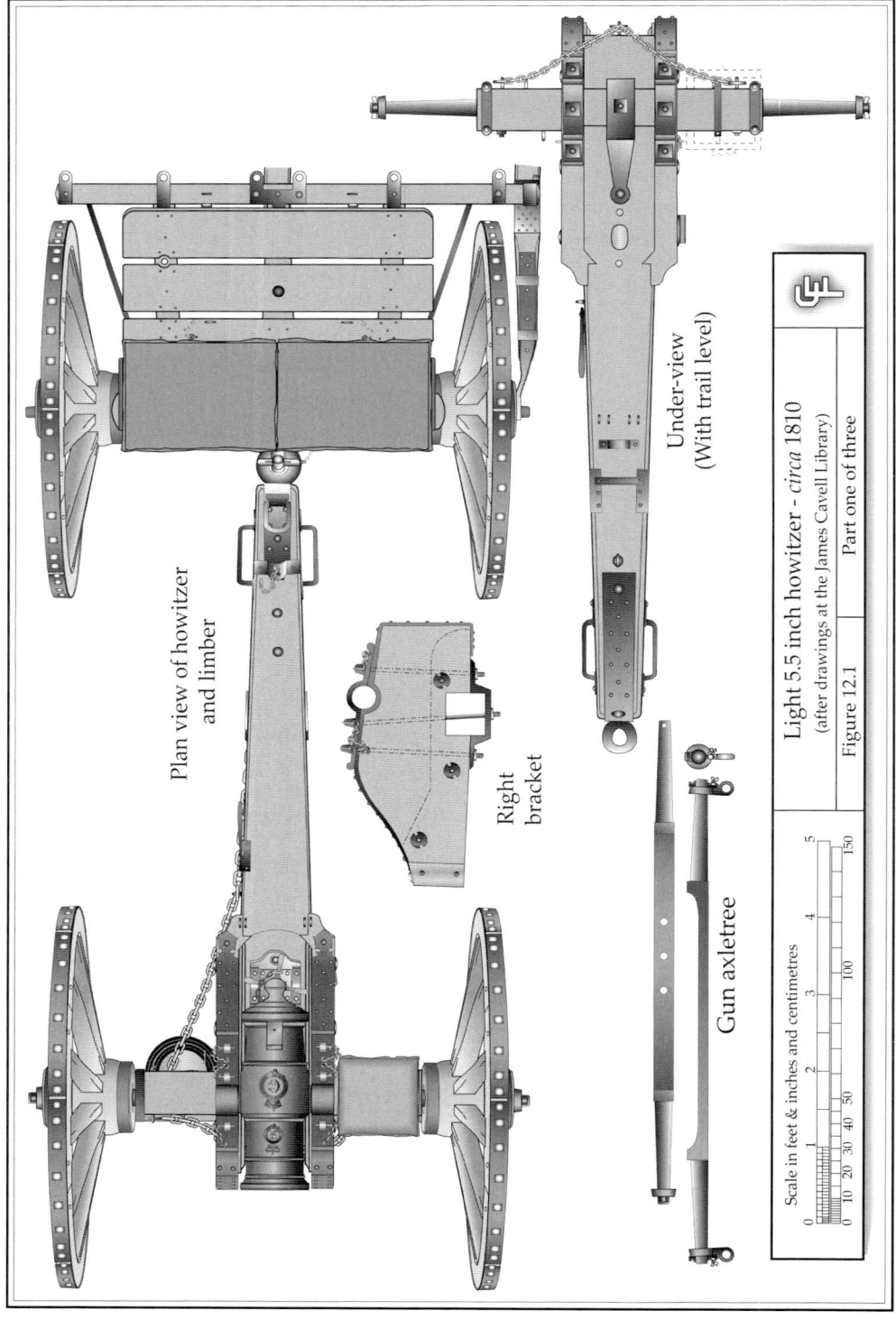

Plan view of howitzer and limber

Under-view
(With trail level)

Right bracket

Gun axletree

Light 5.5 inch howitzer - *circa* 1810
(after drawings at the James Cavell Library)

Figure 12.1   Part one of three

Scale in feet & inches and centimetres

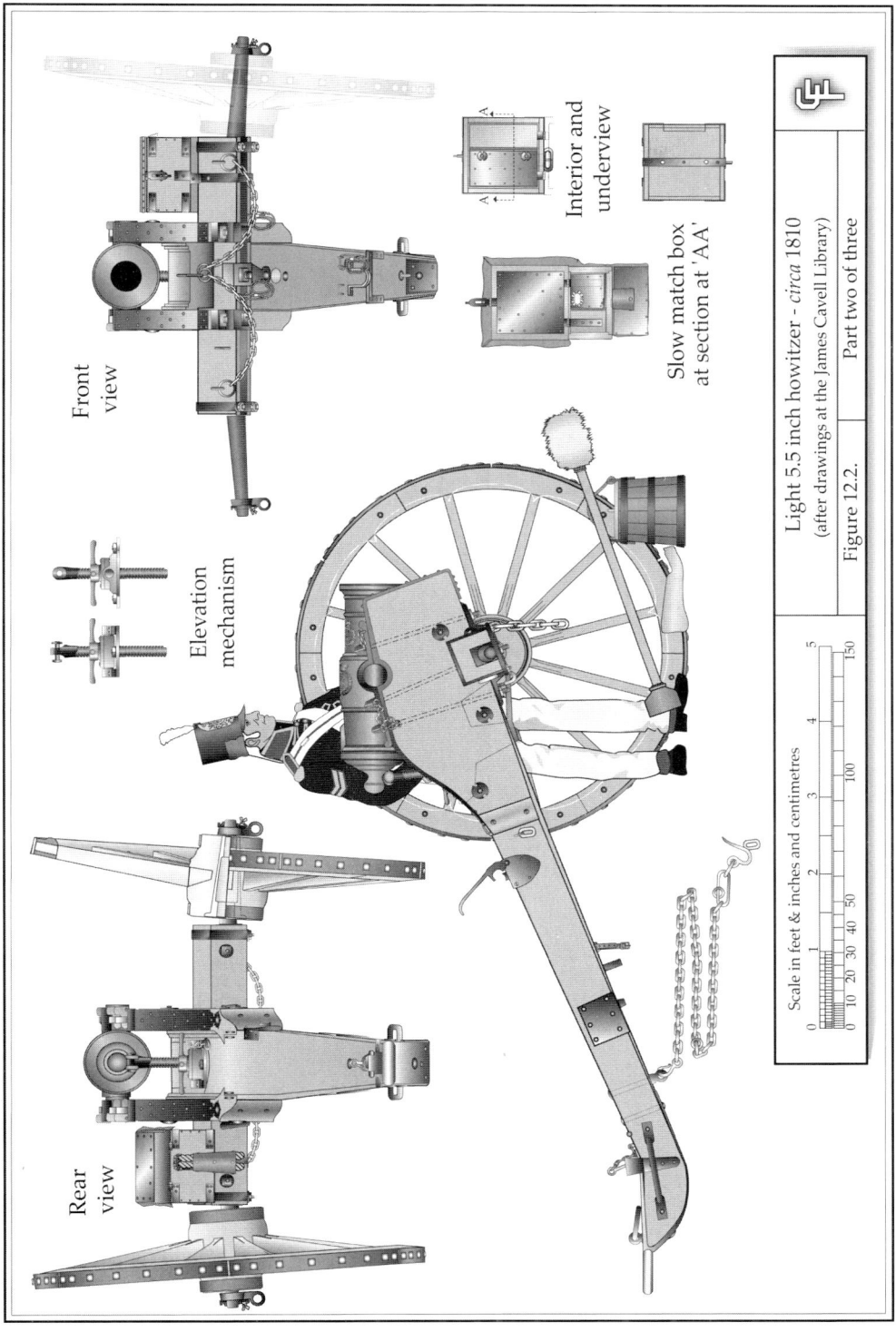

Front view

Interior and underview

Slow match box at section at 'AA'

Elevation mechanism

Rear view

Scale in feet & inches and centimetres

Light 5.5 inch howitzer - *circa* 1810
(after drawings at the James Cavell Library)

Figure 12.2. | Part two of three

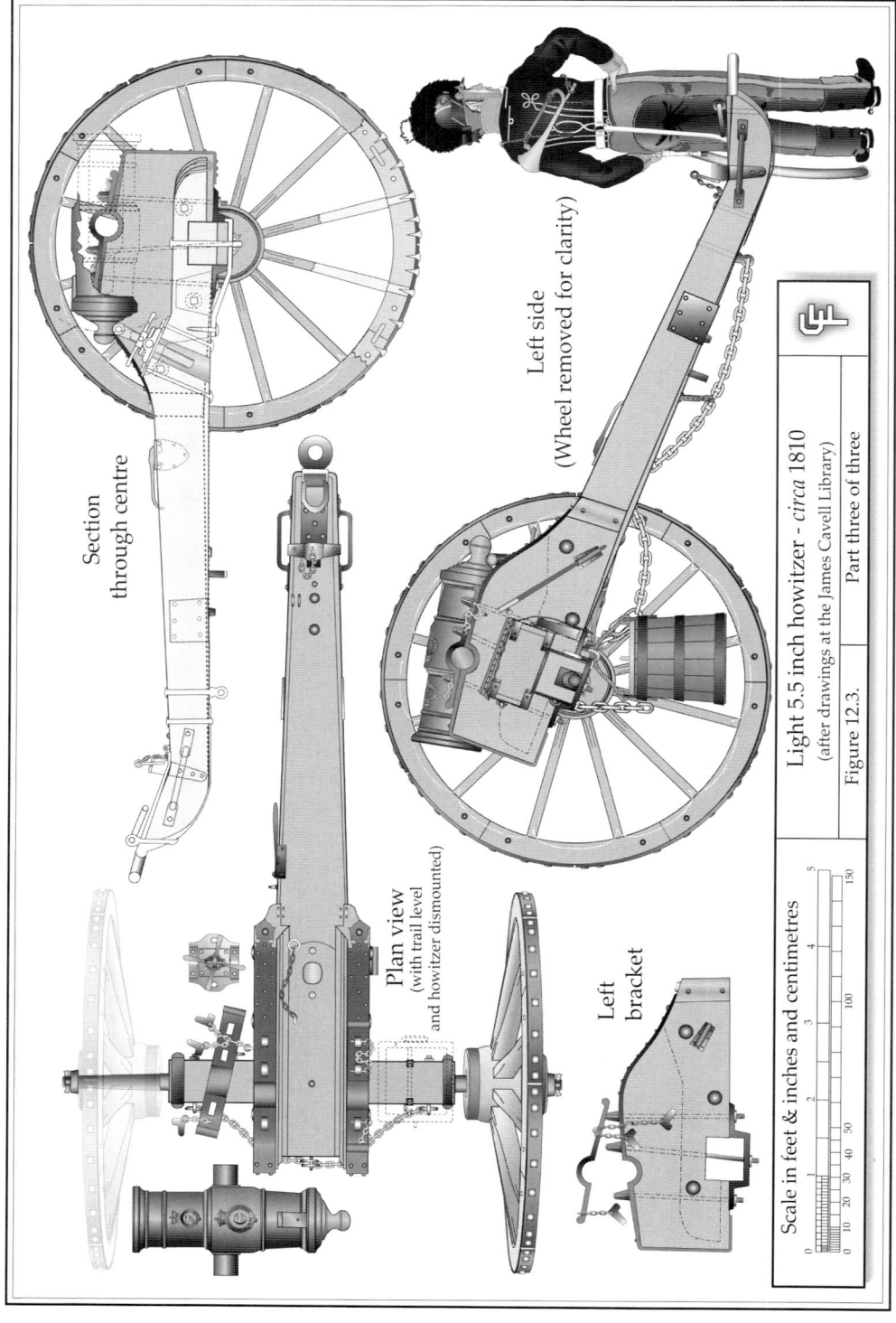

Section through centre

Left side
(Wheel removed for clarity)

Plan view
(with trail level
and howitzer dismounted)

Left bracket

Scale in feet & inches and centimetres

Light 5.5 inch howitzer - *circa* 1810
(after drawings at the James Cavell Library)

Figure 12.3.   Part three of three

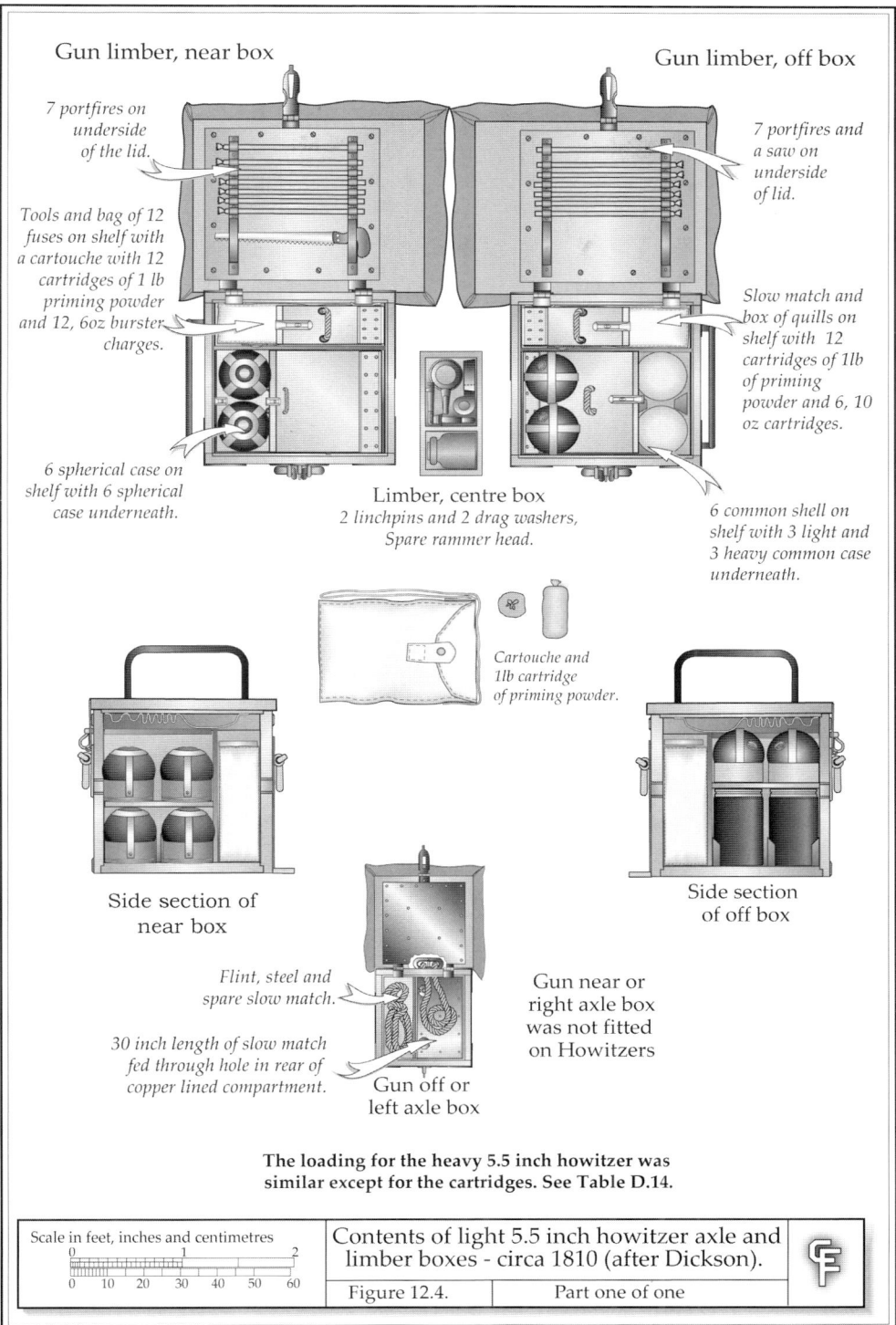

Gun limber, near box

Gun limber, off box

7 portfires on underside of the lid.

7 portfires and a saw on underside of lid.

Tools and bag of 12 fuses on shelf with a cartouche with 12 cartridges of 1 lb priming powder and 12, 6oz burster charges.

Slow match and box of quills on shelf with 12 cartridges of 1lb of priming powder and 6, 10 oz cartridges.

6 spherical case on shelf with 6 spherical case underneath.

Limber, centre box
2 linchpins and 2 drag washers, Spare rammer head.

6 common shell on shelf with 3 light and 3 heavy common case underneath.

Cartouche and 1lb cartridge of priming powder.

Side section of near box

Side section of off box

Flint, steel and spare slow match.

30 inch length of slow match fed through hole in rear of copper lined compartment.

Gun near or right axle box was not fitted on Howitzers

Gun off or left axle box

The loading for the heavy 5.5 inch howitzer was similar except for the cartridges. See Table D.14.

Scale in feet, inches and centimetres

0	1	2

0 10 20 30 40 50 60

Contents of light 5.5 inch howitzer axle and limber boxes - circa 1810 (after Dickson).

Figure 12.4.	Part one of one

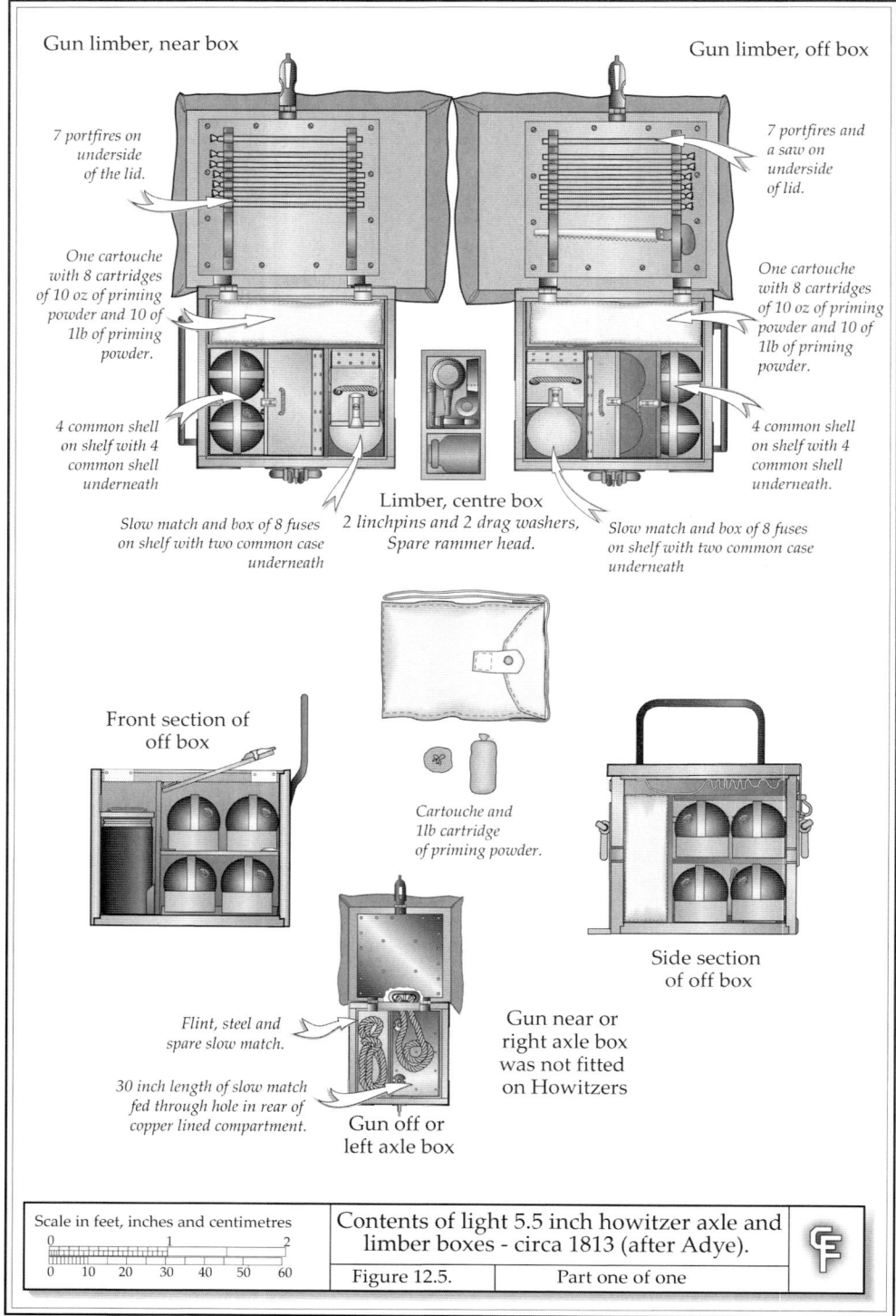

Gun limber, near box

Gun limber, off box

7 portfires on underside of the lid.

7 portfires and a saw on underside of lid.

One cartouche with 8 cartridges of 10 oz of priming powder and 10 of 1lb of priming powder.

One cartouche with 8 cartridges of 10 oz of priming powder and 10 of 1lb of priming powder.

4 common shell on shelf with 4 common shell underneath

4 common shell on shelf with 4 common shell underneath

Slow match and box of 8 fuses on shelf with two common case underneath

Limber, centre box
2 linchpins and 2 drag washers, Spare rammer head.

Slow match and box of 8 fuses on shelf with two common case underneath

Front section of off box

Cartouche and 1lb cartridge of priming powder.

Side section of off box

Flint, steel and spare slow match.

Gun near or right axle box was not fitted on Howitzers

30 inch length of slow match fed through hole in rear of copper lined compartment.

Gun off or left axle box

Scale in feet, inches and centimetres	Contents of light 5.5 inch howitzer axle and limber boxes - circa 1813 (after Adye).		
0 1 2 0 10 20 30 40 50 60	Figure 12.5.	Part one of one	CF

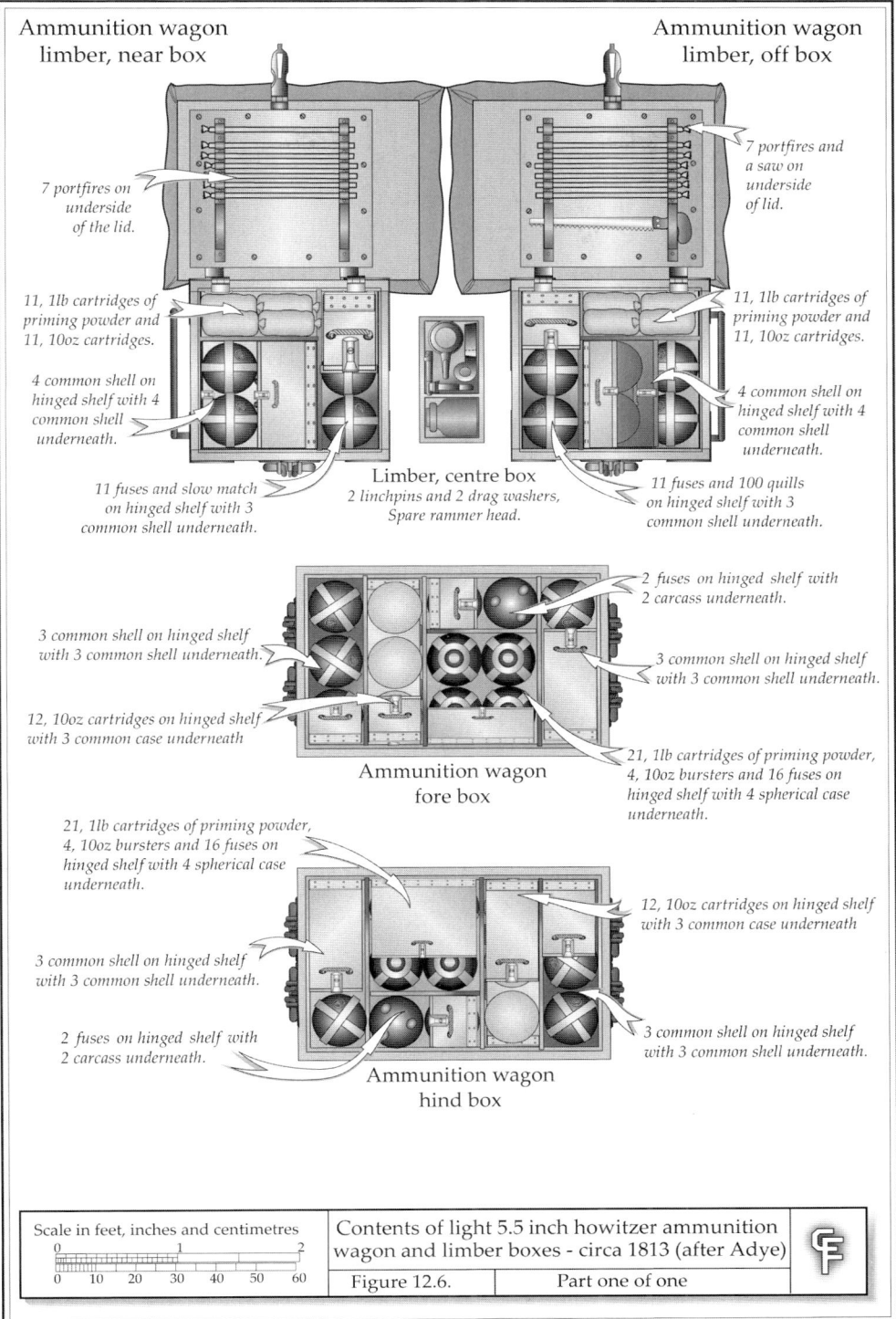

Ammunition wagon
limber, near box

Ammunition wagon
limber, off box

7 portfires on
underside
of the lid.

7 portfires and
a saw on
underside
of lid.

11, 1lb cartridges of
priming powder and
11, 10oz cartridges.

11, 1lb cartridges of
priming powder and
11, 10oz cartridges.

4 common shell on
hinged shelf with 4
common shell
underneath.

4 common shell on
hinged shelf with 4
common shell
underneath.

11 fuses and slow match
on hinged shelf with 3
common shell underneath.

Limber, centre box
2 linchpins and 2 drag washers,
Spare rammer head.

11 fuses and 100 quills
on hinged shelf with 3
common shell underneath.

3 common shell on hinged shelf
with 3 common shell underneath.

2 fuses on hinged shelf with
2 carcass underneath.

3 common shell on hinged shelf
with 3 common shell underneath.

12, 10oz cartridges on hinged shelf
with 3 common case underneath

Ammunition wagon
fore box

21, 1lb cartridges of priming powder,
4, 10oz bursters and 16 fuses on
hinged shelf with 4 spherical case
underneath.

21, 1lb cartridges of priming powder,
4, 10oz bursters and 16 fuses on
hinged shelf with 4 spherical case
underneath.

12, 10oz cartridges on hinged shelf
with 3 common case underneath

3 common shell on hinged shelf
with 3 common shell underneath.

2 fuses on hinged shelf with
2 carcass underneath.

Ammunition wagon
hind box

3 common shell on hinged shelf
with 3 common shell underneath.

Scale in feet, inches and centimetres	Contents of light 5.5 inch howitzer ammunition wagon and limber boxes - circa 1813 (after Adye)	
0 1 2 0 10 20 30 40 50 60	Figure 12.6.	Part one of one

There are drawings of a later 5.5-inch howitzer carriage in the Shuttleworth Papers and it is clear that the recoil from these howitzers was substantial. To permit the minus 6 and plus 12 degrees of elevation required by the howitzer, thicker and taller brackets and additional reinforcement of the bracket to trail joint was essential for the recoil of these pieces. The capsquares were retained by three eye bolts and an additional axle support was fitted under the trail. The height of the trunnions above the trail which still retained the 22 degree angle made for a most unsuitable piece. In many ways the requirements of the howitzer proved a contradiction to the advantages of the block trail and it is hardly surprising that they were replaced soon after the end of the war by the 12-pr and 24-pr howitzers. The earlier versions of the 5.5-inch howitzer had a different type of slow match box that were changed at the same time as the introduction of the improved ammunition wagon and limber boxes.

The ammunition carried at first line varied throughout the period but it is of interest that Adye shows four fewer rounds at the limbers than the probably more accurate figures of Dickson. These showed changes of ammunition allocation and notes the absence of any carcass rounds, the gun limber carrying 12 spherical case, 4 common case and 8 common shells. The wagon limber followed suit and the wagon body carried a further 20 spherical case and 16 common shells. The distribution shown in Figure 12.4 represent the figures of Dickson. The other figures for the ammunition carried at first line are given in Tables D.11 of Appendix D at the end of Part Two.

Performance

In general terms with a charge of 1lb the light 5.5-inch howitzer at point blank ranged 150 yards, each degree up to four degrees increased the range by a further 150 yards. Between four and eight degrees, each degree increased the range by 100 yards and each degree up to twelve degrees increases a further 50 yards.

One inch of fuse burst a shell at 700 yards, two inches at 1,200 yards and three inches to the extreme of the range.[12] The recorded performance figures for the light 5.5-inch howitzer are given in Tables C.16, C.17 and C.18 of Appendix C and the weights for the light 5.5-inch howitzer equipment are given in Table E.8 in Appendix E, both at the end of Part Two.

Heavy 5.5-inch Howitzer

In most respects it was similar to the lighter version with the same calibre but a barrel length of 33 inches, nearly 6 calibres, a bore of 5.62 to 5.66 inches, making it much heavier and weighing some 10cwt, (1,120lb). The diameter of shell was some 5.3 inches and the windage some 0.2 inches. Unlike the light version, it had a cylindrical chamber, 7 inches long and 4.2 inches diameter, and used a 2lb charge. Standard 1lb bags of priming powder were carried in the limbers and wagons, although 2lb cartridges were probably made up in advance from the empty cartridges issued to each unit.

Adye in 1813 noted that the heavy 5.5-inch howitzer had a new-style limber and ammunition wagon that carried a total of 78 rounds of ammunition. There is an example of the piece at the Royal Artillery Museum; it has dolphins at the point of balance and a dispart sight. The Royal Arms are on the chase and the crest of the Master

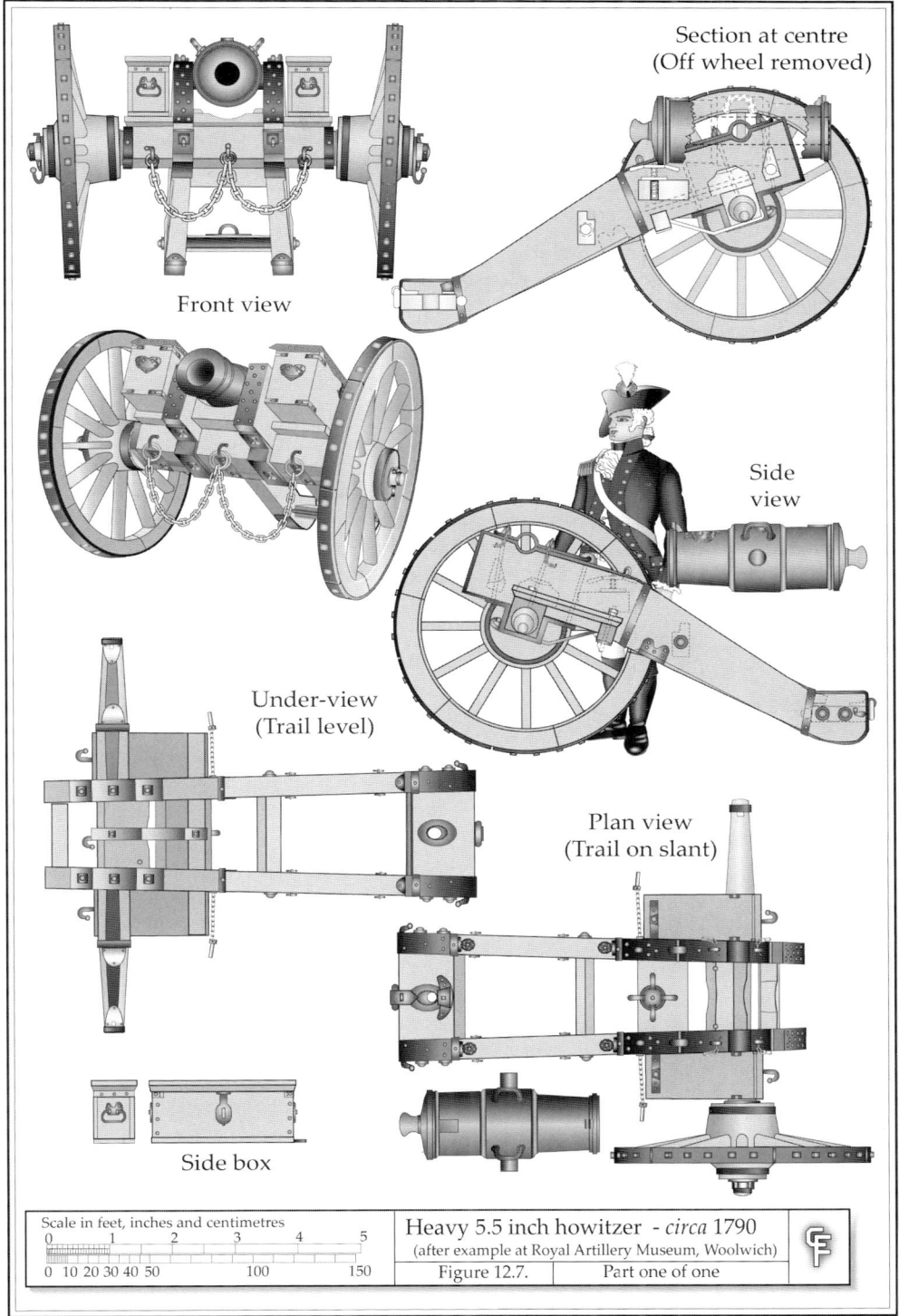

Section at centre
(Off wheel removed)

Front view

Side
view

Under-view
(Trail level)

Plan view
(Trail on slant)

Side box

Scale in feet, inches and centimetres

| 0 | 1 | 2 | 3 | 4 | 5 |

0 10 20 30 40 50   100   150

Heavy 5.5 inch howitzer - *circa* 1790
(after example at Royal Artillery Museum, Woolwich)

| Figure 12.7. | Part one of one |

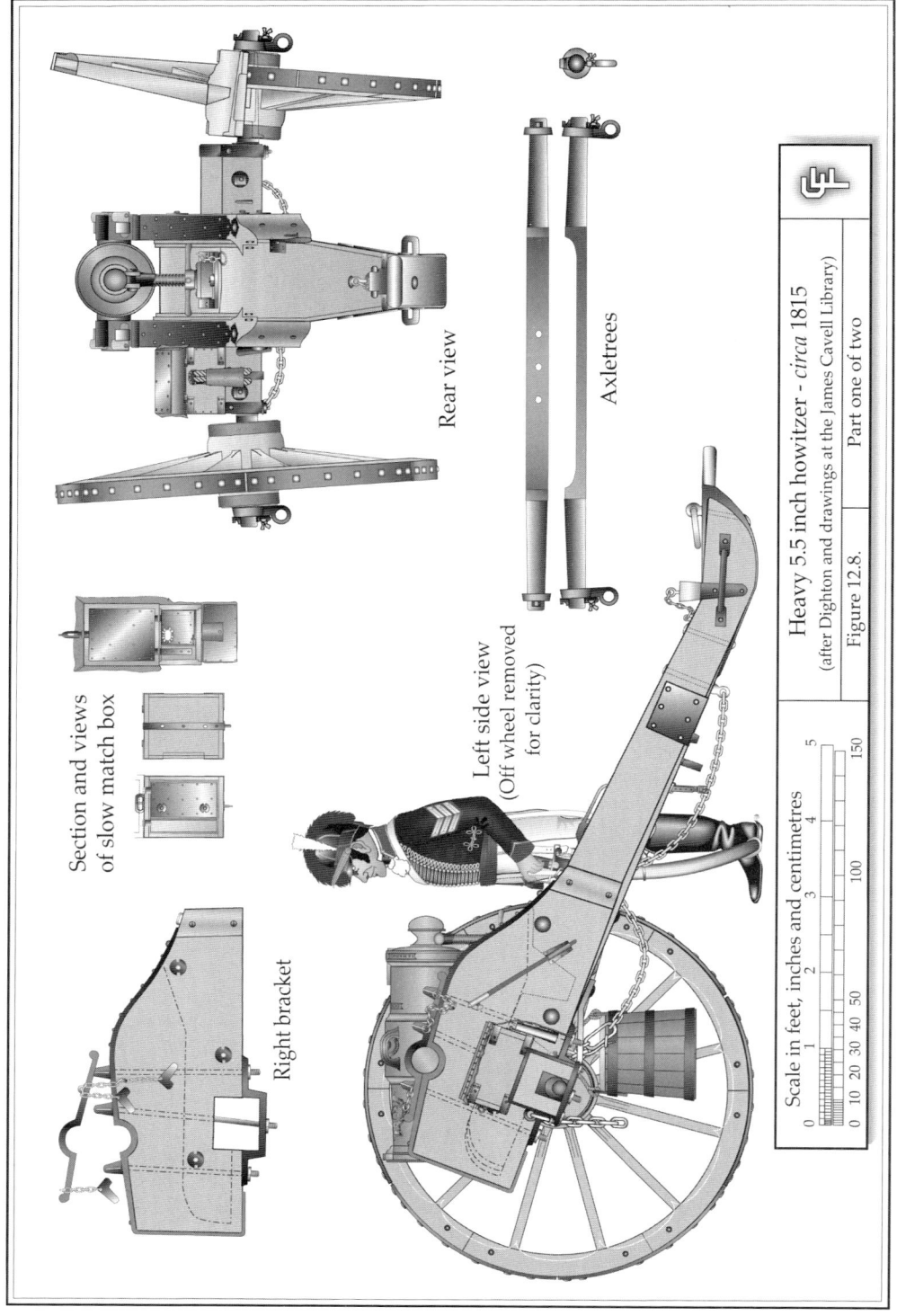

Rear view

Axletrees

Section and views
of slow match box

Right bracket

Left side view
(Off wheel removed
for clarity)

Scale in feet, inches and centimetres

Heavy 5.5 inch howitzer - *circa* 1815
(after Dighton and drawings at the James Cavell Library)

Figure 12.8.   Part one of two

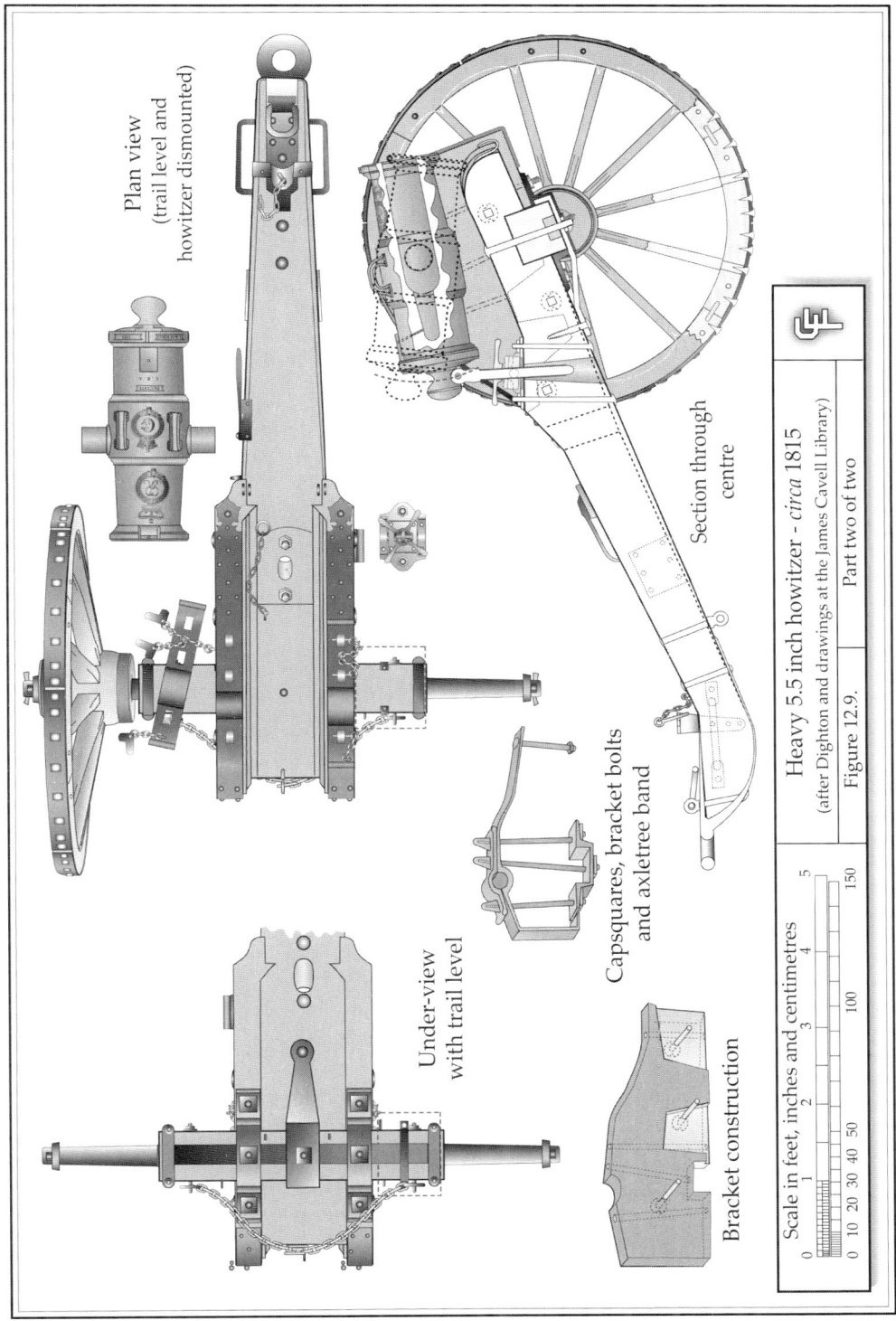

Plan view
(trail level and
howitzer dismounted)

Section through
centre

Capsquares, bracket bolts
and axletree band

Under-view
with trail level

Bracket construction

Heavy 5.5 inch howitzer - *circa* 1815
(after Dighton and drawings at the James Cavell Library)
Part two of two

Figure 12.9.

Scale in feet, inches and centimetres

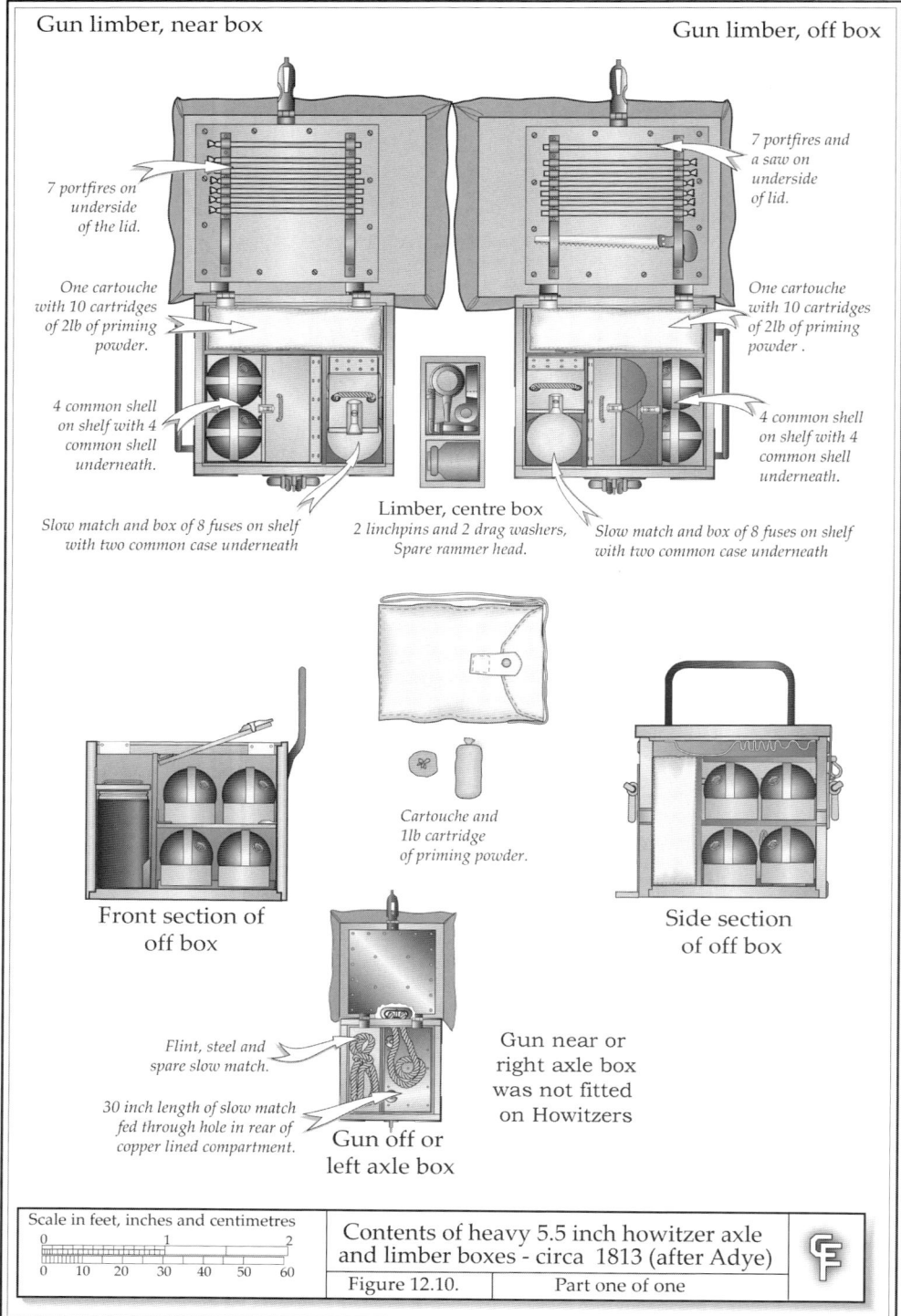

Gun limber, near box

Gun limber, off box

7 portfires on underside of the lid.

7 portfires and a saw on underside of lid.

One cartouche with 10 cartridges of 2lb of priming powder.

One cartouche with 10 cartridges of 2lb of priming powder .

4 common shell on shelf with 4 common shell underneath.

4 common shell on shelf with 4 common shell underneath.

Limber, centre box
2 linchpins and 2 drag washers, Spare rammer head.

Slow match and box of 8 fuses on shelf with two common case underneath

Slow match and box of 8 fuses on shelf with two common case underneath

Cartouche and 1lb cartridge of priming powder.

Front section of off box

Side section of off box

Flint, steel and spare slow match.

Gun near or right axle box was not fitted on Howitzers

30 inch length of slow match fed through hole in rear of copper lined compartment.

Gun off or left axle box

Scale in feet, inches and centimetres

0   1   2
0   10   20   30   40   50   60

Contents of heavy 5.5 inch howitzer axle and limber boxes - circa 1813 (after Adye)

Figure 12.10.   Part one of one

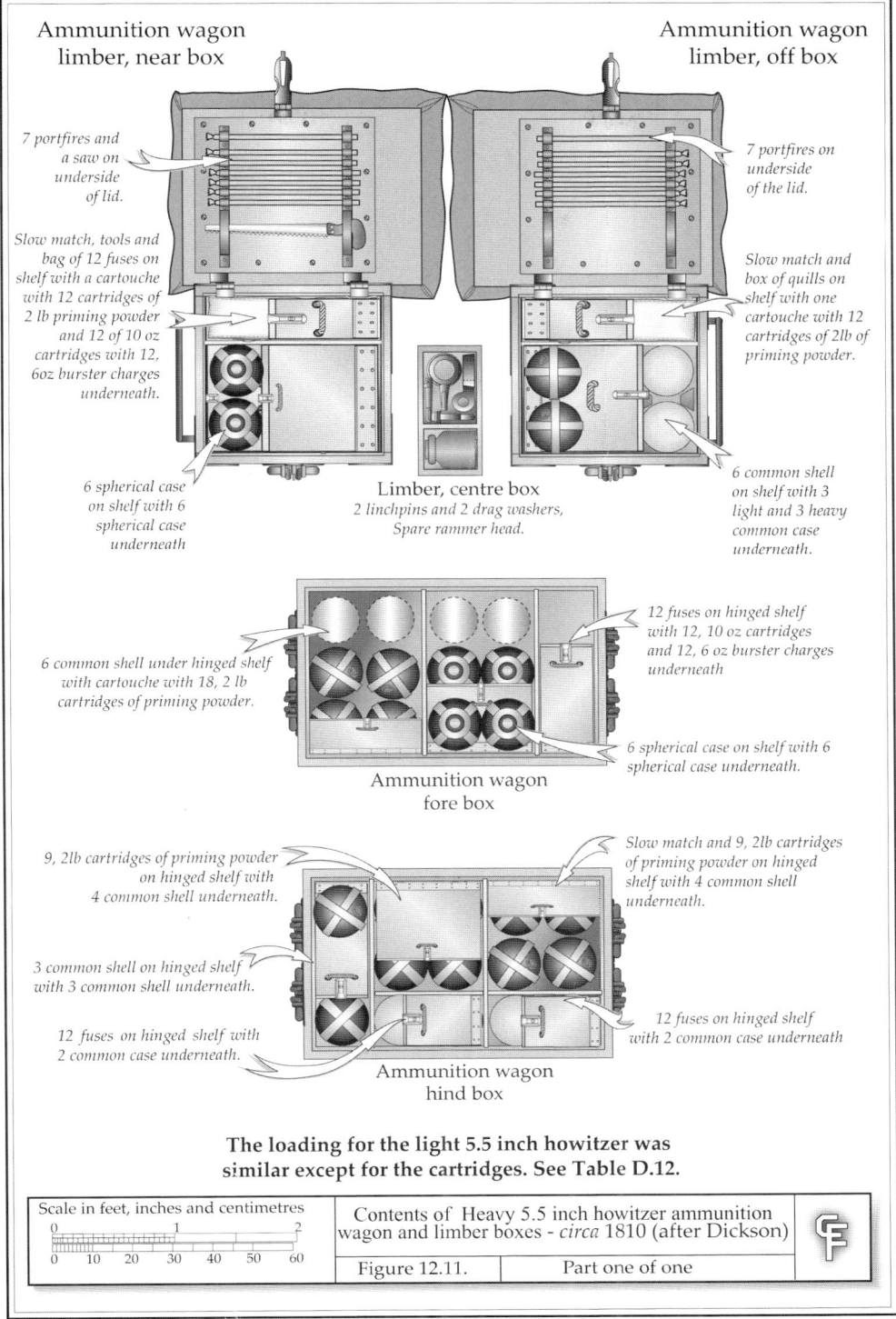

Ammunition wagon limber, near box

7 portfires and a saw on underside of lid.

Slow match, tools and bag of 12 fuses on shelf with a cartouche with 12 cartridges of 2 lb priming powder and 12 of 10 oz cartridges with 12, 6oz burster charges underneath.

6 spherical case on shelf with 6 spherical case underneath

Ammunition wagon limber, off box

7 portfires on underside of the lid.

Slow match and box of quills on shelf with one cartouche with 12 cartridges of 2lb of priming powder.

6 common shell on shelf with 3 light and 3 heavy common case underneath.

Limber, centre box
2 linchpins and 2 drag washers, Spare rammer head.

6 common shell under hinged shelf with cartouche with 18, 2 lb cartridges of priming powder.

12 fuses on hinged shelf with 12, 10 oz cartridges and 12, 6 oz burster charges underneath

6 spherical case on shelf with 6 spherical case underneath.

Ammunition wagon fore box

9, 2lb cartridges of priming powder on hinged shelf with 4 common shell underneath.

3 common shell on hinged shelf with 3 common shell underneath.

12 fuses on hinged shelf with 2 common case underneath.

Slow match and 9, 2lb cartridges of priming powder on hinged shelf with 4 common shell underneath.

12 fuses on hinged shelf with 2 common case underneath

Ammunition wagon hind box

The loading for the light 5.5 inch howitzer was similar except for the cartridges. See Table D.12.

Scale in feet, inches and centimetres	Contents of Heavy 5.5 inch howitzer ammunition wagon and limber boxes - *circa* 1810 (after Dickson)	
0 1 2 0 10 20 30 40 50 60	Figure 12.11.	Part one of one

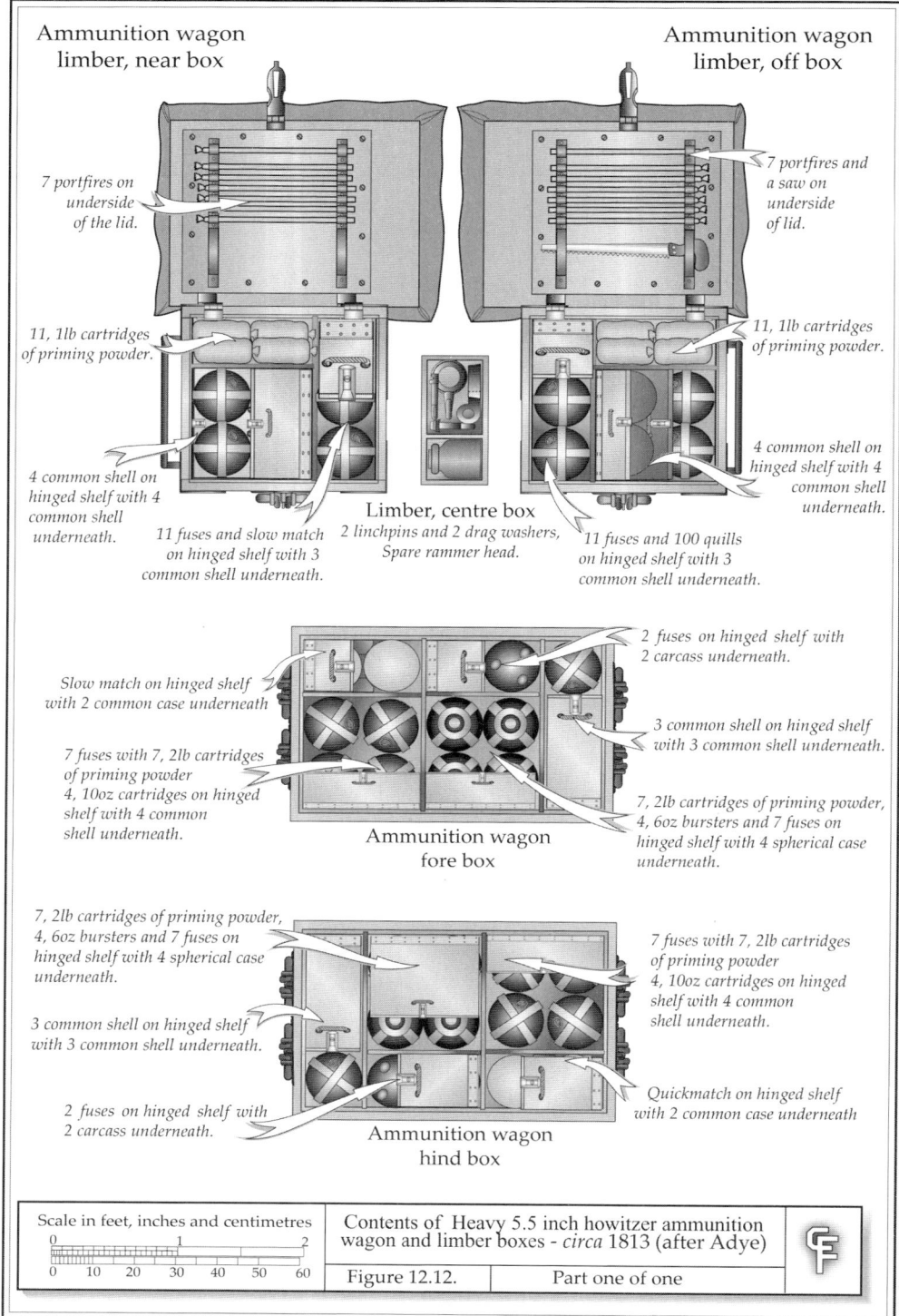

Ammunition wagon
limber, near box

Ammunition wagon
limber, off box

7 portfires on
underside
of the lid.

7 portfires and
a saw on
underside
of lid.

11, 1lb cartridges
of priming powder.

11, 1lb cartridges
of priming powder.

4 common shell on
hinged shelf with 4
common shell
underneath.

4 common shell on
hinged shelf with 4
common shell
underneath.

Limber, centre box
2 linchpins and 2 drag washers,
Spare rammer head.

11 fuses and slow match
on hinged shelf with 3
common shell underneath.

11 fuses and 100 quills
on hinged shelf with 3
common shell underneath.

2 fuses on hinged shelf with
2 carcass underneath.

Slow match on hinged shelf
with 2 common case underneath

3 common shell on hinged shelf
with 3 common shell underneath.

7 fuses with 7, 2lb cartridges
of priming powder
4, 10oz cartridges on hinged
shelf with 4 common
shell underneath.

7, 2lb cartridges of priming powder,
4, 6oz bursters and 7 fuses on
hinged shelf with 4 spherical case
underneath.

Ammunition wagon
fore box

7, 2lb cartridges of priming powder,
4, 6oz bursters and 7 fuses on
hinged shelf with 4 spherical case
underneath.

7 fuses with 7, 2lb cartridges
of priming powder
4, 10oz cartridges on hinged
shelf with 4 common
shell underneath.

3 common shell on hinged shelf
with 3 common shell underneath.

2 fuses on hinged shelf with
2 carcass underneath.

Quickmatch on hinged shelf
with 2 common case underneath

Ammunition wagon
hind box

Scale in feet, inches and centimetres	Contents of Heavy 5.5 inch howitzer ammunition wagon and limber boxes - *circa* 1813 (after Adye)	
0 1 2 0 10 20 30 40 50 60	Figure 12.12.	Part one of one

of Ordnance on the reinforce between the dolphins; it was cast in 1813 by I&H King. A painting by Dighton shows a 5.5-inch howitzer at Waterloo, this is much as expected but the howitzer is shown without dolphins and the carriage has no axle box on the right-hand side. To meet the requirements of the geometry of the piece, the gun carriage would have been generally enlarged on a ratio of 1 to 1.2 but still retaining the 22-degree angle on the trail which was considered the most appropriate to absorb the recoil. It carried the same features as the light howitzers but had a heavier axle 77 inches long and 3.5 inches diameter at the shoulder.

Dickson records the changing ammunition loads carried by the limbers and wagons and also shows the heavy 5.5-inch howitzer with 12 rounds in each limber box and 18 in the fore and hind wagon boxes. His earlier figures show the limbers carried 16 common shells, 4 common case and 4 spherical case. The wagon limber carried the same load and the wagon boxes carried a further 30 common shells, 2 case and 4 carcass rounds.[13]

The weights of the heavy 5.5-inch equipment is given in Table E.9 of Appendix E, the recorded performance in Tables C.19 and C.20 of Appendix C and the ammunition carried at first line, in Tables D.13 and D.14 of Appendix D at the end of Part Two.

Iron 5.5-inch Howitzer also known as the 24-pr Howitzer

In September 1811, it was ordered that iron 5.5-inch howitzers (also referred to as 24-pr howitzers) should be issued to the 9-pr field brigades so that their heavy howitzers could be issued to the horse artillery in lieu of the light howitzers, which were to be 'laid aside'. The intention was to have as heavy ordnance as possible, as the French 6-inch howitzer ranged 'beyond anything the light 5.5-inch howitzer could do'. These iron pieces had a length of 3ft 5in, some 7 calibres, with a weight of 15cwt (1,680lb).[14] They had no chambers and used a 2lb charge of powder with a 10oz separator charge for the spherical case, and in many respects the pieces were of similar performance to the heavy brass 5.5-inch howitzer. They saw limited service and the only record of their use is in the later stages of the Peninsular Campaign. It is said that they were 'specially designed to give the greatest effect to spherical case'.[15]

These howitzers were mounted on block trails and a brigade was formed in August of 1812. The brigade was equipped in the standard manner with the six 24-pr howitzers and limbers drawn by mules, six ammunition wagons, one new pattern forge, one spare wheel carriage and three store carts.[16] No records of their performance have been located.

Little is known of these pieces and there are no records to show the exact nature of the carriages. The illustrations are reconstructions based upon the dimensions of the piece and principles of carriage design as used on the other field howitzers of the period. The width of the trail and the size of the brackets while sufficient to accommodate the trunnions of the piece and allow the maximum elevation meant there was insufficient room on the left of the axle for the usual size of slow match box. It is not known if a special size of box was fitted or if the detachment reverted to the use of a linstock.

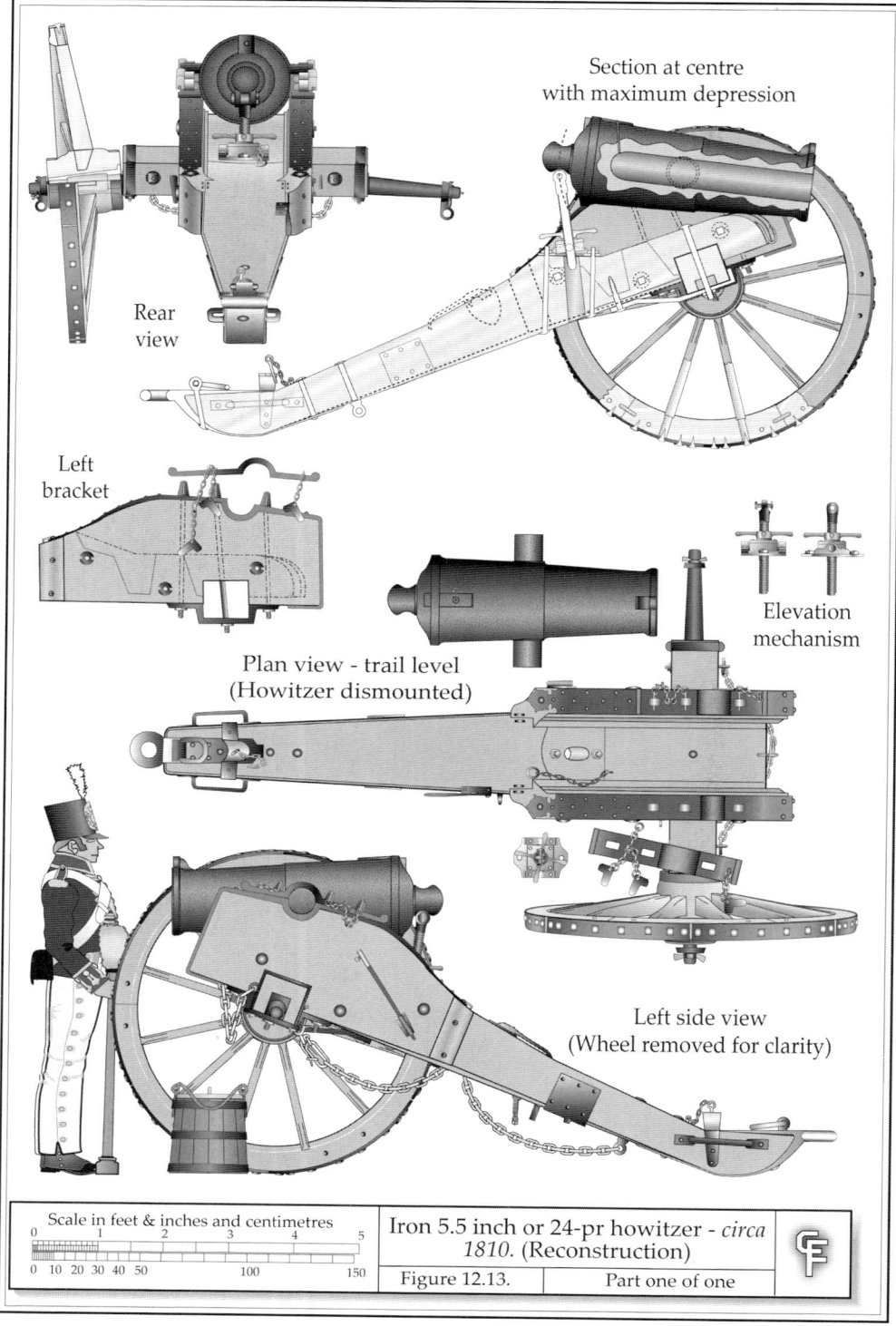

Section at centre
with maximum depression

Rear
view

Left
bracket

Plan view - trail level
(Howitzer dismounted)

Elevation
mechanism

Left side view
(Wheel removed for clarity)

Scale in feet & inches and centimetres

0   1   2   3   4   5

0   10   20   30   40   50   100   150

Iron 5.5 inch or 24-pr howitzer - *circa 1810.* (Reconstruction)

| Figure 12.13. | Part one of one |

Endnotes to Chapter 12

1. Siborne, 1993: p. 227.
2. Duncan, 1872: p. 302.
3. Shuttleworth, 1820: watercolour plates at the James Cavell Library.
4. Caruana, 1980: pp. 9–16.
5. National Archive, WO 1/168: p. 70, dated 6 January 1794; HO 50/368: p. 457.
6. Ibid, WO 55/1194: p. 52.
7. Caruana, 1982: p. 128.
8. Adye, 1801: p. 16.
9. Ibid: p. 10.
10. Ibid: p. 54.
11. Graves, 1982: p. 128.
12. Adye, 1813: p. 194.
13. Dickson, 1908: p. 599.
14. McConnell, 1988: pp. 156–9.
15. Hughes, 1969: p. 42.
16. Dickson, 1908: pp. 462, 463, 642, 652, 820.

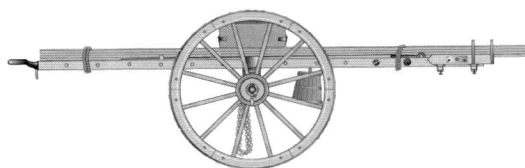

CHAPTER 13

Rocket Equipment

Congreve rockets first saw operational service in 1805, when the British unsuccessfully attacked the French invasion fleet moored in Boulogne harbour basin.[1] By 1806, Congreve had developed cases made of metal and the rockets were classed by weight, the most common sizes being 32-pr and 12-pr, although other sizes were used.[2] It later became general practice to use the 32-pr rockets for bombardment purposes and smaller 12-pr rockets for field service. The main user was the Royal Navy and men from the Royal Marine Artillery became experts in their use. The Royal Artillery only became involved with reluctance and under pressure from the Prince Regent to whom Congreve (the son of Congreve 1st Bart) was an aide and close friend. The artillery was represented by various rocket detachments from the Horse Artillery that served during the Peninsular War and which coalesced to form the 1st and 2nd Rocket Troops of the Royal Horse Artillery in 1815, the foot artillery were never involved.

Two sizes of rockets were carried by the rocket troop, a 12-pr shell rocket and the 32-pr carcass (incendiary) rocket used for bombardment. The 12-pr rockets were fired along the ground from small troughs some 18 inches long. The number 3 of each rocket detachment carried the trough at the rear of his saddle and they were used with varying effect in the Peninsula, at the Battle of New Orleans, during the hundred days and at Waterloo. The performance figures for the Congreve rockets are given in Table C.21 of Appendix C at the end of Part Two.

Rocket Cart or Frame

The heavier 32-pr rocket was fired from a bombarding frame. This frame was in the form of a common land or sea service ladder frame modified for use by the horse artillery as a rocket cart, they were manufactured within the Royal Carriage Department and official descriptions and sketches of the early version still survive. Each rocket cart was accompanied by a standard limber and was the same pattern as that used by the

Royal Horse Artillery. Contemporary descriptions make it clear that the cart taken into service during the Napoleonic era was based upon this early design that had been tested in the Peninsula, it also saw service in Europe, at Leipzig and Waterloo.[3]

The cart consisted of a ladder frame composed of a light ladder, 15 feet long, with two chambers attached to the upper end to hold the rockets, each chamber being fitted with a musket lock and lanyard. The ladder frame was mounted between the wheels of a standard axletree bed as used by a limber or ammunition wagon. Bolted to the top of the axletree bed were two adjustable brackets, which allowed the position of the ladder frame to be adjusted and tightened to lock the ladder frame at different elevations by sliding the ladder through the brackets and lowering the trail end. When on the move the ladder frame itself acted as the perch and was fitted at the lower end with a plate and towing eye to fit over the towing hook of the limber, the rocket sticks, legs or 'pry-poles' and other material being tied by ropes to the ladder-frame. The rockets were carried in special, wagon-style ammunition boxes mounted on the limber. The tools and small stores were carried in the boxes on the axle of the cart and removed when in action, they would have included the special tools for assembling the rockets, pincers, pointed hammers, vices and the wrenches for assembling the sticks. There would have been portfires, portfire igniters, portfire stick, tube box, and pistol locks and cords for the chambers. To swab out the chambers the cart would have also carried buckets, slung beneath the axletree and the side arms as required.[4]

The ladder cart made a very long and cumbersome vehicle that caused considerable difficulty at Waterloo where it was described as 'a great awkward, lumbering carriage with an apparatus called a bombarding frame for heavy rockets'.[5]

When required for action the ladder was unhooked from the limber, the sticks, and other accessories removed from the ladder and axletree bed. The appropriate elevation was applied by tilting the frame upwards while sliding the ladder frame through metal brackets on the axletree bed. The two pry-poles were bolted to the sides of the ladder-frame and acted to support it in the required attitude. A light chain was taken from the axletree of the cart and locked the legs into position, the brackets on the axle were then bolted tight.

Four men were required to bring it into action. Numbers 1 and 2 attached the chambers and locks, while 3 and 4 attached the legs. When ready, all assisted in raising the frame. The proper elevation was applied by moving the legs (a small tape marked in degrees was provided for this purpose). Additionally, a plumb bob was suspended from the ladder to show verticality. Thus prepared, Numbers 1 and 2 waited at the foot of the ladder while 3 and 4, prepared the rockets and fitted the sticks. Number 3 brought the prepared rocket with the vent cover removed and passed it to 2: meanwhile, 1 had ascended the ladder and upon receipt of the rocket from 2, placed the rocket with the stick uppermost in the chamber at the top of the ladder. This process was repeated with the second rocket.

Number 1 then primed and cocked the two locks and descended to the ground. Numbers 1 and 2 each took one of the lanyards and retired obliquely some ten or twelve paces and awaited the order to fire. When the rockets had left the frame, number 1 climbed up the ladder and sponged out the chambers with a wet sponge from the water bucket suspended from the top of the frame. This being done, the cycle was repeated as before. When necessary the ladder could be lowered to facilitate reloading.[6]

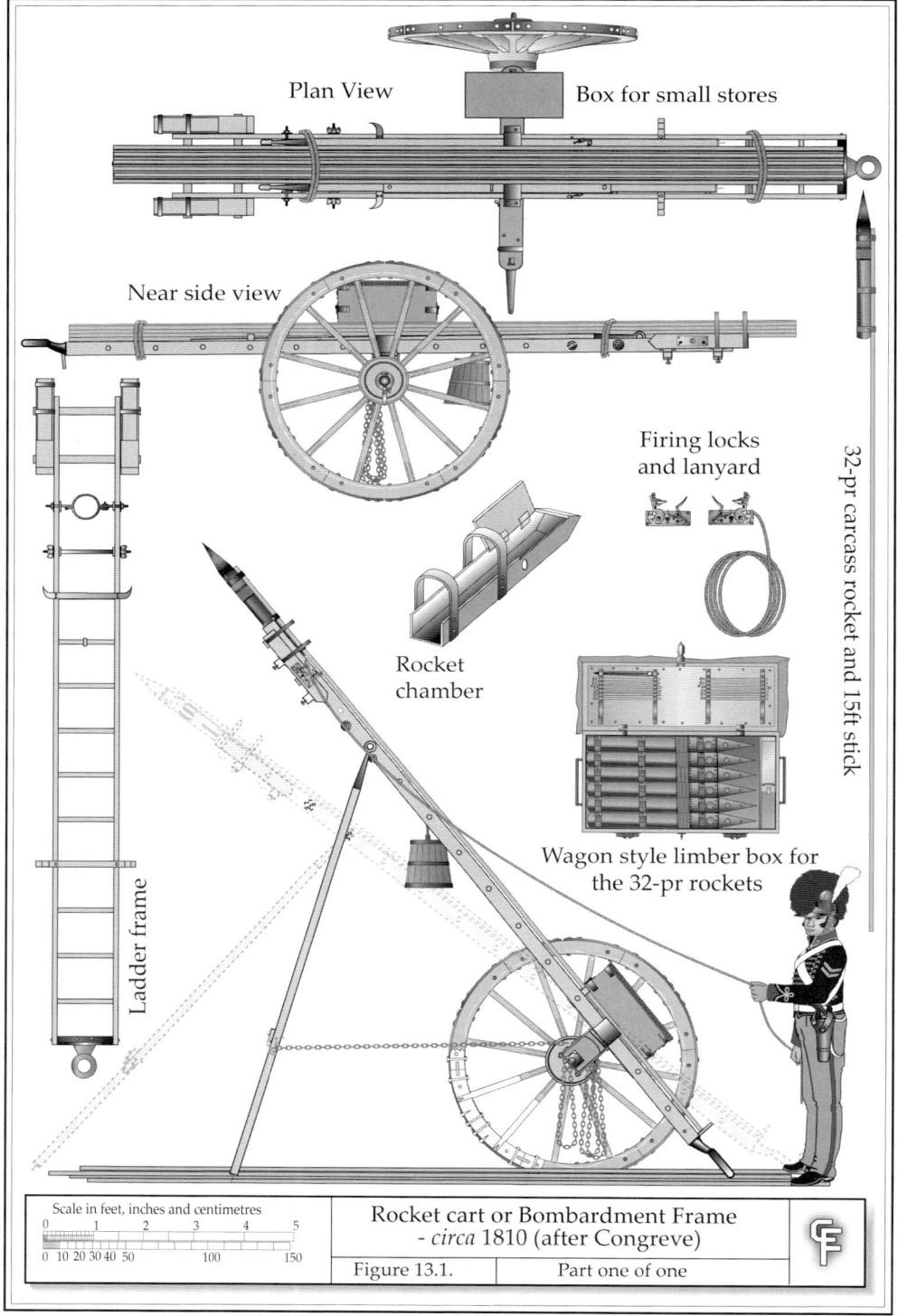

Plan View

Box for small stores

Near side view

Firing locks
and lanyard

32-pr carcass rocket and 15ft stick

Rocket
chamber

Wagon style limber box for
the 32-pr rockets

Ladder frame

Scale in feet, inches and centimetres

0   1   2   3   4   5

0   10 20 30 40 50   100   150

Rocket cart or Bombardment Frame
- *circa* 1810 (after Congreve)

| Figure 13.1. | Part one of one |

Endnotes to Chapter 13

1. Congreve, *W., The Details of the Rocket System*, J. Whiting & Sons, London, 1814: et al.

2. Public Record Office. WO 1/784, 24 April 1806.

3. Franklin, 2005: p. 27; Krigsarkivet, Stockholm. *Kriget I Tyskland 1813–1814*. (Records of the rocket troop when serving under the command of the Swedish army at Leipzig.) The records note that there were six rocket carriages with the Rocket Troop and 1,296 32-pr rockets.

4. Franklin, op. cit: Congreve, W., *Modes of Use and Exercises of Rockets*, 2nd Edn, J. Whiting, London, 1810: pp. 10–21.

5. Siborne, 1891: p. 213.

6. Franklin, 2005: op. cit; Congreve, 1810, op cit.

CHAPTER 14

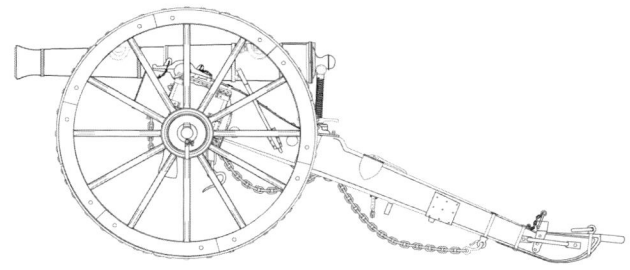

Dimensioned Light 6-pr Gun and Limber

This chapter contains dimensioned drawings of a light 6-pr gun and limber. The dimensions throughout the book are given in feet and inches as this is the measurement used by the source references, but the dimensions on the following drawings are given in millimetres. The original dimensions were taken in 1813 and recorded in Danish feet, inches and lines (Fod, tommer and Linier), for better accuracy and general compliance it was decided to convert the Danish measurements to metric rather than the more imprecise conversion to imperial measurements.

The guns and limbers are currently in the Tøjhusmuseet, Copenhagen and at the Museum of Artillery in Varde. The guns were captured on the 10 December 1813, from the Wiering Battery of the Hanoverian Artillery by the Danish 'Fynske Lette Dragoner' (Funen Light Dragoons) at the Battle of Sehested. Officers of the Danish Artillery, 2nd Lieutenant Carl Christian Shutz and Carl Christian Lundbye, produced the initial drawings in 1813 and 1822.

The gun axles are stamped with the date '1810' and the lack of tire bolts on the wheels clearly date the gun carriage and limber before 1813. The piece of Blomefield design bears the markings 'I.H.King. 1810' on the first reinforce ogee and bears the Royal crest of George III on the second reinforce. The chase is embossed with the crest of the Earl of Chatham who was the Master General of Ordnance at this time. The ring to the second reinforce is embossed MCCCLXXIV and the trunnion end bears the serial number 1379. The pieces are marked with quarter sights and tangent scales are fitted to the breech ring. The length of the piece is given in the convention of 96ths of a calibre and is given as 16 28/96ths calibres and the bore measured as 3.692 inches, slightly oversize for the nominal 3.668 inches.

The gun carriage follows the expected pattern for a block trail carriage but with some differences not previously understood. The complex joint between the brackets, trail and axletree bed is different on the two guns but both have rectangular beds

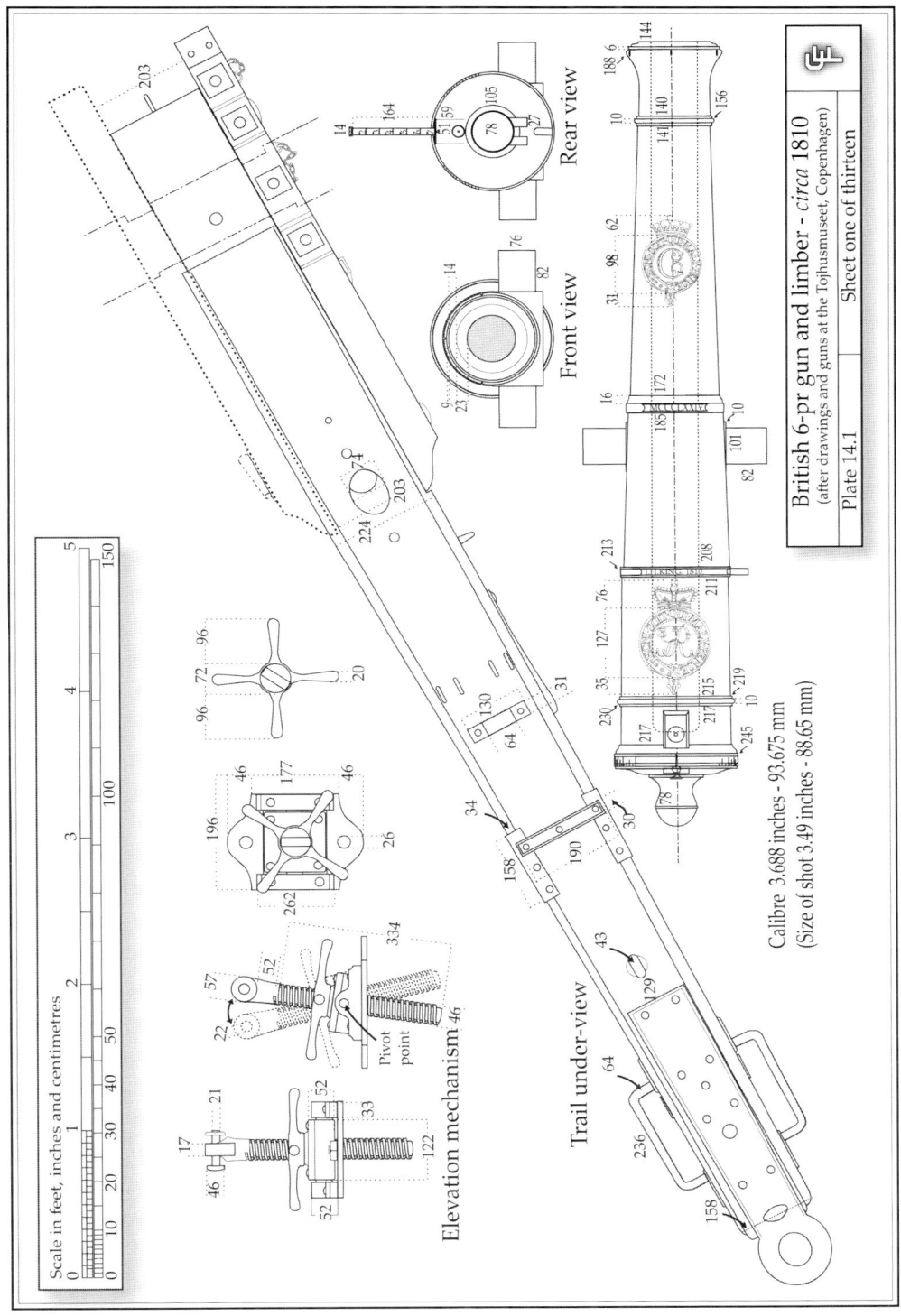

British 6-pr gun and limber - *circa* 1810
(after drawings and guns at the Tøjhusmuseet, Copenhagen)

Plate 14.1   Sheet one of thirteen

Calibre 3.688 inches - 93.675 mm
(Size of shot 3.49 inches - 88.65 mm)

Rear view

Front view

Trail under-view

Elevation mechanism

Pivot point

Scale in feet, inches and centimetres

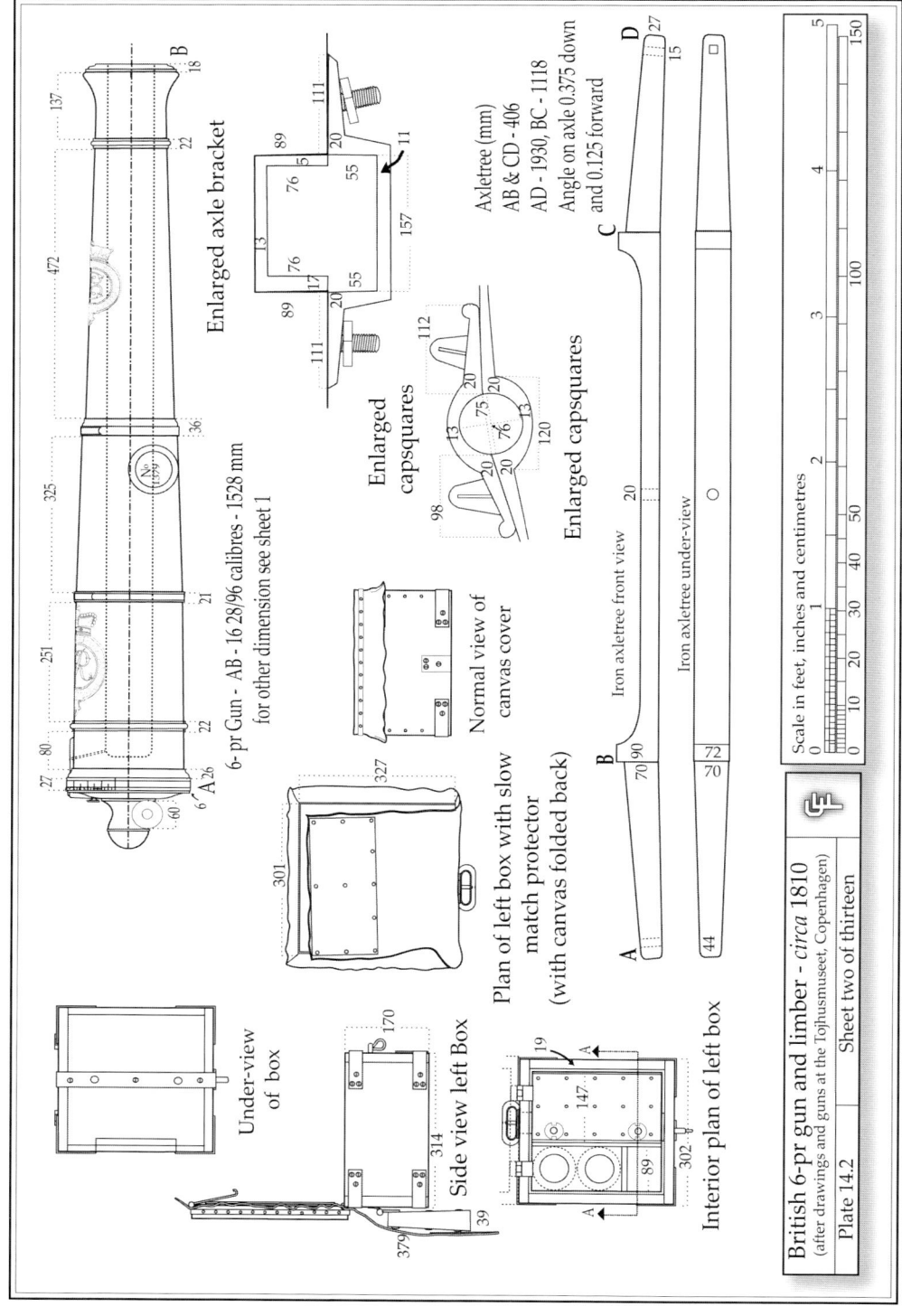

Enlarged axle bracket

6-pr Gun - AB - 16 28/96 calibres - 1528 mm
for other dimension see sheet 1

Enlarged
capsquares

Enlarged capsquares

Axletree (mm)
AB & CD - 406
AD - 1930, BC - 1118
Angle on axle 0.375 down
and 0.125 forward

Iron axletree front view

Iron axletree under-view

Normal view of
canvas cover

Plan of left box with slow
match protector
(with canvas folded back)

Under-view
of box

Side view left Box

Interior plan of left box

Scale in feet, inches and centimetres

British 6-pr gun and limber - *circa* 1810
(after drawings and guns at the Tøjhusmuseet, Copenhagen)

Plate 14.2   Sheet two of thirteen

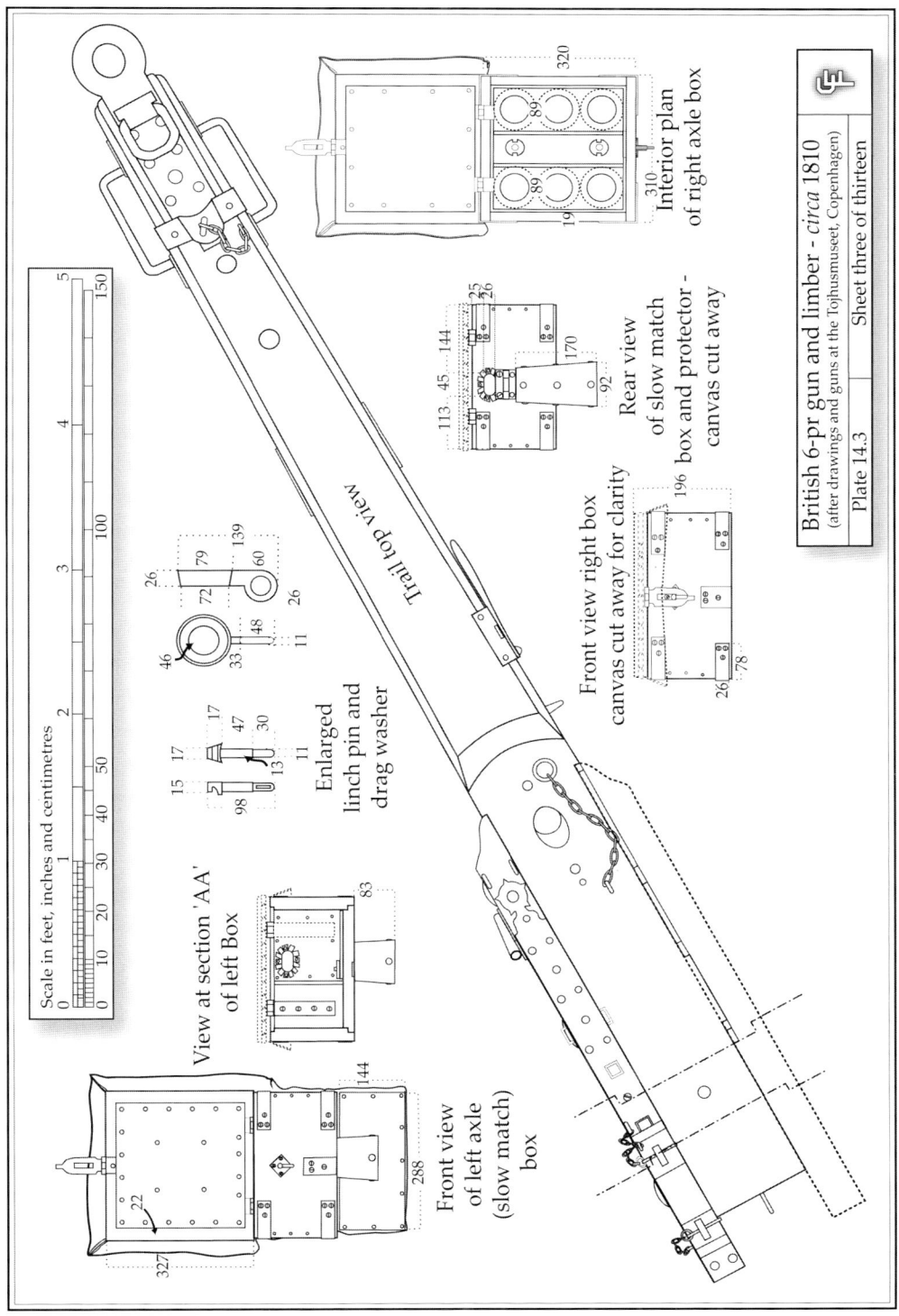

320

89

89

310

19

Interior plan
of right axle box

25
26

144

45

113

170

92

Rear view
of slow match
box and protector -
canvas cut away

196

78

26

Front view right box
canvas cut away for clarity

British 6-pr gun and limber - *circa* 1810
(after drawings and guns at the Tojhusmuseet, Copenhagen)

Plate 14.3   Sheet three of thirteen

5

150

4

100

3

2

50

1

40

30

20

10

0

0

Scale in feet, inches and centimetres

Trail top view

79
139

60

26

72

26

48

11

46

33

11

17

17

47

30

15

17

13

11

5

98

13

Enlarged
linch pin and
drag washer

83

View at section 'AA'
of left Box

144

288

22

327

Front view
of left axle
(slow match)
box

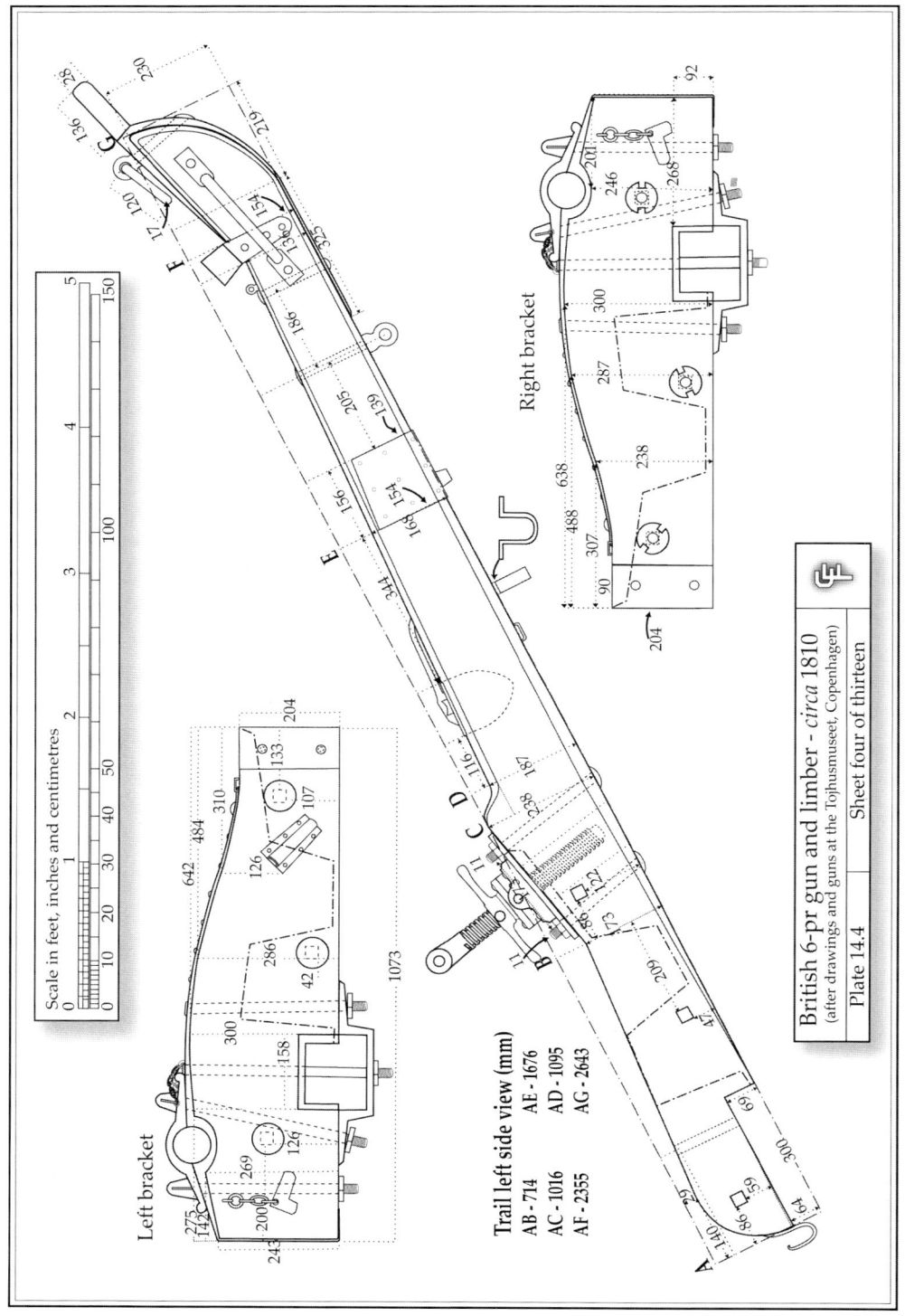

Scale in feet, inches and centimetres

Left bracket

Right bracket

Trail left side view (mm)

AB - 714	AE - 1676
AC - 1016	AD - 1095
AF - 2355	AG - 2643

British 6-pr gun and limber - *circa* **1810**
(after drawings and guns at the Tøjhusmuseet, Copenhagen)

Plate 14.4   Sheet four of thirteen

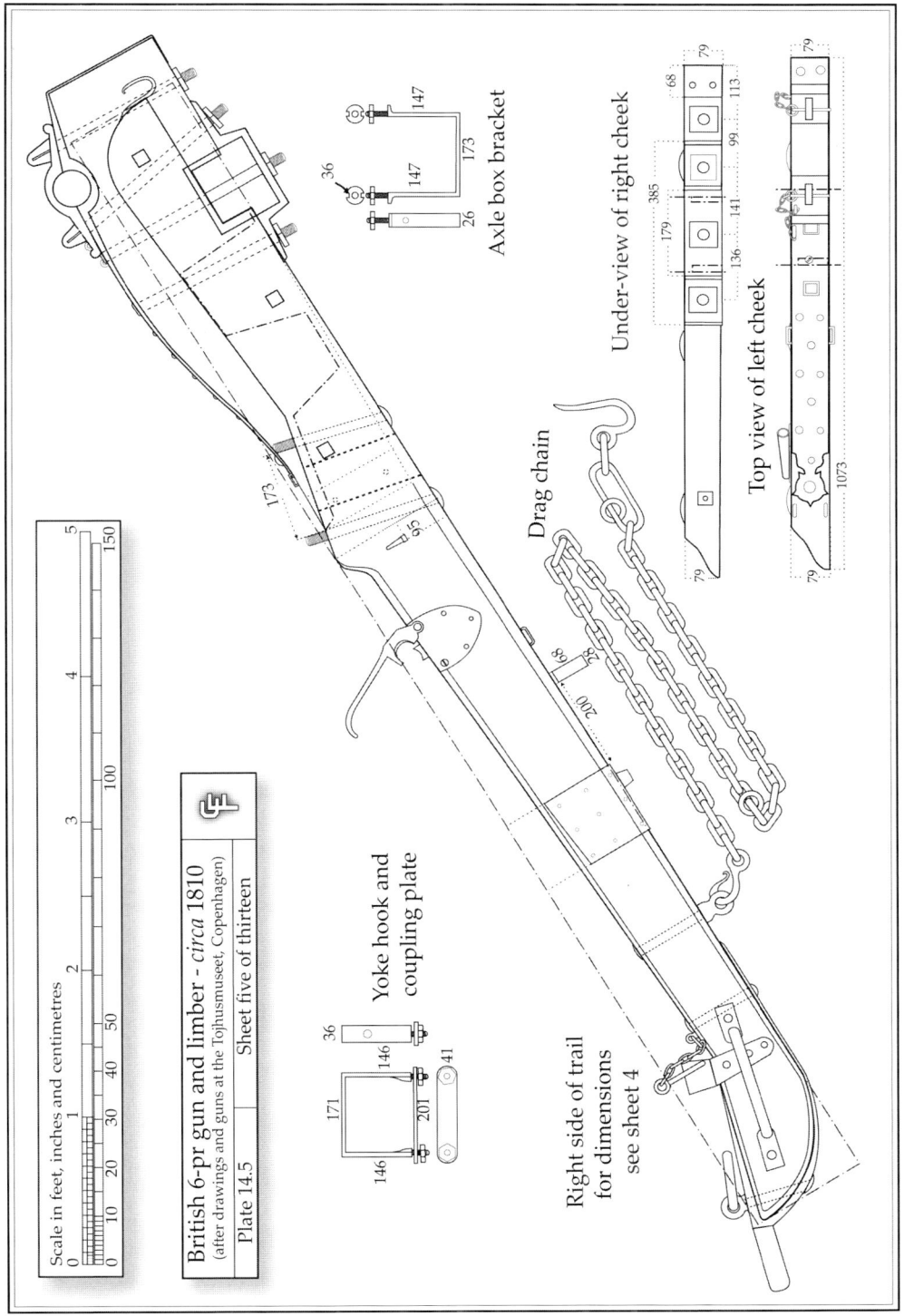

Scale in feet, inches and centimetres

British 6-pr gun and limber - *circa* 1810
(after drawings and guns at the Tøjhusmuseet, Copenhagen)

Plate 14.5   Sheet five of thirteen

Axle box bracket

Under-view of right cheek

Top view of left cheek

Drag chain

Yoke hook and coupling plate

Right side of trail for dimensions see sheet 4

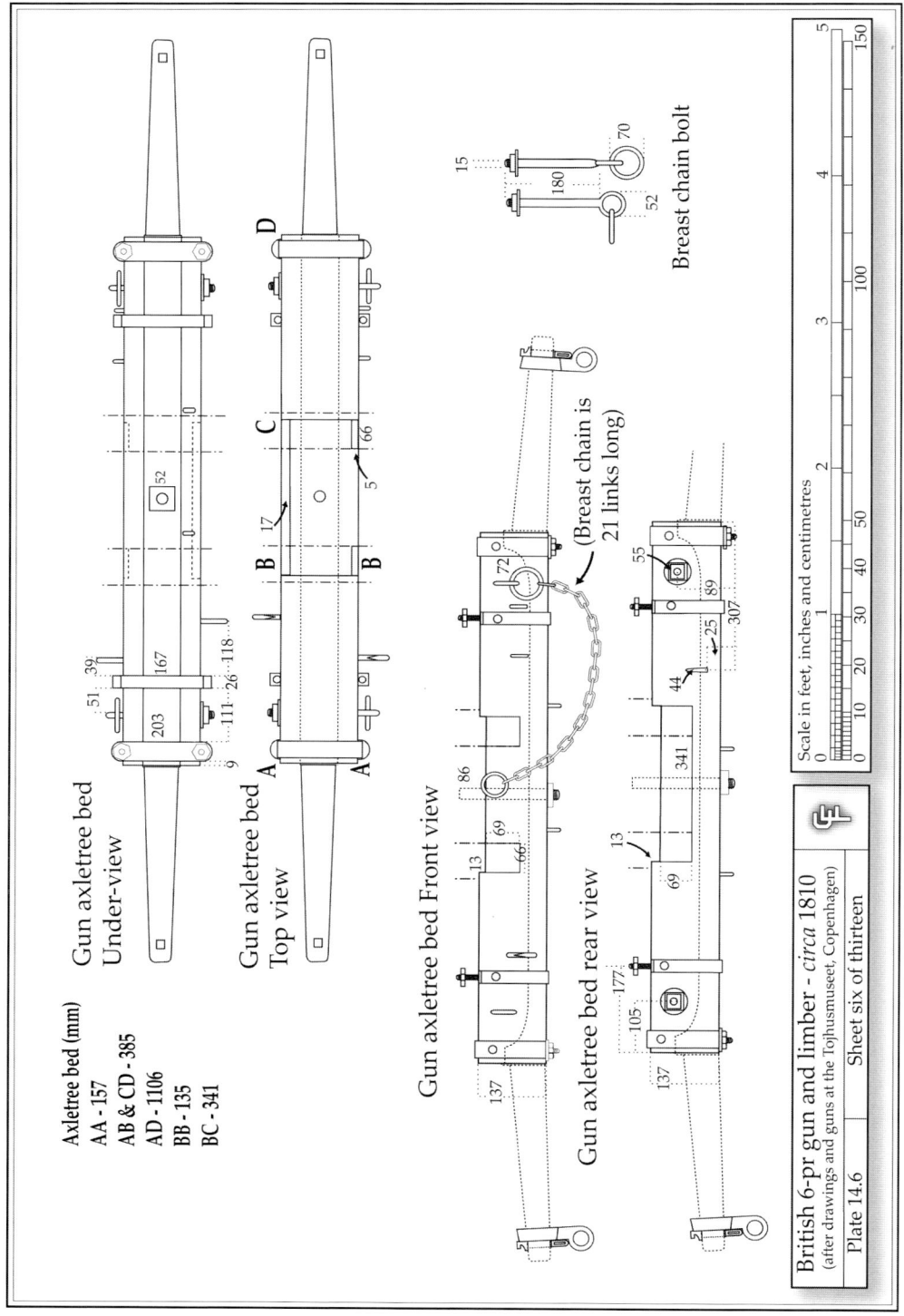

Gun axletree bed
Under-view

Gun axletree bed
Top view

Axletree bed (mm)
AA - 157
AB & CD - 385
AD - 1106
BB - 135
BC - 341

Gun axletree bed Front view

Gun axletree bed rear view

(Breast chain is 21 links long)

Breast chain bolt

Scale in feet, inches and centimetres

British 6-pr gun and limber - *circa* 1810
(after drawings and guns at the Tøjhusmuseet, Copenhagen)

Plate 14.6   Sheet six of thirteen

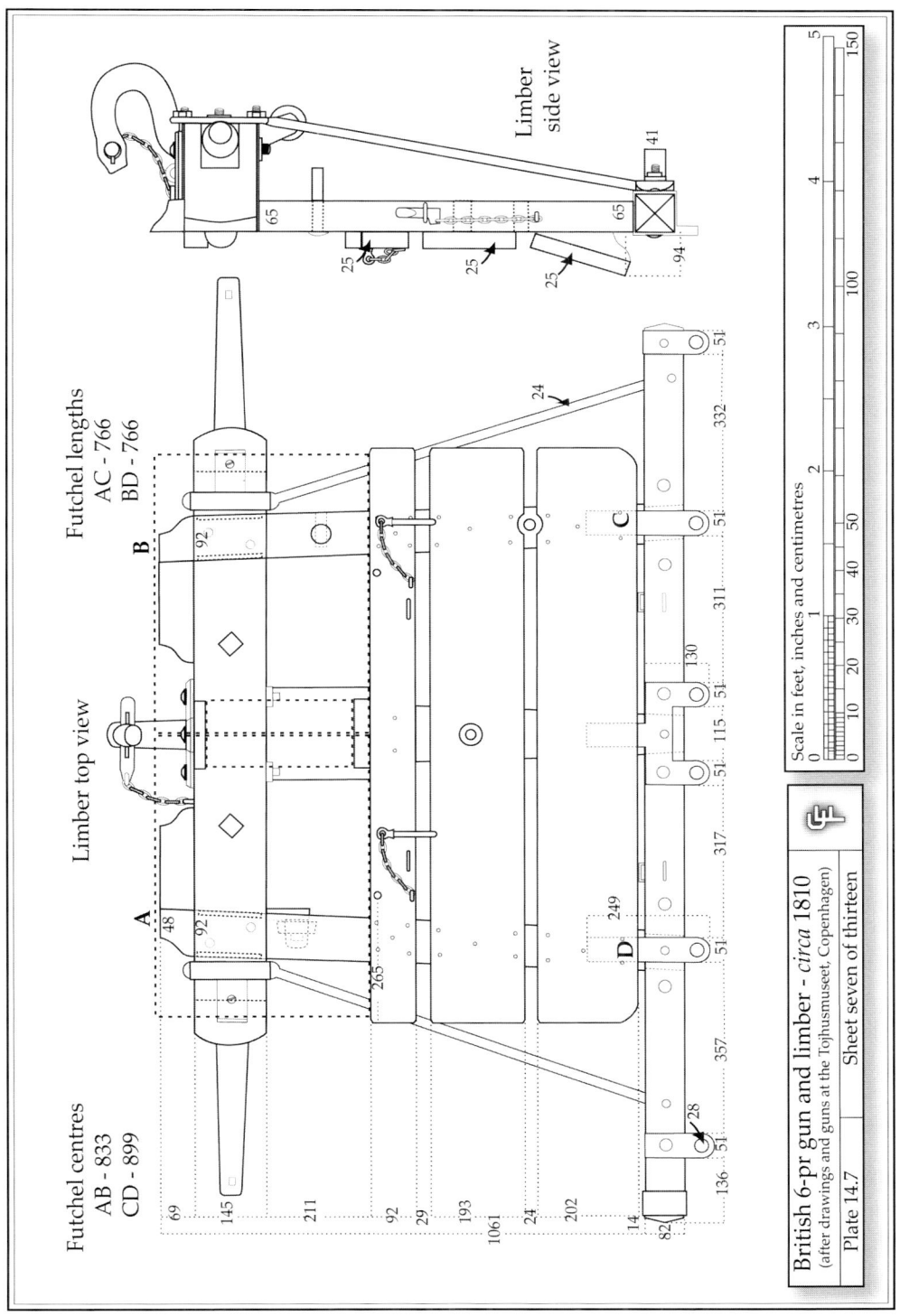

Limber side view

Limber top view

Futchel lengths
AC - 766
BD - 766

Futchel centres
AB - 833
CD - 899

A B

C D

65   65
41
94
25   25   25

24

332   311   317   357

51   51   130 51 115 51 51 51   28   136 51

249
263

92   48   92
92

69   145   211   92   29   193   1061   24   202   14   82

Scale in feet, inches and centimetres

0   1   2   3   4   5

0   10   20   30   40   50   100   150

British 6-pr gun and limber - *circa* 1810
(after drawings and guns at the Tøjhusmuseet, Copenhagen)

Plate 14.7   Sheet seven of thirteen

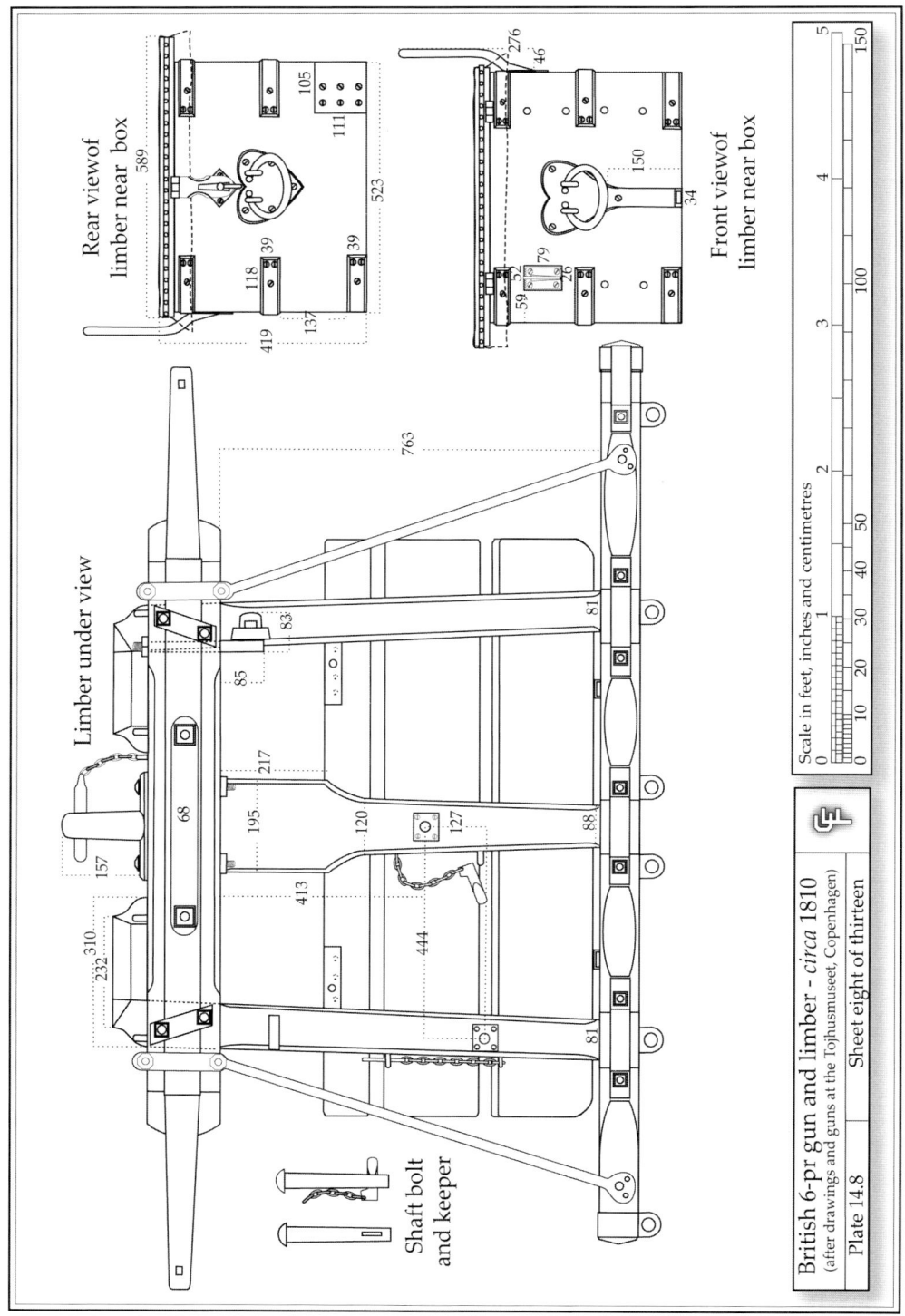

Rear view of
limber near box

Front view of
limber near box

Limber under view

Shaft bolt
and keeper

Scale in feet, inches and centimetres

British 6-pr gun and limber - *circa* 1810
(after drawings and guns at the Tøjhusmuseet, Copenhagen)

Plate 14.8   Sheet eight of thirteen

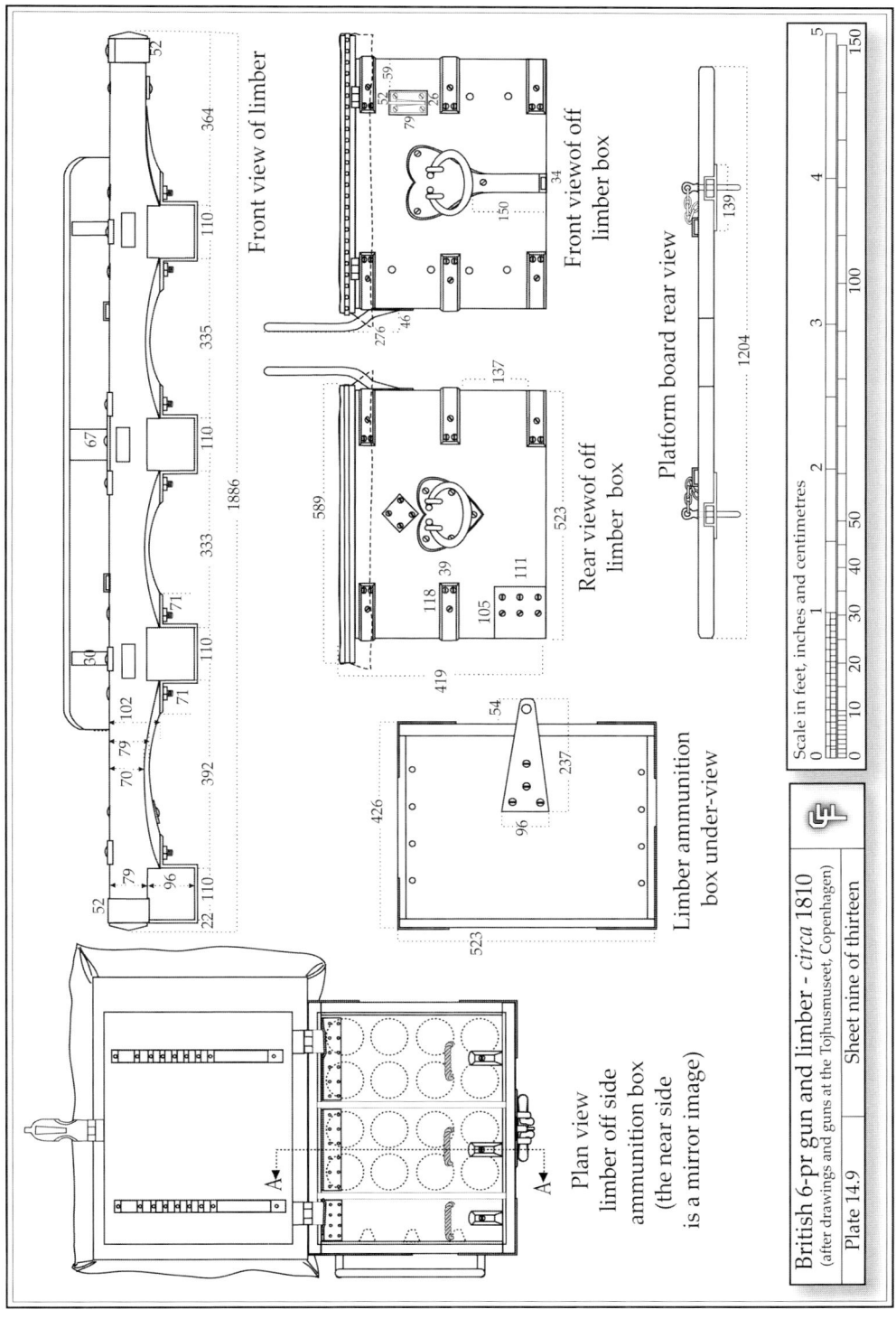

Front view of limber

Front view off limber box

Rear view off limber box

Platform board rear view

Limber ammunition box under-view

Plan view limber off side ammunition box (the near side is a mirror image)

Scale in feet, inches and centimetres

British 6-pr gun and limber - *circa* 1810
(after drawings and guns at the Tojhusmuseet, Copenhagen)

Plate 14.9   Sheet nine of thirteen

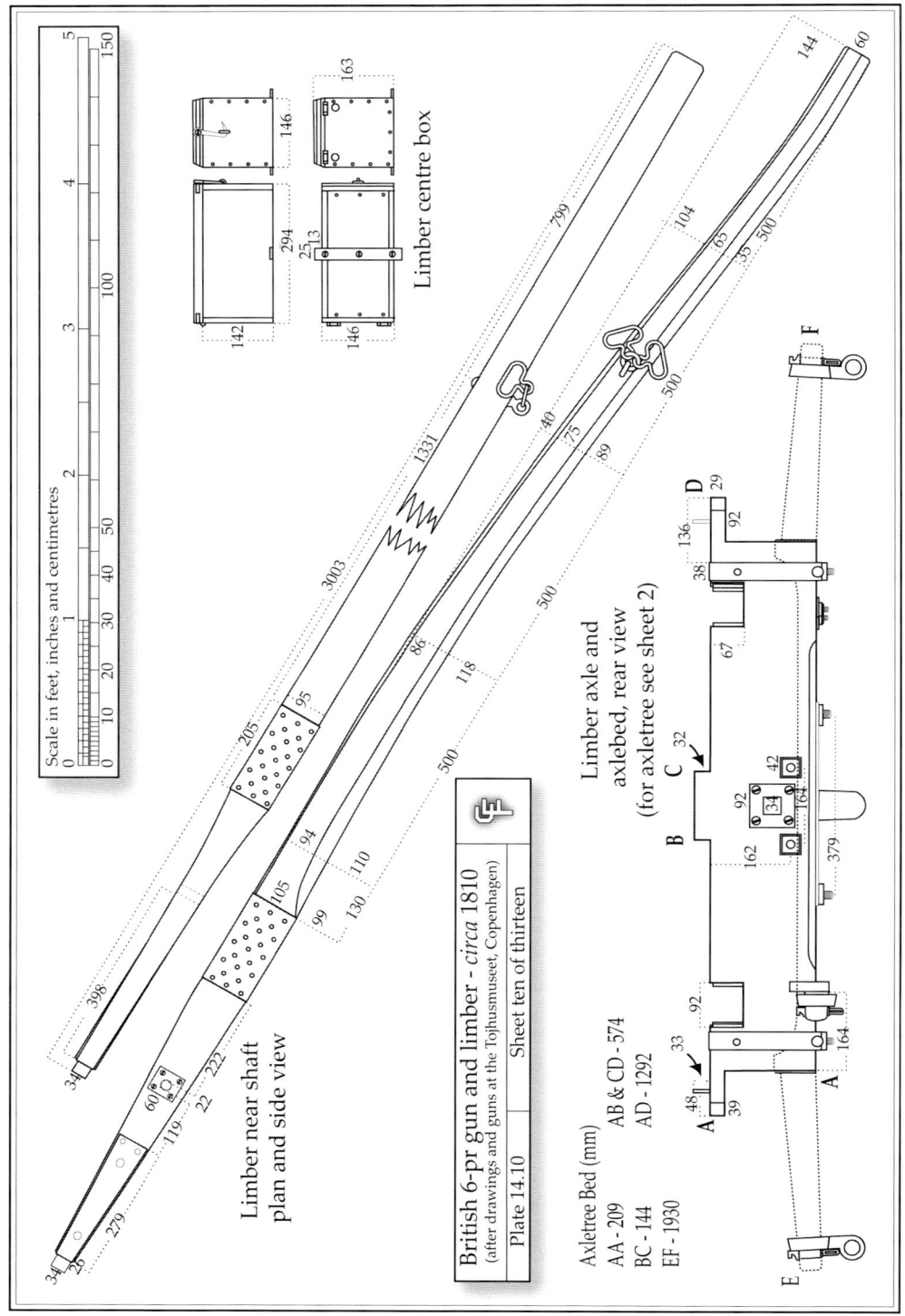

Scale in feet, inches and centimetres

Limber centre box

Limber near shaft plan and side view

Limber axle and axlebed, rear view
(for axletree see sheet 2)

British 6-pr gun and limber - *circa* 1810
(after drawings and guns at the Tøjhusmuseet, Copenhagen)

Plate 14.10	Sheet ten of thirteen

Axletree Bed (mm)
AA - 209   AB & CD - 574
BC - 144   AD - 1292
EF - 1930

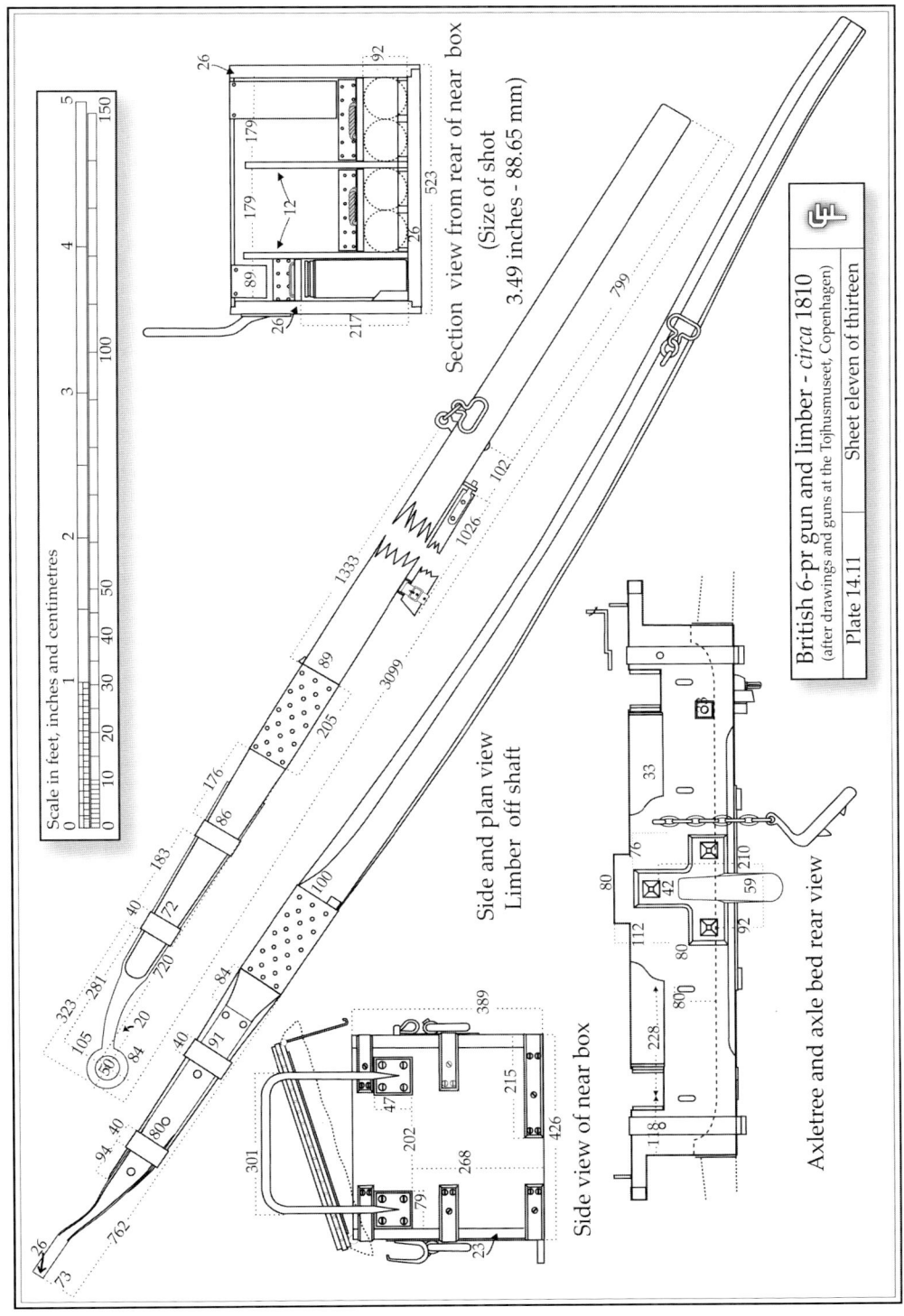

Section view from rear of near box
(Size of shot
3.49 inches - 88.65 mm)

Scale in feet, inches and centimetres

Side and plan view
Limber off shaft

Side view of near box

Axletree and axle bed rear view

British 6-pr gun and limber - *circa* 1810
(after drawings and guns at the Tøjhusmuseet, Copenhagen)

Plate 14.11   Sheet eleven of thirteen

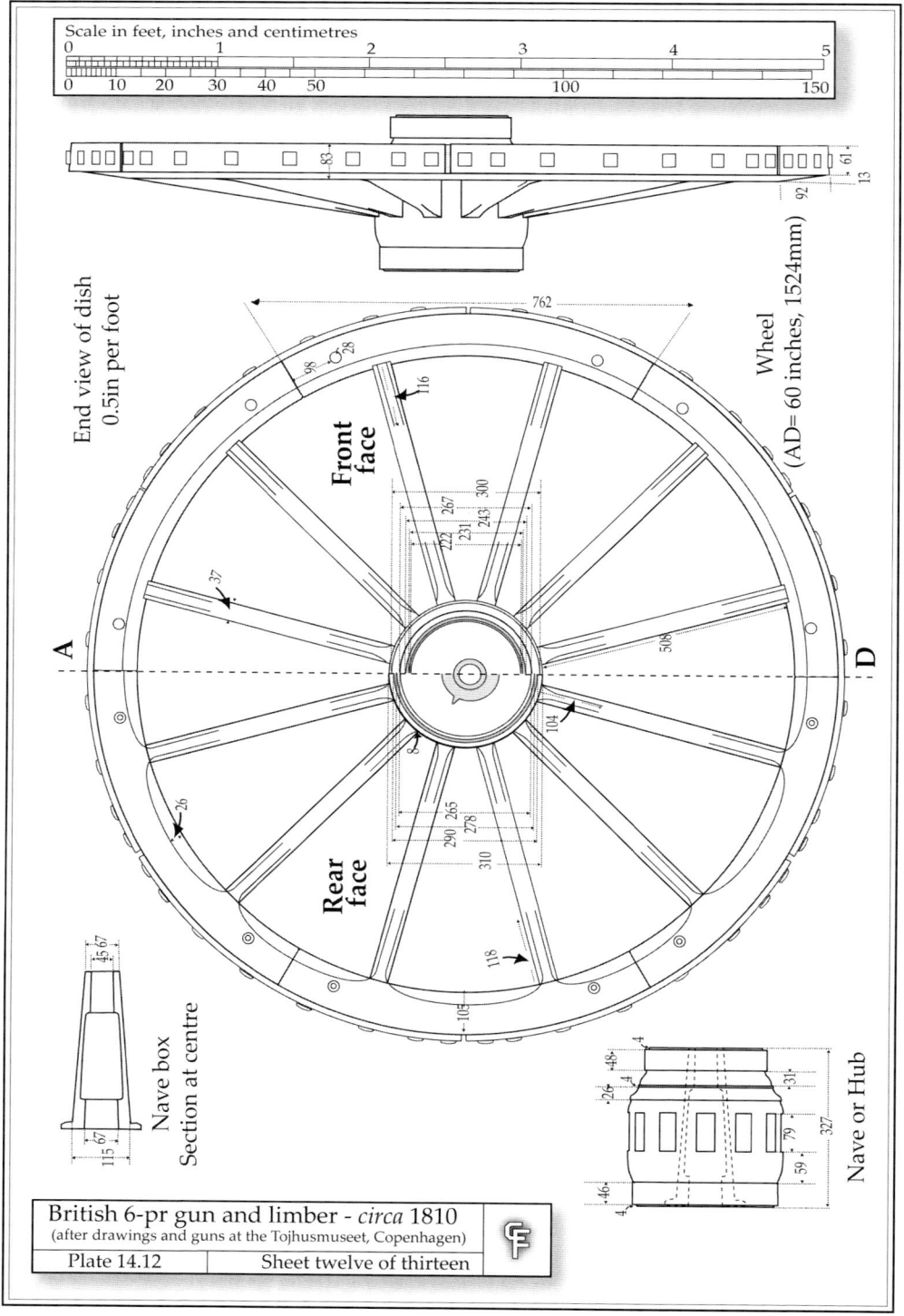

Scale in feet, inches and centimetres

End view of dish
0.5in per foot

Front face

Rear face

Wheel (AD= 60 inches, 1524mm)

Nave box
Section at centre

Nave or Hub

British 6-pr gun and limber - *circa* 1810
(after drawings and guns at the Tojhusmuseet, Copenhagen)

| Plate 14.12 | Sheet twelve of thirteen |

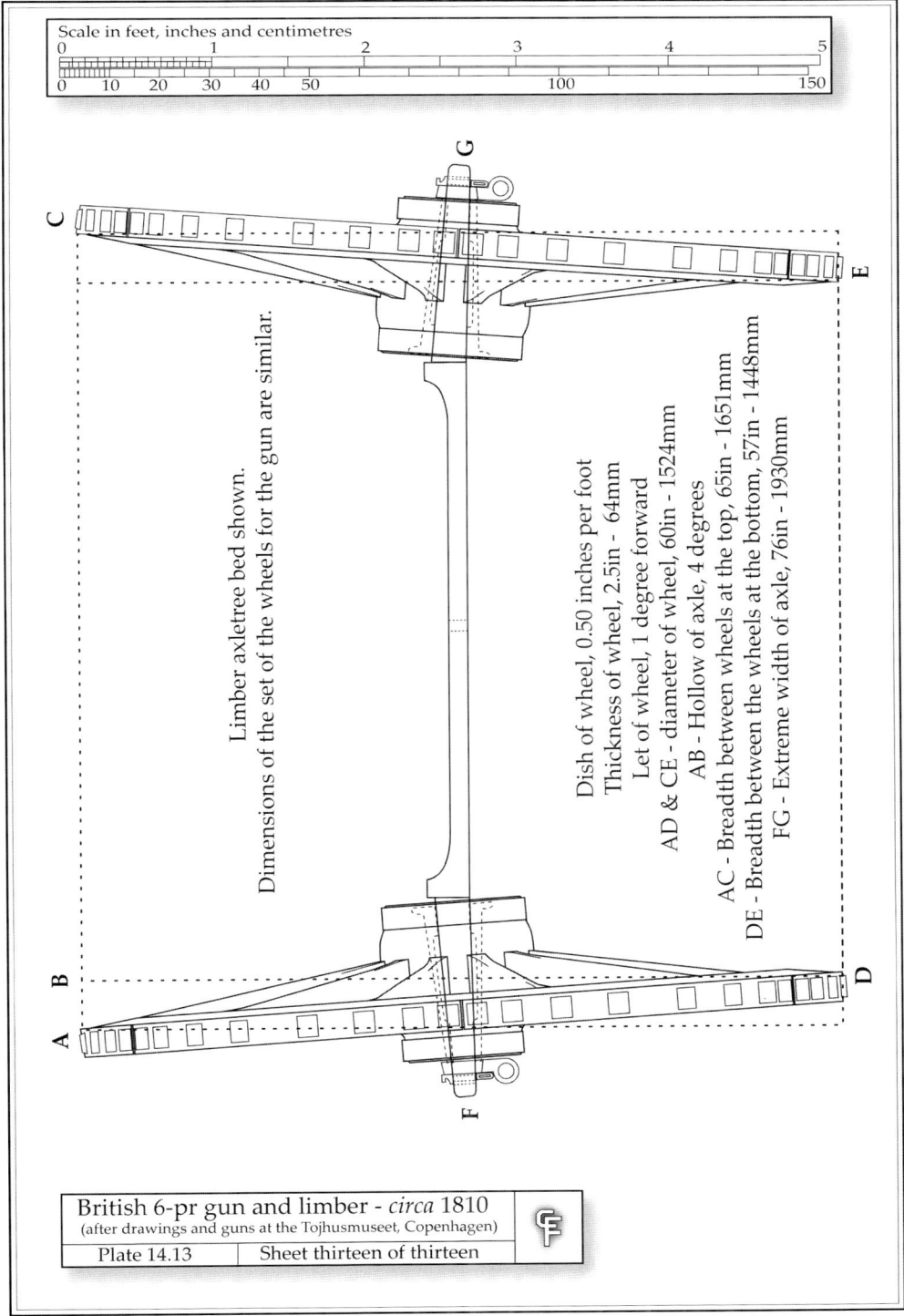

Scale in feet, inches and centimetres

0   1   2   3   4   5

0 10 20 30 40 50   100   150

Limber axletree bed shown.
Dimensions of the set of the wheels for the gun are similar.

Dish of wheel, 0.50 inches per foot
Thickness of wheel, 2.5in - 64mm
Let of wheel, 1 degree forward
AD & CE - diameter of wheel, 60in - 1524mm
AB - Hollow of axle, 4 degrees
AC - Breadth between wheels at the top, 65in - 1651mm
DE - Breadth between the wheels at the bottom, 57in - 1448mm
FG - Extreme width of axle, 76in - 1930mm

British 6-pr gun and limber - *circa* 1810
(after drawings and guns at the Tojhusmuseet, Copenhagen)

| Plate 14.13 | Sheet thirteen of thirteen |

not those shown on the Royal Carriage Department plates of 1870. The elevating mechanism has the pre-1863 elevating mechanism with a brass elevating screw with a thread of three to the inch. The retaining nut and bolt have octagonal ends. On the guns, themselves there are none of the later elaborate fittings for side arms or tools and the right axle box has been replaced by a larger and clearly locally made ammunition box, apparently fitted by the Hanoverian Artillery to provide a supply of ready use ammunition at the gun. On the following drawings, this has been replaced with a conventional box that matches the dispositions according to Adye and Dickson. The left axle box for the slow match is complete in all the details. The drawings in the earlier chapters of this book are based upon these lines and principles of construction as well as other such sources as are quoted. It should be noted by modellers or builders that while the nuts on the bracket bolts and eyebolts are square, those on the yoke hoops and coupling plates are hexagonal.

The limber is complete with clearly unmodified shafts and ammunition boxes. The internal arrangement of the ammunition boxes matches the Adye listing for this period and has no facility for the carriage of spherical case or any form of fixed or semi-fixed ammunition, just common case and round shot without bottoms. The limber arrangement for single, double and triple draft was clearly the same in 1810 as it was in the post-Napoleonic era and follows the pattern quoted in the Treatise on Military Carriages. The other clarification is the way that the ammunition boxes are secured to the limber. Each is fitted with a nib plate on the front edge. This engages in a metal bracket in the rear face of the platform board where it is retained by a chained pin. At the rear, ropes were tied through the handles to staples on the axle-bed and secured the boxes to the limber.

It should be noted that some of the details and dimensions do not concur with those given by some of the contemporary and later sources. This is probably due to manufacturing tolerances or the fact that the surviving equipment was never so fitted. In either event the reader must decide which should be given preference.

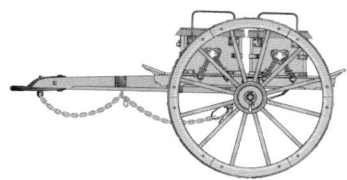

CHAPTER 15

Supporting Equipment

Wagons, Carts and Limbers

Each troop of horse artillery and brigade of foot artillery was supported by a large array of miscellaneous carts, carriages, wagons and limbers. Those that formed a formal part of the unit varied with the nature of the ordnance involved, some had as many as seventeen others only eleven, and this did not include the wagons and carts necessary for the reserve ammunition, baggage, tentage, rations or forage. The combination of gun and limber had provided an articulated four-wheeled vehicle of such excellence that the pattern was copied for the other first-line vehicles that accompanied the guns and rocket carts. In the usual definition of a wagon or cart, they are distinguished in that the wagon has four wheels while a cart has two, curricles being smaller two-wheeled carts. However, in military terminology of the period any two-wheeled vehicle designed to be coupled to another to form an articulated four-wheeled vehicle, was also called a wagon, although perversely this was not applied to rocket or forge carts. Thus, we have at first line a two-wheeled ammunition wagon while at second line, the ammunition and baggage wagons were true wagons, having four wheels. The number of wagons to support an artillery unit is shown in Table F.1 of Appendix F at the end of Part Two.

Ammunition Cars, Wagons and Limbers

Each gun was accompanied at first line by one or more ammunition cars or wagons. Initially the ammunition was carried on two-wheel cars of a similar pattern to the later ammunition wagon but with smaller boxes with separate compartments for each round and less ammunition. That the style of the early ammunition wagons preceded the block trail carriage and limber is referred to in the specifications of the Duke of Richmond, Master General of Ordnance, for the new equipment for the horse artillery which was to *'have wheels and axletree of the same dimension and length of those of the new pattern ammunition wagon'*.[1]

The size of the boxes on these two-wheel cars was given as 28 inches wide, 16 inches high and 17 inches from front to back. Like the later variant, they carried two boxes, known as the fore and hind box. Apart from the design of the car a major difference was in the way the ammunition was packed. The designer of the car observed:

> The lower end of both round and case to be in square cells: the upper tier to be separated by a [pillar] which will, at the same time that the ammunition is kept from shaking in traveling permit the boards to move freely on the hinges … the boards resting on partitions and uprights marked in the plan … The object proposed by this size of body waggon box is to pack the proposed quantity of ammunition in the simplest and safest manner, and in the least possible space, which attending to being a convenient seat for two gunners on each box will permit.[2]

When the change to the new pattern wagon occurred is unclear, but by 1803 the ammunition carried by these early cars is still recorded. However, Adye noted that two-wheel cars were only used until worn out and for all foreign service the new ammunition wagon was used. However, Dickson in September 1810 related that 'This day arrived 8 ammunition carriages of the new construction, 2 for Howitzers, 6 for Light 6 Pr', so perhaps the time to issue throughout the theatres was longer than Adye noted, even by 1811 the old-style ammunition cars were still in use.[3]

The new pattern was one based upon a doubled, standard limber. It was towed by a limber of the same pattern as that of the gun and carrying the same ammunition boxes, so if the gun limber was damaged or destroyed, the limber of the ammunition wagon was a direct replacement.[4] The pattern of the new ammunition wagons was standard except for the internal fittings of the fore and hind ammunition boxes. These were larger and carried more ammunition than the earlier variant and the internal arrangement varied with the nature of the ordnance and the stores carried but conformed in width and height, any variation being accommodated, within certain limits, by adjustment to the size of the platform board just as it was on the limber. These new wagons made the storage of fixed ammunition difficult, as they were not designed for it. Dickson noted this and remarked upon it, 'bottoms occasion an inconvenience when packing the ammunition in the new waggons'.[5] Spare iron axletrees and a camp kettle were also carried, usually under the wagon; often it is said, with the kettle retaining part of the meal.[6]

The ammunition wagon consisted of a framework formed by a short perch, an elm axletree-bed, two sidepieces and three ash platform boards and two footboards. The perch was tenoned through the axletree-bed where it was secured by a large bolt passing down through the bed and the axle. The front end of the perch was fitted with a nose plate and towing eye.

The iron axletree was secured in a groove in the bottom of the bed by yoke hoops and coupling plates, plus two bolts through the bed and secured underneath. Two bolts attached each sidepiece to the axletree-bed, these passed either side of the axletree, the ends being secured by nuts to a coupling plate underneath. To support the side pieces, two metal stays were bolted to the underside of the axletree-bed and across the top of this framework, at either end, was fastened a platform board and an elm footboard raised at the front on small brackets. These were bolted to the sidepieces and the perch at the centre. In the middle of the wagon, above the axletree-bed, was a further centre platform board. Underneath, between the perch and sidepieces, the wagon was fitted with iron brackets to carry the boxes for spare

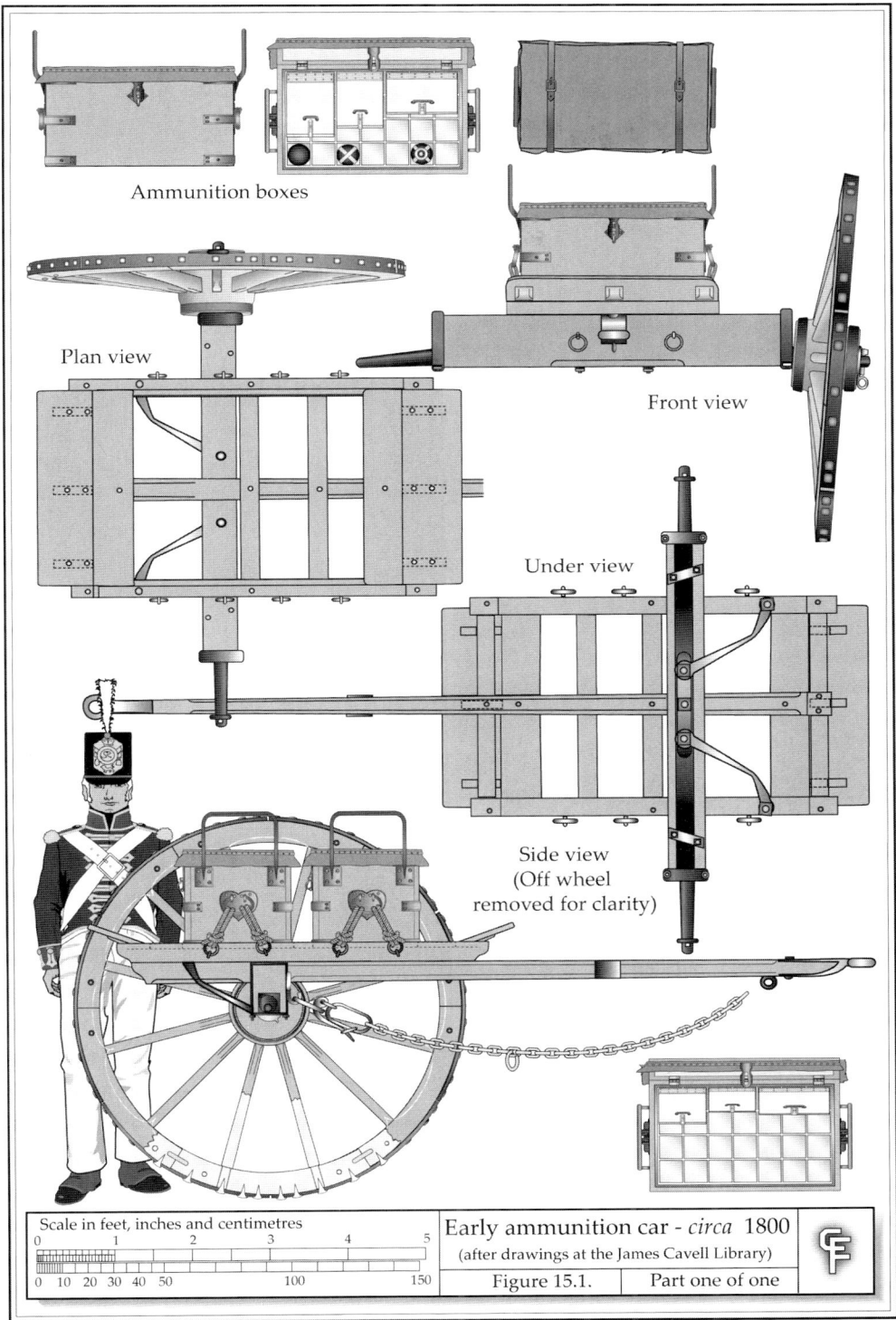

Ammunition boxes

Plan view

Front view

Under view

Side view
(Off wheel
removed for clarity)

Scale in feet, inches and centimetres
0   1   2   3   4   5
0 10 20 30 40 50   100   150

Early ammunition car - *circa* 1800
(after drawings at the James Cavell Library)

Figure 15.1. | Part one of one

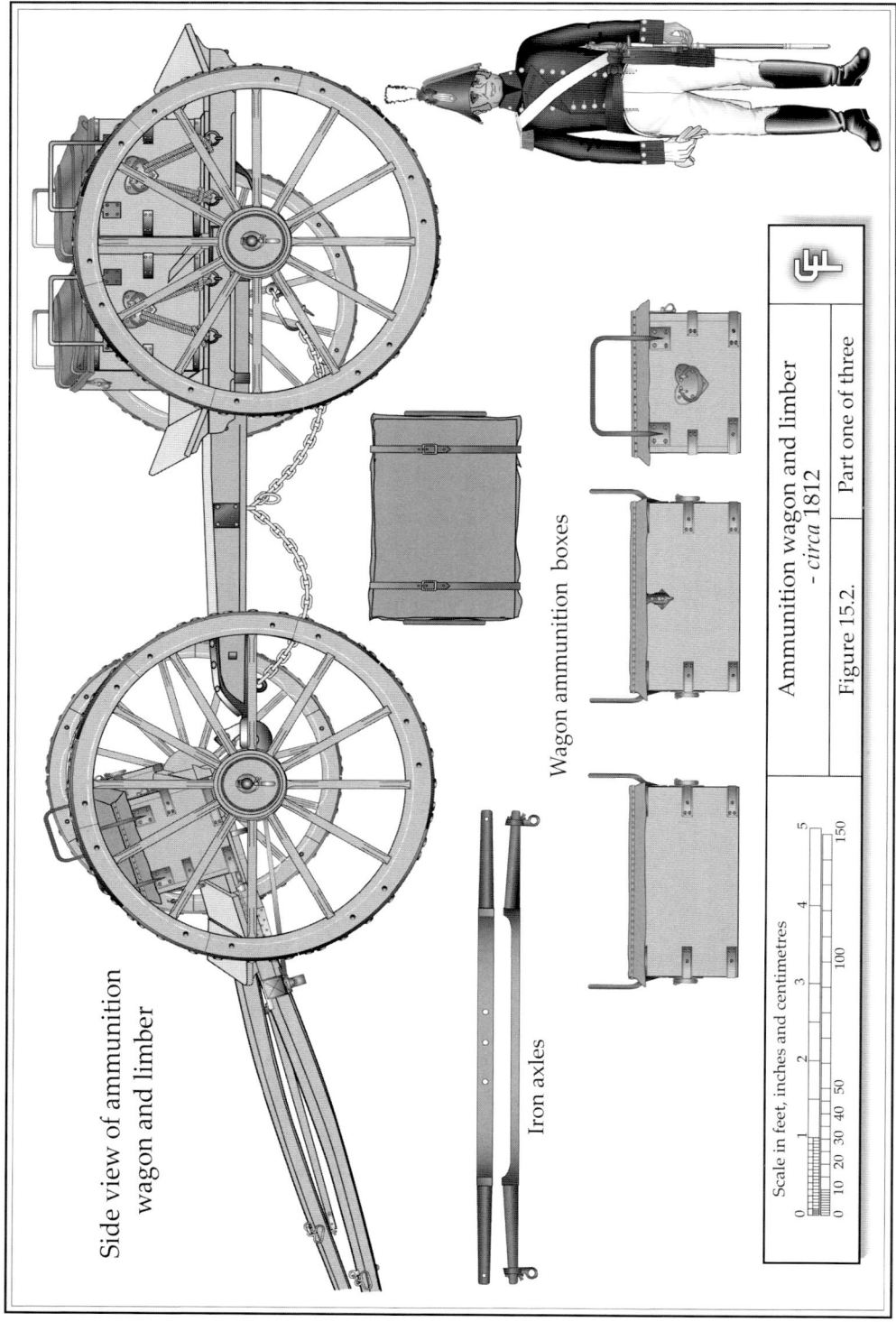

Side view of ammunition wagon and limber

Iron axles

Wagon ammunition boxes

Ammunition wagon and limber - *circa* 1812

Part one of three

Figure 15.2.

Scale in feet, inches and centimetres

5

150

4

100

3

2

50

1

10 20 30 40 50

0

0

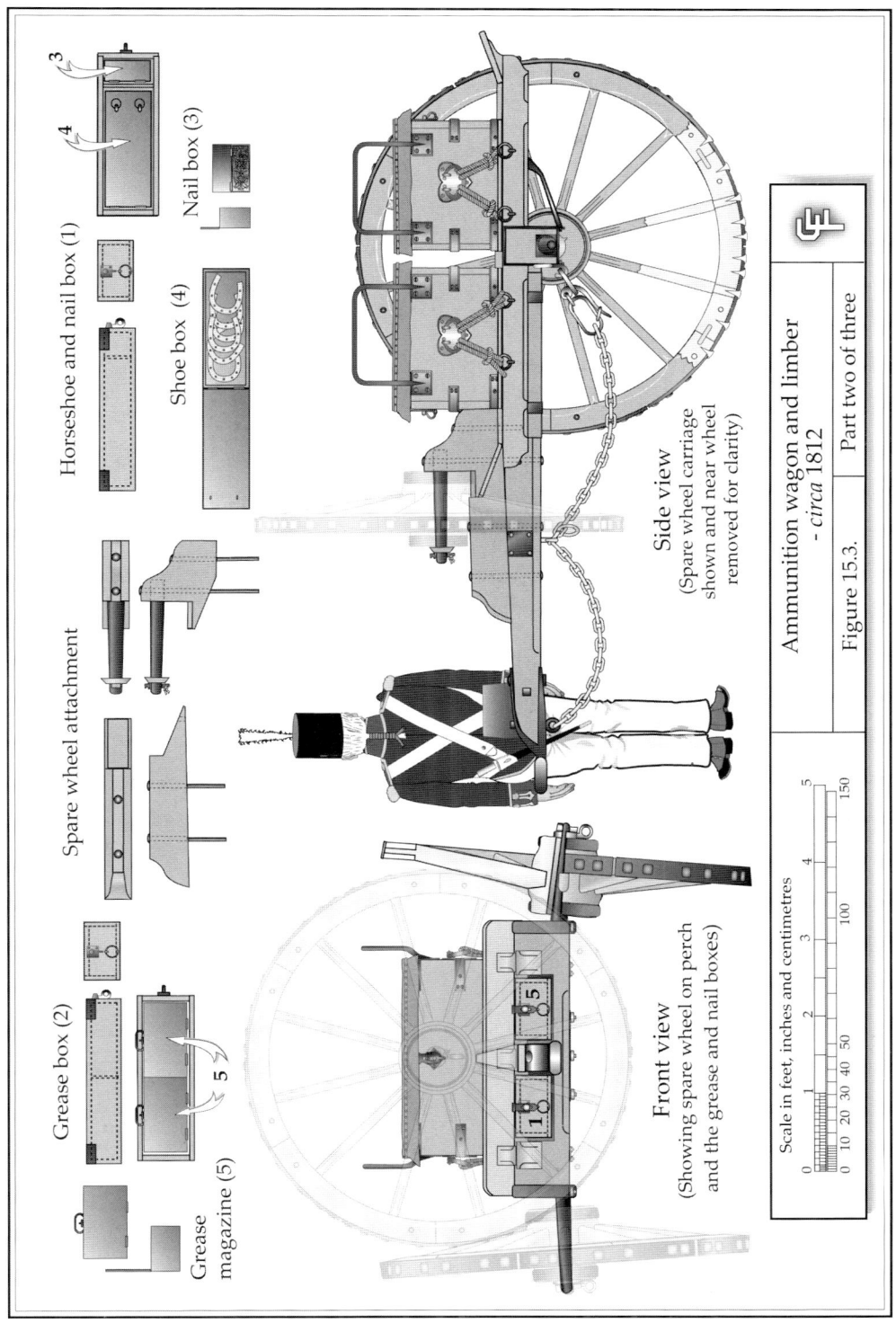

Horseshoe and nail box (1)

Nail box (3)

Shoe box (4)

Spare wheel attachment

Grease box (2)

Grease magazine (5)

Side view
(Spare wheel carriage shown and near wheel removed for clarity)

Front view
(Showing spare wheel on perch and the grease and nail boxes)

Scale in feet, inches and centimetres

Ammunition wagon and limber
- *circa* 1812

Figure 15.3.

Part two of three

horseshoes, grease magazines and nails. A locking chain was secured to an eye under the centre of the perch and when braking was required, the chain was laced through the spokes to lock the wheel. Later, after this period, a drag shoe was placed between the wheel and the road to provide a skid surface and protect the metal tyre from abrasion. Although spare wheels were occasionally fitted to ammunition wagons the modification was not officially approved until about 1825 when the design of the wagon was changed and the front of the perch was fitted with an elm block to carry a spare wheel. The rear stays were also dispensed with and replaced by two extra horseshoe boxes and fittings were attached to carry a spare axle under the perch and spare gun lever on the left of the boxes. These wagons were very successful in the field. Colonel Robe wrote from Lisbon in November of 1808:

> I name the limber waggon as being a perfect four-wheeled carriage, the weight not bearing on the shaft horses, whereas the two-wheeled cars are dreadful when going down a steep hill. No holding on of dragropes will counterpoise the weight on the shaft horse.[7]

The dimensions of the wagons and limber were generally similar to those of the respective gun and limber; the major difference was the size of the wagon ammunition boxes, a shorter distance between the axles and a shorter line of march. The ammunition boxes of the wagon limber were secured in the same manner as the gun limber with metal nibs fitting into metal staples in the platform board where they were pinned through and keyed underneath. At the rear they were secured by rope passing through the carrying handles to iron rings fitted on the wagon axletree bed. The two ammunition boxes of the wagon were made of one-inch deal plank with elm ends, they were strengthened with squares of iron at the corners and carried a guard iron and carrying handle at each end. Generally, they were all of the same size, being 29 inches long, 18 inches high and 21 inches from front to back. They were carried across the wagon between the platform boards and held in place by ropes or straps from the handles at the side to rings or staples on the sidepieces. Extra straps were fitted for the carriage of blankets, grease keg, maul, a camp kettle and a spare off shaft and iron axle.

Some wagons were locally fitted to carry a spare wheel on the perch.[8] No details of this attachment have been located and the structure shown is based upon later practices.

Throughout the period, it is clear that the amount and nature of the ammunition carried in the wagon and the limber boxes varied. The internal fittings were changed and redesigned to suit the needs of the moment and the ammunition available; there appears to be no specific pattern. The records of the period show the ammunition allocated differed regularly and it is probable that the boxes were modified by the unit artificers to suit the local ammunition requirements and availability. The amount and type of ammunition carried is based upon contemporary sources and surviving boxes, with the drawings of 1803 used as guidance for the internal configuration. The details of the ammunition carried in the wagons and limbers are given in the chapters on the respective field pieces. The weights of the ammunition wagons, limbers and associated equipment are given with the appropriate field equipment. A typical loading for a light 6-pr gun was:

Wagon limber, near box.
1. 6 portfires and quickmatch on underside of the lid.
2. Miscellaneous tools and slow match on hinged shelf with 4 heavy, common case underneath.

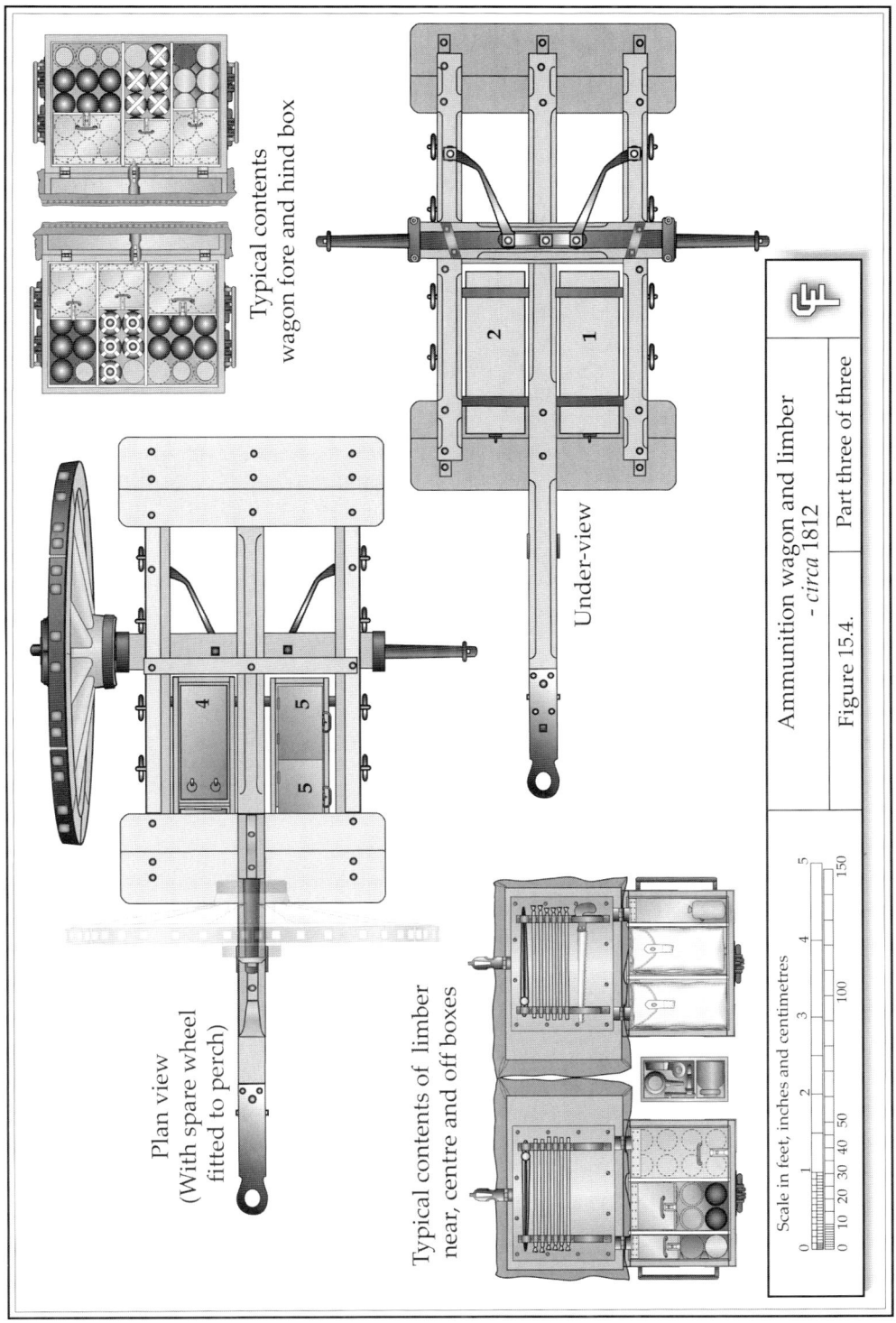

Typical contents wagon fore and hind box

Under-view

Plan view
(With spare wheel fitted to perch)

Typical contents of limber near, centre and off boxes

Scale in feet, inches and centimetres

Ammunition wagon and limber
- *circa* 1812

Part three of three

Figure 15.4.

3. One cartouche with 10 1.5lb cartridges on hinged shelf with 8 round shot underneath.
4. One cartouche with 10 1.5lb cartridges on hinged shelf with 8 round shot underneath.

Wagon limber, centre box.

5. 2 linchpins and 2 drag washers.
6. Spare rammer head.

Wagon limber, off box.

7. 6 portfires on the underside of the lid.
8. One cartouche with 10 1.5lb cartridges on hinged shelf with 8 round shot underneath.
9. One cartouche, with 10 1.5lb cartridges on hinged shelf with 8 round shot underneath.
10. Priming powder, 100 tubes in container and slow match on hinged shelf with 4 light, common case underneath.

Wagon body, fore box.

11. 35 1.5lb cartridges on hinged shelf with 15 round shot underneath.
12. 10 12oz cartridge; 10 2.5oz burster charges of white LG powder and a box of 10 fuses on hinged shelf with 10 spherical case underneath.
13. 10 round shot on hinged shelf with 5 light and 5 heavy common case underneath. Wagon body, hind box.
14. Slow match and 10 round shot on hinged shelf with 10 round shot underneath.
15. 10 12oz cartridges; 10 2.5oz burster charges of and a box of 10 fuses on hinged shelf with 10 spherical case underneath.
16. 35 1.5lb cartridges on hinged shelf with 15 round shot underneath.

Store Wagon and Limber

The establishment of each field brigade and horse troop included one store carriage and limber which was usually allocated four draught horses and two drivers. This was the same pattern as the ammunition wagon but the boxes on the limber and wagon carried the tools of the artificers. There is also evidence that some of these wagons allocated to the heavier brigades were fitted to carry a spare wheel on the perch.[9]

Spare Wheel Carriage and Limber

The establishment of each field brigade and horse troop included one spare gun carriage and limber, usually allocated four draught horses and two drivers. This carriage also served to carry spare wheels while the limber carried specialist tools and spares, they may well have also served as transport for unallocated detachment members. We know that for the 12-pr and heavy 6-pr, each carriage carried one gun wheel and two limber or wagon wheels, for the 6-pr and heavy 3-pr they carried three wheels that could serve both gun and limber.[10] No contemporary illustrations or description of the way that the extra wheels were fitted to the carriage has been found. The only information we have is that the carriage was 'fitted to carry the extra wheels'. Each carriage and limber also carried three iron axles, two handspikes traversing, two shafts, one limber hook, one driving bolt, one nose plate, one trail plate eye, one elevating screw, twenty staples, six linchpins. The limber box carried the tools of the collar maker and wheelwrights; including pincers, axe, adze, draw

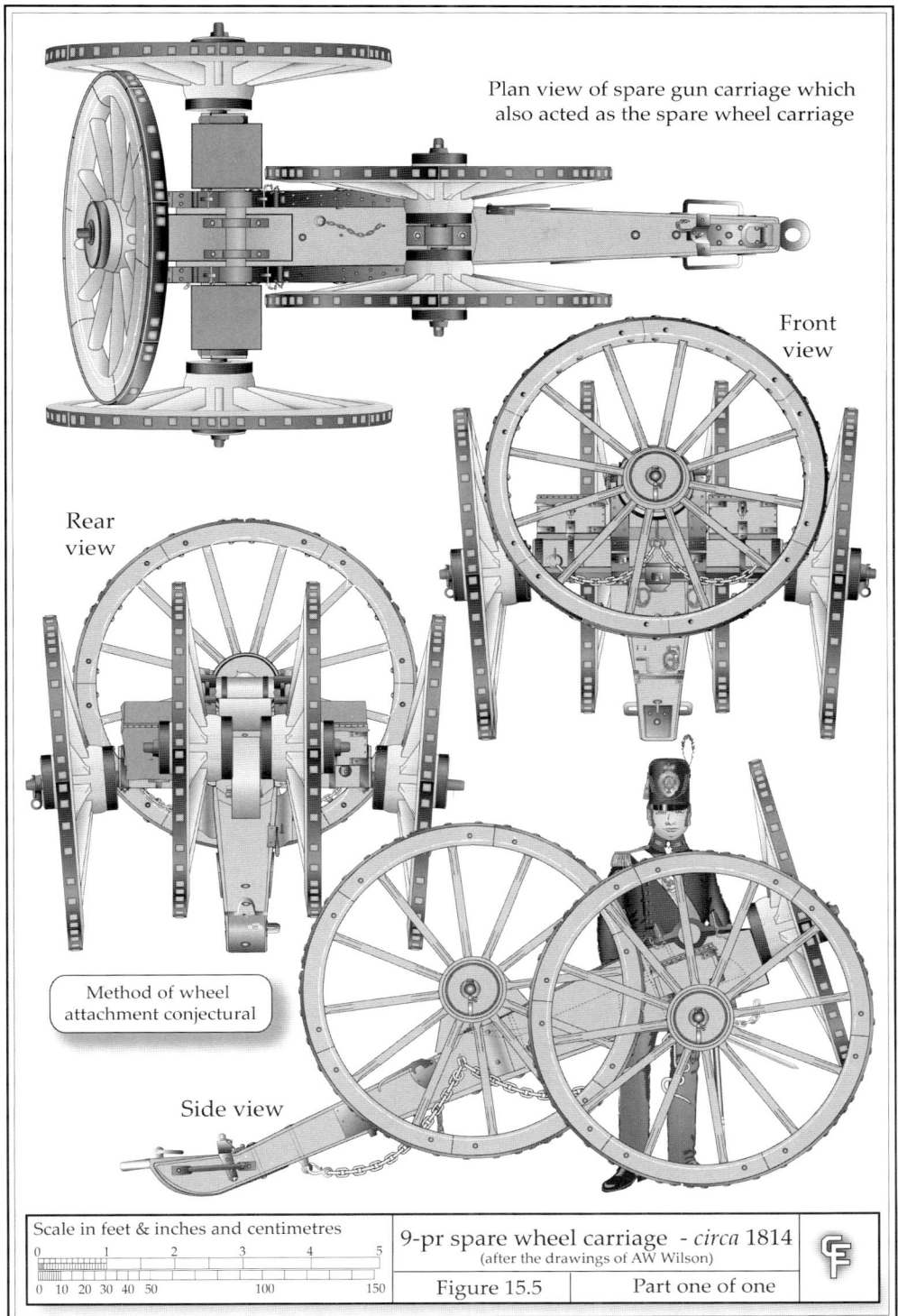

Plan view of spare gun carriage which also acted as the spare wheel carriage

Front view

Rear view

Method of wheel attachment conjectural

Side view

Scale in feet & inches and centimetres

0   1   2   3   4   5

0   10   20   30   40   50   100   150

9-pr spare wheel carriage - *circa* 1814
(after the drawings of AW Wilson)

Figure 15.5

Part one of one

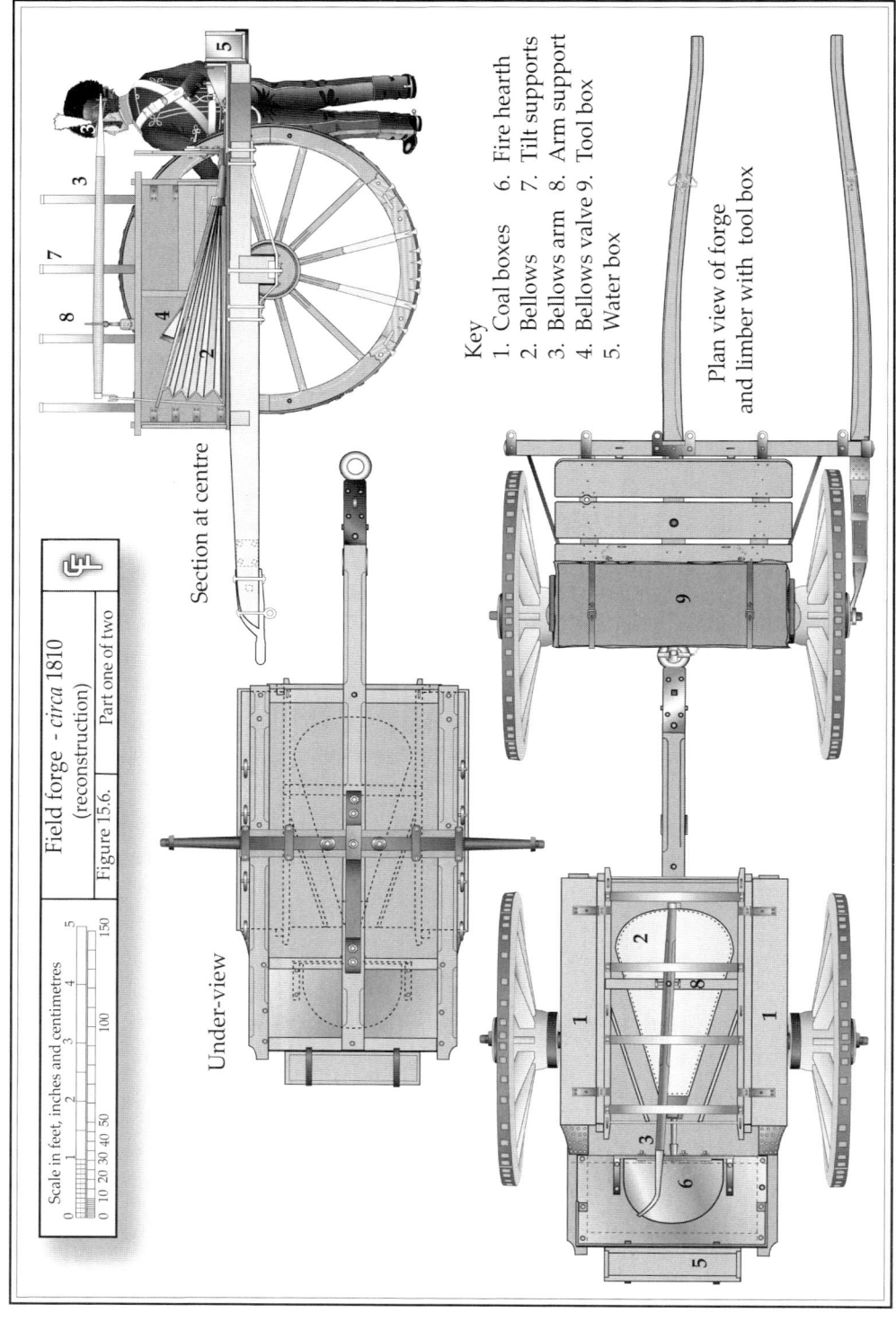

Section at centre

Field forge - *circa* 1810
(reconstruction)

Figure 15.6.   Part one of two

Scale in feet, inches and centimetres

Under-view

Key
1. Coal boxes   6. Fire hearth
2. Bellows   7. Tilt supports
3. Bellows arm   8. Arm support
4. Bellows valve   9. Tool box
5. Water box

Plan view of forge
and limber with tool box

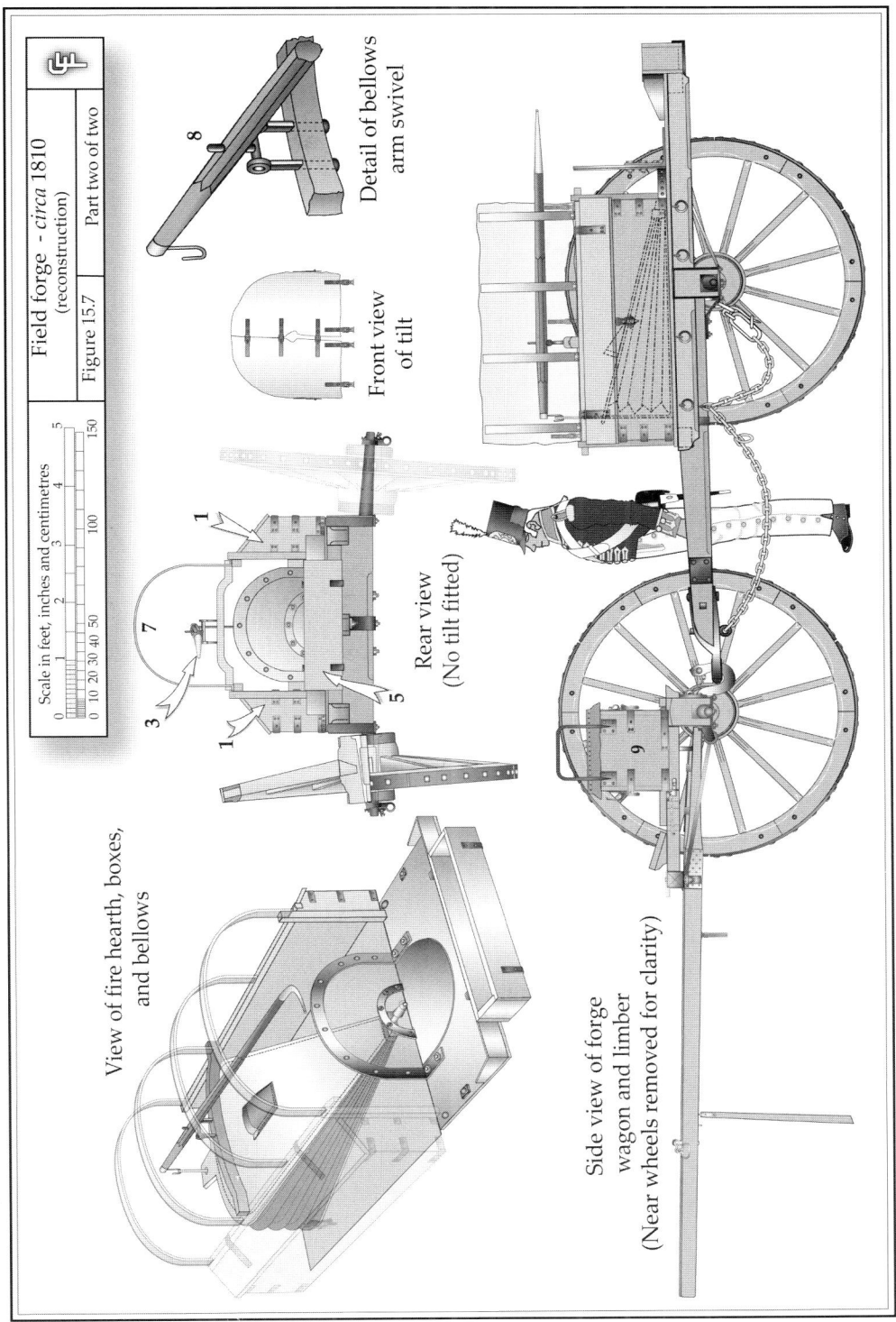

Field forge - *circa* 1810
(reconstruction)

Figure 15.7 | Part two of two

Scale in feet, inches and centimetres

Detail of bellows
arm swivel

Front view
of tilt

Rear view
(No tilt fitted)

View of fire hearth, boxes,
and bellows

Side view of forge
wagon and limber
(Near wheels removed for clarity)

shaves, two spoke shaves, riveting hammer, shoeing hammer, claw hammer, two drive pins and two chisels. The disposition of these spare parts is not known and the accompanying drawing is after AW Wilson. The weights of the spare wheel wagons are given in Table F.4 of Appendix F at the end of Part Two.

Forge Cart and Limbers

At the start of the Napoleonic period the forge wagons were four-wheeled vehicles but with the introduction of the horse artillery a modified ammunition wagon had been adapted for use as a forge cart. Each field brigade and horse troop had a forge cart included in their establishment and the limber carried the tools and spare equipment for the farriers and smiths. The old forge wagon weighed 39.75cwt and would have required a team of at least six horses, the new wagon weighed only 19.5cwt and four horses and two drivers were allocated for the draught.[11]

It was noted in the Peninsula that the forge carts were 'of the oldest pattern and a dead weight upon us', the low wheels at the front were 'abominable. The plan of the frame of the limber wagon is the most proper for the forge cart for field brigades, folding sides being fixed to it, the perch lengthened to facilitate turning and the limber box to carry the tools for the wheeler and collar maker'. A model to the new pattern was to be made locally while six of the approved form had been demanded from Woolwich.[12] In 1809, a new pattern was proposed with the 'forge to be placed on the frame of a small limber waggon', which could 'then follow the brigade which is not the case with the present one'.[13]

No drawing of a forge of this period has been located and the illustrations are reconstructions based upon the practice of the time and earlier and later illustrations.[14] The forge cart shown is a modified ammunition wagon with the extra cross supports necessary for the increased load. Along each outer side was a box for the storage of coal and in the centre of the cart were the leather bellows faced with wood. The bellows were operated by a bellows lever rotating upon a swivel mounted on a crossbeam. The bellows lever was connected to the bottom of the bellows and on the up-stroke, air was forced out the nozzle into the fire hearth. On the down-stroke, air was drawn into the bellows through a flap valve on the top face. At the rear of the wagon was a metal-lined fire hearth with a vertical, semicircular rear face and wind guard around the sides. Attached to the rear edge of the wind guard was a box containing water to quench the hot irons. The wagon was fitted with four tilt brackets and a canvas tilt was fitted as required. Mercer remembers that 'The forge cart and its limber were fitted up in such a manner that, in case of necessity, the farrier could go at his work as they moved on'.[15] The weights of the forge wagons and associated equipment are given with the appropriate field equipment.

Second-line Ammunition Wagons

Ammunition wagons were used to carry the reserve ammunition for the guns and were normally to be found at second line or in the Park of Artillery. It is clear that there were two patterns of ammunition wagon used during the period, one was the older 'rave' pattern and there was a new version. At the time of writing only two contemporary illustrations of these wagons have been located, one drawing by Muller is of the early 'rave' wagon and the only other is an engraving of a burning ammunition wagon at Waterloo. Pyne drew illustrations of baggage wagons in his Peninsular sketches and these have lade boards and ladder extensions at the front and rear to increase the load-carrying capacity. They also show a pronounced curve to the rave rail. These are obviously 'country' wagons hired by the commissariat as required. Hamilton Smith also illustrated wagons in his pictures of the 'Royal Waggon Train' and the 'Corps of Drivers'. In these drawings, the wagons are suspect, they show a large ten-spoke wheel at the rear and a twelve-spoke smaller wheel at the front – a most unlikely combination. The practice of wagon design has been studied in detail by those authors interested in the development of the different patterns of wagon that were found throughout the English counties and much of this work has been used to understand and reconstruct the interpretation of the wagon shown in the drawings.[16]

'Rave' Ammunition Wagon of 1780 – The Old Pattern (see Figure 15.8)

This wagon has a waisted bed to improve the turning circle of the 48-inch ten-spoke front wheels. The rear wheels were 60 inches and had twelve spokes, the same size as that adopted for the newly formed horse artillery. This wagon was made with wooden axles, but by 1800 iron axles may have been fitted. The term 'Rave' is taken from the rail that ran around the top of the wagon body. This wagon was used in single draft with three horses, although it appears that the later models of 1793 were modified to take conventional double draught with four horses and two drivers. The wagons were rated to carry 120 rounds of ammunition for a long 6-pr. Although shown with open rails it was most probably fitted with sideboards to protect the contents. There is a model of this wagon in the reserve collection at the Royal Artillery Museum.

Modified Ammunition Wagon of 1800

General Lawson in his notes of the Egyptian Campaign of 1800 remarked on the old-style ammunition wagon:

> No carriage appears to want reform more than the common artillery waggon. There is too much of it merely for carrying ammunition, and it is too narrow for baggage or bulky stores.[17]

He recalls that some of them were dismantled and the heavier parts put aside – the shafts, side and bolsters. The bottoms were shortened and narrowed to take nine or ten specially modified ammunition boxes. The hoops were lowered and the canvas tilt adjusted to make a better fit. The final change was to install pole draft. This apparently saved over 600lb in weight and made the wagons useable for general use 'hitherto looked upon as out of all question, except the local duties of the park'. A drawing of these modifications was included in Lawson's manuscripts. In November 1811, a carriage to this pattern was made for experimental purposes by the Royal Carriage Department and it may be this that led to the new pattern of ammunition wagon.[18] Congreve noted in 1797 that in lieu of an ammunition wagon for a battalion gun a spare limber was to be used with a change of shafts to provide double draught.[19]

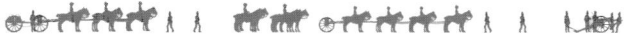

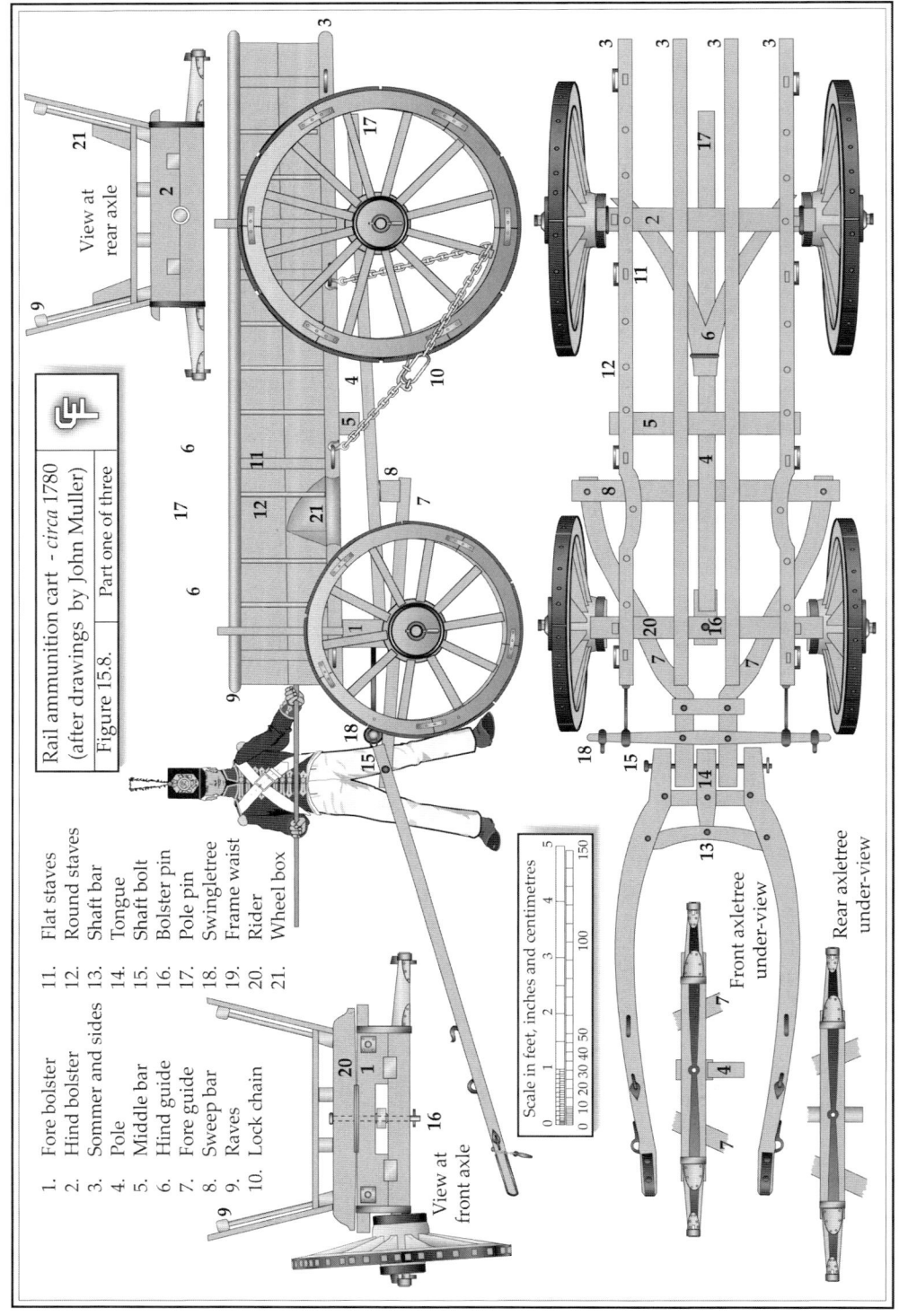

Rail ammunition cart - *circa* 1780
(after drawings by John Muller)
Figure 15.8.   Part one of three

1. Fore bolster
2. Hind bolster
3. Sommer and sides
4. Pole
5. Middle bar
6. Hind guide
7. Fore guide
8. Sweep bar
9. Raves
10. Lock chain
11. Flat staves
12. Round staves
13. Shaft bar
14. Tongue
15. Shaft bolt
16. Bolster pin
17. Pole pin
18. Swingletree
19. Frame waist
20. Rider
21. Wheel box

View at rear axle

View at front axle

Front axletree under-view

Rear axletree under-view

Scale in feet, inches and centimetres

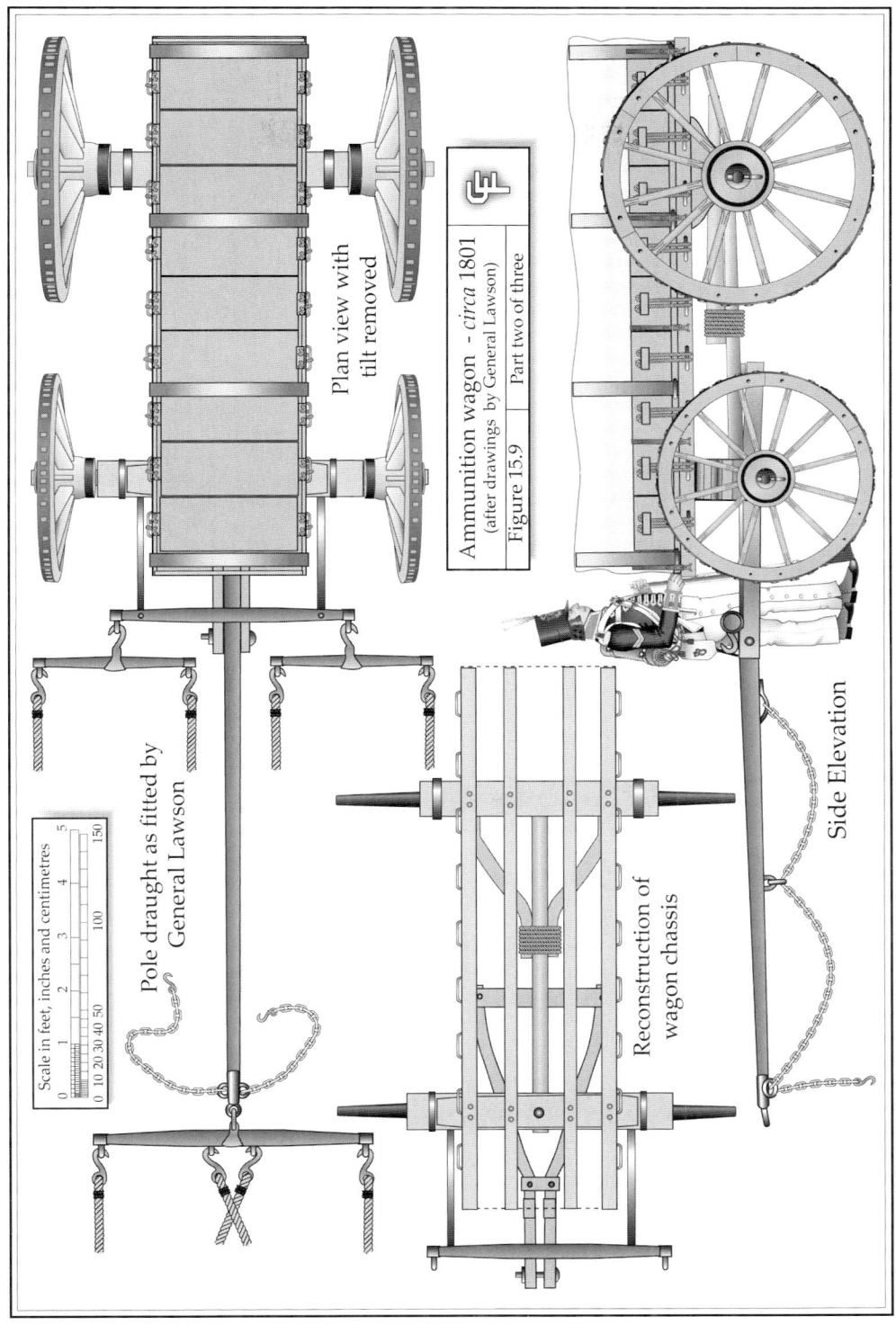

Plan view with tilt removed

Ammunition wagon - *circa* 1801
(after drawings by General Lawson)

Figure 15.9 | Part two of three

Scale in feet, inches and centimetres

Pole draught as fitted by General Lawson

Reconstruction of wagon chassis

Side Elevation

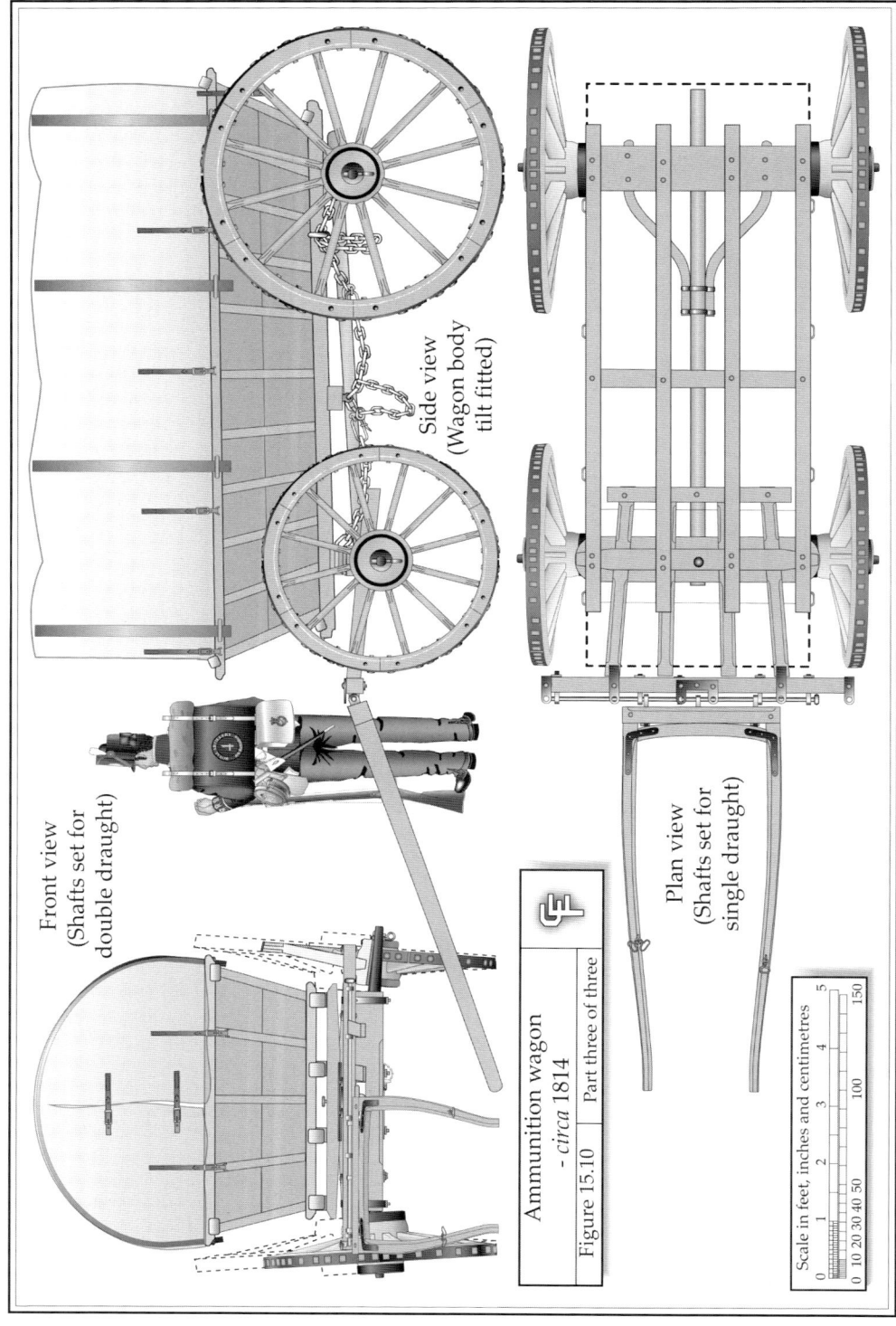

Side view
(Wagon body tilt fitted)

Front view
(Shafts set for double draught)

Plan view
(Shafts set for single draught)

Ammunition wagon
- *circa* 1814

Figure 15.10　Part three of three

Scale in feet, inches and centimetres

New Pattern Ammunition Wagon

This wagon is referred to in the papers of the Ordnance Board. The front and rear tail boards were angled, but it is not clear if the tail board opened or was detachable, but it would seem logical that it was. This wagon had iron axles with the front wheels of 48 inches diameter and the rear wheels of 60 inches, both having twelve spokes. This pattern of wagon was rated to carry 180 rounds of ammunition for the long 6-pr. It was fitted for the standard double or single draught and was allocated a team of six horses and three drivers.

The wagon had sideboards fitted behind the rails and appeared to have a rear axle pole fitted. The main pin on which the fore carriage turned was usually 1.25 inches in diameter and could have been inserted from the top, through the pillow, bolster, pole, and axle bed where it was secured by a spring clip. Alternatively, it could have been fitted from the bottom and a wedge inserted above the pillow. These pins would have had a retaining chain. Splinter bars and draught-pins formed part of the fore carriage members and allowed for the change between single or double draught. There were probably chafing-cleats (metal plates) on the meeting surfaces of the pole and slider bars and between the pillow and bolster at the pivot of the front axle. It is not clear if the new pattern wagon bed was waisted to improve the turning circle of the front wheels. The ammunition carried by the wagons is given in Tables F.2 and F.3 of Appendix F at the end of Part Two.

Country Wagons

The rations, forage and other baggage were often carried in locally hired, country wagons. By this period, the wagons usually had panel boards fitted behind the spokes or rails and this is illustrated in the pictures of Pyne, and after 1800 the use of open sided wagons had declined. The majority of wagons had fixed head boards, although regional variations show some that were removable. The tailboard was always either hinged or removable. The baggage wagons shown by Pyne have an additional out-rail supported by three or four extended standards and they are also shown with a mid-rail supporting the spindles. During the Waterloo Campaign, Flemish wagons were hired for the purpose with locally employed drivers; they came under the control of a Commissariat officer who was employed by the Treasury, but accompanied each horse troop or foot brigade.[20]

Curricle

This was a two-wheeled cart carried on the establishment to carry the baggage of officers. Mercer recalls:

> The Officers were to have no baggage except such as was fixed by regulation, and for this purpose all the articles were furnished by the Board of Ordnance, and of one uniform pattern, viz. a small camp bed with curtains complete, and bedside carpet, all packed in boxes of uniform size; a small round octagonal hair trunk; a small camp table and two large camp stools; the bedding, of course, folded up to put in a painted canvas case. All the above-named articles, constituting the sole baggage of each troop Officer, were to be carried in the curricle cart. This vehicle consisted of a body with a roof like that of a house, with folding doors opening to the rear, mounted on a pair of

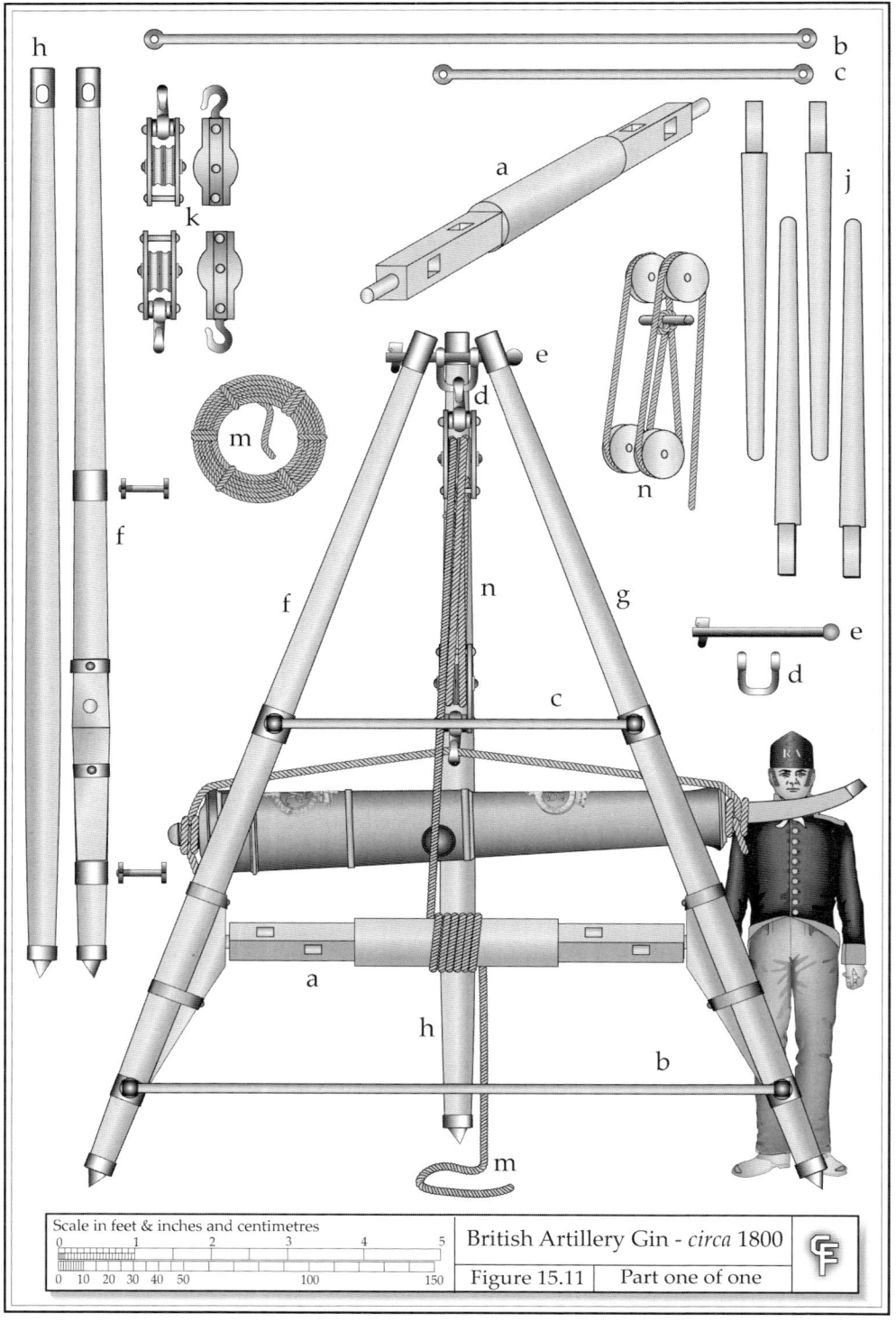

Scale in feet & inches and centimetres

0   1   2   3   4   5

0 10 20 30 40 50   100   150

British Artillery Gin - *circa* 1800

| Figure 15.11 | Part one of one |

wheels the same height as those of the gun, and two horses with a mounted driver. The packing required attention and some skill, for the load was so exactly calculated, and the boxes fitted so nicely, that when the load was finished you could hardly pass a straw between them.[21]

This curricle was also known as the 'Captain's cart' and carried the books of the Sergeant Major, the Pay Sergeant and 'any spare little things he may have, such as shirts, stockings for the men &c'.[22]

British Artillery Gin

Not normally associated with the field artillery this piece of equipment was an essential part of the artillery park where it provided the facility to mount and dismount pieces from their carriages. Although common to all armies, the gin used by the Royal Artillery was somewhat different in construction in that it had three legs, not four. A right cheek (f) and left cheek (g) carried the windlass and the third leg or pry pole (h). Each was some 12 or 13 feet long with the diameters at the lower end about 4 inches. They swelled slightly at the point where the cheeks for the windlass were mounted, to some five inches, then tapered away to some 3 or 3.5 inches at the top end. The windlass (a) was initially round in section, about 7 inches in diameter and six feet long. At each end was a 20-inch square section where the handspikes (j) were fitted. Later windlasses were octagonal or hexagonal in section with holes in each face for the handspikes.

The poles were secured at the top by a gin bolt (e) and secured by a key through a gin loop (d). The cheeks were strengthened by two iron cross bars (b & c) bolted to each cheek above and below the windlass. The gin was also supplied with a rope fall (m) and a pair of hooked, brass blocks. Each had two pulleys (k) and one leg or ring to take the standing part of the fall. The usual arrangement for the four-part fall was as shown (n) with one block hooked to the gin loop and the other hooked to the piece, although other variations were often used. It was the usual practice for pieces without dolphins to use a rope tied around the cascabel and lashed to a handspike inserted in the bore of the gun.[23]

Endnotes to Chapter 15

1. Caruana, 1980: p. 4.
2. James Clavell Library: miscellaneous papers.
3. Adye, 1813: p. 9; Dickson, 1908: pp. 272, 258–9, 411.
4. Siborne, 1891: p. 199.
5. Dickson, 1908: p. 349.
6. Mercer, 1870: p. 161.
7. National Archive, WO 55/1194: p. 48.
8. Dickson, 1908: p. 821.
9. Duncan, 1872: p. 820.
10. Adye, 1813: p. 389.
11. Adye, 1801: p 54.
12. Leslie, 1912: pp. 79, 80.
13. Duncan, 1872: p. 249.
14. Muller, 1780: pp. 138–40; *Aide Memoire*, 1845, plates 52 and 53; *Forge Wagon*, Royal Carriage Department, plate 23, *circa* 1868.

15. Macdonald, 1983: p. 58.

16. Arnold, J: *Farm Waggons and Carts*, David Charles, London, 1977: et al.

17. Duncan, 1872: pp. 119, 124.

18. Hogg, 1963: p. 577; WO/47/2,623, p. 4,321.

19. James Clavell Library, RA 20: p. 266.

20. Mercer, 1870: pp. 52, 127, 140, 193.

21. Macdonald, 1983: p. 58.

22. Dickson, 1908: p. 866.

23. Muller, 1780: pp. 143–5; miscellaneous notes and drawings at the James Clavell Library.

Appendix B – Gun Dimensions

Introduction

This appendix contains tables of the gun dimensions where they are known. Only the information from attributable sources has been included and in some cases, it has not been possible to obtain reliable data.

Table B.1. Dimensions of the Congreve light 6-pr gun of 4ft 6in[1]							
Key	Lengths	inches	mm	Key	Diameters	inches	mm
HA.	Length of the piece	54	1372	H.	Base ring	7.70	196
HB	Length to end of chase	46.48	1181	e.	Maximum at 1st Reinforce	7.04	179
HC	Length to 2nd reinforce junction	27.16	690	E.	Junction of 1st and 2nd reinforce	6.46	164
HD	Length to trunnions	23.92	608	d.	At trunnion shoulders	6.27	159
HE	Length to 1st/2nd reinforce junction	15.04	382	C.	Junction 2nd reinforce and chase	5.59	142
GI	Length to breech from chamber	3.45	88	B.	Junction chase and muzzle swell	5.22	133
GA	Length of bore	51.27	1302	a.	Muzzle lip	6.21	158
-	Trunnion length	2.23	57	A.	Muzzle	3.85	98
-	Trunnions, diameter	2.21	56	J.	Bore	3.668	93

Table B.2. Dimensions of the Blomefield light 6-pr gun of 5ft[2]							
Key	Lengths	inches	mm	Key	Diameters	inches	mm
HA.	Length of the piece	60	1524	H.	Base ring	9.625	244
HB	Length to end of chase	54.07	1373	e.	Maximum at 1st reinforce	8.66	220
HC	Length to 2nd reinforce junction	30.334	423	E.	Junction of 1st and 2nd reinforce	8.29	211
HD	Length to trunnions	26.666	677	d.	At trunnion shoulders	7.8	198
HE	Length to 1st/2nd reinforce junction	16.665	423	C.	Junction 2nd reinforce and chase	7.5	190
GI	Length to breech from chamber	3.45	88	B.	Junction chase and muzzle swell	5.89	139
GA	Length of bore	57.47	1460	a.	Muzzle lip	7.57	192
-	Trunnion length	3.5	89	A.	Muzzle	5.51	140
-	Trunnions, diameter	2.94	75	J.	Bore	3.668	93

Table B.3. Dimensions of the Blomefield heavy 6-pr gun of 5ft 2in[3]							
Key	Lengths	inches	mm	Key	Diameters	inches	mm
HA.	Length of the piece	62.356	1584	H.	Base ring	10.985	279
HB	Length to end of chase	56.156	1426	e.	Maximum at 1st reinforce	10.02	255
HC	Length to 2nd reinforce junction	31.38	797	E.	Junction of 1st and 2nd reinforce	9.575	243
HD	Length to trunnions	27.712	704	d.	At trunnion shoulders	9.13	232
HE	Length to 1st/2nd reinforce junction	17.32	440	C.	Junction 2nd reinforce and chase	8.68	220
GI	Length to breech from chamber	4.94	113	B.	Junction chase and muzzle swell	6.8	173
GA	Length of bore	59.156	1460	a.	Muzzle lip	8.265	210
-	Trunnion length	3.34	85	A.	Muzzle	6.43	163
-	Trunnions, diameter	3.34	85	J.	Bore	3.668	93

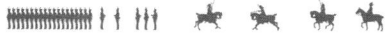

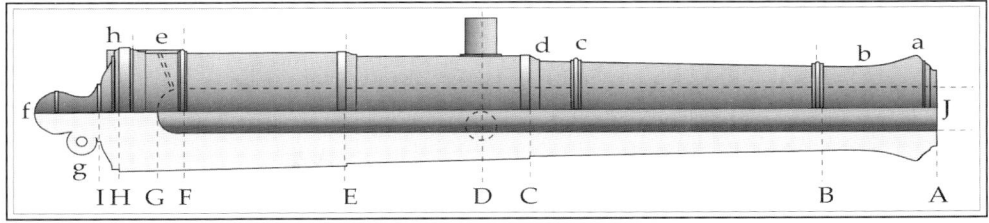

Key	Lengths	inches	mm	Key	Diameters	inches	mm
\multicolumn{8}{c}{**Table B.4. Dimensions of the 9-pr gun[4]**}						
HA.	Length of the piece	71.46	1814	H.	Base ring	12.6	320
HB	Length to end of chase	64.31	1633	F	Vent field end	11.37	289
HC	Length to 2nd reinforce junction	35.96	913	e.	Maximum at 1st reinforce	11.51	292
HD	Length to trunnions	31.76	807	E.	Junction of 1st and 2nd reinforce	11.00	279
HE	Length to 1st/2nd reinforce junction	19.85	504	d.	At trunnion shoulders	10.47	266
HF	Length of vent field	6.3	160	C.	Junction 2nd reinforce and chase	9.485	241
GI	Length to breech from chamber	5.1	130	B.	Junction chase and muzzle swell	7.80	198
GA	Length of bore	67.74	1721	a.	Muzzle lip	9.80	244
-	Trunnion length	3.87	98	A.	Muzzle	7.36	187
-	Trunnions, diameter	3.87	98	J.	Bore	4.20	107

Key	Lengths	inches	mm	Key	Diameters	inches	mm
\multicolumn{8}{c}{**Table B.5. Dimensions of the medium 12-pr gun[5]**}						
HA.	Length of the piece	78.60	1,996	H.	Base ring	13.82	351
HB	Length to muzzle swell junction	70.62	1,799	e.	Maximum at 1st reinforce	12.61	320
HC	Length to 2nd reinforce junction	39.558	1,005	E.	Junction of 1st and 2nd reinforce	12.04	306
HD	Length to trunnions	34.23	887	d.	At trunnion shoulders	11.50	292
HE	Length to 1st/2nd reinforce junction	21.83	554	C.	Junction 2nd reinforce and chase	10.90	277
HF	Length to end of vent field	6.90	176	B.	Junction chase and muzzle swell	8.53	176
GI	Length to breech from chamber	5.90	150	a.	Muzzle lip	10.50	267
GA	Length of bore	74.55	1894	A.	Muzzle	8.05	204
-	Trunnion length	3.5	89	J.	Bore	4.623	118
-	Trunnions, diameter	4.25	108	-	-	-	-

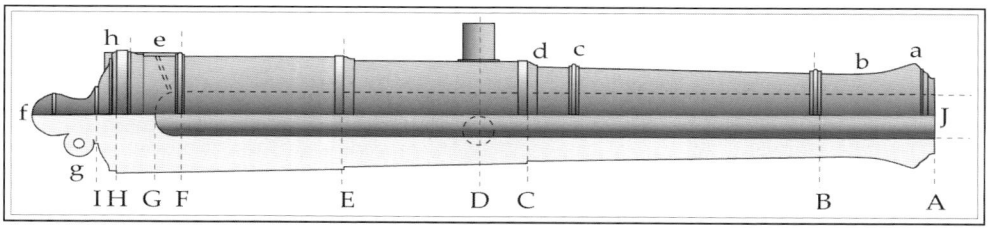

Key	Lengths	inches	mm	Key	Diameters	inches	mm
	Table B.6. Dimensions of the iron 18-pr gun of 9ft [6]						
HA.	Length of the piece	108.0	2,743	H.	Base ring	18.03	457
HB	Length to muzzle swell junction	96.70	2,456	e.	Maximum at 1st reinforce	17.85	453
HC	Length to 2nd reinforce junction	51.582	1,310	E.	Junction of 1st and 2nd reinforce	17.00	432
HD	Length to trunnions	46.29	1,176	d.	At trunnion shoulders	18.62	473
HE	Length to 2nd reinforce junction	30.86	784	C.	Junction 2nd reinforce and chase	15.41	392
HF	Length to end of vent field	-	-	B.	Junction chase and muzzle swell	11.565	294
GI	Length to breech from chamber	-	-	a.	Muzzle lip	14.25	362
GA	Length of bore	101.75	2,584	A.	Muzzle	10.80	274
-	Trunnion length	5.42	138	J.	Bore	5.292	134
-	Trunnions, diameter	5.292	134	-	Weight (cwt)	42	-

Endnotes to Appendix B

1. Rudyerd, 1792: plate 10.
2. Boxer, 1853: plate 21.
3. Ibid: plate 21.
4. Ibid: plate 20.
5. Ibid: plate 19.
6. Ibid: plate 14.

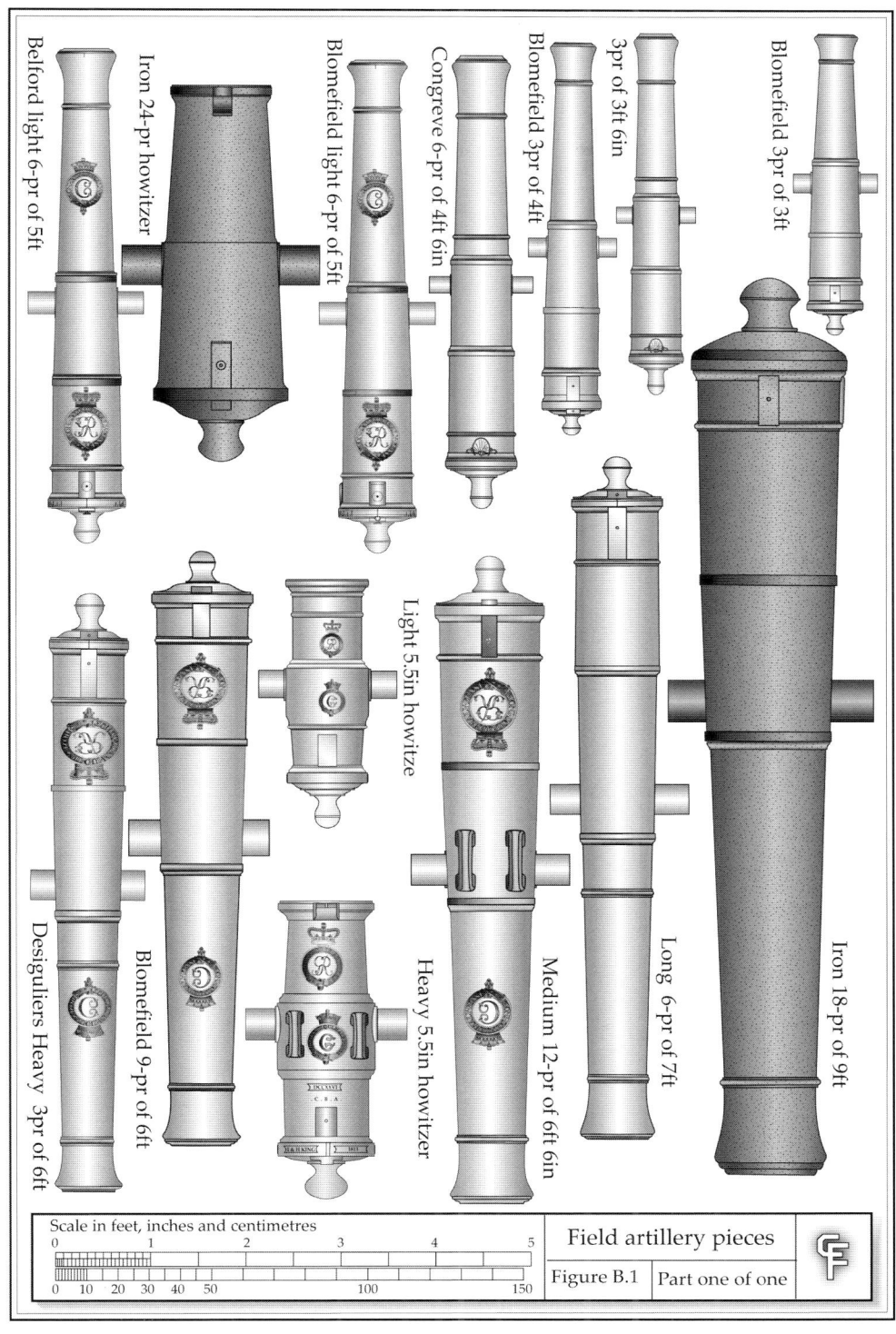

Belford light 6-pr of 5ft

Iron 24-pr howitzer

Blomefield light 6-pr of 5ft

Congreve 6-pr of 4ft 6in

Blomefield 3pr of 4ft

3pr of 3ft 6in

Blomefield 3pr of 3ft

Light 5.5in howitze

Iron 18-pr of 9ft

Desiguliers Heavy 3pr of 6ft

Blomefield 9-pr of 6ft

Heavy 5.5in howitzer

Medium 12-pr of 6ft 6in

Long 6-pr of 7ft

Scale in feet, inches and centimetres

| 0 | | 1 | | 2 | | 3 | | 4 | | 5 |

| 0 | 10 | 20 | 30 | 40 | 50 | | | 100 | | | 150 |

Field artillery pieces

Figure B.1 | Part one of one

Appendix C – Performance Figures

Introduction

The performance figures are based on information published in contemporary documents of the period, but the reader should realize that ranges given to the nearest yard were subject to considerable variation. This was due to the differences in windage and shot size introduced by the contemporary methods of manufacture and the resultant uncertain nature of the ballistics; to this must be added any variation in the power of the powder and burning variations of the fuses. The records are few but those for 1800 suggest range variations of up to 20% were not at all unusual, but the information given is believed to give a reasonable representation of the performance achieved during the period.[1] With the significant improvement in powder and windage achieved in the years after 1815, the reader should be aware that later figures given after the period should not be taken as a direct comparison.[2]

Table C.1. Light 3-pr gun of 3ft. Distance in yards to first graze with round shot[3]									
	Elevation in degrees								
	PB	0.25	0.75	LOM	1.25	1.625	2.125	2.75	3.5
Range to first graze	200	300	400	500	600	700	800	900	1,000

Note: Ranges beyond this were achieved with greater elevation, but visibility in the field was usually limited to the lower elevations as the fall of shot could not be observed and ricochet fire was impracticable due to the angle at which the ball struck the ground.

Table C.2. Heavy 3-pr gun. Distance in yards to first graze with round shot[4]									
	Elevation in degrees and minutes								
	PB	0-15	0-45	1-0	1-23	1-30	2-0	3-15	3-30
Range to first graze	150	238	337	475	500	527	685	835	912

Note: Ranges beyond this were achieved with greater elevation, but visibility in the field was usually limited to the lower elevations as the fall of shot could not be observed and ricochet fire was impracticable due to the angle at which the ball struck the ground.

Table C.3. Long 3-pr gun of 6ft. Hits on target by common case[5]				
Elevation	Point blank	1.0	1.5	2.0
Range in yards	200	300	400	500
Hits on target	15	11	10	9

Common case of 36 balls of 1.25oz fired at a target 9 feet high and 30 yards long by a 1.5lb charge.

Table C.4. Light 6-pr gun of 4ft 6in. Distance to first graze with round shot[6]												
	Elevation in degrees and minutes											
	PB	0-15	0-45	1-0	1-15	1-30	1-45	2-0	2-0*	3-0	4-0	5-0
Recoil in feet	7.5	-	-	8.5	-	-	-	8.5	7.9*	7.0	7.5	8.5
Range to first graze	256	443	548	639	700	750	824	940	729*	1,034	1,500	1,330
Extreme range	1,630	-	-	1,600	-	-	-	1760	1,560*	1,670	1,800	1,825

* Note: Range variations between different sets of recorded data show significant variation, at 2 degrees of elevation the range to first graze varied between 729, 756 and 940 yards.

Table C.5. Light 6-pr gun of 4ft 6in. Hits on target by common case[7]				
Elevation	Point blank	1.0	1.5	2.0
Range in yards	200	300	400	500
Hits on target	35	27	21	11

Common case of 72 balls of 1.25oz fired at a target 9 feet high and 30 yards long by a 1.5lb charge.

Table C.6. Light 6-pr gun of 5ft. Hits on target by common case[8]				
Elevation	Point blank	1.0	1.5	2.0
Range in yards	200	300	400	500

Hits on target	32	28	29	11

Common case of 72 balls of 1.25oz fired at a target 9 feet high and 30 yards long by a 1.5lb charge.

Table C.7. Light 6-pr gun of 5ft. Hits on targets by tiered case at different elevations[9]					
Range	300	400	300**	400**	500**
Point blank	11 – 13*	10 – 12*	-	-	-
0.5	12 – 15*	9 – 10*	6 – 7 **	-	-
1.0	7 – 9*	6 – 8*	3 – 3 **	6 – 6 **	3 – 3 **
1.5	-	-	4 – 6 **	4 – 5 **	3 – 4 **
2.0	-	-	-	4 – 5 **	3 – 4 **

Note: The first hit figure is for infantry, the second for cavalry.
Note: * Tiered canister with 34, 3oz balls, set seven in a tier. Note: ** Tiered canister with 12 8oz balls set three in a tier.

Table C.8. Light 6-pr gun of 5ft. Distance in yards to first graze with round shot[10]													
Elevation	PB	0.25	0.75	LOM	1.00	1.25	1.5	1.75	2	2.25	2.5	2.75	3.00
Light 6-pr	200	300	400	500	600	650	700	750	800	850	900	950	1,000

Note: Ranges beyond this were achieved with greater elevation, but in the field the fall of shot at longer ranges could not be observed and ricochet was impracticable due to the angle at which the ball struck the ground. Due to the windage, the range varied considerably and the spread would have been considerable. LOM is the line of metal range equivalent to an elevation of 58 min 27 sec.

Table C.9. Light 6-pr gun of 5ft. Details of ranges for spherical case[11]											
Approximate elevation (degrees)	1.25	1.75	2 .25	2.75	3. 50	4.00	4.50	5.25	5.75	6.50	7.00
Identifying fuse letter	B	C	D	E	F	G	H	I	K	L	M
Fuse length (inches)	0.2	0.3	0.4	0.5	0.6	0.7	0.8	0.9	1.0	1.1	1.2
Range spread (yards)	570 800	720 980	845 1,045	955 1,145	1,060 1,240	1,160 1,330	1,255 1,415	1,345 1,500	1,450 1,580	1,510 1,655	1,585 1,725

Note: These ranges must have used the standard charge, as they are comparable with the range of first graze given in the table above.

Table C.10. Heavy 6-pr gun. Distance to first graze with round shot[12]													
Elevation (degrees)	PB	0.25	0.5	0.75	1.0	1.25	1.5	1.75	2	2.25	2.5	2.75	3
Range (yards)	300	400	500	600	700	775	850	925	1,000	1,050	1,100	1,150	1,200

Note: Ranges beyond this were achieved with greater elevation, but visibility in the field was usually limited to the lower elevations as the fall of shot could not be observed and ricochet fire was impracticable due to the angle at which the ball struck the ground. Due to the windage, the range varied considerably and the spread of ranges would have been comparable to those in the table below.

Table C.11. Heavy 6-pr gun. Details of ranges for spherical case[13]								
Elevation (degrees)	1.25	1.75	2.25	2.75	3 .25	4.375	5.065	5.75
Length of fuse (inches)	0.2	0.3	0.4	0.5	0.6	0.7	0.8	0.9
Spread of range (yards)	630 880	780 1,070	910 1,120	1,025 1,225	1,130 1,320	1,230 1,410	1,325 1,495	1,413 1,573

Note: These ranges would have used the standard charge, as they are comparable with the range of first graze given in Table C.10 above.

Table C.12. 9-pr gun. Distance to first graze with round shot[14]													
	Elevation (Degrees)												
Elevation	PB	0.25	0.5	0.75	1.00	1.25	1.5	1.75	2.0	2.25	2.5	2.75	3.00
Range (yards)	272	400	500	600	700	775	850	925	1,000	1,050	1,100	1,150	1,200

Note: Ranges beyond this were achieved with greater elevation. In the Peninsula, it is recorded that 9-pr guns fired both round shot and spherical case at ranges of 1,500 yards with good effect. 15 LOM is the line of metal range equivalent to an elevation of 1deg 5 min 56 sec.

Table C.13. 9-pr gun. Details of ranges for spherical case[16]														
Approximate elevation (degrees)	1.25	1.75	2.25	2.75	3 .25	3.75	4.25	5.00	5.75	6.5	7.00	8.25	9.25	10.00
Identifying letter of fuse	B	C	D	E	F	G	H	I	K	L	-	-	-	-
Length of fuse (inches)	0.2	0.3	0.4	0.5	0.6	0.7	0.8	0.9	1.0	1.1	1.2	1.3	1.4	1.5
Spread of range (yards)	640 920	800 1,060	930 1,180	1,050 1,290	1,160 1,390	1,260 1,480	1,360 1,570	1,455 1,655	1,550 1,740	1,640 1,820	1,725 1,895	1,885 2,035	2,030 2,160	2,095 2,215

Note: These ranges would have used the standard charge, as they are comparable with the range of first graze given above.

Table C.14. Medium 12-pr. Distance in yards to first graze with round shot[17]													
	Elevation (Degrees)												
	PB	0.25	0.5	0.75	1	1.25	1.5	1.75	2	2.25	2.5	2.75	3
Medium 12-pr	300	400	500	600	700	775	850	925	1,000	1,050	1,100	1,150	1,200

Note: Ranges beyond this were achieved with greater elevation, but visibility in the field was usually limited to the lower elevations as the fall of shot could not be observed and ricochet fire was impracticable due to the angle at which the ball struck the ground. The range spread would have been similar to those shown in the table below.

Table C.15. Medium 12-pr. Details of ranges for spherical case[18]														
Elevation (degrees)	1.25	1.75	2.25	2.75	3 .25	3.75	4.25	5.00	5.75	6.5	7.00	8.25	9.375	10.00
Identifying fuse letter	B	C	D	E	F	G	H	I	K	L	-	-	-	-
Length of fuse (inches)	0.2	0.3	0.4	0.5	0.6	0.7	0.8	0.9	1.0	1.1	1.2	1.3	1.4	1.5
Spread of range (yards)	660 960	820 1,110	960 1,230	1,080 1,340	1,195 1,445	1,305 1,545	1,415 1,645	1,525 1,740	1,620 1,830	1,720 1,920	1,815 2,005	1,990 2,160	2,140 2,290	2,200 2,340

Note: These ranges would have used the standard charge as they are comparable with the range of first graze given in the table above.

Table C.16. Light 5.5-inch howitzer. Ranges with 1lb charge[19]													
	Elevation (degrees)												
Elevation	PB	1	2	3	4	5	6	7	8	9	10	11	12
Range (yards)	150	300	450	600	750	850	950	1,050	1,150	1,200	1,250	1,300	1,350

Note: Ranges beyond this were achieved with greater elevation, but visibility in the field was usually limited to the lower elevations as the fall of shot could not be observed and ricochet fire was -impracticable due to the angle at which the ball struck the ground. Due to the windage, the range varied considerably and the spread of ranges would have been comparable to those below.

Table C.17. Light 5.5-inch howitzer. Distance in yards to first graze with round shot[20]													
Charge Size	Elevation (degrees)												
	PB	1	2	3	4	5	6	7	8	9	10	11	12
4oz charge	-	66	85	100	110	115	168	144	226	260	279	282	315
Time of flight (sec)	-	1	1	1.5	1.5	2	2	2	2.5	2.5	2.5	2.5	3
8oz charge	96	143	184	258	307	376	408	524	620	642	645	715	797
Time of flight (sec)	1	1.5	1.5	2	2.5	2.5	3	3.5	4.5	5	5.5	5.5	6
12oz charge	140	334	351	500	506	504	581	872	975	911	1,021	1,177	-
Time of flight (sec)	1.5	2	2	2.5	3	3	3.5	5	6.5	7	7	7.5	-
16oz charge	159	225	490	668	728	918	923	975	1,044	1,049	1,104	1,173	1,400
Time of flight (sec)	1	1	2	3	4	5	5.5	6	7	8	8	8	-

Note 1: Captain Congreve observed that a light 5.5-inch howitzer 'at point blank would range its shell to 163 yards to the first graze, and then go after three grazes, to 900 yards'.

Note 2: With a 4oz charge, the extreme of range was 400 to 600 yards; with 8oz the extreme was 700 to 1,000 yards, with 12oz, 1,000 to 1,350 and with 1lb, 1,100 to 1,400 yards.

Table C.18. Light 5.5-inch howitzer. Details of ranges for spherical case[21]											
Elevation (degrees)	2.75	3.25	4.00	4.75	5.75	6.50	7.375	8.25	9.00	10.00	10.75
Identifying letter of fuse	B	C	D	E	F	G	H	I	K	L	-
Fuse length (in)	0.2	0.3	0.4	0.5	0.6	0.7	0.8	0.9	1.0	1.1	1.2
Range spread (yards)	330 590	438 658	534 774	622 852	704 924	782 992	857 1,060	930 1,130	1,002 1,197	1,070 1,262	1,140 1,325

Note: These ranges would have used the standard charge, as they are comparable with the range of first graze given in the tables above.

Table C.19. Heavy 5.5-inch howitzer. Range in yards with 2lb charge[22]													
	Elevation (degrees)												
	PB	1	2	3	4	5	6	7	8	9	10	11	12
5.5-inch howitzer	250	400	550	700	850	975	1,100	1,200	1,300	1,400	1,500	1,600	1,700

Note: Ranges beyond this were achieved with greater elevation, but visibility in the field was usually limited to the lower elevations as the fall of shot could not be observed.

Table C.20. Heavy 5.5-inch howitzer. Distance in yards to first graze with round shot[23]													
	Elevation (degrees)												
	PB	1	2	3	4	5	6	7	8	9	10	11	12
2lb charge	-	453	595	666	847	957	1,173	1,355	1,449	1,585	1,853	1,793	1,686
Time of flight	-	2	4	4	5	5	7	8	9	9	10	9	10
3lb charge	-	479	722	921	1,000	1,325	1,530	1,377	1,721	1,801	1,791	2,013	-
Time of flight	-	3	5	5	5	7	8	9	9	9	9	12	-

Notes. The extreme range with a 2lb charge was 1,400 to 1,900 yards; that with a 3lb charge, 1,400 to 2,000 yards. The ranges for the 3lb charge are comparable with the range of first graze given in the tables above.

Table C.21. Rocket ranges in yards (elevation in degrees)[24]								
	Zero	20–25°	25–30°	30–35°	35–40°	40–45°	45–50°	50–55°
32-pr	1,000 to 1,200			1,000 to 1,500	1,500 to 2,000	2,500 to 3,000	2,500 to 3,000	3,000 to 3,200
24-pr	Nearly the same ranges as 32-pr							
18-pr	1,000		1,000 to 1,500	1,500 to 2,000		2,000 to 2,500		-
12-pr	Nearly the same ranges as 18-pr							
9-pr	800 to 1,000	1,000 to 1,500	1,500 and upwards		2,000 to	2,200	-	-
6-pr	Nearly the same ranges as 9-pr							

Endnotes to Appendix C

1. Hughes, 1969: p. 76.
2. Ibid: p. 76.
3. Adye, 1806: p. 29.
4. Notes of Lt. B.R. Heron of practice in Barbadoes, 14 April 1811.
5. Caruana, 1980: p. 12.
6. Heron, op. cit.
7. Caruana, 1980: p. 12.
8. Caruana, 1977: p. 34.
9. Adye, 1813: p. 207.
10. Adye, 1806: p. 183; Adye 1813: p. 195.
11. Papers in the James Clavell Library; Adye, 1827: p. 351.
12. Adye, 1813: p. 195; Adye, 1827: p. 183.
13. Adye, 1827: p. 347.
14. Adye, 1806: p. 183: Adye, 1813: p. 195.
15. Webber, 1991: p. 112.
16. Adye, 1827: p. 347; Hughes, 1969: p. 78.
17. Adye, 1813: p. 195; Adye, 1827: p. 183.
18. Papers in the James Clavell Library; Adye, 1827: p. 347; Hughes, 1969: p. 78.
19. Adye, 1813: p. 195; and Hughes, 1969: p. 84.
20. Ibid: p. 224.
21. Adye, 1827: p. 351.
22. Ibid: p. 183.
23. Adye, 1813: p. 225.
24. Franklin, 2005: p. 15.

Appendix D – Ammunition Carried

Introduction

This appendix contains tables relating to various parameters mentioned in the chapters of Part Two and contains four groups of tables.

Table D.1 – Heavy 3-pr gun. Ammunition carried at first line in 1813[1]								
Location	Round shot	Light case	Heavy case	Spherical case	Total	Cartridges		
						1lb	8oz	1.5oz
Gun axle boxes	12	-	-	-	12	-	-	-
Gun limber off box	20	5	5	-	30	36	-	-
Gun limber near box	20	5	5	-	30	36	-	-
Total at gun	52	10	10	-	72	72	-	-
Wagon limber off box	20	5	5	-	30	30	-	-
Wagon limber near box	20	5	5	-	30	30	-	-
Wagon fore box	48	-	-	11	59	48	11	11
Wagon hind box	48	-	-	11	59	48	11	11
Total at wagon	136	10	10	22	178	156	22	22
Overall total	188	20	20	22	250	228	22	22

Table D.2. Light 6-pr gun of 4ft 6in (bracket trail). Ammunition and stores carried

Right side box		Fore limber box		Locker under the gun	
Boxes of 80 tubes	2	3oz cartridges	14	Claw hammer	1
Portfires	6	6oz cartridges	11	Lashing rope (fathoms)	2
Portfire stick	1	8oz cartridges	8	*Right side of gun*	
Left side box		Slow match	1	Sponges	2
Portfires	6	*Hind limber box*		Ladle	1
Portfire stick	1	4oz cartridges	14	*Left side of gun*	
Sponge tacks	100	5oz cartridges	10	Straight traversing hand spike	1
Vent punches	1	7oz cartridges	10	Crooked traversing hand spike	1
Vent wires	2	Portfires	24	Wad hook	1
Gun spikes, common	1	Sheep skin	1	*Between the Cheeks*	
Gun spikes, spring	1	*Locker under the limber*		Fork levers	2
Couples for chain traces	2	Rope (fathoms)	45	Linstock on left cheek	1
Spare washers	1	Iron strapped 6-inch blocks	3	Bucket under breast transom	1
Spare linchpins	1	*Behind the Axletree*		Set of men's harness under gun carriage	1
Tarred marlin	1	Felling axe	1	*Lengths of tackles and ropes*	
		Hand bill	1	Tackle long (fathoms)	30
		Pick axe	1	Tackle short (fathoms)	15
		Spades	2	Men's harness (feet)	13

Notes: 1. Cartouches of leather carried on each limber box.
  2. A set of drag ropes on the front of the fore limber box and one set under the gun or the limber.

Table D.3. Light 6-pr gun of 4ft 6in (bracket trail). Ammunition carried at first line[2]

	Fixed ammunition		Unfixed ammunition		Cartridges					
	Case	Round shot	Case	Round shot	3oz	4oz	5oz	6oz	7oz	8oz
Gun off side box	6	6	-	-	-	-	-	-	-	-
Gun near side box	6	6	-	-	-	-	-	-	-	-
Gun locker	-	-	4*	6*	-	-	-	-	-	-
Limber fore box	8	8	-	-	14	-	11	-	-	8
Limber hind box	8**	8**	-	-	-	14	-	10	10	-
Total	28	28	4	6	14	14	11	10	10	8

* When action is expected; ** upon an emergency.

Table D.4. Light 6-pr gun of 5ft (block trail). Ammunition carried at the gun in 1810[3]							
Location	Round shot	Heavy case	Light case	Spherical case	Total	Cartridges		
						1.5lb	12oz	2.5oz
Gun axle boxes	8	-	-	-	8	-	-	-
Gun limber off box	16	4	-	-	21	25	-	-
Gun limber near box	16	-	4	-	21	25	-	-
Total at gun	40	4	4	-	50	50	-	-

Table D.5. Light 6-pr gun of 5ft (block trail). Ammunition carried at first line in 1813[4]							
Location	Round shot	Heavy case	Light case	Spherical case	Total	Cartridges		
						1.5lb	12oz	2.5oz
Gun axle boxes	8 *	-	-	-	8	-	-	-
Gun limber off box	16	5	-	-	21	25	-	-
Gun limber near box	16	-	5	-	21	25	-	-
Total at gun	40	5	5	-	50	50	-	-
Wagon limber off box	16	4	-	-	20	20	-	-
Wagon limber near box	16	-	4	-	20	20	-	-
Wagon fore box	25	5	5	10	45	35	10	10
Wagon hind box	35	-	-	10	45	35	10	10
Total at wagon	92	9	9	20	130	110	20	20
Overall total	132	14	14	20	180	160	20	20

*2 rounds were carried in the slow match box and 6 in the right axle box; the cartridges were carried on the limber.

Table D.6. Heavy 6-pr gun. Ammunition carried at first line in 1813[5]							
Location	Round shot	Heavy case	Light case	Spherical case	Total	Cartridges		
						2 lb	12oz	2.5oz
Gun axle boxes	8 *	-	-	-	8	-	-	-
Gun limber off box	20	5	-	-	25	25	-	-
Gun limber near box	20	-	5	-	25	25	-	-
Total at gun	40	5	5	-	50	50	-	-
Wagon limber off box	20	5	-	-	25	25	-	-
Wagon limber near box	20	-	5	-	25	25	-	-
Wagon fore box	25	5	5	10	45	35	10	10
Wagon hind box	35	-	-	10	45	35	10	10
Total at wagon	100	10	10	20	140	120	20	20

Overall total	140	15	15	20	190	170	20	20

*2 rounds were carried in the slow match box and 6 in the right axle box; the cartridges were carried on the limber.

Table D.7. 9-pr gun. Ammunition carried at first line in 1813[6]							
Location	Round shot	Light case	Heavy case	Spherical case	Total	Cartridges		
						3lb	14oz	3.5oz
Gun axle boxes	-	-	-	-	-	-	-	-
Gun limber off box	13	3	-	-	16	16	-	-
Gun limber near box	13	-	3	-	16	16	-	-
Total at gun	26	3	3	-	32	32	-	-
Wagon limber off box	13	3	-	-	16	16	-	-
Wagon limber near box	13	-	3	-	16	16	-	-
Wagon fore box	12	2	2	12	28	16	12	12
Wagon hind box	24	-	-	-	24	24	-	-
Total at wagon	62	5	5	12	84	72	12	12
Total per gun *	88	8	8	12	116	104	12	12

* Note: There were nine 9-pr ammunition wagons allocated to each battery and troop at Waterloo.

Table D.8. 9-pr gun. Ammunition carried at first line in the Peninsula[7]							
Location	Round shot	Light case	Heavy case	Spherical case	Total	Cartridges		
						3lb	14oz	3.5oz
Gun axle boxes	-	-	-	-	-	-	-	-
Gun limber off box	13	3	-	-	16	16	-	-
Gun limber near box	-	-	3	13	16	3	13	13
Total at gun	13	3	3	13	32	19	13	13
Wagon limber off box	13	3	-	-	16	16	-	-
Wagon limber near box	-	-	3	13	16	3	13	13
Wagon fore box	22	4	-	-	26	26	-	-
Wagon hind box	22	-	4	-	26	26	-	-
Total at wagon	57	7	7	13	84	71	13	13
Overall total	70	10	10	26	116	90	26	26
Reserve wagon limber off box	13	3	-	-	16	16	-	-
Reserve wagon limber near box	-	-	3	13	16	3	13	13
Reserve wagon fore box	12	1	1	12	26	14	12	12

Reserve wagon hind box	26	-	-	-	26	26	-	-
Total at each reserve wagon	51	4	4	25	84	59	25	25
Total per five gun unit	172	18	18	76	284	208	76	76

Note. Each gun was accompanied by one ammunition wagon and each troop or brigade had two further reserve wagons. The ammunition carried changed during the period to suit the nature of the supply and the expected engagement.

Table D.9. Medium 12-pr. Bracket trail carriage. Ammunition carried at first line in 1813[8]

Location	Round shot	Light case	Heavy case	Spherical case	Total	Cartridges		
						4lb	1lb	4.5oz
Gun axle boxes	-	-	-	-	-	-	-	-
Gun limber off box	5	1	-	-	6	6	-	-
Gun limber near box	5	-	1	-	6	6	-	-
Total at gun	10	1	1	-	12	12	-	-
Wagon limber off box	12	-	4	-	16	16	-	-
Wagon limber near box	12	4	-	-	16	16	-	-
Wagon fore box	12	-	-	8	20	12	8	8
Wagon hind box	16	2	2	-	20	20	-	-
Total at wagon	52	6	6	8	72	64	8	8
Overall total	62	7	7	8	84	76	8	8

Table D.10. Medium 12-pr. Block trail carriage. Ammunition carried at first line[9]

Location	Round shot	Light case	Heavy case	Spherical case	Total	Cartridges		
						4lb	1lb	4.5oz
Gun axle boxes	-	-	-	-	-	-	-	-
Gun limber off box	12	-	4	-	16	16	-	-
Gun limber near box	12	4	-	-	16	16	-	-
Total at gun	24	4	4	-	32	32	-	-
Wagon limber off box	12	-	4	-	16	16	-	-
Wagon limber near box	12	4	-	-	16	16	-	-
Wagon fore box	12	-	-	8	20	12	8	8
Wagon hind box	16	2	2	-	20	20	-	-
Total at wagon	52	6	6	8	72	72	8	8
Overall total	76	10	10	8	104	104	8	8

Table D.11. Light 5.5-inch howitzer. Ammunition carried at first line in 1813[10]								
Location	Common shell	Common case	Carcass	Spherical case	Total	Cartridges		
						1lb	10oz	6oz
Gun axle boxes	-	-	-	-	-	-	-	
Gun limber off box	8	2	-	-	10	10	8	
Gun limber near box	8	2	-	-	10	10	8	
Total at gun	16	4	-	-	20	20	16	
Limber off box	11	-	-	-	11	11	11	
Limber near box	11	-	-	-	11	11	11	
Wagon fore box	12	3	2	4	21	21	12	4
Wagon hind box	12	3	2	4	21	21	12	4
Total at wagon	46	6	4	8	64	64	64	8
Total	62	10	4	8	84	84	62	6

Table D.12. Light 5.5-inch howitzer. Ammunition carried at first line in the Peninsula[11]								
Location	Common shell	Common case	Carcass	Spherical case	Total	Cartridges		
						1lb	10oz	6oz
Gun axle boxes	-	-	-	-	-	-	-	-
Gun limber off box	6	6	-	-	12	12	6	-
Gun limber near box	-	-	-	12	12	12	-	12
Total at gun	6	6	-	12	24	24	6	12
Limber off box	6	6	-	-	12	12	6	-
Limber near box	-	-	-	12	12	12	-	12
Wagon fore box	6	-	-	12	18	18	6	12
Wagon hind box	14	4	-	-	18	18	14	-
Total at wagon	26	10	-	24	60	60	26	24
Total	32	16	-	36	84	84	32	36

Table D.13. Heavy 5.5-inch howitzer. Ammunition carried at first line in 1813[12]								
Location	Common shell	Common case	Carcass	Spherical case	Total	Cartridges		
						2lb	10oz	6oz
Gun axle boxes	-	-	-	-	-	-	-	-
Gun limber off box	8	2	-	-	10	10	-	-
Gun limber near box	8	2	-	-	10	10	-	-
Total at gun	16	4	-	-	20	20	-	-

Limber off box	11	-	-	-	11	11	-	-
Limber near box	11	-	-	-	11	11	-	-
Wagon fore box	10	2	2	4	18	14	4	4
Wagon hind box	10	2	2	4	18	14	4	4
Total at wagon	42	4	4	8	58	50	8	8
Total	58	8	4	8	78	70	8	8

Note: The charge of 2lb was made up from 1lb cartridges of priming powder.

Table D.14. Heavy 5.5-inch howitzer. Ammunition carried at first line in the Peninsula[13]							
Location	Common shell	Common case	Carcass	Spherical case	Total	Cartridges		
						2lb	10oz	6oz
Gun axle boxes	-	-	-	-	-	-	-	-
Gun limber off box	6	6	-	-	12	12	-	-
Gun limber near box	-	-	-	12**	12	12	12	12
Total at gun	6	6	-	12	24	24	12	12
Limber off box	6	6	-	-	12	12	-	-
Limber near box	-	-	-	12	12	12	12	12
Wagon fore box	6	-	-	12	18	18	12	12
Wagon hind box	14	4	-	-	18	18	-	-
Total at wagon	26	10	-	24	60	60	24	24
Total	32	16	-	36	84	84	36	36

Note: ** Some common case was added and spherical case removed.

Table D.15. Generic details of ammunition carried in 1813[14]						
	Round shot	Common case, large	Common case, small	Spherical case	Common shell	Rounds per gun
Light and heavy 6-pr guns	60%	5%	5%	30%	-	180
9-pr guns	60%	5%	5%	30%	-	116
Heavy 5.5-inch howitzer	-	5%	5%	50%	40%	84
Total reserve ammunition for each troop or brigade						
Light and heavy 6-pr guns	60%	5%	5%	30%	-	130
9-pr guns	60%	5%	5%	30%	-	84
Heavy 5.5-inch howitzer	-	5%	5%	50%	40%	60

Endnotes to Appendix D

1. Adye, 1813: pp. 9–13, Adye, 1810: p.10.
2. Caruana, 1977: pp. 14–35.
3. Tojhusmuseet, Copenhagen: surviving ammunition boxes.
4. Adye, 1813: pp. 9–13.
5. Ibid: p. 8.
6. Ibid: p. 7, Adye.
7. Dickson, 1908: p. 858.
8. Adye, 1813: p. 6; Adye, 1801: p. 16.
9. Adye, 1813: p.13.
10. Ibid: p. 13.
11. Dickson, 1908: pp. 856–66.
12. Adye, 1813: pp. 9–14.
13. Dickson, 1908: p. 865.
14. Dickson, 1908: p. 858.

Appendix E – Equipment Weights

Being of wooden construction the weight of the equipments would have varied as they seasoned and dried out and the different ammunition allocations of the period had a significant effect upon the total weight. The weights given to the equipments by the various contemporary authorities have been impossible to reconcile as they are based in different periods and do not necessarily include all the same variables. The contemporary figures given by Adye in his various editions seem to confirm those given for the gun carriages and limbers, but they seem too low for the ammunition wagons and limbers if the full weight of the ammunition is calculated from the figures given in his various editions. The figures shown are those that best fit the recorded facts but should be taken as guidance only. The first digit of the table number refers to the chapter to which the information relates. Table E.10 contains the weights for the different equipments given by Adye.

Table E.1. Weights for the heavy 3-pr on a block trail carriage						
	cwt	lb	kg	cwt	lb	kg
Gun	6.00	672	304.8			
Gun carriage	4.87	545	247.2			
Gun wheels	3.60	403	182.8	14.46	1,620	734.8
Gun limber	4.63	519	235.4			
Limber wheels	3.60	403	182.8			
Limber ammunition and stores	2.79	313	142.0	11.03	1,235	560.2
Total weight of gun and limber	25.49	2,855	1,295.0			
Ammunition wagon	7.08	794	359.9			

Wheels	3.60	403	182.8			
Wagon ammunition and stores	4.63	519	235.4	15.32	1,716	778.1
Wagon limber	4.63	519	235.4			
Wagon limber wheels	3.60	403	182.8			
Limber ammunition and stores	2.79	313	142.0	11.03	1,235	560.2
Total weight of ammunition wagon and limber	26.34	2,951	1,338.3			

Table E.2. Weights for the light 6-pr of 4ft 6in (bracket trail) battalion gun						
	cwt	lb	kg	cwt	lb	kg
Gun	6.00	672	304.8			
Gun carriage	4.87	545	247.2			
Gun wheels	3.60	403	182.8	14.46	1,620	734.8
Gun limber	4.63	519	235.4			
Limber wheels	3.60	403	182.8			
Limber ammunition and stores	2.79	313	142.0	11.03	1,235	560.2
Total weight of gun and limber	25.49	2,855	1,295.0			
Ammunition wagon	7.08	794	359.9			
Wheels	3.60	403	182.8			
Wagon ammunition and stores	4.63	519	235.4	15.32	1,716	778.1
Wagon limber	4.63	519	235.4			
Wagon limber wheels	3.60	403	182.8			
Limber ammunition and stores	2.79	313	142.0	11.03	1,235	560.2
Total weight of ammunition wagon and limber	26.34	2,951	1,338.3			

Table E.3. Weights for the light 6-pr gun of 5ft (bracket trail) carriage						
	cwt	lb	kg	cwt	lb	kg
Gun of 5 feet*	5.50*	616*	279.4*			
Gun carriage	3.66	410	186.0			
Gun wheels	2.96	332	150.6	12.13	1,358	616.0
Gun side boxes	0.79	88	39.9			
Gun ammunition	2.28	255	115.7			
Gun side arms and tools	0.79	88	39.9	3.85	431	195.5
Total weight of carriage, ammunition and stores	15.97	1,789	811.5			
Gun limber	2.40	269	122.0			

Limber wheels	2.29	256	116.1	4.69	525	238.1
Limber ammunition boxes	1.31	147	66.7			
Limber ammunition	2.47	277	125.6			
Limber tools and stores	0.53	59	26.8	4.31	483	219.1
Total weight of limber, ammunition and stores	9.00	914	414.6			
Total weight of ammunition wagon and limber	37.45	4,194	1,902.4			

Note: * The piece of 4ft 6in weighed 5.36cwt, 590lb or 268kg, otherwise the weights were similar.

Table E.4. Weights for the light 6-pr of 5ft on a block trail carriage						
	cwt	lb	kg	cwt	lb	kg
Gun	6.00	672	304.8			
Gun carriage	5.50	616	279.2			
Gun wheels	3.60	403	182.8	15.09	1,691	766.8
Gun limber	4.63	519	235.2			
Limber wheels	3.60	403	182.8			
Limber ammunition and stores	3.57	400	181.4	11.80		
Total weight of gun and limber	26.89	3,012	1,366.2			
Ammunition wagon	7.28	815	369.7			
Wheels	3.60	403	182.8			
Wagon ammunition and stores	5.49	615	279.0	16.37	1,322	599.4
Wagon limber	4.63	519	235.2			
Wagon limber wheels	3.60	403	182.8			
Limber ammunition and stores	3.57	400	181.4	11.80	1,322	599.4
Total weight of ammunition wagon and limber	28.17	3,155	1,430.8			

Table E.5. Weights for the heavy 6-pr on a block trail carriage						
	cwt	lb	kg	cwt	lb	kg
Gun	12.39	1,388	629.6			
Gun carriage	7.55	846	383.7			
Gun wheels	3.60	403	182.8	23.54	2,637	1,196.1
Gun limber	4.64	520	235.9			
Limber wheels	3.60	403	182.8			
Limber ammunition and stores	3.26	365	165.6	11.50	1,288	584.2
Total weight of gun and limber	35.04	3,925	1,780.3			

	cwt	lb	kg	cwt	lb	kg
Ammunition Wagon	7.32	820	371.9			
Wheels	3.60	403	182.8			
Wagon ammunition and stores	5.76	645	292.6	16.68	1,868	847.3
Wagon limber	4.64	520	235.9			
Wagon limber wheels	3.60	403	182.8			
Limber ammunition and stores	3.26	365	165.6	11.50	1,288	584.2
Total weight of ammunition wagon and limber	28.18	3,156	1,431.5			

Table E.6. Weights for the 9-pr on a block trail carriage						
	cwt	lb	kg	cwt	lb	kg
Gun	13.50	1,512	685.8			
Gun carriage	7.67	859	389.4			
Gun wheels	4.28	479	217.3	25.44	2,850	1,292.5
Gun limber	4.71	528	239.3			
Limber wheels	3.60	403	182.8			
Limber ammunition and stores	3.65	409	185.5	11.96	1,340	607.6
Total weight of gun and limber	37.40	4,189	1,900.1			
Ammunition wagon	7.35	824	373.5			
Wheels	3.60	403	182.8			
Wagon ammunition and stores	5.47	613	278.1	16.42	1,840	834.4
Wagon limber	4.71	528	239.3			
Wagon limber wheels	3.60	403	182.8			
Limber ammunition and stores	3.65	409	185.5	11.96	1,340	607.6
Total weight of ammunition wagon and limber	28.38	3,179	1,442.0			

Table E.7. Weights for the medium 12-pr on a block trail carriage						
	cwt	lb	kg	cwt	lb	kg
Gun	18.00	2,016	914.4			
Gun carriage	8.42	944	428.0			
Gun wheels	4.28	479	217.3	30.70	3,439	1,559.7
Gun limber	4.88	547	248.1			
Limber wheels	4.28	479	217.3			
Limber ammunition and stores	4.62	517	234.5	13.78	1,543	699.9
Total weight of gun and limber	44.48	4,982	2,259.6			

Ammunition wagon	7.34	822	372.9			
Wheels	3.60	403	182.8			
Wagon ammunition and stores	20.27	2,270	1,029.6	31.21	3,495	1,585.3
Wagon limber	4.88	547	248.1			
Wagon limber wheels	3.60	403	182.8			
Limber ammunition and stores	4.62	517	234.5	13.10	1,467	665.4
Total weight of ammunition wagon and limber	44.30	4,962	2,250.7			

Table E.8. Weights for the light 5.5-inch howitzer on a block trail carriage						
	cwt	lb	kg	cwt	lb	kg
Gun	4.75	532	241.3			
Gun carriage	6.86	768	348.4			
Gun wheels	3.60	403	182.8	15.21	1,703	772.5
Gun limber	4.79	537	243.6			
Limber wheels	3.60	403	182.8			
Limber ammunition and stores	4.42	495	224.5	12.81	1,435	650.9
Total weight of gun and limber	28.02	3,138	1,423.4			
Ammunition wagon	7.18	804	364.7			
Wheels	3.60	403	182.8			
Wagon ammunition and stores	9.26	1,037	470.4	20.04	2,244	1,017.9
Wagon limber	4.79	537	243.6			
Wagon limber wheels	3.60	403	182.8			
Limber ammunition and stores	4.42	495	224.5	12.81	1,435	650.9
Total weight of ammunition wagon and limber	32.85	3,679	1,668.8			

Table E.9. Weights for the heavy 5.5-inch howitzer on a block trail carriage						
	cwt	lb	kg	cwt	lb	kg
Gun	10.00	1,120	508.0			
Gun carriage	9.20	1,030	467.2			
Gun wheels	3.60	403	182.8	22.79		
Gun limber	4.68	524	237.7			
Limber wheels	3.60	403	182.8			
Limber ammunition and stores	4.74	531	240.9	13.02		
Total weight of gun and limber	35.81	4,011	1,819.3			

Ammunition wagon	7.46	836	379.2			
Wheels	3.60	403	182.8			
Wagon ammunition and stores	13.37	1,497	679.0	24.43		
Wagon limber	4.68	524	237.7			
Wagon limber wheels	3.60	403	182.8			
Limber ammunition and stores	4.74	531	240.9	13.02		
Total weight of ammunition wagon and limber	37.45	4,194	1,902.4			

Table E.10. Weights of different ordnance in 1813					
Ordnance		cwt	qtr	lb	lb
Medium 12-pr gun	Gun, gun carriage with limber & ammunition complete	42	0	0	4,704
	Ammunition wagon & limber with ammunition complete	29	0	0	3,248
9-pr gun	Gun, gun carriage with limber & ammunition complete	39	1	0	4,396
	Ammunition wagon & limber with ammunition complete	26	0	0	2,912
Heavy 6-pr gun	Gun, gun carriage with limber and ammunition complete	37	2	0	4,200
	Ammunition wagon & limber with ammunition complete	27	2	0	3,080
Light 6-pr gun	Gun, gun carriage with limber & ammunition complete	27	2	0	3,080
	Ammunition wagon & limber with ammunition complete	26	0	0	2,912
Heavy 3-pr gun	Gun, gun carriage with limber and ammunition complete	26	0	0	2,912
	Ammunition wagon & limber with ammunition complete	23	2	0	2,632
Heavy 5.5-inch howitzer	Howitzer, carriage and limber with ammunition complete	36	1	0	4,060
	Ammunition wagon & limber with ammunition complete	27	1	0	3,052
Light 5.5-inch howitzer	Howitzer, carriage & limber with ammunition complete	27	1	0	3,052
	Ammunition wagon & limber with ammunition complete	27	0	0	3,024
Spare wheel carriage	Carriage and limber complete	27	0	24	3,048
Forge wagon	Forge with limber and stores complete	21	2	23	2,431
Store wagon	Wagon with limber, empty	17	3	21	2,009
These are the weights given by Adye in 1813 (Adye, 1813: pp. 90–1.)					

Appendix F – Supporting Equipment

Introduction

Miscellaneous data relating to the supporting wagons and carts.

Table F.1. Number of wagons with an artillery unit[1]					
Ordnance	Medium 12-pr	9-pr	Heavy 6-pr	Light 6-pr	Heavy 3-pr
Spare wheel carriage	1	1	1	1	1
Ammunition wagons	12	9	8	8	7
Forge & limber	1	1	1	1	1
Store carts	2	1	1	1	1
Curricle	1	1	1	1	1
Total	17	13	12	12	11

Table F.2. Ammunition carried in second-line ammunition carts in 1801[2]						
Ordnance	Medium 12-pr	9-pr	Heavy 6-pr	Light 6-pr	5.5-inch howitzers	3-pr
Case fixed to bottoms	24	-	30	34	24	
Round shot	120	-	120	144	-	
Shell filled	-	-	-	-	24	

Shell empty	-	-	-	-	120	
Carcass	-	-	-	-	4	
Cartridges	144	-	150	190	-	
Tubes/Quills	172	-	178	280	190	
Portfires	18	-	18	31	18	
Total Ammunition	144	-	150	178	172	

Table F.3. Ammunition carried in second-line ammunition carts in 1813[3]						
Ordnance	Round shot	Common case	Spherical case	Shell	Carcass	Total
Medium 12-pr gun	60	12	8	-	-	80
9-pr gun	82	18	10	-	-	110
Both 6-pr guns	112	24	14	-	-	150
Both 5.5-inch howitzers	-	8	8	60	4	80
Both 3-pr guns	210	46	24	-	-	280

Table F.4. Weights of spare wheel carriages and limbers						
	Carriage	Limber	Wheels			Stores
	(lb)	(lb)	Heavy	Light	(lb)	(lb)
Medium 12-pr	1,505	963	1	2	654	371
9-pr	1,400	879	1	2	654	376
Long 6-pr	*	**	1	2	654	376
Heavy 6-pr	1,292	879	1	2	654	376
Light 6-pr	1,075	879	-	3	618	412
Heavy 3-pr	1,023	879	-	3	618	254
Light 3-pr	551	879	-	3	618	254
* Not known; ** assumed the same.						

Endnotes to Appendix F

1. Spearman, 1828: p. 7.
2. Adye, 1801: p. 10.
3. Adye, 1813: p. 14.

PART THREE

The Uniforms of the Royal Regiment of Artillery

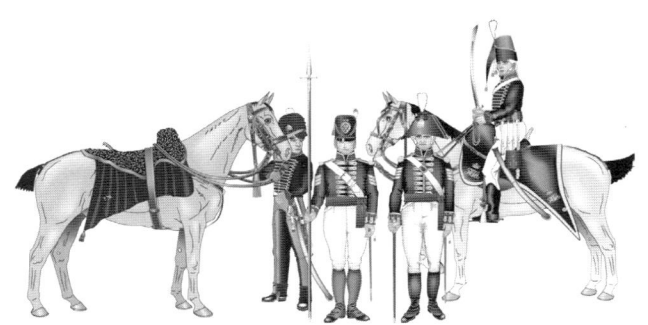

Introduction to Part Three

This part considers the uniforms, dress, accoutrements and weapons of the Royal Regiment of Artillery including the Royal Horse Artillery during the Napoleonic Wars. The Corps of Artillery Drivers were an inherent part of the foot artillery and have been included for completeness. It should be remembered that the artillery answered to the Board of Ordnance, who answered directly to the government and the Prince Regent, and not to the Horse Guards, who regulated the army. The independence of the board was fiercely protected and many, including the Duke of Wellington, were not pleased by this independent role. Throughout the Napoleonic period there was a steady flow of orders issued by the Board of Ordnance concerning the arms, dress and accoutrements of the artillery officers and men. In the main, the board tended to follow, albeit at their own pace, the infantry regulations applicable to a royal regiment where the foot brigades were concerned. The horse artillery was initially dressed to the principles of the light cavalry, but soon adopted their own forms and affectations. In large part, they took up those changes that took their fancy and ignored those that did not.

The dress of the Royal Artillery and its associated arms is one of the most difficult to resolve, as there were no official dress regulations published before 1833, just a random series of Garrison Orders and individual regulations published by the Board of Ordnance, some now recorded in the papers of the National Archive. There are the contemporary illustrations of the period and all the known examples have been consulted during the preparation of this study. A vast amount has been written about artillery uniforms of this period but all draw upon earlier works and give an author's interpretation, often to the better knowledge of the subject. It may be that other regulations may exist in private hands, but those in the public domain have all been consulted. In the light of such diversity, the books and illustrations from which information has been specifically gleaned are listed in the bibliography. To these must be added the unstinting help of the British Library, National Army Museum, the Royal Artillery Museum, the James Clavell Library and the multitude of regimental museums, re-enactors and the many enthusiasts who have so unstintingly provided assistance, both in the UK and abroad.

It was the practice of gunner officers, particularly when away from headquarters, to adopt whatever dress took their fancy and nothing can show this better than the writings of General Cavalier Mercer. His notes and recollections are classic indicators for the attitude of the day and some might suggest that the principle is still practiced by the gunner officer of today, albeit in a more subtle way. It is apparent that whatever the regulations prescribed, the personnel serving away were often dressed in a manner contrary to the current regulations and in many cases the most significant factors were the size of the purse and being dressed à la mode.

Other factors were the time and distances involved and the nature of the supply system for those personnel serving abroad. Wellington was notoriously indifferent to who wore what and the drawings by contemporary artists make it clear that the outfits worn in the Peninsula often reflected the uniforms and equipment well behind the regulations. While the new regulations may have been received, the ability to meet them or even maintain the uniforms they had, was often beyond local resources except for those new arrivals who may well have been dressed in the style prescribed by headquarters. Dickson noted on several occasions the lack of supplies:

> We have never received anything, not even shoes, shirts or stockings … we stand in real need of them. Men obliged to make up suits at their own expense … knapsack also we stand in the greatest need of, as we have nothing but linen [haversacks] which are in a bad state and no security to the men's necessaries against the rain [and] blankets not supplied and greatcoats entirely worn out … as they have neither received blankets or greatcoats for 3 years and then when they did receive greatcoats they were old ones taken from the 4th and 10th Regiments which have worn out long ago.[1]

It seems that it was also practice for the Senior NCOs to sell clothing to the men at a profit:

> to the best of my recollections a profit is allowed at Woolwich to pay-serjeants on the purchase of men's necessaries, with the specious pretence that the price and quality of the articles being fixed the men cannot procure them so good and cheap themselves.[2]

In August 1812, the situation was so bad that Dickson noted that

> 62 French coats and 84 pairs of cap scales … the coats to be altered to jackets for the men and the scales for gunners and drivers.[3]

With these factors in mind, it must be noted that this chapter is only a guide based upon the known regulations and practices. Any references to dress and dates refer to those applicable to the artillery and are often not be the same as those for the army in general. What was actually worn by whom and when, is a peril best avoided and the most one can do is give a generic picture. Readers must make up their own minds as to the implementation or adherence to any given pattern.

Queues

At the start of the period and in common with the army, all the officers and men of the Royal Artillery wore their hair in a queue, but it is not clear if they followed the army by dispensing with powder in 1795.[4] Those men unable to cultivate a queue had to wear an artificial one.[5] The 8- to 10-inch of tail[6] was tied and bound with a ribbon starting at the nape of the neck in line with the collar and ending just short of the end. A rosette and hanging ribbons often covered the tie and dandies of the regiment, and sometimes false extensions with long flowing streamers were worn. One of the best descriptions of the process is from Mercer:

> My first and earliest recollections on this subject … in or about the year 1789 or 1790, …. The operation was to plaster well with grease, whiten with flour, and to roll the hair behind in a club, which was effected by means of a clubbing iron. The hair was rolled up and when the club was made, the instrument was removed by drawing it out sideways. It was fastened by a black leather band, ornamented with a rosette. The whole was made as white as a cauliflower. My next recollection on this subject was at Plymouth, in 1794, when the Officers wore small queues tied with a few turns of riband, and ornamented with a rather large silk rosette. What the men wore, I now forget ; but all were still powdered. 1798, I went to the Royal Academy at Woolwich, and the doctoring my head underwent at that time will give the fashion of the day. On the top the hair was cut close, and the stumps well rubbed back with hard or stick pomatum, a kind of grease made up in hard rolls about an inch in diameter, and three or four inches long, if I recollect right, run into paper moulds, like resin for the violin. The stumpy hair, at first stubborn, by perseverance and pomatum, was after a time quite forced out of its natural direction, and made to grow backwards instead of forwards. The remainder of the hair was gathered into a queue behind, which, according to regulation, should be 10 inches long, and tied close to the head; this we called a rooter, but the dandies affected a loose tye, and began some inches lower down. Those whose hair was not long enough had false queues made of stuffed chamois leather with a brush of hair at the end, and this had to be spliced on to his own hair. For uniformity sake, the gunners, etc., wore false queues of strong black leather, which they cleaned and polished like their shoes ... At the time we went to church in the old Repository, greasing and whitening the head was in full go, and never I forget the stench emanating from so many filthy heads crowded together in the low rooms where service was performed – of course, more particularly in hot weather. The exact year when powder and queues expired, I don't exactly remember. It appears to me that the death-blow was given by the earlier Peninsular campaigns, but there are other things that stagger me in this belief. I remember, for instance, powdering the side locks after putting my helmet on in 1808, and wearing queues in 1809–10, etc.[7]

A general order issued by the Board of Ordnance and dated 1 August 1808 instructed that the order for the Army to dispense with the use of queues, was to be extended to the Artillery. The Commanding Officers of regiments were directed

> to take care that the men's hair be cut close in their neck, in the neatest and most uniform manner, and that their heads be kept perfectly clean, by combing, brushing, and frequently washing them; for the latter essential purpose, a small sponge was ordered to be added to each man's regimental necessaries.[8]

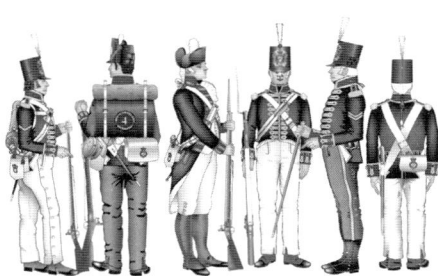

Chapter 16

Royal Artillery – Other Ranks

Introduction

This chapter considers the dress of the gunners and Non-Commissioned Officers throughout the period of the war. The limited information concerning Royal Artillery uniforms fails to explain several anomalies. There is an unresolved disparity in the contemporary illustrations concerning the jackets of the other ranks. Some show red turn backs others white. The braiding shown in the early illustrations is clearly similar to those of the 1st Foot Guards, but the later illustrations show a pattern more representative of a conventional line regiment. The same problem seems to exist where the rear pockets are concerned; the early illustrations show horizontal pockets, the distinction of grenadier and battalion companies, but the line regiments seem to have abandoned this distinction in the later period and the use of the oblique pocket had become general practice. The later drawings suggest the artillery may have followed suit, but one thing is clear: where the Royal Artillery uniforms of this period are concerned, nothing is certain and the best that can be done is to present the different evidence for the reader to consider. There are several suggested explanations for these apparent inconsistencies, one is that different battalions of foot artillery had several uniform distinctions; another is that the variation of dress is more a practice of what was available rather than what was proper and representative of the uniform worn throughout the regiment at this time, and lastly the reliability of the interpretation.

Cocked Hat

At the start of the war the cocked hat was still worn by all ranks, but the shape was now more a bicorn with only two fans folded into two locks instead of the original three of the tricorn. The white lace brim had been removed in 1796 and the hat

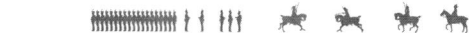

now carried a plain black braid loop and button and a white feather plume, red for the band.[9] It was worn with a loop over the left eye and right wing thrown a little forward so the musket at the shoulder did not knock the hat off. To prevent the hats falling off, two narrow tapes were sewn into the lining and passed down, round the back of the head to be joined by a hook and eye under the queue.[10] The cocked hat was replaced for other ranks in 1804 but continued in use by Senior NCOs until 1813. Mercer recollects that

> when I first went to Woolwich, the latter end of 1797, I remember seeing all the men in cocked hats. Horrid ugly things they were, too, especially the men's, made of very coarse felt and heavy as lead; they turned upwards, instead of drooping, as was afterwards considered the criterion of beauty. Just fitting on the crown of the head, the slightest breeze sufficed to uncover a whole regiment, had it not been for weight and a small string made into a loop, both ends of which being attached to the hat, the bend was passed under the hair behind; so that, on going into church, the men had rather an awkward operation to perform ere they could uncover.[11]

Round Hat

The painting by De Loutherberg of the attack on Valenciennes in 1793 shows artillery gunners wearing a black round hat. This was made of felt with a broad curved brim edged with tape, the crown was about seven inches tall with a yellow band at the base and a red plume and black cockade at the front of the crown. The shape of the brim and the crown seems to have varied and Mercer recalls that

> The first head-dress I remember as worn by the Royal Artillery was at Plymouth, 1794 or 1795 … It was a round hat of the true Mother Shipton breed. Narrow (very narrow) brim, very high crown, going smaller upwards, so that it formed a frustum of an acute cone. This elegant coiffure was ornamented with a broad yellow band, and a cockade in front of the roof, surmounted by a scarlet tuft.[12]

All ranks seem to have adopted the 'Mother Shipton' hat, but no surviving example is known and there are no other known descriptions. It is from these sources that all the interpretations and drawings are based.[13] The hat seems to have remained in used until about 1797 when it was relegated to undress.[14]

Fatigue Hats

When on fatigue duties different hats were worn, some like the standard fatigue cap of line regiments but more commonly a leather cap generally associated with the personnel based at Woolwich. It is described as pork pie shaped with a flap at the back and front flap having a brass badge. The foot artillery version is noted as

> The most ungraceful head-dress that could well be devised, I think, was the fatigue-cap worn by the Foot Artillery when I first entered the regiment, and only required the combination with the loose canvas frock and waistcoat to make it hideously unmilitary. It was of black leather, with a brass ornament in front (G.R. and crown, etc.), the leather not stiff, full of cracks, and looking rusty, for they were never cleaned or expected to be.[15]

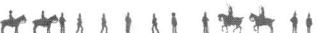

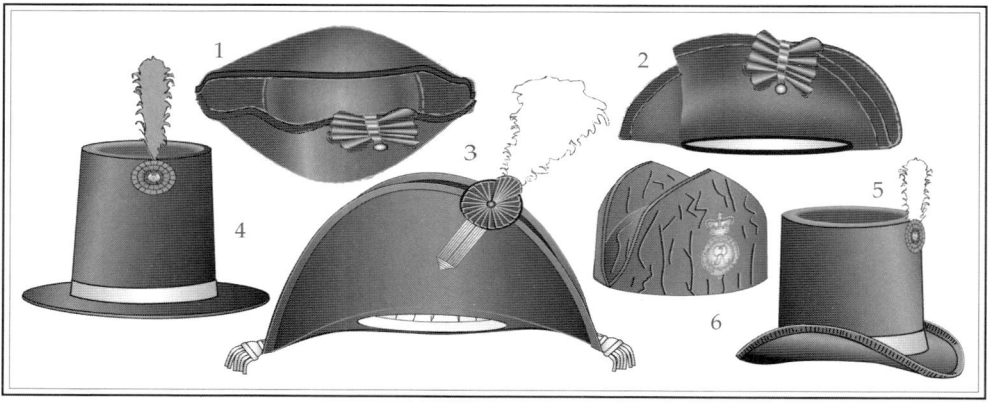

Figure 16.1. Hats of the other ranks of the Royal Artillery. The early black felt bicorn had evolved from the tricorn to a pattern (1 and 2) with two locks and fans instead of the earlier three. The hat changed in shape and size according to the fashion of the day and the later style of hat worn by Staff Sergeants until 1813 (3). The ubiquitous 'Mother Shipton' hat associated with the foot artillery (4), the other ranks' round hat worn during the early part of the period in the Low Countries (5) and the artillery fatigue cap of the style associated with many arms that answered to Woolwich (6).

Stovepipe Shako

The stovepipe shako was introduced for the infantry in 1800 but does not appear to have been adopted by the artillery until about 1804.[16] The shako was similar to those of the infantry being made of lacquered leather with a plain, two-inch wide, flat peak and the cylindrical crown was some 9 inches tall and 7 inches broad at the top. Some of these hats had a rear fall or neck protector made of leather or oilcloth, which was tucked up into the hat or hooked up when not in use. At the front of the crown was a tall white feather plume 10 inches tall,[17] at the base of which was a black cockade that carried a small regimental button at its centre. Those men who had served in Egypt were entitled to wear a small brass 'sphinx' with the word 'Egypt' in lieu of the button,[18] and both 'Peninsula' and 'Waterloo' were granted in the same manner.[19] Senior NCOs and officers wore a 13-inch tall plume until 1808, when it was ordered that the plumes were all to be the same height as those worn by the men, 10 inches.[20] The front of the shako carried a thin brass shako plate with the design die-stamped into the rear. It was a different shape to that of the infantry and smaller at 4.75 inches high and 3.625 inches wide. The plate carried a crown over a garter strap encircling the royal cipher 'GR'. The garter strap carried the title 'ROYAL·REGᵀ OF·ARTILLERY'. Around the outside of the garter belt were arranged trophies of arms and union flags and at the bottom of the plate was a mortar on a sledge between two different-sized piles of shot.[21] On some plates the space at the top, either side of the crown, carried a stamped battalion or company number and there were often small variations in pattern due to the manufacturer or the proclivities of the wearer.

The second, improved, version of the stovepipe shako was introduced in about 1806 to be worn by the other ranks of artillery. It was a lighter pattern, made of felt and slightly shorter, being about eight to nine inches high with a top diameter of seven inches. At the rear of the hat was often stitched the usual fall, or neck protector. The artillery still wore the same plate and the white plume mounted behind a black cockade with a small regimental button at the centre. In 1808, orders dictated that the feather was to be the same height, ten inches, for all ranks.[22]

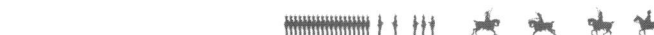

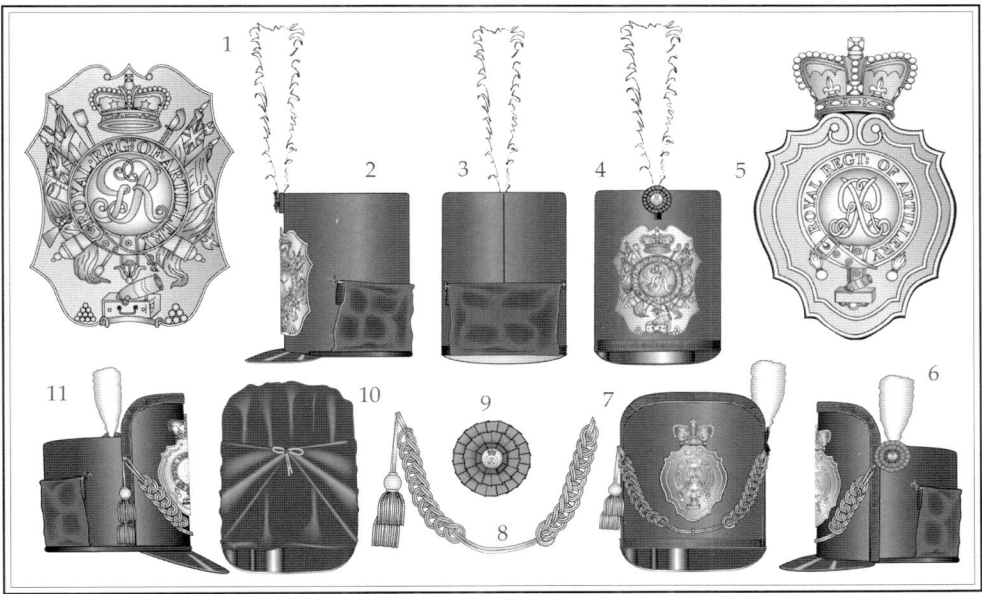

Figure 16.2. Shakos of the other ranks of the Royal Artillery. The 4.75-inch tall artillery brass plate for the stovepipe shako (1), and three views of the shako showing the rear fall and white 10-inch plumes (2, 3 and 4). The 5.5-inch tall brass shako plate for the Belgic-style artillery shako and a side and front view (6 and 7), the yellow cords and black cockade of the other ranks (8 and 9) and a view of the shako with a foul weather cover (10) and a right side view showing the yellow tassels (11).

Belgic Shako

In 1811, a new model shako was ordered as the existing model had many shortcomings and Wellington wished for a head-dress with a plume at the side so that it would not be mistaken for that of the enemy. This hat became know as the Belgic shako, but was not formally adopted by the artillery until August 1813.[23] The crown of the hat was 7 inches in diameter and 6.75 inches high at the sloping back with the false front rising to 8.75 inches. The crown sloped down at the rear and broadened out by another inch or so. The hat was made of felt for the other ranks and coarse beaver for NCOs. The false front was edged with 0.375-inch leather or black braid and there was a 2.25 inch-plain, unedged, lacquered leather peak to the front; around the base of some hats was a black braid. At the rear of some examples was the fall or neck protector of leather or oilcloth; when not in use this was worn tucked up into the hat or suspended from a cord at the rear. The hat carried a white worsted tuft on the left side with a black cockade at its base. At the centre of the cockade was a small regimental button. The hat was issued with an oilskin, foul weather cover and a similar narrow case for the plume. There was no chin strap on this cap but infantry examples exist where they have been added and it may be that the artillery followed suit.

Across the front of the hat, the other ranks wore a yellow, worsted cord with a tassel at each end. This was shortened by a doubled loop knot to form two lengths of chain with an unknotted length at the middle. It was worn with the doubled loop end hooked behind the cockade with the two lengths of loop knots either side of the shako plate and the two tassels on the right with the bottom of the fringe of the lowest, one inch above the bottom of the hat and the shortest two inches.[24]

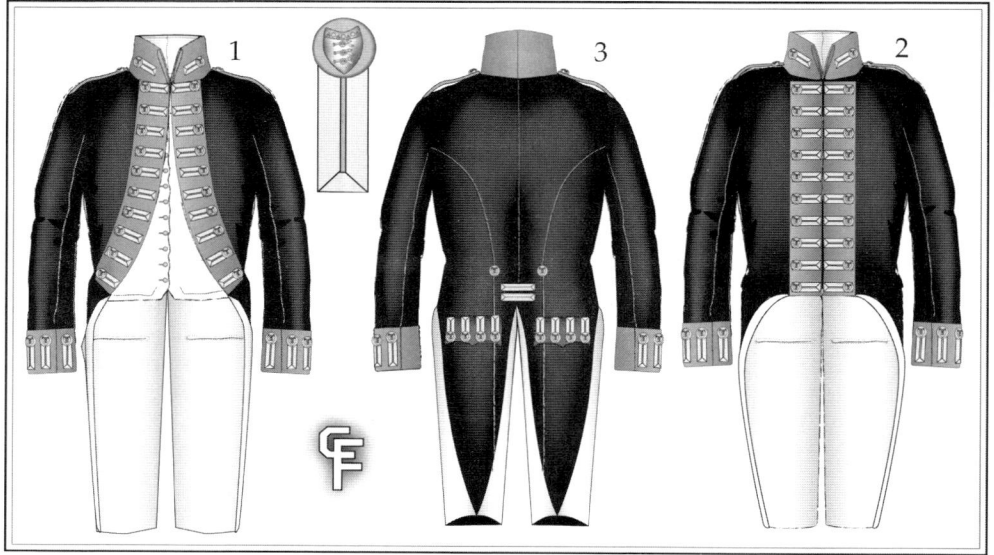

Figure 16.3. Royal Artillery other ranks' long blue coat with red facings of the pre-1797 style, worn hooked at the chest and cut away to show the waistcoat (1) and the early yellow lace and pewter button. The change to the later regulations of 1797 with the coat buttoned to the waist but the lapels retained (2) and a reconstruction of a possible rear view after de Loutherberg (3).

The front of the hat carried a die-stamped shako plate of brass for the other ranks and gilt for the most senior of the NCOs. It was 5.375 inches high by some 3.375 inches wide and was worn about 2.5 inches below the top of the false front. While of a similar shape to that of the infantry, it carried a different design of a crown over a double-edged plate inside which a slightly oval garter belt carried the title 'ROYAL·REG^T OF·ARTILLERY' with a double GR cipher within. Below the garter were two flaming shells either side of a mortar on a sledge.[25] These plates also had small variations in pattern.

Coats and Jackets

At the start of the Napoleonic War, the coats of the Royal Artillery still resembled those worn in the American Revolution. They are illustrated by Dayes in two watercolours, one of a gunner the other of an officer. The long coats were blue, with a scarlet stand-up collar, cuffs, lapels and shoulder straps. The skirt of the coat was lined white. At the chest the lapels were secured together by hooks and below this they were worn open and cut away to show the waistcoat. The coat of the other ranks was more elaborate than that of the officers', having square-ended, equally spaced, yellow-worsted regimental lace. The lapels carried ten laced buttonholes, each with a large regimental button; the cuffs carried four more with the front two astride the front seam of the sleeve and the collar carried one at each side. The long tails of the coat were folded back and secured together to reveal the white linings, the rear pocket of the coat was horizontal with four buttons and vertically laced buttonholes.

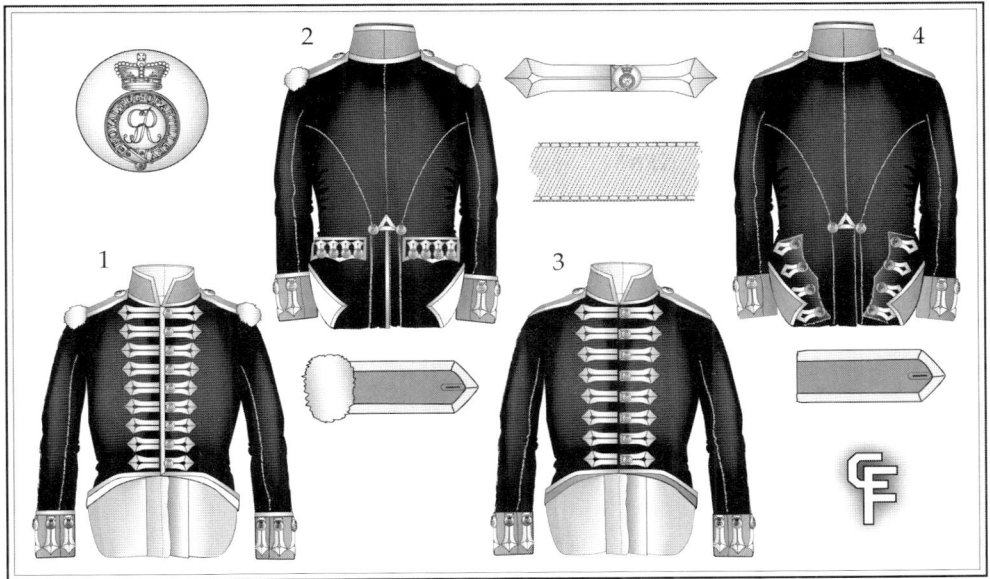

Figure 16.4. Royal Artillery other ranks' blue jackets with red facings. The short jacket introduced by 1800 (1 and 2) after de Bosset, Dighton and Atkinson with white turn backs, horizontal pockets and braid to the top of the cuff. The later jacket, after Hamilton Smith and Dighton (3 and 4), with the red turn-backs, the braid removed from the top of the cuff and the tufts removed from the shoulder straps.

The coats of the Senior NCOs were of a similar pattern to that of the men but with gilt braid and of better quality and cut. De Loutherberg shows the rear of a gunner's coat with two lace bands at the rear waist.

In May 1797, the army ordered that the jackets were to be closed to the waist, and in October the same year the lapels were abolished and the lace and buttons sewn to the front of the now single-breasted coat which also had the skirts cut short to form a jacket. Initially the long coat would have been locally modified, but as time progressed new jackets were issued that better conformed to the new concept. Exactly when the artillery adopted the new-style uniform has not been recorded but it was in general use by 1799.[26]

There are no known examples of this new artillery jacket and we are restricted to the few contemporary illustrations and the limited dress regulations published by the Board of Ordnance. With the change to the new jackets, the pattern of regimental distinction seems to have changed to those closely resembling the 1st Foot Guards but with the reversed colours of a Royal Regiment and yellow lace. The early jackets had the turn backs and lace starting at the bottom button, but later they were cut away at the waist and the white lined, nine-inch long, skirt started further back. The regimental lace while still a yellow, flat worsted braid, half an inch wide, was now set in evenly spaced, bastion-shaped loops. The infantry dress regulations prescribed that, dependent upon the height of the wearer, the front of the jacket should have ten equally spaced, laced buttons on the right side and on the left, ten laced buttonholes; the lace being some four inches long at the neck, reducing to some three inches at the waist. However, it is clear from contemporary notes and illustrations that the tailors found it difficult to fit the required number of bastion-shaped loops in the height between waist and neck and usually, just like the foot guards and other line regiments, only eight or nine buttons and loops were fitted, and these were often longer than the regulated length.[27] The rear pocket flaps were horizontal, as for grenadier or battalion companies, but laced about and with four, equally spaced, buttoned and laced loops pointing upwards; these pockets usually opened, although some may have had the flaps sewn down and pockets on the inside of the skirt, a practice common at the time. At the rear of the waist was a button in a small diamond of lace with the lace extending down the edge of the skirt vent. This form of jacket is illustrated by Atkinson in his picture of 1807.

The 3-inch collar of red serge was lined by one strip of yellow lace and cut away at the front to reveal the black leather stock worn underneath. The shoulder straps were red and edged with yellow lace. They had a crest or roll where they were sewn to the shoulder of the jacket and pointed at the other end, where they were secured, close to the collar, by a small regimental button. The red serge, 3.5-inch deep cuffs were square with the top edge lined by one strip of yellow lace. Each cuff carried four equally spaced, buttoned laced loops with the front pair astride the seam of the sleeve. Dress orders for 1810 noted that

> No part of the waistcoat is to be seen, and the jacket is to come well down, so as to cover the upper part of the breeches. The skirt is to be the same as furnished by the contactor, 9 inches in length.[28]

By 1812 the lace at the back of the waist had changed to 'a triangle of lace, with a large regimental button at each end'; the lace edging to the vent of the skirt appears to have been discontinued but the pocket were still horizontal and the turn backs white. This is the style of uniform illustrated by Dighton in his depiction of the Battle of Waterloo.

The later tunics seem to have abandoned the style of the 1st Foot Guards and followed the pattern of the line regiments as the lace edging to the pockets, the strip of lace to the top of the cuff appears to have been removed, possibly at the same time that oblique pockets were adopted. Hamilton Smith shows gunners with this style of uniform in 1815 with red turn backs to the jacket, no lace to the top of the cuff and no tufts to the shoulder straps. This could be either a late version of the uniform, but the change is also suggested by the drawings of Vernet and Dighton in 1813.[29] (It should be remembered that uniformity was a concept rather than an achievement and the implementation of new dress regulations would have taken considerable time, especially abroad.) Whatever the reasons for these differences, I have found no confirming orders to support them. Until newly discovered evidence clarifies our understanding it appears that up to about 1812 the artillery copied the style of the foot guards, but some time after that the situation changed and a different style was adopted and the colour of the turn backs was changed to red. Coloured illustrations of the coats and jackets of the other ranks are given in the colour plates.

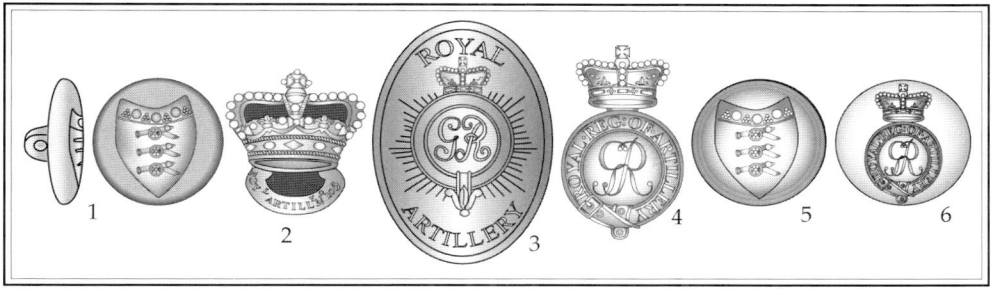

Figure 16.5. Royal Artillery buttons, badges and plates. The early flat pewter button (1), the badge of the early cartridge pouch (2) and an other ranks' brass plate as depicted by Dighton in 1812 (3). The badge of the later cartridge pouch, after Hamilton Smith (4), the brass button pre-1802 (5) and the convex brass button post-1802 (6).

Invalids

Originally, each battalion had companies of invalids, but these were consolidated into a single battalion in about 1784. These companies were made up from gunners who were not fit enough for general service and they were often allocated to guns of position, particularly in garrisons or to training roles. Their uniform was distinctive in that they usually had red facings to the turn backs and little or no braid. Clothing returns of 1792 indicate that they also wore blue waistcoats and breeches.[30] There is some speculation that these may be the uniforms with the red turn backs depicted by Hamilton Smith. It is not clear if the personnel shown are from this cadre or if red turn backs had been adopted by the regiment as a whole.[31]

Buttons, Badges and Belt Plates

Initially, the buttons of other ranks were of pewter, but by the start of the war the pattern on the almost flat brass buttons was the badge of the Board of Ordnance, three cannon in pale and three cannon balls in chief raised on a sunken Norman shield. In about 1802 new buttons were introduced; these were embossed with a crown over a circular garter strap inscribed 'ROYAL REGT OF ARTILLERY'. In the centre of the strap was the royal cypher 'GR'.[32] While there are no surviving references to the subject of the different sizes, it may be assumed they followed infantry regulations with 18 large buttons, some 0.94 inches in diameter, four on each pocket and cuff, plus two at the rear waist. There were also 11 smaller breast buttons, some 0.625 inches in diameter, nine on the front of the jacket and the two on the shoulder straps.

Belt plates do appear to have been worn on the bayonet or sword belt by the other ranks, but their cross straps usually show oval buckles. Other ranks and Senior NCOs who wore the sword belt over the shoulder seem to have worn oval belt plates, but there are few set descriptions or guiding regulations. The pattern may have varied from battalion to battalion like those of the officers.[33]

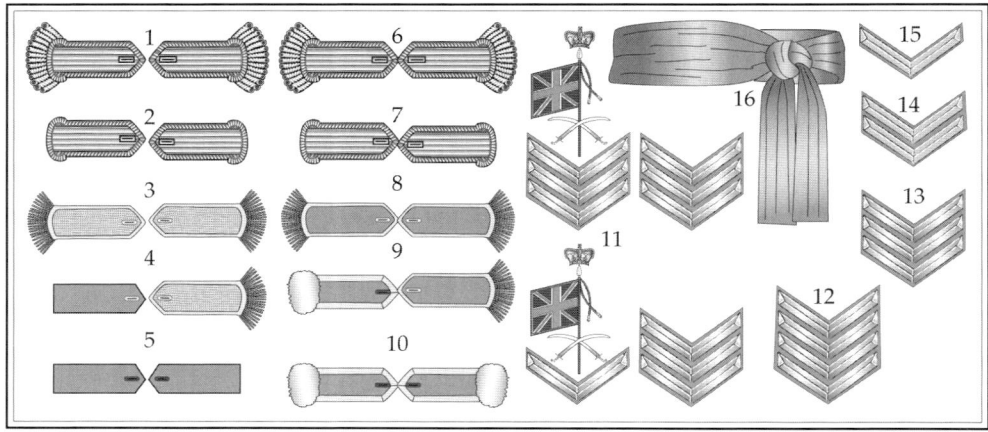

Figure 16.6. Royal Artillery rank distinctions. The rank distinctions for other ranks in 1792; Staff Sergeants and Quarter Master Sergeants (1), Sergeants (2), Corporals (3), Bombardiers (4) and gunners (5). Rank distinctions post-1799; Staff Sergeants (6), Sergeants and Quarter Masters (7), Corporals (8), Bombardiers (9) and gunners (10). Versions of the later rank of Company or Troop Sergeant (11), post-1802 gilt chevrons for Staff Sergeants (12), Sergeants (13), yellow worsted chevrons for Corporals (14), and Bombardiers (15). The crimson worsted sash of the Senior NCO (16).

Rank Distinctions of Non-comissioned Officers

Non-commissioned officers (NCOs) consisted of junior NCOs, Corporals and Bombardiers; Senior NCOs included the ranks of Sergeant Major, Staff Sergeant, Quarter Master Sergeant and the later Colour or Company Sergeant. Senior NCOs wore the same uniform as the other ranks but of 'superior' quality and cut, with gilt lace and loopings.[34] At the start of the war NCOs were distinguished by epaulettes and it was recorded that those for Sergeant Majors and Quarter Master Sergeants

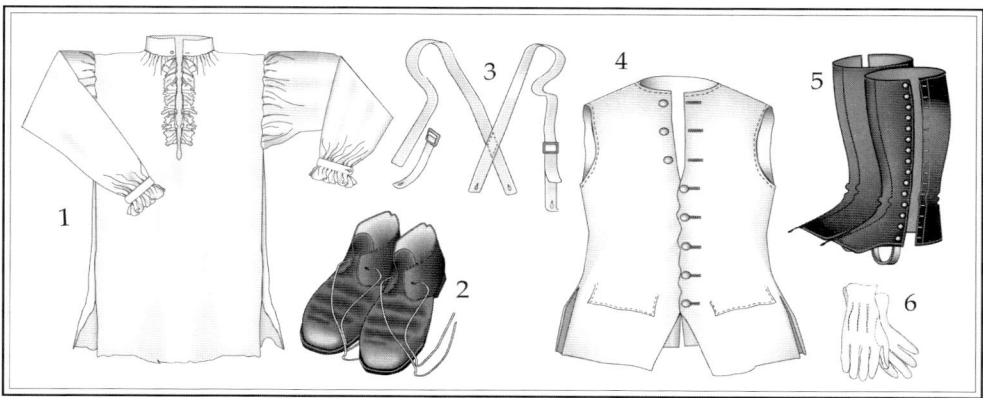

Figure 16.7. The necessaries. A dress shirt with frills at cuff and chest (1) a plainer version would have been worn by the other ranks when not on ceremonial duties. The standard issue straight-lasted shoes issued to other ranks (2), and the canvas or linen suspenders that supported the trousers and breeches (3). The white waistcoat worn by all ranks with the early open coat (4), and the black woollen gaiters worn with the breeches by the other ranks that strapped under the foot and were buttoned on the outer face (5). Dress gloves in white leather for Senior NCOs, for normal duties worsted gloves were issued to the other ranks (6).

 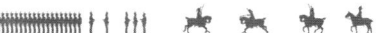

were of gilt, Corporals wore two worsted epaulettes and Bombardiers, one.[35] In 1799 it was confirmed that the Senior NCOs were to wear gold lace on the coat and the rank distinctions were two gold bullion epaulettes for Staff Sergeants, two gold laced shoulder straps for Sergeants, two fringed epaulettes for Corporals, one on the right shoulder only for Bombardiers while the gunner wore two plain, red worsted shoulder straps.[36]

In 1802, chevrons formally replaced the shoulder knots and epaulettes as badges of rank for non-commissioned officers.[37] Exactly when the artillery adopted them is unclear but Atkinson shows them in use by 1807. The style of the chevrons was a double width of regimental lace mounted on cloth of the facing colour with half an inch between them and placed midway between the elbow and the shoulder extending to within half an inch of the sleeve seams. Sergeant Majors and Quarter Master Sergeants wore four chevrons, Sergeants three, Corporals two and Bombardiers one. The chevrons for Senior NCOs were gilt and those of junior NCOs yellow worsted. It may be that the artillery followed infantry practice by only wearing their chevrons on the right arm, since in 1815 it was ordered they should be worn on both arms. In August 1813, the rank of Colour Sergeant was introduced into the army, but in the artillery only after September 1813, where he was termed a Company Sergeant. The badge of rank was a crown over a regimental colour flying to the rear supported by two swords above the chevrons. This changed in 1815 when the Company Sergeant wore the colour on the right over a single chevron and three chevrons on the left as in the infantry.[38] In 1815 the ranks of Senior NCOs in the foot artillery included Staff Sergeant, Brigade Sergeant Major, Brigade Quarter Master Sergeant, Sergeant and Drum Major. The junior NCOs were Corporals and Bombardiers. The other ranks included, Gunners, Drummers, Trumpeters and artificers. The artificers included farriers, collar makers, carriage smiths, shoeing smiths and wheelwrights.

Sashes

Regulations prescribed that Senior NCOs wore a plain crimson worsted sash over the sword belt and tied at the hip. The pattern was the same worsted sash as that supplied to NCOs of the infantry.[39]

Shirts and Stocks

Linen shirts were worn by all ranks. In the early period the front was decorated with a 9-inch frill, puffed out and starched to show protruding between the lapels of the coat. All other ranks wore a 3.5-inch deep black leather stock. For dress false white collars were worn:

> The eighth of inch white shown above the stock was intended for the men, and in their kits were included six false collars. These were narrow strips of linen, which were doubled over the leather stock and confined there by a hook at each end.[40]

Gloves

Worsted gloves of battalion pattern were issued to all other ranks.[41]

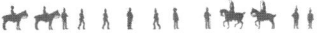

Footwear

Each man was issued with two pairs of shoes but the shoes of the time were generally badly made and survived for only a short time. The shoes and boots of the period were made on straight lasts and it was intended that they were worn on the opposing foot each day, a practice generally ignored. The heels were low and the toes rounded. The military shoes often had large nails punched flat on the soles.

Gaiters

With the breeches, other ranks wore black woollen gaiters buttoned up to the knee-cap and held in place by a button at the back of the knee of the breeches. They were strapped under the boot and buttoned on the outer side with ten to eighteen small equally spaced metal buttons.

> Care is to be taken that the gaiters are of sufficient length to reach the knee-pan, the tops to be cut perfectly straight, and no buttons to be put behind.[42]

When trousers were worn either the normal gaiters or shorter, grey, half-gaiters were worn and strapped under the instep of the boots.

Breeches and Trousers

At the start of the war, white breeches were worn for all occasions except for fatigues and walking out. They were made of a similar material to the coats and fitted to come well up over the hips and below the knees to the calf. At the bottom, each leg had small regimental buttons and tapes to secure it to the leg, to prevent them riding up further, a small button at the rear to support the woollen gaiters. To cover the open fly the breeches were fitted with a flap at the front that buttoned at the waist. The buttons at the knee were discontinued in 1796.

They usually had a pocket at the right side, sometimes on both. Adjustment to the waist was by tapes at the rear and when worn under a jacket, they were usually supported by linen or canvas braces. The trousers introduced into the artillery before the start of the war were, like breeches, not usually tight fitting and the early patterns issued for hot climates were white with a buttoned fly on the outer seam to aid their wear over the breeches or pantaloons; as trousers became wear in their own right the outer fly was discontinued. The trousers were fitted with the same front flap fly as the breeches and they were supported in the same manner. In 1811, grey trousers with half-gaiters worn over the boots formally replaced white trousers for the other ranks and on campaign; for working duties and fatigues, the trousers were usually worn over or in lieu of breeches. Dighton in his painting of 1813 shows loose, white, gaiter-trousers that buttoned at the foot and strapped under the boot; this form of trouser can be traced back to the West Indies where they were often referred to as 'mosquito' trousers. Initially white trousers were for hot climates, grey for cold, but later grey became the standard issue for all climates, and breeches were only worn for dress occasions. In Spain, some artillery men were dressed in blue trousers, the cloth purchased locally.[43] Pantaloons were close fitting and usually

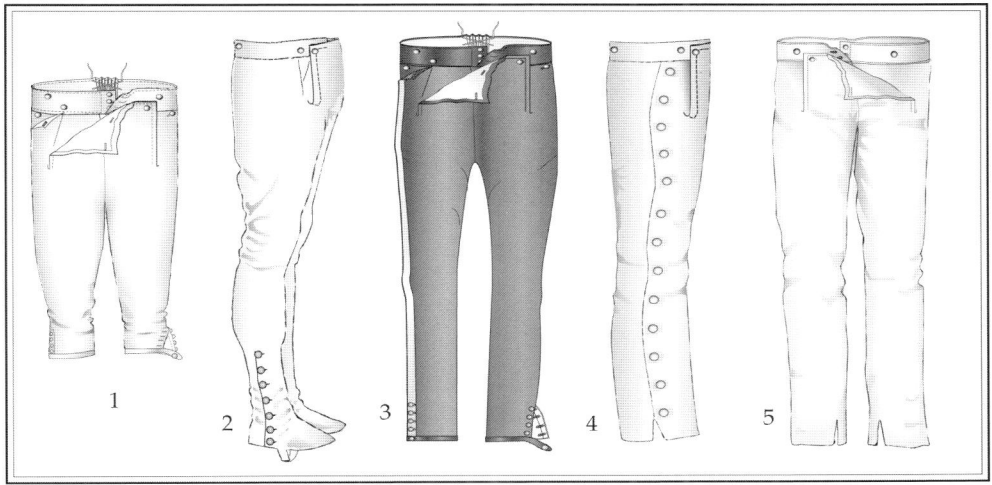

Figure 16.8. Breeches with the front flap to conceal the fly were worn by all ranks in the first part of the war but later relegated to dress occasions (1). The white gaiter-trousers worn buckled at the foot and strapped under the boots (2). Tight pantaloons worn for walking out or undress often shown with stripes down the leg (3). The white overalls worn in hot climates and designed to button over the breeches and gaiters (4) and the pattern when worn as trousers proper, the later grey trousers were similar and issued to all ranks (5).

skin-tight, fastening either below the calf or at the foot. Made of white kerseymere or stocking material they were worn for dress occasions and walking out. By 1802 blue pantaloons began to be worn for informal occasions, but full dress still required white breeches or pantaloons with black woollen gaiters worn strapped under the black boots.

Greatcoats

Each other rank was issued with a dark grey, drab greatcoat.[44] This was a loose, double-breasted coat reaching to the calves and made to come well above the neck with a large cape to the shoulders. The front carried two rows of six large regimental buttons and had vertical pockets in the sides of the skirts. Senior NCOs wore their sword belts and sashes over the greatcoat. In 1808, it was ordered that the greatcoats of artillery NCOs were to have collar and cuffs of facing colour and chevrons were to be worn. Dighton also shows gunners wearing their greatcoats slung diagonally across the back, carried in the straps usually used for the knapsack.

Belts

Senior NCOs who wore the sword usually carried it on a one-piece cross-belt worn over the right shoulder. The sword was carried in a frog and secured by a stud on the scabbard. The belt was made of white buff leather the same width as the bayonet belt and consisted of a short, seventeen-inch, front strap and a longer rear strap some forty-three inches long, both stitched together at the sword frog. The two parts of the straps were held together by a belt plate, probably oval, but there is no specific record of the pattern or style. Other ranks are often shown wearing the artillery sword with a similar belt.

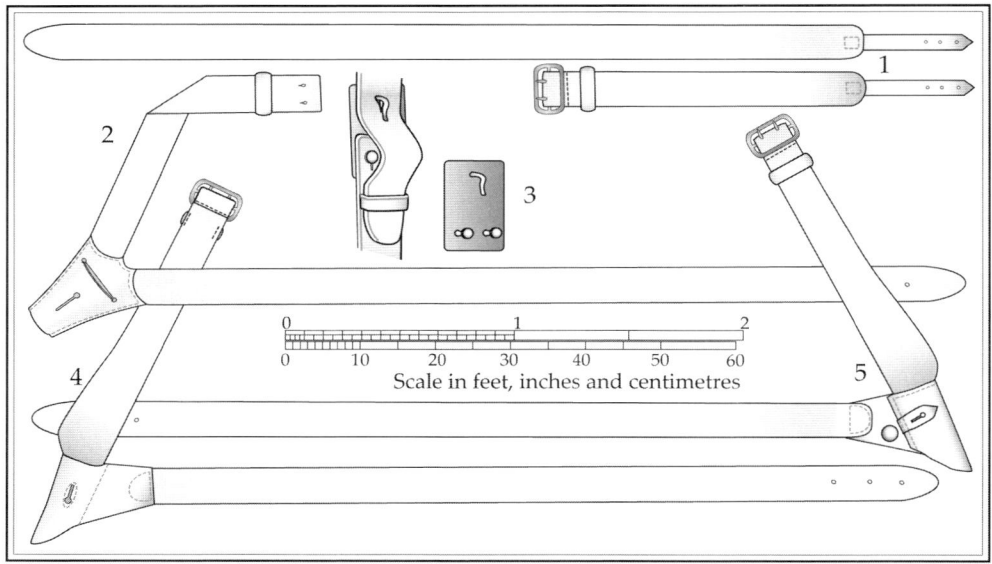

Figure 16.9. White buff sword, cartridge and bayonet belts. The two-piece shoulder belt associated with the later version of the cartridge pouch (1) and the one-piece sword shoulder belt worn by other ranks with the artillery sword (2), with the method of attaching a belt plate (3) and a front (4) and rear view of the bayonet belt. The button at the rear of the frog would have been fitted to attach to a flap on the new form of cartridge box (5).

Bayonet Belt

The bayonet belt was made of white buff (buffalo) leather two and one eighth inches wide. The bayonet belts of artillery personnel are shown to consist of a shorter front strap terminating in an oval buckle and runner with a longer rear strap both stitched to the bayonet frog with a loop and button at the rear. The bayonet belt was worn over the right shoulder and the bayonet frog fastened by the loop to a waist button on the back of the jacket. The bayonet belts of artillery personnel are usually shown worn over the pouch belt at the rear but under it at the front, probably to allow access to the tools on the front of the pouch belt. This practice may not have continued when the new pouch was issued.

Royal Artillery Cartridge Pouch

The artillery pouch has always been a problem in that it seems to have reflected an anachronism well into the period. It is illustrated by Atkinson, Days and Dighton,[45] with the powder flask and red cords, while Hamilton Smith, Dighton and Hull show it still being worn after 1813, but without the flask and cord.[46] This seems quite logical as by then the foot artillery had been supplied with the new pattern limbers, which carried the priming powder as part of the ammunition. De Loutherberg shows a plain black pouch being worn on a plain white strap.[47]

The white artillery pouch was of a quite different construction to the normal infantry pouch of the period. The pouch belt was a separate item, buckled to two pouch straps at the rear of the pouch. The chest part of the strap carried a leather pocket for tools and each end had a brass tip. The pouch is usually shown with a small horn of priming powder retained by a red cord with tassels. Some cords passed through leather keepers on the pouch belt, others through the hammer pocket. The use of priming powder had been superseded by this time by the tube or quill but the illustrations show the priming horn worn earlier in the war.

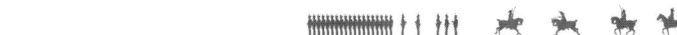

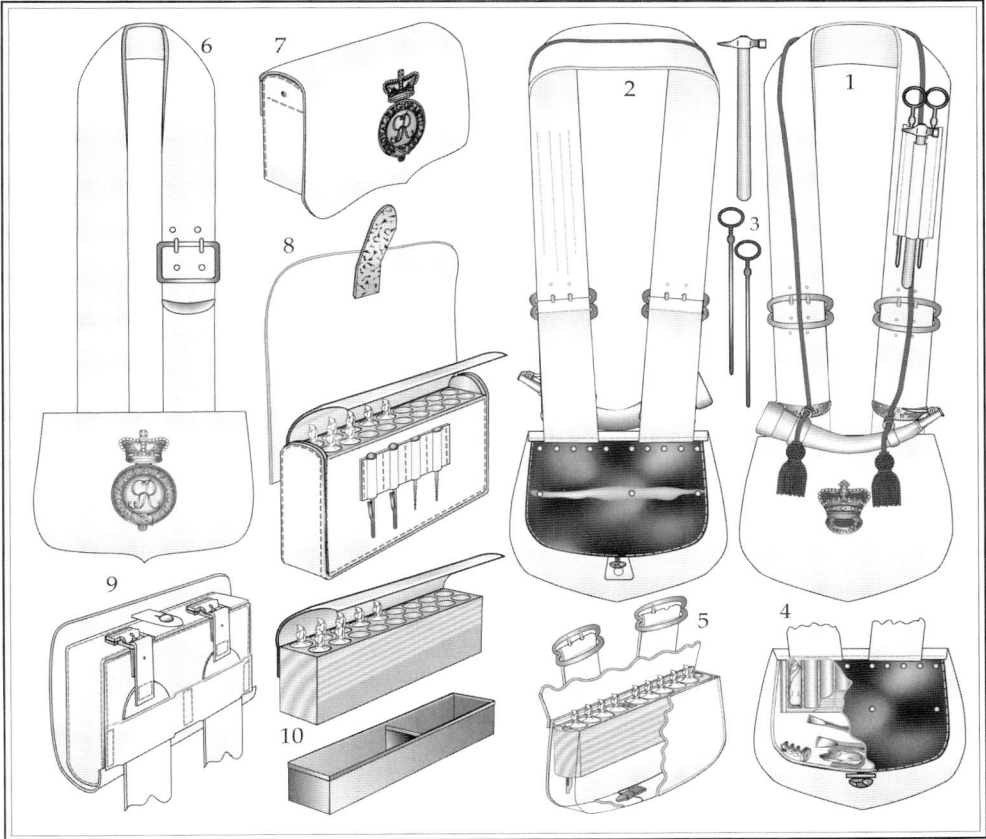

Figure 16.10. Artillery pouches. The early artillery pouch usually associated with the period when priming powder was required and the vent tools were carried by the gunner. A front view (1) and rear view showing the brown leather back of the pouch (2). The tools carried in the pockets on the pouch belt, the vent pins and hammer for the gun spikes (3). A sectioned view of the pouch showing the internal arrangements (4 & 5). Front views of the later pouch (6 & 7), the internal arrangement (8) showing the gun spikes in pockets on the front of the pouch and the method by which the cross-belt was attached (9). The eighteen-round wooden block and tin tray for spare flints and musket tools (10).

The pouch was fitted with a wooden block drilled to take nine cartridges (examples at the Royal Artillery Museum shows eight or nine), two spring gun spikes and a rectangular centre hole to take a vent awl. The cross-belt carried a hammer and two vent pins, these pins would have been used to pierce the bag of the charge prior to priming the vent. The hammer served to drive in the vent spikes in the event the gun was to be disabled. The pouch itself was roughly semi-circular and examples exist with the sides in one or two pieces, a common practice, adopted to save on leather. The wooden block was nailed to the rear face of the pouch, the front face being free to allow access to the space below the block for flints and musket tools etc. The front flap was shaped to a curved point, this and the and the two buckle straps were stitched to the back of the pouch. The front of the pouch carried a brass badge with a crown over a semi-circular scroll often stamped Royal Artillery or some other identifier. On some examples the brass badge has a red cloth underneath that shows through the gaps in the crown and gap above the scroll; the brass tips to the cross-belt and the cap to the powder flask also carry identifiers including the battalion and stores number.[48]

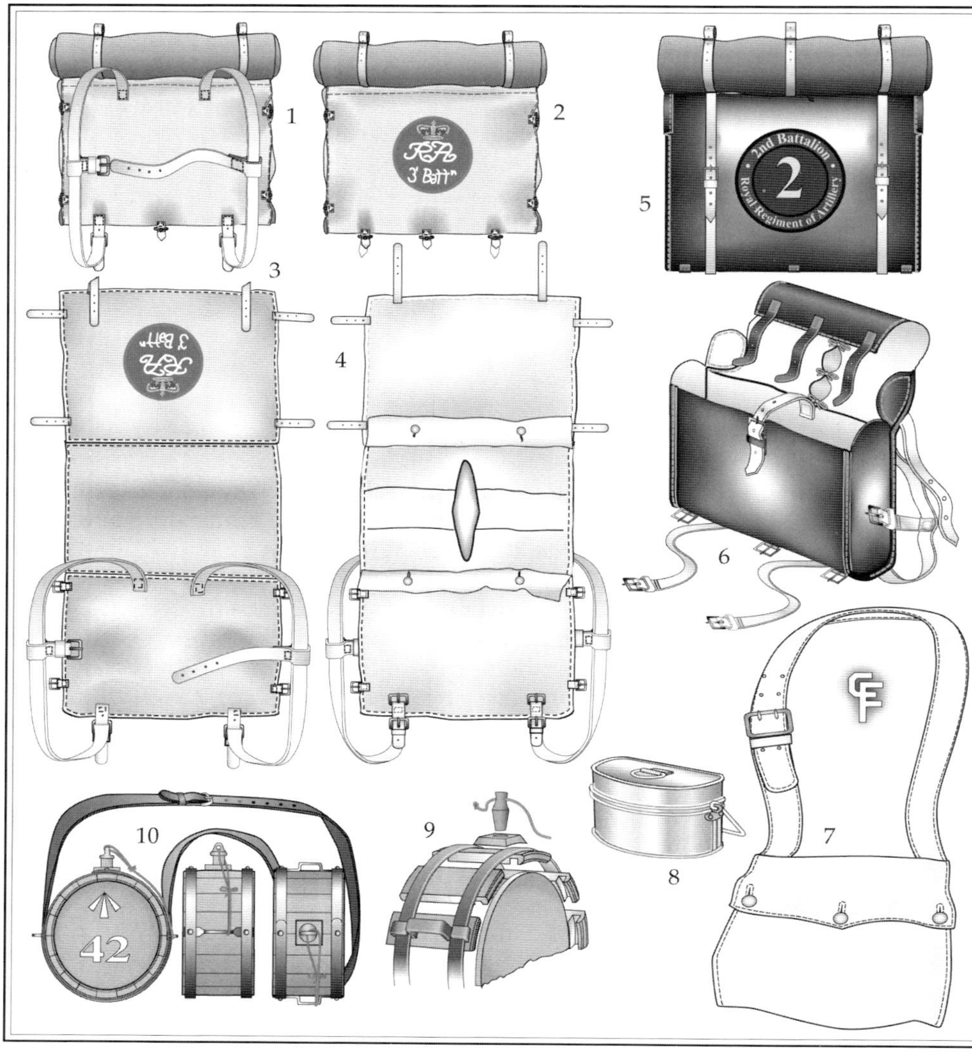

Figure 16.11. Accoutrements – front and rear views of the 'envelope' knapsack (1 & 2) and the view of the pack laid flat and the straps by which it was worn (3) and an interior view showing the two outer and the inner compartments (4). Views of the Trotter knapsack (5 & 6), one of many types of haversack (7) and the later mess tin (8). The water bottle method of construction (9) and views (10).

The later drawings by Hamilton Smith and Hull show a different pouch, which although similar in style is thicker in the body and it no longer carries the obsolete priming horn and red cord. This pouch also has a different badge and is not deep enough to be the 60-round version adopted by the infantry. It is thought that this is an 18-round pouch with the cartridges mounted in a wooden block in two rows of nine over a tin tray. Across the front of the pouch, covered by the flap, were the leather loops for the gun spikes.

No surviving examples of this later artillery pouch have been located, but it may have taken the same form as that of the grenadier company of the 30th Foot (also known as the Fanning pouch). It may well be that this plain pouch came into service when the previous version became obsolete or as the older pouches wore out.

Haversack

Designed to carry three days of rations it was made of light canvas or coarse, unbleached linen. It was worn on a two-inch strap of the same material and secured by a buckle and runner. The flap was fastened with buttons with the exact style varying from maker to maker. The colour seems to have varied between fawn to off-white. On the march, it carried three days' bread or biscuit, salt beef or whatever the owner considered appropriate. This was a standard item of equipment issued to all ranks of the army.

Water Bottle

The standard water bottle was a flat, wooden barrel about four inches deep and seven inches in diameter. Around the outside were two metal bands and the staples for the strap. The cork was secured by a cord or fine chain. Usually painted pale blue it was often marked with the ordnance arrow and often some other unit identifying details painted, chiselled or burnt into it. It was carried on a brown leather strap, one inch wide and sixty inches long and secured by a buckle and runner. The later bottles contained two pints and weighed over three pounds when full. It was usually worn over the haversack. In marching order, gunners with the musket carried the haversack and water bottle slung over the right shoulder to allow ready access to the cartridge pouch. Senior NCOs and men carrying the artillery sword wore them over the left shoulder to give access to the sword. These were also standard-issue items.

Knapsacks

The ubiquitous, and unpopular, British pack had been in service for many years. This early issue was made of canvas or coarse linen with the outside sometimes painted to make it weatherproof and the rear face usually embellished with a regimental badge or identity. The interior had two main 14-inch pockets with buttoned flaps and a 12-inch central hollow compartment that usually held shoes and brushes; when folded out flat it was some 20 inches wide and 40 inches long. When packed it was folded over envelope fashion and the two ends strapped together at the sides and the bottom forming a pack some 18 inches wide, 13 inches high and 4 inches thick. It had no stiffening or rigidity and was usually worn over the cross-belts and shoulder straps. The shoulder straps of the knapsack were secured across the chest by a cross strap that often accorded acute discomfort to the wearer. Several variations in pattern are known and these are probably due to the different manufacturers and the modifications applied by the battalions or gunners in the field. The list of necessaries that every artillery man was expected to keep consisted of a painted canvas knapsack, 4 white shirts, 6 false collars, a leather cap, 2 pairs of shoes, a pair of white stockings, a pair of worsted stockings and 3 pairs of socks. A pair of black cloth gaiters, a pair of shoe buckles, a pair of knee buckles and a stock buckle. He required a check shirt, a canvas frock and canvas trousers for work and the list continued with a black ball, a pair of shoe brushes, a clothes brush, large comb, small comb, powder bag and puff, rosette, leather stock, razor and shaving box. He was also required to have a turn screw and worm, and a brush and picker for the musket.[49] An artillery gunner carried at least 38lb of equipment; this was made up of his greatcoat and straps, knapsack, musket and sling, pouch, belts and cartridges.[50]

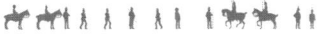

The Trotter knapsack began to replace the envelope pack in 1805, but it was some years before all units were equipped with it and many variations in pattern are known; Dighton shows the Trotter pack being worn by gunners in 1813. The new pack was a significant improvement and while still made of canvas it had boards in the sides to provide rigidity, leather bindings, button-down flaps and extra buckles; there was a space in the flap for the storage of smaller items and a main compartment in the body. After 1808, they were generally painted black, and invariably carried some regimental identifying badge or decoration. The overall size was similar to the earlier model and the initial arrangement of carriage straps was as before, but this changed over time as regiments and men modified the packs to suit their own requirements. The pack and straps weighed some 3 pounds and when full 26 pounds. It was general practice for the artillery to place their knapsacks and accoutrements on the limbers and wagons when serving the guns.[51]

Swords

The more Senior NCOs of artillery may have carried the regulation 1796 infantry sword with a brass hilt and a plain white sword knot, but no appropriate regulations have been located and it may be that they wore the artillery sword. Gunners were known for laying their muskets and pouches aside when serving the guns and in some cases the artillery sword was a preferred method of armament often worn in lieu of the musket and bayonet.[52]

The earlier models, from about 1780 to 1815, had a thick and heavy single-edged, straight blade 25 inches long. The brass hilt had a black leather grip and 'a straight knuclebow and cross guard with shield-shaped languets, cap pommel and backstrap and the pommel having a small beak at the top'. The sword had an overall length of 31 inches and the scabbard was of black leather with brass fittings.[53] Later models, probably after this period, were the more common design with the brass

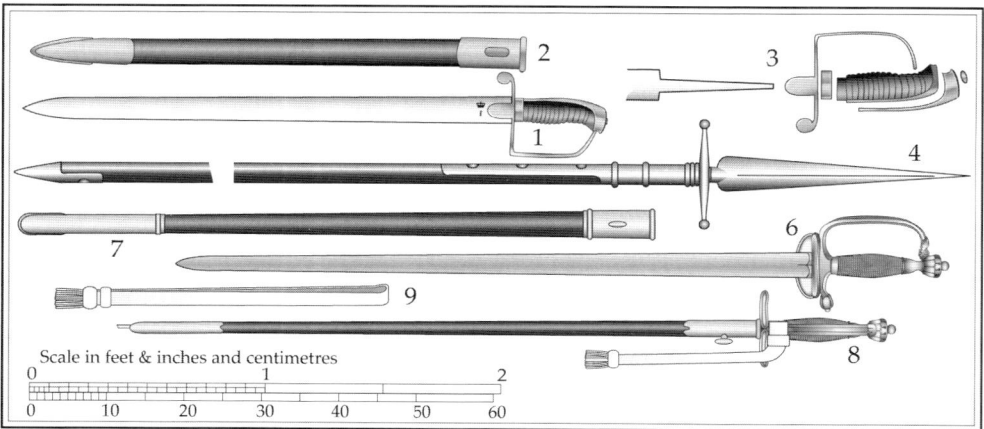

Figure 16.12. Artillery swords. The Royal Artillery straight-bladed sword with the 25-inch blade worn by the other ranks as an alternative to the musket or bayonet, also worn by drivers as an alternative to the light cavalry sword (1), the black leather, brass-bound scabbard (2) and the method of construction (3). Artillery NCOs' 9-foot pike or spontoon not usually carried by gun commanders and more probably only used on parade (4). The brass-hilted version of the 1796, infantry officers' sword that may have been worn by the Senior NCOs at headquarters (6), the scabbard worn in a belt frog (7), a front view of the sword (8) and the plain white sword knot (9).

hilt and grip cast in one piece and driven on to the tang of the blade. The overall length was 29.25 inches and the blade around the slight curve was only 23.5 inches long with the width at the shoulders 1.265 inches tapering to 1.25 inches at four inches from the point. The weight was 1lb 8oz and the scabbard was of black leather with brass mounts. Sword knots were not normally worn.[54] It was referred to as 'A ridiculous kind of cutlass, really only intended for cutting wood'.[55]

Pike or Spontoon

The Senior NCOs of infantry carried the spontoon; this had an ash shaft 9 feet long with a steel butt. The steel blade screwed into a ringed socket some 4.5 inches deep securing the crosspiece that prevented the point penetrating too far. The blade was 12.75 inches long and the cross bar 5.5 inches wide. Two shaft supports extended down from the socket to give added strength. This may have been more an item for parade and ceremonial in the artillery as there are no contemporary illustrations of such an item in use in the field.

Muskets

The standard armament for the gunner was a musket and bayonet and when practicing firing drills the locks were fitted with 'wooden snappers' instead of flints. The weapon in general use was the ubiquitous Brown Bess, it had an effective range of about 200 yards and the weight with the bayonet was some eleven pounds. The barrel was over three feet long and the bullet weighed 490 grains or just under 12 to the pound (in effect almost a twelve-bore shot gun firing a solid shot). A picker and brush to clean the musket lock were worn on a two-part white leather strap and usually attached to a button on the jacket or behind the cross-belt.

The late pattern of the 1770 artillery carbine was effectively the early land pattern with the barrel shortened, a steel ramrod and a later pattern lock; the top of the barrel was often engraved with 'Royal Artillery' and the battalion number. The overall length of the carbine was 52.5 inches. The barrel was 37.125 inches long with a calibre of 0.68 inches.[56] The India pattern artillery carbine began to replace this version after 1807, but there are no records to show which muskets were issued to the different battalions. The overall length of the India carbine was 52 inches. The barrel was 37 inches long with a calibre of 0.65 inches. In all other respects, it was identical to the India pattern sergeants' carbine.

The carbines were fitted with a white buff sling 1.75 inches wide and up to 45 inches long. There were several patterns, some had a lower end pierced with two holes, others four and some carried a stitched leather lace on the inside face, others used a separate lace. The upper end could be fitted with a leather loop, a single buckle or double buckle. The lace end of the sling was passed through the back of the upper swivel, down through the loop or buckle and then to the front of the lower swivel. It was then passed through the swivel and the lace tied, from the back, through the holes to secure it; adjustment to the sling was made by moving the loop or buckle.

The accuracy of these early smooth bore muskets was not good. In a series of tests carried out after the war to determine the effects of the smooth bore musket a target three feet wide and eleven and a half feet high was set up at a range of 150 yards.

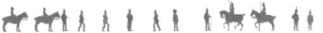

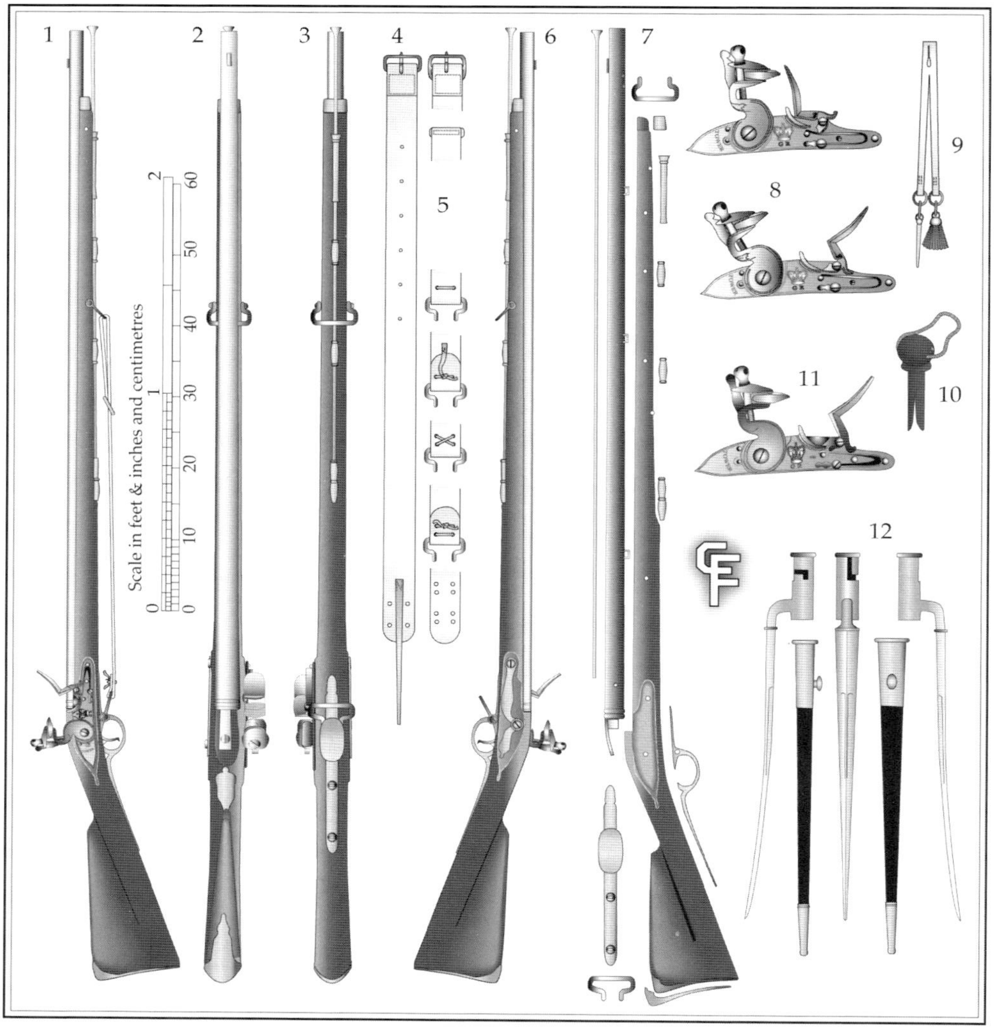

Figure 16.13. Royal Artillery carbines. The late 1770 pattern, effectively an early land pattern with the barrel shortened. The right side view (1), the view from above (2) and the view from below (3). The musket sling (4) and the different methods of attachment to the lower swivel {5). The left side view (6), a view of the musket parts (7). Two views of the land pattern lock of 1770 (8), the lock picker and brush worn on a button on the front of the jacket (9), the muzzle bung to exclude moisture and debris (10), a late land or pre-1808 India pattern lock (11) and views of the bayonet (12).

At this range, only three-quarters of the rounds fired hit the target. The chances of hitting at 250 yards were so poor that the width of the target was increased to 6 feet, but not one in ten rounds hit and at 300 yards, although many rounds were fired, none actually hit the target.

Drummers

Each brigade included at least one drummer on the establishment but little is known about their dress. The regulations for drummers prescribed that the coats were of a

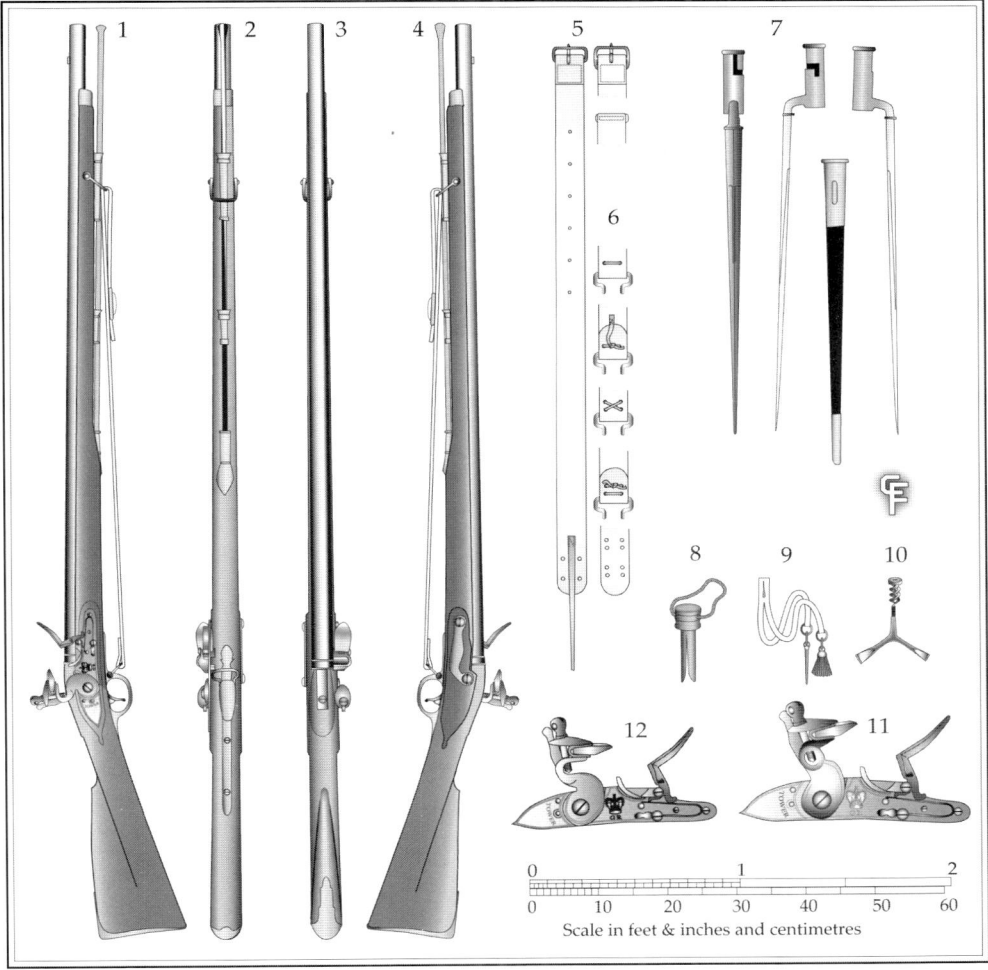

Figure 16.14. Royal Artillery India pattern carbine of 1807. View of the right side of the carbine (1), the view from above (2), the view from below (3) and the left side view (4). The carbine sling (5) and the different attachments to the lower swivel (6). Views of the India pattern bayonet (7), a muzzle plug (8), lock picker and brush (9) and the lock tool and worm (10). Views of the India pattern ring necked locked (11) and the India pattern swan necked lock (12).

superior quality to those of the men and in the colour of the facings. There appears to be no contemporary description of the design and style of the lace and jacket. The regulations prescribed reverse facings until 1831, after which they were to be the same as those of the men but with extra lace. The exact pattern of lace is unknown, but it is recorded that the lace on the drummers' coats was changed from that with the arms of the Board of Ordnance and it was also noted that the coat for each battalion was different.[57] Later the lace was removed from the drummers' hats and for dress the standard twelve-inch tall fur caps were worn, presumably with the standard line infantry drummer plate with a black lacquer ground.[58] The drummers for the invalid battalion were dressed in the same manner as the other drummers.[59] In 1792 the drummers' lace for the Royal Military Artificers was changed from the ordnance arms to a mixture of black, red and yellow with the lace sewn on in the same way as the private soldiers but worsted wings were worn. Fur caps were still worn for dress by the drummers and their coats were different.[60] It could be that the same change occurred for the artillery, although they would have worn a lace of blue, red and yellow.[61] It seems that at the start of the war the coats were not laced, as the cost of a drummers' coat was less than that of a gunner Bombardier.[62] In 1795, they wore cocked hats with a red feather and for dress parades still wore the grenadier-style fur caps.[63] In 1798, the Board of Ordnance was requested to consider a more ornamental form of dress for the artillery band, but this was not carried across to the battalion drummers who retained their red coats with blue facings.[64] Whatever the dress, the effects of bands on those who marched behind seems to have remained unchanged and much like today, Mercer recalls that

> … the earliest peculiarity that I remember is, that when in Guernsey – in the years 1789 and 1790, the 8th and 12th Regiments used, in marching, always to have the band in the centre of the column. By this means, the sound arriving simultaneously at the first and last divisions, the step would be better preserved than in the present mode, since, in a long column with the band marching at its head, I have frequently observed the thump of the long drum marking the time for the left foot of the leading division coincide with the right foot of the rear, so that this last could only preserve the step by disregarding the drum.[65]

The drums were made of wood with red-painted hoops, the body decorated with the arms of the Board of Ordnance and the drum cords were yellow for the marching battalions and blue for the regimental band.[66] The drum was 16 inches in diameter, with the 1.75 inch hoops and was 19.6 inches tall overall. The drums were laced with ten lines of cord. Each drummer wore a sword belt, which came into use in 1789.[67] In 1792, the drummers were issued with plain unlaced buff sword belts; drum carriage, leather girdle and straps.[68] The drummers adopted the stovepipe shako when it was introduced for the rest of the regiment but with a red feather and a brass plate with the ordnance arms.[69] Each Company had at least one drummer on the establishment and each Battalion also had a Drum Major, but these were not on the 'King's' establishment.[70]

There is a drawing by Lawson, which depicts the band and a drummer in 1815. The plate is not coloured but the drummer is shown in a Belgic shako with a white plume, a pale jacket with dark facings and white breeches with black gaiters. The jacket is laced in the same way as that of the other ranks but with blue drummer wings worn at the shoulder, there is no additional lace on the sleeves or jacket. It is not possible to discern any other detail and it may well be a drummer of the band he is depicting rather than that of a marching battalion.[71] Colour illustrations of the drummers' dress are given at Plate 16.

Key to Colour Plates

Plate 9. Royal Artillery – Other ranks – coats and jackets
1. Other ranks' long coat of pre-1792 worn cut away to show the waistcoat.
2. A reconstruction of a possible rear view after Dayes.
3. The change to the later regulations of 1797 with the coat buttoned to the waist.
4. The early flat peweter button with the arms of the Ordnance stamped into the button.
5. Other ranks' short jackets with the red facings and yellow bastion-shaped braid. The regulations prescribed ten rows of lace, but surviving notes show only eight or nine were usual with bastion braid.

6. The jacket of 1815 with the red turn backs and plain shoulder straps, after Hamilton Smith, Vernet and Dighton.
7. The convex brass button, post-1802.
8. A rear view of the 1815 jacket, note the pockets are now oblique and the braid to the top of the cuff has been omitted.
9. Yellow bastion braid introduced with the short jacket.
10. A rear view after de Bosset, Dighton and Atkinson with the horizontal pockets, white turn backs and lace to the skirt.
11. Right side view showing an envelope pack and rolled blanket or greatcoat.
12. Royal Artillery in marching order. Front view with haversack and water bottle carried on the left side to give access to the cartridge pouch, which carries the red flask cord.
13. Detail of the artillery braid.
14. A rear view in full marching order, with later cartridge pouch. The envelope pack is now painted black to prevent the ingress of moisture.
15. The marching order of a Senior NCO with the haversack and water bottle worn on the right side to allow access to the sword; the stripes are shown worn on one arm only.

Plate 11. Royal Artillery – Battalion and brigade drummers
1. The reversed facings of the long coat, probably unlaced after 1795.
2. The front view of the drummer jacket post-1800 shown without extra lace, after Lawson.
3. Similar jacket with sleeve darts after the pattern of line infantry; the exact pattern is not known and the darts in the sleeve are conjectural.
4. Reconstructed rear view of the laced drummer jacket.
5. Artillery drummer wings, after Lawson.
6. Reconstruction of the unlaced drummer jacket, after Lawson.
7. Possible shako plate for the drummer stovepipe shako pre-1813 worn with a red plume.
8. A reconstruction of an artillery drum, after Lawson.
9. A Belgic shako plate worn by the Royal Artillery band based at Woolwich. The plate worn by brigade drummers was probably a standard artillery plate.
10. Front and left view of the drummer dress cap.
11. View of the regulation drummer plate worn with the fur cap by line regiments and the artillery in dress.
12. Front and left views of the twelve-inch dress fur cap worn by artillery drummers in full dress; reconstruction based upon that of a line regiment and Battalion orders.

Plate 12. Uniforms of the Royal Regiment of Artillery and associated arms
1. Early artillery uniforms worn at the start of the war, after Dayes.
2. Horse artillery uniform pre-1800, after MacDonald and Mercer.
3. Horse artillery post-1800 and the introduction of the dolman.
4. Officers and Senior NCOs, early Peninsula period.
5. Gunners, late Peninsula period
6. Foot artillery officers; in full dress, *circa* 1815, in levee dress and in walking out dress.
7. Senior NCO, officer and gunner, post-1813.
8. Early and late versions of drivers, Corps of Artillery Drivers.

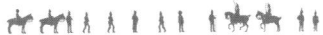

Endnotes to Chapter 16

1. Dickson, 1908: pp. 275, 509, 854.
2. Dickson, 1908: p. 504.
3. Dickson, 1908: p. 739.
4. National Archive, WO 3/14; p. 71, dated 19 July 1795.
5. Framer, 1954: p. 84.
6. National Archive, WO 3/29; p. 32, dated 22 June 1796.
7. Ibid: pp. 37–40.
8. MacDonald, 1985: p. 33.
9. National Archive, WO 55/677.
10. Lawson, 1961: p. 46.
11. MacDonald, 1985: p. 42.
12. Ibid: p. 41.
13. Ibid: pp. 30, 41 and plate VIII; Campbell, 1971: p. 16.
14. General Order, 3 August 1813; MacDonald, 1985: p. 35; Campbell, 1971: p. 16.
15. MacDonald, 1985: p. 46.
16. Campbell, 1971: p. 18.
17. General Order, 10 February 1805; MacDonald, 1985: p. 32.
18. Ibid, 31 October and 1 November 1803; MacDonald, 1985: p. 32.
19. Campbell, 1971: p. 145.
20. General Order, 10 February 1805; MacDonald, 1985: p. 32; Campbell, 1971: p. 18.
21. Reserve collection at the Rotunda, Woolwich. Accession Number BD 0001.
22. Campbell, 1971: p. 18.
23. General Order, 3 August 1813; MacDonald, 1985: p. 35.
24. Campbell, 1971: p. 19.
25. Royal Artillery Museum: reserve collection, BD 0002.
26. MacDonald, 1985: p. 31.
27. Windrow, 1974: p. 48 (an example of a jacket so fitted); Stadler, 1815; Dighton, 1812 and Macdonald, 1899: plate XIII.
28. General Order, 24 January 1810; MacDonald, 1985: p. 34.
29. Dighton. D.: watercolour *'Royal Artillery Dislodging French Cavalry – 1813'*. Royal Collection, RŁ15044.
30. National Archive, WO 47/119: pp. 244–7.
31. Stadler, 1815: *'Royal Artillery'*, after Hamilton Smith.
32. Parkyn, 1956: pp. 55–7: Campbell, 1971: p. 138.
33. Ibid: pp. 54–7; Campbell, 1971: pp. 137–8.
34. National Archive, WO 47/119: pp. 244–7.
35. Ibid, WO 47/2552: p. 338.
36. Campbell, 1971: p. 115.
37. Ibid: p. 115; Duncan, 1872: p. 137.
38. General Order, 3 August 1813; MacDonald, 1985: p. 35; Campbell, 1971: pp. 115–16.
39. National Archive, WO 47/115: p. 43.
40. MacDonald, 1985: p. 53.
41. National Archive, WO 55/677.
42. General Order, 24 January 1810; MacDonald, 1985: p. 34.
43. Dickson, 1908: p. 707.
44. National Archive, WO 47/119: p. 227.
45. Atkinson, 1807; Dayes, 1792 and Dighton 1812; see list of plates in the bibliography.
46. Stadler, 1815; Dighton, 1813; Dighton, 1815 and Hull 1828; see list of plates in the bibliography.
47. De Loutherberg, *Grand Attack on Valenciennes*, 1793.
48. Exhibit 1957.25.1; Charleston Museum, South Carolina, USA.
49. National Archive, WO 47/2553: p. 434.

50. Russell, 2005: p. 132.
51. Siborne, 1993: pp. 233–4.
52. Jones, 1816: *Foot Artillery at Waterloo*.
53. 'Short Swords of the Foot Artillery', *Journal of the Society for Army Historical Research*, No. 226, Vol. 56, pp. 112–18.
54. Wilkinson Latham, 1966: plate 66.
55. Dickson, 1908: p. 1,126.
56. Bailey, 1971: pp. 53 and 60.
57. National Archive, WO 47/111: p. 869.
58. Ibid, WO 47/115: p. 563.
59. Ibid, WO 47/119: p. 227.
60. Ibid, WO 47/119: pp. 244–7.
61. Lawson, 1966: p. 92.
62. National Archive, WO 47/119: p. 453.
63. Farmer, 1954: p. 63; National Archive, WO 47/119: pp. 244–7.
64. Ibid: p. 64.
65. MacDonald, 1985: p. 55.
66. Farmer, 1954: p. 57.
67. Ibid: p. 62.
68. National Archive, WO 47/2225: p. 136.
69. Farmer, 1954: p. 83.
70. National Archive, WO 47/71.
71. Farmer, 1954: p. 106.

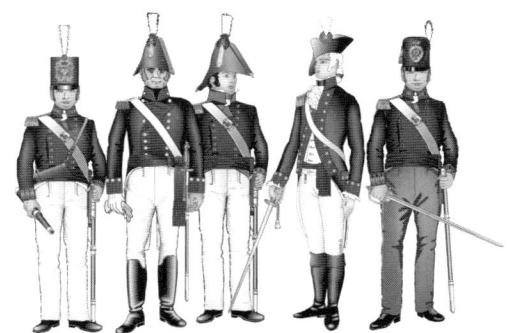

CHAPTER 17

Royal Artillery – Officers

Cocked Hat

At the start of the war, the cocked hat was the standard form of dress for officers but the shape had changed from the original three of the tricorn to a bicorn with two locks (folds) and the two fans folded up. The gilt lace had been removed and the hat now carried just a plain black braid loop and button with a white feather plum. It was worn with the loop over the left eye and right wing thrown a little forward.[1] Mercer recalls:

> The Infantry hat was decorated by a crimson-and-gold rosette in each lock. The cavalry by a pendant tassel of the same material. This, of course, we aped whenever we dared. The regulation mode of wearing this hat was with the loop, etc., perpendicularly over the left eye, and the right corner, or wing, thrown a little forward. What might be termed right shoulders forward. Some of the old men still adhered as nearly as the regulations would admit, to the form of their antique Dettingen hats-triangular. The Navy, instead of wearing their cocked hats square over the brow, like the soldiers, slewed them round, bringing the ends off, as they call it, 'fore and aft'. This the Army soon began to imitate, when off parade, and many a youngster got toko for being caught with his beaver in this unlawful fix. ... Like every other article of clothing, the hat has continually varied its shape within my day. The original cocked hat was triangular, as may be seen in old portraits of the Duke of Cumberland, General Elliot, General Wolfe, and a host of others; then came the broader brim, which made the cocks longer and fan higher, but with the base line straight, or even inclining upwards. ... The droop, once suggested, was gradually increased until, when square, the rosettes interfered with a man's shoulders; when fore and aft, the foremost part hid the face, and the hinder served instead of a 'hand' to scratch between the shoulders behind. Still, the fan was high. By-and-by, id est about 1805 I think, low fans (or lower) became the fashion, which recalls to me what a conceited little puppy I was, when the Cavalry and Horse Artillery adopted the cocked hat as an undress, which was worn with the pelisse. Mine, I remember, was one of the low fans, with the spunge-head feather.[2]

Later a black cockade with a central regimental button with a loop of regimental lace was placed at the base of the all-white plume or feathers. The cords, which originally passed round the crown to tighten it or to pull in the sides, had become purely decorative with those for officers consisting of a gold and crimson cord with tassels or acorns. Each cord now passed around the crown, passing through the loop of the other, with the tassel end hanging from the lock in the hat. The regulations prescribed the hat to be worn across the head, but another version of the story suggests that

> … to show their overseas service, artillery officers returning from abroad wore their hats in the French fashion when off duty. This style soon became de rigueur for all aspiring young subalterns and rapidly became the accepted norm.

During the same period, it was very fashionable to stuff a white silk kerchief into the fold of the hat. As other hats were introduced, the cocked hat retained popularity for walking out and was still worn in full dress.

Round Hat

A different form of hat was worn by artillery officers in the early part of the war and there are several contemporary paintings illustrating it. The De Loutherberg painting of artillery in the Low Countries,[3] shows the round hat worn by Congreve with three gilt chains around the crown, a large black cockade on the left and a black bearskin crest over the top of the hat from brim to brim. The description by Mercer is self-explanatory:

> The hat worn by the Officers at the same period would not even now be considered ungraceful – round, with a brim somewhat broad, and curling up at the sides; low, rounded crown, over all a bearskin in the helmet fashion, cockade, and I think a white feather in the left side – of this last not quite sure. When this was changed for the cocked hat I am also uncertain, but think it must have been about 1797, or perhaps earlier, for in Kane's book there is an order of October 12th, 1796, that the Artillery shall conform to the regulation hat and sword, etc., and when I first went to Woolwich, latter end of 1797, I remember seeing all the men in cocked hats.[4]

Stovepipe Shako

In undress and walking out officers still wore the cocked hat, but many adopted the stovepipe shako on campaign. The style was similar to that of the men, but examples are of better quality beaver, often with black lace around the base, gilt plates and bigger plumes. In 1808, the height of the plume was again ordered to be the same as that of the men.[5] Officers who had served in Egypt were also authorised to wear the 'sphinx' with the word 'Egypt' in the same manner as the men.[6] The gilt shako plate was of a similar style to that of the men, but often with small variations in the pattern; some are known with the battalion number stamped into the plate.

Belgic Shako

Adopted in August 1813,[7] the hat was of a similar style to that of the men, but of better quality with a white feather plume and mixed gilt and red twist cords with tassels.[8]

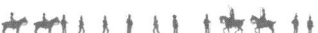

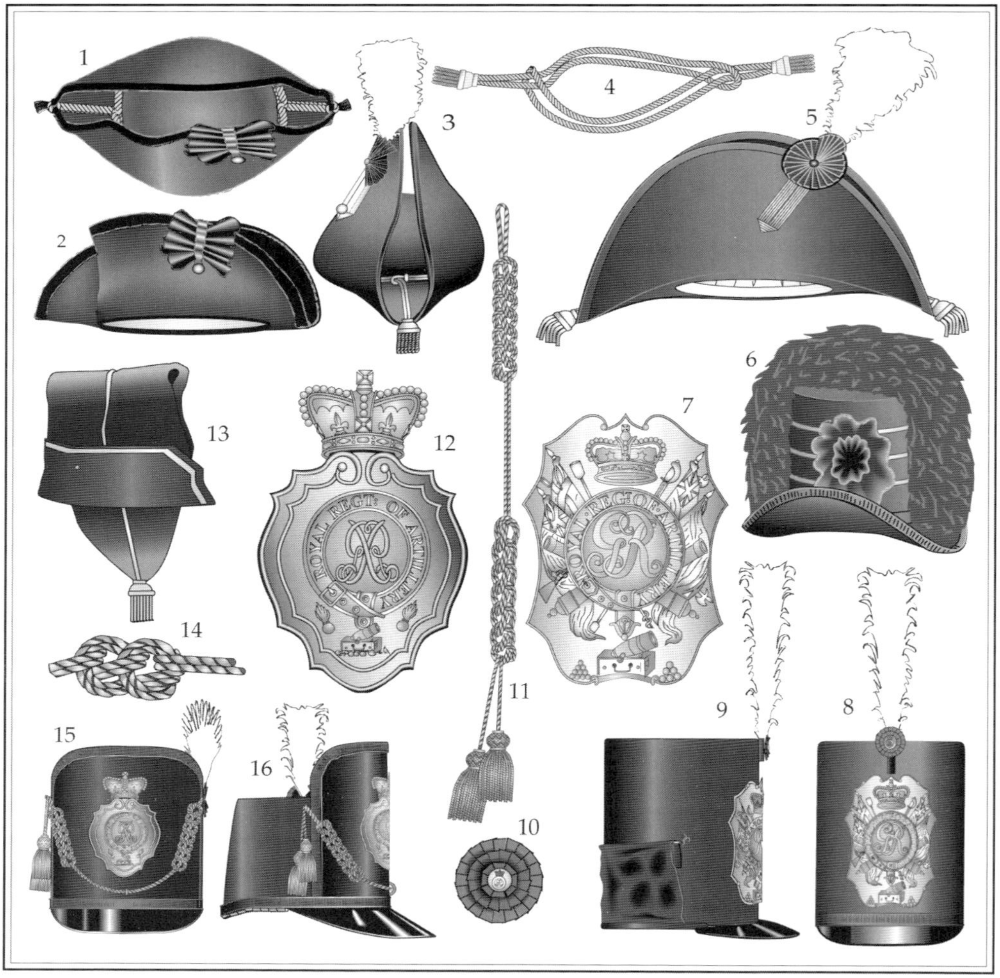

Figure 17.1. Artillery officers' hats. The early versions of the artillery cocked hats or bicorns. These had evolved from the tricorn to a bicorn pattern (1 and 2). The cords that were pulled tight to tighten the hat (4) and the later style of hat worn by artillery officers (3 and 5), the shape and size varied according to the fashion of the day. Black round hat with a black bearskin crest worn by senior officers in the Low Countries (6). The artillery gilt shako plates (7) for the stovepipe shako (8 and 9) with a rear fall or neck protector. The cockade worn at the top of the crown worn over the base of the 10-inch white plume (10). The gilt and red twist cords (11) and gilt plate (12) for an officer's Belgic shako and the fatigue hat associated with foot artillery officers (13). Detail of the gilt and red twist cords of the hat (14) and two views of an officer's Belgic shako (15 and 16).

The shako plate was of gilt and often carried small variations in the pattern. In full dress, the cocked hat was still de rigueur.

Fatigue Hats

Officers of artillery had no approved pattern of fatigue caps, although they seem to have taken into use the form they considered most in fashion. Illustrations exist which show officers wearing a fatigue hat in the style of the French 'bonnet de police'.

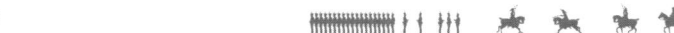

… In those days there was no undress-cap for officers, ergo when off parade they were usually lounging about in round hats, and in some small or slack garrisons I have seen them walking about the streets in them. In the Foot Artillery, at some of our out quarters, we always wore them, with a cockade and button, as substitutes for cocked hats. In the West Indies, I think, they were worn by authority.[9]

Coats and Jackets

The coat worn at the start of the Napoleonic War is illustrated by Dayes and De Loutherberg; it is of a similar style to that of the men but of better quality and cut, and the buttonholes of the lapels and cuffs are marked by red twist lace, those on the rear pocket with blue. These long coats were dark blue with a scarlet unbraided stand-up collar, cuffs and lapels; the turn backs and linings to the skirts were white. The coats were worn hooked together at the chest and the upper part left undone so that the cambric shirt-frill could be pulled out to resemble a cock's comb while the lower part was cut away to show the waistcoat. At the rear, were two plain horizontal pockets, each with four twist buttonholes and buttons. The sash was worn under the coat and over the white waistcoat. The orders stated:

> The Officers lately appointed are informed that the regimental waistcoats are without flaps, and one row of buttons only, the same as the men's. The breeches, which are cloth or kerseymere, are likewise the same as the men's, and buckle at the knee. The tops of the boots are bound and lined with white leather and buckle up with a black strap. The sword has a straight blade, and the length of it as established by his Majesty's regulations; it is to be worn with a crimson and gold sword knot. The lapels of the coat are buttoned back and hooked together, and the skirts hooked up.[10]

Along with the other ranks, the coats of the officers also changed in May 1797 when it was ordered that the jackets were to be closed to the waist. The new long coats were double breasted and buttoned to the waist. They were worn buttoned across or with the lapels turned back to reveal the facings or a combination of the two. The buttonholes were plain twist and there was no lace. An illustration of this form of coat is given in a plate from the British Military Library of 1799.[11]

As Mercer recalls a foot artillery officer could require up to five different coats or jackets; and away from headquarters, less formal dress could be either a laced or unlaced coat of similar style with short tails. Of these earlier coats Mercer recalls:

> From the chief, descending to the middle man and taxing my memory as to its earliest impressions in or about 1795, I remember the gay young officers of Artillery sporting about the streets or dock at Plymouth in blue coats with red facings buttoned back, hooked at the collar, and falling off as they descended, so as to show the white kerseymere waistcoat. Whether the skirts were sewn or hooked back, I cannot remember, but believe the former. A single epaulet decorated this coat, on the right shoulder of captains and lieutenants; field officers alone wearing two. To these coats succeeded the double breasted one, equally plain with the other, which was sometimes worn closely buttoned up; but more generally (and I think such was the order) the three upper buttons undone and the lappels turned back, with the cambric shirt-frill pulled out in the form of a cock's comb. Still no lace, no ornament, save the epaulet. I remember at Clonmel in 1802, venturing (out of the world, as we then considered ourselves) to

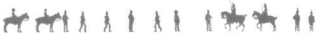

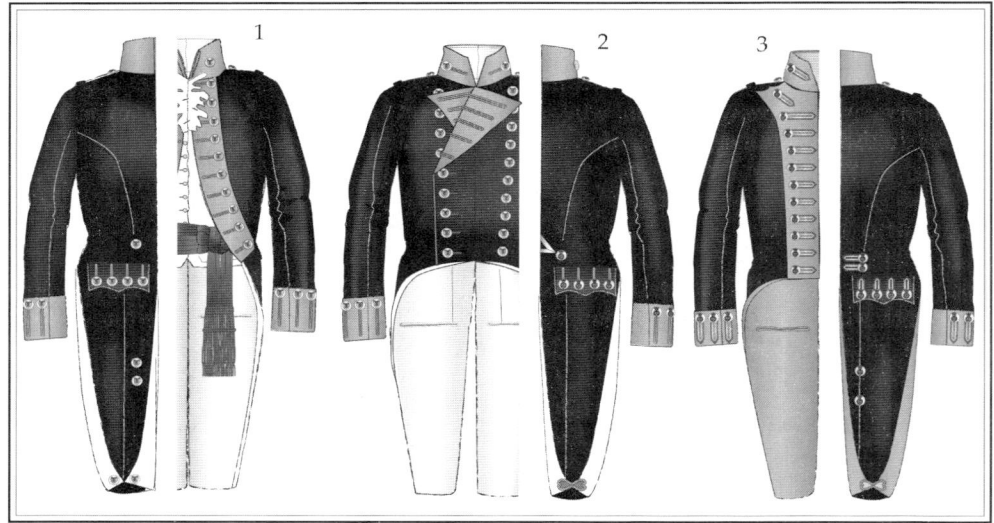

Figure 17.2. Royal Artillery officers' long coats. The long coat with red facings of pre-1797 worn cut away to show the waistcoat (1). An early and late version of the unlaced coat of 1797, this coat was buttoned to the waist and the sash worn over the coat, often with the lapels folded back to reveal the facings (2). The late pattern of a full dress coat with red lining of a pattern similar to the later jackets (3).

stick grenades in our skirts, and thus decorated fancying ourselves uncommonly fine fellows, as we figured away at the balls in the Court-house. After this, I know nothing further of the Foot Artillery, except that their uniform underwent several changes, from coat to jacket, etc. The first lace (beside the epaulet) was an embroidered true lover's knot upon red cloth, as a skirt ornament; then they got cord lace and embroidery – always something very tasteless and ugly.[12]

Officers' Jackets

A general order of 1812 required battalion officers of to wear 'A regimental coat similar to the Private Men, with lace, but with lapels to button over the breast and body'.[13] A further order of August 1812 required that the triangular ornament of a similar pattern to that of the men was to be worn.[14] There is a surviving jacket of this pattern at the Royal Artillery Museum and another in the reserve collection.[15] They are of deep blue with scarlet facings. The coat has short eight-inch long tails that are only nine inches wide at the rear and the jacket is lined throughout in red linen. The narrow scarlet turn backs are false and stitched to the body of the jacket as are the two oblique pockets of dark blue cloth, which are also false. The pocket flaps are plain without edging lace and each carries four 1.75-inch long, buttoned, lace loops. At the rear waist are two regimental buttons set three inches apart with a gold triangular ornament (1.25 inches high and 2.5 inches wide) at the centre. In one jacket, there are two pockets in the plaits at the rear while the other has no pockets. Each jacket has a plain, one-piece, cut-away, scarlet collar, three inches high and lined with red linen; the collar of one jacket carries laced loops and buttons, the other is plain. The scarlet, plastron-shaped lapels are also false and stitched onto the body of the jacket, each carries eight horizontal loops and a ninth, at the top, set at an angle. The one piece scarlet cuffs are 3 inches high with the seam at the rear, each carries four, equally spaced, lace loops with buttons.

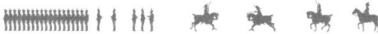

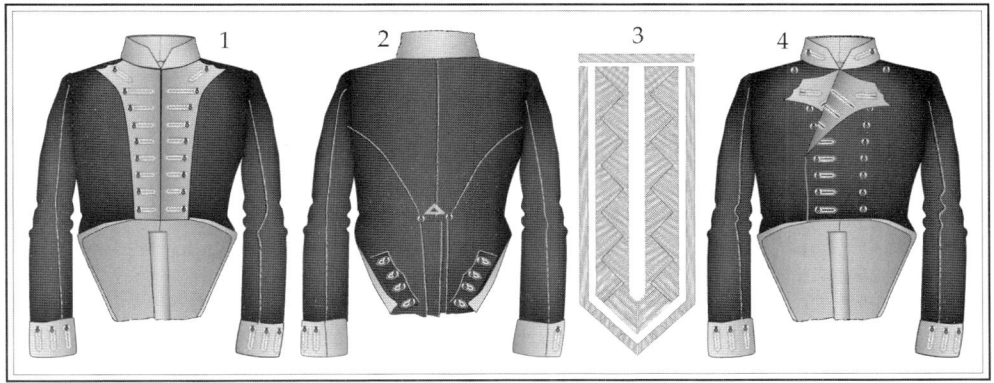

Figure 17.3. Royal Artillery officers' indigo blue jackets with scarlet facings, introduced in 1812. Not all pockets opened and some coats had the false lapels and pocket flaps sewn down with pockets in the plait of the skirts. Front and rear views of surviving jackets in the Royal Artillery Museum (1 and 2). The gilt button holes were not lace, but made from gilt thread stitched directly into the material (3). A jacket after the portrait of General Shrapnel shown with the coat buttoned across and the lapels folded over to reveal the facings and the lace on the reverse of the lapels (4).

The style of the gold lace on the jackets is unusual. Normally gold lace was sewn on to the jacket but in this case, the individual gold threads that comprise the lace pattern are stitched through the material of the jacket to form the pattern. The pattern of the loops is the same on each example and consists of a one-eighth of an inch wide frame to form the outline of a pointed loop. Inside this frame and spaced away from it by a further one-eighth of background material is a pointed loop with the individual threads stitched to form a 'Vandyke' pattern, between the frame and the centre lace is a further clear red light. This practice is repeated on the collar, cuffs, lapels and rear pockets and even the triangular ornament at the rear waist is so formed.

Two portraits, one of Colonel Adye,[16] the other of Lieutenant-General Shrapnel, shows this style of jacket. The portrait of Shrapnel shows that unlike the two examples above, the lapels could be worn buttoned across the chest. In this mode of wear the lace is shown to have been carried through to form laced button holes on the blue side of the lapels; and the scarlet facings have been carried over the lapel to show a clear scarlet strip edging the blue side. The lace shown is of the same pattern as described above with pointed ends and showing a red light at the centre. This jacket has a collar with lace loops. The cuffs carry four, equally spaced, button holes with the front two astride a front seam. The epaulettes are gold bullion with a silver crown. Shrapnel is shown wearing a black silk neck cloth tied at the front. He has white, pointed shirt collars coming well out under the chin.[17]

There was also a long-tailed coat attributed to the Royal Artillery from about 1812 which has since been destroyed. The description of this coatee makes it very similar to those described above, except that the front lapels carried ten buttoned and laced loops and the top of the lapels had another set at an angle. The collar also carried a buttoned and lace loop on either side. The cuffs were the same and the long skirts were lined and faced scarlet with a gold knot on a scarlet ground securing each corner. The waist at the rear carried two pockets, each with four buttoned and laced loops, which pointed upwards. The back of the coat, at the waist, had two loops of

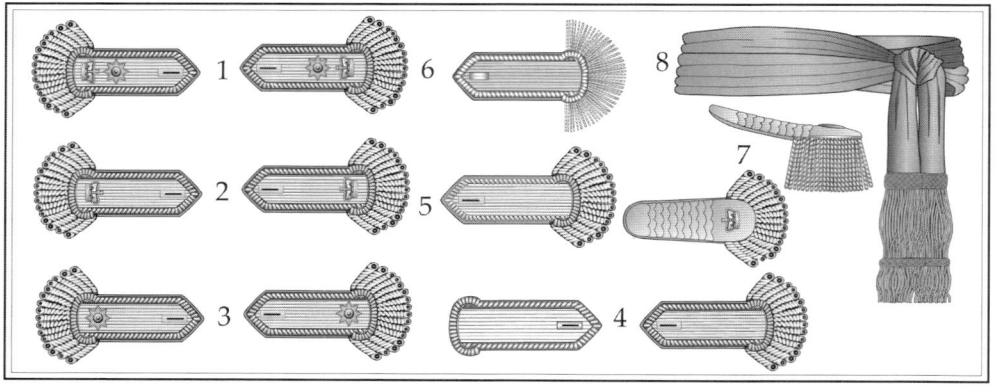

Figure 17.4. Royal Artillery officer's rank distinctions. The gilt epaulettes with silver badges of a Colonel (1), Lieutenant-Colonel (2), Major (3), Adjutant and Quartermaster (4). The single epaulette of a Captain and 2nd Captain – worn on the right shoulder only (5) and that of a Lieutenant, also only worn on the right shoulder (6). Dress scale epaulettes worn at levees and in the dining room by senior and junior officers after Almack (7) and the officer's crimson sash (8).

lace pointing sideways to the centre. This long coat was worn in dress with scale epaulettes with gold bullion fringe and silver crowns.[18] It was worn open over a white waistcoat at levees, balls and when attending the dining room. Colour illustrations of the coats and jackets of the artillery officers are given in the colour plates.

Officers' Rank Distinctions

The officer ranks within the field artillery were Colonel, Lieutenant-Colonel, Major, Captain and Captain-Lieutenant until 1804 when the rank became Second Captain, 1st Lieutenant and 2nd Lieutenant. Also attached to each brigade and troop were officers of the Commissariat who answered to the Treasury, but these carried no rank distinctions or specific uniform. Initially the rank distinctions for officers were gilt bullion epaulettes on the right shoulder for company officers and on each shoulder for those of field rank. These regulations changed in 1810 when the artillery adopted the rank conventions of the infantry and the gilt epaulettes carried badges of silver.[19] The new rank distinctions were pointed, bullion epaulettes. Senior officers (Majors and above) wore an epaulette on each shoulder, Colonels with a crown and star, Lieutenant-Colonels, a crown and Majors, a star. Captains and Second Captains wore one bullion epaulette on the right shoulder while subalterns wore one of gold fringe. Examples of epaulettes of the period at the Royal Artillery Museum show pointed ends to the boards and this concurs with contemporary miniatures. Scale epaulettes with gold fringe were often worn with the long coat for dress occasions. It may also be that senior officers wore additional embellishments to their jackets.

Sashes

The other distinction of rank was the sash. At the start of the war officers wore the crimson net sash around the waist under the coat and tied on the left; originally the sash was large enough to form a hammock stretcher, but later styles were just a distinction of rank. The sashes were usually worn over the sword belt to prevent it

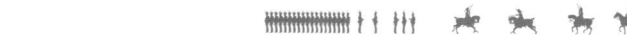

flapping about. In 1798 the officers' sashes were ordered to conform to those of the infantry and were worn over the coat,[20] except for the dining room, balls and levees. Mercer recalls:

> When I got my commission, we wore very large sashes of silk net that went several times round the body, and were admired in proportion. The idea was that, in case of being wounded, an Officer's sash ought to form a hammock to carry him in, by putting a pole through the two holes left next the knots, and then tying the stretched netting over his breast with ends of fringe cut off for the purpose.[21]

The original sash of silk net was six inches wide by eighty-eight inches long with a ten-inch fringe.

Shirts and Stocks

Shirts were worn by all ranks in the early period and those of the officers were profusely decorated with starched and ironed frills, often with lace for dress, which was allowed to show at the neck and cuffs. Mercer recalls:

> In the beginning of my career, the neck was enveloped in a black velvet stock into which a padded stuffing was introduced to keep it up; or it was worn over a sufficient accumulation of white muslin, of which one-eighth of an inch in breadth was to border the upper edge of the stock as a finish. In plain clothes, white muslin cravats were then invariably worn, and none but masters or mates of merchantmen and such-like craft ever dreamed of wearing black. At one period it was fashionable to wear cravats of immense size, or rather an immense number, one put on over the other, so as to form a mass of considerable thickness, in which the chin was buried almost up to the under lip.[22]

Later the shirt collars were worn with the points pulled out under the neck and while officers may have worn the stock for parades, in undress and walking out black neck cloths tied in a knot at the front are often shown in portraits. In dress and in the dining room white silk neck cloths were worn.

Greatcoats

Officers supplied their own greatcoats usually with the backs gathered into pleats with buttons at the waist above the rear slit. In 1807 the colour of the greatcoat was changed to a plain blue cloth with a single row of flat metal buttons,[23] later in 1811 this was changed to a greatcoat made of grey cloth of the same colour as those of the men.[24] It is not clear if they wore collars and cuffs of facing colour.

Breeches, Pantaloons and Trousers

Initially breeches were worn for all occasions, but by 1803 breeches were only worn on dress parades, on guard, under arms, and on Sundays. Blue pantaloons and short boots were permitted at other times with white kerseymere knee breeches worn at levees, balls and when attending the dining room.[25] (Pantaloons were close-fitting breeches that fastened below the calf or at the foot – Kerseymere was a twilled, light woollen cloth, a variant of cashmere.)

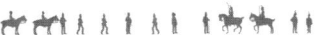

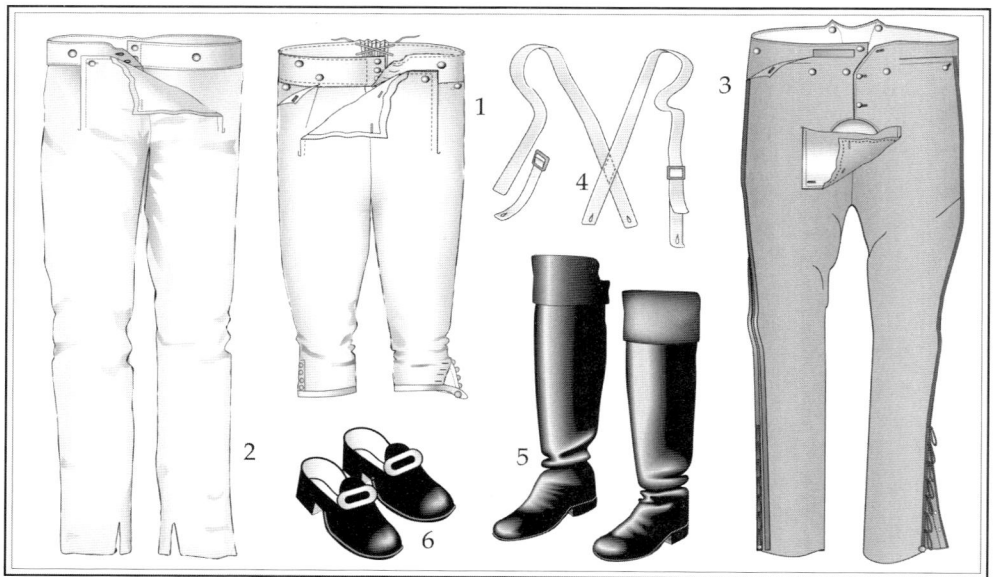

Figure 17.5. Breeches, with the front flap to conceal the fly were most commonly worn, especially for dress (1). White trousers are often shown being worn on campaign and these were replaced by grey before the end of the war (2). The tight fitting, pale blue dress pantaloons of the later period were often made of Kerseymere or stretch worsted with a coloured stripe or stripes, down the outer seam (3). Suspenders were used to retain both breeches and trousers (4). Knee-boots were a common item of dress although the patterns varies (5); for dress occasions and in the dining room shoes were worn (6).

By 1810 breeches were only worn for dress occasions. They were made of doe, buckskin or kerseymere and fitted to come well up over the hips and below the knees to the calf. At the bottom, each leg had four small regimental buttons or tapes to secure it to the leg and prevent it riding up. To cover the open fly the breeches were fitted with a flap at the front, buttoned at the waist. They usually had pockets on both sides. Adjustment to the waist was by tapes at the rear and when worn under a jacket, suspenders of linen or light canvas supported the breeches. For campaign, working duties and fatigues white or later grey trousers were usually worn. The trousers were fitted with the same front-flap fly as the breeches and they were supported in the same manner. In 1812 officers employed on foreign service wore 'grey pantaloons or overalls, with short boots, or with shoes and gaiters, such as the private men's'. There is an example of a late pair of pantaloons at the Royal Artillery Museum. These are of a pale blue cloth with two half-inch wide red strips sewn either side of the outer seam and set a quarter of an inch apart. The front flap, which conceals the centre, three-button fly, is five inches deep, but only seven inches wide; it is secured by three buttons, one at each corner and one at the centre. On each side, there is a five-inch wide pocket, nine inches deep, and buttoned on the outer corner. Also at the waist is a three-inch wide fob pocket. The pantaloons are tight fitting with thirteen-inch bottoms. The bottom ten inches of each leg is open and has seven red-lace loops passing through holes to interlace down the front of the rearmost red stripe to a button at the bottom.

Footwear

In 1792, officers wore black regimental knee boots fastened at the back of the knee with a buckled, black strap. In undress half boots that reached just above the ankle were often worn. For dress and walking out, shoes with gilt or gold buckles were worn, particularly when wearing stockings. Mercer recalls:

> … somewhere in 1798, for I was a Cadet … the first boot I wore myself was the regimental one when I got my commission, up to the knee, with a stiff top, but not cut out behind, which was then a piece of dandyism, and only became regimental afterwards. These boots were made large, and did not fit the leg; but when a Cadet, I remember the Officers wore a more flexible boot, fitting closely and showing the shape of the leg. This was kept up by a tongue attached to the kneeband of the breeches, and a buckle on the calf of the boot. … The half boots then worn were the very reverse of what afterwards came in fashion, for instead of being higher in front, they were cut down and rose to a point behind. … These were made with a single seam down the back, but subsequently it became quizzical not to have a double one, with a broad band between them.[26]

Buttons, Badges and Belt Plates

The buttons for officers were of a similar pattern to those of the men but in gilt and sometimes convex, and versions with battalion numbers are known. Permission to wear belt plates was granted in 1796,[27] and repeated for officers of the first and third battalions in 1799, but the pattern of the plate seems to have varied from battalion to battalion and several different styles are known.[28]

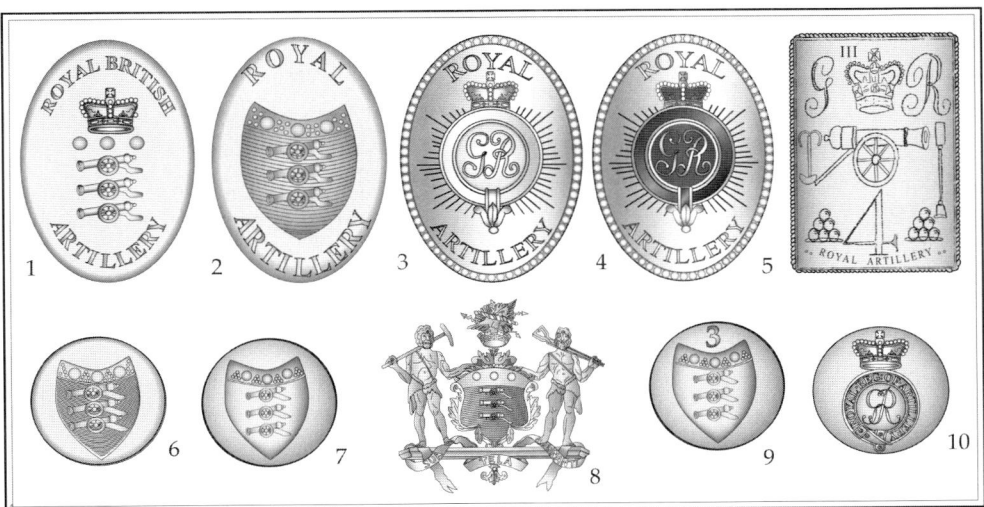

Figure 17.6. Royal Artillery buttons, plates and badges of the officers. A brass plate attributed to before 1801 by Parkyn (1), a brass belt plate attributed to 1790–1805 by Parkyn (2) and an officer's belt plate attributed to 1799 by Parkyn (3). An officer's beaded and enamelled plate, circa 1780–1820, after an example at the Scottish National Museum (4). A belt plate with battalion distinction, circa 1805 (5), one is also known with the figure three. Early flat gilt button (6), gilt convex button pre-1802 (7), the arms of the Board of Ordnance (8), a version of the pre-1802 button with battalion distinction (9) and an officer's convex gilt button post-1802 (10).

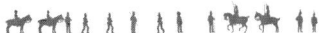

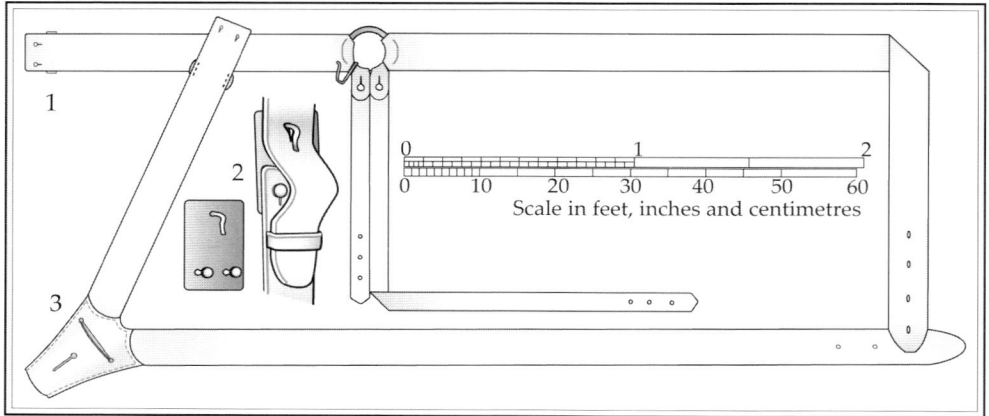

Figure 17.7. The two styles of sword belt adopted by the officers of artillery. A two-piece belt, with ring and sword straps to connect the rings of a scabbard (1). The method of attaching the belt plate (2) and the more common style of shoulder belt with the sword retained in a frog (3).

Sword Cross-belt

Officers usually wore the sword on a two-piece cross-belt worn over the right shoulder. The belt was a similar pattern to that described for the men with a short, seventeen-inch front strap and a long, forty-six-inch rear strap both stitched together at the sword frog. Normally the two belt straps were clipped together by the studs and hooked on the rear of the belt plate. In court dress, balls and other full dress occasions the officers often wore the sword on a waist belt. Mounted officers may have adopted a different style of cross-belt, contemporary illustrations suggest that it was a two-piece cross-belt with the same two straps, but both were stitched to a brass ring, which carried two sword slings and a brass hook to wear the sword up. The sword slings were an inch wide, the front was thirteen inches long and the rear thirty-four inches long. The method of attachment to the scabbard varied. Some patterns had the sling terminating in a buckle and strap in the manner of a harness billot where the strap passed through the rings of the scabbard and back through the buckle of the sling. Another style had the sword sling as a plain strap. A separate, seven-inch strap with a dropped bar buckle was attached through the sword ring and both the strap and sword sling passed through the buckle.

Infantry Sword

Officers of artillery were required to carry the regulation 1796 infantry officers' sword.[29] The hilt consisted of a gilded brass pommel in the shape of a faceted urn topped with acanthus leaves, silver wire-wound grip, a gilt knuckle bow to a quillon with acanthus decoration at its finial and twin gilt shells strengthened around the edges and decorated with acanthus leaves under the shells. These were fixed, but on some examples, the inner shell was hinged to fold up when the sword was sheathed. The straight blade was of flattened diamond section. Most swords of this pattern had straight cut and thrust blades with a single edge and short false edge. The overall length was 39 inches, with the blade 32.5 inches long and 1.125 inches wide at the shoulder. It was carried in a black leather scabbard fitted with rings or a frog stud. The weight was 1lb 10oz and the scabbard weighed 1lb.[30] Mercer remarks on this sword:

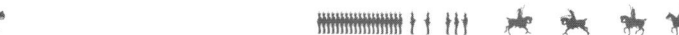

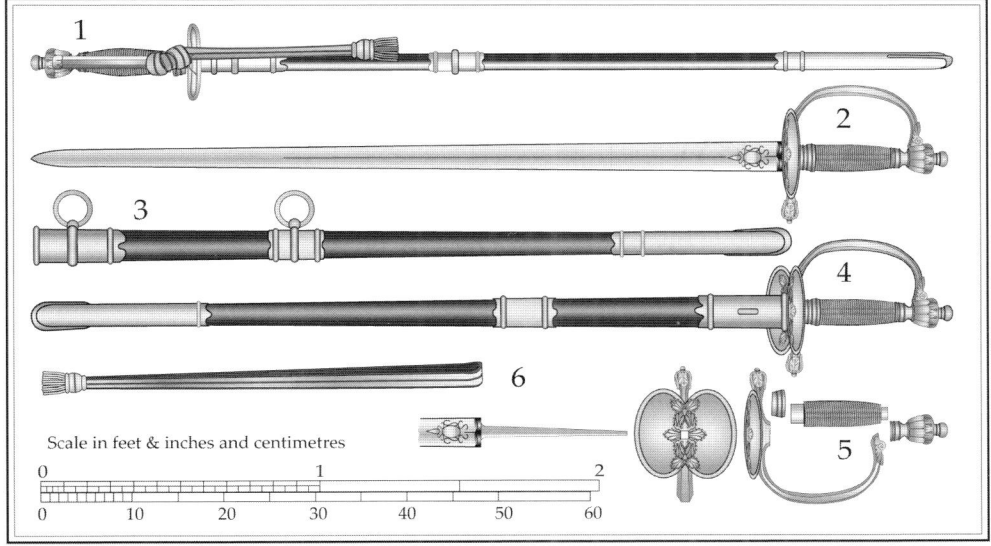

Figure 17.8. Artillery sword. The 1796 infantry officer's sword worn by the officers of the foot artillery. The front view (1), the blade and gilt hilt (2) and a black leather scabbard fitted with gilt fittings and rings for a belt with sword slings (3). The sword in a scabbard for the frog of the shoulder belt (4), a gilt and red sword knot (6) and the method of construction of the sword hilt and guard; some had a hinged guard which folded down to sit better at the waist (5).

Nothing could be more useless or more ridiculous than the old Infantry regulation; it was good neither for cut nor thrust, and was a perfect encumbrance. In the Foot Artillery, when away from headquarters, we generally wore dirks instead of it. Generals, and our Field Officers, seemed to wear what they pleased, and after the Egyptian expedition the Mamaluke sabre was quite the rage.[31]

The sword knot was intended to retain the sword from being knocked out of the hand and was worn looped around the wrist. It consisted of a three-quarter-inch strip of gilt lace with a red centre. This was doubled and terminated in a tassel to form a loop eighteen inches long. It was loop-knotted about the pommel end of the knuckle bow.

Key to Colour Plate

Plate 10. Royal Artillery – Officers – Coats and Jackets
1. The long coat of pre-1797 worn cut away to show the waistcoat.
2. A red thread twist button hole worn on the earlier pattern coat.
3. Not all pockets opened, some coats had false pockets with the flaps sewn down and pockets on the insides of the skirts or in the plait.
4. The late pattern full dress coat for officers of a pattern similar to the later jackets.
5. A front and rear view of an early version of the unlaced coat of 1797. This coat was buttoned to the waist, often with the lapels folded back to reveal the facings and the sash worn over the coat.
6. An early belt plate showing battalion distinctions, *circa* 1800, one is also known with the figure three.

7.　An officer's belt plate attributed to 1799 by Parkyn; a similar other ranks' plate is depicted by Dighton in 1812.

8.　A rear view of the short, laced jacket introduced in 1812, after a surviving example at the Royal Artillery Museum.

9.　A front view of the short, laced jacket introduced in 1812, after a surviving example at the Royal Artillery Museum.

10.　Another version of the short jacket after the portrait of Shrapnel shown with the coat buttoned across and the lapels folded over to reveal the facings and the lace on the reverse of the lapels.

11.　The gilt thread button hole sewn directly into the material of the later jackets and the dress coatee.

12.　A gilt button of the post-1802 pattern, which carried a crowned garter belt with a royal cypher inside.

13.　A version of the pre-1802 button with Battalion distinctions.

14.　An early flat gilt button, which carried the arms of the Board of Ordnance.

15.　Examples of plain, fringed and bullion epaulettes worn by officers.

Endnotes to Chapter 17

1.　Campbell, 1971: p. 16.
2.　MacDonald, 1985: pp. 42–4.
3.　De Loutherberg, *Grand Attack on Valenciennes*, 1793.
4.　MacDonald, 1985: pp. 40, 41.
5.　General Orders, 10 April 1808; MacDonald, 1985: p. 33.
6.　Ibid, 31 October and 1 November 1803; MacDonald, 1985: p. 31.
7.　Ibid, 3 August 1813; MacDonald, 1985: p. 35;
8.　Ibid, 3 August 1813; MacDonald, 1985: p. 35; Campbell, 1971: p. 19.
9.　MacDonald, 1985: p. 47.
10.　Woolwich Garrison Orders, 8 August 1794; MacDonald, 1985: p. 30.
11.　Campbell, 1971: plate II.
12.　MacDonald, 1985: p. 47.
13.　National Archive, WO 54/694: p. 220.
14.　Ibid, WO 54/641: p. 20.
15.　Royal Artillery Museum: reserve collection, UN 310.
16.　Carman, 1973: p. 13.
17.　Hughes, 1984: p. 25, plate 18.
18.　Campbell, 1971: p. 36; Macdonald, 1985: plate 13.
19.　General Order, 2 March 1810; MacDonald, 1985: p. 34.
20.　Ibid, 5 July 1798; MacDonald, 1985: p. 31.
21.　MacDonald, 1985: pp. 53, 54.
22.　Ibid: pp. 51, 53.
23.　General Order, 29 November 1807; MacDonald, 1985: p. 33.
24.　Ibid, 14 January 1812; MacDonald, 1985: p. 35.
25.　General Order, 29 December 1803; MacDonald, 1985: p. 32.
26.　MacDonald, 1985: pp. 50, 51.
27.　General Order, 30 October 1796; MacDonald, 1985: p. 31
28.　Parkyn, 1956: pp. 54–7; Campbell, 1971: pp. 137–9.
29.　General Order, 12 October 1796; MacDonald, 1985: p. 31.
30.　Wilkinson Latham, 1966: plate 10.
31.　MacDonald, 1985: p. 54.

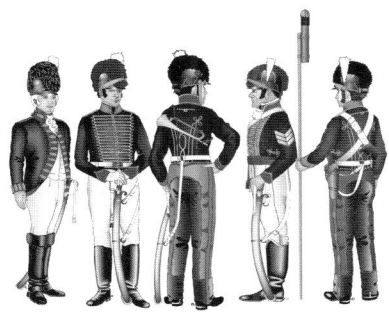

CHAPTER 18

Royal Horse Artillery – Other Ranks

Introduction

The Royal Horse Artillery was formed in 1793. Initially the height of the recruit had to be above five feet, six and three-quarter inches but within six months, this was increased to five feet, eight inches.[1] They were dressed in the manner of light cavalry, as it was the cavalry that they were initially formed to support, although their role soon widened to that of a mobile field artillery. There were no 'official' troop distinctions of dress, although there is some evidence that they occurred; the exception was the Rocket Troop, but even this unit was dressed in the same manner as the rest of the horse artillery with any individuality of appearance limited to their ancillary equipment, weapons and horse furniture – the dress and equipment of this unit have already been considered in detail elsewhere.[2] There was no specific distinction of rank for officers of the Royal Horse Artillery, but it is most probable that the more senior wore more elaborate embellishments to the uniform. Officers were generally (or perhaps more accurately – supposed to be) dressed in the same manner as the men but with items of better quality. The surviving jackets in the Royal Artillery Museum are those of officers, there are no known surviving jackets of the other ranks and for these we must rely upon those depicted by the artists of the period.

Head-dress

The helmet worn by the horse artillery was the light cavalry Tarleton helmet. The early patterns had a low crown with the base of the skull forming a straight line to the peak, a sparse crest and a two-inch high turban originally intended to fold down for additional protection in foul weather but soon to become just an item of decoration. The crown of the helmet carried a black bearskin comb secured by laces through holes in the crown either side of the centre seam. The helmets were often

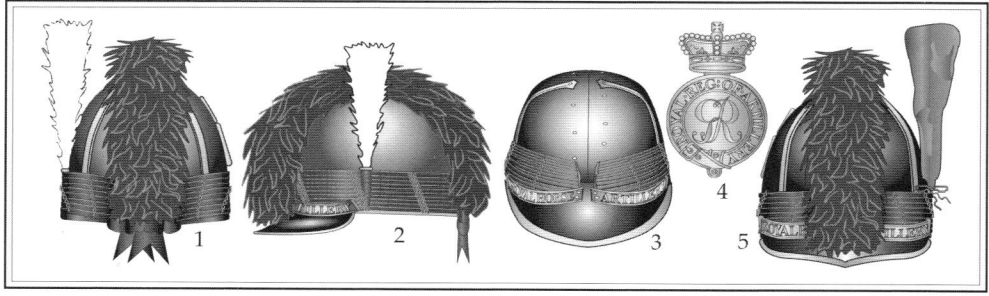

*Figure 18.1. Early versions of the Tarleton helmet recognised by the straight edge to the bottom of the crown.
A rear view showing the turban tied in a bow at the rear (1). Mercer recalls that the turban was originally
leopard skin then changed to red silk (2) before the change to black. The helmet crown showing the early brass
two-piece title strip and the holes by which the crest was tied to the crown (3). A front view with foul weather
cover to the plume (5). The early version of the horse artillery helmet badge worn on the right side above the
turban (4).*

fitted with cords or ribbons that tied under the queque to keep the helmet in place.
After 1799, a more elegant pattern appeared with a pronounced curve to the base
of the helmet. This had a higher 8.5-inch crown and was some 10 inches from peak
to back with a leather edging to the base of the crown. The skull was formed from
leather, with brass skull guard strips to ward off sabre cuts. The slightly pointed
peak was formed as an integral part with the crown and edged with brass. Secured
around each side of the crown by fine yellow metal chains was a black silk turban
tied at the rear in a rosette. Mercer recalls that it was originally black velvet and
finally black silk.[3] Across the front, above the peak, was a brass metal band carrying
the embossed title 'ROYAL HORSE ARTILLERY'. On the right side of the helmet,
above the turban, was the brass regimental badge. Originally this consisted of a
crown over the Royal Cypher 'GR' within a garter belt inscribed 'ROYAL·REG·OF·
ARTILLERY'.

After about 1811, the inscription was changed to 'ROYAL HORSE ARTILLERY' and
the cypher changed to a reversed version. Below, or to either side of this, on separate

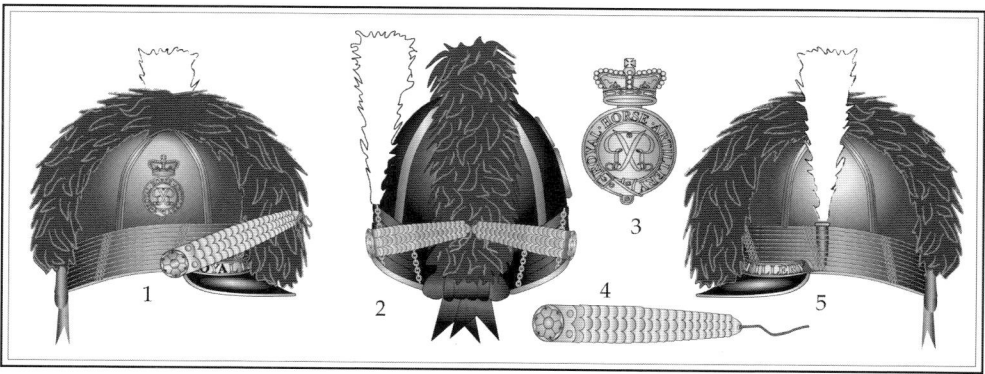

*Figure 18.2. Later versions of the Tarleton helmet recognised by the curved edge to the bottom of the crown.
A right side view showing the turban tied in a bow at the rear (1); it was common practice to tie the chin scales
up to the front or back of the helmet (2). The later style of horse artillery helmet badge (3) and the style of the
later chin scales that were not always worn on the earlier helmets (4). A right side view of the helmet showing the
plume holder (5).*

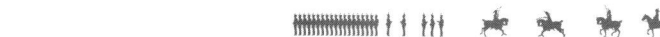

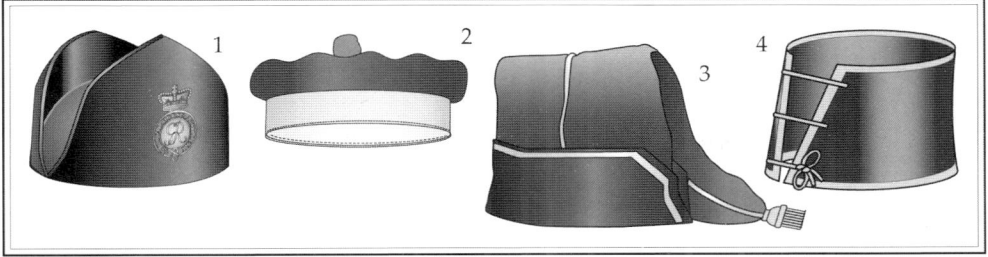

Figure 18.3. The black leather 'Woolwich'-style cap of the horse artillery (1) was also worn by the early drivers. The standard issue light cavalry forage cap with a blue top and yellow band (2), the blue fatigue hat worn by the horse artillery copied from the French 'bonnet de police' (3) and the blue-laced, red fatigue-hat worn for undress parades and watering order (4).

small scrolls were any battle honours awarded to the wearer.[4] On the left side of the helmet, above the turban, was a brass plume holder, carrying a 10-inch white feather plume, which could be encased in a waterproof cover when on active service. In spite of the many modern illustrations showing otherwise, most of the Tarleton helmets of the period had no chin scales,[5] but some surviving examples show them. They were the fashion for those who could afford them, but for most other ranks they were not fitted. Mercer mentions in his Waterloo Diaries that his men had to hold on to their helmets during a strong wind and he also recalls:

> At the same time, the bearskins were raised and made fuller. The first time this was done for the non-commissioned officers and men, I remember, we made the alteration ourselves (i.e. our collar-maker did it) by uniting the bearskin of the old helmet to the new one just served out, and a monstrous improvement it made in the appearance of our parades. There is nothing like a lofty head-dress to make soldiers look imposing, particularly so when drawn up in a body. The feathers worn in the helmets of officers differed like those for the cocked hats; those of the men, I believe, were always the same, for the feather-case was always of the same form and dimensions.[6]

Fatigue-hats

There are two types of fatigue-hat attributed to the RHA at this time. One is the ubiquitous black leather fatigue-hat commonly worn by many of the arms associated with Woolwich. It is described as being of pork pie shape with a flap at the back and front. In the case of the RHA it was kept polished and in good order and carried a RHA badge on the front flap; another hat attributed to the horse artillery is a laced blue cloth cap and it seems that the French 'bonnet de police' was also used. The descriptions by Mercer are interesting:

> It was of black leather, with a brass ornament in front (G.R. and crown, etc)… The Horse Artillery and drivers had a similar mitre-shaped cap, but better, inasmuch as, being made of thick stiff leather, it was kept polished, and looked smart. This was used for undress parades, watering order, etc. But for common stable parades, fatigues, etc., the Horse Artillery had a blue cloth cap edged with red, and tied behind with red ferreting. This was also worn night by stable sentries and others. The captains of troops must have been greater men, and have enjoyed much more latitude formerly, than in the present day. Many circumstances which I call to mind make me think this, but among

other, the circumstance that Duncan, in 1804, took it into his head to give his troop a new and Frenchified forage-cap, such a one as until then was only known to us through the medium of costumes, etc., although familiar to him, a service officer. Numerous were the fancies he and I tried, some in sketches, some he actually had made up, until at last we pitched upon the annexed as the most elegant ; and the tailors were forthwith set to work making them up. In a short time they were finished, Duncan delighted ; inspected the watering-order parade himself, and contemplated the beautiful effect of his Frenchified troop with rapture.[7]

Coats and Jackets

Initially the horse artillery were dressed in the manner of the French chasseurs with the short-tailed coat worn open from the neck showing the waistcoat and worn 'hooked at the collar, it sloped away towards the little skirts which terminated it behind and had red half facings, collar and cuffs'. There are no records or details of the pattern adopted for the other ranks, but there is a painting in the Royal Collection showing the Honourable Artillery Company wearing a similar jacket.[8] The jacket fits the description and the rear view shows two white turn backs with the standard light cavalry braid and tassels from buttons at the waist. The cuffs are square and the half lapels unadorned by braid and fringed shoulder wings are worn. This coat was replaced by the hussar-style jacket, but the date this change was implemented is unclear, it may have been when the light cavalry jacket was

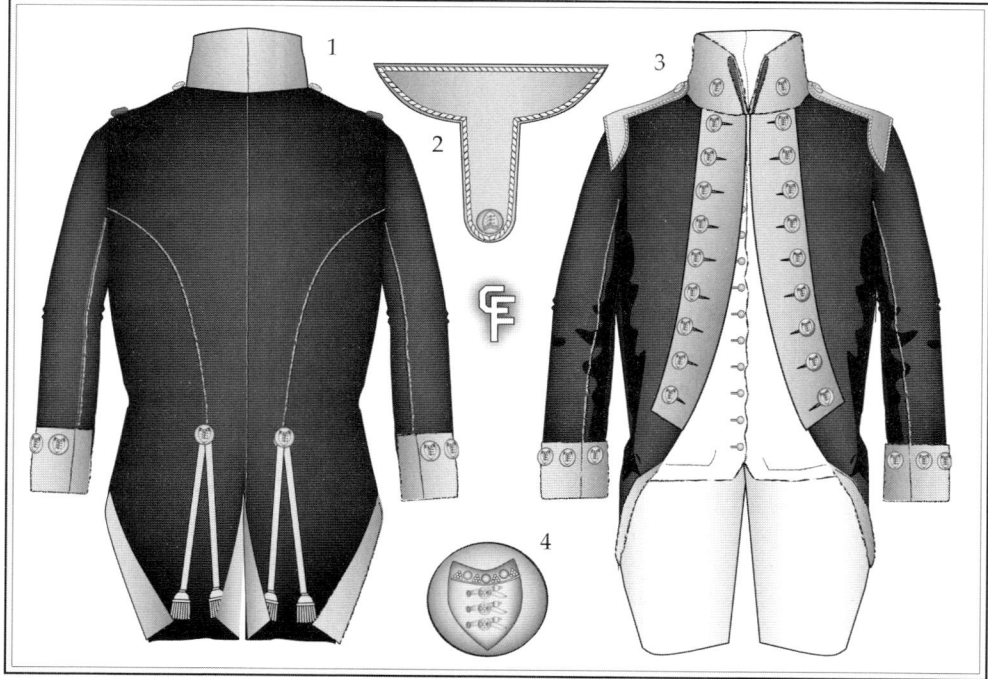

Figure 18.4. The early blue coats with red facings of the other ranks of the Royal Horse Artillery. No illustration or description exists for this coat. This reconstruction of the coatee originally worn in 1793 (1) is based upon the description by Mercer and the uniforms of the period. The shoulder wings (2) and a possible front view (3) and the button worn until 1802 (4).

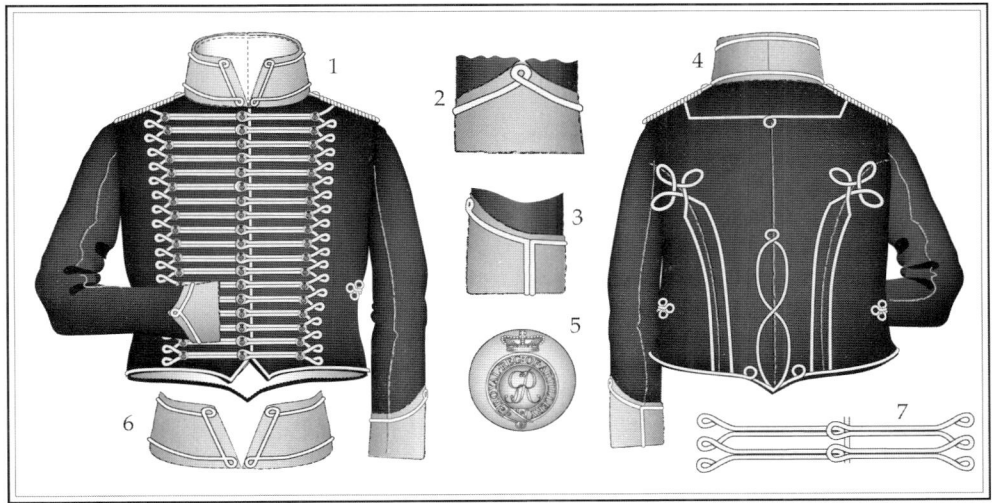

Figure 18.5. The later blue jacket with red facings of the other ranks of the Royal Horse Artillery. Front view of the later hussar-style jacket adopted in about 1805 (1), with the cuff lace detail (2 & 3) and the rear view, after Dighton (4). The button pattern adopted in 1802 (5) and the collar detail (6) and the lace pattern of yellow lace for the other ranks but in gilt for the Senior NCOs (7).

changed by the General Order in July 1796, but no records are available to confirm this.

The new jacket was waist length in the style recently adopted by the light cavalry in 1796; it was dark blue and single breasted, with the scarlet collar and cuffs of a Royal Regiment. Just below the hip, each edge of the jacket was extended to form a point.

The jacket was laced on the chest and around the front and bottom edges with a flat, yellow worsted lace, carried in an elaborate crow's foot pattern on the rear seams with false pockets also outlined in lace, just above the hips on both sides.[9] The front of the jacket had three rows of buttons and the chest lacing ran in equally spaced pairs, which were joined, outside the buttons, at each end by a small loop. At the rear the seams at the waist were decorated with two four-looped cord knots. The scarlet cuffs were pointed on the outside and square on the inside and laced about by yellow lace, placed away from the edge to show a clear red border to the cuff. The lace had a loop to the outside at the seam, which opened at the cuff with two small buttons. The red cut-away collar was 3.5 inches deep, and laced about by yellow worsted cord placed away from the edge to show a clear red border to the collar. At each corner and turn, the cord had a small loop to the outside. Under the collar was worn a black leather stock, in dress, the stock for men was required to show an eighth of an inch of white at the top, and for this purpose they were issued with six false collars of linen that attached to the stocks by hooks.

By 1805 the jacket changed to the style of the hussars, the bottom now sloped away to the front and rear to form shallow points but in other respects it remained similar to that worn previously, except the lace was changed from flat to round. This is the jacket illustrated in Dighton's painting in the Royal Collection, the jacket had three rows of buttons some six inches apart at the collar and about four inches apart at the waist, the chest lacing remained much as before. Hamilton Smith shows the new jacket with eighteen and fourteen rows of lace, Sauerweid shows at least seventeen and a surviving jacket (now lost) had twenty-two. On each shoulder, there was a twisted or plaited braid shoulder strap secured by a button. Colour illustrations of the coats and later jackets of the other ranks of the horse artillery are given in the colour plates.

Rank Distinctions

Initially, with the early coat, it would seem that the horse artillery followed the light cavalry in the way that the ranks were identified. Rank distinctions changed to chevrons, although the date authorised by the Board is not recorded. Initially they may have been worn on the right arm only but by 1815, they were worn on both arms. Sergeant Majors and Quarter Master Sergeants wore four gilt chevrons on a scarlet background and Sergeants wore three. Corporals wore two yellow chevrons on a red background and Bombardiers, one.[10] Senior Non-commissioned Officers wore gilt braid or a combination of both and they probably wore additional embellishments to the pattern of lacing at the collar and cuffs. In 1810, the rank of Company Sergeant was introduced for the horse artillery with the same rank distinctions as those of the rest of the regiment. NCOs rank distinctions also included a crimson sash, made of silk after 1795, tied about the waist with the knot at the right hip.

Buttons, Badges and Belt Plates

The original horse artillery buttons were of brass or yellow metal with the ordnance arms die stamped into them. In 1802, the pattern changed to a convex brass button die stamped with a badge similar to that of the helmet, a crown over a garter belt inscribed 'ROYAL REGT OF ARTILLERY' with the 'GR' cypher at the centre. In 1811, the button carried a similar design but the cypher was doubled and the inscription varied between 'Royal Horse Artillery', 'Royal Horse Artil' or 'Royal Horse Arty'. The centre buttons were ball shaped, the outer ones were half round.[11]

The horse artillery wore belt plates when they wore the sword on a cross-belt and there are several illustrations which show square plates while others show oval.

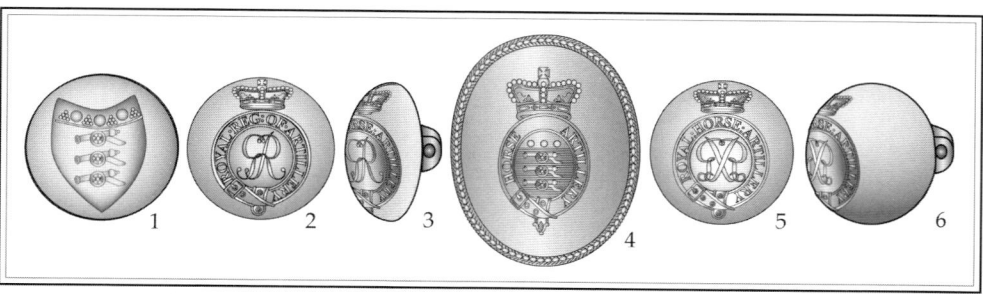

Figure 18.6. Royal Horse Artillery buttons. The early brass button pre-1802 (1), the brass button after 1802, but before 1812 (2) and the later convex shape (3). A brass sword plate with husked rim and the arms of the board of ordnance attributed to the horse artillery by Almack and Parkyn (4). The horse artillery button after 1811 (5) and later ball button (6).

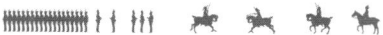

No regulation or order relating to the pattern has been located, but there is a possible example from Almack of an oval brass plate with a husked border and a crown over the arms of the ordnance within a garter belt for the early period.[12]

Breeches, Overalls and Trousers

Initially white buckskin breeches that buckled at the knee were the standard form of dress.[13] The breeches were made and fitted to come well up over the hips and below the knees to the calf. At the bottom, each leg had a small regimental button and tapes to secure it to the leg and prevent it riding up. To cover the open fly the breeches were fitted with a flap at the front that buttoned at the waist. They usually had a pocket at the right side, sometimes on both. Adjustment to the waist was by tapes at the rear and when worn under a jacket, they were worn with suspenders of linen or light canvas.

By 1802 other ranks generally wore grey, later 'pepper and salt' overalls for working duties, marching order, undress and on active service; for fatigues white or grey trousers were usually worn and breeches only worn on full dress parades, on guard and on Sundays. The original overalls were worn suspended from canvas braces and had a front flap that buttoned at the waist in a similar manner to the breeches. To prevent the overalls riding up they were strapped at the bottom, under the instep of the boot. To save on wear they were often faced with leather around the bottoms and down the inside of the thigh and seat (this was changed from black to brown

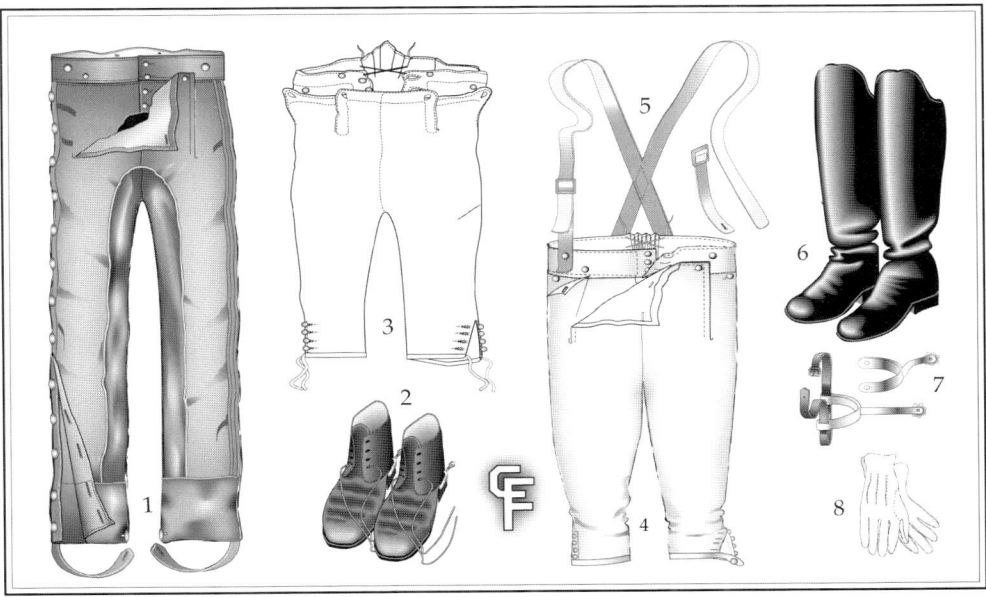

Figure 18.7. The necessaries of the other ranks of the horse artillery. The grey or pepper and salt overalls (1) shown with and without the red-laced buttoned fly. The straight-lasted ankle boots often worn with overalls or pantaloons by the other ranks (2) and the doe or buckskin breeches worn for formal parades (3). The white breeches worn for dress and walking out (4), the suspenders of canvas or linen (5). The early 'Hessian' type boots worn by the other ranks (6) and the early straight spurs and the later swan-necked spurs that screwed into the heel of the boot (7) and the worsted gloves worn by the men (8).

in about 1810). Initially, overalls were worn over the breeches or pantaloons and a buttoned fly was provided down the outer seam to facilitate putting them on. (Thus they were worn over-all, hence the name 'overalls'.) About 1810 it became practice to edge the outer fly with a stripe of facing material and when overalls became a standard item of dress in their own right, the outer fly with the buttons was abandoned but the decorative stripes retained.

Dighton shows a horse artillery detachment with two thin stripes of facing colour either side of the outer seam,[14] but others suggest that the overalls carried a single red stripe down the outer seam,[15] the exact pattern seems to have varied from unit to unit, or even man to man. It was only in 1823 that white breeches and hessian boots were abolished for the horse artillery and blue-grey overalls and Wellington boots were adopted for all orders of dress.[16]

Boots, Shoes and Spurs

With the light dragoon uniform, other ranks wore black leather boots, which reached to the knee. With the change to the hussar jacket in 1799, black leather hussar or hessian boots were worn. Long or short boots were worn with overalls and with pantaloons, short boots or shoes. The horse artillery first wore a long straight spur with a spiked rowel strapped to the boot,[17] but by the later Napoleonic period, the steel, curved or swan-necked spur, which screwed directly into the heel of the boot, was in common use. The quality of the boots and shoes was no better than that described for the foot artillery, but as the horse artillery were mounted the wear may not have been such a problem.

Pouch and Sword Belt

All the sources agree that while the men of the Rocket Troop wore a pouch belt over the left shoulder the other ranks of the horse artillery did not.[1] Some troops of horse artillery carried the sword on a waist belt while others wore it from a shoulder belt across the right shoulder, both forms are illustrated in the contemporary illustrations, and Mercer recalls:

> ... we {D troop} were ordered to give up our white cross-belts to G troop, in exchange for their waist-belts – exhibiting thus our old worn jackets in all their nakednes.[19]

This makes it quite clear that there were at least two patterns of the sword belt. Contemporary illustrations suggest that there were two patterns of cross-belt, each worn over the right shoulder. One was a two-piece belt made of white buff leather, two and one eighth inches wide, with a short, seventeen-inch front strap and a longer, forty-six-inch rear strap, both stitched to a brass ring which carried two sword slings and a brass hook to wear the sword up. The free ends were clipped together by the studs and hooked on the rear of a cross-belt plate. The slings were one inch wide and the front was some thirteen inches long, the rear some thirty-four inches long. The method of attachment to the scabbard varied. Different patterns had the sling terminating in a buckle and strap in the manner of a harness billet, the strap passing through the rings of the scabbard and back through the buckle of the sling. Another style had the sling as a plain strap. A separate, seven-inch strap and buckle was attached through the sword ring and both the strap and sword sling

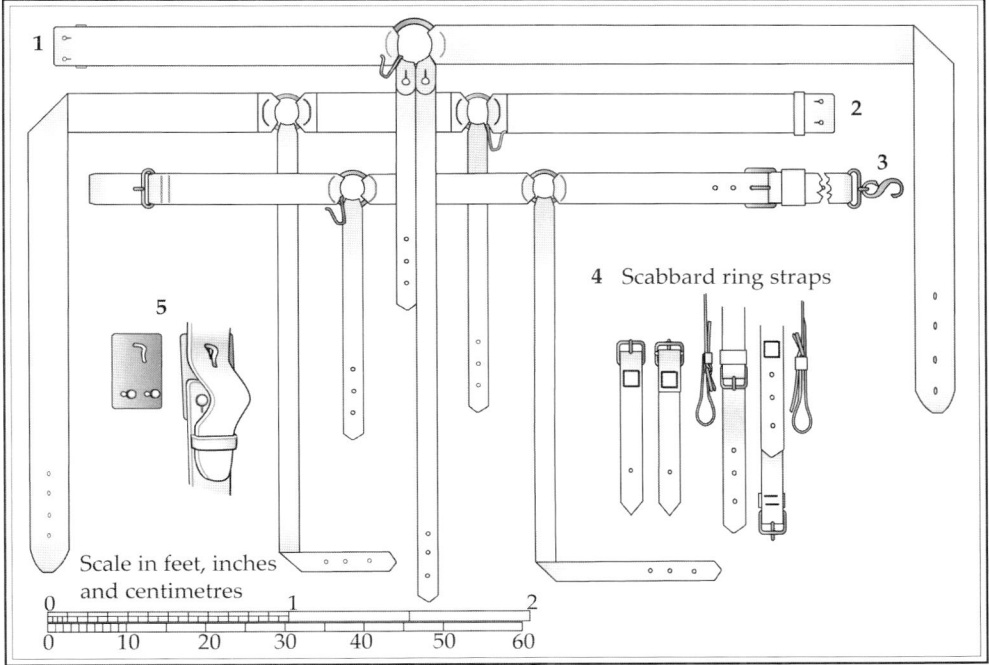

Figure 18.8. Royal Horse Artillery sword belts. The cross-belt worn with the original uniform and later by some Troops(1) and a three-piece version of this belt (2). The standard waist belt more usually associated with this arm (3). The different methods of attaching the sword slings to the scabbard rings (4) and the method of attaching the belt plate for the cross-belt (5).

passed through the buckle. The other pattern of shoulder belt was similar but with two rings joined by a third strap, nine inches long – the length of the rear strap being reduced accordingly. The front ring carried the standard short sword sling and the hook to wear the sword up while the long sling was carried on the rear ring.

The standard issue waist belt was similarly made but only one and a half inches wide with size adjustment by a reversed buckle on the right-hand side of the belt. The standard sword slings were carried, one on each ring. As with the three-piece shoulder belt the centre section was nine inches long, the left was some eight inches. The right-hand section was sixteen inches long with a further eight inches of adjustment.

Pistol

It was intended that the horse artillery should be armed with a version of the Nock pistol.[20] Henry Nock was asked to supply double-barrelled pistols at £8 each. They can be positively identified from his bill book, which reads: 'Pistols for the Horse Artillery. Double barrelled, one of the barrels rifled 18 ins long, one detent trigger, a slide in the left-hand tumbler, folding elevating sight, a shifting butt & a steel Rammer & the barrels browned.' The twin barrels were placed side by side. Only the left-hand barrel was rifled, with nine grooves, and its lock released by the rear trigger. The steel ramrod was housed in an unusually large brass trumpet pipe.

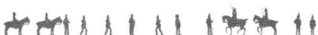

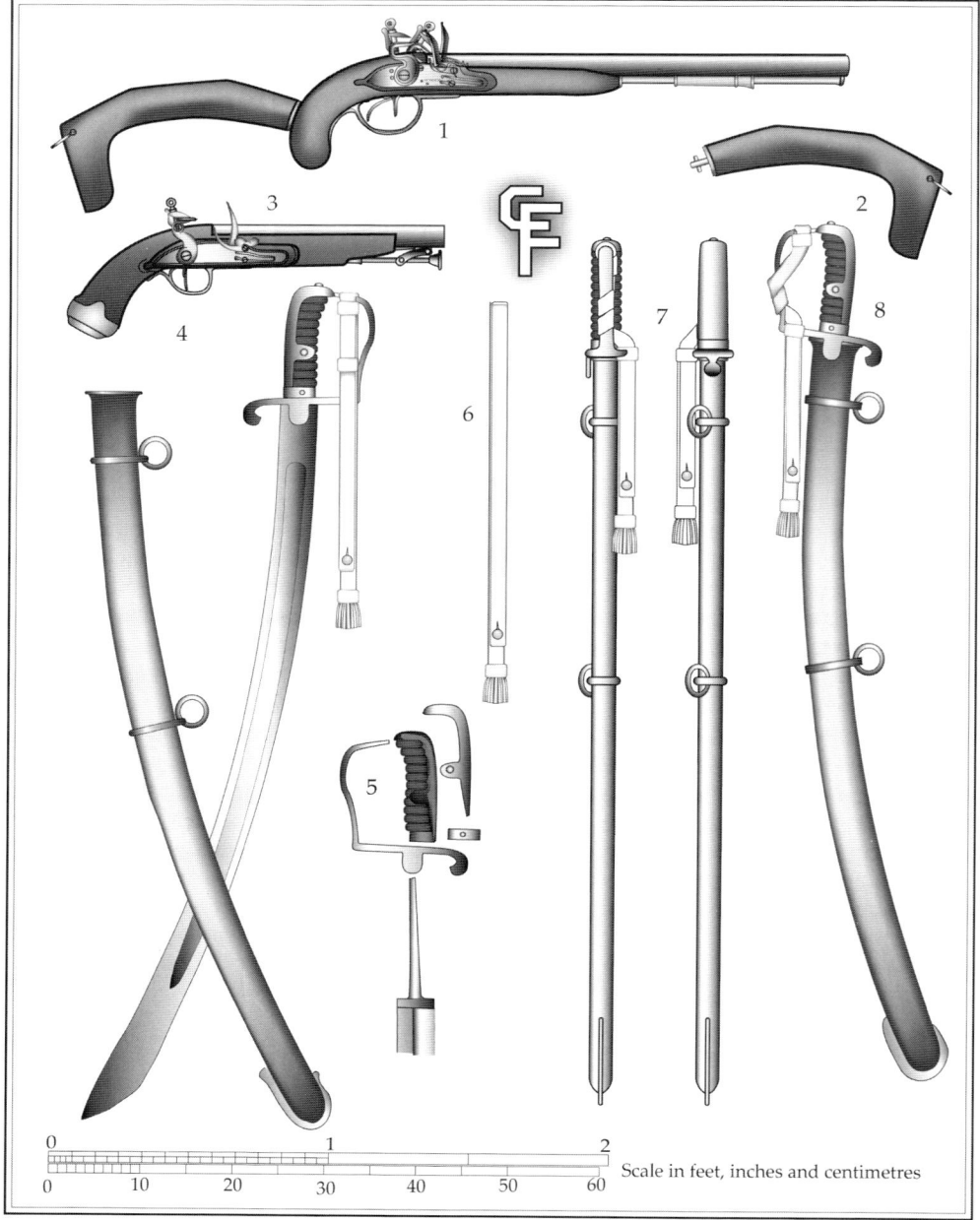

Figure 18.9. The early Knock, double-barrelled pistol with extended butt attached (1) and the detachable butt (2). A standard form of light cavalry pistol of the time (3). The standard issue 1796 light cavalry sabre used throughout the war by the horse artillery (4). One of the methods of construction for the blade and hilt components (5) and an other ranks' white sword knot (6). Different views from the front and rear (7) of the other ranks' sabre in the metal scabbard (8).

The holster could be used as an extension to the butt to form a longer weapon. The pistol weighed 7lb 12oz, the barrel length was 17.8 inches. It had a barrel marking of a royal crown over the 'GR' cipher, all over downward pointing WD arrow. The calibre was 0.72 inches – 13 balls to the pound and the lock was marked H. NOCK. The stock was of walnut, detachable and serial numbered with the gun. The overall length was 23.9 inches but with the 10.2 inch butt fitted, the pistol was 34.1 inches long. Nock died in 1804 and his bill book indicates that by 1783 he had made only 80 of the pistols, hardly enough for one troop. Examination of surviving examples make it clear that the pistols are so large and heavy, and have such a small curved butt, that it is practically impossible to use them single-handed,[21] but they may have initially been carried in the manner of the light dragoons carbine. It must be concluded that if this pistol was issued it was later replaced by the standard light cavalry 'New Land Service' pistol or any other of the many variants available at the time.[22] In 1813, two pistols were carried in holsters at the front of the saddle and covered by bearskin flounces but there is no information as to the type.[23]

Sword

The weapon used by the Royal Horse Artillery before 1796 is unclear, after this date it was the standard 1796 Light Cavalry Pattern. It had a curved blade with a deep fuller towards the back edge and terminated in almost a hatchet point. The total length of the sword was 37.5 inches and the blade around the curve was 32.5 inches from shoulder to point. The blade was 1.625 inches wide at the shoulder tapering to 1.375 inches at 18 inches from the point, widening again to 1.5 inches some 3 inches from it. It was carried in a heavy steel scabbard with two loose rings, one near the mouthpiece and the other 9 inches down the scabbard. The weight of the sword was 2lb 9oz and the scabbard nearly the same. It had a stirrup hilt with semi-circular languet on the cross guard and ears on the back piece, protruding round and riveted to the grip which was made of wood covered with leather. The sword knot was of a three-quarter inch wide strip of white buff leather doubled and terminating in a leather tassel to form a loop 18 inches long. It was loop-knotted about the pommel end of the knucklebow. The loop was passed around the wrist to retain the sword if it was knocked from the grasp.

Accoutrements

A gunner's personal marching equipment would also have included a haversack and a water bottle. These were standard items issued to all arms and have been described earlier in Chapter 16. When mounted, the gunner wore these items of equipment on shortened straps, tight under the left armpit, to prevent them flapping around.

Trumpeters

Until 1797 each troop of horse artillery was established with two drummers, which were in fact issued with bugle horns and acted as orderlies. With the change to the new uniform jacket in 1796, they were issued with trumpets and shown on the establishment as trumpeters. The dress of the early drummers is not known but the later trumpeters were dressed as the rest of the horse artillery with no known distinctions of dress other than their trumpets and cords.

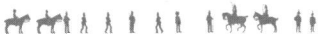

Key to Colour Plate

Plate 13. Royal Horse Artillery – other ranks' uniforms
1. Early version of the Tarleton helmet showing the straight edge to the crown and the early red turban.
2. Rear view of the later helmet showing the black turban and ribbons.
3. The helmet crown with the brass two-piece title strip and the holes by which the crest was tied on.
4. A reconstruction of the rear view of the early Chasseurs' coat worn in 1793, after Mercer and MacDonald.
5. View of the early helmet badge worn on the left side of the helmet.
6. A front view of the early Chasseurs' coat, after Mercer and Macdonald.
7. A reconstruction of the shoulder wings, after MacDonald.
8. Lacing of the short jacket adopted in about 1796. The lacing for Senior NCOs was gilt with embellishments to the collar and cuff.
9. Front view of the later jacket, *circa* 1810.
10. Rear view of the jacket, after Dighton, *circa* 1813.
11. Detail of collar braid of the short jacket, *circa* 1810.
12. Detail of cuff detail of the short jacket, *circa* 1810.
13. Detail of the rear cuff detail.
14. Early brass, horse artillery button, pre-1802.
15. Later brass button post-1802 but pre-1812.

Endnotes to Chapter 18
1. Duncan, 1892; p. 41.
2. Franklin, 2005: pp. 210–27.
3. Mercer, 1883: p. 45.
4. On 10 May 1815, the battle honour 'Leipzig' was authorized for those members of the Rocket Troop who had served there and the battle honours 'Waterloo' and 'Peninsula' were granted in a similar manner.
5. Mercer, 1883: p. 18: 'the gunners leaning to windward, with one hand generally upraised holding on to their helmets'.
6. MacDonald, 1983: pp. 45, 46.
7. Ibid: p. 45.
8. *'The Honourable Artillery Company, about 1796'*, painting in the Royal Collection, Catalogue no. 343.
9. Dighton, Denis, 'Royal Horse Artillery coming into action, *circa* 1815'. Paintings in the Royal Collection. Catalogue no. RL 0195.
10. Campbell, 1971: p. 115.
11. Parkyn, 1956: pp. 55–7: Campbell, 1971: p. 138.
12. Almack, 1900: plate 66.
13. National Archive, WO 47/2557: p. 340.
14. Dighton, op. cit.
15. Stadler and Sauerweid, op. cit.
16. MacDonald, 1985: p. 60.
17. National Archive, WO 47/2557: p. 400.
18. Franklin, 2005: p. 214.
19. Mercer, 1883: p. 375.
20. Blackmore, 1967: p. 106.
21. Royal Armouries, Leeds: object no. XII 843–44.
22. Blackmore, 1967: p. 106.
23. Adye, 1813: p. 359.

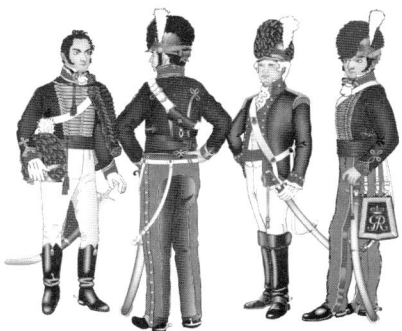

CHAPTER 19

Royal Horse Artillery – Officers

Introduction

Officers were generally dressed in the same manner as the men but with clothing of better quality , cut and gold lace. The officers went to some effort to ape the style of the light cavalry, the hussars in particular, and when away from headquarters they were well known for adopting almost any manner of dress that took their fancy and the extent of their embellishment was more often a function of the purse than regulations. In fact regulations referring to dress of the horse artillery of this period are very few and often their meaning or intent is unclear. Orders of 1806 required that

> Except at dress parades the blue Regimental overalls are to be worn until dinner-time in place of the blue pantaloons, which is to be the afternoon dress when at home. At all parades, whether mounted or dismounted, and during the day, the black velvet stock is to be worn, with an inch of shirt collar over it: no other white to be shown. In the evenings, it is requested that black silk handkerchiefs may be substituted with the same proportion of shirt collar over them. When officers are dressed for a ball, evening party, or dine out, they are to wear the jacket open, white pantaloons, plain white waist-coat (with sash over it), light sword, regulation sword-knot, black belt, with cocked hat and feather. In common a white leather sword-knot is to be worn. Spurs with horizontal rowels to be worn at all times.[1]

Head-dress

Officers' Tarleton helmets were of a similar pattern to that of the men but with gilt fittings, double or treble chains and a fuller bearskin crest. There are more examples with chin scales and while the later pattern helmets had them fitted, some of the officers must have purchased their own. Dighton's illustrations of the fashionable

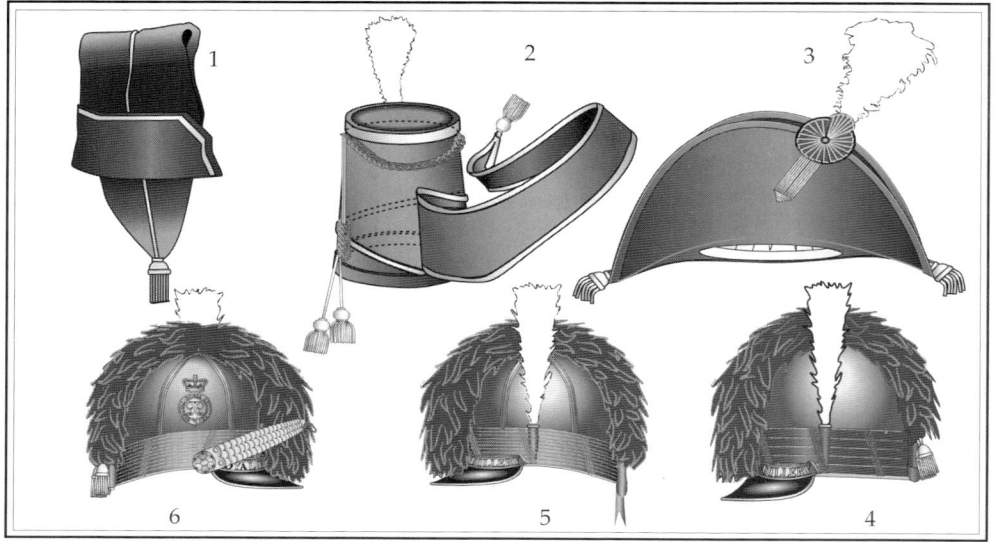

Figure 19.1. Hats of the officers of the horse artillery. The fatigue hat worn by both the horse and foot artillery and copied from the French 'police' (1). The 'Mirleton' adopted by the light cavalry and apparently worn by the horse artillery early in the century (2). The bicorn worn at levees and other formal dress occasions (3). The early version of the horse artillery helmet worn with a red turban (4), after a portrait of General Lawson. Views of the late versions of the Tarleton helmet recognised by the curved edge to the crown and the chin scales (5 & 6).

light cavalry bucks of the day show no such attachments, although some yeomanry officers are shown with them.[2] When worn, the chin scales were attached to each side of the helmet by large metal rosettes and tied together under the chin. They were often worn tied up by the leather laces at the front or back of the helmet. Mercer's recollections on the helmet noted that

> ... the helmet in the course of years varied in ornament and form, and although essentially the same, yet latterly was a very different, and far more elegant article of dress than when I first saw it in 1797. Here I confess in one point to be uncertain – I mean as to the nature of the turban or ornamental fillet, surrounding the lower part ; but I think it was of leopard-skin similar to the helmets of the Light Dragoons. This, however, could not have lasted long, for my first distinct recollection is of a crimson silk turban. On or about 1805 we succeeded ... in getting turbans of black velvet; for all the Light Dragoons wore black silk turbans, and, alas! even in those days the mania for imitating the Cavalry existed. The drivers (or Wee Gee Corps) had dark-blue turbans, which was a sad nuisance to us, so nearly resembling our own, that another change was obtained in a few months, to black silk, which delighted us all, for the Cavalry wore black silk. This might have been about the latter part of 1805, or beginning of 1806, and afterwards no alteration took place until their abolition. The form of the helmet formerly was very ugly, straight line at bottom, with the shade or peak sticking straight out, and very large. The bearskin low and poor. By degrees all this was changed, until, from an ugly, it became really an elegant article of dress. Like the cocked hat, one of its principal improvements consisted in an alteration of the base line from straight to curved, which, with the shade, made it droop over the face in front, and into the neck behind, thus at once improving its appearance and its qualities as a defence for the knowledge-box. At the same time, the bearskins were raised and made fuller. ... The helmet was latterly decorated, and perhaps rendered more perfect, by gilt scales attached to the sides. When not worn down, these were turned to and tied in rear of the bearskin.[3]

Other Hats

There are two paintings in the Royal Collection showing an officer and gunner of horse artillery wearing 'mirliton' bonnets. While there is no reference or authority for this mode of dress and the artist is unknown, it was very popular among the light dragoon and hussar officers of the period and it well may be that the horse artillery also adopted the fashion; the colour plates include an illustration after these paintings. Cocked hats continued as wear for horse artillery officers for dismounted dress occasions such as levees, balls, the dinning room and walking out with the vagaries of style and fashion being closely followed. Officers also wore fatigue hats in undress and in camp; they are known to have adopted those of a French pattern known as the 'bonnet de police'.[4]

Coats and Jackets

The first coat adopted by the horse artillery was in the same style as that worn by the French Chasseurs. This had a short-tailed coat worn open from the neck showing the waistcoat and worn 'hooked at the collar, it sloped away towards the half skirts which terminated it behind and had buttoned, red half facings, collar and cuffs. On the shoulders, officers wore a sort of wing made of interlinked rings and scales.[5] According to Mercer:

> the 1st Horse Artillery jacket, or at least the first I recollect. I never remember seeing any other English troops wear such a one, but think it was the Chasseur jacket in the French Army. Hooked at the collar, it sloped away toward the little skirt which terminated it behind, and had half facings. On the shoulders a sort of wing, made of interwoven rings; with leather breeches, long boots, and the helmet; this was rather a soldier-like service dress.[6]

The Royal Artillery Museum has a portrait of General Lawson who commanded the first troop of horse artillery in 1793. It shows the old style of Tarleton helmet with no chin scales and gold tassels at the rear of the turban. The jacket has a scarlet cutaway collar with a button at the front. The scarlet lapels are unlaced and secured to the jacket by a series of gilt buttons. The cuffs are unlaced but have a button at the centre with another on the sleeve above. He is wearing a sword belt over his right shoulder with an oval belt plate carrying a crown over a garter belt with the ordnance arms inside. On each shoulder is a red, bullion-fringed wing covered by rings and gilt scales.[7]

In about 1799, in common with the other ranks the officers adopted the short, single-breasted jacket laced across the front in the style adopted by the light cavalry regiments in 1796. This became the standard form of dress for the horse artillery, although the style was adapted by the younger officers of the regiment.[8] The jacket was of better quality and cut and more elaborately decorated than those of the other ranks and without shoulder cords.[9] Regulation braiding was rarely adhered to and there are no surviving regulations regarding the style of braid on the cuffs or collars and it seems that the purse and the wishes of the tailor were the most significant factors, as Mercer records:

> The Horse Artillery, which I joined in 1804, wore flat lace on their jackets, although the Light Dragoons had been wearing the cord lace for some years. The regulation jacket was to have on the breast equal blue and lace, that is, the space between the lace was to

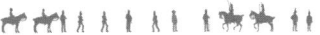

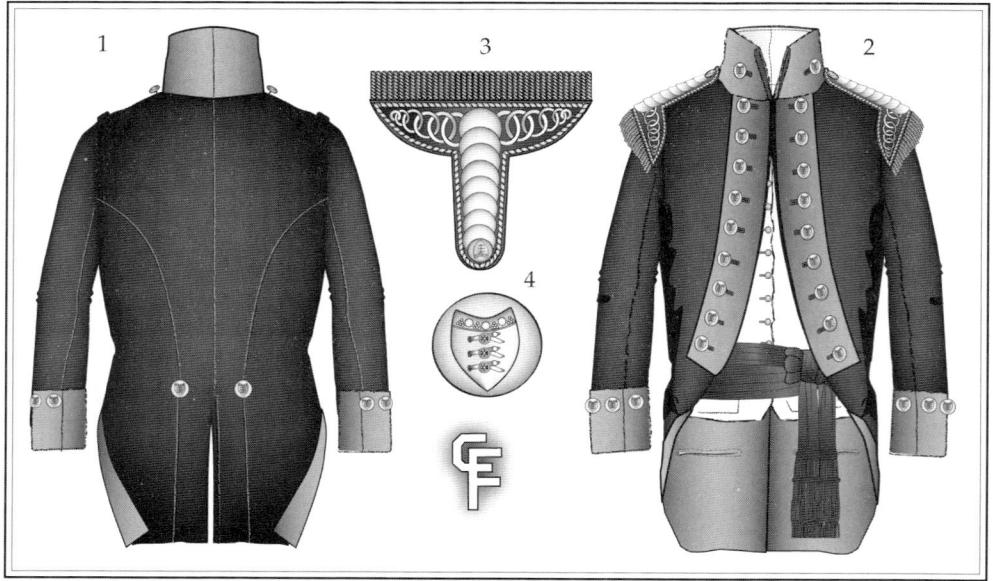

Figure 19.2. The early blue coatee with red facings of the officers of the horse artillery (1), after the description by Mercer and a reconstructed rear view (2). The shoulder wings, after Macdonald and Mercer, and the portraits of Lawson (3) and the early gilt button (4).

be of the same breadth as the lace itself. This, however, was too poor to satisfy us; and as regulations in those days were little adhered to away from headquarters, every one put on as much more lace as his fancy dictated or his purse permitted. For my part, my first jacket resembled a furze-bush in full blossom, for it was one mass of gold from the collar to the sash. No great space, after all, for the waists were then worn so exceedingly short that my sash was nearly under my arms ; and other jackets which I had afterwards, of more modest description, had only six loops of lace on the breast. ... Long before this we had got rid of our flat lace – once thought so fine, now so mean – and our jackets were laced with the cord as at present. I think this change took place in 1806.[10]

Mercer also recalls that closed collars were a novelty and the horse artillery affected collars that were low, very sloping and cut down in the front'.[11]

In 1812, regulations prescribed that

The officers of the Royal Horse Artillery are to wear jackets similar to the private men, with an aiguillette. In parade dress, they are to wear white leather pantaloons, and Hussar boots, with gold binding. Ordinary duties or on the march, they are to wear overalls of a colour similar to the private men's, and short surtout, which is calculated to be worn likewise as a pelisse on service. When attending the drawing room or levée, they may appear in long coats, with lapels and aiguillettes, the same as are worn with the jacket, but without lace on the seams: or in the Regimental jacket, as they may prefer. The officers of the Horse Artillery are likewise to wear cocked-hats, with the star loop, with dress regimentals.[12]

In these orders the term 'aiguillettes' is confusing; while the modern meaning is clear, the meaning in the orders is not understood. The use of such an embellishment was not general within any arm of the British army at this time and the exact meaning

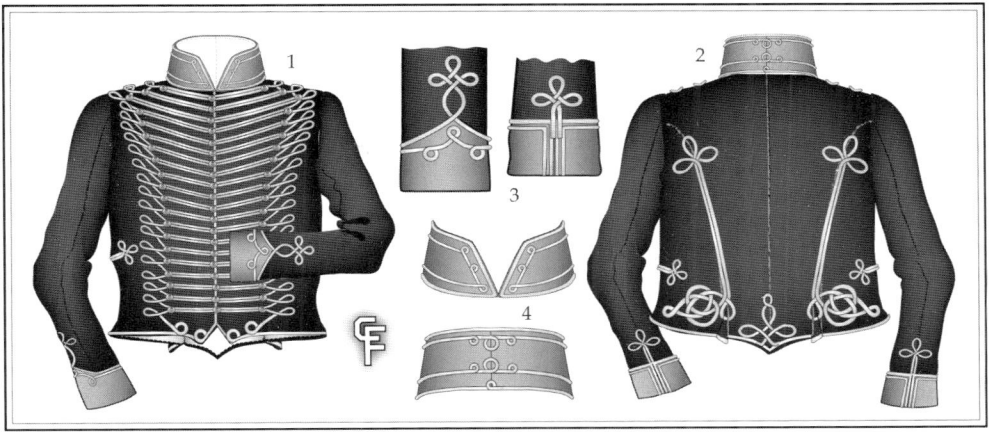

Figure 19.3. The blue, hussar-style jacket with scarlet facings of the officers of the horse artillery. The front view of the jacket with gold lace (1) based upon an existing jacket in the Royal Artillery Museum and contemporary portraits (1) and the rear view (2). The cuff details (3), note that the braid is set forward towards the front of the cuff and the braid at the front and rear of the collar (4).

is still unclear and there is no representation of any such decoration being worn. There is a surviving jacket, attributed to 1807, in the Royal Artillery Museum. This has three rows of ball buttons with 23 rows of flat gold lace from the waist to the opening at the neck and one further set of lace set equally spaced but nearer the shoulder. The lace at the neck slopes upwards and is six inches long from the centre to the outer button; that at the waist is set square and two and one half inches long. The jacket edge is laced all round and has two false pockets above the hips, outlined in gold lace and at the rear the jacket has two stitched flaps, known as pleats, which appear to be a deliberate style feature. The collar and cuffs are of scarlet superfine material and decorated in gold lace. The cuffs are pointed and the point and lace embroidery are set forward from the centre of the sleeve nearer the front seam. The patterns of lace shown are from this jacket, Campbell and surviving portraits of horse artillery officers.[13]　Illustrations of the coats and jackets of the horse artillery officers are given in the colour plates.

Buttons

The officers' buttons and badges were of a similar pattern to those of the men but in gilt. There are no recorded patterns for the use of belt plates, but they may have been worn when the sword was carried on a cross-belt with the first uniform.[14]

Rank Distinctions and Sashes

With the early uniforms the horse artillery wore gilt shoulder scales, but there are no records of the distinction of rank for officers of the Royal Horse Artillery. It seems that epaulettes may have been used when the hussar-style jacket was first adopted – a portrait of Quartermaster Wightman shows a bullion shoulder strap.[15] It is most probable that the senior officers had additional embellishments to the lacing on their uniforms and that rank distinctions were not worn.

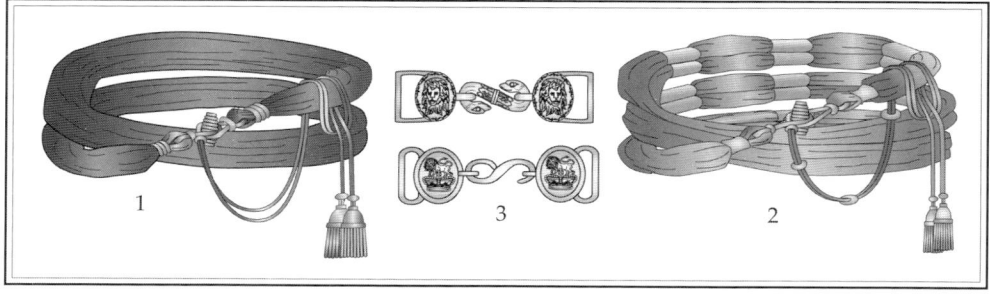

Figure 19.4. Initially the horse artillery used the standard crimson sash of a similar style to that of the foot artillery but they are recorded as soon adopting the whip sash (1) along with all the other accoutrements associated with the light cavalry. Later, by 1815 the barrel sash (2) was copied from the hussar regiments. Also shown are two gilt waist belt clasps of the period (3).

When the horse artillery was first formed the officers were required to wear the crimson silk net sash, which went several times round the waist and tied at the left hip with fringed ends. They soon adopted the whip pattern secured with cords and tassels and by 1815, the barrel sashes of the hussars were a commonly adopted item.

Stocks and Handkerchiefs

Stocks were worn and fashion dictated that the chin be buried in elaborate white linen; in the evenings black silk handkerchiefs were worn tied at the neck.[16] The portrait of Captain Bogue shows him wearing a black silk neck cloth tied at the front. Shirt collars were later substituted and the peaks or dog-ears were required to be worn out under the chin:

> The exact period when the shirt-collar began to be substituted in the shape of 'dog's ears,' I cannot precisely say, but think it must have been about 1810. In the Horse Artillery these became almost regulation, but I took it into my head that all black was more soldier-like, consequently would not wear them. One day when our two splendid troops were drawn up on Rushmere Heath, by Ipswich, ranks open, and every moment expecting the arrival of His Royal Highness George Prince Regent, by whom we were to be reviewed, Sir Augustus Frazer (then only Captain), who was one of the most precise little men in the world, happening to turn his head toward the lines to see that all was right, perceived me in front of G troop, all black, no dog's ears ! Hastening to me, he begged that I would make myself like the rest by pulling up my collar, as the Royal Family were noted for their quick perceptions in all matters of military uniform. I told him my collar was too low. Dilemma! Frazer was not to be refused, and it ended by his tearing off the blank leaf of a letter he luckily had in his sabretasche, with which we fitted up a pair of dog's ears which answered perfectly to receive and march past His Royal Highness, and were thrown away as soon as we began to manoeuvre.[17]

Breeches, Overalls and Pantaloons

Dress required white breeches or pantaloons worn with hussar boots usually with gold bindings. Dark blue cloth trousers were introduced in about 1802, with

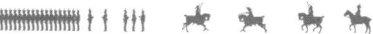

black leather down inside and about the leg in the shape of hessian boots. These buttoned down the outside and were usually worn over pantaloons. (Pantaloons were close-fitting breeches that fastened below the calf or at the foot.) These original overalls were strapped under the instep to prevent them from riding up the leg and it was common for the officers to use chains and these were often worn 'très à la mode' hooked up behind the knee. Blue pantaloons were popular for undress and walking out, and white kerseymere knee breeches were worn at levees and balls. Officers wore blue overalls until dinnertime in lieu of blue pantaloons,[18] and for evening dress, they had white pantaloons or breeches and hussar boots with gold binding.[19] Mercer's recollections on these various forms of dress are explicit and comprehensive:

> When I first got my commission, the Horse Artillery Officer clad his thighs in well-pipe clayed doe or buckskins; the Padnagge [this meaning is not known] in well-whitened kerseymere, fastened at the knee with four small buttons and a buckle. These, for aught I can remember, constituted the one only pair of thigh-cases for each service. Morning parade, evening parade, wet weather or fine, breakfast, dinner, tea-party, ball or court – always white breeches.

Mercer continues on the subject of legware:

> It was a sort of innovation when after a time the Foot Artillery assumed to themselves the skins, which eventually became also their uniform. Dark blue pantaloons (cloth)

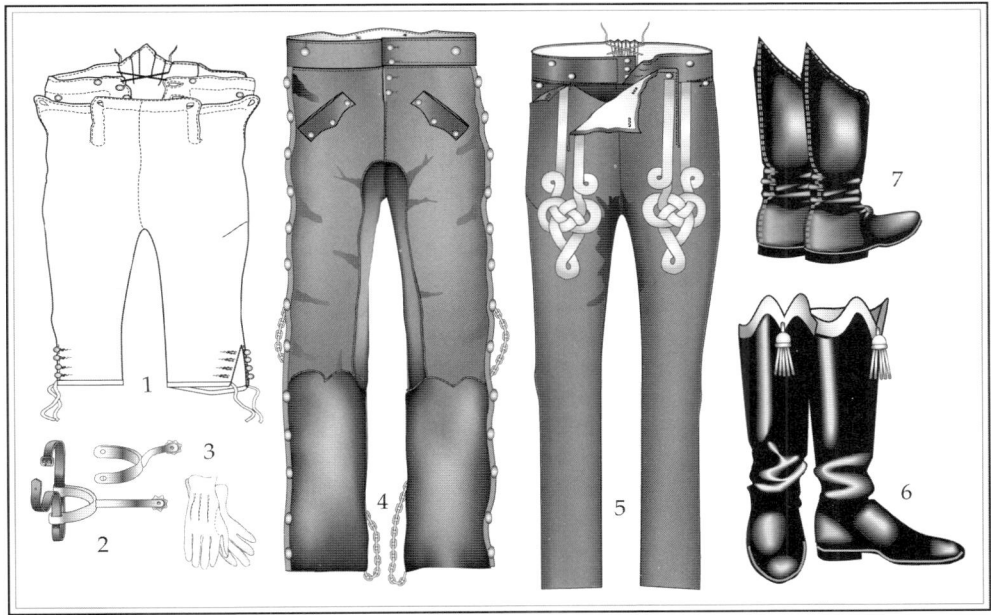

Figure 19.5. The necessaries of the horse artillery officer. The white doe or buckskin breeches (1), the early straight spurs and the later swan-necked spurs that screwed into the heel of the boot (2) and the white kid gloves of the officers (3). The early horse artillery blue overalls with red stripes, black leather strapping simulating hessian boots and worn with chains (4) later replaced by grey or pepper and salt overalls strapped with brown leathers. The dress blue pantaloons with gold lace on the thigh (5); red pantaloons are also recorded. The black leather hessian boots with gold tassels worn by officers (6) and the half-boots with the raised rear (7).

began to creep in about 1802 (though they had always been worn by Officers on expeditions, etc.), and we were very proud of ourselves when at out quarters we could thus dress, as it looked so like service. So far is all I know of the Foot Artillery. [Blue pantaloons permitted by a General Order in 1803 ; see Kane.] In the Horse Artillery, besides our leather breeches, we wore the blue cloth pantaloons for common undress parades, and the same with gold lace for full dress, etc. The fronts of these were profusely decorated nearly halfway down the thigh, in the same style as worn by drum-majors of aujourd'hui [1840]. For marching order, we had blue cloth overalls, having leather down the inside of the thighs, and about the whole of the leg, in the shape of Hessian boots. These articles were then what the name implied, really overalls, being worn over pantaloons and buttoning from top to bottom outside; the pockets were in front of the groin, set slopingly. To keep the overall down, instead of straps, we used chains, about the size and made like curb-chains, which, when walking about, instead of being under the foot, were suspended across the back of the leg by one of the buttons near the knee, as in the annexed. These chains, being kept highly polished, really looked very well, at least, to eyes of those days. The dandyism of the day consisted in having them very long, half a yard, par exemple (for undress parades and common wear). For dress, foot parades, etc., we had white stocking-net fitting quite as tight as the blue mentioned below. One of the Buenos Ayres Hussars fell desperately in love with a pair I wore at a ball, and teased me the whole night to sell them to him.[20]

It was only after the war that white breeches and hessian boots were abolished for the horse artillery and blue-grey overalls and Wellington boots were adopted for all orders of dress.[21] There are also records of scarlet pantaloons embroidered with gold lace being worn.[22] Mercer recalls:

At a subsequent period pepper-and-salt coloured overalls were worn, and the shades or tints of grey were altered more than once; but when this took place I know not now, nor can I call to mind when the red stripe down the side was introduced – I think somewhere about 1810 or 1811. At the same time the black leather inside the thighs, and boot below, gave place to brown leather, and instead of finishing in a boot, there was only a band of 3 or 4 inches round the bottes to save the cloth from the stirrup. The present purply half-tint was introduced in 1815. I remember Frazer showing me some of it one day at Paris, as a new thing.[23]

Boots, Shoes and Spurs

Initially, with the light dragoon uniform, black leather knee boots were worn which reached to the knee. With the change to the hussar jacket, black leather hussar or hessian boots were worn. With overalls, long or short boots were worn and with pantaloons short boots or shoes. The quality of this footwear was probably better as most of the officers had them made to measure or purchased their own. On this subject again, Mercer is very descriptive:

The first time I saw the Hussar boot, it was worn by a very handsome, well-made man, and I thought it grand. Captain Foy had just arrived from Vienna, and I saw him at practice in the Warren, somewhere in 1798, for I was a Cadet … (The heels worn in 1804 by exquisites were very high and very small, tapering too; just such as women used to wear some forty or fifty years before, par exemple.) The Hussar boot is well known at the present day, rising in front, decorated with a silk tassel, and having a seam down each side. A sort of half-boot, rising in front like this, but having the double

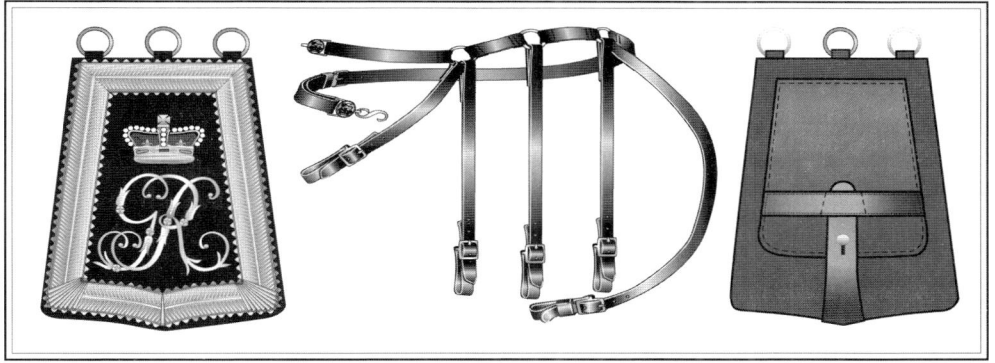

Figure 19.6. Reconstruction of a horse artillery sabretache. The pocket at the rear was used to carry papers and maps. Officers wore their swords on a waist belt and a black version is described in the orders for dress occasions. These belts would have been fitted with extra straps for the sabretache.

seam behind, became fashionable about the beginning of the century, and I shall not in a hurry forget the sensation caused at Plymouth Dock by Lieutenant Anderson (afterwards Colonel Morehead) making his appearance at the promenade in front of Government House one Sunday evening in a pair of these. 'Oh, the puppy!' was heard on all sides. 'If he has not silk tassels to his boots! Only think! silk tassels on boots'. The greatest of all comforts and improvements, in my opinion, was when (after the general adoption of the trousers in imitation of overalls) we ceased casing our poor legs in leather, and substituted the short or ankle boot for the high Hussar … before dismissing the boot and its appendages I must say a word about the iron heels, which, like many other parts of our military costume, have been borrowed from the Germans. In 1802, the Hompesch Chasseurs a Cheval were quartered at Cork, and long shall I remember the impression produced whenever I met a party of these (dismounted) marching through the streets, the heavy tread of so many iron heels on the pavement, accompanied by regular clang of their steel scabbards and jingling of their carbine slings, the solemn unvarying features of their bronzed and mustachioed faces. To me there was something exquisitely picturesque and imposing in all this. We did not begin to wear iron heels for a year or two after this, my first recollection of them being in 1804.[24]

Originally, the horse artillery wore a long straight spur with a spiked rowel strapped to the boot,[25] but by the end of the Napoleonic period the steel curved or swan-necked spur, which screwed directly into the heel of the boot, was in common use.

Spurs … Like all other articles of dress, they went through a great variety of vagaries in the course of forty years … The Horse Artillery (and I believe the Cavalry) used to wear a plated spur (the men's steel), with a long straight neck. It was not until 1805 or 1806 that we first began to wear spurs screwed on the heel of the boot. The form I do not remember, but think they had crooked necks.[26]

Sabretache

The sabretache was a fashionable item of hussar wear and while there was no standard pattern or regulations relating to them, official records clearly record their use after 1808,[27] and Mercer recalls wearing his at Waterloo.[28] No surviving examples are known to exist and the illustrations of the sashes, sabretache and

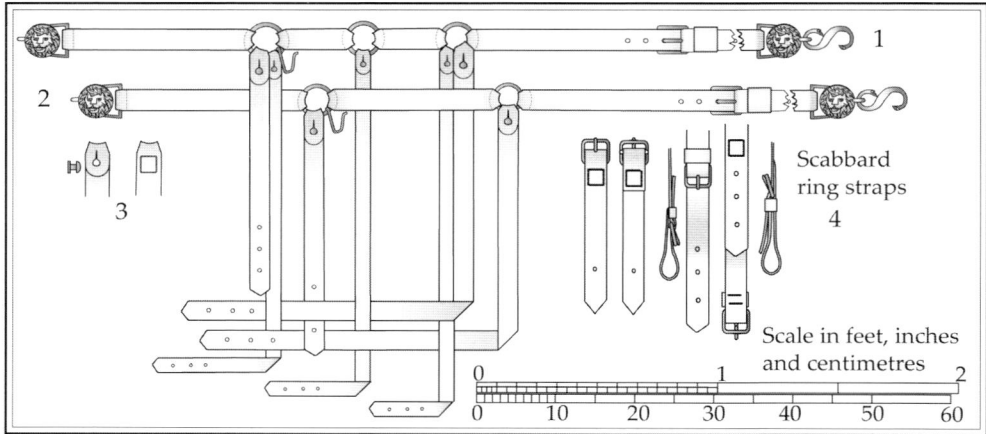

Figure 19.7. Officers' sword belts. A four-piece waist belt fitted with straps for a sabretache (1); a black version was worn for dress. A three-part waist belt with two slings for the sword (2). Different methods of attaching the sword slings (3) and the different method of attaching the scabbard rings to the sword slings (4).

pelisse worn by the horse artillery officers given above and in the colour plates are based upon the practices of the time and the paintings that depict these items worn by horse artilllery officers.

Pouch Belt and Sword Belt

There is no evidence that pouch belts were worn in this period by other than the Rocket Troop, but individual officers may well have affected their use. With the first uniform the officers used the cross-belt with an oval plate, but when they changed to the hussar-style sword it was worn from a waist belt. The belt would have followed the pattern of that described for the other ranks but would have been of better quality and fittings. When the sabretache was worn, extra slings were needed and the pattern of waist belt worn may have followed that of the light cavalry with two slings for the sword and three extra slings for the sabretache. Black leather sword belts were worn for dress in the evenings.[29]

Pelisse

Mercer also recalls wearing his pelisse at Waterloo.[30] There is a watercolour portrait of Captain Bogue who commanded the Rocket Troop in 1813, which clearly shows him wearing a dark blue pelisse with black braid and black cord barrels instead of buttons, the fur being grey astrakhan. A similar pelisse is depicted in a later portrait of Colonel Frazer.[31] In 1806 there are records of a blue pelisse richly laced in gold, lined with crimson plush with a scarlet waistcoat.[32] Mercer recalls:

> About 1805 we first began to wear pelisses, and poor shabby concerns they would be thought in the present day, although we then looked upon them as marvelously fine. They were trimmed with some brown fur, such as was then in common use for ladies' tippets, etc., perhaps sable – don't know; the braiding on the breast also was sparse and of very small cord. Altogether it was a shabby thing. Somewhere about 1808 the pelisse,

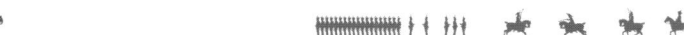

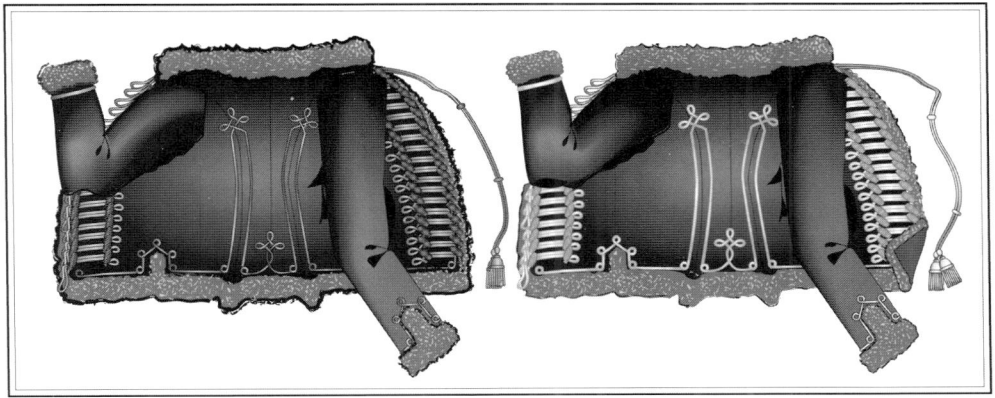

Figure 19.8. Officers' pelisses after contemporary portraits and descriptions. In the watercolour of Captain Bogue by Slater he is shown wearing the pelisse with black braid and black barrels. The use of black braid and barrel buttons seems to have been a pattern adopted by horse artillery officers, although both styles are recorded. The lining was red silk and the fur grey, astrakhan.

only tolerated before, became a regular and authorized part of our uniform. The sable fur gave place to the grey astrachan, the braiding became richer with barrel buttons, and the whole affair more Hussarish.[33]

Sword

Officers used a slightly more elaborate version of the light cavalry sword, the hilt was a little lighter than the regulation, of better quality and the curved blade was decorated, often being blued and having gold-filled engraving. Officers chose to wear swords of a variety of styles and were apparently permitted to do so; on dress occasions, horse artillery officers carried a sword with a very curved blade and Mameluke-style ivory hilt. It was a purely decorative weapon and Mercer remarks on the weapon at length:

> In the Horse Artillery, besides the large regulation sabre, we had a small undress one; but in the form of this we were not particular, every one adopting that most pleasing to his fancy, and this was usually so crooked as to be useless as anything but a reap-hook. The regulation itself, though an excellent sword for cutting, was bad for using the point, which was not so much insisted on in the drills then as now, since we have experienced the efficacy of the long French straight pusher. Dandyism with the sword was to wear it trailing along the ground, and some Cavalry beaux used to have a little treek or wheel in the end of the scabbard. It was common, nay, almost general, to have the points of the scabbards worn out by this trailing.[34]

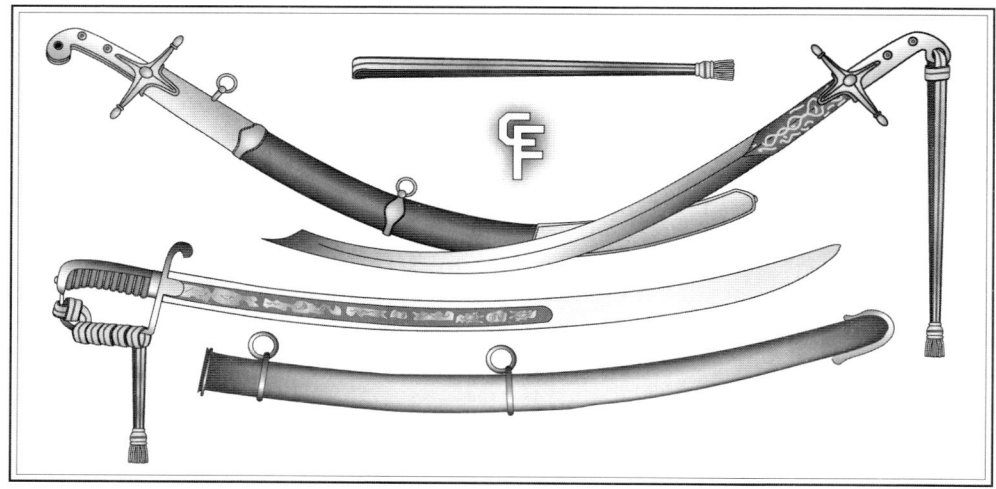

Figure 19.9. Mameluke type of sabre affected by officers of the horse artillery for dress and walking out and the scarlet and gilt sword knot of an officer. An officer's version of the 1796 light cavalry sabre, although some used the standard issue version.

Key to Colour Plates

Plate 14. Royal Horse Artillery – officers' uniforms, part 1
1. The early pattern Tarleton helmet without chin scales and with the straight edge to the crown.
2. A late pattern helmet with the curved edge to the crown and the black turban.
3. A right side view of the late pattern helmet with chin scales attached.
4. Rear view of the early chasseurs' coat, after MacDonald and Mercer.
5. The gilt wings with scales and rings, attributed to the early coat by Mercer.
6. Front view of the early pattern chasseurs' coat, after MacDonald and Mercer.
7. The early pattern gilt button.
8. The later pattern gilt button adopted at the same time as the jackets changed.
9. Collar detail of the short jacket.
10. Rear view of the hussar-style short jacket, after Campbell.
11. Front and rear cuff detail after a surviving jacket, after Campbell.
12. The front view of the later hussar-style jacket with gold lace, based upon the style in contemporary portraits.

Plate 15. Royal Horse Artillery – officers' uniforms, part 2
1. French-style fatigue cap adopted by the horse artillery, after Mercer.
2. The cocked hat worn by horse artillery officers on formal dismounted duties.
3. Mirleton-type cap shown worn by the early horse artillery, after paintings in the Royal Collection.
4. Records clearly show that horse artillery officers carried sabretaches in dress and when on campaign, and while there is no surviving example a possible reconstruction of the front view has been made.
5. Officers wore their swords on a waist belt and a black version is described in orders for dress. These belts would have been fitted with the extra straps for the sabretache and the standard buckles of the period.
6. Typical rear view of a sabretache showing the pocket used to carry maps and papers.

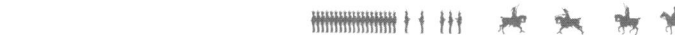

7. Initially the horse artillery used the standard sash of a similar style to that of the foot artillery, but they are recorded as soon adopting the early whip sash.
8. Officers' pelisses, after contemporary portraits. In the watercolour of Captain Bogue by Slater he is shown wearing the pelisse with black braid and black barrels; the use of black braid and barrel buttons seems to have been a pattern adopted by horse artillery officers.
9. Early and later-style officers' gilt ball buttons.
10. Dress pattern of a pelisse; both styles are recorded. The lining was red silk and the fur grey astrakhan.
11. Hussar-type sash adopted later by the horse artillery, after Campbell.
12. Different styles of waist belt clasps.

Endnotes to Chapter 19

1. Duncan, 1872; pp. 42–3.
2. Portrait of Lt William Palgrave, Yarmouth Volunteer Cavalry, 1799.
3. MacDonald, 1983: pp. 45–6.
4. Mercer, 1883: p. 52.
5. MacDonald, 1983: p. 49 and plate VII.
6. Ibid: pp. 48–9.
7. Royal Artillery Museum, Reference PT 1365.
8. MacDonald, 1983: p. 48.
9. Campbell, 1971: p. 30.
10. MacDonald, 1983: pp. 47–8.
11. Mercer, 1883: p. 231.
12. Duncan, 1872: p. 43.
13. Campbell, 1971: pp. 30–1.
14. Parkyn, 1956: pp. 54–7; Campbell, 1971: pp. 137–9.
15. Campbell, 1971: plate VI.
16. General Orders, 1 November 1806; Macdonald, 1985: p. 33.
17. MacDonald, 1985: p. 53.
18. General Orders, 1 November 1806; Macdonald, 1985: p. 33.
19. MacDonald, 1985: pp 34–50.
20. Ibid: pp 49–50.
21. Ibid: p. 60.
22. 'King Georges wardrobe accounts': *Journal of Army Historical Research*, Vol. 25, 1947.
23. MacDonald, 1985: p. 50.
24. Ibid: pp. 51–2.
25. General Orders, 1 November 1806; Macdonald, 1985: p. 33.
26. MacDonald, 1985: p. 51.
27. Ibid: p 49.
28. Mercer, 1883: pp. 58, 129.
29. Campbell, 1971: p. 61.
30. Mercer, 1883: p. 178.
31. Campbell, 1971: p. 13.
32. 'King Georges wardrobe accounts': *Journal of Army Historical Research*, Vol. 25, 1947.
33. MacDonald, 1985: p. 49.
34. Ibid. pp. 54.

CHAPTER 20

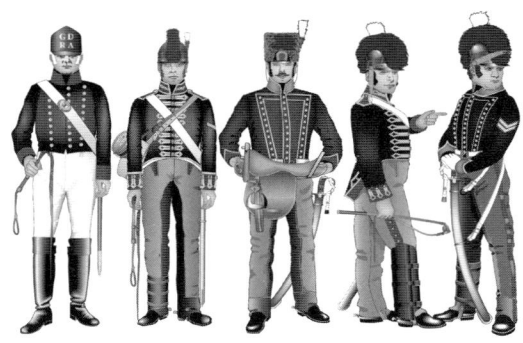

Royal Artillery Drivers

Introduction

At the start of the Napoleonic period the Foot brigades of the field artillery still hired civilian drivers and horses to move their guns, but this proved so unsatisfactory that in September 1794 a permanent corps of 'Captains, Commissaries and Drivers' was established and the men attested as soldiers and called drivers instead of wagoners.[1] Parties of men and horses of this corps were attached to field artillery brigades as the situation demanded. This corps was found to be unsatisfactory and was disbanded in 1801 and replaced by a similar body, the 'Corps of Gunner Drivers'. This proved equally unsatisfactory and was soon disbanded and replaced in 1806 by the 'Corps of Royal Artillery Drivers'. This corps answered directly to the Board of Ordnance but continued to remain as a separate entity to the artillery. It was administered by its own officers for pay and subsistence but answered to the brigade commander in all other respects. The Corps of Royal Artillery Drivers was disbanded in 1822 and their duties were taken over by 'gunner-drivers' of artillery. Throughout the Napoleonic period the foot artillery had to rely upon horses and drivers belonging to another corps, only the horse artillery having their own drivers.

Known by the nickname the 'Wee Gee Corps', the drivers were not highly regarded by the foot artillery with whom they served and the artillery personnel often resented the similarity of dress. The uniform of the drivers changed several times and there are at least four uniforms attributed to them during the Napoleonic Wars, but in comparison with other arms, little is known of their uniform and there are few orders and regulations to give guidance.

The first comes from the early period of the Captains, Commissaries and Drivers, the second is that adopted by the Corps of Gunner Drivers and the third is attributed to the Corps of Royal Artillery Drivers and is similar to that worn by the Royal

Artillery. The fourth, similar in style to that of the Royal Waggon Train, is attributed to the corps after 1815 and may have been introduced to make a clear distinction between the drivers and artillery personnel.

A battery inspection of 1798 notes that each gun was drawn by three horses in file with hired drivers in white smocks with blue collar and cuffs. A print by Carrington Bowles in the British Museum shows a plain frock but with a Mother Shipton hat. Mercer remarks:

> The first brigades … were formed by Major Spearman in 1800, … They consisted of medium 12-prs, I think six each (there were two brigades), drawn by six horses each, two and two, the drivers (then a new corps) mounted as postillions – quite a novelty … At the same time Lieutenant (now Colonel) Wallace was drilling another brigade of light 6-prs. for the same destination, but to be attached as battalion guns to the Guards. The equipment of these was entirely different from Spearman's brigades. The guns were drawn by three horses each, with common cart harness and chain traces. These were conducted by contract drivers, dressed in canvas frocks, like our gunners' undress, with blue fall-down collars. One walked by the leader, the other by the wheelers, and both carried long waggon whips.[2]

It seems clear that there was a considerable variation in the dress of the drivers as the field artillery evolved from the early battalion guns to the later brigades present at Waterloo.

There are few contemporary illustrations of drivers and those that exist present a confusing picture. The early dress is not clear but in 1793, they were issued with leather caps and frocks, both at much less expense than hats and jackets of the foot artillery.[3] In 1794, they were issued with coats, waistcoats, shirts, stocks etc.[4] Pyne in his illustrations of 1800 shows a driver in frock-coat and leather cap; he is leading the horses of a battalion gun but the picture also shows a mounted gunner in a Tarleton helmet and the early horse artillery jacket. Atkinson in 1807 shows a plain blue jacket with red collar and cuffs, the hat being versions of the Woolwich leather fatigue cap. Both these pictures contain unexplained anomalies. Vernet gives two views of drivers in the artillery-style jacket, one showing a mounted driver and the other a driver and an infantry private. These two pictures generally agree but again present certain anomalies. There are illustrations by Hamilton Smith and Sauerweid and these show a later version of the uniform, apparently based upon that of the Royal Waggon Train.[5]

Several schools of thought have attempted to clarify this confusion. One suggests that different battalions may have worn different uniforms, another that one style was worn by the drivers of the foot artillery and another by those of the horse artillery. The most commonly accepted view is that the uniform evolved from the frock to the plain blue jacket when they became 'Gunner–Drivers' in 1801 and then to the artillery jacket after they became 'Royal Artillery Drivers' in 1806, coming under the auspices of the Board of Ordnance.[6]

Where drivers are concerned little is certain, but on balance, it seems that it was intended they adopted the wagon train style of jacket at the very end of the war. The horse artillery, formed in 1793, recruited their own drivers and horses as an integral part of their establishment and this was formalised by a Royal Warrant of 1801 when it was ordered they be mustered and paid with the troop to which they

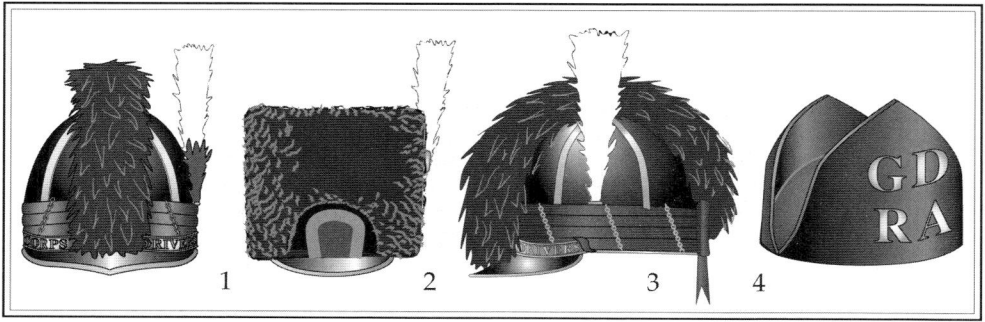

Figure 20.1. Corps of Drivers' hats. Front view of early pattern Tarleton helmet with blue turban and red base to plume after Vernet (1). Farrier busby after Sauerweid (2) and side view of driver helmet (3) and the Woolwich style leather fatigue cap (4).

were attached.[7] It may be, before 1799, the drivers were dressed differently; but when the horse artillery changed their uniform to the dolman, it seems that their drivers followed suit; after this the drivers of the horse artillery were dressed in the same uniform as the rest of that arm.[8] However, it must be remembered that drivers from the Corps of Drivers were commonly attached to the horse artillery to supplement their numbers and it seems improbable that these attached personnel were issued with different uniforms, so both forms could be present when this occurred.

Headware

The drivers of the early period are shown wearing the Woolwich leather fatigue-hat, common to the artillery and Woolwich-associated arms. In 1795 they were issued with helmets,[9] these were the light cavalry Tarleton helmet, but they are generally shown as those of the older style. This helmet was similar to the early pattern worn by the horse artillery except that it had a dark blue turban and the brass band above the peak carried the embossed title 'Corps of Artillery Drivers'.[10] Generally, the plume is shown as white, but Vernet shows white-over-red. According to Sauerweid, the farrier wore a black busby of a style commonly worn by farriers of the light cavalry.

Jacket, *circa* 1794

The early illustrations suggest the jacket worn by the drivers was a short blue one; it had a plain red collar and cuffs and the unlaced front carried buttons in three columns of eight that narrowed to the waist. The only illustration of this jacket is in the watercolour by Atkinson.[11]

Artillery-style Jacket

The jacket shown in the two illustrations by Vernet from 1815 is similar to that of the foot artillery. The other ranks' jackets were single breasted with short skirts and lined with white linen. The skirts of the jacket are shown with oblique pockets and

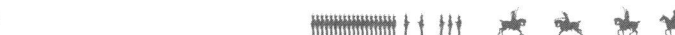

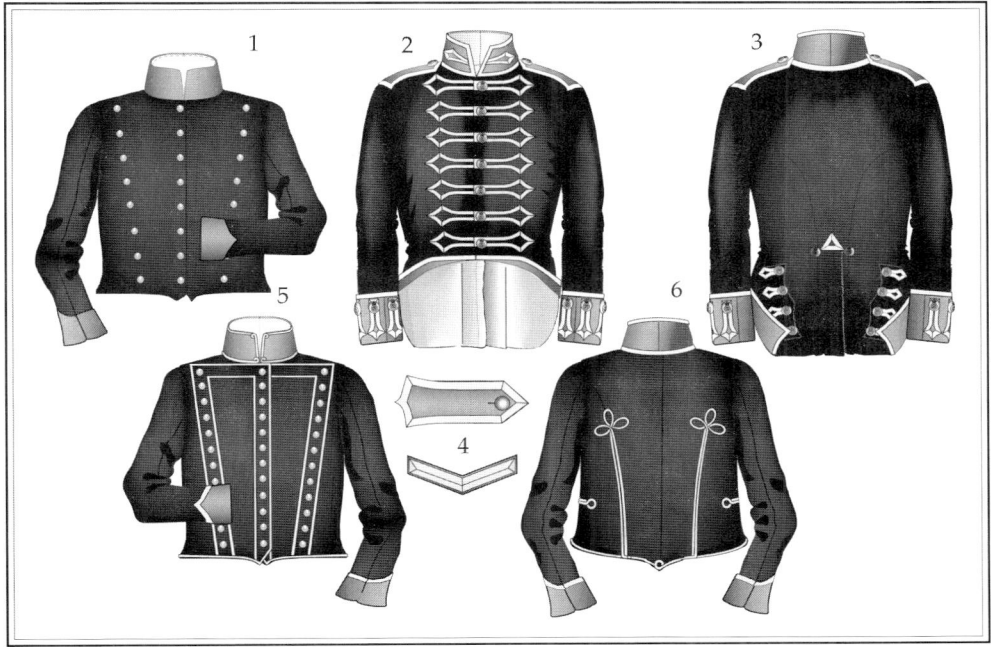

Figure 20.2. Corps of Drivers' blue jacket with red facings and yellow lace. Front view of early jacket after Atkinson (1). The front view of the artillery style jacket after Vernet in 1815 (2) and rear view (3). Bastion shaped shoulder strap after Vernet with the single chevron of the 2nd Corporal (4). Front view of later jackets after Sauerweid and Hamilton Smith (5) and possible rear view (6).

the rear of the jacket was decorated by a triangle of lace between the hip buttons. The turnbacks were faced with red serge and edged with yellow lace. Dependent upon the height of the wearer the coat front had some eight equally spaced, bastion-laced buttonholes. The regulation yellow lace loops were some four inches long at the neck reducing to some three inches long at the waist, but those shown by Vernet are considerably longer and wider and the red shoulder straps are shown as bastion shaped at the outer edge and lined about with yellow lace. The collar is shown red, three to four inches deep and cut away at the front to reveal the black leather stock worn underneath. It is lined about by flat yellow worsted lace and had a bastion loop of yellow lace at each front edge. The cuffs of red serge are square, four inches deep. They carried the same distinction as the artillery: four, equally spaced buttoned loops of yellow lace with the front pair astride the sleeve seam and a yellow lace edging to the top of the cuff. In 1796 it was noted that the drivers' coats

> Might be converted to the use of the marching battalions by altering the linings and facings, which would cost 7 shillings and 2 pence each coat.[12]

Later Jacket

Another jacket is attributed to the corps in 1815 or 1816. This is taken from the painting by Alexander Sauerweid in the Royal Collection and from the plate of Hamilton Smith; the style of the jacket illustrated was similar to that shown for the Royal Waggon Train, but is blue-faced red. The front carries three vertical rows of twelve, small brass buttons lined about by a frame of yellow lace to form a plastron-shaped front. There are no details of the reverse of the jacket, but it is probable that the rear seams would have been lined with a simple pattern with crow's feet in yellow lace, and any side pockets would have been similarly figured. No shoulder straps are shown. The red cuffs are shown pointed and edged with plain, flat, yellow lace showing no border to the cuff. The collar is shown as red, three and a half to four inches deep and cut away at the front to reveal the black leather stock. It was lined about the edge with flat, yellow lace, figured at each corner.

Buttons

No surviving description exists of the buttons worn by this corps, but artillery or ordnance buttons may have been worn with the later jackets.

Rank Distinctions of Non-commissioned Officers

What rank distinctions were worn is not known but the drivers may have adopted the same system as used by the artillery. When chevrons were formally introduced they were probably also worn in the same manner as the artillery, except the single chevron denoted a rank of Second Corporal, a rank peculiar to the Corps of Drivers. Junior NCOs wore yellow worsted chevrons mounted on a red background; Senior Non-commissioned officers probably wore a gilt lace of better quality. In the Peninsula, Dickson awarded his better drivers the distinction of wearing a red stripe on their left arm.[13]

Sashes

Regulations prescribed that senior NCOs wore a crimson worsted sash over the sword belt and tied at the hip.

Breeches, Overalls and Trousers

Ceremonial and dress occasions dictated white breeches and black hessian boots, but for marching order, undress and active service, grey pepper and salt overalls were generally worn over ankle-length boots with boxed, swan-necked spurs. The exact pattern may well have varied from man to man or troop to troop, but the pattern most usually shown suggests that the overalls were lined and cuffed with brown leather and carried one red stripe down the outer, buttoned, fly. In all respects, they were similar to those described earlier.

Greatcoats

Drivers were issued with greatcoats and these were probably carried strapped to the top front arch of the saddle. The example illustrated by Sauerweid shows a large, loose-fitting garment with a large collar, pointed cuffs and a cape at the shoulders.

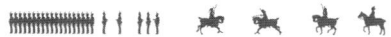

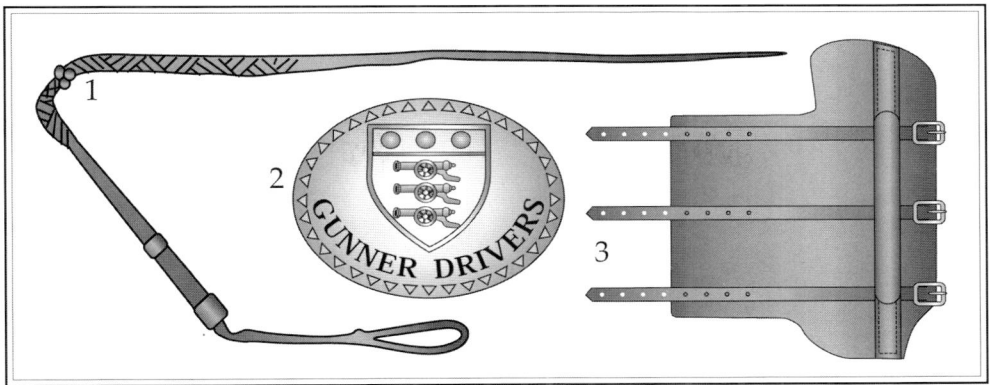

Figure 20.3. Corps of Drivers. Short leather whip used to control the off horse (1), driver's belt plate, after Parkyn (2), and the driver's leg protector worn on the right leg to prevent it being crushed between the horses in double or triple draught (3).

Leg Protector and Whip

Drivers were issued with a special leg protector. This was worn on the right leg strapped over the foot and leg below the knee. The purpose was to prevent the leg on the off side from being crushed between the horses when riding in double draught. It was made of black leather and secured by three straps around the lower leg; with a leather-covered, 20-inch iron plate secured on the outside. Each driver also carried a short leather whip, used when mounted, to control the off horse.

Weapons

Drivers were equipped with the 1796 light cavalry sabre or the artillery sword. Drivers mounted on riding horses are shown with pistols in holsters carried at the front of the saddle.

Sword Belt

The drivers are usually shown with the sword worn on a hanger carried over the left shoulder. This terminated in a ring from which the two sword slings were suspended. NCOs are shown wearing the waist belt.

Belt Plates

There are no records of any official pattern worn by the drivers. There is one brass plate that may have been worn on the helmet or as a belt plate. This carried the inscription 'GUNNER DRIVERS' below a shield containing the Ordnance arms of three cannon balls over three cannon. It is believed to originate from the Peninsula period.[14]

Valise

The drivers carried their personal effects in a blue valise strapped to the cantle of the saddle.

Accoutrements

These were standard items issued to all arms. They were usually worn by mounted personnel, tight up under the left arm with the straps short, to prevent them bouncing about when on the move, but Vernet shows them hanging loose. The two-pint 'Italian' water bottle was a flat wooden barrel seven inches in diameter and four inches deep, with iron hoops and a one-inch wide, brown leather strap secured by brackets. It was usually painted blue and carried the Board or Ordnance cipher (the Broad Arrow) and usually some individual troop or regimental marking. The haversack or bread bag was of canvas or linen with a two-button flap and a three-inch wide strap of the same material. It was usually fawn or off white in colour and adjusted by a buckle and loop on the left strap. Both were worn over the left shoulder.

Riding Saddle

The riding saddle shown by Vernet is the Hungarian type and probably dates to 1815, as it is shown with a white sheepskin shabraque with red Van Dyke edging. The blue valise is carried strapped at the rear of the saddle and the harness is brown with a double bridle and head collar.

Endnotes to Chapter 20

1. Duncan, 1872: p. 58.
2. MacDonald, 1985: p. 56.
3. National Archive, WO 47/2556: p. 409.
4. Ibid, WO 47/2557: p. 283.
5. Sauerweid, AI: *Driver and Farrier, Corps of Drivers*, painting in the collection of Her Majesty the Queen; Stadler: *Corps of Drivers and Royal Waggon Train*, aquatint after Hamilton Smith, Colnaghi & Co., 1815.
6. MacDonald, 1985: pp. 30–6.
7. Duncan, 1872: p. 136.
8. Hamilton Smith, 1815.
9. National Archive, WO 47/2559: p. 1,413.
10. MacDonald, 1985: p. 45.
11. Atkinson, 1807: *Artillery on the Move.*
12. National Archive, WO 47/2561: p. 609.
13. Dickson, 1908: p. 720.
14. Parkyn, 1956: pp. 55–7.

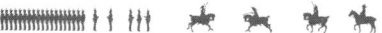

Glossary

This glossary supplies a definition of terms appropriate to the period and the artillery in particular; they may not have the same meaning in other contexts. One example is the carbine; in this period it is the generic term for a weapon usually shorter than the standard, later the term was more specific and referred to a small arm where the round did not complete one full revolution before leaving the barrel.

Accoutrements	Parts of military equipment other than clothing or weapons.
Advance chains	Chains fitted to the front of the axletree to facilitate manhandling the gun carriage.
Ammunition	All forms of powder, cartridges, artillery rounds, rockets and small arms ammunition.
Artificer	Specialist tradesman who repaired and maintained equipment.
Astragal	Decorative raised ring or section at various places on the outside of the piece.
Axle band	Bracket used to retain the axle bracket of the gun carriage.
Axletree	The part to which the wheels are attached. Initially axletrees were made of wood; later they were made of iron.
Axletree bed	Wooden housing for the iron axletree.
Base ring	The rearmost ring of metal that encircles the breech and maximum diameter of a piece. It is from the rear of this to the muzzle that the length of the piece was measured.
Battery	Later generic term used for a grouping of guns but not used during this period.
Ball	Inert sphere of lead or cast iron fired from a piece of ordnance or small arm.
Battalion gun	Field piece attached to infantry.
Battery	Description for a group of guns positioned to form a set defensive or siege role. Not used at this time to describe a group of guns in a field role.
Belford	General William Belford (1709–80) designer of the widely used light 6-pr gun.
Block Trail	Trail of a gun carriage made from single piece of wood.
Blomefield	Sir Thomas Blomefied, Bart (1744–1822), designer of ordnance, later Inspector-General of Artillery.
Bomb	Alternative name for a common shell also a vessel for discharging mortars.
Bombardier	In the artillery context a rank between corporal and gunner designated by one chevron.

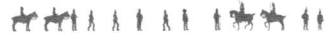

Bore	See cylinder.
Bottom	See wooden bottom.
Bracket	That part of a gun carriage that supported the trunnions of the gun also known as cheeks.
Bracket Trail	Gun carriage with two parallel or diverging cheeks that formed the trail.
Breast	The front part of the cheeks or the leading transom of a gun carriage.
Breast chains	See advance chains.
Breech	The rear of the piece between the vent and the base ring, but not including the cascable.
Bricole	French term for a rope used as a drag rope for a gun.
Brigade	Collective name for an established number of men and guns within the foot arm of the Royal Artillery.
Button	The rounded end of the cascabel at the very rear of the piece.
Calibre	Usually the size or diameter of the bore of the piece.
Canister	Also known as 'common case'. A tin container of musket balls packed in sawdust.
Cannon	Smooth bore, muzzle-loading weapon that uses gunpowder to discharge a projectile.
Cannon lock	Lock working on the same principle as a musket and fitted to an artillery piece. Not used in field artillery of the period.
Cap	Piece of sheepskin, leather or canvas placed over the mouth of a mortar when in action to prevent the inside of the piece from getting wet in inclement weather.
Capsquare	Metal bracket placed over the trunnions of a piece to hold it in position on the gun carriage.
Carbine	Musket with a shorter than normal barrel.
Carcass	Incendiary device considered impossible to extinguish, fired from howitzers and mortars.
Cart	Usually a two-wheeled vehicle.
Cartouche	Linen or canvas container used to carry cartridges.
Cartridge	Paper, serge or flannel container used to carry a designated charge of gunpowder.
Case shot	Alternative term for canister.
Centre horses	The horses behind the leaders and in front of the wheelers, there were two or more for each team.
Chamber	In field artillery, the rear area of the bore into which the powder charge was rammed. Chambers were cast in howitzers and mortars.
Charge	The measure of powder for one round of artillery ammunition.
Cheeks	See brackets.
Coat	Generally a long-tailed garment that reached to about the back of the knee.
Coatee	Coat, which ends at the waist in front and extends to about the knee behind. It can be either double or single breasted.
Common case	Tin container of musket balls used at short range.
Common colour	Another term for the grey paint used on artillery equipment.
Common shell	Hollow spherical round filled with a bursting charge and fitted with a fuse.
Congreve	Sir William Congreve, 1st Bart, also known as 'the elder' (1741–1814). He was Comptroller of the Royal Laboratory, Colonel-commandant of the Royal Artillery and should not be confused with his son of the same name and title (1772–1828) who was better known for his development of the rocket as a weapon of war.
Counter battery	Firing at the artillery unit that is firing at you.
Cylinder	The bored-out cylinder down the axis of the gun into which the round was inserted and rammed for firing. The contemporary name used for the barrel or bore of a piece in the Napoleonic period.
Dead ground	Ground in front of a battery that cannot be observed or struck by fire.
Depress	To decrease the elevation of the piece.
Desaguliers	General Thomas Desaguliers (1721–80), more well known as designer of guns and gun carriages, Chief Firemaster 1748–80.

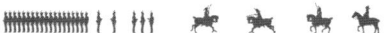

Discharge	To fire a piece.
Dolphins	The handles on top of the gun barrel that were used to lift it from the carriage. Originally quite ornate, and shaped like dolphins (hence the name); by this period they were quite plain and functional.
Drivers	Personnel who managed and rode the horse teams in the foot artillery.
Drag rope	Length of rope attached to the gun by the crew, by which they could pull it around the battlefield.
Drag washer	Washer fitted between the linchpin and the wheel and made with a loop or hook for drag ropes.
Elevating screw	Screw assembly mounted through a swinging block used for elevating and depressing the gun.
Elevation	The angle of the piece about the trunnions.
Encastrement	The practice of having two sets of trunnion plates on the gun carriage. The second set was only used for travelling.
Enfilade	To engage from the side or flank.
Eye bolts	Bolts with shaped eyes to receive the locking pins holding the capsquares in position.
Facings	The colour and regimental distinction of the collar, cuffs, turn backs and lapels of a uniform.
Felloes	The curved wooden segments that formed the circumference of a wheel.
Fire	The command to ignite the charge of a gun.
First graze	The point where a round first strikes the ground.
First line	Where the action is, the scene of battle.
Fixed ammunition	Ammunition with the charge sealed in the cartridge, later used as a term for ammunition that was pre-fitted with a cartridge so that it could be quickly loaded.
Foot artillery	Companies of artillery in which the individual gunners marched alongside their guns.
Forge	Vehicle equipped for making or repairing ironwork in the field. It was attached at the front to a limber.
Former	Wooden rod or tube around which paper or linen was wrapped to form a cartridge.
Foundry	A place where cannon are cast and bored out.
Fuse	See fuze.
Futchell	Lengthwise timber supporting the splinter bar of a limber.
Fuze	Wooden device filled with quick match and used to initiate a shell or spherical case at a predetermined time after it had been fired. The contemporary spelling of the word in the Napoleonic period.
Gauges	Metal rings, which prescribe the maximum and minimum diameter of shot.
Gin	Tripod assembly with attached block and tackle for lifting guns on and off carriages.
Grapeshot	Anti-personnel round, using much larger, and fewer, balls than canister. Not fired from brass ordnance.
Graze	Round hitting the ground after being fired. At low elevations, a round could graze three or four times.
Gun	See piece.
Gun carriage	The carriage on which the piece was mounted for firing or transportation.
Gunmetal	Another term for brass in the ratio of 100 parts of copper to 8 or 9 parts of tin.
Gunner	Any artilleryman; one who serves the guns; a member of a gun crew or any member of the Royal Artillery.
Gun of position	Term used during the Napoleonic period to describe a gun in a fixed battery.
Gunpowder	Propellant charge for all ordnance of the day, composed of sulphur, charcoal, and saltpetre.
Handles	See dolphins.
Hand mallet	Hammer used to drive fuses into shells.
Handspike	Wooden lever used for traversing or moving the gun carriage.

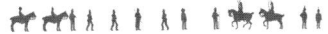

Horse artillery	Field artillery in which all of the gunners were mounted on horses, wagons or limbers.
Howitzer	Short-barreled gun that fired common shell and canister, often at high angles.
Jacket	Generally a short-tailed coat.
Kerseymere	Twilled, light woollen cloth, a variant of cashmere.
KLG	King's German Legion.
Knapsack	Back pack.
Laboratory	Place where explosives and ammunition are manufactured.
Leaders	The pair of horses leading a wagon or artillery gun team.
Lead	The common name for the colour of artillery paint.
Limber	Two-wheeled cart attached to the draught horses and used to form an articulated four-wheeled vehicle with a gun carriage or other cart.
Linchpin	Pin that passed through the arms of the axletree to retain the wheels.
Line of metal	The axis of the piece also the point at which the shot first descends though the axis of the piece.
Linstock	Wooden stick, pointed at one end, to stick in the ground, the other end being split and carrying the slow match for bracket trail guns. If the supply of portfires ran out, the linstock could be used to fire the gun.
Load	The command and process of putting the ammunition into the piece for firing.
Locking chain	Chain carried on the near side and used to stop the near wheel of a vehicle from rotating.
Locking-plates	Metal plates nailed to the sides of a carriage to prevent damage from the metal tires of a limber in a tight turn.
Magazine	Place of storage or manufacture of powder, shot, and other ammunition items.
Match	Rope impregnated with chemicals to retain ignition and burn at a given rate. There were two types, slow match and fast match.
Muzzle	The open end of the piece into which the round was loaded.
Muzzle swell	Projection behind the muzzle moldings.
Nature	Classification by weight, type or function of artillery material.
Nave	Wooden hub of a wheel.
Necessaries	Officially those items of personal equipment supplied at the expense of the recipient.
Neck	The piece of metal joining the button to the breech.
Ogee	Ornamental molding on the surface of artillery pieces.
Ordnance	General term for any weapon and its ammunition, not normally applied to small arms.
Overalls	Additional protective outer garments worn over the breeches or pantaloons, worn 'over all'.
Pantaloons	Close fitting breeches that fastened below the calf or at the foot.
Park	The field artillery headquarters where the spare vehicles, guns, and carriages were kept and maintained, and where artificers and reserve ammunition were usually stationed.
Perch	Single central pole or shaft of a carriage.
Picker	Small, sharp needle-like tool used to clean the touch hole of a gun or musket.
Piece	A general term for a gun, cannon, howitzer, or other item of artillery ordnance, derivation – fieldpiece.
Pintle	Spike on a limber over which the bracket trail of the gun was attached when moving.
Pintlehole	The hole in the trail transom of the gun carriage through which the pintle was placed.
Projectile	Round of ammunition of any type.
Pomatum	Hair dressing made from fat, lard or grease; as pomade.
Portfire	Pyrotechnic used to ignite the quill and fire the piece.
Pr – Pounder	The weight of the round shot fired by the piece.

Prime	To prepare a piece for firing by inserted a quill into the vent.
Priming powder	Fine-grain powder that was readily ignited but not as powerful as large-grain powder.
Prolonge	Rope that was run from the trail of the piece to the limber and allowed the gun to be moved by the horses without 'limbering up'.
Proof	Testing the piece to see if it was fit for service by firing a larger charge than that normally used.
Prop stick	Fitted to the off shaft to prop up a limber without horses.
Quadrant	Graduated tool that was used by gunners to check and fix the elevation of the piece before firing. Also gunner's quadrant.
Queue	Wearing the hair tied into a tail at the rear.
Quill	Goose quill filled with priming powder and inserted into the vent to penetrate the cartridge and make the piece ready for firing.
Quoin	Shaped wedge used to adjust the elevation of a gun or mortar.
Ram	The process of pushing the round down the bore of the piece to the chamber.
Rammer	Long wooden rod with a wooden, flat head at one end and a sponge on the other, used to ram the round.
Ramming	Act of forcing a projectile and cartridge into the bore of a piece.
Range	The distance from the piece to the target.
Recoil	Sudden and very violent movement rearward that a piece performs when fired.
Reinforce	Thicker layer of metal around the bore intended to make the piece stronger there in order to resist the force of explosion when a round was fired.
Red LG	The large-grain, best and most powerful form of British gunpowder. When loaded in an 8-inch howitzer a charge of two ounces would project a ball weighing 64 pounds to 180 feet. Pit powder achieved 150 feet and re-dried powder about 110 feet.
Ricochet	Solid shot used with a trajectory that would cause the round to bounce along the ground on the way to the target.
Round	One piece of ammunition.
Round shot	Inert, cast-iron ball fired from ordnance.
Sabot	See wooden bottom.
Salute	Firing of artillery in honor of a person, occasion or event. Originally used to show the guns were discharged.
Salvo	Round fired from all the guns, ideally simultaneously or on command.
Searcher	Long-handled tool used to find defects on the inside of a gun bore.
Second line	Place where the support services and reserve ammunition were grouped. See park.
Serve	To load and fire the piece.
Shot	Projectile fired from a piece. Also called round shot or solid shot.
Shell	Hollow ball filled with explosive, and exploded after a certain time by a wooden, pre-cut fuse.
Spherical case	Hollow shell filled with musket balls and a separating charge. Developed by Henry Shrapnel.
Side arms	General term for the accoutrements used to serve the gun, for example handspikes, rammers, and sponges.
Solid shot	Round shot.
Spent	A round was said to be spent when it has past the range at which it can cause significant effect.
Spike	To hammer a spike into the vent and render a piece of ordnance unable to fire.
Sponge	Lamb's wool used to swab out the bore and extinguish any burning remnants after the gun had fired.
Spring key	Two-layer locking key. They were driven through the eyebolts and the ends splayed out.
Stocking net	Elastic knitted material.
Streak	Metal, segmented tyre nailed to the rim of a wheel.

Swingletree	Wooden bar used to transfer the effort from two traces to a single point.
Tampion	Wooden muzzle-plug inserted in the bore when a gun was not in use.
Tarleton	General Banastre Tarleton (1754–1833) after whom the Tarleton helmet was named.
Thumbstall	Leather or woollen covering for the thumb. It protected the thumb from the hot metal of the vent.
Tiered Case	As common case but the musket balls are arranged in regular tiers or layers.
Touch hole	Hole by which the means of ignition was transferred to the main charge, see vent.
Traces	Harness that transfers the effort of one horse to that of another or to the carriage.
Trail	The end of the gun carriage that rested on the ground or was attached to the limber.
Trajectory	The path of a projectile in flight.
Transom	Pieces of wood that held the brackets together.
Traverse	To move the gun in azimuth by moving the trail of the piece.
Troop	Collective name for an established number of men and guns within horse artillery.
Trunnions	Cylindrical projections from the side of the piece by which it was retained on the carriage and allowed to change elevation.
Trunnion plate	Metal strapping on the underside of the trunnions.
Tube	Tin tube filled with priming powder; because of its tendency to rust and damage the priming powder it was replaced by the quill.
Tumbrels	Two-wheeled, covered ammunition carts.
Vent	Hole inclined at 110 degrees and connecting to the chamber of a piece and by which the charge was ignited.
Vent pin	Tool used to pass through the vent and pierce the cartridge to ensure ignition from the quill to the powder.
Vent field	The section of the vent that extended from the base ring to the first reinforce astragal.
Volley	The act of firing all the pieces of a battery at once. Something akin to a salvo.
Wagon	More usually a four-wheeled vehicle.
Water-deck	Painted, waterproof canvas cover, used to cover the saddle and harness.
Watering cap	Fatigue hat used when watering the horses.
Wheeler	Horses connected to the shafts of the limber or wagon. They were usually the strongest and steadiest pair in the gun team.
Windage	Distance between the round and the wall of the bore. The smaller the distance, the greater the accuracy.
Wooden bottom	Circular disc of wood fitted to ammunition to stop it turning in the barrel and damaging the fuse or to facilitate ready use ammunition.
Woolwich	The location of the Royal Arsenal, Royal Carriage Department and home of the Royal Regiment of Artillery.
Worm	Tool with a corkscrew-like tip, used to extract excess material out of the bore. It screwed into the end of the rammer.

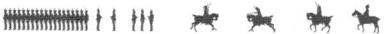

Bibliography

The list below gives the books and illustrations used for reference and from which information has been gleaned but not necessarily referred to in the endnotes to each chapter. Where reference is made, it is limited to the author and date, a full description being given below.

Adye, R.W.
  The Little Bombardier and Pocket Gunner, 1801, London
  The Bombardier and Pocket Gunner, 2nd edn, London, 1802
  The Bombardier and Pocket Gunner, 3rd edn, London, 1803
  The Bombardier and Pocket Gunner, 4th edn, London, 1804
  The Bombardier and Pocket Gunner, 5th edn, London, 1806
  The Bombardier and Pocket Gunner, 6th edn, London, 1810
  The Bombardier and Pocket Gunner, 7th edn, London, 1813
  The Bombardier and Pocket Gunner, 8th edn, London, 1827
Almack, E.
  Regimental Badges worn in the British Army 100 years ago, Blades, East & Blades, London, 1900
Anon.
  'The Honourable Artillery Company, about 1796'. Painting in the Royal Collection, Windsor Castle, *Catalogue No. 343*
Atkinson, A.J.
  'Royal Artillery': A *Picturesque Representation of the Naval, Military and Miscellaneous Costumes of Great Britain*, London, 1807
  'Royal Artillery on the move': A *Picturesque Representation of the Naval, Military and Miscellaneous Costumes of Great Britain*, London, 1807
Bailey, D.W.
  British Military Longarms, 1715–1815, Arms & Armour Press, London, 1971
Blackmore, H.L.
  British Military Firearms 1650–1850, Herbert Jenkins, London, 1967
Boxer, E.M., Capt
  Treatise on Artillery, Section 2, Part 2, HMSO, & Eyre & Spottiswoode, London, 1853

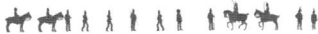

Brown, O.C., Capt
  Ammunition, A Descriptive treatise of the different Projectile, Charges Fuzes, Rockets etc, Eyre &
  Spottiswoode, London, 1870
Campbell, D.A., Maj
  Dress of the Royal Regiment of Artillery, Royal Artillery Press, Woolwich, 1971
Carman, W.Y.
  Richard Simkin's Uniforms of the British Army, 2 Vols, Web & Bower, Exeter, 1985
  Royal Artillery, Osprey, Reading, 1973
Caruana, A.
  'A Note on British Field Artillery Equipments of the War of 1812', *Arms Collecting*, Vol. 20, No. 4,
  1982
  'British Artillery Drill in the 18th Century', *Arms Collecting*, Vol. 16, No. 2, 1978
  Grasshoppers and Butterflies, Museum Restoration Service, Ontario, 1979
  'The Introduction of the Block Trail Carriage', *Arms Collecting*, Vol. 18, No. 1, 1980
  'The Aiming of Artillery', *Arms Collecting*, Vol. 18, No. 3, 1980
  The Light Battalion Gun of 1776, Museum Restoration Service, Ontario, 1977
Chappell, M.
  British Cavalry Equipments 1800–1914, Osprey, London, 1983
  British Infantry Equipments (1), Osprey, Oxford, 1999
Committee of Engineers
  Aide-Memoire to the Military Sciences, Vol. 1, 1st edn, John Weale, London, 1847
  Aide-Memoire to the Military Sciences, Vol. 1, 2nd edn, John Weale, London, 1853
  Aide-Memoire to the Military Sciences, Vol. 2, John Weale, London, 1850
  Aide-Memoire to the Military Sciences, Vol. 3, John Weale, London, 1852
De Loutherberg
  'Grand Attack on Valenciennes, 1793'. Engraving by W. Bromley. National Museum of Scotland,
  Ref. A6338
Dayes, E.
  'Officer, Royal Artillery', *circa 1792*, watercolour painting
  'Gunner, Royal Artillery', *circa 1792*, watercolour painting
Dickson, A.
  'Artillery Services in North America 1814–15', *Journal of the Society for Army Historical Research*,
  Vol. VIII, 1929
  '*The Dickson Manuscripts. 1809–1818*', Royal Artillery Institute Press, Woolwich, 1908
Dighton, D.
  'Royal Horse Artillery Coming into Action', 1814: Painting in the Royal Collection,
  Reference RL 15405
  'Royal Artillery, 1812': Painting in the Royal Collection, Reference RL 15041
  'British Artillery Dislodging French Cavalry', 1813: Painting in the Royal Collection,
  Reference RL 15044
  'Battle of Waterloo, 1815': Details not known.
Duncan, F.
  History of the Royal Regiment of Artillery, Vol. II, 1892; reprint by Naval & Military Press, Uckfield,
  2005
Farmer, H.G.
  History of the Royal Artillery Band, Royal Artillery Institute, London, 1954
Fortune, T.
  The Artillerist Companion, London, 1778
Fraser, A., Col Sir
  Letters written during the Peninsular and Waterloo Campaigns, Longmans, London, 1859
Franklin, C.E.
  Rockets of the Napoleonic and Colonial Wars, Spellmount Ltd, Staplehurst, 2005
Graves, D.E.
  'A note on British Field Artillery of the War of 1812', *Arms Collecting*, Vol. 20, 1982

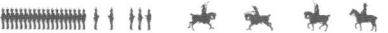

Griffiths, F.A., Capt
  Artillerists Manual and Compendium, E. Jones, Woolwich. Published in 8 edns between 1839 to 1859.
Hamilton Smith, C.
  Costume of the Army of the British Empire, 1815; see Stadler
Haswell Miller, A.E. & Dawnay, N.P.
  Military Drawings and Paintings in the collection of Her Majesty The Queen, 2 Vols, Phaidon, London, 1966
Headlam, J., Maj-Gen Sir
  History of the Royal Artillery, Vol. 3, Woolwich, 1940
Henry, C.
  British Napoleonic Artillery 1793–1815, Vols 1 and 2, Osprey, Oxford, 2003
Hime, H.W.L., Lt Col
  History of the Royal Regiment of Artillery from 1815 to 1853, Longmans, London, 1908
HMSO:
  *Treatise on Military Carriage*s, 8 edns between 1865 and 1900
  Treatise on Ammunition, 7 edns between 1865 and 1902
  List of Changes in Artillery Materiel, Small arms and other Military Stores, published on a calendar basis after 1860
Hogg, O.F.G., Brig
  *Artillery, its Origins, Heyday and Dec*line, Hurst, London, 1970
  The Royal Arsenal, Oxford University Press, London, 1963
Hughes, B.P., Maj Gen
  British Smooth Bore Artillery, Arms and Armour Press, 1996
  Open Fire, Antony Bird Publications, 1983
  Regimental Heritage, Europa Press, London, 1984
Hull, E.
  Battalion Bombardier, 1828: coloured lithograph
James Clavell Library, see the Royal Artillery Historical Trust
  Instructions and Regulations for the Exercise and Movement of the Royal Horse Artillery, Royal Artillery, 1833, 1854 and 1855
  'Artillery Harness, 1865', Royal Carriage Department Plate 37 and 38, May 1870
  'Forge Wagon, 1860', Royal Carriage Department Plate 23, October, 1868
  'Field Carriage for 6-pr SB Gun', Royal Carriage Department Plate 13, July 1867
  'Field Carriage for 9-pr SB Gun', Royal Carriage Department Plate 14, December 1867
  Miscellaneous manuscript notes of the cadets at the Royal Military Academy at Woolwich. The James Clavell Library, Royal Artillery Historical Trust. Some of these notes are not attributable but others are. Where reference is made the name is given if known.
Jocelyn, J.R.J., Col
  History of the Royal Regiment of Artillery, Murray, London, 1911
Jones, G., Capt
  'Foot Artillery at Waterloo', etching by S. Mitan, 1816
Kemmis, R.A., Capt
  Treatise on Military Carriages, London, 1874
Longford, E.
  Wellington, the Years of the Sword, World Books, London, 1971
Lawson. C.C.P.
  A History of the Uniforms of the British Army, Vols 3, 4 and 5, Norman Military Publications, London, 1961, 1966 and 1967
Lawson, H., Capt
  Abstract of the Exercises of the Field Artillery, Stainton, London, 1821
  Handbook for Field Service, London, 1857
Lefroy, J.H., Capt
  Field Service or Field Pocket Book, Parker Furnivalt, Woolwich, London, 1854
  Handbook for Field Service, Woolwich, London, 1857

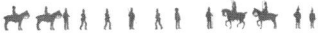

Le Mesurier, C.B., Capt
   Notes on the Manufactures of the Royal Carriage Department, HMSO, London, 1858
Leslie, J.H., Maj
   Services of the Royal Artillery in the Peninsular War, 3 Vols, Royal Artillery Press, Woolwich,
   1912
Lunbye, C.C.
   Dimensioned Drawings of Light 6-pr Gun and Limber, 1816, Artillery Museum, Varde and the
   Tøjhusmuseet, Copenhagen
MacDonald, R.J., Capt
   The History of the Dress of the Royal Regiment of Artillery, Henry Southern, London, 1899
Majendie, V.D., Capt
   Ammunition, a Descriptive Treatise, Mitchell & Co., London, 1867
McConnell, D.
   British Smooth Bore Artillery, Canadian Parks Services, Ottawa, 1988
Mercer, C.
   Journal of the Waterloo Campaign, 2 vols, Blackwood & Sons, London, 1870
Muller, J.
   A Treatise of Artillery, 3rd edn, London, 1780
National Archive
   (formerly known as the Public Record Office) Letters and papers relating to the War Office,
   Home Office and Ordnance Board. Usually suffixed as WO, HO etc.
Nelson, R.J.
   Gun Carriages, Museum Restoration Services, Ontario, 1972
Nock, H.
   Horse Artillery Pistol. Exhibits at the Royal Armouries, Leeds; reference XII – 843 and 844
Parkyn, H.G.
   Shoulder-belt Plates and Buttons, Gale & Polden, London, 1956
Pyne, W.H.
   A Picturesque Delineation of the Arts, Agriculture and Manufactures &c of Great Britain, W. Millar,
   London, 1802
Reserve collection at the Rotunda. See Royal Artillery Historical Trust
Rogers, H.C.B.
   Artillery through the Ages, Seeley Service & Co., London, 1971
Royal Artillery Historical Trust
   The Royal Artillery Museum (Firepower), The James Clavell Library and the Reserve collection at
   the Rotunda, Woolwich, all form part of this trust.
Royal Artillery Museum, see the Royal Artillery Historical Trust
Royal Collection
   A series of drawings and paintings in the collection at Windsor Castle
Rudyerd, C.W.
   A Course of Artillery, 1792. Reprinted by the Museum Restoration Service, Ottawa, 1970
Russell, J., Lt
   *A series of Military Exercises of Attack and Defence Made in Hyde Park in 1802 and the Island
   of Jersey in 1805*, T. Egerton, London, 1806: reprint by Naval and Military Press, Uckfield, 2005
Sauerweid, A.I.
   'Driver and Farrier, Corps of Drivers', painting in the collection of Her Majesty The Queen
   'Private, Mounted Rocket Corps', painting in the collection of Her Majesty The Queen
Shrapnel, H.
   Spherical Case Shot, London, 1803
Siborne, H.T., Maj-Gen
   The Waterloo Letters, Cassell, London, 1891: reprint by Greenhill Books, 1993
Schutz, Lt
   Dimensioned Drawings of Light 6-pr Gun and Limber, 1816, Artillery Museum, Varde and the
   Tøjhusmuseet, Copenhagen

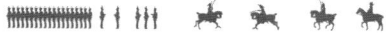

Shuttleworth, A.A.
> Watercolour plates of ordnance and carriages, *circa* 1820, at the James Clavell Library.
> Ashton Suttleworth was an artillery cadet at Woolwich between 1819 and 1821

Spearman, J.M.
> *The British Gunner*, 2nd edn, Woolwich, 1828

Stadler, I.C.
> 'Royal Horse Artillery', aquatint after Hamilton Smith, Colnaghi & Co., London, 1815
> 'Royal Artillery. Mounted Rocket Corps', aquatint after Hamilton Smith. Colnaghi & Co., 1815
> 'Royal Horse Artillery', aquatint after Hamilton Smith, Colnaghi & Co., London, 1815
> 'Gunners, Royal Artillery', aquatint after Hamilton Smith, Colnaghi & Co., London, 1815
> 'Corps of Drivers and Royal Waggon Train', aquatint after Hamilton Smith, Colnaghi & Co., London, 1815

Tylden, G., Maj
> 'Horses and Saddlery', J.A. Allen, London, 1965

Tøjhusmuseet, Copenhagen and the Artillery Museum, Varde, Denmark
> Two 6-pr Guns and Limbers, *circa* 1810

Vernet, C.
> 'Driver, Royal Horse Artillery', watercolour, *circa* 1815
> 'Driver and Infantry man', watercolour, *circa* 1813

Vigors, D.D.
> 'Voices from the Napoleonic Wars', *Journal of the Royal Artillery*, Vol. 111, No. 2, September 1984

Webber, W., Capt
> *With the Guns in the Peninsula*, Greenhill Books, London, 1991

Whinyates, F.A., Col
> *From Corunna to Sevastopol, The History of C Battery. RHA*, Royal Artillery Press, 1893

Widrow, M. and Embleton, E.
> *Military Dress of the Peninsular War*, Ian Allen, London, 1975

Wilkinson-Latham, L.
> *British Military Swords*, Hutchinson & Co., London, 1966

Wilkinson-Latham, R.
> *British Artillery on Land and Sea*, David & Charles, Newton Abbot, 1973
> *Crimean Uniforms, 2. British Artillery*, Historical Research Unit, Adlard & Sons, Dorking, 1973

Wilson, A.W.
> *The Story of the Gun*, Royal Artillery Institution, Woolwich, 1944

Index

References in **bold** refer to illustrations and those in *italics* to tables. A full list of illustrations follows the Contents.

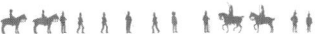

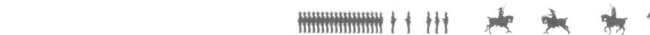